D0993781

British Qualifications 2017

47TH EDITION

A Complete Guide to Professional,
Vocational & Academic Qualifications
in the United Kingdom

KoganPage

LONDON   NEW YORK   NEW DELHI

Publisher's note

Every possible effort has been made to ensure that the information contained in this book is accurate at the time of going to press, and the publishers and authors cannot accept responsibility for any errors or omissions, however caused. No responsibility for loss or damage occasioned to any person acting, or refraining from action, as a result of the material in this publication can be accepted by the editor, the publisher or any of the authors.

First published in Great Britain in 1966

Forty-seventh edition published in Great Britain and the United States in 2017 by Kogan Page Limited

Apart from any fair dealing for the purposes of research or private study, or criticism or review, as permitted under the Copyright, Designs and Patents Act 1988, this publication may only be reproduced, stored or trans-mitted, in any form or by any means, with the prior permission in writing of the publishers, or in the case of reprographic reproduction in accordance with the terms and licences issued by the CLA. Enquiries concerning reproduction outside these terms should be sent to the publishers at the undermentioned addresses:

2nd Floor, 45 Gee Street	c/o Martin P Hill Consulting	4737/23 Ansari Road
London EC1V 3RS	122 W 27th St, 10th Floor	Daryaganj
United Kingdom	New York NY 10001	New Delhi 110002
www.koganpage.com	USA	India

© Kogan Page, 2017

British Library Cataloguing-in-Publication Data

A CIP record for this book is available from the British Library.

ISBN 978 0 7494 7949 7
E-ISBN 978 0 7494 7950 3
ISSN 0141-5972

Typeset by AMA DataSet Ltd, Preston
Print production managed by Jellyfish
Printed and bound by CPI Group (UK) Ltd, Croydon, CR0 4YY

PUBLISHER'S NOTE

This 47th edition of *British Qualifications* has been considerably revised and updated to reflect the many changes in degree, diploma and certificate courses and to take account of legislative reforms affecting the structure of higher and further education over the past year.

The editor and compilers are most grateful to the academic registrars and the secretaries of the many bodies they have contacted for information and advice. Without their cooperation, the revision and updating of *British Qualifications* would not have been possible.

Class: 378.013 REf
Accession No: 141494
Type: REfERENCE

CONTENTS

Contents

Contents

Contents

Contents

Contents

REFERENCES

Association of MBAs (AMBA) (annual) *AMBA – Financial Times Guide to Business Schools*, AMBA, London

Committee of Vice-Chancellors and Principals (CVCP) (annual) *University Entrance: The official guide*, CVCP, London

Department for Education and Skills (DfES) (2003) *The Future of Higher Education*, The Stationery Office, London [online] http://www.dfes.gov.uk/hegateway/strategy/hestrategy/foreword.shtml

DfES (2004) *Five-Year Strategy for Children and Learners*, DfES, London

Qualifications and Curriculum Authority (QCA) (2004) *New Thinking for Reform: A framework for achievement*, QCA, London (July)

HOW TO USE THIS BOOK

You may find these notes helpful when using the book.

Part 1 presents an overview of the further and higher educational systems currently in operation in the United Kingdom, including a discussion of the major reforms that have taken place over the past year and their impact.

Part 2 takes a look at the teaching establishments whose qualifications are listed in Part 4 of the book, offering an explanation of the different types of institution, their place in the overall system and the levels of qualification that they award.

Part 3 presents a detailed description of vocational qualifications awarded by many of the professional associations included in Part 5, including an explanation of validating, examining and awarding bodies.

Part 4 is a directory of qualifications awarded by universities in the United Kingdom (ordered by university name). There is a brief introduction detailing admission to degree courses, degree structure and the various categories of degree available.

Part 5 is a directory of qualifications awarded by professional, trade and specialist associations in the United Kingdom (ordered by profession / discipline), including certificates, diplomas, NVQs and SVQs. A short introduction explains the functions of professional associations and how to gain membership.

Part 6 describes various bodies involved in the accreditation of colleges in the independent sector of further and higher education.

Part 7 is a list of study associations and learned societies.

Also included (at the beginning of the book) is a list of all abbreviations and designatory letters used throughout *British Qualifications*.

INDEX OF ABBREVIATIONS AND DESIGNATORY LETTERS

AAB	Associate of the Association of Book-keepers
AACB	Associate of the Association of Certified Bookkeepers
AACP	Associate of the Association of Computer Professionals
AAFC	Associate of the Association of Financial Controllers and Administrators
AAIA	Associate of the Association of International Accountants
AAMS	Associate of the Association of Medical Secretaries, Practice Managers, Administrators and Receptionists
AASI	Associate of the Ambulance Service Institute
AASW	Advanced Award in Social Work
AAT	Association of Accounting Technicians
ABC	Awarding Body Consortium
ABDO	Associate of the British Dispensing Opticians
ABE	Association of Business Executives
ABEng	Associate Member of the Association of Building Engineers
ABHA	Associate of the British Hypnotherapy Association
ABIAT	Associate Member of the British Institute of Architectural Technologists
ABIPP	Associate of the British Institute of Professional Photography
ABMA	Associate of the Business Management Association
ABPR	Association of British Picture Restorers
ABRSM	Associated Board of the Royal Schools of Music
ABS	Association of Business Schools
ABSSG	Associate of the British Society of Scientific Glassblowers
ACA	Associate of the Institute of Chartered Accountants in England and Wales
ACA	Associate of the Institute of Chartered Accountants in Ireland
ACB	Association of Certified Bookkeepers
ACC	Accredited Clinical Coders
ACCA	Associate of the Association of Chartered Certified Accountants
ACCA	Association of Chartered Certified Accountants
ACE	Association for Conferences and Events
ACEA	Associate of the Institute of Cost and Executive Accountants
ACertCM	Archbishop of Canterbury's Certificate in Church Music
ACGI	Associate of City and Guilds of London Institute
ACIArb	Associate of the Chartered Institute of Arbitrators
ACIB	Associate of the Chartered Institute of Bankers
ACIBS	Associate of the Chartered Institute of Bankers in Scotland
ACIBSE	Associate of the Chartered Institution of Building Services Engineers
ACIH	Associate of the Chartered Institute of Housing
ACII	Associate of the Chartered Insurance Institute
ACILA	Associate of the Chartered Institute of Loss Adjusters
ACIM	Associate of the Chartered Institute of Marketing
ACIOB	Associate of the Chartered Institute of Building
ACIS	Associate of the Institute of Chartered Secretaries and Administrators
ACIT	Advanced Certificate in International Trade
ACLIP	Certified Affiliate of CILIP
ACMA	Associate of the Chartered Institute of Management Accountants
ACP	Association of Child Psychotherapists
ACP	Associate of the College of Preceptors

ACP	Association of Computer Professionals
ACPM	Associate of the Confederation of Professional Management
ACPP	Associate of the College of Pharmacy Practice
ACT	Associate of the College of Teachers
ACYW	Associate of the Community and Youth Work Association
ADCE	Advanced Diploma in Childcare and Education
ADCM	Archbishop of Canterbury's Diploma in Church Music
AdDipEd	Advanced Diploma in Education
ADI	Approved Driving Instructor
AECI	Association Member of the Institute of Employment Consultants
AEWVH	Association for the Education and Welfare of the Visually Handicapped
AFA	Associate of the Faculty of Actuaries
AFA	Associate of the Institute of Financial Accountants
AFBPsS	Associate Fellow of the British Psychological Society
AFCI	Associate of the Faculty of Commerce and Industry Ltd
AffBMA	Affiliate of the Business Management Association
AffIManf	Affiliate of the Institute of Manufacturing
AffIMI	Affiliate of the Institute of the Motor Industry
AffIMS	Affiliate of the Institute of Management Specialists
AffInstM	Affiliate of the Meat Training Council
AffIP	Affiliate of the Institute of Plumbing
AffProfBTM	Affiliate of Professional Business and Technical Management
AFIMA	Associate Fellow of the Institute of Mathematics and its Applications
AFISOL	Aerodrome Flight Information Service Officer's Licence
AFPC	Advanced Financial Planning Certificate
AFRCSEd	Associate Fellow of Royal College of Surgeons of Edinburgh
AGCL	Associate of the Guild of Cleaners and Launderers
AGI	Associate of the Greek Institute
AGSM	Associate of the Guildhall School of Music and Drama
AHCIMA	Associate of the Hotel and Catering International Management Association
AHFS	Associate of the Council of Health Fitness and Sports Therapists
AHRIM	Associate of the Institute of Health Record Information and Management
AIA	Associate of the Institute of Actuaries
AIA	Association of International Accountants
AIAgrE	Associate of the Institution of Agricultural Engineers
AIAT	Associate of the Institute of Asphalt Technology
AIBCM	Associate of the Institute of British Carriage and Automobile Manufacturers
AIBMS	Associate of the Institute of Biomedical Science
AICB	Associate of the Institute of Certified Book-Keepers
AIChor	Associate of the Benesh Institute of Choreology
AICHT	Associate of the International Council of Holistic Therapists
AICM(Cert)	Associate Member of the Institute of Credit Management
AICS	Associate of the Institution of Chartered Shipbrokers
AICSc	Associate of the Institute of Consumer Sciences Incorporating Home Economics
AIDTA	Associate of the International Dance Teachers' Association
AIE	Associate of the Institute of Electrolysis
AIEM	Associate of the Institute of Executives and Managers
AIExpE	Associate of the Institute of Explosive Engineers
AIFA	Associate of the Institute of Field Archaeologists
AIFBQ	Associate of the International Faculty of Business Qualifications
AIFireE	Associate of the Institution of Fire Engineers
AIFP	Associate of the British International Freight Association

AIGD	Associate of the Institute of Grocery Distribution
AIHort	Associate Member of the Institute of Horticulture
AIIMR	Associate of the Institute of Investment Management and Research
AIIRSM	Associate of the International Institute of Risk and Safety Management
AIL	Associate of the Institute of Linguists
AILAM	Associate of the Institute of Leisure and Amenity Management
AIMBM	Associate of the Institute of Maintenance and Building Management
AIMC	Associate of the Institute of Management Consultancy
AIMgt	Associate of the Institute of Management
AIMIS	Associate of the Institute for the Management of Information Systems
AIMM	Associate of the Institute of Massage and Movement
AInstAM	Associate of the Institute of Administrative Management
AInstBA	Associate of the Institute of Business Administration
AInstBCA	Associate of the Institute of Burial and Cremation Administration
AInstBM	Associate of the Institute of Builders' Merchants
AInstCM	Associate of the Institute of Commercial Management
AInstM	Associate of the Meat Training Council
AInstPkg	Associate of the Institute of Packaging
AInstPM	Associate of the Institute of Professional Managers and Administrators
AInstSMM	Associate of the Institute of Sales and Marketing Management
AInstTA	Associate of the Institute of Transport Administration
AInstTT	Associate Member of the Institute of Travel and Tourism
AIOC	Associate of the Institute of Carpenters
AIOFMS	Associate of the Institute of Financial and Management Studies
AIP	Associate of the Institute of Plumbing
AIQA	Associate of the Institute of Quality Assurance
AIS	Accredited Imaging Scientist
AISOB	Associate of the Incorporated Society of Organ Builders
AISTD	Associate of the Imperial Society of Teachers of Dancing
AISTDDip	Associate Diploma of the Imperial Society of Teachers of Dancing
AITSA	Associate of the Institute of Trading Standards Administration
AIVehE	Associate of the Institute of Vehicle Engineers
AIWSc	Associate Member of the Institute of Wood Science
ALCM	Associate of the London College of Music
ALI	Associate of the Landscape Institute
ALS	Associate of the Linnean Society of London
AMA	Associate of the Museums Association
AMABE	Associate Member of the Association of Business Executives
AMAE	Associate Member of the Academy of Experts
AMASI	Associate Member of the Architecture and Surveying Institute
AMBA	Association of MBAs
AMBA	Non-Teacher Associate Member of the British (Theatrical) Arts
AMBCS	Associate Member of the British Computer Society
AMBII	Associate Member of the British Institute of Innkeeping
AmCAM	Associate of the Communication Advertising and Marketing Education Foundation
AMCT	Associate of the Association of Corporate Treasurers
AMCTHCM	Associate Member of the Confederation of Tourism, Hotel and Catering Management
AMI	Association Montessori Internationale
AMIA	Affiliated Member of the Association of International Accountants
AMIAgrE	Associate Member of the Institution of Agricultural Engineers
AMIAP	Associate Member of the Institution of Analysts and Programmers

AMIAT	Associate Member of the Institute of Asphalt Technology
AMIBC	Associate Member of the Institute of Building Control
AMIBCM	Associate Member of the Institute of British Carriage and Automobile Manufacturers
AMIBE	Associate Member of the Institution of British Engineers
AMIBF	Associate Member of the Institute of British Foundrymen
AMICE	Associate Member of the Institution of Civil Engineers
AMIChemE	Associate Member of the Institution of Chemical Engineers
AMIED	Associate Member of the Institution of Engineering Designers
AMIEE	Associate Member of the Institution of Electrical Engineers
AMIEx	Associate Member of the Institute of Export
AMIHIE	Associate Member of the Institute of Highway Incorporated Engineers
AMIHT	Associate Member of the Institution of Highways and Transportation
AMIIE	Associate Member of the Institution of Incorporated Engineers
AMIIExE	Associate Member of the Institution of Incorporated Executive Engineers
AMIIHTM	Associate Member of the International Institute of Hospitality Tourism & Management
AMIISE	Associate Member of the International Institute of Social Economics
AMIM	Associate Member of the Institute of Materials
AMIManf	Member of the Institute of Manufacturing
AMIMechE	Associate Member of the Institution of Mechanical Engineers
AMIMechIE	Associate Member of the Institution of Mechanical Incorporated Engineers
AMIMI	Associate Member of the Institute of the Motor Industry
AMIMinE	Associate of the Institute of Mining Engineers
AMIMM	Associate Member of the Institution of Mining and Metallurgy
AMIMS	Associate Member of the Institute of Management Specialists
AMInstAEA	Associate Member of the Institute of Automotive Engineer Assessors
AMInstBE	Associate Member of the Institution of British Engineers
AMInstE	Associate Member of the Institute of Energy
AMInstR	Associate Member of the Institute of Refrigeration
AMInstTA	Associate Member of the Institute of Transport Administration
AMIPlantE	Associate Member of the Institution of Plant Engineers
AMIPR	Associate Member of the Institute of Public Relations
AMIPRE	Associate Member of the Incorporated Practitioners in Radio and Electronics
AMIQ	Associate Member of the Institute of Quarrying
AMIQA	Associate Member of the Institute of Quality Assurance
AMIRTE	Associate Member of the Institute of Road Transport Engineers
AMISM	Associate Member of the Institute for Supervision & Management
AMIStrutE	Associate Member of the Institution of Structural Engineers
AMITD	Associate Member of the Institute of Training and Development
AMIVehE	Associate Member of the Institute of Vehicle Engineers
AMNI	Associate Member of the Nautical Institute
AMPA	Associate Member of the Master Photographers Association
AMProfBTM	Associate Member of Professional Business and Technical Management
AMRAeS	Associate Member of the Royal Aeronautical Society
AMRSH	Associate Member of the Royal Society for the Promotion of Health
AMS	Associate of the Institute of Management Services
AMS(Aff)	Affiliate of the Association of Medical Secretaries, Practice Managers, Administrators and Receptionists
AMSE	Associate Member of the Society of Engineers (Inc)
AMSPAR	Association of Medical Secretaries, Practice Managers, Administrators and Receptionists

AMusEd	Associate Diploma in Music Education
AMusLCM	Associate in Music of the London College of Music
AMusTCL	Associate in Music of Trinity College of Music
AMWES	Associate Member of the Women's Engineering Society
ANAEA	Associate of the National Association of Estate Agents
ANCA	Advanced National Certificate in Agriculture
AOP	Association of Photographers
AOR	Association of Reflexologists
APA	Accreditation of Prior Experience
APC	Assessment of Professional Competence
APCS	Associate of the Property Consultants Society
APMI	Associate of the Pensions Management Institute
APMP	Association for Project Management Professional
AQA	Assessment & Qualifications Alliance
ARAD	Associate of the Royal Academy of Dancing
ARAM	Associate of the Royal Academy of Music
ARB	Architects Registration Board
ARCM	Associate of Royal College of Music
ARCO	Associate of the Royal College of Organists
ARCS	Associate of the Royal College of Science
AREC	Associate of the Recruitment and Employment Confederation
ARELS	Association of Recognised English Language Services
ARELS-FELCO	Association of Recognised English Language Teaching Establishments in Britain
ARIBA	Associate of the Royal Institute of British Architects
ARICS	Associate of the Royal Institution of Chartered Surveyors
ARIPHH	Associate of the Royal Institute of Public Health and Hygiene
ARPS	Associate of the Royal Photographic Society
ARSC	Associate of the Royal Society of Chemistry
ARSCM	Associate of the Royal School of Church Music
ARSM	Associate of the Royal School of Mines
AS	Advanced Supplementary level
ASCA	Associate of the Institute of Company Accountants
ASCT	Associate of the Society of Claims Technicians
ASDC	Associate of the Society of Dyers and Colourists
ASE	Associate of the Society of Engineers (Inc)
ASI	Ambulance Service Institute
ASI	Architecture and Surveying Institute
ASIAffil	Affiliate of the Ambulance Service Institute
ASIS	Accredited Senior Imaging Scientist
ASLC	Advanced Secretarial Language Certificate
ASMA	Associate of the Society of Sales Management Administrators Ltd
ASNN	Associate of the Society of Nursery Nursing
AssCI	Associate of the Institute of Commerce
AssociateCIPD	Associate of the Chartered Institute of Personnel and Development
AssociateIEEE	Associate of the Institution of Electrical and Electronics Engineers Incorporated
AssociateIIE	Associate of the Institution of Incorporated Engineers
AssocIMechIE	Associate of the Institution of Mechanical Incorporated Engineers
AssocIPD	Associate of the Institute of Personnel & Development
AssocIPHE	Associate of the Institution of Public Health Engineers
AssocMIWM	Associate Member of the Institute of Wastes Management
AssocTechIIE	Associate Technician of the Institution of Incorporated Engineers
ASTA	Associate of the Swimming Teachers' Association

ASVA	Associate of the Incorporated Society of Valuers and Auctioneers
ATC	Art Teacher's Certificate
ATCL	Associate of Trinity College of Music
ATCLicence	Air Traffic Controller's Licence
ATCLTESOL	Associate Diploma in the Teaching of English to Speakers of Other Languages, Trinity College
ATD	Art Teacher's Diploma
ATI	Associate of the Textile Industry
ATII	Associate of the Chartered Institute of Taxation
ATPL	Airline Transport Pilot's Licence
ATSC	Associate of the Oil and Colour Chemists' Association
ATSC	Associate in the Technology of Surface Coatings
ATT	Association of Taxation Technicians
ATT	Member of the Association of Taxation Technicians
ATTA	Association of Therapy Teachers Associate
ATTF	Association of Therapy Teachers Fellow
ATTM	Association of Therapy Teachers Member
AWeldI	Associate of the Welding Institute
BA	Bachelor of Arts
BA(Econ)	Bachelor of Arts in Economics & Social Studies
BA(Ed)	Bachelor of Arts (Education)
BA(Lan)	Bachelor of Languages
BA(Law)	Bachelor of Arts in Law
BA(Music)	Bachelor of Music
BABTAC	British Association of Beauty Therapy and Cosmetology Ltd
BAC	British Accreditation Council for Independent Further and Higher Education
BAC	British Association for Counselling
BAcc	Bachelor of Accountancy
BACP	British Association for Counselling Psychotherapy
BADA	British Antique Dealers' Association
BADN	British Association of Dental Nurses
BAE	British Association of Electrolysists Ltd
BAGMA	British Agricultural and Garden Machinery Association
BAgr	Bachelor of Agriculture
BAO	Bachelor of Obstetrics
BAP	British Association of Psychotherapists
BArch	Bachelor of Architecture
BASELT	British Association in State English Language Teaching
BBO	British Ballet Organisation
BChD	Bachelor of Dental Surgery
BChir	Bachelor of Surgery
BCL	Bachelor of Civil Law
BCom	Bachelor of Commerce
BCombStuds	Bachelor of Combined Studies
BComm	Bachelor of Communications
BCS	Bachelor of Combined Studies
BCS	British Computer Society
BD	Bachelor of Divinity
BDA	British Dietetic Association
BDes	Bachelor of Design
BDS	Bachelor of Dental Surgery
BEconSc	Bachelor of Economics

BECTU	Broadcasting, Entertainment, Cinematograph and Theatre Union
BEd	Bachelor of Education
BEng	Bachelor of Engineering
BEng and Man	Bachelor of Mechanical Engineering, Manufacture and Management
BER	Board for Engineers' Regulation
BFA	Bachelor of Fine Arts
BFin	Bachelor of Finance
BHA	British Hypnotherapy Association
BHI	British Horological Institute Ltd
BHS	British Horse Society
BHSAI	British Horse Society's Assistant Instructor's Certificate
BHSI	British Horse Society's Instructor's Certificate
BHSII	British Horse Society's Intermediate Instructor's Certificate
BHSIntSM	British Horse Society's Intermediate Stable Manager's Certificate
BHSSM	British Horse Society's Stable Manager's Certificate
BIA	Beauty Industry Authority
BIAT	British Institute of Architectural Technologists
BIBA	Bachelor of International Business Administration
BIE	British Institute of Embalmers
BIFA	British International Freight Association
BIPP	British Institute of Professional Photography
BIS	British Interplanetary Society
BKSTS	British Kinematograph Sound and Television Society
BLD	Bachelor of Landscape Design
BLE	Bachelor of Land Economy
BLEng	Bi-Lingual Engineer
BLib	Bachelor of Librarianship
BLing	Bachelor of Linguistics
BLitt	Bachelor of Letters
BLS	Bachelor of Library Studies
BM	Bachelor of Medicine
BMA	British Medical Association
BM, BCh	Conjoint degree of Bachelor of Medicine, Bachelor of Surgery
BM, BS	Conjoint degree of Bachelor of Medicine, Bachelor of Surgery
BMedBiol	Bachelor of Medical Biology
BMedSci	Bachelor of Medical Sciences
BMedSci(Speech)	Bachelor of Medical Sciences (Speech)
BMet	Bachelor of Metallurgy
BMid	Bachelor of Midwifery
BMidwif	Bachelor of Midwifery
BMSc	Bachelor of Medical Sciences
BMus	Bachelor of Music
BN	Bachelor of Nursing
BNNursing	Bachelor of Nursing, Nursing Studies
BNSc	Bachelor of Nursing
BNurs	Bachelor of Nursing
BOptom	Bachelor of Optometry
BPA	Bachelor of Performing Arts
BPharm	Bachelor of Pharmacy
BPhil	Bachelor of Philosophy
BPhil(Ed)	Bachelor of Philosophy (Education)
BPL	Bachelor of Planning

BSc	Bachelor of Science
BSc(Archit)	Bachelor of Science (Architecture)
BSc(DentSci)	Bachelor of Science in Dental Science
BSc(Econ)	Bachelor of Science in Economics
BSc(MedSci)	Bachelor of Science (Medical Science)
BSc(Social Science)	Bachelor of Science (Social Science)
BSc(Town & Regional Planning)	Bachelor of Science (Town & Regional Planning)
BSc(VetSc)	Bachelor of Science (Veterinary Science)
BScAgr	Bachelor of Science in Agriculture
BScEng	Bachelor of Science in Engineering
BScFor	Bachelor of Science in Forestry
BScTech	Bachelor of Technical Science
BSocSc	Bachelor of Social Science
BSSc	Bachelor of Social Science
BSSG	Member of the British Society of Scientific Glassblowers
BTEC	Business and Technology Education Council
BTech	Bachelor of Technology
BTechEd	Bachelor of Technological Education
BTEC HC	Business and Technology Education Council Higher Certificate
BTEC HD	Business and Technology Education Council Higher Diploma
BTEC HNC	Business and Technology Education Council Higher National Certificate
BTEC HND	Business and Technology Education Council Higher National Diploma
BTechS	Bachelor of Technology Studies
BTh	Bachelor of Theology
BTheol	Bachelor of Theology
BTP	Bachelor of Town Planning
BVC	Bar Vocational Course
BVetMed	Bachelor of Veterinary Medicine
BVMS	Bachelor of Veterinary Medicine
BVM&S	Bachelor of Veterinary Medicine
BVSc	Bachelor of Veterinary Science
C&G	City and Guilds
CA	Member of the Institute of Chartered Accountants of Scotland
CAA	Civil Aviation Authority
CABE	Companion of the Association of Business Executives
CACHE	Council for Awards in Children's Care and Education
CAE	Certificated Automotive Engineer
CAE	Companion of the Academy of Experts
CAM	Communication Advertising and Marketing Education Foundation
CAS	Certification of Accountancy Studies
CASS	Certificate of Applied Social Studies
CAT	Certificate for Accounting Technicians
CAT	College of Advanced Technology
CATS	Postgraduate Qualification by Credit Accumulation and Transfer
CBA	Companion of the British (Theatrical) Arts
CBAE	Companion of the British Academy of Experts
CBIM	Companion of the British Institute of Management
CBiol	Chartered Biologist
CBLC	Certificate in Business Language Competence
CBSSG	Craft Member of the British Society of Scientific Glassblowers
CCETSW	Central Council for Education and Training in Social Work

CChem	Chartered Chemist
CCol	Chartered Colourist
CCST	Certificate of Completion of Specialist Training
CDBA	Certified Doctor of Business Administration
CDipAF	Certified Diploma in Accounting and Finance
CEE	Extended European Command Endorsement
CeFA	Certificate for Financial Advisers
CEM	Certificate in Executive Management
CeMAP	Certificate in Mortgage Advice and Practice
CEng	Chartered Engineer
CertAMed	Certificate in Aviation Medicine
CertArb	Certificate in Arboriculture
CertBibKnowl	Certificate of Bible Knowledge
CertCIH	Chartered Institute of Housing recognised Housing Qualification
CertCM	Certificate of Cash Management
CertDesRCA	Certificate of Designer of the Royal College of Art
CertEd	Certificate in Education
CertEPK	Certificate of Essential Pensions Knowledge
CertHE	Certificate of Higher Education
CertHSAP	Certificate in Health Services Administration Practice
CertHSM	Certificate in Health Services Management
CertMFS	Certificate in the Marketing of Financial Services
CertOccHyg	Certificate in Operational Competence in Comprehensive Occupational Hygiene
CertRP	Certificate in Recruitment Practice
CertTEL	Certificate in the Teaching of European Languages
CertTESOL	Certificate of Teaching of English to Speakers of Other Languages
CertTEYL	Certificate of Teaching of English to Young Learners
CertYCW	Certificate in Youth and Community Work
CETHV	Certificate of Education in Training as Health Visitor
CEYA	Council for Early Years Awards
CFS	Certificate in Financial Services
CFSP	Certificate in Financial Services Practice
CGeol	Chartered Geologist
CGLI	City & Guilds of London Institute
CHARM	Centre for Hazard and Risk Management
ChB	Bachelor of Surgery
CHD	Choral-Training Diploma
ChM	Master of Surgery
CHP	Certificate in Hypnosis and Psychology
CHRIM	Certified Member of the Institute of Health Record Information and Management
CIAgrE	Companion of the Institution of Agricultural Engineers
CIArb	Chartered Institute of Arbitrators
CIB	Chartered Institute of Bankers
CIBM	Corporate Member of the Institute of Builders' Merchants
CIBS	Chartered Institute of Bankers in Scotland
CIBSE	Chartered Institution of Building Services Engineers
CIC	Construction Industry Council
CIEx	Companion of the Institute of Export
CIFE	Conference for Independent Further Education
CIH	Chartered Institute of Housing
CII	Chartered Insurance Institute
CILA	Chartered Institute of Loss Adjusters

CILIP	Chartered Institute of Library and Information Professionals
CIM	Chartered Institute of Marketing
CIMA	Chartered Institute of Management Accountants
CIMediE	Companion of the Institution of Mechanical Engineers
CIMgt	Companion of the Institute of Management
CIOB	Chartered Institute of Building
CIP	Certificate of Institute Practice
CIPD	Chartered Institute of Personnel and Development
CIPFA	Chartered Institute of Public Finance & Accounting
CIPS	Chartered Institute of Purchasing and Supply
CISOB	Counsellor of the Incorporated Society of Organ Builders
CIT	Certificate in Information Technology
CIWEM	Chartered Institution of Water and Environmental Management
CL(ABDO)	Diploma in Contact Lens Practice of the Association of British Dispensing Opticians
CLAC	Commercial Language Assistant Certificate
CLAIT	Computer Literacy & Information Technology
CLC	Council for Licensed Conveyancers
CLE	Limited European Command Endorsement
ClinPsyD	Doctorate in Clinical Psychology
CMA	Certificate in Management Accountancy
CMathFIMA	Fellow of the Institute of Mathematics and its Applications
CMBA	Certified Master of Business Administration
CMBHI	Craft Member of the British Horological Institute
CMC	Certified Management Consultants
CMet	Chartered Meteorologist
CMIWSc	Certified Member of the Institute of Wood Science
CMS	Certificate in Management Studies
CNAA	Council for National Academic Awards
COA	Certificate of Accreditation
COBC	Certificate of Basic Competence
CoEA	Certificate of Educational Achievement
COES	Certificate of Educational Studies
CofE	Church of England
CofS	Church of Scotland
CompBCS	Companion of the British Computer Society
CompIAP	Companion of the Institution of Analysts and Programmers
CompIEE	Companion of the Institution of Electrical Engineers
CompIGasE	Companion of the Institution of Gas Engineers
CompIManf	Companion of the Institute of Manufacturing
CompIMS	Companion of the Institute of Management Specialists
CompIP	Companion of the Institute of Plumbing
CorporateIRRV	Corporate Member of the Institute of Revenues, Rating and Valuation
COSCA	Confederation of Scottish Counselling Agencies
CPA	Chartered Patent Agents
CPC	Certificate of Professional Competence, the Institute of Transport Administration
CPD	Continuing Professional Development
CPE	Common Professional Exam
CPEA	Certificate of Practice in Estate Agency
CPFA	Member of Chartered Institute of Public Finance and Accountancy
CPhys	Chartered Physicist of the Institute of Physics
CPIM	Certificate in Production and Inventory Management

CPL	Commercial Pilot's Licence
CPM	Certified Professional Manager
CPP	Certificate of Pre-school Practice
CPR	Chartered Professional Review
CProfBTM	Companion of Professional Business and Technical Management
CPS	Certificate in Pastoral Studies and Applied Theology
CPSC	Certificate of Proficiency in Survival Craft
CPsychol	Chartered Psychologist, British Psychological Society
CPT	Continuing Professional Training
CPVE	Certificate of Pre-Vocational Training
CRAeS	Companion of the Royal Aeronautical Society
CRAH	Central Register of Advanced Hypnotherapists
CRCW	Church Related Community Workers
CRNCM	Companion of the Royal Northern College of Music
CSCT	Central School for Counselling Training
CSD	Chartered Society of Designers
CSE	Certificate of Secondary Education
CSM	Certificate in Safety Management
CSMGSM	Certificate in Stage Management (Guildhall School of Music and Drama)
CStat	Chartered Statistician
CSYS	Certificate of Sixth Year Studies
CTABRSM	Certificate of Teaching of the Associated Board of the Royal School of Music
CTextATI	Associate of the Textile Institute
CTextFTI	Fellow of the Textile Institute
CTHCM	Confederation of Tourism, Hotel and Catering Management
CVA	Certificated Value Analyst
CVM	Certificated Value Manager
CVT	Certified Vehicle Technologist
DA	Diploma in Anaesthetics
DAdmin	Doctor of Administration
DAES	Diploma in Advanced Educational Studies
DArch	Doctor of Architecture
DAvMed	Diploma in Aviation Medicine
DBA	Doctor of Business Administration
DBE	Diploma in Business Engineering
DBO	Diploma of the British Orthoptic Society
DBS	Diploma in Business Studies
DCC	Diploma of Chelsea College
DCDH	Diploma in Child Dental Health
DCE	Dangerous Cargo Endorsements
DCE	Diploma in Childcare and Education
DCG	Diploma in Careers Guidance
DCH	Diploma in Child Health
DChD	Diploma of Dental Surgery
DChM	Diploma in Chiropodial Medicine, Institute of Chiropodists and Podiatrists
DCHT	Diploma in Community Health in Tropical Countries
DCL	Doctor of Civil Law
DCLF	Diploma in Contact Lens Fitting
DClinPsych	Doctor of Clinical Psychiatry
DCLP	Diploma in Contact Lens Practice
DCR(R)or(T)	Diploma of the College of Radiographers
DD	Doctor of Divinity

DDH(Birm)	Diploma in Dental Health, University of Birmingham
DDOrthRCPSGlas	Diploma in Dental Orthopaedics of the Royal College of Physicians and Surgeons of Glasgow
DDPHRCS(Eng)	Diploma in Dental Public Health, Royal College of Surgeons of England
DDS	Doctor of Dental Surgery
DDSc	Doctor of Dental Science
DEBA	Diploma in European Business Administration
DEdPsy	Doctor of Educational Psychiatry
DEM	Diploma in Executive Management
DEng	Doctor of Engineering
DES	Department of Education and Science (now the Department for Education)
DETR	Department of the Environment, Transport and the Regions
DFin	Doctor of Finance
DFSM	Diploma in Financial Services Management
DGA	Diamond Member of the Gemmological Association and Gem Testing Laboratory of Great Britain
DGDPRCSEng	Diploma in General Dental Practice, Royal College of Surgeons of England
DGM	Diploma in Geriatric Medicine
DGO	Diploma in Obstetrics and Gynaecology
DHC	Doctorate in Healthcare
DHE	Diploma in Horticulture, Royal Botanic Garden, Edinburgh
DHMSA	Diploma in the History of Medicine, Society of Apothecaries of London
DHP	Diploma in Hypnosis and Psychotherapy
DIA	Diploma of Industrial Administration
DIB	Diploma in International Business
DIC	Diploma of Membership of Imperial College of Science and Technology, University of London
DIH	Diploma in Industrial Health
DipABRSM	Diploma of the Associated Board of the Royal Schools of Music
DipAD	Diploma in Art and Design
DipAdvHYP	Diploma in Advanced Hypnotherapy
DipAE	Diploma in Adult Education
DipAgrComm	Diploma in Agricultural Communication
DipArb	Diploma in Arbitration
DipArb	Diploma in Arboriculture
DipArch	Diploma in Architecture
DipASE(CofP)	Graduate Level Specialist Diploma in Advanced Study in Education, College of Preceptors
DipASSc	Diploma in Arts and Social Sciences
DipAT	Diploma in Accounting Technology
DipAvMed	Diploma in Aviation Medicine
DipBA	Diploma in Business Administration
DipBldgCons	Diploma in Building Conservation
DipBMA	Diploma in Business Management
DipCAM	Diploma in the Communication Advertising and Marketing Education Foundation
DipCD	Diploma in Community Development
DipCHM	Diploma in Choir Training, Royal College of Organists
DipClinPath	Diploma in Clinical Pathology
DipCOT	Diploma of the College of Occupational Therapists
DipCP	Diploma of the College of Teachers
DipCT	Diploma in Corporate Treasury Management
DipDerm	Diploma in Dermatology

DipEd	Diploma in Education
DipEF	Diploma in Executive Finance
DipEH	Diploma in Environmental Health
DipEM	Diploma in Environmental Management
DipEMA	Diploma in Executive and Management Accountancy
DipEngLit	Diploma in English Literature
DipFD	Diploma in Funeral Directing, National Association of Funeral Directors
DipFS	Diploma in Financial Services
DipGAI	Diploma of the Guild of Architectural Ironmongers
DipGrTrans	Diploma in Greek Translation
DipGSM	Diploma of the Guildhall School of Music and Drama
DipHE	Diploma of Higher Education
DipHS	Diploma of the Heraldry Society
DipIEB	Diploma of the International Employee Benefits
DipISW	Diploma of the Institute of Social Welfare
DipLE	Diploma in Land Economy
DipLP	Diploma in Legal Practice
DipM	Postgraduate Diploma in Marketing
DipMedAc	Diploma in Medical Acupuncture
DipMetEng	Diploma in Meteorological Engineering
DipMFS	Diploma in the Marketing of Financial Services
DipMth	Diploma in Music Therapy
DipOccH	Diploma in Occupational Health
DipOccHyg	Diploma of Professional Competence in Comprehensive Occupational Hygiene
DipPDTC	Diploma in Professional Dancers Teaching Course
DipPharmMed	Diploma in Pharmaceutical Medicine
DipPhil	Diploma in Philosophy
DipProjMan	Diploma in Project Management
DipPropInv	Diploma in Property Investment
DipRAM	Diploma of the Royal Academy of Music
DipRCM	Diploma of the Royal College of Music
DipRMS	Diploma of the Royal Microscopical Society
DipSc	Diploma in Science
DipSM	Diploma in Safety Management
DipSurv	Diploma in Surveying
DipSW	Diploma in Social Work
DipTCL	Diploma of the Trinity College of Music, London
DipTCR	Diploma in Organ Teaching
DipTESOL	Diploma in Teaching of English to Speakers of Other Languages
DipTHP	Diploma in Therapeutic Hypnosis and Psychotherapy
DipTM	Diploma in Training Management, Institute of Personnel and Development
DipTransIoL	Diploma in Translation, Institute of Linguists
DipUniv	Diploma of the University
DipVen	Diploma in Venereology, Society of Apothecaries of London
DipWCF	Diploma of the Worshipful Company of Farriers
DIS	Diploma in Industrial Studies
DLang	Doctor of Language
DLit(t)	Doctor of Letters or Literature
DLO	Diploma of Laryngology and Otology
DLORCSEng	Diploma in Laryngology and Otology, Royal College of Surgeons of England
DLP	Diploma in Legal Practice
DM	Doctor of Medicine

DMedRehab	Diploma in Medical Rehabilitation
DMedSc	Doctor in Medical Science
DMet	Doctor of Metallurgy
DMJ(Clin) or DMJ(Path)	Diploma in Medical Jurisprudence (Clinical or Pathological), Society of Apothecaries of London
DMRD	Diploma in Medical Radio-Diagnosis
DMRT	Diploma in Radiotherapy
DMS	Diploma in Management Studies
DMU	Diploma in Medical Ultrasound
DMus	Doctor of Music
DMusCantuar	Archbishop of Canterbury's Doctorate in Music
DNSc	Doctor in Nursing Science
DO	Diploma in Ophthalmology
DO	Diploma in Osteopathy
DocEdPsy	Doctorate in Educational Psychology
DOpt	Diploma in Ophthalmic Optics
DOrth	Diploma in Orthoptics
DOrthRCSEdin	Diploma in Orthodontics, Royal College of Surgeons of Edinburgh
DOrthRCSEng	Diplomate in Orthodontics, Royal College of Surgeons of England
DP	Diploma in Psychotherapy
DPA	Diploma in Public Administration
DpBact	Diploma in Bacteriology
DPD(Dund)	Diploma in Public Dentistry, University of Dundee
DPH	Diploma in Public Health
DPharm	Diploma in Pharmacy
DPhil	Diploma in Philosophy
DPHRCSEng	Diploma in Dental Public Health, Royal College of Surgeons of England
DPM	Diploma in Psychological Medicine
DPodM	Diploma in Podiatric Medicine
DProf	Doctor of Professional Studies
DPS	Diploma in Professional Studies
DPSE	Diploma in Pastoral Studies and Applied Theology
DPsychol	Doctor of Psychology
DrAc	Doctor of Acupuncture
Dr(RCA)	Doctor of the Royal College of Art
DRCOG	Diploma of the Royal College of Obstetricians and Gynaecologists
DRDRCSEd	Diploma in Restorative Dentistry, Royal College of Surgeons of Edinburgh
DRE	Diploma in Remedial Electrolysis, Institute of Electrolysis
DRI	Diploma in Radionuclide Imaging
DRSAMD	Diploma in the Royal Scottish Academy of Music and Drama
DSA	Diploma in Secretarial Administration
DSc	Doctor of Science
DSc(Econ)	Doctor of Science (Economics) or in Economics
DSc(Eng)	Doctor of Science (Engineering)
DSc(Social)	Doctor of Science in the Social Sciences
DScEcon	Doctor in the Faculty of Economics and Social Studies
DSCh(Ox)	Diploma in Surgical Chiropody (Oxon), Oxford School of Chiropody and Podiatry
DScTech	Doctor of Technical Science
DSocSc	Doctor of Social Science
DSSc	Doctor of Social Science
DSTA	Diploma Member of the Swimming Teachers' Association
DTCD	Diploma in Tuberculosis and Chest Diseases

DTech	Doctor of Technology
DTI	Department of Trade and Industry
DTMH	Diploma in Tropical Medicine and Hygiene
DTM&H	Diploma in Tropical Medicine and Hygiene
DTp	Department of Transport
DUniv	Doctor of the University
DVetMed	Doctor of Veterinary Medicine
DVM	Doctor of Veterinary Medicine
DVM&S	Doctor of Veterinary Medicine and Surgery
DVS	Doctor of Veterinary Surgery
DVSc	Doctor of Veterinary Science
ECBL	European Certification Board for Logistics
ECDL	European Computer Driving Licence
ECG	Executive Group Committees (of the Board for Engineers Registration)
EDBA	Executive Diploma in Business Accounting
EdD	Doctor of Education
EDH	Efficient Deck Hand
EdPsyD	Doctor of Educational Psychology
EEAC	European Executive Assistant Certificate
EFB	English for Business
EFL	English as a Foreign Language
EHO	Environmental Health Officer
EIS	Educational Institute of Scotland
EITB	Engineering Industry Training Board
EMBA	European Master of Business Administration
EMBS	European Master of Business Sciences
EMFEC	East Midland Further Education Council
EN	Enrolled Nurse
EN(G)	Enrolled Nurse (General)
EN(M)	Enrolled Nurse (Mental)
EN(MH)	Enrolled Nurse (Mental Handicap)
ENB	English National Board
EngC	Engineering Council
EngD	Doctor of Engineering
EngTech	Engineering Technician
ENS	Electronic Navigational System
ESD	Executive Secretary's Diploma
ESOL	English for Speakers of Other Languages
ESSTL	Engineering Services Training Trust Ltd
EurIng	European Engineer
EuroBiol	European Biologist
FABE	Fellow of the Association of Business Executives
FACB	Fellow of the Association of Certified Bookkeepers
FACP	Fellow of the Association of Computer Professionals
FAE	Fellow of the Academy of Experts
FAFC	Fellow of the Association of Financial Controllers and Administrators
FAIA	Fellow of the Association of International Accountants
FAMS	Fellow of the Association of Medical Secretaries, Practice Managers, Administrators and Receptionists
FAPM	Fellow of the Association for Project Management
FASI	Fellow of the Ambulance Service Institute
FASI	Fellow of the Architecture and Surveying Institute

FASP	Fellow of the Association of Sales Personnel
FBA	Fellow of the British Academy
FBA	Fellow of the British (Theatrical) Arts
FBCS	Fellow of the British Computer Society
FBDO	Fellow of the Association of British Dispensing Opticians
FBDO(Hons)	Fellow of the Association of British Dispensing Opticians with Honours Diploma
FBDO(Hons)CL	Fellow of the Association of British Dispensing Opticians with Honours Diploma and Diploma in Contact Lens Practice
FBEI	Fellow of the Institution of Body Engineers
FBEng	Fellow of the Association of Building Engineers
FBHA	Fellow of the British Hypnotherapy Association
FBHI	Fellow of the British Horological Institute
FBHS	Fellow of the British Horse Society
FBID	Fellow of the British Institute of Interior Design
FBIDST	Fellow of the British Institute of Dental and Surgical Technologists
FBIE	Fellow of the British Institute of Embalmers
FBIPP	Fellow of the British Institute of Professional Photography
FBIS	Fellow of the British Interplanetary Society
FBMA	Fellow of the Business Management Association
FBPsS	Fellow of the British Psychological Society
FCA	Fellow of the Institute of Chartered Accountants in England and Wales
FCAM	Fellow of the Communication Advertising and Marketing Education Foundation
FCB	Fellow of the British Association of Communicators in Business Ltd
FCBSI	Fellow of the Chartered Building Societies Institute
FCCA	Fellow of the Association of Chartered Certified Accountants
FCEA	Fellow of the Institute of Cost and Executive Accountants
FCGI	Fellowship, City & Guilds
FChS	Fellow of the Society of Chiropodists and Podiatrists
FCI	Faculty of Commerce and Industry
FCI	Fellow of the Institute of Commerce
FCIArb	Fellow of the Chartered Institute of Arbitrators
FCIB	Fellow of the Chartered Institute of Bankers
FCIBS	Fellow of the Chartered Institute of Bankers in Scotland
FCIBSE	Fellow of the Chartered Institute of Building Services Engineers
FCIH	Fellow of the Chartered Institute of Housing
FCII	Fellow of the Chartered Insurance Institute
FCIJ	Fellow of the Chartered Institute of Journalists
FCILA	Fellow of the Chartered Institute of Loss Adjusters
FCIM	Fellow of the Chartered Institute of Marketing
FCIOB	Fellow of the Chartered Institute of Building
FCIPD	Fellow of the Chartered Institute of Personnel and Development
FCIPS	Fellow of the Chartered Institute of Purchasing and Supply
FCIS	Fellow of the Institute of Chartered Secretaries and Administrators
FCIT	Fellow of the Chartered Institute of Transport
FCLIP	Chartered Fellow of CILIP
FCLS	First Certificate for Legal Secretaries
FCMA	Fellow of the Chartered Institute of Management Accountants
FCMA	Fellow of the Institute of Cost and Management Accountants
FCMC	Fellow Grade Certified Management Consultants
FCOphth	Fellow of the College of Ophthalmology
FCOptom	Fellow of the College of Optometrists
FCoT	Ordinary Fellow of the College of Teachers

FCPM	Fellow of the Confederation of Professional Management
FCPP	Fellow of the College of Pharmacy Practice
FCSP	Fellow of the Chartered Society of Physiotherapy
FCT	Fellow of the Association of Corporate Treasurers
FCoT	Fellow of the College of Teachers
FCTHCM	Fellow of the Confederation of Tourism, Hotel and Catering Management
FCYW	Fellow of the Community and Youth Work Association
FDSRCPSGlas	Fellow in Dental Surgery of the Royal College of Surgeons of Glasgow
FDSRCSEd	Fellow in Dental Surgery of the Royal College of Physicians and Surgeons of Edinburgh
FDSRCSEng	Fellow in Dental Surgery of the Royal College of Surgeons of England
FE	Further Education
FEANI	Fédération Européene d'Associations Nationales d'Ingénieurs
FECI	Fellow of the Institute of Employment Consultants
FEFC	Further Education Funding Council
FEIS	Fellow of the Educational Institute of Scotland
FFA	Fellow of the Faculty of Actuaries
FFA	Fellow of the Institute of Financial Accountants
FFARCSEng	Fellow of the Faculty of Anaesthetists of the Royal College of Surgeons in England
FFARCSIrel	Fellow of the Faculty of Anaesthetists of the Royal College of Surgeons in Ireland
FFAS	Fellow of the Faculty of Architects and Surveyors (Architects)
FFCA	Fellow of the Association of Financial Controllers and Administrators
FFCI	Fellow of the Faculty of Commerce and Industry
FFCS	Fellow of the Faculty of Secretaries
FFHom	Fellow of the Faculty of Homeopathy
FFPHM	Fellow of the Faculty of Public Health Medicine, Royal College of Physicians of London and Edinburgh and Royal College of Physicians and Surgeons of Glasgow
FFPHMIrel	Fellow of the Faculty of Public Health Medicine, Royal College of Physicians of Ireland
FFRRCSIrel	Fellow of the Faculty of Radiologists, Royal College of Surgeons in Ireland
FFS	Fellow of the Faculty of Architects and Surveyors (Surveyors)
FGA	Fellow of the Gemmological Association and Gem Testing Laboratory of Great Britain
FGCL	Fellow of the Guild of Cleaners and Launderers
FGI	Fellow of the Greek Institute
FGSM	Fellow of the Guildhall School of Music and Drama
FHCIMA	Fellow of the Hotel and Catering International Management Association
FHFS	Fellow of the Council of Health, Fitness and Sports Therapists
FHG	Fellow of the Institute of Heraldic and Genealogical Studies
FHRIM	Fellow of the Institute of Health Record Information and Management
FHS	Fellow of the Heraldry Society
FHSM	Fellow of the Institute of Health Services Management
FHT	Federation of Holistic Therapies
FIA	Fellow of the Institute of Actuaries
FIAB	Fellow of the International Association of Book-keepers
FIAEA	Fellow of the Institute of Automotive Engineer Assessors
FIAgrE	Fellow of the Institution of Agricultural Engineers
FIAP	Fellow of the Institution of Analysts and Programmers
FIAT	Fellow of the Institute of Asphalt Technology
FIBA	Fellow of the Institution of Business Agents
FIBC	Fellow of the Institute of Building Control

FIBCM	Fellow of the Institute of British Carriage and Automobile Manufacturers
FIBCO	Fellow of the Institute of Building Control Officers
FIBE	Fellow of the Institution of British Engineers
FIBF	Fellow of the Institute of British Foundrymen
FIBiol	Fellow of the Institute of Biology
FIBM	Fellow of the Institute of Builders' Merchants
FIBMS	Fellow of the Institute of Biomedical Science
FIBMS	Fellow of the Institute of Medical Laboratory Sciences
FICA	Fellow of the Institute of Company Accountants
FICB	Fellow of the Institute of Certified Book-Keepers
FICE	Fellow of the Institution of Civil Engineers
FIChemE	Fellow of the Institution of Chemical Engineers
FIChor	Fellow of the Benesh Institute of Choreology
FICHT	Fellow of the International Council of Holistic Therapies
FICM	Fellow of the Institute of Credit Management
FICorr	Fellow of the Institute of Corrosion
FICS	Fellow of the Institute of Chartered Shipbrokers
FICW	Fellow of the Institute of Clerks of Works of Great Britain Incorporated
FIDTA	Fellow of the International Dance Teachers' Association
FIED	Fellow of the Institution of Engineering Designers
FIEE	Fellow of the Institution of Electrical Engineers
FIEM	Fellow of the Institute of Executives and Managers
FIEx	Fellow of the Institute of Export
FIExpE	Fellow of the Institute of Explosives Engineers
FIFBQ	Fellow of the International Faculty of Business Qualifications
FIFireE	Fellow of the Institution of Fire Engineers
FIFM	Fellow of the Institute of Fisheries Management
FIFST	Fellow of the Institute of Food Science and Technology
FIGasE	Fellow of the Institution of Gas Engineers
FIGD	Fellow of the Institute of Grocery Distribution
FIGeol	Fellow of the Institute of Geologists
FIHEc	Fellow of the Institute of Home Economics Ltd
FIHIE	Fellow of the Institute of Highway Incorporated Engineers
FIHort	Fellow of the Institute of Horticulture
FIHT	Fellow of the Institution of Highways and Transportation
FIIE	Fellow of the Institution of Incorporated Engineers
FIIHTM	Fellow of the International Institute of Hospitality Tourism & Management
FIIM	Fellow of the International Institute of Management
FIIMR	Fellow of the Institute of Investment Management and Research
FIIRSM	Fellow of the International Institute of Risk and Safety Management
FIISE	Fellow of the International Institute of Social Economics
FIISec	Fellow of the International Institute of Security
FIL	Fellow of the Institute of Linguists
FILAM	Fellow of the Institute of Leisure and Amenity Management
FILT	Fellow of the Institute of Logistics and Transport
FIM	Fellow of the Institute of Materials
FIMA	Fellow of the Institute of Mathematics and its Applications
FIManf	Fellow of the Institute of Manufacturing
FIMarE	Fellow of the Institute of Marine Engineers
FIMatM	Fellow of the Institute of Materials Management
FIMBM	Fellow of the Institute of Maintenance and Building Management
FIMechE	Fellow of the Institute of Mechanical Engineers

FIMechIE	Fellow of the Institute of Mechanical Incorporated Engineers
FIMF	Fellow of the Institute of Metal Finishing
FIMgt	Fellow of the Institute of Management
FIMI	Fellow of the Institute of the Motor Industry
FIMIS	Fellow of the Institute for the Management of Information Systems
FIMM	Fellow of the Institute of Massage and Movement
FIMM	Fellow of the Institution of Mining and Metallurgy
FIMM	International Federation of Manual Medicine
FIMS	Fellow of the Institute of Management Specialists
FIMunE	Fellow of the Institution of Municipal Engineers
FInstAEA	Fellow of the Institute of Automotive Engineer Assessors
FInstAM	Fellow of the Institute of Administrative Management
FInstBA	Fellow of the Institute of Business Administration
FInstBCA	Fellow of the Institute of Burial and Cremation Administration
FInstBM	Fellow of the Institute of Builders' Merchants
FInstBRM	Fellow of the Institute of Baths and Recreation Management
FInstCh	Fellow of the Institute of Chiropodists
FInstCM	Fellow of the Institute of Commercial Management
FInstD	Fellow of the Institute of Directors
FInstE	Fellow of the Institute of Energy
FInstLEx	Fellow of the Institute of Legal Executives
FInstMC	Fellow of the Institute of Measurement and Control
FInstNDT	Fellow of the British Institute of Non-Destructive Testing
FInstP	Fellow of the Institute of Physics
FInstPet	Fellow of the Institute of Petroleum
FInstPkg	Fellow of the Institute of Packaging
FInstPM	Fellow of the Institute of Professional Managers and Administrators
FInstPS	Fellow of the Institute of Purchasing and Supply
FInstR	Fellow of the Institute of Refrigeration
FInstSMM	Fellow of the Institute of Sales and Marketing Management
FInstTA	Fellow of the Institute of Transport Administration
FInstTT	Fellow of the Institute of Travel and Tourism
FInstWM	Fellow of the Institute of Wastes Management
FInstWM	Fellowship of the Institute of Wastes Management
FIntMC	Fellow of International Management Centre
FIOC	Fellow of the Institute of Carpenters
FIOM	Fellow of the Institute of Operations Management
FIOP	Fellow of the Institute of Plumbing
FIOP	Fellow of the Institute of Printing
FIOSH	Fellow of the Institution of Occupational Safety and Health
FIPA	Fellow of the Institute of Practitioners in Advertising
FIPD	Fellow of the Institute of Personnel Development
FIPI	Fellow of the Institute of Professional Investigators
FIPlantE	Fellow of the Institution of Plant Engineers
FIPR	Fellow of the Institute of Public Relations
FIQ	Fellow of the Institute of Quarrying
FIQA	Fellow of the Institute of Quality Assurance
FIR	Fellow of the Institute of Population Registration
FIRSE	Fellow of the Institution of Railway Signal Engineers
FIRTE	Fellow of the Institute of Road Transport Engineers
FIS	Fellow of the Institute of Statisticians
FISM	Fellow of the Institute for Supervision & Management

FISOB	Fellow of the Incorporated Society of Organ Builders
FISTC	Fellow of the Institute of Scientific and Technical Communicators
FISTD	Fellow of the Imperial Society of Teachers of Dancing
FIStrucE	Fellow of the Institution of Structural Engineers
FISW	Fellow of the Institute of Social Welfare
FIT	Foundation Insurance Test
FITD	Fellow of the Institute of Training and Development
FITSA	Fellow of the Institute of Trading Standards Administration
FIVehE	Fellow of the Institute of Vehicle Engineers
FIWM	Fellow of the Institute of Wastes Management
FLAW	Foreign Languages at Work
FLCM	Fellow of the London College of Music
FLCSP	Fellow of the London and Counties Society of Physiologists
FLI	Fellow of the Landscape Institute
FLIC	Foreign Languages for Industry and Commerce
FLS	Fellow of the Linnean Society of London
FMA	Fellow of the Museums Association
FMAAT	Fellow Member of the Association of Accounting Technicians
FMPA	Fellow of the Master Photographers Association
FMR	Fellow of the Association of Health Care Information and Medical Records Officers
FMS	Fellow of the Institute of Management Services
FMusEd	Fellowship in Music Education
FN	Fellow of the Nautical Society
FNAEA	Fellow of the National Association of Estate Agents
FNAEAHon	Honoured Fellow of the National Association of Estate Agents
FNCP	Fellow of the National Council of Psychotherapists
FNI	Fellow of the Nautical Institute
FNIMH	Fellow of the National Institute of Medical Herbalists
FPC	Financial Planning Certificate
FPC	Foundation for Psychotherapy and Counselling
FPCS	Fellow of the Property Consultants Society
FPMI	Fellow of the Pensions Management Institute
FPodS	Fellow of the Surgical Faculty of the College of Podiatrists
FProfBTM	Fellow of Professional Business and Technical Management
FRAeS	Fellow of the Royal Aeronautical Society
FRAS	Fellow of the Royal Astronomical Society
FRCA	Fellow of the Royal College of Anaesthetists
FRCGP	Fellow of the Royal College of General Practitioners
FRCM	Fellow of the Royal College of Music
FRCO	Fellow of the Royal College of Organists
FRCO(CHM)	Fellow of the Royal College of Organists (Choir-training Diploma)
FRCOG	Fellow of the Royal College of Obstetricians and Gynaecologists
FRCP	Fellow of the Royal College of Physicians of London
FRCPath	Fellow of the Royal College of Pathologists
FRCPEdin	Fellow of the Royal College of Physicians of Edinburgh
FRCPsych	Fellow of the Royal College of Psychiatrists
FRCR	Fellow of the Royal College of Radiologists
FRCS(Irel)	Fellow of the Royal College of Surgeons in Ireland
FRCSEd	Fellow of the Royal College of Surgeons of Edinburgh
FRCSEd(C/TH)	Fellow of the Royal College of Surgeons of Edinburgh, specialising in Cardiothoracic Surgery

FRCSEd(Orth)	Fellow of the Royal College of Surgeons of Edinburgh, specialising in Orthopaedic Surgery
FRCSEd(SN)	Fellow of the Royal College of Surgeons of Edinburgh, specialising in Surgical Neurology
FRCSEng	Fellow of the Royal College of Surgeons of England
FRCSEng(Oto)	Fellow of the Royal College of Surgeons of England, with Otolaryngology
FRCSGlasg	Fellow of the Royal College of Physicians and Surgeons of Glasgow
FRCVS	Fellow of the Royal College of Veterinary Surgeons
FREC	Fellow of the Recruitment and Employment Confederation
FRHS	Fellow of the Royal Horticultural Society
FRIBA	Fellow of the Royal Institute of British Architects
FRICS	Fellow of the Royal Institution of Chartered Surveyors
FRIN	Fellow of the Royal Institute of Navigation
FRINA	Fellow of the Royal Institution of Naval Architects
FRIPHH	Fellow of the Royal Institution of Public Health and Hygiene
FRNCM	Fellow of the Royal Northern College of Music
FRPharmS	Fellow of the Royal Pharmaceutical Society of Great Britain
FRPS	Fellow of the Royal Photographic Society
FRS	Fellow of the Royal Society
FRSC	Fellow of the Royal Society of Chemistry
FRSCM	Fellow of the Royal School of Church Music
FRSH	Fellow of the Royal Society for the Promotion of Health
FRTPI	Fellow of the Royal Town Planning Institute
FSAPP	Fellow of the Society of Advanced Psychotherapy Practitioners
FSBP	Fellow of the Society of Business Practitioners
FSBT	Fellow of the Society of Teachers in Business Education
FSCT	Fellow of the Society of Claims Technicians
FSDC	Fellow of the Society of Dyers and Colourists
FSE	Fellow of the Society of Engineers (Inc)
FSElec	Fellow of the Society of Electroscience
FSG	Fellow of the Society of Genealogists
FSG(Hon)	Honorary Fellow of the Society of Genealogists
FSGT	Fellow of the Society of Glass Technology
FSIAD	Fellow of the Society of Industrial Artists and Designers
FSMA	Fellow of the Society of Martial Arts
FSMA	Fellow of the Society of Sales Management Administrators Ltd
FSNN	Fellow of the Society of Nursery Nursing
FSS	Fellow of the Royal Statistical Society
FSSCh	Fellow of the British Chiropody and Podiatry Association
FSSF	Fellow of the Society of Shoe Fitters
FSTA	Fellow of the Swimming Teachers' Association
FSVA	Fellow of the Incorporated Society of Valuers and Auctioneers
FTCL	Fellow of the Trinity College of Music
FTI	Fellow of the Textile Institute
FTII	Fellow of the Chartered Institute of Taxation
FTSC	Fellow of the Oil and Colour Chemists' Association
FTSC	Fellow in the Technology of Surface Coatings
FWeldI	Fellow of the Welding Institute
FYDA	Associate Fellowship of the Youth Development Association
GAGTL	Gemmological Association and Gem Testing Laboratory of Great Britain
GAI	Guild of Architectural Ironmongers
GASI	Graduate Member of the Ambulance Service Institute

GBSM	Graduate of the Birmingham School of Music
GCE	General Certificate of Education
GCE A	General Certificate of Education Advanced Level
GCE O	General Certificate of Education Ordinary Level
GCGI	Graduateship, City & Guilds
GCL	Guild of Cleaners and Launderers
GCSE	General Certificate of Secondary Education
GDC	General Dental Council
GIBCM	Graduate of the Institute of British Carriage and Automobile Manufacturers
GIBiol	Graduate of the Institute of Biology
GIEM	Graduate of the Institute of Executives and Managers
GIMA	Graduate of the Institute of Mathematics and its Applications
GIMI	Graduate of the Institute of the Motor Industry
GInstP	Graduate of the Institute of Physics
GIntMC	Graduate of the International Management Centre
GIS	Graduate Imaging Scientist
GLCM	Graduate Diploma of the London College of Music
GMAT	Graduate Management Admissions Test
GMC	General Medical Council
GMDSS	Global Maritime Distress & Safety System
GMInstM	Graduate Member of the Meat Training Council
GMus	Graduate Diploma in Music
GMusRNCM	Graduate in Music of the Royal Northern College of Music
GNSM	Graduate of the Northern School of Music
GNVQ	General National Vocational Qualifications
GradAES	Graduate of the Royal Aeronautical Society
GradBEng	Graduate Member of the Association of Building Engineers
GradBHI	Graduate of the British Horological Institute
GradDip	Graduate Diploma
GradIAP	Graduate of the Institution of Analysts and Programmers
GradIBE	Graduate of the Institution of British Engineers
GradIElecIE	Graduate of the Institution of Electrical and Electronics Incorporated Engineers
GradIIE	Graduate of the Institution of Incorporated Engineers
GradIISec	Graduate of the International Institute of Security
GradIManf	Graduate of the Institute Manufacturing
GradIMF	Graduate of the Institute of Metal Finishing
GradIMS	Graduate of the Institute of Management Specialists
GradInstNDT	Graduate of the British Institute of Non-Destructive Testing
GradInstP	Graduate of the Institute of Physics
GradInstPS	Graduate of the Institute of Purchasing and Supply
GradIOP	Graduate of the Institute of Printing
GradIPD	Graduate of the Institute of Personnel and Development
GradIS	Graduate of the Institute of Statisticians
GradISCA	Graduate of the Institute of Chartered Secretaries and Administrators
GradMechE	Graduate of the Institution of Mechanical Engineers
GradMIWM	Graduate Member of the Institute of Wastes Management
GradRNCM	Graduate of the Royal Northern College of Music
GradRSC	Graduate of the Royal Society of Chemistry
GradSMA	Graduate of the Society of Martial Arts
GradStat	Graduate Statistician
GraduateCIPD	Graduate of the Chartered Institute of Personnel and Development
GraduateIEIE	Graduate of the Institution of Electrical and Electronics Incorporated Engineers

GradWeldI	Graduate of the Welding Institute
GRC	General Readers Certificate
GRC	Grade Related Criteria
GRIC	Graduate Membership of the Royal Institute of Chemistry
GRSC	Graduate of the Royal Society of Chemistry
GRSM	Graduate Diploma of the Royal Manchester School of Music
GRSM(Hons)	Graduate of the Royal Schools of Music
GSMA	Graduate of the Society of Sales Management Administrators Ltd
GSNN	Graduate of the Society of Nursery Nursing
GTC	General Teaching Council
HABIA	Hairdressing and Beauty Industry Authority
HC	Higher Certificate
HCIMA	Hotel and Catering International Management Association
HD	Higher Diploma
HDCR (R) or (T)	Higher Award in Radiodiagnosis or Radiotherapy, College of Radiographers
HEFCE	Higher Education Funding Council for England
HFInstE	Honorary Fellow of the Institute of Energy
HNC	Higher National Certificate
HND	Higher National Diploma
HonASTA	Honorary Associate of the Swimming Teachers' Association
HonDrRCA	Honorary Doctorate of the Royal College of Art
HonFAE	Honorary Fellow of the Academy of Experts
HonFBID	Honorary Fellow of the British Institute of Interior Design
HonFBIPP	Honorary Fellow of the British Institute of Professional Photography
HonFCP	Charter Fellow of the College of Preceptors
HonFEIS	Honorary Fellow of the Educational Institute of Scotland
HonFHCIMA	Honorary Fellow of the Hotel, Catering and Institutional Management Association
HonFHS	Honorary Fellow of the Heraldry Society
HonFIEE	Honorary Fellow of the Institution of Electrical Engineers
HonFIExpE	Honorary Fellow of the Institute of Explosives Engineers
HonFIGasE	Honorary Fellow of the Institution of Gas Engineers
HonFIMarE	Honorary Fellow of the Institute of Marine Engineers
HonFIMechE	Honorary Fellow of the Institution of Mechanical Engineers
HonFIMM	Honorary Fellow of the Institution of Mining and Metallurgy
HonFInstE	Honorary Fellow of the Institute of Energy
HonFInstMC	Honorary Fellow of the Institute of Measurement and Control
HonFInstNDT	Honorary Fellow of the British Institute of Non-Destructive Testing
HonFIQA	Honorary Fellow of the Institute of Quality Assurance
HonFIRSE	Honorary Fellow of the Institution of Railway Signal Engineers
HonFIRTE	Honorary Fellow of the Institute of Road Transport Engineers
HonFPRI	Honorary Fellow of the Plastics and Rubber Institute
HonFRIN	Honorary Fellow of the Royal Institute of Navigation
HonFRINA	Honorary Fellow of the Royal Institution of Naval Architects
HonFRPS	Honorary Fellow of the Royal Photographic Society
HonFSE	Honorary Fellow of the Society of Engineers (Inc)
HonFSGT	Honorary Fellow of the Society of Glass Technology
HonFWeldI	Honorary Fellow of the Welding Institute
HonGSM	Honorary Member of the Guildhall School of Music and Drama
HonMIFM	Honorary Member of the Institute of Fisheries Management
HonMInstNDT	Honorary Member of the British Institute of Non-Destructive Testing
HonMRIN	Honorary Member of the Royal Institute of Navigation
HonMWES	Honorary Member of the Women's Engineering Society

HonRAM	Honorary Member of the Royal Academy of Music
HonRCM	Honorary Member of the Royal College of Music
HonRNCM	Honorary Member of the Royal Northern College of Music
HonRSCM	Honorary Member of the Royal School of Church Music
HSC	Higher School Certificate
HSE	Health & Safety Executive
HTB	Hairdressing Training Board
HTC	Higher Technical Certificate
IAAP	International Association for Analytic Psychology
IAB	International Association of Book-Keepers
IABC	International Association of Business Computing
IAC	Investment Advice Certificate
IAgrE	Institution of Agricultural Engineers
IAP	Institution of Analysts and Programmers
IAQ	Investment Administration Qualification
IAT	Institute of Asphalt Technology
IBA	Institute of Business Administration
IBC	Institute of Building Control
IBE	Institution of British Engineers
IBF	Institute of British Foundrymen
IBMS	Institute of Biomedical Science
ICAEW	Institute of Chartered Accountants in England and Wales
ICAI	Institute of Chartered Accountants in Ireland
ICAS	Institute of Chartered Accountants of Scotland
ICB	Institute of Certified Book-Keepers
ICE	Institution of Civil Engineers
ICEA	Institute of Cost and Executive Accountants
ICG	Institute of Careers Guidance
IChemE	Institution of Chemical Engineers
ICIOB	Incorporated Member of the Chartered Institute of Building
ICM	Institute of Commercial Management
ICM	Institute of Complementary Medicine
ICM	Institute of Credit Management
ICMQ	International Capital Markets Qualification
ICSA	Institute of Chartered Secretaries and Administrators
ICSF	Intermediate Certificate of the Society of Floristry
IDA	Improvement and Development Agency
IDTA	International Dance Teachers' Association Ltd
IED	Institution of Engineering Designers
IEE	Institution of Electrical Engineers
IEM	Institute of Executives and Managers
IEng	Incorporated Engineer
IETTL	Insulation and Environmental Training Trust Ltd
IEx	Institute of Export
IExpE	Institute of Explosives Engineers
IFA	Institute of Field Archaeologists
IFA	Institute of Financial Accountants
IFA	Insurance Foundation Certificate
IFBQ	International Faculty of Business Qualifications
IFM	Institute of Fisheries Management
IFST	Institute of Food Science and Technology (UK)
IHBC	International Health & Beauty Council

IHIE	Institute of Highway Incorporated Engineers
IHort	Institute of Horticulture
IHT	Institute of Highways and Transportation
IIA	Institute of Internal Auditors
IIE	Institution of Incorporated Engineers
IIExE	Institution of Incorporated Executive Engineers
IIHHT	International Institute of Health & Holistic Therapies
IIHTM	International Institute of Hospitality Tourism & Management
IIRSM	International Institute of Risk and Safety Management
ILAM	Institute of Leisure and Amenity Management
ILE	Institution of Lighting Engineers
ILEX	Institute of Legal Executives
ILT	Institute of Logistics and Transport
IMarE	Institute of Marine Engineers
IMBM	Institute of Maintenance and Building Management
IMC	Institute of Management Consultancy
IMechE	Institution of Mechanical Engineers
IMF	Institute of Metal Finishing
IMI	Institute of the Motor Industry
IMIBC	Incorporated Member of the Institute of Building Control
IMInstAEA	Incorporated Member of the Institute of Automotive Engineer Assessors
IMIS	Institute for the Management of Information Systems
IMM	Institution of Mining and Metallurgy
IMS	Institute of Management Specialists
IncMWeldI	Incorporated Member of the Welding Institute
InstAEA	Institute of Automotive Engineer Assessors
InstAM	Institute of Administrative Management
InstBCA	Institute of Burial and Cremation Administration
InstE	Institute of Energy
InstPet	Institute of Petroleum
IOB	Institute of Brewing
IOC	Institute of Carpenters
IoD	Institute of Directors
IOM	Institute of Operations Management
IOP	Institute of Packaging
IOSH	Institution of Occupational Safety and Health
IOTA	Institute of Transport Administration
IPA	Institute of Practitioners in Advertising
IPD	Initial Professional Development
IPD	Institute of Personnel and Development
IPFA	Member of the Chartered Institute of Public Finance and Accountancy
IPlantE	Institution of Plant Engineers
IPR	Incorporated Professional Review
IPR	Institute of Public Relations
IPSM	Institute of Public Service Management
IQ	Institute of Quarrying
IQA	Institute of Quality Assurance
IRMT	International Register of Massage Therapists
IRRV	Corporate Member of the Institute of Revenues, Rating and Valuation
IRRV	Institute of Revenues, Rating and Valuation
IRSE	Institution of Railway Signal Engineers
IRTE	Institute of Road Transport Engineers

ISEB	Information Systems Examinations Board
ISM	Incorporated Society of Musicians
ISM	Institute for Supervision & Management
ISMM	Institute of Sales and Marketing Management
ISRM	Institute of Sport and Recreation Management
ISTD	Imperial Society of Teachers of Dancing
IStructE	Institution of Structural Engineers
ITEC	International Therapy Examination Council
ITIL	IT Infrastructure Library
ITSA	Institute of Trading Standards Administration
IVehE	Institute of the Vehicle Engineers
IVM	Institute of Value Management
IWSc	Institute of Wood Science
JEB	Joint Examination Board
JET	Jewellery, Education and Training
JP	Justice of the Peace
LA	Library Association
LABAC	Licentiate Member of the Association of Business and Administrative Computing
LAE	Licentiate Automotive Engineer
LAEx	Legal Accounts Executive
LAMDA	London Academy of Music and Dramatic Art
LAMRTPI	Legal Associate Member of the Royal Town Planning Institute
LASI	Licentiate of the Ambulance Service Institute
LASI	Licentiate of the Architecture and Surveying Institute
LBEI	Licentiate of the Institution of Body Engineers
LBIDST	Licentiate of the British Institute of Dental and Surgical Technologists
LBIPP	Licentiate of the British Institute of Professional Photography
LCCI	London Chamber of Commerce and Industry
LCCIEB	London Chamber of Commerce and Industry Examinations Board
LCEA	Licentiate of the Association of Cost and Executive Accountants
LCFI	Licentiate of CFI International (Clothing and Footwear Institute)
LCGI	Licentiate, City & Guilds
LCIBSE	Licentiate of the Chartered Institution of Building Services Engineers
LCP	Licentiate of the College of Preceptors
LCSP	London and Counties Society of Physiologists
LCSP(Assoc)	Associate of the London and Counties Society of Physiologists
LCSP(BTh)	Member of the London and Counties Society of Physiologists (Beauty Therapy)
LCSP(Chir)	Member of the London and Counties Society of Physiologists (Chiropody)
LCSP(Phys)	Member of the London and Counties Society of Physiologists (Physical and Manipulative Therapy)
LCT	Licentiate of the College of Teachers
LDS	Licentiate in Dental Surgery
LDSRCPSGlas	Licentiate in Dental Surgery of the Royal College of Physicians and Surgeons of Glasgow
LDSRCSEd	Licentiate in Dental Surgery of the Royal College of Surgeons of Edinburgh
LDSRCSEng	Licentiate in Dental Surgery of the Royal College of Surgeons of England
LFA	Licentiate of the Institute of Financial Accountants
LFCI	Licentiate of the Faculty of Commerce and Industry
LFCS	Licentiate of the Faculty of Secretaries
LFS	Licentiate of the Faculty of Architects and Surveyors (Surveyors)
LGCL	Licentiate of the Guild of Cleaners and Launderers
LGSM	Licentiate of the Guildhall School of Music and Drama

LHCIMA	Licentiate of the Hotel and Catering International Management Association
LHG	Licentiate of the Institute of Heraldic and Genealogical Studies
LI	Landscape Institute
LicentiateCIPD	Licentiate of the Chartered Institute of Personnel and Development
LicIPD	Licentiate of the Institute of Personnel & Development
LicIQA	Licentiate of the Institute of Quality Assurance
LICW	Licentiate of the Institute of Clerks of Works of Great Britain Incorporated
LIDPM	Licentiate of the Institute of Data Processing Management
LIEM	Licentiate of the Institute of Executives and Managers
LIIST	Licentiate of the International Institute of Sports Therapy
LILAM	Licentiate of the Institute of Leisure and Amenity Management
LIM	Licentiate of the Institute of Materials
LIMA	Licentiate of the Institute of Mathematics and its Applications
LIMF	Licentiate of the Institute of Metal Finishing
LIMIS	Licentiate of the Institute for the Management of Information Systems
LInstBCA	Licentiate of the Institute of Burial and Cremation Administration
LInstBM	Licentiate of the Institute of Builders' Merchants
LIOC	Licentiate of the Institute of Carpenters
LIR	Licentiate of the Institute of Population Registration
LISTD	Licentiate of the Imperial Society of Teachers of Dancing
LISTD(Dip)	Licentiate Diploma of the Imperial Society of Teachers of Dancing
LittD	Doctor of Letters
LIWM	Licentiate of the Institute of Wastes Management
LLB	Bachelor of Law
LLCM	Performers Diploma of Licentiateship in Speech, Drama and Public Speaking
LLCM(TD)	Licentiate of the London College of Music and Media (Teachers' Diploma)
LLD	Doctor of Law
LLM	Master of Law
LM	Licentiate in Midwifery
LMIFM	Licentiate Member of the Institute of Fisheries Management
LMInstE	Licentiate Member of the Institute of Energy
LMPA	Licentiate Member of the Master Photographers Association
LMRTPI	Legal Member of the Royal Town Planning Institute
LMSSALond	Licentiate in Medicine, Surgery and Obstetrics & Gynaecology, Society of Apothecaries of London
LMusEd	Licentiate Diploma in Music Education
LMusLCM	Licentiate in Music of the London College of Music
LMusTCL	Licentiate in Music, Trinity College of Music
LNCP	Licentiate of the National Council of Psychotherapists
LPC	Legal Practice Course
LRAD	Licentiate of the Royal Academy of Dancing
LRAM	Licentiate of the Royal Academy of Music
LRCPEdin	Conjoint Diplomas Licentiate of the Royal College of Physicians of Edinburgh
LRCPSGlasg	Conjoint Diplomas Licentiate of the Royal College of Physicians and Surgeons of Glasgow
LRCSEdin	Conjoint Diplomas Licentiate of the Royal College of Surgeons of Edinburgh
LRCSEng	Licentiate of the Royal College of Surgeons in England
LRPS	Licentiate of the Royal Photographic Society
LRSC	Licentiate of the Royal Society of Chemistry
LRSM	Licentiate Diploma of the Royal Schools of Music
LSBP	Licentiate of the Society of Business Practitioners
LSCP(Assoc)	Associate of the London and Counties Society of Physiologists

LTCL	Licentiate of Trinity College of Music
LTh	Licentiate in Theology
LTI	Licentiate of the Textile Industry
LTSC	Licentiate of the Oil and Colour Chemists' Association
LVT	Licentiate Vehicle Technologist
MA	Master of Arts
MA(Architectural)	Master of Arts (Architectural Studies)
MA(Econ)	Master of Arts in Economic and Social Studies
MA(Ed)	Master of Arts in Education
MA(LD)	Master of Arts (Landscape Design)
MA(MUS)	Master of Arts (Music)
MA(RCA)	Master of Arts, Royal College of Art
MA(SocSci)	Master of Arts (Social Science)
MA(Theol)	Master of Arts in Theology
MAAT	Member of the Association of Accounting Technicians
MABAC	Member of the Association of Business and Administrative Computing
MABE	Member of the Association of Business Executives
MAcc	Master of Accountancy
MACP	Member of the Association of Computer Professionals
MAE	Member of the Academy of Experts
MAgr	Master of Agriculture
MAgrSc	Master of Agricultural Science
MAMS	Member of the Association of Medical Secretaries, Practice Managers, Administrators and Receptionists
MAMSA	Managing & Marketing Sales Association Examination Board
MAnimSc	Master of Animal Science
MAO	Master of Obstetrics
MAP	Membership by Assessment of Performance
MAPM	Member of the Association for Project Management
MAppSci	Master of Applied Science
MAQ	Mortgage Advice Qualification
MArAd	Master of Archive Administration
MArb	Master of Arboriculture
MArch	Master of Architecture
MArt/RCA	Master of Arts, Royal College of Art
MasFCI	Master of the Faculty of Commerce and Industry
MASHAM	Management and Administration of Safety and Health at Mines
MASI	Member of the Architecture and Surveying Institute
MBA	Master of Business Administration
MBAE	Member of the British Association of Electrolysists
MB, BCh	Conjoint Degree of Bachelor of Medicine, Bachelor of Surgery
MB, BChir	Conjoint Degree of Bachelor of Medicine, Bachelor of Surgery
MB, BS	Conjoint Degree of Bachelor of Medicine, Bachelor of Surgery
MB, ChB	Conjoint Degree of Bachelor of Medicine, Bachelor of Surgery
MBChA	Member of the British Chiropody and Podiatry Association
MBCO	Member of the British College of Ophthalmic Opticians
MBCS	Member of the British Computer Society
MBEng	Member of the Association of Building Engineers
MBHA	Member of the British Hypnotherapy Association
MBHI	Member of the British Horological Institute
MBIAT	Member of the British Institute of Architectural Technologists
MBID	Member of the British Institute of Interior Design

MBIE	Member of the British Institute of Embalmers
MBII	Member of the British Institute of Innkeeping
MBioc	Master of Biochemistry
MBKS	Member of the British Kinematograph, Sound and Television Society
MBM	Master of Business Management
MBMA	Member of the Business Management Association
MBSc	Master in Business Science
MBSSG	Master of the British Society of Scientific Glassblowers
MCAM	Member of the Communication Advertising and Marketing Education Foundation
MCB	Mastership in Clinical Biochemistry
MCB	Member of the British Association of Communicators in Business
MCBDip	Member of the British Association of Communicators in Business who hold the Association's Certificate and Diploma
MCC	Master of Community Care
MCCDRCS(Eng)	Member of the Royal College of Surgeons of England, Clinical Community Dentistry
MCD	Master of Civic Design
MCDH	Master of Community Dental Health
MCGI	Membership, City & Guilds
MCGPIrel	Member of the Irish College of General Practitioners
MCh	Master of Surgery
MChD	Master of Dental Surgery
MChem	Master of Chemistry
MChemA	Master of Chemical Analysis
MChemPhys	Master of Chemical Physics
MChemPST	Master of Chemistry Polymer Science and Technology
MChir	Master of Surgery
MChOrth	Master of Orthopaedic Surgery
MChS	Member of the Society of Chiropodists and Podiatrists
MCIArb	Member of the Chartered Institute of Arbitrators
MCIBS	Member of the Chartered Institute of Bankers in Scotland
MCIBSE	Member of the Chartered Institution of Building Services Engineers
MCIH	Corporate Member of the Chartered Institute of Housing
MCIJ	Member of the Chartered Institute of Journalists
MCIM	Member of the Chartered Institute of Marketing
MCIOB	Member of the Chartered Institute of Building
MCIPD	Member of the Chartered Institute of Personnel and Development
MCIPS	Member of the Chartered Institute of Purchasing and Supply
MCIT	Member of the Chartered Institute of Transport
MCIWEM	Member of the Chartered Institution of Water and Environmental Management
MCLIP	Chartered Member of CILIP
MCom	Master of Commerce
MCommH	Master of Community Health
MComp	Master of Computer Science
MCOptom	Member of the College of Optometrists
MCoT	Member of the College of Teachers
MCPM	Member of the Confederation of Professional Management
MCPP	Member of the College of Pharmacy Practice
MCQ	Multiple Choice Question paper
MCSD	Member of the Chartered Society of Designers
MCSP	Member of the Chartered Society of Physiotherapy
MCT	Member of the Association of Corporate Treasurers

MCTHCM	Member of the Confederation of Tourism, Hotel and Catering Management
MCYW	Member of the Community and Youth Work Association
MD	Doctor of Medicine
MDA	Master of Defence Administration
MD; ChM	Conjoint Doctorate in Medicine, Doctorate in Surgery
MDCR	Management Diploma of the College of Radiographers
MDent	Master of Dental Science
MDes	Master of Design
MDes(RCA)	Master of Design, Royal College of Art
MDORCPSGlas	Membership of Dental Orthopaedics, Royal College of Physicians and Surgeons of Glasgow
MDra	Master of Drama
MDS	Master of Dental Surgery
MDSc	Master of Dental Science
MEBA	Master of European Business Administration
MECI	Member of the Institute of Employment Consultants
MEd	Master of Education
MEd(EdPsych)	Master of Education (Educational Psychology)
MEdStud	Master of Educational Studies
MEng	Master of Engineering
MEnv	Master of Environmental Studies
MEnvSci	Master of Environmental Science
MESc	Master of Earth Sciences
MFA	Master of Fine Art
MFC	Mastership in Food Control
MFCM	Member of the Faculty of Community Medicine
MFDO	Member of the Faculty of Dispensing Opticians
MFDS	Member of the Faculty of Dental Surgery
MFGDPEng	Membership in General Dental Practice, Royal College of Surgeons of England
MFHom	Member of the Faculty of Homeopathy
MFM	Master of Forensic Medicine
MFPHM	Member of the Faculty of Public Health Medicine, Royal College of Physicians of London and Edinburgh and Royal College of Physicians and Surgeons of Glasgow
MFPHMIrel	Member of the Faculty of Public Health Medicine, Royal College of Physicians of Ireland
MFTCom	Member of the Faculty of Teachers in Commerce
MGDSRCSEd	Membership in General Dental Surgery, Royal College of Surgeons of Edinburgh
MGDSRCSEng	Membership in General Dental Surgery, Royal College of Surgeons of England
MGeog	Master of Geography
MGeol	Master of Geology
MGeophys	Master of Geophysical Sciences
MHCIMA	Member of the Hotel and Catering International Management Association
MHM	Master of Health Management
MHort(RHS)	Master of Horticulture, Royal Horticultural Society
MHSM	Member of the Institute of Health Services Management
MIAB	Member of the International Association of Book-keepers
MIAEA	Member of the Institute of Automotive Engineer Assessors
MIAgrE	Member of the Institution of Agricultural Engineers
MIAP	Member of the Institution of Analysts and Programmers
MIAT	Member of the Institute of Asphalt Technology
MIBC	Member of the Institute of Building Control

MIBCM	Member of the Institute British Carriage and Automobile Manufacturers
MIBCO	Member of the Institution of Building Control Officers
MIBE	Member of the Institution of British Engineers
MIBF	Member of the Institute of British Foundrymen
MIBiol	Member of the Institute of Biology
MIBM	Member of the Institute of Builders' Merchants
MICB	Member of the Institute of Certified Book-Keepers
MICE	Member of the Institute of Civil Engineers
MIChemE	Member of the Institution of Chemical Engineers
MICHT	Member of the International Council for Holistic Therapies
MICM	Member of the Institute of Credit Management
MICM(Grad)	Graduate Member of the Institute of Credit Management
MICorr	Member of the Institute of Corrosion
MICS	Member of the Institute of Chartered Shipbrokers
MICSc	Corporate Member of the Institute of Consumer Sciences Incorporating Home Economics
MICW	Member of the Institute of Clerks of Works of Great Britain Incorporated
MIDTA	Member of the International Dance Teachers' Association
MIED	Member of the Institution of Engineering Designers
MIEE	Member of the Institution of Electrical Engineers
MIEM	Member of the Institute of Executives and Managers
MIEx	Member of the Institute of Export
MIEx(Grad)	Graduate Member of the Institute of Export
MIExpE	Member of the Institute of Explosives Engineers
MIFA	Member of the Institute of Field Archaeologists
MIFireE	Member of the Institution of Fire Engineers
MIFM	Registered Member of the Institute of Fisheries Management
MIFST	Member of the Institute of Food Science and Technology
MIGasE	Member of the Institution of Gas Engineers
MIGD	Member of the Institute of Grocery Distribution
MIHEc	Member of the Institute of Home Economics
MIHIE	Member of the Institute of Highway Incorporated Engineers
MIHM	Member of the Institute of Healthcare Management
MIHort	Member of the Institute of Horticulture
MIHT	Member of the Institution of Highways and Transportation
MIIA	Member of the Institute of Internal Auditors
MIIE	Member of the Institution of Incorporated Engineers
MIIExE	Member of the Institution of Incorporated Executive Engineers
MIIHTM	Member of the International Institute of Hospitality Tourism & Management
MIIM	Member of the Institute of Industrial Managers
MIIM	Member of the International Institute of Management
MIIRSM	Member of the International Institute of Risk and Safety Management
MIISE	Member of the International Institute of Social Economics
MIISec	Member of the International Institute of Security
MIL	Member of the Institute of Linguists
MILAM	Member of the Institute of Leisure and Amenity Management
MILT	Member of the Institute of Logistics and Transport
MIM	Professional Member of the Institute of Materials
MIMA	Member of the Institute of Mathematics and its Applications
MIManf	Member of the Institute of Manufacturing
MIMarE	Member of the Institute of Marine Engineers
MIMatM	Member of the Institute of Materials Management

MIMBM	Member of the Institute of Maintenance and Building Management
MIMC	Member of the Institute of Management Consultancy
MIMechE	Member of the Institution of Mechanical Engineers
MIMechIE	Member of the Institution of Mechanical Incorporated Engineers
MIMF	Member of the Institute of Metal Finishing
MIMI	Member of the Institute of the Motor Industry
MIMinE	Member of the Institution of Mining Engineers
MIMIS	Member of the Institute for the Management of Information Systems
MIMM	Member of the Institute of Massage and Movement
MIMM	Member of the Institution of Mining and Metallurgy
MIMS	Member of the Institute of Management Specialists
MInstAEA	Member of the Institute of Automotive Engineer Assessors
MInstAM	Member of the Institute of Administrative Management
MInstBA	Member of the Institute of Business Administration
MInstBCA	Member of the Institute of Burial and Cremation Administration
MInstBE	Member of the Institution of British Engineers
MInstBM	Member of the Institute of Builders' Merchants
MInstCF	Master Fitter of the National Institute of Carpet and Floorlayers
MInstChP	Member of the Institute of Chiropodists & Podiatrists
MInstCM	Member of the Institute of Commercial Management
MInstD	Member of the Institute of Directors
MInstE	Member of the Institute of Energy
MInstLEx	Member of the Institute of Legal Executives
MInstMC	Member of the Institute of Measurement and Control
MInstNDT	Member of the British Institute of Non-Destructive Testing
MInstP	Member of the Institute of Physics
MInstPet	Member of the Institute of Petroleum
MInstPkg	Member of the Institute of Packaging
MInstPkg(Dip)	Diploma Member of the Institute of Packaging
MInstPM	Member of the Institute of Professional Managers and Administrators
MInstPS	Corporate Member of the Institute of Purchasing and Supply
MInstPSA	Member of the Institute of Public Service Administrators
MInstR	Member of the Institute of Refrigeration
MInstSMM	Member of the Institute of Sales and Marketing Management
MInstTA	Member of the Institute of Transport Administration
MInstTT	Full Member of the Institute of Travel and Tourism
MInstWM	Member of the Institute of Wastes Management
MIOC	Member of the Institute of Carpenters
MIOFMS	Member of the Institute of Financial and Management Studies
MIOM	Member of the Institute of Operations Management
MIOP	Member of the Institute of Printing
MIOSH	Member of the Institution of Occupational Safety and Health
MIP	Member of the Institute of Plumbing
MIPA	Member of the Institute of Practitioners in Advertising
MIPD	Member of the Institute of Personnel and Development
MIPI	Member of the Institute of Professional Investigators
MIPlantE	Member of the Institution of Plant Engineers
MIPR	Member of the Institute of Public Relations
MIPRE	Member of the Incorporated Practitioners in Radio & Electronics
MIQ	Member of the Institute of Quarrying
MIQA	Member of the Institute of Quality Assurance
MIR	Member of the Institute of Population Registration

MIRRV	Member of the Institute of Revenue, Rating and Valuation
MIRSE	Member of the Institution of Railway Signal Engineers
MIRTE	Member of the Institute of Road Transport Engineering
MISM	Member of the Institute for Supervision & Management
MISOB	Member of the Incorporated Society of Organ Builders
MISTC	Member of the Institute of Scientific and Technical Communicators
MIStrucE	Member of the Institution of Structural Engineers
MISW	Member of the Institute of Social Welfare
MITAI	Member of the Institute of Traffic Accident Investigators
MITSA	Member of the Institute of Trading Standards Administration
MIVehE	Member of the Institute of Vehicle Engineers
MIWM	Member of the Institute of Wastes Management
MIWPC	Member of the Institute of Water Pollution Control
MJur	Master of Jurisprudence
MLA	Master of Landscape Architecture
MLang	Master of Languages
MLangEng	Master of Language Engineering
MLD	Master of Landscape Design
MLE	Master of Land Economy
MLI	Member of the Landscape Institute
MLing	Master of Languages
MLitt	Master of Letters
MLPM	Master of Landscape Planning and Management
MLS	Master of Library Science
MM	Master of Midwifery
MMA	Master of Management and Administration
MMAS	Master of Minimal Access Surgery
MMath	Master of Mathematics
MMedE	Master of Medical Education
MMedSci	Master of Medical Science
MMet	Master of Metallurgy
MML	Master of Modern Languages
MMS	Member of the Institute of Management Services
MMSc	Master of Medical Sciences
MMus	Master of Music
MMus(Comp)	Master of Music (Composition)
MMus(Perf)	Master of Music (Performance)
MMus, RCM	Master of Music, Royal College of Music
MMusArt	Master of Musical Arts
MN	Master of Nursing
MNAEA	Member of the National Association of Estate Agents
MNatSc	Master of Natural Science
MNCP	Member of the National Council of Psychotherapists
MNeuro	Master of Neuroscience
MNI	Member of the Nautical Institute
MNIMH	Member of the National Institute of Medical Herbalists
MNRHP	Full Member of the National Register of Hypnotherapists and Psychotherapists
MNRHP(Eqv)	Full Member (Equivalent) of the National Register of Hypnotherapists and Psychotherapists
MNTB	Merchant Navy Training Board
MObstG	Master of Obstetrics and Gynaecology
MOptom	Master of Optometry

MOrthRCSEng	Membership in Orthodontics, Royal College of Surgeons of England
MPA	Master of Public Administration
MPaedDenRCSEng	Membership in Paediatric Dentistry, Royal College of Surgeons of England
MPC	Master of Palliative Care
MPH	Master of Public Health
MPharm	Master of Pharmacy
MPharmSci	Master of Pharmaceutical Science
MPhil	Master of Philosophy
MPhil(Eng)	Master of Philosophy in Engineering
MPhys	Master of Physics
MPhysGeog	Master of Physical Geography
MPlan	Master of Planning
MPPS	Master of Public Policy Studies
MPRI	Member of the Plastics and Rubber Institute
MProf	Master of Professional Studies
MProfBTM	Member of the Professional Business and Technical Management
MPS	Member of the Pharmaceutical Society of Northern Ireland
MPsychMed	Master of Psychological Medicine
MPsychol	Master of Psychology
MQB	Mining Qualifications Board
MRad	Master of Radiology
MRad; MRad(D)	Master of Radiology (Radiodiagnosis) or (Radiotherapy)
MRAeS	Member of the Royal Aeronautical Society
MRCGP	Member of the Royal College of General Practitioners
MRCOG	Member of the Royal College of Obstetricians and Gynaecologists
MRCP	Member of the Royal College of Physicians of London
MRCP(UK)	Member of the Royal College of Physicians of the United Kingdom
MRCPath	Member of the Royal College of Pathologists
MRCPEdin	Member of the Royal College of Physicians of Edinburgh (superceded by MRCP(UK))
MRCPGlasg	Member of the Royal College of Physicians of Glasgow (superceded by MRCP(UK))
MRCPIrel	Member of the Royal College of Physicians of Ireland
MRCPsych	Member of the Royal College of Psychiatrists
MRCSEd	Member of the Royal College of Surgeons of Edinburgh
MRCSEng	Member of the Royal College of Surgeons of England
MRCVS	Member of the Royal College of Veterinary Surgeons
MRDRCS	Membership in Restorative Dentistry, Royal College of Surgeons of England
MREC	Member of the Recruitment and Employment Confederation
MREHIS	Member of the Royal Environmental Health Institute of Scotland
MRes	Master of Research
MRIN	Member of the Royal Institute of Navigation
MRINA	Member of the Royal Institution of Naval Architects
MRIPHH	Member of the Royal Institute of Public Health and Hygiene
MRPharmS	Member of the Pharmaceutical Society of Great Britain
MRSC	Member of the Royal Society of Chemistry
MRSH	Member of the Royal Society for the Promotion of Health
MRSS	Member of the Royal Statistical Society
MRTPI	Member of the Royal Town Planning Institute
MS	Master of Surgery
MSA	Marine Safety Agency
MSAPP	Member of the Society of Advanced Psychotherapy Practitioners

MSBP	Member of the Society of Business Practitioners
MSBT	Member of the Society of Teachers in Business Education
MSc	Master of Science
MSc(Econ)	Master of Science in Economics
MSc(Ed)	Master of Science in Education
MSc(Eng)	Master of Science in Engineering
MSc(Entr)	Master of Entrepreneurship
MSc(Mgt)	Master of Science in Management
MScD	Master of Dental Science
MScEcon	Master in Faculty of Economic and Social Studies
MSCi	Master of Natural Sciences
MScTech	Master of Technical Science
MSE	Member of Society of Engineers (Inc)
MSF	Member of the SMAE Institute
MSFA	Advanced Financial Planning Certificate
MSIAD	Member of the Society of Industrial Artists and Designers
MSMA	Member of the Society of Martial Arts
MSocSc	Master of Social Science
MSSc	Master of Social Science
MSSc	Master of Surgical Science
MSSCh	Member of the British Chiropody and Podiatry Association
MSSF	Member of the Society of Shoe Fitters
MSt	Master of Studies
MSTA	Member of the Swimming Teachers' Association
MSTI	Certificate of Insurance Work
MSurgDentRCSEng	Membership in Surgical Dentistry, Royal College of Surgeons of England
MSW	Master of Social Work
MTCP	Master of Town and Country Planning
MTD	Master of Transport Design
MTech	Master of Technology
MTh	Master of Theology
MTheol	Master of Theology
MTP	Master of Town Planning
MTPI	Master of Town Planning
MTropMed	Master of Tropical Medicine
MTropPaediatrics	Master of Tropical Paediatrics
MUniv	Master of University (Honorary)
MURP	Master of Urban and Regional Planning
MusB	Bachelor of Music
MusD	Doctor of Music
MVC	Management Verification Consortium
MVM	Master of Veterinary Medicine
MVSc	Master of Veterinary Science
MWeldI	Member of the Welding Institute
MWES	Member of the Women's Engineering Society
MYD	Member of the Youth Development Association
NACOS	National Approval Council for Security Systems
NAEA	National Association of Estate Agents
NAG	National Association of Goldsmiths
NAMCW	National Association for Maternal and Child Welfare
NC	National Certificate
NCA	National Certificate in Agriculture

NCC	National Computing Centre
NCC	Navigational Control Course
NCDT	National Council for Drama Training
NCTJ	National Council for the Training of Journalists
NCVQ	National Council for Vocational Qualifications
ND	Diploma in Naturopathy
NDD	National Diploma in Design
NDF	National Diploma in Forestry
NDH	National Diploma in Horticulture
NDSF	National Diploma of the Society of Floristry
NDT	National Diploma in the Science and Practice of Turfculture and Sports Ground Management
NEBOSH	National Examination Board in Occupational Safety and Health
NEBS	National Examining Board for Supervision & Management
NFTS	National Film and Television School
NICCEA	Northern Ireland Council for the Curriculum, Examinations and Assessment
NID	National Intermediate Diploma
NIM	Northern Institute of Massage
NNEB	National Nursery Examination Board
NRHP	National Register of Hypnotherapists and Psychotherapists
NRHP(Affil)	Affiliate of the National Register of Hypnotherapists and Psychotherapists
NRHP(Assoc)	Associate of the National Register of Hypnotherapists and Psychotherapists
N-SHAP	National School of Hypnosis and Psychotherapy
NTTG	National Textile Training Group
NUJ	National Union of Journalists
NVQ	National Vocational Qualifications
NWRAC	North Western Regional Advisory Council for Further Education
OCR	Oxford, Cambridge & RSA Examinations
ODLQC	Open & Distance Learning Quality Council, formerly CACC, Council for Accreditation of Correspondence Colleges
ONC	Ordinary National Certificate
OND	Ordinary National Diploma
OSCE	Objective Structured Clinical Exam
PBTM	Professional Business and Technical Management
PCN	Personnel Certification in Non-Destructive Testing Ltd
PDP	Professional Development Programme
PESD	Private and Executive Secretary's Diploma, London Chamber of Commerce and Industry
PgC	Postgraduate Certificate
PGCE	Postgraduate Certificate in Education
PGCert	Postgraduate Certificate
PgD	Postgraduate Diploma
PGDip	Postgraduate Diploma
PGDip(Comp)	Postgraduate Diploma in Composition
PGDip(LCM)	Postgraduate Diploma of the London College of Music
PGDip(Perf)	Postgraduate Diploma in Performance
PGDip(RCM)	Postgraduate Diploma of the Royal College of Music
PGDipMin	Postgraduate Diploma in Ministry
PGDipMus	Postgraduate Diploma in Music
PhD	Doctor of Philosophy
PhD(RCA)	Doctor of Philosophy (Royal College of Art)
PIC	Professional Investment Certificate

PIFA	Practitioner of the Institute of Field Archaeologists
PIIA	Practitioner of the Institute of Internal Auditors
PInstNDT	Practitioner of the British Institute of Non-Destructive Testing
PJDip	Professional Jewellers' Diploma
PJGemDip	Professional Jewellers' Gemstone Diploma
PJManDip	Professional Jewellers' Management Diploma
PJValDip	Professional Jewellers' Valuation Diploma
PPL	Private Pilot's Licence
PPRNCM	Professional Performance Diploma of the Royal Northern College of Music
PQS	Professional Qualification Structure
PQSW	Post-Qualifying Award in Social Work
PRCA	Public Relations Consultants Association
PSC	Private Secretary's Certificate
PSD	Private Secretary's Diploma
PTA	Pianoforte Tuners' Association
PVM	Professional in Value Management
QC	Queen's Counsel
QCA	Qualifications and Curriculum Authority
QCG	Qualification in Careers Guidance
QDR	Qualified Dispute Resolver
QICA	Qualification in Computer Auditing
QIS	Qualified Imaging Scientist
QPA	Qualification in Pensions Administration
QPSPA	Qualification in Public Sector Pensions Administration
RA	Royal Academician
RAD	Royal Academy of Dancing
RADA	Royal Academy of Dramatic Art
RAM	Royal Academy of Music
RANA	Royal Animal Nursing Auxiliary
RAS	Royal Astronomical Society
RBS	Royal Ballet School
RC	Roman Catholic
RCM	Royal College of Midwives
RCN	Royal College of Nursing
RCSLT	Royal College of Speech and Language Therapists
RCVS	Royal College of Veterinary Surgeons
REA	Regional Examining Body
REC	Recruitment and Employment Confederation
Ret'dABID	Retired Associate of the British Institute of Interior Design
Ret'dFBID	Retired Fellow of the British Institute of Interior Design
Ret'dMBID	Retired Member of the British Institute of Interior Design
RGN	Registered General Nurse
RHS	Royal Horticultural Society
RHV	Registered Health Visitor
RIBA	Royal Institute of British Architects
RICS	Royal Institution of Chartered Surveyors
RINA	Royal Institution of Naval Architects
RJDip	Diploma for Retail Jewellers
RJGemDip	National Association of Goldsmiths Gemstone Diploma
RM	Registered Midwife
RMN	Registered Mental Nurse
RMS	Royal Microscopical Society

RNMH	Registered Nurse for the Mentally Handicapped
RP	Registered Plumber
RPS	Royal Photographic Society
RSA	Royal Society of Arts
RSBEI	Registered Student of the Institution of Body Engineers
RSC	Royal Society of Chemistry
RSCN	Registered Sick Children's Nurse
RSP	Registered Safety Practitioner
RTO	Recognised Training Organisation
RTPI	Royal Town Planning Institute
SA	Salvation Army Management
SBP	Society of Business Practitioners
SCAA	School Curriculum and Assessment Authority
ScD	Doctor of Science
SCE	Scottish Certificate of Education
SCLS	Second Certificate for Legal Secretaries
SCMT	Ship Captain's Medical Training
SCOTVEC	Scottish Vocational Education Council
SCPL	Senior Commercial Pilot's Licence
SE	Society of Engineers
SEE	Society of Environmental Engineers
SEFIC	Spoken English for Industry and Commerce
SenAWeldI	Senior Associate of the Welding Institute
SEng	Qualified Sales Engineer
SenMWeldI	Senior Member of the Welding Institute
SF	Society of Floristry Ltd
SFA	Securities and Futures Authority
SFInstE	Senior Fellow of the Institute of Energy
SG	Society of Genealogists
SGT	Society of Glass Technology
SHNC	Scottish Higher National Certificate
SHND	Scottish Higher National Diploma
SIEDip	Securities Industry Examination Diploma
SInstPet	Student of the Institute of Petroleum
SITO	Security Industry Training Organisation Ltd
SLC	Secretarial Language Certificate
SLD	Secretarial Language Diploma
SNC	Scottish National Certificate
SND	Scottish National Diploma
SNNEB	Scottish Nursery Nurses Examination Board
SPA	Screen Printing Association
SPRINT	Sport Play and Recreation Industries National Training Executive
SQA	Scottish Qualifications Authority
SRD	State Registered Dietician
SRN	State Registered Nurse
SSC	Secretarial Studies Certificate, London Chamber of Commerce and Industry
STA	Specialist Teacher Assistant (CACHE)
STA	Swimming Teachers' Association
STAT	Society of Teachers of the Alexander Technique
StudentIEE	Student of the Institution of Electrical Engineers
StudentIIE	Student of the Institution of Incorporated Engineers
StudentIMechE	Student of the Institution of Mechanical Engineers

StudIAP	Student of the Institution of Analysts and Programmers
StudIManf	Student Member of the Institute of Manufacturing
StudIMS	Student of the Institute of Management Specialists
StudProfBTM	Student of the Professional Business and Technical Management
StudSE	Student of the Society of Engineers (Inc)
StudSElec	Student of the Society of Electroscience
StudWeldI	Student of the Welding Institute
SVQ	Scottish Vocational Qualification
TC	Technician Certificate
TCA	Technician in Costing and Accounting
TCA	Technician of the Institute of Cost and Executive Accountants
TCert	Teacher's Certificate
TD	Technician Diploma
TDCR	Teacher's Diploma of the College of Radiographers
TechICorr	Technician of the Institute of Corrosion
TechMIWM	Technician Member of the Institute of Wastes Management
TechRICS	Technical Surveyor of the Royal Institution of Chartered Surveyors
TechRMS	Technological Qualification in Microscopy, Royal Microscopical Society
TechRTPI	Technical Member of the Royal Town Planning Institute
TechSP	Technician Safety Practitioner
TechWeldI	Technician of the Welding Institute
TEMOL	Training in Energy Management through Open Learning
TI	Textile Institute
TIMBM	Technician of the Institute of Maintenance and Building Management
TMBA	Teacher Member of the British (Theatrical) Arts
TnIMBM	Technicians of the Institute of Maintenance and Building Management
TOEFL	Test of English as a Foreign Language
TPP	Test of Professional Practice
TVM	Trainer in Value Management
UCAS	Universities and Colleges Admissions Service
UCL	University College London
UEB	United Examining Board
UKCC	United Kingdom Central Council
UKCP	United Kingdom Council for Psychotherapy
UMIST	University of Manchester Institute of Science and Technology
URC	United Reformed Church
VetMB	Bachelor of Veterinary Medicine
VTCT	Vocational Training Charitable Trust
WCMD	Welsh College of Music and Drama
WES	Women's Engineering Society
WJEC	Welsh Joint Education Committee
WMAC	West Midlands Advisory Council for Further Education
WSA	West of Scotland Agricultural College
YHAFHE	Yorkshire and Humberside Association for Further and Higher Education
ZSL	Zoological Society of London

Part 1

Introduction

INTRODUCTION

Since its first publication in 1970, *British Qualifications* has charted a number of fundamental changes in further and higher education provision in the UK. Major advances in technology and more flexible delivery and attendance patterns have created different types of learning opportunity, encouraging an ever more diverse student population to access education at all levels. The range of subjects delivered has grown beyond all recognition. New areas of research have been established and developed into major subject specialisms. Employers and professional bodies have collaborated to develop subject areas aligned to changing industry requirements. Flexibility and choice are the hallmarks of today's system, and anyone new to higher education may well be bewildered by the sheer variety of degree pathways available. The capacity to combine and mix modules and subjects has in fact grown beyond anything that could have been imagined in 1970.

Traditional boundaries between academic and vocational pathways continue to break down, and today most degrees have a vocational slant. Extended industry and professional placements, sponsored research projects, practitioner input and field-based assignments are common features in many degrees, and provide an important link into practice at the early stages of learning. Overall, in 20 years universities have doubled in size and the responsibilities they have taken on have expanded considerably. Collaboration between further education (FE) and higher education (HE) institutions has enabled a substantial amount of HE-level provision to be delivered in FE institutions. Clear progression routes have been established for some time. Considerable breadth of provision is now available in FE: not only has the sector grown to accommodate sub-degree provision, it has also continued to deliver a wide range of pre- and post-18 vocational qualifications, which include technical, occupational and professional awards.

Today, certain types of external qualification cross the boundaries between further and higher education. Several higher education institutions (HEIs) – particularly those that gained university status in the 1990s and in 2005 – deliver advanced professional qualifications and higher national diplomas or certificates from awarding bodies like Edexcel, OCR and SQA. At the same time there has been a significant shift towards FE's involvement in delivery of these types of qualification, and a greater input from private sector colleges.

EDUCATION REFORM

The Higher Education Act 2004 introduced in 2006/07 brought new student support and tuition fee arrangements. Following the Browne Review of 2010, universities are able to charge full-time UK and EU undergraduate students up to £9,000 a year as part of a reorganization of HE funding and student finance. You will find further authoritative, official information about universities and colleges in the UK at the Unistats website: http://unistats.direct.gov.uk/. The Unistats website enables you to compare data and information on UK university and college courses, as well as providing useful information on cost and financial support. Information on student finance and how to apply for it can be found at www.gov.uk, and this site also gives information about university and higher education courses.

As well as implementing reforms, the further and higher education sectors contribute to UK economic performance and the delivery of the government's policies on HE. As part of this shared responsibility a great deal of effort is being made to increase access to and participation in education, particularly among individuals who have not had much involvement in the past. The general availability of modular study programmes and related credit recognition of units, and greater use of ICT and e-learning resources, have done a lot to create more flexible methods of delivery and attendance requirements in further and higher education.

Foundation degrees

Foundation degrees (FDs) were established to give people the intermediate technical and professional skills that are in demand from employers, and to provide more flexible and accessible ways of studying. They are a higher-level qualification awarded by universities. A foundation degree is the equivalent of two thirds of a full honours degree and is a fully flexible qualification allowing students to study part-time or full-time to fit their lifestyle. Unlike full degrees, there are no set entry requirements for foundation degrees. The qualification can be 'built up' from a range of relevant learning experiences, to allow for extremely flexible and adaptable qualifications that can be 'tailored' by employers to support their workforce and business development needs. They offer opportunities for employment and career advancement. Progression routes include links with associated professional qualifications and/or direct entry to the final year of a relevant Honours-level degree. FDs are offered by universities, colleges and other providers.

The first FDs in 2001 were studied by 4,000 students. In 2014–15, 2.3% of the higher education qualifications awarded were FDs. There are now hundreds of FD courses available, both full- and part-time.

- Information about FDs can be found on the UCAS website: www.ucas.com/ucas/undergraduate/getting-started/what-study/foundation-degrees
- Information, advice and guidance resources for work-based learners and their advisers are hosted by unionlearn at www.unionlearn.org.uk/higher-learning-work
- Foundation Degree Forward (fdf) offered e-learning resources to support the delivery of work-based higher education in sectors such as retail, travel and low carbon energy but closed at the end of July 2011. The Higher Education Academy hosts publications produced by fdf so that they remain available to the higher education community at www.heacademy.ac.uk/fdf

Policy and regulation

The UK and Scottish parliaments and the Welsh and Northern Ireland assemblies set national priorities for further and higher education. Policy development, planning and implementation rest with the government departments responsible for each national education brief – the Department for Education (DfE, website: www.gov.uk/government/organisations/department-for-education), the Department for the Economy (DfENI, website: www.economy-ni.gov.uk) for Northern Ireland (covering further and higher education), the Scottish Government (www.gov.scot), and The Department for Education and Skills (DfES, website: http://gov.wales/topics/educationandskills) in Wales.

In England, delivery of FE is subject to external audit and public reporting by the Office for Standards in Education, Children's Services and Schools (Ofsted, website: www.gov.uk/government/organisations/ofsted).

In Scotland, the Scottish Funding Council (SFC, website: www.sfc.ac.uk) is the national, strategic body that is responsible for funding teaching and learning provision, research and other activities in Scotland's 26 colleges and 19 universities and higher education institutes. Inspection is carried out by Education Scotland (www.educationscotland.gov.uk/inspectionandreview).

DfES is responsible for planning, funding and promotion of all post-16 education in Wales. Estyn (the Welsh-language acronym for Her Majesty's Inspectorate for Education and Training in

Wales, website: www.estyn.gov.uk) is the appointed authority for audit of the quality of provision and related areas.

The Department for the Economy (DfE) is responsible for planning and funding of further education provision in Northern Ireland. The Education and Training Inspectorate (ETI) (www.etini.gov.uk) undertakes inspection and audit on behalf of the Department.

QUALITY ASSURANCE

A degree of convergence exists in the quality assurance of qualifications at level 3 and below. England, Wales and Northern Ireland share a common qualifications system, and the regulators in each country (listed below) work together in regulating qualifications for use across the three countries. Scotland has a separate qualifications system, although there is close correlation across all four countries, particularly in the area of vocational qualifications.

The following four bodies are responsible for the accreditation and standards of external qualifications and for curriculum and assessment for ages 3–16:

- *England*: Office of the Qualifications and Examinations Regulator (Ofqual, website: www.gov.uk/government/organisations/ofqual);
- *Northern Ireland*: Council for Curriculum, Examinations and Assessment (CCEA*, website: http://ccea.org.uk);
- *Scotland*: Scottish Qualifications Authority (SQA**, website: www.sqa.org.uk);
- *Wales*: Qualifications Wales, which was established through the Qualifications Wales Act 2015 (website: http://qualificationswales.org) and is organised to focus on: recognising awarding bodies and approving and designating qualifications; regulating awarding bodies and reviewing qualifications already in existence; developing and commissioning new qualification requirements for Wales; and research to provide the evidence base for regulatory decision-making.

*CCEA is also an Awarding Body for qualifications in Northern Ireland, offering a diverse range of qualifications, such as GCSEs, including the GCSE Double Award specifications in vocational subjects, GCE A and AS levels, Entry Level Qualifications, and Online Language Assessment (OLA).

**SQA is also an Awarding Body that develops and validates SQA-branded qualifications including National Qualifications, Skills for Work, Scottish Baccalaureates, National Progression Awards and National Certificates, Higher National Certificates and Diplomas, Scottish Vocational Qualifications and Modern Apprenticeships, and Scottish Professional Development Awards. The Scottish Credit and Qualifications Framework (SCQF) is Scotland's national qualifications framework.

In HE the responsibility for standards and quality rests firmly with each institution. All institutions work with the independent Quality Assurance Agency for Higher Education (QAA) for England, Northern Ireland, Scotland and Wales. Institutional audits and subject-level reviews have been undertaken by QAA since 2001. It publishes its findings on its website (www.qaa.ac.uk) as publicly accessible information.

Given the current scale and diversity of degree provision in the HE sector, there has been a need to clarify what can reasonably be expected from undergraduate and postgraduate programmes. QAA has responded to this requirement and developed the Quality Code for HE providers (www.qaa.ac.uk/assuring-standards-and-quality/the-quality-code), and subject benchmark statements indicating the expected standards of degrees across a range of subjects.

QUALIFICATION FRAMEWORKS

In further response to the breadth and diversity of qualifications available, a number of national qualification frameworks have been introduced. The framework concept is closely associated with greater transparency and comparability between types of qualification, particularly between those that were traditionally classified as academic or vocational. The frameworks allow comparison with qualifications in different countries by grading them into levels based on the learning outcomes.

The framework for Higher Education Qualifications in England, Wales and Northern Ireland (FHEQ) applies to degrees, diplomas, certificates and other academic awards by higher education providers (see Figure 1.1). Further information can be found at www.qaa.ac.uk/assuring-standards-and-quality/the-quality-code/qualifications.

The Scottish Credit and Qualification Framework (SCQF) was developed by SQA, the Scottish Executive, QAA (Scottish Office) and Universities for Scotland. It provides an overview of all levels of national and higher qualifications provision in Scotland (see Figure 1.2). Further information and the database of courses can be found at http://scqf.org.uk

The Regulated Qualifications Framework was introduced in October 2015 (find more information at: https://ofqual.blog.gov.uk/2015/10/01/explaining-the-rqf).It is the new framework for recognizing and accrediting general and vocational qualifications in England and vocational qualifications Northern Ireland. It is intended to act as a simple tool for describing qualifications. Ofqual regulates this framework, and more information can be found at https://www.gov.uk/what-different-qualification-levels-mean and http://register.ofqual.gov.uk/, which is a searchable database of qualifications and organizations.

For current information about qualifications offered in Wales, please go to the Qualifications in Wales website, www.qiw.wales

The European Qualifications Framework (EQF) compares the level of qualifications across Europe to make it easier for employers and educational establishments to compare their value. More information can be found at the website of the European Commission: https://ec.europa.eu/ploteus/en

Part 2

Teaching Establishments

INTRODUCTION

The statutory responsibility for the provision of education in the United Kingdom lies with the Department for Education (DfE) (www.gov.uk/government/organisations/department-for-education) in England, the Welsh Assembly Government's Department for Education and Skills (DfES) (http://gov.wales/topics/educationandskills), the Education Department of the Scottish Government (www.gov.scot/Topics/Education) and the Department of Education (DENI) (www.education-ni.gov.uk) and the Department for the Economy (DfENI) (www.economy-ni.gov.uk), which is responsible for further and higher education, in Northern Ireland.

In the United Kingdom the statutory system of public education has three progressive stages: primary education (up to the age of 11 or 12), secondary education (up to age 16), and further education (post-16).

The Education and Skills Act 2008 introduced a new requirement that all young people in England must continue in education or training at least part-time until they are 18 years old, and this applies to any person born on or after 1 September 1997 (see www.gov.uk/know-when-you-can-leave-school). The website www.ucas.com/ucas/after-gcses gives useful information on the options available and the government website www.gov.uk/further-education-courses also gives information on courses and funding.

This section briefly describes further and higher provision and the main types of institution.

FURTHER AND HIGHER EDUCATION

'Higher education' (HE) is a term that broadly defines any course of study leading to a qualification at level 4 and above in the Regulated Qualifications Framework for England, Wales and Northern Ireland, and level 6 and above in the Scottish Credit and Qualifications Framework.

HE incorporates study towards a wide range of qualifications including Foundation, undergraduate and postgraduate degrees, certificates and diplomas awarded by individual universities and other higher education institutions (HEIs) with degree-awarding powers. It can also include study towards general, technical or occupationally-related diplomas and certificates awarded by the large unitary awarding bodies. Unitary awarding bodies are characterized by their breadth of provision, from NVQs and BTEC courses and A levels through to qualifications at level 5 and above in the national frameworks.

The other category that can be characterized as HE, includes post-experience education above level 4 (and level 7 in Scotland). This includes qualifications available from awarding bodies that represent a particular sector, occupation or technical/craft area, and professional institutions that are also approved as awarding bodies.

HE can take place in universities and HE colleges (which continue to provide the majority of undergraduate and postgraduate courses). It can also take place in colleges of further education (FE). A significant number of colleges deliver parts of, and in some cases entire, Foundation and undergraduate degree courses in agreement with a selected university partner that is responsible for quality assurance and final awards.

In general terms, FE is available for students who are over the age of 16 and still in full-time education, and for adults aged 19 and over. FE provision includes GCSEs, A levels and other types of general and vocational qualifications below level 4 (and level 6 in Scotland) in the National Qualifications Frameworks.

All qualifications are awarded by approved external awarding bodies that include AQA, City & Guilds, Edexcel, LCCI, OCR, OCN and SQA in Scotland. This also includes qualifications below level 4 (level 6 in Scotland) that have a craft or technical focus or are related to an occupation/sector. At the time of writing, readers who want to find out more about approved qualifications below level 4 will find The Register of Regulated Qualifications website informative (http://register.ofqual.gov.uk). It contains details of all regulated qualifications in England (Ofqual), Wales (Welsh Government) and Northern Ireland (Ofqual and CCEA).

FURTHER AND HIGHER EDUCATION INSTITUTIONS

England and Wales

There is a wide range of further and higher education establishments, including colleges with various titles. There are also a number of independent specialist establishments, like secretarial and correspondence colleges.

In 2016 there were 161 universities and colleges that were allowed to award degrees. All institutions that are recognized as having degree-awarding powers in the UK can be found on the government website (www.gov.uk/check-a-university-is-officially-recognised/recognised-bodies).

There were also over 600 colleges and other institutions that could not award degrees themselves, but provided courses leading to UK degrees. Institutions offering courses leading to a degree from a recognized body can be found at www.gov.uk/check-a-university-is-officially-recognised/listed-bodies. For general information on UK degrees visit www.gov.uk/recognised-uk-degrees.

Courses include those for first and second degrees, certain graduate-equivalent qualifications, and the examinations of the principal professional associations. These institutions also provide courses leading to important qualifications below degree level, such as Foundation degrees, Higher National Diplomas and Certificates, and Diplomas of Higher Education. Most FE colleges specialize in providing courses that lead to qualifications below degree level, such as A levels and BTEC qualifications. Some offer degree courses, including in many cases Foundation degrees.

Students aged 16–18 who have been ordinarily resident in the UK for three years and, while the UK is still part of the European Union, European Economic Area nationals normally have the right to attend a full-time course without paying tuition fees. More detailed information on tuition fees for international students can be found at www.ukcisa.org.uk. Colleges are free to determine fee levels for students who do not qualify for 'home fees'.

Further Education choices can be searched on www.gov.uk/government/statistical-data-sets/fe-choices-performance-indicators and also http://findfe.com. The 2016 figures show there were 348 FE colleges in England (of which 94 were sixth-form colleges) 19 in Wales, 40 in Scotland and 6 in Northern Ireland.

Scotland

There are 26 FE colleges in Scotland that provide a broad mix of courses, many awarded by the Scottish Qualifications Authority (SQA). Most HE courses at or near degree level and beyond are provided by the 18 universities/HE institutions and The Open University in Scotland (www.universities-scotland.ac.uk; www.studyinscotland.org). These institutions offer a range of vocationally-oriented courses ranging from science, engineering and computing to health care, art and design, music and drama, and teacher training, as well as the more traditional 'academic' courses. The Scottish Funding Council funds all the universities and HE institutions in Scotland.

Northern Ireland

Responsibility for the FE sector in Northern Ireland rests with the Department for the Economy (DfENI) which directly funds colleges. There are six further and higher education colleges, offering a wide range of vocational and non-vocational courses for both full- and part-time students. Details can be found at www.anic.ac.uk

Queen's University Belfast and the University of Ulster receive Quality-related Research (QR) funding from the Department for the Economy. Many of the courses in both universities are designed to suit the needs of industry, commerce and the professions. Agricultural, horticultural and food colleges in Northern Ireland are administered through the Department of Agriculture, Environment and Rural Affairs (DAERA, website: www.daera-ni.gov.uk), which works with the College of Agriculture, Food and Rural Enterprise (CAFRE, website: www.cafre.ac.uk) to offer a range of further and higher education courses.

UNIVERSITIES AND HE COLLEGES

Universities are self-governing bodies, largely financed by the government through the Higher Education Funding Councils in the UK. They generally derive their rights and privileges from Royal Charter or Act of Parliament, and any amendment of their charters or statutes is made by the Crown acting through the Privy Council on the application of the universities themselves. The universities alone decide what degrees they award and the conditions on which they are awarded; they alone decide which students to admit and which staff to appoint. However, government policies have started to influence admission criteria, particularly in terms of widening access and participation in HE. Student fees set by universities are also subject to strict guidelines set by the government.

The Higher Education Funding Council (www.hefce.ac.uk) funds HE, research and related activities in English HE institutions and FE colleges. In 2016–17 it funded 132 HE institutions (including University Campus Suffolk, established and validated by the Universities of East Anglia and Essex) and 214 FE colleges.

Institutions receiving funding from Higher Education Funding Council for England

The schools and institutes of the University of London which receive funds directly from the HEFCE are marked *.

Anglia Ruskin University; Aston University; University of Bath; Bath Spa University; University of Bedfordshire; Birkbeck College, University of London*; University of Birmingham; Birmingham City University; University College Birmingham; Bishop Grosseteste University; University of Bolton; Arts University Bournemouth; Bournemouth University; University of Bradford; University of Brighton; University of Bristol; British School of Osteopathy; Brunel University; Buckinghamshire New University; University of Cambridge; Institute of Cancer Research*; Canterbury Christ Church University; University of Central Lancashire; University of Chester; University of Chichester; City University, London; Conservatoire for Dance and Drama; Courtauld Institute of Art*; Coventry University; Cranfield University; University for the Creative Arts; University of Cumbria; De Montfort University; University of Derby; University of Durham; University of East Anglia; University of East London; Edge Hill University; University of Essex; University of Exeter; Falmouth University; University of Gloucestershire; Goldsmiths' College,

University of London*; University of Greenwich; Guildhall School of Music and Drama; Harper Adams University; University of Hertfordshire; Heythrop College, University of London*; University of Huddersfield; University of Hull; Imperial College London; Keele University; University of Kent; King's College London*; Kingston University; University of Lancaster; University of Leeds; Leeds College of Art; Leeds Beckett University; Leeds Trinity University; University of Leicester; University of Lincoln; University of Liverpool; Liverpool Hope University; Liverpool Institute for Performing Arts; Liverpool John Moores University; Liverpool School of Tropical Medicine; University of the Arts, London; University of London; London Business School*; London School of Economics and Political Science*; London School of Hygiene and Tropical Medicine*; London Metropolitan University; London South Bank University; Loughborough University; University of Manchester; Manchester Metropolitan University; Middlesex University, London; National Film and Television School; University of Newcastle upon Tyne; Newman University; University of Northampton; University of Northumbria at Newcastle; Norwich University of the Arts; University of Nottingham; Nottingham Trent University; The Open University; University of Oxford; Oxford Brookes University; Plymouth University; Plymouth College of Art; University of Portsmouth; Queen Mary, University of London*; Ravensbourne; University of Reading; Roehampton University; Rose Bruford College; Royal Academy of Music*; Royal Agricultural University; Royal Central School of Speech and Drama*; Royal College of Art; Royal College of Music; Royal Holloway, University of London*; Royal Northern College of Music; Royal Veterinary College*; St George's, University of London*; University of St Mark and St John; St Mary's University, Twickenham; University of Salford; University of Sheffield; Sheffield Hallam University; School of Oriental and African Studies, University of London*; University of Southampton; Southampton Solent University; Staffordshire University; University Campus Suffolk; University of Sunderland; University of Surrey; University of Sussex; Teesside University; Trinity Laban Conservatoire of Music and Dance; University College London (including UCL Institute of Education)*; University of Warwick; University of the West of England, Bristol; University of West London; University of Westminster; University of Winchester; University of Wolverhampton; University of Worcester; Writtle College; University of York; York St John University.

(*Source*: Higher Education Funding Council for England)

Universities receiving funding from the Department for Employment and Learning in Northern Ireland

Queen's University Belfast; University of Ulster.

(*Source*: Higher Education Funding Council for England)

Higher Education Institutions receiving funding from the Scottish Funding Council

University of Aberdeen; Abertay University; University of Dundee; Edinburgh Napier University; University of Edinburgh; Glasgow Caledonian University; Glasgow School of Art; University of Glasgow; Heriot-Watt University; The Open University in Scotland; Queen Margaret University; Robert Gordon University; Royal Conservatoire of Scotland; SRUC; University of St Andrews; University of Stirling; University of Strathclyde; University of the Highlands and Islands; University of the West of Scotland. They also fund 25 colleges.

(*Source*: Scottish Funding Council, www.sfc.ac.uk/funding/funding.aspx)

Institutions receiving funding from the Higher Education Funding Council for Wales

Aberystwyth University; Bangor University; Cardiff University; Cardiff Metropolitan University; The Open University in Wales; University of South Wales; Swansea University; University of Wales; University of Wales Trinity Saint David; Wrexham Glyndwr University.

(*Source*: Higher Education Funding Council for Wales, www.hefcw.ac.uk)

OTHER HE ORGANIZATIONS

There are a number of other organizations involved in shaping the HE sector. You can find a full list of these organizations on the Universities UK website: www.universitiesuk.ac.uk

Part 3

Qualifications

INTRODUCTION

Definition of Common Terms

A number of terms are commonly used as synonyms for qualifications, for example 'examinations' and 'courses'. This can hide important differences of meaning and lead to confusion and mis-understanding. In some contexts it may be important to make these differences explicit to guard against exaggerating or diminishing the level of achievement, which is an essential core of the concept of qualification. It is especially important to clarify the difference in meaning between 'examination', 'course' and 'qualification'.

Examination

An examination is a formal test or assessment. It can focus on one or more of the following: knowledge, understanding, skill or competence. An examination may be set as a written test, an oral test, an aural and oral test (e.g. a foreign language test) or a practical test. In the past, most forms of external assessment in FE were based on a model of examination dominated by the psychometric model, designed to discriminate between individuals – normative referencing – and took the form of written tests. There was considerable variation in different kinds of written examination, including essays, question and answer, and 'multiple response'. Today, largely as a result of the introduction of National Vocational Qualifications (NVQs), the purpose and format of many examinations have been reappraised, and criterion-referenced examinations that focus on achievement (and in the case of NVQs, competence) are increasingly common. Many forms of assessment are now an integral part of the learning process, with a formative as well as a summative function rather than a separate, terminal, summative function.

Course

A course implies an ordered sequence of teaching or learning over a period of time. A course is governed by regulations or requirements, frequently imposed by an external awarding body and sometimes by the institution providing the course. An important distinguishing feature between different courses is the length of time allocated to study: it can vary from a few days to several years. Some courses offer a terminal award on the basis of course completion, and these courses are set for a given period of time. Other 'set period' courses may prescribe examinations; these can include continuous assessment, terminal testing or a combination of both. In other courses, the programme of study may be accomplished at a faster or slower rate; such courses normally enjoin continuous assessment or a terminal examination, or both. Many courses require attendance at an institution, while distance learning, correspondence courses, and various forms of flexible-learning courses are usually free of these requirements, although some may require occasional attendance for residential components or face-to-face tutoring. A successful examination result usually confers a qualification or an award.

Qualification

A qualification is normally a certificated endorsement, from a recognized awarding body, that a level or quality of accomplishment has been achieved by an individual. Qualifications are usually conferred on successful completion of an examination, although not all examinations necessarily offer qualifications. An examination may offer an award that is a part-qualification. For example, an NVQ candidate may acquire a unit of competence that is a part-qualification building towards a full statement of competence – an NVQ. A first-year student on an HND course may be required to pass all first-year examinations to be permitted to continue into the second year: in a sense that student is 'qualified' to continue the course but no qualification is awarded. Some award-bearing examinations may be fully recognized and certificated qualifications in themselves (e.g. a BTEC HNC) but only part-qualifications for a profession (e.g. chartered engineer).

Apparent anomalies do exist. Some professional bodies and trade associations award qualifications that are recognized within the profession or association but are not obtained by examination. They are usually awarded on the basis of experience, and payment of a fee, and denote membership or acceptance. When the body also offers an examination route to the same qualification, successful examinees are usually known as 'graduate members'.

There are a number of accreditation authorities that approve qualifications. There are also many specialist and general validating, examining and awarding bodies that are responsible for the design and assessment of qualifications.

ACCREDITING REGULATORY BODIES

England

Sector Skills Councils

Federation for Industry Sector Skills and Standards (FISSS)
Tel: 0300 303 4444 E-mail: info@fisss.org Website: www.fisss.org
The Federation for Industry Sector Skills and Standards, is an organization that supports the network of licensed UK Sector Skills Councils (SSCs). These are employer-led, independent organizations that cover specific work sectors across the UK (currently accounting for approximately 90 per cent of the UK workforce). With the influence granted by licences from the governments of England, Scotland, Wales and Northern Ireland, and with private and public funding, this independent network engages with the education and training supply-side such as universities, colleges, funders and qualifications bodies to increase productivity at all levels in the workforce. There are 20 Sector Skills Councils who work with over 550,000 employers to define skills needs and skills standards in their industry. There are also 19 National Skills Academies. Details of the Sector Skills Councils are listed in the following table.

Table 3.1

Cogent skills	**Creative & Cultural Skills**
Sector: Science industries	*Sector:* Craft, cultural heritage, design,
Tel: 01925 515 200	literature, music, performing and visual arts
E-mail: info@cogentskills.com	Tel: 020 7015 1800
Website: www.cogentskills.com	E-mail: info@ccskills.org.uk
	Website: www.ccskills.org.uk
Construction Skills	
Sector: Construction	**Creative Skillset**
Tel: 0344 994 4400	*Sector:* TV, film, radio, interactive media,
E-mail: call.centre@cskills.org	animation, computer games, facilities, photo
Website: www.cskills.org	imaging, publishing, advertising and fashion
	and textiles
	Tel: 020 7713 9800
	E-mail: info@creativeskillset.org
	Website: www.creativeskillset.org

continued

Table 3.1 *Continued*

Energy & Utility Skills
Sector: Gas, power, waste management and water industries
Tel: 0845 077 9922
E-mail: enquiries@euskills.co.uk
Website: www.euskills.co.uk

ecITB
Sector: Engineering
Tel: 01923 260000
E-mail: ecitb@ecitb.org.uk
Website: www.ecitb.org.uk

Financial Skills Partnership
Sector: Finance, accountancy and financial services
Tel: 0114 261 5800
E-mail: info@financialskillspartnership.org.uk
Website: www.financialskillspartnership.org.uk

IMI The Institute of the Motor Industry
Sector: Retail motor industry
Tel: 01992 519039
E-mail: comms@theimi.org.uk
Website: www.theimi.org.uk

Instructus Group
Sector: Business and administration, customer service, enterprise and business support, human resources and recruitment, industrial relations, leadership and management, marketing and sales
Tel: 0207 091 9620
E-mail: info@skillscfa.org
Website: www.skillscfa.org

Lantra
Sector: Land management and production, animal health and welfare and environmental industries
Tel: 024 7669 6996
E-mail: connect@lantra.co.uk
Website: www.lantra.co.uk

National Skills Academy for Food and Drink
Sector: Food and drink manufacturing and associated supply chains
Tel: 0845 644 0558
E-mail: info@insafd.co.uk
Website: www.nsafd.co.uk

People 1st
Sector: Hospitality, leisure, passenger transport, travel and tourism and retail
Tel: 020 3074 1222
E-mail: info@people1st.co.uk
Website: www.people1st.co.uk

SEMTA
Sector: Science, engineering and manufacturing technologies
Tel: 0845 643 9001
E-mail: customerservices@semta.org.uk
Website: www.semta.org.uk

Skills Active
Sector: Sport, fitness, outdoors, playwork, caravans and hair and beauty
Tel: 0207 840 1900
E-mail: skills@skillsactive.com
Website: www.skillsactive.com

Skills for Care & Development
Sector: Social care, children, early years and young people's workforces in the UK
Tel: 01133 241 1240
E-mail: sscinfo@skillsforcareanddevelopment.org.uk
Website: www.skillsforcareanddevelopment.org.uk

Skills for Health
Sector: UK Health
Tel: 0117 922 1155
E-mail: office@skillsforhealth.org.uk
Website: www.skillsforhealth.org.uk

continued

Table 3.1 *Continued*

Skills for Justice	**Summit Skills**
Sector: Community Justice, Courts Services, Custodial Care, Fire and Rescue, Forensic Science, Policing and Law Enforcement and Prosecution Services	*Sector:* Building Services Engineering
Tel: 0114 261 1499	Tel: 0207 313 4890
E-mail: info@skillsforjustice.com	E-mail: enquiries@summitskills.org.uk
Website: www.skillsforjustice.com	Website: www.summitskills.org.uk
Skills for Security	**Tech Partnership**
Sector: Security	*Sector:* Software, internet and web, IT services, telecommunications and business change
Tel: 01905 744000	Tel: 020 7963 8920
E-mail: info@skillsforsecurity.org.uk	E-mail: info@thetechpartnership.com
Website: www.skillsforsecurity.org.uk	Website: www.thetechpartnership.com

In October 2013, in response to the Richard Review of Apprenticeships (2012), the government set out its plans to reform Apprenticeships in England by replacing the existing Apprenticeship frameworks with employer-defined standards, putting employers in control and giving them a high degree of freedom to develop these standards to best meet the needs of their occupations and sectors. To support this reform, they established 'trailblazers' – groups led by employers and professional bodies – to develop the first of these new Apprenticeship standards (www.gov.uk/government/publications/future-of-apprenticeships-in-england-guidance-for-trailblazers).

The Government plan to introduce new standards for all occupations by 2017. A number of new Apprenticeship standards have already been government approved with the number growing all the time. Information on the new standards can be found at www.apprenticeships.org.uk/standards. The Federation for Industry Sector Skills and Standards (http://fisss.org) is developing a series of practical tools and guides for employers and employer-led partnerships to support the development of a new Apprenticeship standard and the detail of the implementation requirements which go with it – assessment, training and governance. The Federation currently manages the following certification systems for apprenticeships: ACE (England), ACW (Wales), MA Online v1 (Scotland) and MA Online v2 (Scotland).

The National College for Teaching and Leadership

The National College for Teaching and Leadership (NCTL) is part of the Department for Education and is involved in the exam administration function. The NCTL can be found at www.gov.uk/nctl, General enquiries, Ministerial and Public Communications Division, Department for Education, Piccadilly Gate, Store Street, Manchester, M1 2WD; Tel: 0370 000 2288. Information about the administration of exams can be found at www.gov.uk/exams-administration-information-for-exam-centres. The Department for Education is also a useful source of information, www.gov.uk/government/organisations/department-for-education.

Standards and Testing Agency (STA)

The Standards and Testing Agency is responsible for the development and delivery of all statutory assessments from early years to the end of Key Stage 3; Standards and Testing Agency,

53–55 Butts Road, Earlsdon Park, Coventry, CV1 3BH; National Curriculum assessments helpline: 0300 303 3013; E-mail: assessments@education.gov.uk; Website: www.gov.uk/sta

Ofqual: Office of Qualifications and Examinations Regulation

Contact details for Ofqual are: Ofqual, Spring Place, Herald Avenue, Coventry, CV5 6UB; Tel: 0300 303 3344; E-mail: public.enquiries@ofqual.gov.uk; Website: www.gov.uk/government/organisations/ofqual. Vocational qualifications that are only provided in Northern Ireland are regulated by the Council for the Curriculum, Examinations and Assessment, 29 Clarendon Road, Clarendon Dock, Belfast BT1 3BG; Tel: 02890 261200; E-mail: info@ccea.org.uk; Website: http://ccea.org.uk/

Ofqual is the regulator of qualifications, examinations and tests in England and a wide range of vocational qualifications in both England and Northern Ireland. Ofqual also regulates the National Curriculum Assessments in England. It monitors organizations that deliver qualifications and assessments as set out in the Apprenticeship, Skills, Children and Learning Act (2009) and Education Act (2011). Ofqual's role is to ensure all learners get the results they deserve, standards are maintained, and qualifications are correctly valued and understood, now and in the future.

Ofqual is accountable to parliament rather than to government ministers and advises the Government on qualifications and assessment based on their research into these areas.

Scotland

Scottish Qualifications Authority (SQA)

Customer Contact Centre, Tel: 0345 279 1000; Fax: 0345 213 5000; E-mail: customer@sqa.org.uk; Website: www.sqa.org.uk

The Scottish Qualifications Authority (SQA) is the national accreditation and awarding body in Scotland. It is an executive non-departmental public body (NDPB) sponsored by the Scottish Government's Learning Directorate and is fully committed to working with other organizations, agencies and institutions in Scotland to help meet the Scottish Government's National Outcomes, strategies, policies and priorities.

SQA works in partnership with schools, colleges, universities and industry to provide high-quality, flexible and relevant qualifications and assessments, embedding industry standards where appropriate. It strives to ensure that SQA qualifications are inclusive and accessible to all, that they provide clear progression pathways, facilitate lifelong learning and recognize candidate achievement. The National Qualifications have been designed to meet the aims, purposes and values of Curriculum for Excellence.

People take SQA qualifications at all stages of their lives – at school, at college, at work and in their leisure time. There are qualifications at all levels of attainment. SQA is responsible for three main types of qualification: units, courses and group awards. Most SQA-awarded qualifications are made up of a combination of units, which can also be used in their own right. Each unit represents approximately 40 hours of teaching with additional study. Units are achieved by passing an assessment.

National Courses

There are seven levels of National Courses – National 1–5, Higher, and Advanced Higher and there are at present four Scottish Baccalaureates, which are awarded at Pass and Distinction.

National Courses are designed to develop skills and knowledge in a specific subject area as well as skills for learning, skills for life and skills for work. Achieving a National Course shows that a learner has demonstrated the specified knowledge and skills in a particular subject at the defined national standard. Some of the new Awards cover work from across different subject areas, are shorter than traditional courses and recognize success at different levels of difficulty, meaning they are suitable for young people of all abilities.

Higher National Courses

Higher Courses provide progression from National 5 and lead on to Advanced Higher and are designed to develop skills and knowledge in a specific subject area. Offered by colleges, some universities and many other training centres, Higher National Certificates (HNCs) and Higher National Diplomas (HNDs) are specially designed to meet the needs of employers. HNCs are usually made up of 12 Higher National Unit credits (one credit represents roughly 40 hours of timetabled learning and 40 hours of self-guided learning and study) and usually take one year to complete; HNDs are made up of 30 credits and usually take two years to complete.

Advanced Higher National Courses

Advanced Higher awards are designed to meet the aims, purposes and values of Curriculum for Excellence, and provide progression from Higher Courses. These courses, which are designed to develop skills and knowledge in a specific subject area, are usually made up of three National Units and an external assessment by means of an examination and a project. Advanced Highers tend to be taken in the sixth year at school or college by students who have normally passed Highers.

Skills for Work

There are also Skills for Work Courses from National 3 to National 5. These are vocational courses for pupils in third and fourth year of secondary school and above. Normally pupils following the Skills for Work courses will spend some of their time at a local college or another training provider or with an employer. The courses are intended to provide progression pathways to further education, training and employment.

Skills for Work courses, National 3, 4 and 5 and Higher are designed to develop skills and knowledge in a broad vocational area, as well as an understanding of: the workplace skills and attitudes for employability, Core Skills, and other transferable skills. They involve a strong element of learning through involvement in practical activities which are directly related to a particular vocational area. National 3 is usually made up of three 40-hour units and National 4, 5 and Higher are usually made up of four 40-hour units.

Other SQA Courses

National Qualification Group Awards – National Certificates (NCs), Higher National Certificates and Diplomas (HNCs and HNDs) and National Progression Awards (NPAs) – are designed to be taken at college; Scottish Vocational Qualifications (SVQs), Professional Development Awards (PDAs), QCF (Qualifications and Credit Framework) registered Awards, Certificates and Diplomas and Functional Skills, and Customized Awards are designed for the workplace. A private company or training provider must become an 'approved centre' to deliver SQA qualifications, or work in partnership with a college or training provider. SQA also offer Modern Apprenticeships.

SQA Qualifications

Higher National Certificates (HNCs) and **Higher National Diplomas** (HNDs) are developed by SQA in partnership with FE colleges, universities, and industry and commerce. They are credible, flexible qualifications that are designed to deliver skills and knowledge to meet the needs of today's businesses. Some HNCs allow direct entry into the second year of a degree programme, and some HNDs allow direct entry to the third year. Higher National qualifications can also give you the knowledge and understanding required for Scottish Vocational Qualifications (SVQs).

National Progression Awards (NPAs) are designed to assess a defined set of skills and knowledge in specialist vocational areas. They are mainly used by colleges for short programmes of study.

National Certificates are primarily aimed at 16–18-year olds and adults in full-time education. They prepare candidates for employment or further study by developing a range of knowledge and skills.

Scottish Vocational Qualifications (SVQs) are based on job competence, and recognize the skills and knowledge people need in employment. SVQs can be attained in most occupations and are available for all types and levels of job. They are primarily delivered to candidates in full-time employment and in the workplace.

Professional Development Awards (PDAs) are qualifications for people who are already in a career and who wish to extend or broaden their skills. In some cases they are designed for people wishing to enter employment. PDAs can be taken at college or the workplace.

Customized Awards are specially designed vocational qualifications at any level to meet an organization's need for skills and expertise and provide recognition and development opportunities for individuals. They can also help a company meet regulatory requirements and demonstrate the competence of its employees to external parties.

Scottish Credit and Qualifications Framework

The SQA is a partner in a 'credit' system called the Scottish Credit and Qualifications Framework (SCQF), which sets out the Scottish qualifications and how they relate to one another by making clear the credit value of each type of qualification available in Scotland. The framework has 12 levels, from Level 1 for very basic education to Level 12 for doctoral degrees.

More information about SQA and its qualifications can be found at its website: www.sqa.org.uk

Validating, examining and awarding bodies/organizations

A large number of external bodies provide qualifications recognized by accrediting and regulatory bodies. Not all qualifications are available across the entire FE sector: some colleges specialize in particular vocational areas while others are involved in more general adult education provision.

The Federation of Awarding Bodies (FAB) is a trade federation and membership organization for vocational awarding bodies. At the time of writing there are around 120 Ofqual-recognized awarding bodies that are full members of FAB. It also has associate members. Find more information at www.awarding.org.uk.

It is important to contact the examining or awarding bodies directly to find which colleges deliver the qualifications desired. However, most colleges deliver courses leading to qualifications awarded by the sample selection of organizations listed below.

ABC Awards

Robins Wood House, Robins Wood Road, Aspley, Nottingham NG8 3NH; Tel: 0115 854 1620; Fax: 0115 854 1617; E-mail: centresupport@abcawards.co.uk; website: www.abcawards.co.uk

ABC Awards is a vocational awarding organization with accredited QCF qualifications in all sectors. It is a registered charity and part of the EMFEC Group. ABC has a portfolio of Ofqual regulated qualifications covering 16 industry sectors as well as functional skills and is designed for all ages and abilities post-14. ABC Awards' qualifications give learners the skills they need to find employment, progress within education and training or enhance their skills within their current job roles.

AQA

Stag Hill House, Guildford, Surrey GU2 7XJ; Tel: 0800 197 7162; Exams Office Support e-mail: eos@aqa.org.uk; website: www.aqa.org.uk

AQA is an independent education charity and the largest of the exam boards, currently setting and marking the papers for around half of all GCSEs and A-levels in England, Wales and Northern Ireland. AQA qualifications are internationally recognized and are taught in 30 countries around the world. As an awarding body AQA offers a broad range of academic qualifications for 14–19-year olds including GCEs, GCSEs, AQA iGCSEs, the Extended Project Qualification and the AQA Baccalaureate.

ASDAN

Wainbrook House, Hudds Vale Road, St George, Bristol BS5 7HY; Tel: 0117 941 1126; e-mail: info@asdan.org.uk; website: www.asdan.org.uk

ASDAN is a curriculum development organization and awarding body, offering programmes and qualifications that explicitly grow skills for learning, for employment and for life. ASDAN is established as a registered charity for the 'advancement of education, by providing opportunities for all learners to develop their personal and social attributes and levels of achievement through ASDAN awards and resources, and the relief of poverty, where poverty inhibits such opportunities for learners'.

   ASDAN qualifications contribute towards school/college performance measures and Ofsted requirements. ASDAN offers a range of nationally approved qualifications based around the development of personal, social and employability skills:

- Entry 1, 2 and 3 (Access) qualifications meet the needs of learners working below GCSE (Intermediate) level
- Levels 1 and 2 (Intermediate) qualifications are comparable to GCSEs
- Level 3 (Higher) qualifications are A/AS-level comparable
- Level 4 accreditation represents a Certificate of Higher Education

Ofqual, Qualifications Wales and CCEA approve ASDAN qualifications for pre-and post-16 provision. ASDAN qualifications sit within the Regulated Qualifications Framework (RQF) and the Qualifications and Credit Framework (QCF), and some have approval within the SCQF in Scotland. ASDAN also offers a wide choice of activity-based curriculum programmes that can be used in a variety of educational settings with learners working at a range of levels, offering imaginative ways of developing, recording and certificating young people's personal achievements. Through Customised Accreditation ASDAN also accredits programmes that are already being offered or has been written by another organization.

The following ASDAN qualifications are available:
- Qualifications in Personal Progress: Entry 1
- Personal and Social Development (PSD): Entry 1–3, Levels 1 and 2
- Employability: Entry 2 to Level 3
- Diplomas in Life Skills: Entry 1–3
- Event Volunteering Qualifications: Entry 3 to Level 3
- Wider Key Skills: Levels 1–4
- Certificate of Personal Effectiveness (CoPE): Levels 1–3
- Award of Personal Effectiveness (AoPE) Levels 1–3

City & Guilds

1 Giltspur Street, London EC1A 9DD; Tel: Customers: 0844 543 0000, Main switchboard: 0207 294 2468; e-mail: centresupport@cityandguilds.com; website: www.cityandguilds.com

City & Guilds is a leading vocational educational organization, offering hundreds of work-related qualifications worldwide. City & Guilds' qualifications, which span from basic skills to the highest level of professional achievement, are delivered in more than 80 countries across the world.

With over 130 years of experience, City & Guilds offers a wide range of vocational qualifications, apprenticeships and traineeships from agriculture to engineering; hairdressing to health and social care; IT to tourism; and photography to catering. They are developed with the help of industry experts and are workplace-relevant, so these qualifications equip people for doing a real job – benefiting them and their employer.

City & Guilds qualifications develop both knowledge and practical skills. They are available at nine levels, from Entry Level to Level 8, and are suitable for anyone, whether they are beginners or advanced in their career or area of study. Assessment is based on any combination of examination, projects or coursework. The organizations that offer City & Guilds qualifications include schools, colleges, training organizations, companies and adult education institutes. Depending on the organization, it is possible to study full time, part time or through distance learning.

City and Guilds offer the following qualifications: National Vocational Qualifications (NVQs) and Scottish Vocational Qualifications (SVQs), Functional Skills, Core Skills and Essential Skills, International Vocational Qualifications (IVQs), Single Subject Qualifications, International English Qualifications (IEQs), Institute of Leadership and Management (ILM) qualifications, Professional Recognition Awards, Tech Levels, TechBac, Apprenticeships and Traineeships.

Pearson (Edexcel, BTEC and LCCI)

190 High Holborn, London WC1V 7BH; website: https://qualifications.pearson.com, online contact form for students: http://qualifications.pearson.com/en/support/support-for-you/students/contact-us.html

Edexcel, of Pearson Education Limited, is the UK's largest awarding organization, offering academic and vocational qualifications and testing to schools, colleges, employers and other places of learning in the UK and internationally. Edexcel academic qualifications include GCSE,

GCE (A level) and International GCSE (Edexcel Certificate for UK state schools). Edexcel vocational qualifications include NVQ and BTEC from entry level to Higher National Diplomas.

Pearson acquired EDI, a leading provider of education and training qualifications and assessment services and the EDI qualifications have been rebranded as Pearson material. The qualifications selected from EDI have been redeveloped or reaccredited to be delivered through Pearson's brands including: Pearson Edexcel, Pearson BTEC and Pearson LCCI.

LCCI International Qualifications are widely used in South East Asia and over 100 countries around the world. LCCI International Qualifications, vocational qualifications available as single subjects or diplomas, cover the key areas of business, language and teaching.

NCFE

Q6, Quorum Business Park, Benton Lane, Newcastle upon Tyne NE12 8BT; Tel: 0191 239 8000; e-mail: service@ncfe.org.uk; website: www.ncfe.org.uk

NCFE is a national awarding organization and registered educational charity. It currently offers over 500 nationally accredited qualifications from Entry level up to and including level 4 as well as NVQs, Functional Skills, Apprenticeships and Traineeships. Further qualifications are constantly in development. The NCFE website has a qualifications finder search facility: www.ncfe.org.uk/ qualification-search

OCR

1 Hills Road, Cambridge CB1 2EU;
General qualifications: Tel: 01223 553998; e-mail: general.qualifications@ocr.org.uk;
Vocational qualifications: Tel: 02476 851 509; e-mail: vocational. qualifications@ocr.org.uk;
website: www.ocr.org.uk

OCR is a leading UK awarding body, committed to providing qualifications that engage learners of all ages at school, college, in work or through part-time learning programmes to achieve their full potential. OCR offers a wide range of general and vocational qualifications, from GCSEs, A levels and Diplomas to OCR Nationals, NVQs and specialist qualifications. You can find a full index of OCR qualifications at: www.ocr.org.uk/qualifications/index.aspx

WJEC

245 Western Avenue, Cardiff CF5 2YX; Tel: 029 2026 5000; e-mail: info@wjec.co.uk; website: www.wjec.co.uk

A registered charity with members from the 22 local authorities in Wales, WJEC is a leading awarding organization providing assessment, training and educational resources in England, Wales, Northern Ireland and elsewhere; WJEC CBAC Ltd is a company limited by guarantee, registered in England and Wales. WJEC offers the following major qualifications: GCSE; Entry Level (EL) and Advanced (A)/Advanced Supplementary (AS) levels and the Welsh Baccalaureate, which is available at different levels and incorporates GCSEs, A Levels and NVQs. In addition, WJEC provides Essential Skills Wales, Project and Extended Project, Pathways QCF, Principal Learning and Wider Key Skills qualifications. The reformed GCSE and GCE qualifications in England are provided via Eduqas, the new brand from WJEC (www.eduqas.co.uk).

Part 4

Qualifications Awarded or Validated by Universities

ADMISSION TO DEGREE COURSES

Higher Education Institutions (HEIs)

Most institutions have a general requirement for admission to a degree course; special requirements may be in force for particular courses. Requirements are usually expressed in terms of subjects passed at GCE A level and the Higher Grade of the SQC. UCAS is the clearing house for the universities and it handles applications for university courses (www.ucas.com).

All intending students who live in the UK may obtain information on application procedures from their schools or colleges, or directly from UCAS. The scheme covers all universities and all medical schools. UCAS also has specialist services: the UCAS Teacher Training www.ucas.com/ucas/teacher-training, the UK Postgraduate Application and Statistical Service (www.ucas.com/ucas/postgraduate) and the UCAS Conservatoires (www.ucas.com/ucas/conservatories). HEIs have specific schemes to encourage access and participation in higher education. These can include partnerships with further education colleges that run access to higher education courses.

The Open University

For admission to most first-degree courses, no formal educational qualifications are necessary. However, students who have successfully completed one or more years of full-time study at the higher education level (or its equivalent in part-time study) may be eligible for exemption from some credit requirements of the BA degree. The Open University handles its own admissions.

Business schools

The degrees awarded by the various university business schools are postgraduate and therefore normally require an Honours degree as part of their entrance qualification.

AWARDS

The awards made by the universities may be separated into the following categories: first degrees; higher degrees; honorary degrees; first diplomas and certificates; higher diplomas and certificates.

First degrees

Nomenclature

Various names are given to first degrees at British universities. At most universities the first degree in Arts is the BA (Bachelor of Arts) and the first degree in Science is the BSc (Bachelor of Science), but at the universities of Oxford and Cambridge and at several new universities, the BA is the first degree gained by students in both arts and science. Although the first degree in most faculties in Scottish universities is a Bachelor's degree, the first degree in Arts in the four 'ancient' universities and Dundee University is MA or Master of Arts. Heriot-Watt University also offers some 'first degree' MAs, but at Honours level only.

There are numerous variations on the bachelor theme, for example BSc (Econ) (Bachelor of Science in Economics), BCom (Bachelor of Commerce), BSocSc (Bachelor of Social Science), BEng (Bachelor of Engineering) and BTech (Bachelor of Technology). The first award in medicine is the joint degrees of MB, ChB (Bachelor of Medicine, Bachelor of Surgery), the designatory letters of which vary from university to university.

Structure of courses

First-degree courses vary considerably in structure, not only between one university and another but also between faculties in a single university. The degree examination is usually in two sections, Part I coming after one or two years of the course and Part II, 'finals, at the end of the course. The first-degree system at some Scottish universities differs substantially from that in English and Welsh universities (see below).

Bachelor degrees

These degrees, sometimes known as 'ordinary' or 'first' degrees, lead to qualifications such as Bachelor of Arts (BA), Bachelor of Science (BSc) or Bachelor of Medicine (MB). Each university decides the form and content of its own degree examinations. These vary from university to university.

The first-degree structure in all British universities is based on the honours degree. Successful candidates in honours degree examinations are placed in different classes according to their performance, first class being the highest. The other classes given vary from university to university, but the classification most often used is: Class I; Class II (Division 1); Class II (Division 2); Class III. Most graduates who go on to higher academic qualifications and those entering, for example, the higher grades in the Civil Service or research, normally have a good class honours degree.

You can find out more about recognized UK degrees at the Government website: www.gov.uk/recognised-uk-degrees.

Number of subjects studied

Excluding medicine and dentistry, the broad subject areas are Arts (or Humanities), Social Science, Pure Science and Applied Science. Most students study one main subject selected from one of these areas. It is possible to distinguish many types of degree course according to the number of subjects studied; these types are a variation on three main categories:

1. Honours course in one to three subjects with or without examinable subsidiary subjects.
2. Pass or ordinary courses in one to three subjects with or without examinable subsidiary subjects.
3. Common studies for pass and Honours in one to three subjects, with or without examinable subsidiary subjects.

Length of degree course

First-degree courses may be preceded by a preliminary year, from which students with the appropriate entry qualifications may be exempted. At most universities Honours and pass courses in arts, social science, pure and applied science last three or four years, but courses in architecture, dentistry and veterinary medicine usually last five years, and complete qualifying courses in medicine up to six years. Courses in fine arts and pharmacy may last four years; four-year courses exist mainly in double Honours schools, especially when they involve foreign languages and a period of study abroad, and in the technological universities where some courses include a period of integrated industrial training (sandwich courses).

The Scottish first degree

Undergraduate Honours degrees in Scotland are usually four years in duration and are structured to ensure a great deal of flexibility during the first two years of study. Most students only confirm their major in the final two years of study, which usually allows the student to choose a variety of subjects. This is different from the English system of undergraduate education, which is normally three years in duration and is more specialized from the beginning. After three years study students can gain a Bachelor or Ordinary degree or obtain the Honours degree by studying for a further year.

The Medicine and Veterinary Medicine degrees and MA Fine Art degree all take five years. In several science and engineering subjects there are opportunities to study for a five-year MChem, MChemPhys, MEng or MPhys degree. These degrees entail in-depth study, often with a research focus, but are undergraduate degrees and not equivalent to postgraduate Master's.

Aegrotat degrees

Candidates who have followed a course for a degree but have been prevented from taking the examinations by illness may be awarded a degree certificate indicating that they were likely to have obtained the degree had they taken the examinations.

Higher degrees

These comprise:
- some Bachelor's degrees: BPhil, BLitt, etc;
- Master's degrees: MA, MSc, etc;
- Doctor of Philosophy: PhD or DPhil;
- Higher Doctorates: DLitt, DSc, etc.

At Oxford and Cambridge the degree of MA is conferred on any BA of the university without any further course of study or examination after a specified number of years and on payment of a fee.

Candidates for a Master's degree at other universities (and at some for the degrees of BPhil, BLitt and BD, which are of equivalent standing) are normally required to have a first degree, although it need not have been obtained in the same university. Master's degrees are taken after one or two years' full-time study. The PhD requires at least two or more – usually three – years of full-time study.

In some universities and faculties students may be selected for a PhD course after an initial year's study or research common to both a PhD and a Master's degree. Candidates for a Master's degree are required either to prepare a thesis for presentation to examiners, who may afterwards question candidates on it orally, or to take written examination papers; they may be required to do both. All PhD students present a thesis; some may be required to take an examination paper as well. MPhil, MSc and similar degrees are usually awarded at the end of a one- or two-year course in a specific topic on the results of a written examination or a thesis. Higher doctorates are designated on a faculty basis, eg DLitt (Doctor of Letters) and DSc (Doctor of Science). Candidates are usually required to have at least a Master's degree of the awarding university. Senior doctorates are conferred on more mature and established people, usually on the basis of published contributions to knowledge.

Foundation degrees

Foundation degrees were established to give people the intermediate technical and professional skills that are in demand from employers and to provide more flexible and accessible ways of studying. Increasing opportunities for employment and career advancement are priorities; Foundation degree content and assessment are therefore designed in consultation with employers. Additional progression routes include links with associated professional qualifications and/or direct entry to the final year of a relevant Honours-level degree. Provision is available across a range of FE colleges and a number of HEIs.

Honorary degrees

Most universities confer honorary degrees on people of distinction in academic and public life, and on others who have rendered service to the university or to the local community. Normally degrees awarded are at least Foundation level.

Diplomas and certificates of higher education

Courses for first diplomas and certificates are relatively simple in structure; they usually reach a level lower than that required for the award of a degree. There is usually a carefully defined course in a specialized or vocational subject, lasting one or two years, followed by all candidates. Most courses are full time.

Postgraduate diplomas and certificates

Diplomas (eg in public health, social administration, medicine and technology) are awarded either on a full-time or, less often, part-time basis according to the subject and the university. Candidates must usually be graduates or hold equivalent qualifications. Diplomas are awarded after formal courses of instruction and success in written examinations. A Certificate or Diploma in Education is awarded to graduates training to become teachers after one year's full-time study and teaching practice.

Postgraduate courses

A number of courses for graduates or people with equivalent qualifications are offered in FE establishments. They include short specialist courses in management and business studies and secretarial courses for graduates.

Business schools

A Master of Business Administration (MBA) is an internationally recognized postgraduate qualification intended to prepare individuals for middle to senior general managerial positions. Most programmes contain as their core a number of subjects considered essential for understanding the operations of any enterprise. These are: accounting and finance, operations management, business policy, economics, human resource management, marketing, information systems and strategic planning.

Unlike any other Master's programme, the MBA is not only postgraduate, it is also strongly post-experience. A minimum of three years' (often more) work experience at an appropriate level of responsibility is generally expected of applicants. The requirement for a first degree (or equivalent) is sometimes waived for those holding an impressive track record of over five years at managerial level. Approximately one-third of MBA students have an engineering or information technology background. Many undertake the qualification to facilitate change from technical or specialist positions to more general ones.

The MBA was conceived originally in the United States at the beginning of the twentieth century. Introduced in the United Kingdom in the late 1960s, it did not grow in popularity until the late 1980s. The popularity of this degree in the United Kingdom can be seen in the rapid expansion in the number of providers.

The Association of MBAs (AMBA) operates a system of accreditation. The accreditation process, which is internationally recognized for all MBA, DBA and Master's in Business and Management (MBM) programmes, measures individual MBA programmes against specific accreditation criteria.

Further information, including a list of accredited MBA programmes, can be obtained from the Association of MBAs, 25 Hosier Lane, London EC1A 9LQ; Tel: 020 7246 2686; e-mail: info@mbaworld.com; website: www.mbaworld.com.

The Chartered Association of Business Schools (CABS)

3rd Floor, 40 Queen Street, London EC4R 1DD; Tel: 020 7236 7678; website: www.associationof-businessschools.org.

The CABS is the representative body for management and business education and all the United Kingdom's leading business schools and acts as a hub for sharing new ideas and developing best practice.

The CABS works broadly in three main areas: policy development, promotion and representation, and training and development. The CABS is able to provide general information about the wide range of courses and programmes provided by the United Kingdom's business schools.

First awards

- **BA, BEd, BEng, LLB, BSc, BBA, BMedSci:** with 1st Class, 2nd Class (Divisions 1 and 2), 3rd Class Honours or Pass; or unclassified with or without Distinction.

- **MEng:** awarded to students who successfully complete a course of study that is longer and more demanding than the BEng first degree course in engineering.
- **GMus (Graduate Diploma in Music):** awarded to those students who complete three years' approved full-time study (or equivalent) in music and who demonstrate competence in musical performance.

- **M.Ost (Master of Osteophathy):** M.Ost is an undergraduate degree of four years' full-time study.
- **DipHE (Diploma of Higher Education):** equivalent in standard and often similar in content to the first two years of an Honours degree course.
- **Certificates of Higher Education:** equivalent to the first year of an Honours degree course.

Higher awards

- **MA, MBA, MEd, MSc:** for successful completion of an approved postgraduate course of full-time study of three trimesters duration (or the part-time equivalent).
- **MPhil, PhD:** for successful completion of approved programmes of supervised research.
- **DSc, DLitt, DTech:** for original and important contributions to knowledge and/or its applications.
- **Postgraduate Diploma:** awarded for the successful completion of an approved postgraduate course of study of 30 weeks' duration (or the part-time equivalent).

- **Postgraduate Certificate:** awarded for the successful completion of postgraduate/post-experience courses of 15 weeks' duration (or the part-time equivalent).
- **Postgraduate Certificate in Education (PGCE):** awarded on completion of a one-year full-time course; candidates must be British graduates or hold another recognized qualification.
- **Diploma in Professional Studies:** available in the fields of education and nursing, health visiting, midwifery and sports coaching. Students normally hold an initial professional qualification. A minimum of two years' experience is normally expected.

UNIVERSITY OF ABERDEEN
www.abdn.ac.uk

College of Arts and Social Sciences; www.abdn.ac.uk/about/social-sciences/php

Aberdeen Business School; www.abdn.ac.uk/business
accounting, applied economics (finance/health), digital management leadership, economics, finance, financial mathematics, real estate, accounting & finance, applied economics, international business management, management consultancy, marketing management, energy management, finance & real estate/management, petroleum, energy economics & finance/management, MBA programmes, MBA/HRM; MA(Hons), MBA, MRes, MSc, MPhil, PGCert, PhD

School of Divinity, History & Philosophy; www.abdn.ac.uk/sdhp
divinity, history of art, history, philosophy, biblical studies, ministry studies, theological ethics, systematic theology, ancient Greek, Islamic studies, art and business, medieval and early modern studies, Scandinavian studies, modern history, Irish & Scottish history; BD, BTh, DMin, LicTh, MA(Hons), MLitt, MTh, PGDip, PhD, DPS, PGCert, ProfDoc

School of Education; www.abdn.ac.uk/education
education, childhood practice, professional development, teaching qualification further education, counselling skills, autism and learning, inclusive practice, pastoral care, guidance and pupil support, person-centred counselling, community learning and development, studies in mindfulness, early years, Streap: Gaelic medium education, leadership in professional contexts, teaching qualification further education, social and educational research, teaching & learning in the primary context; MA(Hons), BA(Hons), BEd(-Hons), MEd, MPhil, MRes, MSc, BMus(Hons), PGCert, PGDE, PGDip, PhD, EdD

School of Language & Literature,Music; www.abdn.ac.uk/sll

Celtic and Anglo-Saxon studies, English, ethnology & folklore, film and visual culture, French and Francophone studies, Gaelic studies, German studies, Hispanic studies, language and linguistics, literature in a world context, professional communication, TESOL, translation studies, creative writing, English literary studies, Irish and Scottish literature, literature, science and medicine, the novel, visual culture, music, sonic arts, vocal music; MA, MA(Designated), MA(Hons), MLitt, PhD, MSc, MMus, TESOL

School of Law; www.abdn.ac.uk/law

law, law with English law/Spanish law/French law/German law/Belgian law, law with options in French language/German language/Spanish language/Gaelic language/music, energy law, oil & gas law /with professional skills, energy and environmental law, international law, public international law, private international law, international law and international relations, international law and strategic studies, criminal justice, human rights, criminal justice & human rights; LlB(Hons), LlM, MPhil, PhD

School of Social Science; www.abdn.ac.uk/ socsci

anthropology, genderising of global governance, people & the environment, politics & international relations, international law, social anthropology, religion & society, sex, gender & violence, museum studies, sociology; MA(Hons), MA, MLitt, MPhil, MRes, MSc, PGDip, PhD

College of Life Sciences and Medicine; www.abdn.ac.uk/clsm

School of Biological Sciences; www.abdn.ac.uk/biologicalsci

animal behaviour, behavioural biology, biological sciences, marine biology, conservation biology, ecology, ecological & environmental ecology, environmental science/microbiology, animal, marine & fisheries ecology, forestry, plant & soil science, zoology; BSc, MSci

School of Medicine, Medical Science, and Nutrition; www.abdn.ac.uk/sms

biochemistry, biomedical sciences, biotechnology, dentistry, exercise and health science, genetics, genetics (immunology), human embryology & developmental biology, immunology, immunology & pharmacology,medicine, medical science, microbiology, molecular biology, neuroscience with

psychology, pharmacology, physiology, sports & exercise science; BSc(Hons), MSc, MPhil, PGDip/Cert, PhD/MD, MRes, MSci, MBChB, BDS

School of Psychology; www.abdn.ac.uk/ psychology

psychology, social/cognition, perception & attention, behavioural studies; BSc(Hons), MA, MRes, MSc, PhD

Rowett Institute of Nutrition and Health Studies; www.abdn.ac.uk/rowett

impacts on human health

CLSM (College of Life Sciences & Nutrition) Graduate School; www.abdn.ac.uk/clsm/ graduate

public health, research methods for health, health psychology, global health and management, health economics, human nutrition, applied marine & fisheries ecology, ecology & conservation, environmental science, environmental & forest management, soil science, bio-business and medical sciences, clinical pharmacology, drug discovery/and development, genetics, immunology, stratified medicine and pharmacological innovation in medical education, research methods for health, medical education, physician associate studies, clinical pharmacology, medical imaging, medical physics, psychological studies, psychology; BDS, BSc(Hons), MA, MBChB, MMedSci, MPhil, MSc, PhD, PGDip/Cert, MD, MRes, MPH

College of Physical Sciences; www.abdn.ac.uk/about/physical-sciences.php

School of Engineering; www.abdn.ac.uk/ engineering

chemical engineering, civil/structural engineering, electrical & electronic engineering, mechanical engineering, project management, reservoir engineering, process safety, renewable energy engineering, subsea engineering, oil & gas/structural/engineering, petroleum engineering, safety & reliability engineering for oil & gas; BEng(Hons), EngD, MEng, MSc, PhD

School of Geosciences; www.abdn.ac.uk/ geosciences

archaeology, geography, geology and petroleum geology, geoscience, geoscience and geography, geology and physics, geology and archaeology, archaeology of the north, GIS, geophysics, land economy (rural surveying), hydrocarbon exploration, integrated petroleum geoscience, oil & gas enterprise management, petrophysics and formation evaluation; BSc, MA, MSc, PhD, MLE

Dept of Archaeology; www.abdn.ac.uk/archaeology

archaeology, with Celtic civilization/history/geography, archaeology of the north; BSc(Hons), MA(Hons), MPhil, PhD, MSc

Dept of Geography & the Environment; www.abdn.ac.uk/geography

geography, physical/human geography, geographical information systems(GIS), data analysis, environmental partnership management, marine & coastal resource management, urban/rural planning, land economy (rural surveying/change), sustainable rural development, environmental management/hydrology; BSc(Hons), MA, MSc, PGDip, PhD, MRes

Dept of Geology & Petroleum Geology; www.abdn.ac.uk/geology

oil & gas enterprise management, geology, geology & archaeology/geoscience/physics/petroleum geology, integrated petroleum geoscience, petrophysics & formation evaluation; BSc(Hons), MA(Hons), MRes, MSc, PGDip/Cert, PhD, MGeol

School of Natural & Computing Sciences; www.abdn.ac.uk/ncs

Chemistry; www.abdn.ac.uk/ncs/chemistry

chemistry, environmental/ analytical chemistry, chemistry, oil & gas chemistry, jt degrees; BSc(Hons), MChem, MSc, PGDip, PhD

Computing; www.abdn.ac.uk/ncs/computing

computing (with numerous joint degrees), computing science/&mathematics/physics, data & visualisation communication, information systems/& data management, information technology, oil & gas computing, software entrepreneurship; BSc(Hons), MA(Hons), MSc/PGDip, MSci, PhD, PGDip, MPhil, MEng

Institute of Mathematics; www.abdn.ac.uk/ncs/mathematics

mathematics (with numerous jt degrees), applied mathematics, statistics, topology of high dimension manifolds; BSc(Hons), MA(Hons), MSc, PhD, MPhil

Physics; www.abdn.ac.uk/ncs/physics

physical sciences, physics (with numerous jt degrees), physics education, physics with chemistry/geology/philosophy/ engineering/ mathematics/ modern language; BSc(Hons), MSc(Hons), PhD

UNIVERSITY OF ABERTAY, DUNDEE
www.abertay.ac.uk

School of Arts, Media & Computer Games; www.abertay.ac.uk/studying/schools/amg

School of Science, Engineering & Technology; www.abertay.ac.uk/studying/schools/set

Dundee Business School; www.abertay.ac.uk/studying/schools/dbs

The School of Social & Health Sciences; www.abertay.ac.uk/studying/schools/shs

Undergraduate Courses

accounting and finance, biomedical science, business management, civil and environmental engineering, civil engineering, computer arts, computer game applications developments/technology, game design & production management, ethical hacking, criminology, English, environmental science and technology, food, nutrition & health, food & consumer science, psychology and forensic biology, forensic sciences, law, marketing & business, nursing (mental health nursing), psychology, psychology and forensic biology counselling, social science, sociology, sound and music for games, sport & management/psychology, strength and conditioning, physical activity & health, development and coaching, sport and exercise science, sport and exercise; BA(Hons), BSc(Hons),BBA(Hons), LlB(Hons)

Postgraduate Taught Courses

international finance and accounting, international human resource management, international management, oil & gas accounting and management, games development, computer games technology, ethical hacking & cyber security, counselling, counselling skills, English, energy, water & environmental management, food & drink innovation, EU security and transnational criminal justice, mental health nursing, energy, water and environmental management, oil & gas accounting and management, psychology; MSc,

MEng, BEng,MProf, LlM, PGDip/Cert, Grad Cert, MBA

ABERYSTWYTH UNIVERSITY
www.aber.ac.uk

School of Art; www.aber.ac.uk/en/art
art, art history, fine art, creative arts; BA(Hons), MA, MPhil, PhD

Institute of Biological, Environmental & Rural Sciences; www.aber.ac.uk/en/ibers
agriculture/with animal science/countryside management/business studies, animal science/zoology, biochemistry, biology, conservation/countryside management, environmental bioscience & ecology, microbiology, equine science, food & water security, genetics, life sciences, livestock science, marine & freshwater biology/systems, microbiology, green biotechnology & innovation management, managing the environment – environmental sustainability/bioenergy & environmental change/habitat restoration & conservation, sport & exercise science,equine science, equine studies, equine and veterinary bioscience; BSc(Hons), MPhil, MSc, PhD, DAg

Dept of Computer Science; www.aber.ac.uk/en/cs
computer science/& AI, AI & robotics, computer graphics vision and games, internet computing & systems administration, business information technology, software engineering, space science & robotics, intelligent autonomous systems, intelligent systems, ICT & computer science, statistics for computational biology; BEng, BSc(Hons), HND, MEng, MSc, PhD, MRes

School of Education & Lifelong Learning; www.aber.ac.uk/en/sell
childhood studies, lifelong learning, education/& international development, PGCE secondary education (English, drama, geography, ICT & modern languages, computer science, behavioural science, chemistry, history, lifelong learning), Welsh for adults; BA(Hons), BSc(Hons), MPhil, PGCE, PGDip, PhD

Dept of English & Creative Writing; www.aber.ac.uk/en/english
literature &/creative writing, literary/classical studies, American literature, 18th century writing &

romanticism, post modernist writing & Welsh writing in English; BA(Hons), MA, PhD

Dept of European Languages; www.aber.ac.uk/en/eurolangs
French, modern German, Italian, European culture, Romance languages, modern languages with business & management, numerous post-graduate modules, applied translation, Spanish; BA(Hons), MA, PhD

Institute of Geography & Earth Sciences; www.aber.ac.uk/en/iges
physical geography/ education/ statistics/mathematics, environmental change, impact and adaptation, environmental monitoring and analysis, food and water security, geography and earth sciences, glaciology, practising human geography, remote sensing & GIS/living environment, regional & environmental policy,river system dynamics and management; BSc(Hons), MPhil, MRes, MSc, PhD, BA(Hons), MA, PGCE

Dept of History & Welsh History; www.aber.ac.uk/en/history
art history, European history, history, economic and social history, history and media, history and Welsh history, international politics and international/military history, medieval and early modern history,,modern and contemporary history, politics and modern history, numerous joint honours and Welsh medium degrees
eighteenth century Britain, history and heritage, history of Wales, medieval Britain & Europe, modern British history,modern European history, modern history; BA(Hons), MA, PhD, MPhil, NQPG

Dept of Information Studies; www.aber.ac.uk/en/dis
information and library studies, archive administration, digital curation, digital information services, information and library studies, information management and leadership, international archives, records and information management, management of library and information services, information management, information governance & assurance;

BA(Hons), BSc(Econ), Dip/Cert, MPhil, MSc(Econ), PhD, MA(Econ), Dip, MSc, MPhil

Dept of International Politics; www.aber.ac.uk/en/interpol
international politics/& strategic studies/international history/military history/intelligence studies/non-western world, intelligence & strategic studies, security studies, political studies, critical international politics, food & water security, intelligence and strategic studies, international relations, politics, media and performance, post-colonial policy; BSc(Econ), MA, MSc, MSc(Econ), PhD

Dept of Law and Criminology; www.aber.ac.uk/en/law-criminology
law, business law, criminal law, criminology with applied psychology/law, European law, human rights, law with criminology, criminology & criminal/international justice, climate change & human rights, democracy, human security & international law, information technology law, international commercial law and the environment/human rights/ criminology of armed conflict, internet commerce & law, human rights & development/humanitarian law, rights, gender & international law, law with languages; BA(Hons), BSc(Econ), LlB, LlM, MSc,PhD

School of Management and Business; www.aber.ac.uk/en/smb
business & management, accounting & finance/ economics/French/Spanish, business finance, business economics, economics, economics/marketing, marketing, marketing economics, adventure tourism management, tourism management, management, international business management, management &

marketing, international business, international finance/& banking; BSc(Econ), MBA, MSc(Econ), PhD

Dept of Mathematics; www.aber.ac.uk/en/maths
mathematics, mathematical theoretical physics, applied mathematics, pure mathematics/& statistics, financial mathematics, statistics/for computational biology; BSc(Hons), MSc, PhD,MPhil,

Dept of Physics; www.aber.ac.uk/en/physics
physics, planetary and space physics, space science & robotics, mathematical & theoretical physics, astrophysics, robotics; BSc(Hons), MMath, MPhys, PhD

Dept of Psychology; www.aber.ac.uk/en/psychology
psychology/& criminology,
Postgrad; only MPhil and PhD by research; BSc(Hons), MPhil, PhD

Dept of Theatre, Film & Television Studies; www.aber.ac.uk/en/tfts
drama & theatre studies, documentary, film/& television studies, media & communication, studies, scenography/theatre design, scriptwriting, Welsh medium courses, politics, media & performance; BA(Hons), MA, MPhil, PhD

Dept of Welsh; www.aber.ac.uk/en/cymraeg
Celtic studies, professional Welsh, Welsh, Welsh and the Celtic languages, computer science and Welsh (for beginners), creative writing and Cymraeg, Irish / fine art, Irish language and literature /English literature, Welsh /education; BA(Hons), MA, PhD

ANGLIA RUSKIN UNIVERSITY
www.anglia.ac.uk

Faculty of Arts, Law and Social Sciences; www.anglia.ac.uk/en/home/faculties/ alss.html

Department of English and Media; www.anglia.ac.uk/arts-law-and-social sciences/department-of-english and-media
drama and English literature/ film studies, English language and English language teaching/linguistics, English language studies, English literature, film studies/and media studies, media studies,

philosophy and English literature, writing and English literature/film studies
Postgrad; applied linguistics and TESOL, creative writing, English literature, intercultural communication, publishing, TESOL and materials development; BA(Hons), MA, MPhil, PhD

Anglia Law School; ww.anglia.ac.uk/ ruskin/en/home/faculties/alss/deps/law
international business/commercial law, law, legal practice, medical law & ethics; BA(Hons), LlB, LlD, LlM, PGDip, MPhil, PhD, PGDip, ProfDoc

Cambridge School of Art;
www.anglia.ac.uk/ruskin/en/home/
faculties/alss/deps/csoa

animation, children's book illustration & book arts, computer games art, fashion/interior design, film & TV production, fine art, illustration, photography, printmaking, graphic design & typography, computer games development; BA(Hons), FdA, MA, MFA

Dept of Humanities & Social Sciences;
www.anglia.ac.uk/ruskin/en/home/
faculties/alss/deps/hss

criminology, forensic science, history, English, English literature, international relations, philosophy, public service, sociology; BA(Hons), FdA, MPhil, PhD

Dept of Music & Performing Arts;
www.anglia.ac.uk/ruskin/en/home/
faculties/alss/deps/music

creative music technology, drama/& English literature/film studies, music/drama therapy, performing arts, pop music, body psychotherapy, psychodrama; BA(Hons), FdADip, MA, MPhil, PhD

Lord Ashcroft International Business
School; www.anglia.ac.uk/ruskin/en/
home/faculties/aibs

accounting, accounting and financial management, banking & finance, business administration, business and finance, business and HRM, business economics, business management, business management and finance, business management and leadership, data centre leadership & management, entrepreneurship management, finance and economics/business analytics, international business management, management, marketing, international hospitality & tourism management, tourism management, business administration (MBA), leadership & management, supply chain management; BA(Hons), BSc(Hons), LlB, UnivDip, MA, MBA, MSc, CertHE, FdA, PGDip, DBA

Faculty of Health, Social Care &
Education; www.anglia.ac.uk/ruskin/
en/home/faculties/fhsce

School of Nursing & Midwifery;
www.anglia.ac.uk/health-social-care-
and-education/about/school-of-nursing-
and-midwifery

acute care (top-up), children and young people, community specialist practitioner (district nursing), counselling (child and young person), early childhood professional studies, international nursing studies, mental health, midwifery, nursing (adult, child, mental health), paediatric intensive care nursing, palliative care, specialist community public health nursing (health visiting or school nursing)

School of Education and Social-Care;
www.anglia.ac.uk/health-social-care-
and-education/about/school-of-
education-and-social-care

counselling (child and young person), early childhood studies, early years, playwork and education, education and childhood studies, education studies, education, technology and computing, education, management of social and affordable housing, social care and well-being, social care and well-being (older person), social policy

postgrad; early childhood education, education, educational leadership and management, global military veteran and family studies, international social welfare and social policy, learning and teaching (higher education), student affairs in higher education

Veterans and Families Institute;
www.anglia.ac.uk/study/postgraduate/
military-veterans-and-families-studies

global military veteran and family studies, military veteran & family affairs; BA(Hons), BSc(Hons) MA, MSc, FdA, FdSc, MBA, DipHE, PGCert, EdD, MPhil, ProfDoc, GradCertHE, DipPGCE, PGDip/Cert, Dips Grad Cert, Professional Practice, MBA

Faculty of Science and Technology;
www.anglia.ac.uk/ruskin/en/home/
faculties/fst

Dept of Engineering & Built Environment;
www.anglia.ac.uk/ruskin/en/home/
faculties/fst/departments/eng_builtenv

architecture/technology, building surveying, civil engineering, conservation of buildings, construction/project management, engineering management, engineering & tribology, integrated/engineering, manufacturing systems, mechanical engineering, mobile telecommunications, motorsport engineering, project management, property & facilities management, quantity surveying, town planning, sustainable building engineering, urban design; BSc(Hons), BEng, FdSc, MSc, PGCert, PGDip, FdSc, GradCert

Dept of Computing & Technology; www.anglia.ac.uk/ruskin/en/home/faculties/fst/departments/comptech

audio music technology, business information systems, cloud computing, computer gaming technology/science, computer games technology (computing), computer networks, cyber security, networking, software development, sound engineering, telecommunications multimedia, electronic/ & electrical engineering, information & communication technology; BEng(Hons), BSc(Hons), MBA, FdSc, MSc

Dept of Biomedical and Forensic Science

analytical chemistry, biomedical science, bioscience biotechnology, crime and investigative studies, forensic science, molecular biology; BSc(Hons), MSc, MPhil, PhD

Dept of Vision and Hearing Sciences; www.anglia.ac.uk/ruskin/en/home/departments/vision_hearing

hearing aid audiology, hearing sciences, ophthalmic dispensing/assistants, optometric clinical assistant, optometry, optometry and vision sciences;
BOptom(Hons), BSc(Hons), MOptom, FdSc, UnivCert), FdSc, UnivCert, MPhil, PhD

Dept of Psychology; www.anglia.ac.uk/ruskin/en/home/faculties/fst/departments/psychology

applied positive psychology, psychology, abnormal & clinical psychology, clinical child psychology, cognitive & clinical neuroscience, psychology & criminology, foundations in clinical psychology, research methods in psychology; BSc(Hons), MSc, MPhil, PhD

Dept of Life Sciences; www.anglia.ac.uk/ruskin/en/home/faculties/fst/departments/lifesciences

Sport & Exercise Science

coaching for performance in football, sport and exercise science, sports coaching and physical education, sports science; BSc(Hons), MSc, PhD

Animal & Environmental Biology

animal and environmental sciences, animal behaviour, applications for conservation, applied wildlife conservation, equine science, equine science with rehabilitation therapies, marine biology with biodiversity and conservation, marine biology with biodiversity and conservation, sustainability, veterinary nursing and applied animal behaviour, zoology; BSc(Hons), FdSc, MSc, PGDip

Faculty of Medical Science; www.anglia.ac.uk/medical-science

Department of Allied and Public Health

clinical medicine, decontamination sciences, doctor of medicine by research, health care management, healthcare science, leadership and management in health and social care, leadership practice in health and social care, magnetic resonance imaging, management and leadership in health and social care, medical and healthcare education, medical science, medical technology, minimally invasive and robotic surgery, nutrition, health, urology; BSc(Hons), MSc, FdSc, MPhil, PhD, MD, MBA, MCh,BOst, MOst, MCh, DipHE, MPhil, PhD

Dept of Medical & Healthcare Science

decontamination sciences, health care management, healthcare science, leadership and management in health and social care, magnetic resonance imaging, medical and healthcare education, medical science, minimally invasive and robotic surgery, nutrition, operating department practice, orthopaedics. osteopathy, paramedic science, pharmaceutical science, physician associate, plastic and aesthetic surgery practice, pre-hospital care, health, public health, surgical care practice, urology; BSc(Hons), FdSc, MSc, MD(Res), BOst, MOst, MCh, DipHE, MBA, MPhil, PhD

Degrees validated by Anglia Ruskin University offered at:

COLCHESTER INSTITUTE
www.colchester.ac.uk

business innovation and applied management, counselling studies, 3D design and craft, art and design with foundation year, creative performance (acting), digital film production, early years, education studies, fashion and textiles, film music and soundtrack production, fine art, graphic design, health and social care, management, music education, musical theatre, photography, popular music, sport management, technical theatre, construction management (commercial management/ site management), IT systems and applications, business administration, construction, management of sport, photography, education, business administration (MBA), project

management, reflective management and leadership, business environment, person-centred counselling; BSc(Hons), BA(Hons), CertHE, FD, MA, MBA, DipHE

ASHRIDGE
www.ashridge.ac.uk

---

executive MBA, management, executive coaching, advanced coaching & supervision, global executive, international business/marketing management, key account management,sustainability & responsibility,

organisational change, leadership, social entrepreneurship; Doc Orgn Change, ExecMBA, MBA, MSc, Masters, PGCert, B Business Admin

---

ASTON UNIVERSITY
www.aston.ac.uk

Aston Business School; www1.aston.ac.uk/aston-business-school

Undergrad; accounting for management, business & management, business computing & IT, economics & management, finance, human resource management, international business & management/economics, marketing, law with management, law, international business & modern languages, business and psychology, business and mathematics, mathematics with economics, sociology and business, politics and business, international relations and business, public policy, business and management, business management and English language

Postgrad; business analytics, business & management, information systems & business analysis, services innovation, supply chain management, international business, entrepreneurship and international business, accounting & finance, business economics & finance, finance,,international accounting & finance, investment analysis, strategic marketing management, HRM & business, organisational behaviour, work psychology & business, social responsibility & sustainability; BSc(Hons), DBA, LlB, LlM, MBA, PhD, FD,MSc, GradCert

School of Engineering and Applied Science; www1.aston.ac.uk/eas

Chemical Engineering & Applied Chemistry; www1.aston.ac.uk/eas/about-eas/academic-groups/ceac

applied/biological chemistry, chemical engineering, chemistry, professional engineering; BEng, MEng, MChem

Computer Science; www1.aston.ac.uk/eas/about-eas/academic-groups/computer-science

computing science/& mathematics, computing for business, data communication networks, multimedia computing, IT project management, software engineering, professional engineering; BSc, MSc

Electrical, Electronic & Power Engineering; www1.aston.ac.uk/eas/about-eas/academic-groups/electronic-engineering/

communications engineering, data communications networks, electronic & electrical engineering, electrical & electronic engineering/computer science, telecommunications systems, professional engineering; BEng, MEng, MSc

Engineering Systems & Management; www1.aston.ac.uk/eas/about-eas/academic-groups/esm

construction project management, engineering leadership & management, industrial enterprise management, logistics with supply chain management/

transport management, logistics management, purchasing management; BSc, MSc, FD

Mathematics; www1.aston.ac.uk/eas/about-eas/academic-groups/mathematics

mathematics, mathematics with computing/business/economics, mathematics of complex systems; BSc, MSc

Mechanical Engineering & Design; www1.aston.ac.uk/eas/about-eas/academic-groups/med

electromechanical engineering, mechanical engineering/modelling, design engineering, transport product design, product design/enterprise/innovation, professional engineering, transport product design, industrial product design, product design & management; BEng, MEng, MSc

School of Life and Health Sciences; www1.aston.ac.uk/lhs

Undergraduate courses;

Audiology; hearing aid audiology healthcare science (audiology), audiological science

Biology & Biomedical Science; biological sciences/cell and molecular biology/ human biology/ microbiology and immunology

Biomedical Engineering; biomedical engineering

Neuroscience; neuroscience

Optometry; optometry

Pharmacy; pharmacy

Psychology; psychology, psychology & business/sociology

Masters level study

Biology & Biomedical Sciences; biomedical sciences, health and disease, molecular biotechnology, stem cells and regenerative medicine

Pharmacy & Pharmaceutical Science; drug delivery, pharmaceutical sciences, pharmacokinetics,pharmacology

Psychology & Cognitive Neuroscience; cognitive neuroscience, health psychology, health psychology

Postgraduate and doctoral level study for Healthcare Professionals

Allied Health Professions; advanced clinical practice; clinical science (neurosensory sciences)

Neurophysiology; clinical neurophysiology practice/neurophysiology

Optometry; optometry/ophthalmic science

Pharmacy; pharmacist independent prescribing, overseas pharmacists, psychiatric pharmacy, psychiatric pharmacy practice

BSc(Hons), GradDip, FD, MPharm, MRes, MSc, PGCert/Dip, PhD, M/DOptom, DOptSci, Dip,Sci, PharmD, MBiol, BEng, MEng

School of Languages and Social Sciences; www1.aston.ac.uk/lss

Modern Languages

French, German, Spanish, translation studies, international business & modern languages studies, TESOL, applied linguistics, translation in European context, English language with French/German/Spanish, sociology with Spanish/French, international relations/politics/business with French

English language

business management/international relations/politics/social policy/sociology and English language, English with Modern Languages

Politics and International Relations

politics with international relations,business/English language/social policy/ sociology and international relations, business/ economics/English language/ social policy/sociology and politics, international relations and French/German/Spanish

Sociology and Social Policy

sociology,sociology and social policy/French/Spanish/international relations/politics/business/psychology/English language, sociology/international relations./politics/English language and social policy/business, management and public policy

Business Combinations

international business and modern languages, social science and business combinations, business management and English language, business and sociology/management and public policy/international relations, politics, politics and economics

Taught postgraduate

TESOL, translation studies, translation in a European context, the EU/multilevel governance & international relations/global governance, EU & international relations, Europe & the world, governance & international politics, social research/public policy & social change, sociology, TESOL, TESP, TEYL, ELT EMT; BA(Hons), BSc(Hons), MA, MPhil, MRes, MSc, PhD

BANGOR UNIVERSITY
www.bangor.ac.uk

College of Arts and Humanities; www.bangor.ac.uk/cah

Creative Studies & Media; www.bangor.ac.uk/creative_industries

Chinese and creative studies, creative and professional writing, creative practice, creative studies,,creative studies and English language/Italian, creative writing and media studies, English language with film studies, English literature with journalism, English literature with theatre and performance, film studies,film studies and Chinese/theatre, fine art, French with journalism/media studies, German with creative writing, history with film studies/journalism, journalism and English language,/media studies, media, media studies, media studies and English/ French/German/Italian Spanish/theatre, music and creative writing/film studies, professional writing

Postgrad; filmmaking: concept to screen, fine art, international media and management, creative practice, film studies, media and practice, professional writing; BA(Hons), MA, MRes, MSc, PhD, MPhil, MArts, PGCert/Dip

English Literature; www.bangor.ac.uk/english

creative and professional writing, English literature, English literature with creative writing, English language and English literature, English literature and Chinese/Italian/English language/journalism/ theatre and performance, law with English literature, linguistics with English literature, media studies and English, philosophy & religion and English literature

Postgrad; Arthurian literature, creative writing, English literature,,literatures of Wales, medieval studies; BA(Hons), MA, MArts, PGDip, PhD, MPhil, LlB

History, Welsh History & Archaeology; www.bangor.ac.uk/history

archaeology, heritage, archaeology and history, history, history and economics/Italian, philosophy & religion & Welsh/history, Welsh history with archaeology, history with film studies/journalism, medieval and early modern history, modern and contemporary history, social policy and history, sociology, politics & history, the Celts, Welsh history; BA(Hons), MA, PGDip, MPhil, PhD

School of Linguistics & English Language; www.bangor.ac.uk/linguistics

English language, English language with creative writing/English literature/media studies, English literature with English language, international English language, linguistics/with English literature/English language, numerous joint degrees, bilingualism, cognitive linguistics, international English language for TEFL, applied linguistics for TEFL; BA(Hons), MA, MPhil, PhD, MSc

School of Modern Languages & Cultures; www.bangor.ac.uk/ml

French, German, Italian, Spanish, or in joint degrees with European law, accounting, banking, business studies, creative studies, criminology & criminal justice, economics, English literature, journalism, creative writing, marketing, media studies, psychology, linguistics, management, sport science, philosophy & religion, music, history; Chinese and business studies/Cymraeg/linguistics/economics/English language/English literature/film studies, joint degrees between French, German, Italian, Spanish, history and Italian; European languages and cultures, translation studies; LlB(Hons), BA(Hons), BSc(Hons), MA, MPhil

School of Music; www.bangor.ac.uk/music

music, composition, electroacoustics, early music, 20/ 21st century music, performance, sonic arts, composition, composition, numerous joint degrees, music with education; BA, BMus, BSc, MA, PGDip/Cert, MMus/Dip

School of Philosophy & Religion; www.bangor.ac.uk/spar

philosophy & religion, study of religion, theology, numerous joint degrees; BA, MA, MTh, MRes, MARes

School of Welsh; www.bangor.ac.uk/ysgolygymraeg

details of courses provided in Welsh language; Welsh, Welsh with creative writing/journalism/theatre studies and the media, creative Welsh with popular music, the Celt, Welsh /Celtic studies; MA, MA/Diploma, MPhil/PhD, BA(Hons), BD, BMus, Dip, MMus, MTh, PGDip, PhD, MSc

College of Business, Social Sciences & Law; www.bangor.ac.uk/cbss

Bangor Business School; www.bangor.ac.uk/business

accounting and banking/economics/finance/Italian banking and finance,banking and finance/Italian, business and computer information systems/law, business economics, business studies, business studies and Chinese/finance/Italian/marketing/ French/ German/Spanish, economics and Italian/economics and Spanish, financial economics, French and economics/marketing/ history and economics, Italian and management, management with accounting, marketing/with mod languages, psychology with business, social policy and economics, sociology and economics

Postgraduate Courses; law and banking, banking and finance/law, business and marketing/finance,/management and finance, accounting, accounting and banking/finance, banking and finance, business with consumer psychology, finance, international banking/ finance/media and management, investment management, Islamic banking and finance, management and finance, leadership for collaboration MBA; banking and finance, law, chartered banker, environmental management, finance, information management, international business, international marketing, Islamic banking and finance, law and management, management

MBA; banking and finance, law, chartered banker, environmental management, finance, information management, international business, international marketing, Islamic banking and finance, law and management, management; BA(Hons), BSc(Hons), MA, MSc, MBA, MPhil, PhD, LlM, PGCert

School of Social Sciences; www.bangor.ac.uk/so

childhood studies and social policy, criminology & criminal justice/and Italian, cymdeithaseg a pholisi cymdeithasol (sociology and social policy), health & social care and social policy/social care, social policy and criminology & criminal justice/economics/history/history, sociology, sociology and economics/ social policy, social studies, criminology and law, social work, societal health, comparative criminology and criminal justice, criminology and sociology; BA(Hons), MA/PGDip/Cert, PhD, MPhil, MARes

School of Law; www.bangor.ac.uk/law

(European) law with French/German/Italian/Spanish, business and law, English law and French law, law,

law with accounting and finance, law with business studies/contemporary Chinese studies/ criminology law with English literature/ professional English/ social policy, law with Welsh, graduate conversion course, international intellectual property law, international law, international law – specialising in European law/ global trade law, international criminal law and international human rights law, law and banking, law and criminology, law of the sea, maritime law, public procurement law and strategy, international commercial and business law, law, criminology and law, law and management; BA(Hons), MBA, DBA, HND, LlB, LlM(Res/Dip), MA, MSc, MPhil, PGDip, PhD

School of Education; www.bangor.ac.uk/ addy

childhood studies, design & technology secondary education with QTS, education studies, product design, secondary education, early childhood & learning support studies, primary education, PGCE primary/secondary, preparing to teach, graduate teaching program, music with education
BA(Hons) Cert, Dipl, FdA, EdD, MA, MEd, MPhil, PhD

Academic Development Unit; www.bangor.ac.uk/adu

Welsh for adults; PGCertHE, BSc(Hons), EdMed, FdA, MA, MEd, MMusD, MPhil, MTh, PGCE, PhD

College of Natural Sciences; www.bangor.ac.uk/cns

CNS School of Biological Sciences; www.bangor.ac.uk/biology

biology, biology with biotechnology, marine biology and zoology, zoology, zoology with animal behaviour (animal behaviour)/(climate change), zoology with conservation, zoology with evolution, zoology with herpetology/ marine zoology, molecular biology with biotechnology, wetland science and conservation/pollution control, biological sciences
BSc(Hons), Dipl, MA, MBiol, MPhil, MRes, MScRes, MZool, PhD

School of Environment, Natural Resources, & Geography; www.bangor.ac.uk/senrg

applied terrestrial and marine ecology, environmental conservation, environmental management, environmental science, geography, agroforestry, conservation and land management/with forestry, environmental and business management, environmental forestry, forestry/ and environmental

management, sustainable forest and nature management, food security in the changing environment, tropical/forestry
BA(Hons), BSc(Hons), MA, MBA, MPhil, MSc, PhD, MEnvSci, MGeog

School of Ocean Sciences; www.bangor.ac.uk/sos

applied marine biology, coastal geography, computing and oceanography, geological oceanography, marine biology/and oceanography/ zoology, marine environmental studies, marine vertebrate zoology, marine biology, marine geography, marine science, ocean science, physical oceanography, applied marine geoscience, physical oceanography, marine biology, marine environmental protection, marine renewable energy
BSc(Hons), MMBiol, MMSci, MOcean, MPhil, MSc, PhD

Welsh Institute for Natural Resources; www.bangor.ac.uk/winr

College of Health & Behavioural Sciences; www.bangor.ac.uk/cohabs

School of Healthcare Sciences; www.bangor.ac.uk/healthcaresciences

children's/learning disability/adult/mental health nursing, diagnostic radiography, advanced healthcare practice, dementia studies, advanced clinical practice, health and social care leadership, public health and health promotion, implementing evidence in health & social care, ageing and dementia studies, health economics, health services research
BA(Hons), BSc(Hons), BMidw, DipHE, GradCert/ Dip, MPhil, PhD, MSc, MRes

School of Medical Sciences; www.bangor.ac.uk/sms

medical sciences/biology, biomedical science, clinical sciences, medical molecular biology with genetics, medical education practice; MSc, PGDip/Cert(HE), BMedSci, BSc, PhD, MBiol

School of Psychology; www.bangor.ac.uk/ psychology

psychology, psychology with business/ clinical and health psychology/psychology with neuropsychology, neuropsychology, psychology and childhood studies/criminology and criminal justice/English language/linguistics/social policy/sociology, clinical psychology, consumer psychology with business, mindfulness-based approaches, applied behaviour analysis, clinical and health psychology, foundations of clinical neuropsychology, neuroimaging, psychological research; BSc(Hons),BA(Hons) MSc, PhD, MRes, MA, PGDip/Cert, MPsych, DClinPsych, MSci

School of Sport, Health & Exercise Science; www.bangor.ac.uk/sport

sport science, sport, health and exercise science, sport science (outdoor activities), sport, health and physical education, sport and exercise psychology, applied sport science, applied sport and exercise physiology/ psychology/outdoor activities, exercise rehabilitation, sport and exercise psychology, exercise rehabilitation, applied sport science (outdoor activities)
BSc(Hons), MPhil, MSc, PhD, MRes, MA, MSci

Institute of Medical & Social Care Research; www.bangor.ac.uk/imscar

ageing & dementia studies, health economics, health services research; PhD, MPhil, MSc

College of Physical and Applied Sciences; www.bangor.ac.uk/copas

School of Chemistry; www.bangor.ac.uk/ chemistry

analytical chemistry, chemistry, environmental/chemistry, industrial/European experience; BSc, MChem, MSc, MRes, PGDip, PhD, MPhil

School of Computer Science; www.bangor.ac.uk/cs

computer science for business, computer information systems/for business, creative technologies, information & communications technology, computing & oceanography, advanced visualization, virtual environments and computer animation
BA(Hons), BEng(Hons), MEng(Hons), MPhil, MRes, MSc, PhD

School of Electronic Engineering; www.bangor.ac.uk/eng

computer systems engineering, control and instrumentation engineering, critical safety engineering, electronic engineering, electronic engineering and music, broadband and optical communications, nanotechnology and microfabrication, electronic engineering (bio-electronics/micromachining/microwave devices/ nanotechnology, optical communications/optoelectronics/organic electronics/polymer electronics/VLSL design; BEng(Hons), BSc(Hons), MEng(Hons), MSc, PhD

UNIVERSITY COLLEGE, BARNSLEY
www.hud.ac.uk/barnsley

interdisciplinary art & design, construction & project management, early years, teacher training, lifelong learning, education & professional development, digital film & visual effects, film production, animation, music, music production & sound recording, mechanical/electrical/electronic engineering technology, popular music & promotion, teacher training; CertEd, PGCE, BA(Hons), BSc(Hons), MA/PGDip/PGCert

UNIVERSITY OF BATH
www.bath.ac.uk

Faculty of Engineering and Design; www.bath.ac.uk/engineering

Architecture & Civil Engineering; www.bath.ac.uk/ace
architectural engineering: environmental design, architecture, civil engineering, conservation of historic buildings, civil & architectural engineering, civil engineering: innovative structural materials, professional practice, modern building design; BEng, BSc, EngD, MArch, MEng, MPhil, MSc, PGCert, PhD

Chemical Engineering; www.bath.ac.uk/chem-eng
chemical engineering, biochemical engineering, sustainable chemical engineering; BEng, EngD, MEng, MPhil, MSc, PhD

Electronic & Electrical Engineering; www.bath.ac.uk/elec-eng
electrical & electronic/electrical power engineering, computer systems engineering, electrical power engineering, electronic systems engineering, mechatronics, space science & technology; BEng, EngD, MEng, MPhil, MSc, PhD

Mechanical Engineering; www.bath.ac.uk/mech-eng
aerospace engineering, integrated design engineering, mechanical with automotive engineering, mechanical engineering/ with manufacturing and management, automotive engineering, engineering design, innovation and technology management, mechatronics, orthopaedic engineering; EngD, MEng, MPhil, MSc, PhD, PGCert

Faculty of Humanities and Social Science; www.bath.ac.uk/hss

Dept of Economics; www.bath.ac.uk/economics
economics/& finance/politics/mathematics, international money & banking, economics; BSc(Hons), MPhil, MRes, PhD

Dept of Education; www.bath.ac.uk/education
education, international education & globalisation, education with psychology, TESOL; BA(Hons), EdD, FdSc, MA, MPhil, MRes, PGCE, PhD, ProfPGCE

Dept for Health; www.bath.ac.uk/health
sport & exercise science/medicine, sports physiotherapy, research in health practice, health & wellbeing; BSc, MPhil, MRes, MSc, PhD, ProfDoc, MD, MS, MSci

Dept of Politics, Languages & International Studies; www.bath.ac.uk/polis
international relations & European politics, contemporary European studies, interpreting & translation, politics/ & economics/international relations/international studies, translating, international security, international management & modern languages, language & politics, politics & international relations, translation & professional language skills/with business interpreting(Chinese), modern languages & European Studies; BA(Hons), BSc(Hons), MA, MPhil, PGDip, PhD

Dept of Psychology; www.bath.ac.uk/psychology
psychology, health psychology, clinical psychology, environment, energy & resilience; BSc(Hons), MPhil, MSc, PhD, MRes, DClin Psych

Dept of Social & Policy Science; www.bath.ac.uk/sps

sociology, social sciences, social policy, international development/public policy analysis, wellbeing in public policy & international development, European social policy, global political economy: transformations and policy, analysis, international development security, conflict & justice; BSc(Hons), MSc, MRes, MPhil, PhD

Faculty of Science; www.bath.ac.uk/science

Dept of Biology & Biochemistry; www.bath.ac.uk/bio-sci

biology, biochemistry, biomedical sciences, biosciences, molecular & cellular biology, developmental biology, evolutionary & population biology, molecular plant sciences, molecular microbiology, protein structure & function, regenerative medicine; BSc(Hons), MPhil, MRes, PhD

Dept of Chemistry; www.bath.ac.uk/chemistry

chemistry/for drug discovery, management, education; BSc(Hons), MChem, MSci, PhD

Dept of Computer Science; www.bath.ac.uk/comp-sci

computer science/with maths/business, software systems, digital entertainment systems, human-computer interaction; BSc(Hons), EngD, MComp, MSc, PhD

Dept of Mathematics; www.bath.ac.uk/math-sci

mathematical sciences, mathematics, modern applics of mathematics, statistics, mathematical biology; BSc(Hons), MMath, MSc, PhD

Dept of Natural Sciences; www.bath.ac.uk/nat-sci

multidisciplinary studies include biology, chemistry, pharmacology, physics, mathematics; BSc(Hons), MSci

Dept of Pharmacy & Pharmacology; www.bath.ac.uk/pharmacy

primary/secondary care, pharmacy, clinical pharmaceutical practice, pharmacology, pharmacy, advanced & specialist healthcare practice, pharmaceutical prescribing, medicinal chemistry, medicine management pharmacy, clinical specialist, medicines information, teacher/practitioner, pharmacy manager, prescribing support; MPharm, MPharmacol, PhD, CPD

Dept of Physics; www.bath.ac.uk/physics

physics, mathematics/astrophysics and physics, physics/with computing, nanoscience, photonics; BSc, MSc, MPhil, MPhys, PhD

School of Management; www.bath.ac.uk/management

accounting/& finance, business administration, international management & languages, management/marketing, business analytics, operations, logistics & supply chain management, accounting & finance, entrepreneurship & management, finance, finance with banking/ risk management, human resource management & consulting, innovation & technology management, international management, management, marketing, sustainability & management; BSc(Hons), DBA, EngD, MBA, MPhil, MRes, MSc, PhD

BATH SPA UNIVERSITY
www.bathspa.ac.uk

Bath School of Art & Design; www.artbathspa.com

history of art & design, textile design for fashion and interiors, contemporary arts practice, creative arts,,- fashion design, fine art, graphic communication, photography, textile design for fashion and interiors, three dimensional design,fashion portfolio, design: ceramic/fashion and textiles, curatorial practice, fine art, visual communication; BA(Hons), FdA, MFA, MA, MPhil, PhD

Institute of Education; www.bathspa.ac.uk/schools/education

Undergraduate; early years education, early years education (primary teaching/work-based), education (primary teaching), education studies, international education/primary teaching, youth and community studies

Postgraduate; professional master's, learning and innovation, education studies, education: international education, PMP: specific learning difficulties /

dyslexia/PMP: counselling and psychotherapy, professional practice in HE, education: leadership and management, education: early years, education: learning technology, TESOL, national award for special educational needs coordination, early years initial teacher training, subject knowledge enhancement courses mathematics/modern languages/physics, foundation; early years, education studies for teaching assistants;
PGCE (primary (3-11)/middle years (7-14)/secondary (11-16); range of subjects), TESOL, international education & global citizenship
FD, GradCert, MA/MTeach, PGCE, PGCert/Dip

School of Humanities & Cultural Industries; www.bathspa.ac.uk/schools/humanities- and-cultural-industries

Undergraduate; creative arts, creative computing, creative computing (animation/gaming/software development), creative media practice, creative writing, English literature, film and screen studies, film, TV and digital production, heritage, history,media communications, philosophy and ethics, publishing, religion, philosophy and ethics, study of religions
Postgraduate; arts management, creative technologies and enterprise, creative writing, feature filmmaking, heritage management, independent filmmaking, Jane Austen's England, literature, landscape and environment, scriptwriting, travel and nature writing, writing for young people
BA(Hons), MPhil, PhD, MA,FD

Music & the Performing Arts; www.bathspampa.com

commercial music, contemporary circus, creative arts, creative music technology, musical theatre, dance, drama, acting, music, composition, performance Shakespeare, songwriting, creative & media technology, performance, performing arts, theatre production/for young audiences, pop; BA(Hons), FdA, FdMus, MA, PhD

School of Society, Enterprise & Environment; www.bathspa.ac.uk/schools/ society-enterprise-and-environment

accounting, biology, global development & sustainability, business & management, geography, HRM, counselling, environmental science, food & nutrition, GIS, health studies, tourism management, psychology, sociology; BA(Hons), BSc(Hons), MPhil, MSc, PhD, FdA, DipHE, FD

UNIVERSITY OF BEDFORDSHIRE
www.beds.ac.uk

Faculty of Creative Arts, Technologies & Science; www.beds.ac.uk/departments/ cats

Art & Design

Undergraduate; advertising and branding design, animation, animation for industry, art and design,- contemporary fine art practice, creative and editorial photography, fashion and surface pattern design, fashion design, fine art, graphic design, graphic design and advertising, illustration, interior architecture, interior design and retail branding, photography and video art; Postgraduate; art and design, fashion design, styling and promotion
BA(Hons), FD, MA

Computer Science and Technology

Undergraduate; artificial intelligence and robotics, building services and sustainability, building technology, business information systems, computer animation and visual effects, computer games development, computer networking, computer science, computer science and robotic software engineering/ forensics, computer systems engineering, computing and mathematics, construction management, data science, electronic engineering, information systems, interactive digital technologies, IT networking and security, mathematics and finance, network management, product design, software engineering, sustainable construction, telecommunications and network engineering web design and software development
Postgraduate; applied computing and information technology, business information systems, computer networking, computer science, computer security and forensics, cyber security, electronic engineering, information management and security, sensors and smart cities, telecommunications management; BSc(Hons), FdSc, MSc, BEng, MPhil, PhD

Journalism and Communications

broadcast journalism, creative writing, creative writing & journalism, journalism, journalism and PR, magazine journalism, media communications, media and PR, sport journalism; BA(Hons), FdA, MA, MRes, PhD, PGCert

Life Sciences

Undergraduate; animal science; biochemistry, biomedical science, biological science, forensic science; Postgraduate; pharmacology, biotechnology, biomedical engineering, environmental management; BSc(Hons), FdSc, MSc, PGCert, PGDip, MPhil, PhD

Media Arts and Production

Undergraduate; broadcast TV and radio, film and TV production, film production, media production, media production (moving image/radio), music technology, TV production. Postgraduate; creative digital film production, digital film technologies and production, documentary, international cinema; FD, BA(Hons), MA, PGDip

Performing Arts & English

Undergraduate; acting, dance and professional practice, education studies and English, English and theatre studies, English language and literature, English literature, English studies performing arts, technical theatre and stage management, theatre and professional practice

Postgraduate; community dance leadership, dance performance and choreography, dance science,English literature, performing arts: creative practice and leadership; BA(Hons), FdA, MA, MRes, PhD, PGCert

The Faculty offers postgraduate courses in Art & Design, Biological & Biomedical Sciences, Computing & Engineering

Faculty of Health and Social Sciences; www.beds.ac.uk/departments/ healthsciences

Nursing, Midwifery & Health

sport and exercise rehabilitation, public health, nursing, midwifery and health; nursing studies, advanced nursing studies; BA(Hons), BSc(Hons), MSc

Social Sciences

applied social studies, child and adolescent studies, criminology/and sociology, health and social care; BA(Hons), BSc(Hons)

Sports Therapy

sports therapy; BA(Hons), BSc

Dept of Clinical Education & Leadership

Healthcare

short courses on health-related issues

Medical and Dental Education

medical education, medical education leadership, dental education, medical simulation, dental law and ethics; MSc, PGCert/Dip

Post qualifying health

advanced nursing studies, hospitals and health, services management, specialist community public health nursing (health/school nursing), specialist practitioner community district nursing; MSc/ PGCert/Dip, MBA

Public Health

public health; MSc, PGCert/Dip,MBA

Dept of Applied Social Studies; www.beds.ac.uk/departments/ appliedsocialstudies

Undergraduate; applied social studies, child and adolescent studies, child and family studies, children, families and community health, criminology/and sociology, early years studies, integrated city urban planning & design, social work, sociology, systemic practice (child focused practice/families and couples) youth and community work

Postgraduate; applied social work practice: children and families/leadership and management/ education, childhood and youth: applied perspectives, criminology, family and systemic psychotherapy, intermediate child focused systemic practice, intermediate systemic practice with families and couples, international social work and social development, professional practice, social work, systemic leadership and organisational development

BSc(Hons), FdA, FdSc, MSc, ProfDoc, PGCert/Dip, BA(Hons), MA, MSocWkPract,GradCert

Dept of Healthcare Practice

Undergraduate; healthcare practice, midwifery, nursing with registered nurse adult/mental health, operating department practice, paramedic science

Postgraduate; nursing with registration (adult/mental health); FD, DipHE, BSc(Hons), MSc

Div of Psychology; www.beds.ac.uk/departments/ psychology

Undergraduate; applied psychology, health psychology, psychological studies, psychology, psychology and crime/criminal behaviour/criminology/psychology, counselling and therapies, Postgraduate; applied psychology, forensic psychology, health psychology, psychological approaches to health and management, BSc(Hons), BA(Hons), CertHE, FdA, MSc, PhD

Div of Sports Therapy; www.beds.ac.uk/departments/spoth
sports therapy/& exercise rehabilitation, physical exercise for sport & exercise rehabilitation; BSc(Hons), PGDip/Cert, FD, MSc

Institute for Health Research; www.beds.ac.uk/research/ihr
psychological approach to health & management, public health; MSc, PhD, MPhil

Institute of Applied Social Research; www.beds.ac.uk/research/iasr
applied social studies, psychology; ProfDoc, MA

University of Bedfordshire Business School; www.beds.ac.uk/departments/ubbs

Accounting and Finance
accounting, accounting and finance, accounting with management, business economics, international finance and banking; Postgrad; accounting and business finance, economics of international business, international finance and banking

Business, Management and HRM
beauty therapy and spa management, business administration, business management, business studies, business studies (business analytics/decision modelling/finance/HRM/ international/ marketing/ project management), HRM, international business, international business with languages; Postgrad; business and management, business information, engineering business management business administration executive, finance and business management, HRM, information systems and business management, international business and management, international HRM, logistics and supply chain management, MBA /marketing/finance/information technology management/(hospital and health services management/HRM), project management

Law
law Postgrad; international business law, international commercial and dispute resolution law

Marketing, Tourism and Hospitality
advertising and marketing communications, event management, hospitality and tourism management, marketing, PR, PR in practice, travel and tourism, international tourism management; Postgrad; intercultural communication, international relations, international tourism management, marketing and business management, marketing communications, tourism and events management
BA(Hons), BSc(Hons), MBA, DBA, FdA, LlB, LlM, MA, MSc, PGCert, LLM

Faculty of Education, Sport & Tourism; www.beds.ac.uk/departments/es

Dept of English Language & Communication
applied linguistics, premasters courses in business, certificate in English language teaching, English language and linguistics, applied linguistics TEFL, ELT management, teaching & assessment

Dept of Teacher Education
disability studies, early years studies, educational practice, applied disability studies, applied early years studies, applied education studies, mathematics with secondary education (with QTS), PE secondary, with QTS, primary education (with QTS), primary years education, PGCE primary, early years and PE, and numerous secondary subjects, all with QTS, and PGCE early years teaching with EYTS, and PGCE early years birth to 5 with EYTS, post compulsory education, university certificate of continuing professional development in TESOL, continuing professional development in mathematics

Dept of Educational Studies
Undergraduate; childhood and youth studies, early years education, education studies, special needs and inclusive education Postgraduate; behavioural issues in schools, difficulties in literacy development and dyslexia, education, education (early years/leadership/national award for special educational needs coordination/social justice, international development

Dept of Sport Science & Physical Activity
football studies, health, nutrition and exercise, sport and exercise science, sport and physical education, sport development and management, sport science and coaching, sport science and personal training, sports studies, sport science and physical education, clinical exercise physiology, physical activity, nutrition and health promotion, physical education and sport pedagogy, sport science & PE, sport development management, sports performance, sports studies, strength & conditioning; PGCE, BA(Hons), BEd(Hons), MA, MSc, PGCert/Dip, FdA, PGCSMT, Univ Adv Cert, QTS, FdA

THE QUEEN'S UNIVERSITY OF BELFAST
www.qub.ac.uk

School of Biological Sciences; www.qub.ac.uk/schools/schoolofbiologicalsciences

agricultural technology, biochemistry, biological sciences, food science and security, food quality, safety and nutrition, land use & environmental management, energy, environment and sustainability; marine biology, microbiology, zoology, Postgraduate; microbes and pathogen biology, ecosystem biology and sustainability; BSc(Hons), MSc, PhD, MPhil

School of Chemistry and Chemical Engineering; www.ch.qub.ac.uk

chemistry, chemistry with French/Spanish, medicinal chemistry, chemical engineering, chemical research, chemical technology, pharmaceutical analysis, process engineering, professional studies; BSc(Hons), MSci, BEng, MEng, MSc, PGDip, PhD, MSci

School of Creative Arts; www.qub.ac.uk/schools/SchoolofCreativeArts

arts management, music, music technology/& sonic arts, drama/& English, film studies, film & visual studies, arts management, musicology; BA, MA, BMus, BSc, MPhil, PhD

School of Education; www.qub.ac.uk/schools/schoolofeducation

appl behavioural analysis, autism spectrum disorders, children's rights, initial teacher education (PGCE in wide range of secondary education subjects), educational leadership, Irish medium post primary PGCE, educational studies, inclusion and special needs education, teaching English to speakers of other languages (TESOL), professional development, quantitative methods in educational research; AdvCertEd, DASE, EdD, MA, MEd, MSc, MSSc, PGCE, PGDip/Cert, UnivCert, BA(Hons), EdD(TESOL)

School of Electronics, Electrical Engineering and Computer Science; www.qub.ac.uk/schools/eeecs

business IT, computing and IT, computer science, cyber security, electrical & electronic engineering, electronics, software/engineering & electronic systems engineering, software development; BEng, BSc, MEng, MSc, MPhil, PhD

School of English; www.qub.ac.uk/schools/SchoolofEnglish

English literature and language, English with creative writing, Postgraduate; creative writing, English literary studies, poetry: creativity and criticism, speech and language; BA(Hons), MA, PhD

School of Geography, Archaeology and Palaeoecology; www.qub.ac.uk/schools/gap

geography, geography with extended studies in Europe, archaeology, palaeoecology and geography, archaeology, archaeology jt degrees, archaeology-palaeoecology, archaeology-palaeoecology and geography, Postgraduate; cultural heritage and GIS, human geography: society, space and culture; BA(Hons), BSc(Hons), MSc, PhD, PGDip/Cert, MSci

School of History and Anthropology; www.qub.ac.uk/schools/SchoolofHistoryandAnthropology

history, anthropology, history & archaeology/ theology/philosophy/politics/sociology/modern languages, anthropology and languages, history & international studies, history
Postgraduate; history, anthropology, social anthropology, Irish Studies
BA(Hons), GradDip, MA, MPhil, PhD

School of Law; www.law.qub.ac.uk

law, law/with politics/languages, human rights, Postgraduate; human rights, human rights & criminal justice, European law and governance, international business and law, criminal justice, environmental law and governance, international corporate governance, criminal justice and criminology; LlB, LlM, MSSc, MLSc, PGDip, MPhil, PhD, JD, MLaw

Queens University Management School; www.qub.ac.uk/schools/QueensUniversityManagementSchool

accounting/& finance, actuarial science & risk management, business information technology, politics, philosophy & economics, economics
Postgraduate; accounting and finance, finance, computational finance and trading, risk and investment management, economics, management, international business, marketing, HRM, executive/international; MBA, BSc(Hons), MSc, MScs, MBA, PhD, MSSc

School of Mathematics and Physics; www.qub.ac.uk/schools/SchoolofMathematicsandPhysics

mathematics, applied mathematics/& physics, plasma physics, materials science, pure & applied mathematics, applied physics, theoretical physics, mathematics with finance; BSc(Hons), GradDip, MSc, MSci, PhD

School of Mechanical and Aerospace Engineering; www.qub.ac.uk/schools/SchoolofMechanicaland AerospaceEngineering

adv/aerospace engineering, adv/mechanical engineering, product design engineering; BEng, MEng, MSc, PhD

School of Medicine, Dentistry and Biomedical Sciences; www.qub.ac.uk/schools/mdbs

medicine, biomedical science, clinical education, clinical anatomy, dentistry, dental surgery, human biology, surgery, bioinformatics and computational genomics, translational medicine, public health, mental health, obstetrics; BCh, BAO, BSc(Hons), BDS, DAO, MB, MD, MSc, MPH, PGDip/Cert

School of Modern Languages; www.qub.ac.uk/schools/SchoolofModernLanguages

French/Irish/Spanish & Portuguese studies, interpreting & translation, business/law/science with a language, arts & humanities; BA(Hons), MA, PhD

School of Nursing and Midwifery; www.qub.ac.uk/schools/SchoolofNursingandMidwifery

nursing adult/children/learning disability/mental health/midwifery sciences, caring for children & young people with complex health needs, continuing professional development, clinical practice, neonatal studies, non-medical prescribing, health studies and health & clinical studies, specialist practice in nursing, professional studies in midwifery, enhanced/neonatal studies, trauma studies, advanced professional practice, advanced professional & clinical practice, practice development, cognitive behaviour therapy, introduction to counselling skills; BSc(Hons), Diploma, MPhil, PhD, DNursingPractice

School of Pharmacy; www.qub.ac.uk/schools/SchoolofPharmacy

adv pharmaceutical practice, pharmaceutical analysis, clinical pharmacy, community pharmacy, non medical prescribing, pharmaceutical science/biotechnology, adv pharmacy practice; MPharm, MSc, PGCert/Dip, MPhil

School of Planning, Architecture and Civil Engineering; www.qub.ac.uk/schools/SchoolofPlanningArchitectureand CivilEngineering

architecture, building & regeneration, building information modelling project management, environmental/& civil engineering, construction/ & project management, environmental engineering/planning, environmental & civil engineering, planning and regeneration, planning environment & design, portfolio guidance, urban & rural design, structural engineering with architecture,design & management sustainable practice in the built environment; BSc(Hons), MSc, MArch, MPhil, PhD, PGDip/Cert,MPlan

School of Politics, International Studies and Philosophy; www.qub.ac.uk/schools/SchoolofPoliticsInternationalStudies andPhilosophy

international relations, politics, philosophy, legislative studies & practice, philosophy, politics & economics, international politics & conflict studies, violence, terrorism and security, public policy; BA(Hons), LlB, MA, MRes, MPhil, PhD

School of Psychology; www.psych.qub.ac.uk

atypical child development, applied psychology (clinical specialism), psychology, educational child & adolescent psychology, political psychology, politics, clinical psychology, psychology of childhood adversity; BSc(Hons), MSc, DocClinPsych, PhD DocEducational

School of Sociology, Social Policy and Social Work; www.qub.ac.uk/schools/SchoolofSociologySocialPolicySocialWork

applied social studies, criminology, childhood studies, social work, social policy, social research methods, sociology, sociology with quantitative methods, cognitive behavioural therapy; BA(Hons), BSW, MA, MSc, DChild, MRes

UNIVERSITY OF BIRMINGHAM
www.bham.ac.uk

College of Arts and Law;
www.birmingham.ac.uk/schools/
historycultures/departments/caha/
index.aspx

Birmingham Law School; www.birmingham.ac.uk/schools/law/index.aspx

law, international law and globalisation, law with business studies/criminology/French law/German law, LlB for graduates; international law, international law: crime, justice & human rights, commercial law, international commercial law, criminal law & criminal justice, health, bioethics & law; GradDip, LlB, LlM, MPhil/MJur/PhD

English, Drama and American & Canadian Studies; www.birmingham.ac.uk/schools/edacs/index.aspx

American & Canadian literature/studies & culture, English language & applied linguistics, English, film/ & creative writing, directing, drama & theatre arts, English language/literature, creative writing, directing, film and television, Shakespeare and creativity, English literature, medieval studies, Shakespeare and education, Shakespeare studies, Shakespeare and theatre, applied linguistics, English language and applied linguistics, language, culture and communication, TESOL; BA(Hons), BSc(Hons), MPhil, PhD, MA, MRes

School of History and Cultures; www.birmingham.ac.uk/schools/historycultures/index.aspx

African Studies and Anthropology

African studies, African studies with anthropology/ development, archaeology and anthropology, anthropology and classical literature and civilisation. anthropology and history,anthropology and political science; Postgraduate; Africa and development, African studies, Caribbean literature, social research (African studies)

Classics, Ancient History and Archaeology

classics, classical literature & civilisation, and ancient history; Postgraduate; Byzantine studies, antiquity(-classical archaeology/classics and ancient history/ Egyptology), archaeology(cultural archaeology/ landscape archaeology), ancient history, archaeology, Byzantine studies, classics, Egyptology, Greek

archaeology, late antiquity, modern East Mediterranean history,

History

ancient and medieval history, history, history & American and Canadian studies/anthropology/ archaeology & ancient history/education/English/ French studies/geography/German studies/Hispanic studies/history of art/political science/ Russian studies/theology; Postgraduate; contemporary history, early modern history, global history, history of warfare, Holocaust and genocide, medieval studies, military history, modern British studies, social research (economic and social history), medieval history, modern European history, twentieth Century British history

Ironbridge international Institute for Cultural Heritage

Postgraduate;world heritage studies, international heritage management, cultural heritage; BA(Hons), MA, MPhil, PGDip, PhD/Dip/Cert, MRes

School of Languages, Cultures, Art History and Music; www.birmingham.ac.uk/schools/lcahm/index.aspx

History of Art

history of art, art history, curating and visual studies, English/history/modern languages and history of art Postgraduate; art History and curating, history of art

Modern Languages

modern languages with business management, French studies and geography/history/mathematics, geography/history and German studies, Hispanic studies and history, history and Russian studies, modern languages and English, Russian studies and international relations; Postgraduate; colonial and postcolonial studies, Holocaust and genocide, translation Studies, modern languages, sexuality and gender studies

Music

music, mathematics/modern languages and music; Postgraduate; music, British music studies, choral conducting, critical musicology, early music, electroacoustic composition/sonic art, global popular music, instrumental/vocal composition, mixed composition, performance, performance practice; BA, MA, BMus, MPhil, PhD

The School of Philosophy, Theology and Religion; www.birmingham.ac.uk/schools/ptr/index.aspx

Philosophy

philosophy, philosophy, religion and ethics, politics, religion and philosophy, classical literature & civilisation and philosophy, English /history/mathematics and philosophy, philosophy and sociology, political science and philosophy; Postgraduate; philosophy, philosophy of health and happiness, philosophy of mind and cognitive science, philosophy of religion and ethics, health, bioethics and law, international law, ethics and politics, global ethics, human values and human rights

Theology and Religion

theology & religion, philosophy, religion and ethics, politics, religion and philosophy, history and theology; Postgraduate; evangelical and charismatic studies, philosophy of religion and ethics, religion, politics and society, theology and religion, interreligious relations, Islamic studies, Pentecostal and charismatic studies, religion and culture, Sikh studies, theology and religion; BA(Hons), BMus, MA, MPhil, PhD, MRes, Dip/Cert, BD, MDiv, DPT D

School of Chemistry; www.birmingham.ac.uk/schools/chemistry/index.aspx

chemical biology & biochemical imaging, chemistry/with pharmacology/business management, drug discovery & mediscience, physical science for health, chemistry for biomedicine; BSc, MSci, MSc, PhD/MPhil

School of Chemical Engineering; www.birmingham.ac.uk/schools/chemical-engineering/index.aspx

adv/chemical engineering, biochemical engineering, efficient fossil energy technologies, energy engineering, food safety, hygiene & management, industrial project management, food quality & health; BEng, MEng, Masters/MSc/Diploma/PG Certificate

School of Civil Engineering; www.birmingham.ac.uk/schools/civil-engineering/index.aspx

civil engineering/& energy engineering, civil engineering & management, civil & railway engineering, geotechnical engineering & management/international experience/international study, railway systems engineering & integration, railway risk & safety management, construction management, road management & engineering, structural engineering &

practice; BEng, MEng, Masters/MSC/Diploma/Certificate, PhD

School of Computer Science; www.cs.bham.ac.uk

artificial intelligence, & computer science, adv/computer science, computer science & business management/software engineering, cyber security, natural computation, human/computer interaction, cognitive robotics & psychology, mathematics & computer science, robotics; BSc, MEng, MSc, MRes, PhD, MSci

School of Electronic, Electrical and Computer Engineering; www.birmingham.ac.uk/schools/eece/index.aspx

communications engineering & networks, electrical engineering & business management, electrical & energy/electronic engineering, electrical power systems, electromagnetic sensor networks, electrical & railway engineering/with business management, electronic & computer engineering, electronic transportation systems & infrastructure, radio engineering, RF & microwave engineering, computer systems engineering, embedded systems, industrial experience; BEng, MEng, MSc, MRes, PhD

School of Mathematics; www.birmingham.ac.uk/schools/mathematics/index.aspx

mathematics, mathematics & computer science/French studies/music/philosophy/business management pure/applied mathematics, mathematics/with engineering, operational research, statistics, theoretical physics & applied mathematics, computer science, management mathematics, mathematic modelling, financial engineering, OR, statistics & econometrics, statistics; BA, BSc, MSci, MSc, MRes, PhD

School of Mechanical Engineering; www.birmingham.ac.uk/schools/mechanical-engineering/index.aspx

adv/mechanical/automotive engineering, engineering/project/operations management; BEng, MEng, Masters/MSc, PhD/MSc

School of Metallurgy and Materials; www.birmingham.ac.uk/schools/metallurgy/index.aspx

biomaterials, materials/for sustainable energy technologies, materials science & technology/engineering/business management,/energy engineering metallurgy, biomaterials, mechanical & materials engineering, science & engineering of materials, nuclear science & engineering, sports & materials science; BSc, BEng, MEng, MRes, PhD/MSc

School of Physics and Astronomy; www.birmingham.ac.uk/schools/physics/index.aspx

physics, physics & astrophysics/particle physics & cosmology, theoretical physics, & applied mathematics, physics & technology of nuclear reactors, nuclear decommissioning & waste management; BEng, BNatSci, BSc(Hons), DEng, MEng, MPhil, MRes, MSc, MSci, PGDip/Cert, PhD

College of Life and Environmental Sciences; www.birmingham.ac.uk/university/colleges/les/index.aspx

School of Biosciences; www.birmingham.ac.uk/schools/nces/index.aspx

biochemistry/with biotechnology/molecular & cellular biology, biological sciences, biochemistry (genetics), bioscience with management, medical biochemistry, biological sciences (biotechnology/environmental biology/genetics/microbiology/plant biology/zoology), human biology, natural sciences, toxicology, zoology, medical biology, microbiology & infection, molecular mechanistic toxology/biotechnology; BSc, MSci, MSc, MPhil, PhD

School of Geography, Earth and Environmental Sciences; www.birmingham.ac.uk/schools/gees/index.aspx

geography (jt degrees), geology/& physical geography, applied & petroleum micropalaeontology, environmental geology, environmental & biological nanoscience, air pollution management & control, applied meteorology & climate, geology/physical geography, human geography (res), hydrogeology, environmental science/health, nuclear decommissioning & waste management, palaeobiology & palaeoenvironment, public & environmental health science, river environments their management, science of occupational health, safety & the environment, urban & regional planning, urban regeneration & renewal; BA, BSc/MSci, MSci, MSc, MRes

School of Psychology; www.birmingham.ac.uk/schools/psychology/index.aspx

psychology, clinical psychology, cognitive robotics/neuroscience cognitive behaviour therapy, compassion focused therapy, forensic/clinical psychology,

human neuroscience, psychology & psychological practice/res, psychology & brain imaging, rational emotional behaviour therapy; BSc, MSci, MSc/Dip/Cert, ForClinPsyD, PhD

School of Sport, Exercise and Rehabilitation Sciences; www.birmingham.ac.uk/schools/sport-exercise/index.aspx

adv practice, adv manipulative physiotherapy, clinical health research, exercise & sport medicine (football), health studies/research, sport & exercise sciences, sports & materials science, sport PE & coaching science, PE, physical education & sport pedagogy, sport, exercise & rehabilitation science, sport & materials science, sport coaching, golf coaching, applied golf management studies physiotherapy, sport policy, business & management; BSc(Hons), MPhil, MRes, MSc, PhD, FdSc, PGDip, PGCert

College of Medical and Dental Sciences; www.birmingham.ac.uk/university/colleges/mds/index.aspx

The Five Schools of the College are: Cancer Sciences, Clinical & Experimental Medicine, Dentistry, Health & Population Sciences, Immunity & Infection

biomedical materials science, biomedical science, dental hygiene and therapy, dental surgery, medicine and surgery, medicine and surgery, nursing, pharmacy, clinical science, health management and leadership, healthcare ethics and law, history of medicine, international health, medical sciences, psychological medicine, public health & population sciences

Postgraduate; advanced clinical practice, advanced critical care practitioner, advanced general dental practice, biomedical research: integrative and translational, cancer sciences, cardiovascular science, clinical health research, clinical neuropsychiatry, clinical oncology, clinical primary and community care, clinical research, functional and clinical anatomy, genomic medicine, health economics and econometrics, health economics and health policy, health research methods, immunology and immunotherapy, multidisciplinary healthcare simulation, musculoskeletal ageing and health, occupational health, pharmaceutical enterprise, physician associate studies, physicians assistant (anaesthesia), pharmacy, public health, public health (health technology assessment/international), trauma science, biomedical research: integrative and translational, cancer sciences, cardiovascular science, clinical health research; BDS,

BMedSci, BSc(Hons), BNurs, DDS, MBChB, MD, MPharm, DPharm, MEd, MSc, MRes, PGDip/Cert, MPH

College of Social Sciences; www.birmingham.ac.uk/university/ colleges/socsci/index.aspx

Birmingham Business School; www.birmingham.ac.uk/schools/business/ index.aspx

accounting and finance, accountancy, economics, money, banking and finance, mathematical economics and statistics, economics with language, money, banking and finance with language, geography and economics, economics and political science, policy, politics and economics, planning and economics, business management, business management with communications, international business with communications, business management with marketing, international business with languages,, money, banking and finance, money, banking and finance with modern language, mathematical economics and statistics; Postgraduate; financial management, international accounting and finance, investments, economics, development economics, economics, environmental and natural resource economics, financial economics, international economics,,international money and banking, mathematical finance, money, banking and finance, HRM, international business, management, management, entrepreneurship and innovation, management: operations, management: organisational leadership and change, management: strategy, international marketing, marketing communications, marketing, strategic marketing and consulting, business administration; MBA; international business, global banking and finance, strategy and procurement management; BSc(Hons), Dip, MSc, MBA, DBA, MPhil, PhD, PGCert, PGDip, UCert

School of Education; www.birmingham.ac.uk/schools/ education/index.aspx

autism (adults), autism (children), autism spectrum disorders (webautism), bilingualism in education, education for health professionals, initial teaching education, education (qts), subject knowledge enhancement courses (physics, mathematics), school direct (qts), teaching studies; Postgraduate; autism (adults), autism (children), autism spectrum disorders (webautism), bilingualism in education, character education, education for health professionals, education of learners with multisensory impairment

(deafblindness),inclusion and special educational needs, international studies in education, language, literacies and dyslexia, management of special education in developing countries, school improvement and educational leadership, severe, profound and multiple learning difficulties, special educational needs coordination, special educational needs and disabilities, social, emotional and behavioural difficulties, teachers of children with hearing impairment, teaching English as a foreign language TEFL, visual impairment: mandatory and non-mandatory qualification for teachers of children and young people with a visual impairment, educational studies, MA by research, educational psychology; education; AdvCert, BA(Hons), BPhil, ChildPsyD, EdD, EdPsychD, MEd, MPhil, PGCE, PGCert/Dip, PhD, PGDE, CertHE

School of Government and Society; www.birmingham.ac.uk/schools/ government-society/index.aspx

society & economics, international relations with French/German/Spanish, political economy, political science, sociology, international relations with economics/political science, political science with economics/history/sociology/social policy/philosophy, sociology & social policy/philosophy/education/political science

Postgraduate; global cooperation and security, aid management, human resources and development management, public economic management and finance, development management, international development, environment, sustainability and politics, conflict, security and development, governance and statebuilding, international political economy and development, poverty, inequality and development, urban development, international development, conflict, security and development, poverty, inequality and development, political science, British politics and the state, political theory, social and political theory, research methods, contemporary Asia pacific, diplomacy, gender, global cooperation and security, international peacekeeping, security, terrorism and political violence, research methods, social and political theory, public management, local policy and leadership, health and social care, public service commissioning, public administration, poverty, inequality and development; BA(Hons), BSc(Hons), PGDipGDipGCert, MA, MEd, AdvCert, MPhil, MSc, PhD, MPA

The School of Social Policy (The Health Services Management Centre; Institute of Applied Social Studies); www.birmingham.ac.uk/schools/social-policy/index.aspx
policy, politics and economics, social work, social policy, social policy: health and social care/ housing and communities, policy, politics and economic, social policy and criminology/ sociology, political science/planning and social policy, mental health and deafness

Postgraduate; health care policy and management, leadership for health services improvement, healthcare commissioning, migration, superdiversity and policy, policy into practice, policy into practice with integrated placement, social policy, social research (social policy/social work and professional practice), leadership and management for social work/ social care, social work, social work with children, young people, their families and carers, specialist social work with adults, social research; BA(Hons), MA, MSc, PGDip, SocScD, PhD

Degrees validated at the University of Birmingham offered at:

SCHOOL OF EDUCATION, SELLY OAK
www.education.bham.ac.uk Refer to School of Education in University of Birmingham entry, above

UNIVERSITY COLLEGE BIRMINGHAM
www.ucb.ac.uk

applied food and nutrition, aviation and airport management, bakery and confectionery technology, beauty therapy management, business enterprise, childhood studies, culinary arts management/ science, digital marketing, events management, food development and innovation, health and social care, hospitality and restaurant management, hospitality and tourism management, hospitality business management, hospitality with events management, international hospitality and tourism management, international tourism/business management, managing in service industries, marketing management, marketing with events management, spa management, specialist hair and media, sport and fitness studies, sports management/ therapy, youth, community and families; Postgraduate; culinary arts management, early years initial teacher training, global meetings and events management, hospitality with tourism management, international hospitality management/ tourism business administration, learning and teaching, marketing management for events, hospitality and tourism, PGCE primary QTS (qualified teacher status) (primary 3-7 and primary 5-11 years pathways), PGCE direct pathway (primary 3-7 and primary 5-11 years), tourism destination management, youth/work and community development; BA(Hons), BSc(Hons), FdA, Dip HE, FdSc, MA, MSc, PGCE, PGDip/Cert

BIRMINGHAM CITY UNIVERSITY
www.bcu.ac.uk

Faculty of Arts, Design & Media; www.bcu.ac.uk/arts-design-and-media

Birmingham School of Acting
acting, acting (the British tradition), creative drama (adults), professional voice practice, stage management

Birmingham School of Architecture & Design
3D design:3D designer maker, architectural practice, architecture; art and design, conservation of the historic environment, design innovation management, design management, interior design, landscape architecture, luxury brand management, luxury product management, product design, zero carbon architecture and retrofit design

Birmingham Conservatoire; www.bcu.ac.uk/conservatoire

jazz, music, composition, conducting (choral or orchestral), conservatoire research degrees, instrumental performance, music technology, musicology, orchestral performance (strings), professional performance, vocal performance

School of Art

art and design: interdisciplinary practices, arts and education practices, arts, wellbeing and mindfulness, contemporary arts china, contemporary curating, fine art, history and theory in art and design, queer studies in arts and culture, radical media arts philosophy

School of Fashion & Textiles; www.bcu.ac.uk/fashion-textiles

art and design, cosmetics branding and promotion, fashion accessory design, fashion business and promotion, fashion design, fashion design with design for performance/ fashion accessories, fashion communication, garment technology, fashion management, fashion media management/promotion/ fashion retail management, surface design textile design, textile design (constructed textiles/embroidery/printed textiles and surface design/retail management), textile management

School of Jewellery; www.bcu.ac.uk/ jewellery

gemmology and jewellery studies, horology, jewellery and silversmithing – design for industry, jewellery and silversmithing, jewellery design and related products, gemmology and jewellery studies; BA(Hons), BSc(Hons)

School of Visual Communication

art and design, design for theatre, performance and events, visual communication (film and animation/ graphic communication/ illustration), visual communication, visual communication – photography; BA(Hons), MA, PGDip/Cert, MArch, Cert/DipHE, MPhil, PhD, BMus, MMus, MFA, FD

Faculty of Business, Law & Social Sciences; www.bcu.ac.uk/business-law-and-social-sciences

Birmingham City Business School; www.bcu.ac.uk/business-school

accountancy, accountancy and business, accountancy and finance, arts and project management, business, business (professional practice), business administration/research, business and economics, business and finance, business and HRM, business and management, business and marketing, data analytics and management, design innovation management, economics and finance, executive MBA (internal audit and risk), fashion management, global media management (advertising industry), global education management, global media management (the news/music business), HRM internal audit practice, internal auditing and management & consultancy, international business, international finance, international HRM, international marketing, leadership and management practice, luxury brand management, luxury jewellery management, luxury product management, management and finance, management and international business/entrepreneurship, management and marketing, marketing, marketing (professional practice), marketing, psychology with business/marketing, risk management, advertising and PR, Master of Business Administration International, multi-unit leadership and strategy, textile management; BA(Hons), MBA, DBA, MPhil, MSc, PhD, MA, PGDip

The School of Law; www.bcu.ac.uk/law

international business law, international human rights, law, legal studies/practice, law with American legal studies/business law/criminology/marketing/ psychology/sociology, legal practice, oil & gas management; Grad Dip, MPhil, PhD, LlB(Hons), LlM, PGDip/Cert, LPC, MSc

School of Social Sciences; www.bcu.ac.uk/ socialsciences

conductive education, criminology, criminology and security studies, criminology, policing and investigation, forensic psychology, health psychology, law with psychology, integrative psychotherapy, psychology/with sociology/business/criminology/marketing/ sociology sociology/& criminology, public sociology, social sciences; BA(Hons), BSc(Hons), LlB, CertHE, FDA, MA, MPhil, MSc, PGCert/Dip, PhD

Faculty of Health Education & Life Sciences; www.bcu.ac.uk/

School of Allied & Public Health Professions

advanced healthcare, advanced practice, community health nursing specialist practitioner, diagnostic radiography, dimensions in healthcare, habilitation work, working with children and young people, health and social care, medical ultrasound, mental health – approved mental health practitioner, mental health studies, operating department practice, pain management, paramedic science, professional studies in health and social care, public health, radiography, radiotherapy, rehabilitation work (visual impairment), specialist community public health nurse, speech and language therapy; BSc(Hons), DipHE, FdA, MPhil, MSc, PGDip/Cert, PQ, PhD

School of Defence Healthcare Education; www.bcu.ac.uk/defence-healthcare-education

defence healthcare studies; BSc(Hons)

School of Education; www.bcu.ac.uk/school-of-education

Initial Teacher Training; primary education with QTS / specialism in mathematics with QTS, post-compulsory education and training, primary and early years education, secondary art and design/computer science/drama/design and technology: food, textiles and product/mathematics/music/religious education, subject knowledge enhancement in mathematics, subject knowledge enhancement

Education, Childhood and Youth; children and integrated professional care, conductive education, early childhood studies, early years, education, global education management, international education, education

Professional Development; education, global education management, international education; BA(Hons), FD, MPhil, PGCert/Dip, PGCE, PhD, MTL, EdD, MA,MEL, ProfDocEd

School of Life Sciences; www.bcu.ac.uk/life-sciences

occupational therapy, biomedical engineering, biomedical sciences, sports therapy, dietetics, physical education and school sport, nutrition science, sport and exercise science, sports therapy, physiotherapy, sport and exercise nutrition; BSc(Hons), MSc, BEng, MEng

School of Nursing, Midwifery & Social Work; www.bcu.ac.uk/nursing-midwifery-and-social-work

midwifery, nursing, adult/child/learning disability/ mental health, dimensions in healthcare, mental health studies, advanced healthcare, advanced clinical practice, community health nursing specialist practitioner, dimensions in healthcare, graduate practice nursing, rehabilitation work working with children and young people, professional studies in health and social care, medical ultrasound, public health, nursing studies, radiography, specialist community public health nursing, specialist complex needs rehabilitation (visual impairment); BSc(Hons), MSc, PGDip/Cert, AdvDip

Faculty of Performance, Media & English; www.bcu.ac.uk/pme

Birmingham School of Media; www.bcu.ac.uk/media

international/broadcast/online journalism,/PR creative industries & cultural policy, interactive entertainment (digital art/marketing/games development), film distribution & marketing, freelance photography/media, event & exhibition management, film futures, global media (advertising industry/music business/news business) media & creative enterprises/cultural studies/communication/events & exhibitions,online journalism, video games development, media photography/music industry (PR/radio/TV/online), radio & audio production, TV production, screen studies, social media, video games; BA(Hons), PGDip, MA, MPhil, PhD, Adv Cert, MSc

Birmingham School of Acting; www.bsa.bcu.ac.uk

acting/British tradition, acting training, professional voice practice, stage management, applied performance (community & education); BA(Hons), MPhil, PhD, MA, MFA, FD

School of English; www.bcu.ac.uk/English

English with creative writing/literature/drama/ media, English language/literature/linguistics; BA(Hons), Dip, MA, MPhil, PhD

Faculty of Computing, Engineering & the Built Environment; www.bcu.ac.uk/computing-engineering-and-the-built-environment

Digital Media Technology; digital broadcast technology, film production technology, film technology & visual effects, music technology, sound engineering & production; BSc(Hons), MSc, PhD

Built Environment

architectural technology, building information modelling and management, building surveying, built environment research, civil engineering, construction management/project management, environmental sustainability (strategy and management), planning built and natural environments, planning law (built and natural environments), quantity surveying, real estate, real estate management; BSc(Hons), BEng/ MEng, MSc, PGDip/Cert, LlM, FD, MA, PhD

Computing & Digital Technology

big data analytics, business computing, business information technology, computer networks, computer networks and security, computer science, computing, cyber security, data analytics and management, data networks and security, electronic engineering (microelectronics/foundation), forensic computing, information and communications technology; BSc(Hons), BEng, MEng, MSc, PGDip/Cert, PhD

School of Engineering and the Built Environment

automotive engineering, electronic engineering (microelectronics/telecommunications), engineering, design and manufacturing systems research, enterprise information systems/ integration, international logistics and supply chain management., international project management, logistics and supply chain management, mechanical engineering, oil and gas management, project management; BSc(Hons), FdSc, MSc, MPhil, PGCert/Dip, BEng, MEng, PhD

BISHOP GROSSETESTE UNIVERSITY
www.bishopg.ac.uk

archaeology, business (team entrepreneurship) counselling, drama, early childhood studies, education studies, history, mathematics, primary education, psychology, special educational needs, sport, theology & ethics, community health & social care, education, English, sociology, PGCE (primary/secondary), theology & ethics in society; BA(Hons), FdA, GradDip, MA, PhD, EdD, PGCE

BLACKBURN COLLEGE
www.blackburn.ac.uk

Vocation qualifications (BTEC, City & Guilds etc)

accounting, business accounting, financial services; retail management, business studies, business with HRM, retail management, management studies; hospitality management, hospitality management (events management); positive practice with children & young people, early childhood studies; computing (software development/networking & forensics/software development); construction sustainable design/project management/building surveying; photography, photographic media, contemporary textiles, contemporary fashion, contemporary design for interiors, graphic design, fine art (integrated media), graphic communication; illustration and animation, photographic media, contemporary textiles, contemporary design for interiors, contemporary fashion; education and training, teaching & learning support (primary), coaching & mentoring, education studies, PGCE (education & training); mechanical engineering, robotics & mechatronics, electrical and electronic engineering; Health, social care, disability studies (inclusive practice), counselling, disability studies (inclusive practice), applied psychology (counselling & health); criminology & criminal justice, criminology, paralegal studies, law; public service management, public service management (uniformed services/housing), fire & rescue service management, community policing & justice management, public service management; English language & literary studies, history & politics/sociology/English language/literary studies, sociology & English language/literary studies, politics & English language/literary studies, social science; health & personal training, community coaching & sports development, sports coaching & performance, professional practice/in complementary therapies; BA(Hons, Ord), BEng(Hons, Ord), BSc(Hons, Ord), DMS (validated externally), FdA/Sc, LlB (validated by Lancaster), LlB, LlM, MBA, MSc, EDMS, CertEd

BOURNEMOUTH UNIVERSITY
www.bournemouth.ac.uk

Faculty of Science & Technology; www.bournemouth.ac.uk/schools-and-faculty/faculty-science-technology

Department of Archaeology, Anthropology & Forensic Science

archaeology, archaeology & anthropology/forensic sciences, forensic investigation, forensic science; Postgraduate: applied sciences by research, biological anthropology, forensic archaeology/anthropology, forensic osteology, forensic toxicology by research, archaeological practice, maritime archaeology, osteoarchaeology

Department of Computing & Informatics

business information technology, computer networks, computing, forensic computing & security, information technology management, software engineering; Postgraduate; applied data analytics, computer games technology, cyber security and human factors, cyber security networks/security management, information technology

Department of Creative Technology

games technology, games programming, music & audio technology, music & sound production technology; Postgraduate: computer games technology, digital music & audio production

Department of Design & Engineering

design engineering, industrial design, product design, engineering; Postgraduate: mechanical engineering design, engineering project management, industrial design, product design

Department of Life & Environmental Sciences

biological sciences, ecology & wildlife conservation, environmental science, geology; Postgraduate: biodiversity conservation, biological anthropology, green economy

Department of Psychology

psychology; Postgraduate: foundations of clinical psychology, clinical & developmental neuropsychology, forensic & neuropsychological perspectives in face processing
All departments conduct applied sciences by research
BSc(Hons), BA(Hons), MSc, PhD, FD, MRes, BEng(Hons), MEng(Hons)

The Faculty of Management; www.bournemouth.ac.uk/schools-and-faculty/faculty-management

The Business School;
www.business.bournemouth.ac.uk

Dept of Accounting, Finance & Economics

acounting & business/finance/law/taxation, economics, finance and business/economics; Postgraduate; corporate governance, finance, international accounting/ economics and finance, international finance, international investment/international risk management/international taxation and finance

Dept of Leadership, Strategy & Organisation

business & management; business studies, business studies with economics/enterprise/finance/HRM/law/marketing/operations and project management, international business studies/& management; Postgraduate; the Bournemouth MBA, professional development (loss adjusting/HRM), innovation management and entrepreneurship, international management, management with human resources/project management

Dept of Events & Leisure

events management, events & leisure marketing; Postgraduate; events management, events marketing

Dept of Marketing

marketing, retail management; Postgraduate; retail management and marketing, consumer behaviour, marketing management

Dept of Sports & Physical Activity

sport development & coaching sciences, sports management, sports management (golf), sports psychology & coaching sciences; Postgraduate; sports management

Dept of Tourism & Hospitality

international hospitality management, tourism management, international hospitality & tourism management, Postgraduate; hotel and food services management, international hospitality and tourism management, tourism management, tourism management & marketing; BA(Hons), LIB(Hons), BSc(Hons), LlM, MA, MBA, MPhil, MSc, PhD, PGCert/Dip, Grad Dip(Law), MBA

Faculty of Media & Communication; www.bournemouth.ac.uk-schools-and-faculty/faculty-media-communication

Department of Corporate & Marketing Communications

advertising, marketing, politics, PR, Postgraduate; advertising, corporate communication, international political communications

Dept of Law

law, law with economics/& taxation, business law, entertainment law; Postgraduate; law/CPE, international commercial law, intellectual property, international tax law, public international law, legal practice; BA(Hons), BSc(Hons), FdA, MBA, MPhil, MSc, PhD, ProfDoc, LlB, LlM

Dept of Media Production

film, film production & cinematography, history, media production, photography, scriptwriting for film and television, television production; Postgraduate; cinematography for film and TV, creative media arts: data and innovation, directing film and TV, post production editing, producing film and TV, radio production, scriptwriting, sound design for film and TV

Faculty of Health & Social Sciences; www.bournemouth.ac.uk-schools-and-faculty/faculty-health-social-sciences

Dept of Human Science & Public Health

clinical exercise science, midwifery, nutrition, occupational therapy, physiotherapy, operating department practice, paramedic science; Postgraduate; midwifery, nutrition & behaviour, public health, public health with professional registration as a specialist community public health nurse (health visiting)

Department of Nursing & Clinical Sciences

adult/children & young people's/mental health nursing; Postgraduate; advanced nurse practitioner, adult/children & young people's/mental health nursing (with professional registration)

Dept of Social Work and Social Sciences

social work, sociology, sociology & anthropology/criminology; Postgraduate; advanced mental health practice, advanced practice (child & family social work), advanced practice (vulnerable adults), social care, social work, social work (children & families) BA(Hons), LlB(Hons), BSc(Hons), LlM, MA, MBA, MPhil, MSc, PhD, PGCert, Grad Dip(Law), CPE, MBA

UNIVERSITY OF BRADFORD
www.bradford.ac.uk

School of Engineering & Informatics
www.brad.ac.uk/ei

Faculty of Engineering & Informatics

School of Electrical Engineering and Computer Science

Computer Science; business computing, computer science, computer science for games, ICT with business; Postgraduate; advanced computer science, big data science and technology, computing, cyber security, mobile applications, software engineering Electrical and Electronic Engineering; electrical and electronic engineering, medical electronics engineering, engineering and technology; Postgraduate; electrical and electronic engineering, personal, mobile and satellite communications, telecommunications engineering and entrepreneurship

School of Engineering

Chemical Engineering; chemical engineering; Postgraduate; chemical and petroleum engineering
Civil and Structural Engineering; civil and structural engineering; Postgraduate; civil and structural engineering
Mechanical and Automotive Engineering; mechanical engineering, mechanical and manufacturing engineering; Postgraduate; automotive engineering; mechanical engineering, information technology management, manufacturing management
Medical Engineering; Postgraduate; clinical technology, medical engineering, medical electronics engineering
Healthcare Technology; Postgraduate; medical engineering

School of Health Studies; www.brad.ac.uk/acad/health

clinical nursing practice, clinical practice, critical care, dementia studies, diagnostic radiography, health, wellbeing and social care, midwifery studies, nursing (adult/child/mental health), occupational therapy, paramedic science, physiotherapy, sport rehabilitation; Postgraduate; adult cardiology, examination, assessment and intervention module, advanced care of the older person, advanced care of the older person, advanced practice (clinical practitioner),advanced practice (critical care), advanced practice (midwifery), advanced practice (minor injuries and minor illness),advancing transdisciplinary practice, applied physiotherapy, continence for physiotherapists, dementia studies, dementia studies (arts and activities/training in dementia care),diagnostic hysteroscopy and therapeutic diversity management, health and social care management, health wellbeing and social care, international health management, leadership, management and change in health and social care, leading service improvement, learning and talent development, managing health and social care, medical imaging, medical imaging (computed tomography/magnetic resonance imaging/medical image reporting/international), midwifery, musculoskeletal physiotherapy practice, nursing studies (international), patient safety, physiotherapy in women's health, professional healthcare practice, professional healthcare practice (cancer care), professional healthcare practice (children and young people/cognitive behavioural therapy/collaborative mental health care/diabetes care/end of life care/long term conditions/practice nursing/psychological therapies/public health/tissue viability), professional support, rehabilitation studies (continence for physiotherapists/musculoskeletal physiotherapy practice/physiotherapy in women's health/sports physiotherapy), sexual health, sports physiotherapy
AdvDip, BSc(Hons), CertHE, DipHE, FD, MSc, MPhil, PGDip/Cert, PhD, MPH

Faculty of Life Sciences; www.brad.ac.uk/acad/lifesci

Archaeological Sciences; archaeology, archaeological sciences, forensic archaeology and anthropology; Postgraduate; archaeological prospection, archaeological sciences, archaeology, forensic archaeology and crime scene investigation, human osteology & palaeopathology; Chemistry and Forensic sciences; chemistry, chemistry (analytical/materials/(medicinal), chemistry with industrial experience/research

experience, integrated science; Postgraduate; analytical sciences, materials chemistry, science and entrepreneurship; Forensic and Medical sciences; forensic and medical sciences, forensic science, biomedical science), healthcare science (life sciences); healthcare science (life sciences); clinical sciences; clinical sciences/medicine, clinical sciences; Postgraduate; biomedical science, cancer drug discovery, cancer pharmacology, cellular pathology laboratory practice, drug toxicology and safety pharmacology, science and entrepreneurship; Optometry and Vision Science; optometry, career progression programme; Pharmacy; pharmacy; Postgraduate; clinical pharmacy (community), clinical pharmacy (secondary care), pharmaceutical technology
BSc(Hons), MPhil, PhD, MChem, MPharm, CertHE, MSc, MSci(Hons), DPharm

Bradford School of Management; www.brad.ac.uk/management

Management; business and management studies, HRM, marketing, international business & management; Accounting and Finance; accounting and finance; Corporate management and business; Postgraduate; European and international business management, finance, accounting and management, international business and management, management, marketing and management, sustainable operations and management, applied management and entrepreneurship, innovation, enterprise and the circular economy: marketing and management, strategic marketing, media and entrepreneurship, science and entrepreneurship, telecommunications engineering and entrepreneurship
Executive MBA, MBA; BA(Hons), BSc(Hons), DBA, LlB, LlM, GradDip(Law), MBA, MRes, PhD, MSc, PGCert/Dip

School of Media, Design & Technology

Animation and Games; computer animation and visual effects, game design and development, graphics for games,
Film, TV and Media; film and TV production, film and media studies,
Web Design; web design and technology,
Postgraduate; digital filmmaking
BEng(Hons), BSc(Hons), BA(Hons), FD, MEng, MPhil, MSc, PhD

Faculty of Social Sciences; www.brad.ac.uk/acad/ssis

Economics; economics, business economics, financial economics

Peace Studies; development and peace studies, international relations and security studies, history and politics, politics, peace studies; PostGrad;African peace and conflict studies, applied dual-use biosecurity education, conflict resolution, conflict, security and development, international politics and security studies, peace studies, peace, conflict and development, politics, violence & terrorism, Middle East violence & security studies

Psychology; psychology, psychology with counselling
Sociology & Criminology; applied criminal justice studies, sociology, sociology and psychology, psychology and crime
Social Work & Social Care; social work, working with children, young people and families; Postgraduate; social work
BA(Hons), BSc(Hons), MA, MPhil, PhD, PGDip, MPA

Degrees validated by University of Bradford offered at:

BRADFORD COLLEGE
www.bradfordcollege.ac.uk

accountancy, beauty therapy management, business management (HRM), business management (marketing), business management, childhood and youth studies, computer networks and systems support, computing and information systems, computing, construction management, counselling and psychology in community settings, education and training, early years, early years practice, education studies, fashion, film, games and digital media, graphic media design, health and social welfare, hospitality and travel management, interior design, internet applications, law (accountancy/marketing/social welfare), law and legal practice, law, lifelong learning, management and leadership, media make-up with special effects, photography, physical activity, health and well-being, primary education with QTS, public services management, secondary education (physics), social nutrition and health, sports coaching, supporting and managing learning in education, surface design and textile innovation, teaching and learning in the primary phase with QTS,visual arts, youth and community development; Postgraduate; applied business,PGCE (14-19), computing, education and training, education/leadership & management/inclusive education/early childhood/ICT, health and social care GCE (14-19), international business management, management, primary PGCE, youth and community development; BSc(Hons), CertHE, DipHE, BA(Hons), LlB(Hons), BEngTech, MA, MEd, PGDipCert, MSc, PGCE, FD, LawPGDip, LlM

UNIVERSITY OF BRIGHTON
www.brighton.ac.uk

College of Arts & Humanities;
www.arts.brighton.ac.uk
Architecture & Interiors; architecture, interior architecture/design, architecture & urban design, arts & cultural research
Design; 3D design & craft, craft, sustainable design
English Language Teacher Education; TESOL, English language teaching, TESOL with HCT
Literature; English literature & media studies, history, literature & culture, English literature, English language & English literature, media & English literature, creative writing
Fashion & Textile Design; fashion/communication with business studies, textiles with business studies

Fine Art Practices; art & design by independent practice, digital media arts, sequential design/illustration, fine art, fine art (painting/printmaking/sculpture/critical practice), moving images, sequential design/illustration, performance & visual practice
Fine Art Performance, Music, Theatre Dance; theatre performance, visual art, music & visual art, performance & visual performance
History of Art & Design; fashion & dress history, history of decorative arts & crafts, history of decorative art & craft, history of design/art & design, museum & heritage studies, fashion & dress/visual culture, philosophy, politics & art, arts & cultural research, history of design & material culture

Humanities: History, Philosophy, Culture & Politics; politics, philosophy & ethics, globalisation, history, humanities/politics, craft & human rights, cultural & craft theory, politics/literature & culture, humanities, war, history & politics, applied ethics, culture & cultural theory, cultural history, memory & identity, arts & cultural research, literary culture, philosophy, politics & art

Language & Linguistics; English language, English language & linguistics, arts & cultural research, linguistics, English literature & language/media, philosophy of language, creative writing

Media; media and English literature, film and screen studies, TV and digital media production, English literature and media studies, environment and media studies, media, industry and innovation, multimedia broadcast journalism, media studies, English language and media, digital film, broadcast media, TV production, arts and cultural research, digital/& creative media

Photography, Moving Image & Sound; photography, digital music & sound arts, moving image, film & screen studies arts & cultural research; BA(Hons), FdSA, Grad Dip, MA, MDes, MFA, MPhil, MRes, PGDip/Cert, PhD, MArch

College of Social Sciences

School of Education; www.brighton.ac.uk/education

Studies in Education; education – early childhood education and care, media studies and education, education and English literature, computing and education, education and sociology, mathematics and education, human biology and education, environmental biology and education; Working with children and young people; early childhood practice, professional studies in learning and development, supporting learning 5-11 years, 11-19 years, working with children and young people, youth work; Working with adults; professional studies in learning and development; Postgraduate; Professional Development; education; Professional Education Studies; mathematics for secondary school teachers, mentoring and coaching: maximising potential, primary mathematics specialist teacher programme, science education for primary and secondary school teachers, strategies for working with autistic learners, specific learning difficulties (dyslexia), education, education (leadership and management), education (international education),education (higher education), education (mathematics

education), education (early childhood), MPhil/PhD programme, Professional Doctorate in Education programme; BA(Hons), BSc(Hons), MSc, MA, FdA, CertEd, PGCert/Dip, QTS, PGCE, EdD, MPhil, PhD

School of Sport & Service Management; www.brighton.ac.uk/sasm

hospitality, international hospitality management, retail management, retail marketing, journalism, sport journalism, sport and exercise science, sport and fitness, applied exercise physiology, applied sport physiology, sport coaching/and development, sport studies, sport business management/studies, sport and international development, sport and society, sport and social anthropology, physical education, international event management, international travel management, international tourism management with travel business, tourism and international development, PE with QTS degree/PGCE, PE (secondary), dance (secondary) PGCE; BA(Hons), BSc(Hons), FdA, MA, MSc, PhD, PGCert/Dip

Centre for Learning and Teaching; www.brighton.ac.uk/clt

higher education, learning & teaching in HE; MA, PGCE

School of Applied Social Science; www.brighton.ac.uk/sass

applied psychology/& criminology/sociology, applied social science, approved mental health practice, criminology & social policy/sociology/substance misuse interventions/social justice, community psychology, psychotherapy, mental health, approved mental health practice, politics, sociology, social policy, social work, public admin, social policy, sociology, adv/social work, social science, sociology & social policy, substance misuse, humanistic/psychodynamic therapeutic counselling; BA(Hons), MA, MPhil, MSc, PGDip/Cert, PhD, MPA, FD, Prof Doc, BSc(Hons), MRes

Brighton Business School; www.brighton.ac.uk/bbs

accounting/ & finance, business, business & business management, business with economics/finance/HRM/marketing, business management with economics/finance/HRM/marketing, international business, economics and finance, finance & investment, business management with economics/finance, marketing; Postgraduate; accounting, international management, international retail management, logistics and supply chain management, management,

management (entrepreneurship/HR/innovation), retail management, change management, managing change and innovation, HRM, economics and finance, finance and accounting, finance and banking, finance and investment, finance and risk management, HRM, postgraduate diploma in law, Common Professional Examination, CPE, marketing, marketing (branding and communications/digital marketing/international marketing/ social marketing), MBA; general management, international management, knowledge and innovation management, leadership, public service management; BA(Hons), LlB, MBA, MSc, PGCert/Dip, CPE, BSc(Hons)

College of Life, Health & Physical Science; www.brighton.ac.uk/scieng

School of Computing, Engineering & Mathematics; www.brighton.ac.uk/cem

Computing and Digital Media; business computer system, business information systems, computer science/games, computer systems and communication, digital media/development, European computing, software engineering; Postgraduate; information systems, digital media production, user experience design, computer science, computing, internet and distributed systems; Engineering; aeronautical engineering, mechanical engineering, electrical and electronic engineering, electronic and computer engineering, electronic engineering; Postgraduate; automotive electronic engineering, automotive engineering
Product Design; product design technology/sport product design with professional experience
Mathematics and Data Analytics; mathematics, mathematics with business/economics/finance; Postgraduate; data analytics
BSc(Hons), FdSc, MA, MComp, MPhil, MSc, PGDip/Cert, MEng, BEng

School of Environment and Technology; www.brighton.ac.uk/set

architectural technology, building surveying, construction management, project management for construction, civil engineering/with environmental engineering/construction management, environmental sciences/media studies, geography, physical geography & geology, geography & archaeology/geoinformatics, earth & ocean science, geology; Postgraduate; civil engineering, construction management, environmental assessment and management, GIS and

environmental management, project management for construction, town planning, water and environmental management; BA/BSc(Hons), BEng(Hons), BSc(Hons), FdSc, FdEng, MEng, MPhil, PGDip/Cert, PhD

School of Pharmacy and Biomolecular Sciences; www.brighton.ac.uk/pharmacy

biomedical/biological sciences, cellular sciences, chemistry, clinical/general pharmacy practice, pharmacy, pharmacology, ecology, industrial pharmaceutical studies/sciences, blood sciences, infection sciences, chemical sciences, pharmaceutical & chemical biomedical science, supplementary prescribing for pharmacists; BSc(Hons), MSc, MPharm(Hons), MPhil, MRes, PGDip, PhD

Brighton and Sussex Medical School; www.bsms.ac.uk

medicine, surgery, anaesthesia and perioperative medicine, cardiology, clinical radiology, dementia studies, diabetes in primary care, global health, leadership & commissioning, medical education, medical research, paediatrics & child health, psychiatry,public health; BMBS,MD,MPhil, MSc, PGDip/Cert, PhD

School of Health Science; www.brighton.ac.uk/about-us/contact-us/academic-departments/school-of-health-sciences.aspx

acute clinical practice, community specialist practice, health studies, nurse practitioner, professional practice, specialist community public health nursing; Postgraduate; advanced practice (health), clinical research, community health, community specialist practice health, health and education/ management, health promotion, health promotion and education/ management, international health promotion, neuromusculoskeletal physiotherapy, occupational therapy, occupational therapy and education, occupational therapy and management, physiotherapy, physiotherapy and education/ management/ independent prescribing, podiatry, podiatry and education/management/clinical biomechanics/diabetes, podiatry with independent prescribing, podiatry with rheumatology, principles of podiatric surgery, specialist community public health nursing, sports injury management; BSMS, BSc(Hons), MSc, MA, PGDip/Cert

UNIVERSITY OF BRISTOL
www.bris.ac.uk

Faculty of Arts; www.bris.ac.uk/arts

School of Arts
archaeology/& anthropology, film and television, film and English, film & modern European language, theatre & film; music, music and French/German/Italian, philosophy, English and philosophy, mathematics and philosophy, philosophy and economics/modern European language/politics/theology/physics/sociology, theatre and performance studies, theatre and English/film/modern European language

School of Humanities
ancient history, classics, classical studies, English, English literature and community engagement, English and classical studies/philosophy/film/theatre, history, history of art, history of art and modern European language, religion and theology, theology and sociology, philosophy and theology

School of Modern Languages
modern languages; French, Spanish and Portuguese, French, Spanish and Italian, French, Spanish and German, French, German and Italian, French, German and Russian, German, Russian and Czech

Master Programmes in the Faculty of Arts
Chinese-English translation, comparative literatures and cultures, composition of music for film and TV, English literature, film and TV, history, history of art, logic and philosophy of mathematics, music, philosophy, philosophy and history of science, philosophy of biological and cognitive sciences, religion, translation; BA(Hons), BSc(Hons), LlB, MA, MLitt, MPhil, PGDip, PhD, MSci

Faculty of Engineering; www.bris.ac.uk/engineering

Queen's School of Engineering

Dept of Aerospace Engineering; www.bris.ac.uk/aerospace
aeronautical engineering, advanced composites, aerospace engineering

Dept of Electrical and Electronic Engineering; www.bris.ac.uk/eeng
image & video communications & signals processing, communication networks & signal processing, computer science & electronics, electrical & electronic engineering, electronics & communication engineering, microelectronics & systems, wireless communication systems & signal processing, adv microelectronic & systems engineering, biomedical engineering

Dept of Engineering Mathematics; www.enm.bris.ac.uk
complexity sciences, systems engineering, adv engineering robotics & autonomous systems, neural dynamics, engineering mathematics

Merchant Venturers' School of Engineering

Dept of Civil Engineering; www.bris.ac.uk/civilengineering
civil engineering, water & environmental management

Dept of Computer Science; www.cs.bris.ac.uk
computer science/& electronic/mathematics, adv computing (internet technologies with security/machine learning & data mining & high performance computing/creative technologies), adv microelectronic systems engineering, computer science with innovation

Dept of Mechanical Engineering; www.bris.ac.uk/mecheng
mechanical engineering, adv mechanical engineering, engineering design
BSc(Hons), BEng, EngD, PGCert, MEng, MSc, PhD

Faculty of Medical and Veterinary Science; www.bris.ac.uk/mvs

Dept of Biochemistry; www.bris.ac.uk/biochemistry
biochemistry/with molecular biology & biotechnology, biophysics & molecular life sciences, medical biochemistry, biomedical sciences

Dept of Cellular and Molecular Medicine; www.bris.ac.uk/cellmolmed
cancer biology and immunology, cellular and molecular medicine, medical microbiology, virology and immunology, biomedical sciences research, biochemistry with dynamic cell biology, transfusion & transplantation sciences

Dept of Physiology & Pharmacology; www.bris.ac.uk/phys-pharm
biomedical science research systems, neuroscience, pharmacology, physiological science; BSc(Hons), BVSc, MD, MSc, MSci, PhD

Bristol Veterinary School; www.bris.ac.uk/vetscience
animal behaviour & welfare science, meat science & technology, veterinary nursing & bioveterinary science, veterinary science, global wildlife health & conservation, animal welfare & behaviour & rehab, gateway to veterinary science

Faculty of Medicine and Dentistry; www.bris.ac.uk/fmd

medicine, gateway to medicine, surgery, child medicine, dentistry, dental implantology/hygiene/therapy, molecular neuroscience, orthodontics, reproduction & development, stem cells and regeneration, teaching & learning for health professionals, translational cardiovascular medicine, health science research, global wildlife & health & conservation, dental postgrad study; MB, BDS, BSc(Hons), ChB, ChM, BDS, Diploma, DPDS, MClinDent, MD, MMedEd, MSci, PhD, DipDent

Faculty of Science; www.bris.ac.uk/science

School of Biological Sciences; www.bris.ac.uk/biology
biology, botany, geology, zoology, palaeontology & evolution, palaeobiology, research biological sciences

School of Chemistry; www.chm.bris.ac.uk
chemistry, chemical physics, inorganic & materials chemistry, organic & biological chemistry, physical & theoretical chemistry, chemical synthesis

School of Earth Sciences; www.bris.ac.uk/earthsciences
environmental geoscience, geology/& biology, geophysics, palaeobiology, volcanology, palaeontology & evolution, earth sciences

Dept of Experimental Psychology; www.bristol.ac.uk/exppsych.ac.uk
clinical neuropsychology, clinical/applied neuropsychology, psychology, neuropsychological research, research methods, experimental psychology, psychology with innovation

School of Geographical Sciences; www.ggy.bris.ac.uk
geography, human/physical geography, human geography, society & space, geographical science, environmental policy & management, climate change science & policy, geography with innovation/quantitative research

Dept of Mathematics; www.maths.bris.ac.uk
applied/pure mathematics, mathematics, mathematics & philosophy/physics/statistics/computer science, statistics & probability, statistics, mathematical science, applied/pure mathematics

Dept of Physics; www.bris.ac.uk/physics
astrophysics, physics, mathematics and physics, physics with innovation, nanoscience & functional nanomaterial particle physics, physics/& philosophy, theoretical physics, nuclear science & engineering; BSc(Hons), DSc, LlB, MRes, MSci, MSc, PhD, UGCert

Faculty of Social Science and Law; www.bris.ac.uk/fss

Graduate School of Education; www.bris.ac.uk/education
education, psychology of education, education management, policy and international development, leadership and policy, learning, technology and society, mathematics education, neuroscience and education, psychology of education, science education, special and inclusive education, teaching and learning, neuroscience & education, PGCE/School Direct/Teach First TESOL, educational leadership, educational research

School for Policy Studies; www.bristol.ac.uk/sps
social policy, social policy with management/quantitative research methods, social policy and politics/sociology/criminology, childhood studies, childhood studies with management/quantitative research methods, global health, disability studies: inclusive theory and research, nutrition, physical activity and public health, public policy, policy research, social work research, social work, advanced social work with children and families

School of Economics, Finance & Management; www.bristol.ac.uk/efm
accounting, finance, management, econometrics, economics, public policy, accounting and finance, economics pathways, finance and investment, economics and finance, accounting, finance and management, economics, accounting and finance, economics, finance and management, management, strategy, change and leadership

School of Law; www.bris.ac.uk/law
law, law and French/ German, socio-legal studies, adv studies legal system; Postgraduate; commercial

law, European legal studies, human rights law, international commercial law, international law, international law and international relations, public law, advanced study, law, socio-legal studies

School of Sociology, Politics & International Studies; www.bristol.ac.uk/spais

Politics and International relations; politics and international relations/sociology/quantitative research methods, economics/philosophy/social policy and politics, politics & modern European language; Postgraduate; European and global governance, gender and international relations, international relation, international security, social science research methods (politics)

Sociology; sociology, sociology with quantitative research methods, social policy and sociology, sociology and philosophy, theology and sociology; Postgraduate; contemporary identities, ethnicity and multiculturalism, social and cultural theory, social science research methods (sociology), sociology Development; European and global governance, gender and international relations, international relation, international security, social science research methods (politics); Postgraduate; development and security, East Asian development and the global economy, international development,

School of Geographical Sciences; www.bris.ac.uk/geography

geography, human geography, physical geography, geography with quantitative research methods, human geography,society & space, environmental policy & management, climate change science & policy, geographical sciences

BA(Hons), BSc(Hons), DSocSci, EdD, LlB, LlD, LlM, MEd, MPhil, MSc, MSci, PGCE, PhD, Dip, MEd, DEdPsY

UNIVERSITY OF THE WEST OF ENGLAND, BRISTOL
www.uwe.ac.uk

Faculty of Business & Law; www.uwe.ac.uk/bl

Bristol Business School; www.uwe.ac.uk/bbs

accounting and finance, banking and finance, business (team entrepreneurship), business management practice, business management and leadership/accounting and finance/economics/marketing, business and events management/HRM/management, economics, international business, marketing, marketing communications; Postgraduate; accounting and financial management, business management, events management, global trade, HRM, HRM (International), innovation and applied entrepreneurship, international management, leadership and management (coaching and mentoring), leadership and management, leadership and media production management, marketing, marketing communications, Business Administration (Bristol/Executive MBA),project management (professional development); BA(Hons), BSc(Hons), MA, MBA, MSc, PhD, MBA, PGDip/Cert, LlM

Bristol Law School; www1.uwe.ac.uk/bl/bls

adv legal practice, business & law, commercial law, environmental law & sustainable development, European/ & international law, international banking & financial/trade law/economic law, international trade & economic law, global trade, law, bar professional training, legal practice, law & psychology; LlB, LlM, PhD, PGDip

Faculty of Arts, Creative Industries & Education; www.uwe.ac.uk/cahe

Dept of Arts & Cultural Industries; www1.uwe.ac.uk/cahe/arts.aspx

creative media design, creative & professional writing, English, English language and linguistics/English, games & animation production, language/history/writing, history, history with heritage, literature and film studies, media culture and practice; Postgrad; English and drama, European studies, film studies, history, linguistics; BA(Hons), FdA, MA, MPhil, PhD

Dept of Art & Design; www1.uwe.ac.uk/cahe/artanddesign

drawing and print, fashion, fashion communication, fine arts, graphic design, illustration, interior design; Postgrad; curating, design, fine art, graphic arts, multi-disciplinary printmaking; BA(Hons), MA, PGDip/Cert, MFA

Dept of Education; www1.uwe.ac.uk/cahe/edu

early childhood, early years, education, education in professional practice, initial teacher education, primary/early years, primary education, PGCE primary early years initial teacher education (3-7) – primary initial teacher education (5-11), secondary initial teacher education art and design/English/mathematics with business education/ modern languages/ physics with mathematics/science with biology/ science with chemistry/physics,post-compulsory education; ASR, BA(Hons), CertEd, DipHE, MA, MPhil, MSc, PGCert/Dip, PhD, FD, MEd, EdD

Dept of Film & Journalism; www1.uwe.ac.uk/cahe/film and journalism

animation, filmmaking, journalism, journalism and PR, media and journalism, photography, documentary and features; BA(Hons), MA, PGDip/Cert

Faculty of Environment and Technology; www.uwe.ac.uk/et

Dept of Architecture & the Built Environment; www.uwe.ac.uk/et/cp

architecture, architectural technology & design, architecture & environmental engineering/planning, building information modelling, building services engineering, creative product design, interior architecture, international construction law, professional practice & management in architecture, quantity surveying & commercial management, building surveying/information modelling, construction/project management, property development & planning, real estate finance & investment/management; FdA, BA(Hons), BSc(Hons), MSc, MPhil, PhD, BEng(Hons), MArch, GradDip, MPlan

Dept of Computer Science & Creative Technologies; www.uwe.ac.uk/et/cst

applied computing, audio & music technology, broadcast audio & music technology, computer science for games & security, computer systems integration, computing, creative music technology, digital media, forensic computing & security, games technology, IT management for business, information management/technology, mobile technology, software development for business, software engineering; BSc(Hons), MSc, MPhil, PhD, PGDip/Cert, FdSc

Dept of Engineering Design & Mathematics; www.uwe.ac.uk/et/edm

aerospace engineering/manufacture/with pilot studies, automation & computer vision, automotive engineering, creative product design, electrical & electronic engineering, electronic & computer engineering, engineering/management, engineering operations & improvement, electronics & communications, embedded systems & wireless networks, mathematics/&statistics, mechanical engineering, mechatronics, professional engineering, robotics, statistics; BEng, MEng, BSc(Hons), MPhil, PhD

Dept of Geography & Environmental Management; www.uwe.acf.uk/et/gem

civil & environment engineering, geography/& planning, geology, applied GIS, civil/& environmental engineering, environmental resource management, river & coastal engineering, sustainable development in practice, traffic engineering, transport engineering/ & planning, uniformed & public services, urban/& rural planning; BA(Hons), BSc(Hons), PGradDip, MPhil, PhD, FD,MPlan

Faculty of Health & Life Sciences; www.uwe.ac.uk/hls

Dept of Allied Health Professions; www.uwe.ac.uk/hls/ahp

diagnostic imaging, applied/paramedic science, health professions, physiotherapy, health professions, occupational therapy, radiotherapy & oncology, medical ultrasound, nuclear medicine, physical activity & community health, physician associate studies, sports rehabilitation; FdSc, BSc(Hons), MSc, PGDip/Cert, MPhil, PhD

Dept of Biological, Biomedical & Analytical Sciences; www.uwe.ac.uk/hls/as

adv forensic analysis, biological science, biomedical sciences, environmental health/science, forensic science, healthcare science (life sciences/physiological sciences), integrated wildlife conservation, adv wildlife conservation in practice, biosensing technologies, premedical science, practical science communication, wildlife & conservation science/in practice; FdSc, BSc(Hons), MSc, MRes, ProfDoc, PGCert/Dip, MPhil, PhD, CertHE, MSci

Dept of Health & Social Sciences; www.uwe.ac.uk/hls/hass

criminology/& criminal justice/sociology/psychology, counselling/occupational psychology, environmental health, health psychology, integrated professional development (social work), philosophy, public health, social work/with adults, politics & international relations, professional development, psychology with criminology/law/sociology, sociology, specialist community public health/& environmental health, occupational psychology, professional development (practical skills/therapeutic education/psycho-social studies/social work), public health, public health (specialist community public health nursing), social work, sport & exercise science, therapeutic work with children & young people, music therapy; FdA, BSc(Hons), BA(Hons), MSc, PGDip/Cert, GradDip, MPhil, PhD

Dept of Nursing & Midwifery; www.uwe.ac.uk/hls/nm

care management in the community, health and social care practice, midwifery, nursing (adult nursing/children's nursing/learning disabilities nursing/mental health nursing), professional studies, specialist practice, advanced practice, health and social care; FdSc, BSc(Hons), MSc, PGDip/Cert, ProfDoc, MPhil, PhD

Dept of Psychology; www.uwe.ac.uk/hls/psychology

psychology, psychology & criminology/law/sociology, psychological therapy (cognitive behaviour/relational psychotherapy), counselling psychology, occupational psychology, psychological; BA(Hons), BSc(Hons), MSc, DPS, ProfDoc, MPhil, PhD

Hartpury College (Associate Faculty); www.hartpury.ac.uk

agriculture, bioveterinary science, animal behaviour and welfare, animal management, animal science and management, applied animal science/with therapy, equestrian sports coaching, equine science with therapy, equestrian sports science, equine business management, equine management, equine science/performance/science and management, sports therapy (equestrian) and exercise nutrition, sports business management, PE and school sport, sports coaching, strength and conditioning, sport performance/therapy/coach development, sport and exercise sciences, equine veterinary nursing science, veterinary nursing science, equine veterinary nursing science

animal behaviour & veterinary science/welfare, equine performance & rehabilitation/behaviour & welfare/science, coaching science, PE & school sport, physiology, sport management/studies/injury management/business management/coaching performance/therapy, professional development (coaching science), sport & exercise nutrition, sport conditioning & injury management, sport management (equine/golf), equine veterinary nursing, veterinary nursing/science; BA(Hons), BSc(Hons), FdSc, FdA, MA, MSc, PGDip/Cert

BRUNEL UNIVERSITY
www.brunel.ac.uk

College of Business, Arts and Social Sciences; www.brunel.ac.uk/cbass

Department of Arts and Humanities; www.brunel.ac.uk/cbass/arts-humanities

composition, creative writing, English and film and TV studies, English, English with creative writing, music, performance, sonic arts, theatre and creative writing/English, theatre and film and TV studies, theatre; Postgraduate; contemporary performance making, creative writing/the novel, experimental music

Brunel Business School; www.brunel.ac.uk/cbass/bbs

business and management (accounting/marketing), business and management, international business, business administration, accounting and business management, applied corporate brand management, business intelligence and social media, global supply chain management, HRM, human resources and employment relations, international business, management, marketing; BSc, MSc, MBA, PhD

Dept of Economics & Finance; www.brunel.ac.uk/cbass/economics-finance

economics and accounting, economics and business finance/management, economics, finance and accounting, politics and economics

Postgraduate; banking and finance, business finance, finance and accounting, finance and investment; BSc, MSc, PhD

Dept of Education; www.brunel.ac.uk/cbass/education

education, contemporary education,teaching (MAT), PGCE (PGCert) primary education (5-11 years)/computer science and information and communications technology, PGCE (PGCert) secondary education (English/mathematics/physical education/ physics with mathematics/science with biology/ science with chemistry/ science with physics) with recommendation for QTS; BA, MA, PhD

Politics, History and the Brunel Law School; www.brunel.ac.uk/cbass/politics-history-law

history, international politics, law, law with criminal justice/international arbitration & commercial law, politics and economics/ history/ sociology, politics Postgraduate; law, intellectual property law, intelligence and security studies, international commercial law, international financial regulation and corporate law, international human rights law, international intellectual property law, international relations, law, military history, public affairs and lobbying; BA, BSc, LlB, LlM, PGCert, MSc, GradDip, CPE, PGCert, PhD, MPhil

Department of Social Sciences, Media and Communications; www.brunel.ac.uk/cbass/social-sciences-me

anthropology/and sociology, communication and media studies, English/ and film and TV studies, games design/and creative writing/film and TV studies, journalism, sociology/and media studies, theatre and film and television studies; Postgraduate; anthropology of childhood, youth and education, anthropology of international development and humanitarian assistance, digital games theory and design, documentary practice, international journalism, media and communications/PR, medical anthropology, psychological and psychiatric anthropology, social anthropology; BA, MA, MSc, MRes, PhD

College of Engineering, Design & Physical Sciences; www.brunel.ac.uk/cedps

Department of Computer Science; www.brunel.ac.uk/cedps/computer-science

business computing (ebusiness)/human computer interaction/social media, business computing computer science (artificial intelligence/digital media and games/network computing/software engineering), computer science, information systems, computing and mathematics; Postgrad; business systems integration, data & analytics, digital service design, information systems management

Department of Design; www.brunel.ac.uk/cedps/design

industrial design and technology, product design, product design engineering; Postgrad; design & branding strategy, design strategy & innovation, integrated product design

Department of Electronic and Computer Engineering; www.brunel.ac.uk/cedps/electronic-computing

computer systems engineering (networks/software), computer systems engineering digital design, electrical engineering with renewable energy systems, electronic and communications engineering, electronic and computer engineering, electronic and electrical engineering, engineering, professional development, visual effects and motion graphics; Postgrad; advanced electronic and electrical engineering, advanced multimedia design and 3D technologies, computer communication networks, digital design and branding, distributed computing systems engineering, sustainable electrical power, wireless communication systems

Department of Mathematics; www.brunel.ac.uk/cedps/mathematics

financial mathematics, information systems, computing and mathematics, professional development, mathematics and statistics with management mathematics, mathematics with computer science

Department of Mechanical, Aerospace and Civil Engineering; www.brunel.ac.uk/cedps/mechanical-aerospace

aerospace engineering, automotive engineering, aviation engineering, aviation engineering with pilot studies, civil engineering, civil engineering/with sustainability, engineering, professional development, mechanical and energy engineering, mechanical engineering, mechanical engineering, mechanical engineering with aeronautics/automotive design,/ building services motorsport engineering

Postgraduate; advanced electronic and electrical engineering, advanced engineering design, advanced manufacturing systems, advanced mechanical engineering, aerospace engineering, automotive and motorsport engineering, bioengineering, biomedical genetics and tissue engineering, building services engineering, building services engineering with sustainable energy, engineering management, oil and gas engineering, project and infrastructure management renewable energy engineering, structural engineering, structural integrity, sustainable

electrical power, sustainable energy – technologies and management, water engineering
BA(Hons), BEng, BSc(Hons), EngD, MEng, MPhil, MSc, PhD, MMath, FdSc, MA, PGDip/Cert

College of Health and Life Sciences; www.brunel.ac.uk/chls

Dept of Clinical Sciences; www.brunel.ac.uk/chls/clinical-sciences

occupational therapy, physiotherapy, social work, specialist community public health nursing
Postgraduate; children, youth and international development, neurorehabilitation, occupational therapy, physiotherapy, public health and health promotion, social work, specialist community public health nursing, public health
BSc, BA, MA, PGCert, DPh, Ph

Dept of Life Sciences; www.brunel.ac.uk/chls-life-sciences

biomedical sciences (biochemistry)/genetics/human health/biomedical sciences immunology), biomedical sciences, psychology and anthropology/sociology, psychology, sport, health and exercise sciences (coaching/human performance/ sport development), sport, health and exercise sciences/with business studies
Postgraduate; ageing studies, children, youth and international development, climate change impacts and sustainability, cross-cultural psychology, environmental science – environment and monitoring, evolutionary psychology, functional neuroimaging, molecular medicine and cancer research, molecular medicine, psychoanalysis and contemporary society, psychological sciences, psychology, health and behaviour, public health and health promotion, sport and exercise psychology, sport, health and exercise sciences (human performance/sport psychology), sport, health and exercise sciences, sustainability, entrepreneurship and design, toxicology and risk assessment; BSc, MSc, MA, BA, PGDip/Cert, PhD

University Specialist Research Institutes offer postgraduate degree opportunities

UNIVERSITY OF BUCKINGHAM
www.buckingham.ac.uk

Buckingham Business School; www.buckingham.ac.uk/business

business and management, marketing, accounting and financial management, business enterprise;
Postgrad; MBA, accounting and finance, entrepreneurial consultancy & practice, finance and investment management in a global service economy,,continuous improvement in public services, lean enterprise; BSc(Econ)(Hons), BSc(Hons), CMS, MBA, MSc/Diploma

School of Humanities; www.buckingham.ac.uk/humanities

Department of Art History and Heritage Studies; www.buckingham.ac.uk/art-history

art history and heritage management/English literature/French/history/journalism/Spanish
Postgraduate; decorative arts and historic interiors, history of art: Renaissance to modernism; BA(Hons), MA

School of Education; www.buckingham.ac.uk/education

Teacher Training: primary/secondary PGCE with QTS, educational leadership, middle leadership; qualified teacher; primary/secondary; MEd, BA(Hons), MPhil, DPhil, PGCert, CML

Dept of Economics & International Studies; www.buckingham.ac.uk/economics-international

Politics, Security & International Studies; international relations/politics with applied computing/economics/English language studies/French/journalism/Spanish, international studies with politics and economics/history/ applied computing/English language studies/French/journalism/Spanish/law, law enforcement security & intelligence, economics and law, international affairs security and intelligence studies, security, intelligence and diplomacy economics/international studies
Economics; business economics, economics, economics with applied computing/English language studies/French/history/journalism/politics/ Spanish, economics, business and law

Postgraduate; economics; BA(Hons), BSc(Econ)Hons, DPhil, MA, MPhil, MSc

Dept of Modern Foreign Languages; www.buckingham.ac.uk/mfl

French/Spanish as minor subject with business and range of languages taught for part of joint degrees; art history with French/Spanish, accounting with French/Spanish, business and management with French/Spanish, economics with French/Spanish, English literature with French/Spanish, international studies with French/Spanish, journalism with French, law with French/Spanish/Spanish, marketing with French/Spanish, psychology with French/Spanish; BA(Hons), BSc(Hons), LlB(Hons)

Dept of English; www.buckingham.ac.uk/ english

Literature; English literature/with English language studies (EFL), English literature with French/history/journalism/psychology/Spanish, English studies, English studies (EFL), English studies for teaching/(EFL) English studies with journalism/media communications, Postgrad; English literature, biography Journalism; communication (EFL) and media studies, communication, media and journalism, journalism with communication studies/English literature/French/international relations/international studies/Spanish; BA(Hons), MA

London Programmes; www.buckingham.ac.uk/london

archaeology, applied research in urban design, English country house 1485-1945, history of sport, Stonehenge a landscape, international affairs,biography, decorative arts & historic interiors, history of art renaissance to modernism, modern war studies, the art market & history of collecting, contemporary military history, human rights, history; MA

Buckingham Law School; www.buckingham.ac.uk/law

law, international trade, maritime law, oil & gas law, financial services law, commercial law; LlB, LLM, MPhil, DPhil, PGDip

Medical School; www.buckingham.ac.uk/ medicine

undergraduate medicine; PG medical school, general internal medicine, clinical science; Clinical MD, MBChB, MSc, BDS

School of Science; www.buckingham.ac.uk/science

Dept of Applied Computing; www.buckingham.ac.uk/applied computing

computing and software entrepreneurship/accounting and finance/ business and management/communication studies/economics
Postgraduate; computing, innovative computing, applied computing; BSc(Hons), MSc, MPhil, PhD, GradDip/Cert

Dept of Psychology; www.buckingham.ac.uk/psychology

psychology/with applied computing, media communications/business & management/Spanish/French/English literature/marketing; BSc(Hons), MPhil, MSc, PhD

Clore Laboratory; www.buckingham.ac.uk/clore

diabetes, obesity & metabolic research, molecular genetics, biochemistry, biochemical informatics, nutrition, dermatology; DPhil, MPhil, MSc

BUCKINGHAMSHIRE NEW UNIVERSITY
www.bucks.ac.uk

School of Arts & Creative Industries; www.buck.ac.uk/whowho/school-of arts-and creative industries

Creative & Visual Communication
creative advertising, fashion design, graphic arts, graphic design, illustration, textiles and surface design, art design and media, design and make for interiors, kitchen design; Postgrad; advertising, art and design practice

Design & Craft
interior and spatial design, product design, product design: interior product
Media Production
animation and visual effects, audio and music production, creative writing for publication, film and television production; Postgrad; animation

Music & Event Management

event and festivals management, music and live events management, music business, music management and studio production, music performance management

Performance & Dance

dance and fitness, dance and performance, performing arts (film, tv and stage); Postgrad; performing arts

School of Health & Social Sciences; www.buck.ac.uk/whowho/school-of-health-and-social-sciences

Department of Advanced Health Science

exercise, health and fitness management, sport and exercise science, sports development and coaching, sports therapy, advanced practice, health exercise and wellbeing, health rehabilitation and exercise, cancer care, cardiac disease: prevention and management for non specialists, critical practice in child protection and adult safeguarding, cytotoxic chemotherapy: principles management and care, dementia management, developing a portfolio for accredited prior experiential learning diabetes management, ear care, emergency and unscheduled care, end of life care and symptom management, enhancing practice through work related learning, essentials of spinal care, foundations of current service issues for healthcare practitioners, haematooncology, independent and supplementary nurse prescribing, intensive care, intravenous drug administration refresher, introduction to cognitive behavioural therapy, introduction to critical care, leadership and business skills for healthcare practitioners, leadership and management in practice, learning through critical reflection, leg ulcer management, management of long term conditions for general practice nurses, mentorship in professional practice, minor illness management, neonatal special care, personal and professional development in mental health practice, physical assessment of the adult practice teacher award, principles and practice of infection prevention & control, principles and practices of anaesthetics and surgery, professional clinical practice skills for general practice nursing, recovery and social inclusion, recovery postoperative care in the perioperative environment, respiratory care, return to practice (adult, stroke management and care, supporting emotional needs of children, surgical care perioperative practice, theoretical concepts in renal care, transition to community, community nursing, wound care management, trauma care,

understanding dementia, professional practice (healthcare), nursing, renal care

[a large proportion of the above are obtained by part-time study]

Department of Community Health, Education & Social Sciences

health and social science, community health care nursing (district nursing/community children's nursing), professional practice (early years)/primary education and education)working with children and young people), working with children and young people), early years practice, policing, working with children and young people, education, child and adolescent studies, mentorship in professional practice, criminology communities and disorder, community health care nursing (community children's and district nursing/school nursing and health visiting), learning and teaching in higher education

Department of Psychology

criminological psychology, psychology, psychology and criminology, sports psychology, cognitive behavioural therapy, applied positive psychology

Department of Social Work & Integrated Care

social work, health and social care, child protection and adult safeguarding; BSc(Hons), BA(Hons), FD, PGCE, PGCert/Dip, MA, MSc

School of Management & Professional Studies; www.buck.ac.uk/whowho/school-of-management-and-professional-studies

Bucks Business School

accounting and finance, advertising management and digital communications, business and finance, business and HRM, business management, marketing, sport business management, sport marketing, sports business and coaching, international accounting & finance, marketing communications, leadership and management international master of business administration MBA online executive

Department of Computing

computing, computing and web development, games development, independent games production, technology-enhanced learning, commercial law

Department of Security & Resilience

security management, crowd safety management, organisational resilience

Dept of Travel and Aviation

air transport with helicopter pilot training, air transport management for aviation professionals, air transport with commercial pilot training, airline and airport management, international tourism management with air travel, international travel and tourism management, air transport with commercial pilot training, Private Pilot Training; BA(Hons), BSc(Hons), LlB, MA, MSc, FdA

School of Pre-Qualifying Nursing & Vocational Health Care; www.buck.ac.uk/whowho/school-of-pre-nursing-and-vocational-health-care

operating department practice, assistant practitioner (acute rehabilitation/child care/immediate critical and peri-operative care/longer term care and Care of older people/maternity and newborn/mental health nursing (adults/children/mental health), the Care Certificate; BSc(Hons), FdSc, DipHE, PGDip

UNIVERSITY OF CAMBRIDGE
www.cam.ac.uk

Arts and Humanities; www.csah.cam.ac.uk

Faculty of Architecture and History of Art; www.aha.cam.ac.uk

architecture/and urban design/practice, professional practice, interdisciplinary design in the built environment, British architecture, building history, history of art, medieval art & architecture,Medieval English and/or French art, Renaissance Italy, Early Modern British art and architecture, nineteenth- and twentieth-century Modern art, and Surrealism, Renaissance art & architecture, sustainable building, conflict in the city, 20th-century art & theory, western & non-western cultural exchange; BA, MPhil, MSt, PhD

Faculty of Asian & Middle Eastern Studies; www.ames.cam.ac.uk

Chinese studies, Hebrew and Semitic studies, Japanese studies, Korean studies, Arabic & Persian studies, East Asia, Middle Eastern/Southern Asia studies, Assyriology, Egyptology, Indian studies; BA, MPhil, PhD

Faculty of Classics; www.classics.cam.ac.uk

classics & Latin literature, history, philology and linguistics, philosophy, Greek & Roman studies, Greek and Latin literature, ancient/philosophy, philology and linguistics, classical art & archaeology; BA, MPhil, PGCE, PhD

Faculty of Divinity; www.divinity.cam.ac.uk

biblical studies, history of Christianity, Jewish, early Christian studies, history of Christianity, Hebrew, religious studies, late antiquity, Old Testament/New Testament Christian theology, systematic theology, religious studies, the philosophy of religion, world religions/Christianity, ministry, patristics, scriptural language; BA, MPhil, PhD, PGDip

Faculty of English; www.english.cam.ac.uk

American literature, Anglo-Saxon, Norse & Celtic, English & applied linguistics, medieval/English literature studies, European languages & literatures, English studies: criticism & culture/18th-century & romantic studies/medieval & renaissance literature, literary theory, middle English, modern & contemporary literature; BA, MLitt, MPhil, PhD

Faculty of Modern and Medieval Languages; www.mml.cam.ac.uk

French, German & Dutch, Italian, Spanish & Portuguese, European literature, theoretical & applied/linguistics, modern Greek, neo-Latin, Polish, Russian studies, screen & media cultures, Slavonic studies, Ukrainian, European & comparative literatures & cultures; BA, MPhil, PhD

Faculty of Music; www.mus.cam.ac.uk

ethnomusicology, choral studies, music studies, music/with education studies, analysis, jazz & pop music, performance studies, recitals, tonal compositions & analysis & repertoire, musical composition, choral studies, Western classical tradition, cultural musicology, ethnomusicology, historical musicology, music and science, music before 1600, nineteenth-century music, opera studies, popular and media music, theory and analysis; theory, analysis and criticism, performance studies; BA, MPhil, PhD, MMusD

Faculty of Philosophy; www.phil.cam.ac

ethics, experimental psychology, history of philosophy, logic, metaphysics, philosophy of science, political philosophy, aesthetics, mathematical logic, ancient philosophy; BA, MPhil, PhD, MLitt

Humanities & Social Sciences; www.cshss.cam.ac.uk

Faculty of Human, Social & Political Science

Dept of Archaeology and Anthropology; www.hsps. cam.ac.uk

archaeological heritage & museum/science, archaeology, Aegean prehistory, archaeology, archaeology of the Americas, biological anthropology, Egyptian archaeology, Egyptology, Assyriology, European prehistory, human evolutionary studies, medieval archaeology/Britain, Mesopotamian studies, palaeolithic & mesolithic archaeology, social anthropology, south Asian archaeology; BA, MPhil, PhD

Dept of Politics & International Relations; www.hsps. cam.ac.uk

politics/and international relations/sociology, social anthropology & sociology/politics; MPhil, PhD

Dept of Sociology; www.sociology/cam.ac.uk

sociology, social theory, economic and political sociology, media, culture and new technologies, gender, reproduction and family life, public health and biomedicine; MA, MPhil, PhD

Centre of Latin American Studies; www.latin-america. cam.ac.uk

Latin American studies; MPhil, PhD

Centre of African Studies; www.africa.cam.ac.uk

African studies; MPhil

Centre of South Asian Studies

modern South Asian studies; MPhil

Dept of Social Sciences

Centre of Development studies; www.devstudies.cam. ac.uk

development studies; MPhil, PhD

Centre for Family Research; www.cfr.cam.ac.uk

bioethics & the family, early social development & the family, genetics, health & families, non-traditional families, parent, children & family relationships, psychotherapeutics, social & cognitive development & the family, genetics, health and the family, new families, social & developmental psychology; MPhil, PhD

The Psychometrics Centre; www.psychometrics.cam.ac.uk

MPhil, PhD

Faculty of Economics; www.econ.cam.ac.uk

asset pricing, behavioural economics, economic theory, finance & economics, microeconomics, quantitative methods, microeconomics, macroeconomics, macroeconometrics, economics, economics research; BA, Adv Diploma, MPhil, PhD

Faculty of Education; www.educ.cam.ac.uk

philosophy, psychology, sociology or history of education, children and literature, creativity and thinking, educational inclusion and diversity, PGCE in early primary, primary, secondary subject specialities in: art, classics, design and technology, English, geography, history, mathematics, modern languages, music, science with biology, chemistry or physics, religious studies educational research, arts culture and education, critical approaches to children's literature, educational leadership and school improvement, mathematics education, perspectives on inclusive and special education, politics, development and democratic education, psychology and education, research in second language, education, researching practice, science teacher researchers and practitioners; BA, MEd, PGCE, PGDip/Cert, PhD, MPhil

Faculty of History; www.hist.cam.ac.uk

American history, British/early modern history, economic, social & cultural history, mid/European history, modern European history, ancient & medieval history, political thought & intellectual history, world history, modern British history, early modern history, modern European history, world history, history & politics/modern languages; BA, MPhil, PhD

History and Philosophy of Science; www.hps.cam.ac. uk

general philosophy of science, history of ancient and medieval science, technology and medicine, history of early modern science, history of modern science, technology and medicine, history, philosophy and sociology of the life sciences, history, philosophy and sociology of the physical and mathematical sciences, history, philosophy and sociology of the social and psychological sciences, history, philosophy and sociology of medicine, ethics and politics of science, history and methodology of history, philosophy and sociology of science, technology and medicine; BA, MPhil, PhD

Faculty of Law; www.law.cam.ac.uk

criminological research, criminology, international law, law, legal studies, civil law, communication law, European law, large range of legal topics at Master level; BA, Diploma, LLD, LLM, MLitt, MPhil, PhD, MCL

Institute of Criminology; www.crim.cam.ac.uk

applied/criminology, penology/& management, police management; MPhil, MSt, PhD

Dept of Land Economy; www.landecon.cam.ac.uk

land economy, planning, growth & regeneration, real estate finance, environmental policy, environment, law & economics; BA, MPhil, PhD

School of Biological Sciences; www.cam.ac.uk/sbs

Faculty of Biology; www.cam.ac.uk

Biochemistry; www.bio.cam.ac.uk

biology of cells, biological science, computational biology, systems biology, evolution & behaviour, biochemistry & molecular biology

Psychology; www.psych.cam.ac.uk

psychology & human behaviour, experimental psychology, social & developmental psychology, neuropsychology, psychology by research, psychology & behavioural science, natural science

Genetics; www.gen.cam.ac.uk

mathematical biology, molecules in medical science, cells & developmental biology, genetics, ecology, systems biology, biology of cells

Centre for Family Research; www.cfr.cam.ac.uk

early social development & the family, non-traditional families, genetics, health and family, bioethics & the family, social development & the family

Pathology; www.path.cam.ac.uk

graduate clinical course in medicine

Pharmacology; www.pha.ca.ac.uk

pharmacology, medicinal chemistry, design/use of medicine

Physiology, Development & Neuroscience; www.pdn.cam.ac.uk

biological & biomedical sciences, physiology, neuroscience, neurobiology, developmental biology, stem cell biology, ageing, integrative biology, basic translational neuroscience

Plant Science; www.plantsci.cam.ac.uk

bioenergy, cell biology and development, crop improvement and protection, epidemiology, ecology and evolution, systems biology, mathematical modelling, plant/ bial science, cell & developmental biology, ecology, plant & microbiological science, biology of cells

Zoology; www.zoo.cam.ac.uk

animal biology, biological sciences, cell & developmental biology, ecology, evolution & behaviour, zoology, neurobiology/science, mathematical/molecular biology; BA, MPhil, PhD

Faculty of Veterinary Medicine

Department of Veterinary Medicine; www.vet.cam.ac.uk

Clinical Course: veterinary science, preclinical course; MPhil, VetMB

Wellcome Trust Centre for Stem Cell Research; www.cscr.cam.ac.uk

stem cell biology, mammalian stem cells, infection & immunology, mathematical genomics & medicine; PhD

Wellcome Trust/Cancer Research UK Gurdon InstituteTechnology; www.gurdon.cam.ac.uk

cellular & molecular biology, developmental, cell & cancer biology; PhD

School of Technology; www.tech.ac.uk

Faculty of Engineering; www.eng.cam.ac.uk

Academic Divisions; energy, fluid mechanics and turbomachinery, electrical engineering mechanics, materials and design, civil engineering, manufacturing and management, information engineering; aerospace and aerothermal engineering, bioengineering, civil, structural and environmental engineering, electrical and electronic engineering, electrical and information sciences, energy, sustainability and the environment, information and computer engineering, instrumentation and control, mechanical engineering, manufacturing engineering, chemical engineering, management studies, energy, fluid mechanics & turbomechanics, materials design, civil, structural and environmental engineering, construction engineering, geotechnology & environmental structures, interdisciplinary design/future interaction and/ for the built environment, engineering sustainability, engineering for sustainable development, applied mechanics, manufacture & management, industrial systems, practice & management, gas turbine aerodynamics, graphene technology, information engineering, engineering for life sciences, turbomachines, energy & fluid mechanics, electrical engineering, energy technologies, mechanics, materials & design, manufacture & management, manufacturing engineering, nuclear engineering, sustainable development, production processes, integrated photonic & electronic systems, ultra precision; BA(Hons), MEng, MPhil, PhD

Faculty of Business & Management (Judge Business School); www.jbs.cam.ac.uk

MBA; accounting, corporate finance, Cambridge venture project, management praxis, microeconomics, management science, organisational behaviour, cost management and control, marketing, negotiation skills, operations management, strategy, corporate governance and ethics, macroeconomics Master of Finance; introduction to derivatives, econometrics, economic foundations of finance, financial institutions & markets, financial reporting & analysis, fundamentals of credit, principles of finance, management practice, financial modelling workshops Cambridge Executive MBA; corporate finance, accounting, operations management, management practice, marketing Professional Practice Masters & Diplomas; management, entrepreneurship technology policy, social innovation, PhD Pathways; business economics, finance, marketing, operations & technology management, organisational behaviour, organisational theory & information systems, strategic management; MBA, MFin, MPhil, MSt, PhD, PGDip

Faculty of Computer Science & Technology; www.cl.cam.ac.uk

adv/computer science, AI, computer architecture, computer science, digital technology, graphics & integrated action, natural language & information, network architecture, internet user interface, forensic signal analysis, language processing, embedded systems, programming logic & semantics, security, systems research; BA, MPhil, PhD, MEng

Department of Chemical Engineering & Biotechnology; www.ceb.cam.ac.uk

advanced/ chemical engineering, biotechnology, innovation, materials, measurement, metrology, bioscientific enterprise, modelling, processes, sensor technology & enterprise; BA/MEng, MPhil, PhD

Cambridge Programme for Sustainability Leadership; www.cpi.cam.ac.uk

sustainability, health & care, innovation, sustainable business/leadership/value chains; MSt, PGCert

School of Physical Sciences; www.physci.cam.ac.uk

Faculty of Earth Sciences & Geography; www.physci.cam.ac.uk

Dept of Earth Sciences; www.esc.cam.ac.uk

petrology (rocks), mineralogy and volcanology, climate, science and oceanography, surface processes and sedimentology, palaeobiology (the history of life), geophysics, tectonics and seismology, geochemistry, geology in the field; Postgraduate climate change and earth-ocean atmosphere systems, geodynamics, geophysics and tectonics, mineral sciences, palaeobiology, igneous, metamorphic and volcanic studies; BA, MPhil, PhD

Dept of Geography; www.geog.cam.ac.uk

3rd Year Topics; the geographies of global urbanism, knowledge, policy and expertise, political ecology in the global south, the political geography of postcolonialism, changing cultures of risk, geographies of discipline and social regulation, historical demography, the glacial and quaternary records, glaciology, volcanology, biosedimentary coastal systems, biogeography; Postgraduate; conservation leadership, geographical research, geography, polar studies; BA, MPhil, PhD

Faculty of Mathematics; www.maths.cam.ac.uk

Dept of Applied Mathematics & Theoretical Physics; www.physci.cam.ac.uk/about the school/damtp

mathematical science, applied mathematics, statistical science, theoretical physics, computational biology, quantum mechanics, relativity, fluid dynamics, numerical analysis

Dept of Pure Mathematics & Mathematical Statistics

pure mathematics & mathematical statistics, statistical science; BA, MPhil, PhD, MMath, MAdvStud, MASt

Faculty of Physics & Chemistry; www.cam.ac.uk/physchemfaculty

Institute of Astronomy; www.ast.cam.ac.uk

structure and evolution of stars, principles of quantum mechanics, physical cosmology, relativity, astrophysical fluid dynamics, statistical physics, stellar dynamics and structure of galaxies, physics of astrophysics, astronomy, astrophysics

Dept of Chemistry; www.ch.cam.ac.uk

physical, theoretical, organic, inorganic biochemistry, synthesis, materials chemistry, chemistry, theoretical modelling & information

Dept of Material Science & Metallurgy; www.physci.cam.ac.uk/abouttheschool/materialsscience

materials science, metals, alloys, ceramics, polymers, semiconducting/magnetic/superconducting/ferroelectric/biomedical materials, composites, micro & nanotechnology enterprises, device materials, electron microscopy, materials chemistry, medical & pharmaceutical materials, structural materials, clean energy & sustainability, nuclear energy

Dept of Physics; www.phy.cam.ac.uk
experimental & theoretical physics, astrophysics, scientific computing, nanoscience & technology, atomic/high energy/quantum & condensed matter/ thin film magnetism, scientific computing, astrophysics, atomic, mesoscopic and optical physics, biological and soft systems, high energy physics, nanophotonics, optoelectronics, microelectronics, quantum matter, quantum sensors, semiconductor physics, structure and dynamics, surfaces, microstructure and fracture, theory of condensed matter, thin film magnetism
astrophysics, atomic, molecular engineering, scientific computing, semiconductor physics, surfaces; BA, MPhil, MSci, PhD, MASt, MSC, EngD

School of Clinical Medicine; www.medschl.cam.ac.uk

Dept of Clinical Biochemistry (Metabolic Research Laboratories); www.clbc.cam.ac.uk
biomedical research, diabetes, molecular cell biology of membrane traffic pathways, obesity & other related endocrine and metabolic disorders; PhD

Dept of Clinical Neurosciences (Cambridge Centre for Brain Repair; Neurology Unit; Neurosurgery; Wolfson Brain Imaging Centre); www.neurosciences.medschl.am.ac.uk
brain repair, neurology, neurosurgery, anaesthesia, opthomology, stem cell neurology; MB/PhD

Dept of Haematology; www.haem.cam.ac.uk
transfusion medicine diagnostics development, structural medicine & thrombosis, haematopoiesis & leukaemia; PhD

Dept of Medical Genetics; www.cimr.cam.ac.uk/medgen
diabetes inflammation, genome informatics, statistical and non-Mendelian genetics, renal genetics (acid base homeostasis), Cancer genetics, genomic imprinting, autosomal recessive disease, autophagy and neurodegeneration and the biological effects of triplet repeat diseases, applying genomic methods to X-linked learning disability, studies on axonal degenerative disorders, Renal genetics (autosomal dominant polycystic kidney disease) and genetics of autoimmune liver disease, genetic cause of primary biliary cirrhosis, genetic cause of primary sclerosing cholangitis, cancer genetics. genetic testing in epithelial ovarian cancer, autosomal recessive primary microcephaly; Mendelian disorders of painlessness, genetic testing in epithelial ovarian cancer; BChir, MB, MD, PhD

Dept of Medicine; www.med.cam.ac.uk
anaesthesia, cardiovascular medicine, diabetes and endocrinology, experimental medicine and immunotherapeutics, gastroenterology and hepatology, immunology, infectious diseases, metabolic medicine, renal medicine, respiratory medicine, rheumatology

CAMBRIDGE INTERNATIONAL COLLEGE
www.cambridgecollege.ac.uk

Numerous courses are provided under the following subject categories: bookkeeping, accounting, finance, business studies, economics, commerce, trade, English, secretarial, communication, hotel, tourism, travel, hospitality, management administration, leadership, marketing, sales, advertising, personnel, HR, organisation, stores, logistics, purchasing, materials

The following are awarded in respect of the above courses; Diploma, Mastery of Management Graduate Diploma, Honours Diploma, Baccalaureate, Executive Business Administration (EBA), Advanced Mastery of Business Administration (AMBA)

CANTERBURY CHRIST CHURCH UNIVERSITY
www.canterbury.ac.uk

Faculty of Arts and Humanities; www.canterbury.ac.uk/arts-humanities

Humanities
American studies, archaeology, arts and humanities, catholic theology, creative and professional writing, English literature, history, religion, philosophy and ethics, theology for Christian ministry, theology; Postgraduate; American studies, creative writing: prose fiction, English literature, history, theology and religious studies; BA(Hons), MA, MPhil, PhD

School of Language Studies and Applied Linguistics; www.canterbury.ac.uk/arts-and-humanities,/language-studies-and-applied-linguistics
English language and communication, French, Spanish, modern foreign language modules in French, Spanish, German, Italian and Mandarin, Postgraduate; applied linguistics, language teacher education,- TESOL; BA(Hons),MA, MPhil, PhD

Media, Art & Design; www.canterbury.ac.uk/arts-and-humanities/media-art-and-design
broadcast & interactive TV, digital media, film, radio & TV studies, multimedia journalism/design, journalism, graphic design, web design, fine & applied arts, film & digital video production, media & communication, cultural studies, PR, media marketing, photography, research in media, art & design, web design

Music & Performing Arts; www.canterbury.ac.uk/arts-and-humanities/music-and-performing-arts
creative theatre production, dance education, dance, drama, music, music: commercial music/ creative music technology, performing arts; Postgraduate; music, arts and cultural management
BA, BSc, MA, MPhil, PhD, PGDip, FD, BMus, MMus

Faculty of Education; www.canterbury.ac.uk/education
supporting children's learning, childhood studies, counselling, coaching and mentoring, early childhood studies/education & care, early years, education and learning, education and professional training, education studies, education: global and international education studies, learning and teaching, mathematics with secondary education, PE and physical activity/ sport & exercise science, primary education, social pedagogy, special educational needs and inclusion studies, supporting young people, youth work; Postgraduate; learning and teaching, primary mathematics specialist teacher, primary physical education, career management, early childhood education, education (specialist pathways), global and international education, myth, cosmology and the sacred, professional learning and education, transformational leadership, teaching and learning, research guidance & support; BA, MA, GradDip/Cert, FdA, BSc, DipHE, EdD, PGCert/Dip, BA(Hons), BSc(Hons), PGCE, EYPS, FdA, MA, MPhil/PhD, UnivDip

Faculty of Health and Wellbeing; www.canterbury.ac.uk/health-and-wellbeing

Department of Allied Health Professions; www.canterbury.ac.uk/health/allied-health-professions
advanced/occupational therapy, clinical reporting/imaging, dance movement therapy, diagnostic radiography, health & wellbeing, medical imaging, operating dept practice, ophthalmic dispensing, paramedic science, range of post-graduate programmes, speech & language therapy

School of Nursing; www.canterbury.ac.uk/health-and-wellbeing/nursing
adult nursing, child nursing, mental health nursing, return to practice

The School of Public Health, Midwifery and Social Work; www.canterbury.ac.uk/health-and-wellbeing/public-health-midwifery-and-social-work
public health promotion and public health, health studies/public health /health promotion, midwifery, social work, specialist community public health nursing, Postgraduate; specialist community public health nursing, social work, public health, mental health and approved mental health professional practice, continuing professional development, applied practice (health & social care), public health, CPD

Centre for Work Based Learning and Continuing Development

health and social care/studies, Continuing Development; Applied practice (health and social care), public health; Postgraduate; health and wellbeing

Institute of Medical Sciences

Postgraduate; anaesthesia (perioperative, cardiology, minimally invasive surgery (general surgery/ orthopaedics/urology)
BA(Hons), BSc(Hons), FD, EdD, MPhil, PhD, MA, MSc, PGCert, CertHE

Faculty of Social and Applied Sciences; www.canterbury.ac.uk/social-and-applied-science

Dept of Psychology, Politics & Sociology; www.canterbury.ac.uk/social-and-applied-sciences/psychology-politics-and-sociology

environment, society and sustainability, European politics, international relations, politics, psychology, psychology (sport and exercise), sociology; Postgraduate; applied psychology, clinical psychology, cognitive behavioural therapy, European politics, international relations, politics, politics and international relations, psychology, professional practice: psychological perspectives, sociology (by research); BA/BSc, MSc, MPhil, PhD, DClinPsych, PGDip

The Business School; www.canterbury.ac.uk/business-management/business-school

accounting, accounting and management, advertising, business management, business studies, digital marketing communications, finance, hotel management, HRM, marketing, PR, media and marketing; Postgraduate; collaborative transformation, education leadership and management, healthcare leadership and management, HRM, international business, management studies; BSc, BA, MSc, MA, Adv Dip, MBA, PGCert/Dip, MPhil, PhD

School of Law, Criminal Justice and Computing; www.canterbury.ac.uk/social-and-applied-sciences/law-criminal-justice-and-computing

applied criminology, business information systems, computer forensics and security, computing, forensic investigation, information technology, international policing, law, policing, policing (crime science/criminal investigation/criminal psychology/critical incidents/cybersecurity/public administration/, policing, politics and governance, web technology; Postgraduate; computing, criminal justice, criminology, criminology and criminal justice, cybercrime forensics, digital forensics and cybersecurity, forensic computing, forensic investigation, law, policing and criminal justice, policing; BSc(Hons), BA/BSc, MSc, FD, LlB, MA, LPC

School of Human & Life Sciences; www.canterbury.ac.uk/social-and-applied-sciences/human-and-life-sciences/human-and-life-sciences.aspx

Sport and Exercise Sciences; PE and sport & exercise science, psychology (sport and exercise), sport and exercise psychology, sport and exercise science, sport coaching science; Postgraduate; applied health and fitness, sport and exercise science, sport and exercise psychology, sport policy and development
Geography, Events, Leisure and Tourism; ecology and conservation, environment, society and sustainability events management, geography, sport and leisure management tourism and leisure studies, tourism management; Postgraduate; cartography and infographics, environmental geography, events, geospatial analysis, human geography, leisure, tourism, urban and regional studies
Life Sciences; animal science, biosciences, environmental biology, environmental science, integrated science, plant science, science foundation; Postgraduate; bioscience, ecology; PhD/ MPhil; biological sciences, geography, sport and exercise science
PE & psychology (sport and exercise), sport and exercise psychology, sport and exercise science, sport coaching science; ecology and conservation, environment, society and sustainability, events management, geography, tourism and leisure studies, tourism management, sport and leisure management; animal science, biosciences, environmental biology, environmental science, integrated science, plant science, science foundation; Postgraduate; biological sciences, geography, sport and exercise science

Centre for Sport, Physical Education & Activity Research; www.canterbury.ac.uk/SPEAR

Olympic & Paralympic research, physical education & activity in schools, sport, physical activity & health; Sport and Exercise Sciences; PE and sport & exercise science, psychology (sport and exercise), sport and exercise psychology, sport and exercise science, sport coaching science; Postgraduate; applied health and fitness, sport and exercise science, sport and exercise psychology, sport policy and development

Geography, Events, Leisure and Tourism; ecology and conservation, environment, society and sustainability events management, geography, sport and leisure management, tourism and leisure studies, tourism management; Postgraduate; cartography and infographics, environmental geography, events, geospatial analysis, human geography, leisure, tourism, urban and regional studies

Life Sciences; animal science, biosciences, environmental biology, environmental science, integrated science, plant science, science foundation; Postgraduate; bioscience, ecology; PhD / MPhil; biological sciences, geography, sport and exercise science; BA/BSc, MBA, MSc, MA, Adv Dip, Grad Cert, PGDip, FD, DipHE, MPhil, PhD, MRes(Ed)

CARDIFF UNIVERSITY
www.cs.cardiff.ac.uk

College of Arts, Humanities & Social Sciences; www.cardiff.ac.uk/ahss

Cardiff Business School; www.business.cardiff.ac.uk

accounting, accounting with finance/modern languages, accounting & economics/management, finance & management, business management, business management (HRM, international management/logistics & /operations/marketing/modern languages),banking & finance/economics with French/German/Spanish, business economics/with modern languages, economics, economics/& finance/management studies/modern foreign languages, history/philosophy/politics & economics, Cardiff/Media Management/Executive MBA Postgrad; accounting & finance, finance, international economics, banking & finance, HRM, international management/HRM, international transport, lean systems, logistic & operations management, marine policy & shipping management, business strategy & entrepreneurship, strategic marketing & shipping management; BSc(Hons), BSc(Econ), MSc, MBA, MPA, PhD, Dip

Cardiff School of Planning & Geography; www.cardiff.ac.uk/cplan

human geography/& planning, urban planning & development; Postgraduate; ecocities, food, space & society, geography, policy & practice, international planning & development, spatial policy & planning, sustainability, planning & environmental policy, transport & planning, urban & regional development, urban design, planning practice, European spatial planning, environmental policies & regional development, environmental planning; BSc, MSc, MA, PGCert, PhD

School of English, Communication & Philosophy; www.cardiff.ac.uk/encap

philosophy, English language/literature; Postgraduate; analytical & modern European philosophy, creative writing, critical & cultural theory, English literature, ethics & social philosophy, applied linguistics, language and communication research, forensic linguistics; BA, Dip, MA/Dip, MPhil, PhD

School of History, Archaeology & Religion; www.cardiff.ac.uk/share

Ancient History; ancient history, archaeology and ancient history, philosophy, ancient and medieval history, ancient history and history, ancient history and various modern languages; Postgraduate; ancient history, history and archaeology of the Greek and Roman world, ancient and medieval warfare, late antique and Byzantine studies

History; history, ancient history and history, archaeology and history, history and religious studies French/German and history, history and economics, history and Italian, history and music/ philosophy/sociology, history and Spanish/Welsh, modern history and politics, history with Welsh history, ancient and medieval history, archaeology and medieval history, English literature and history; Postgraduate; medieval warfare, medieval British studies or Welsh history, medieval British studies, Welsh history, history, ancient and medieval

Archaeology & Conservation; archaeology, archaeology and ancient history, archaeology and medieval history/ history/philosophy/religious studies, archaeology and French/German/Italian/Welsh, English literature and archaeology, archaeology; Postgraduate; archaeology, archaeology: prehistoric Britain/early medieval society and culture European neolithic, early Celtic studies, history and archaeology of the Greek and Roman world Conservation; Conservation of Objects in Museums and Archaeology;

Postgraduate; care of collections, conservation practice, professional conservation

Religious Studies and Theology; archaeology and religious studies/history/English literature and religious studies, religious studies and German/Italian/Spanish/Welsh, religious studies and music/philosophy/politics; Postgraduate; Islam in contemporary Britain, religious studies/myth, narrative and theory/religion in late antiquity/Asian religions, religious studies, late antique and Byzantine studies; Chaplaincy & MTh Programmes; theology, chaplaincy studies, chaplaincy studies: military route, myth, narrative and theory, religion in late antiquity, Asian religions, late antique and Byzantine studies; BA, BSc, BScEcon, MA, MPhil, MSc, PhD,PGDip/Cert, MTh

Cardiff School of Journalism, Media and Cultural Studies; www.cardiff.ac.uk/jomec

journalism/media, media, journalism and culture, journalism, communications and politics, journalism, media and English literature/sociology, Welsh and journalism; Postgraduate; broadcast journalism, computational and data journalism, digital media and society, international journalism, international PR and global communications management, journalism, media and communications, magazine journalism, media management, news journalism, political communication, science, media and communication; BA, MA, MPhil, MSc, PhD, PGDip, MBA

Cardiff Law School; www.law.cf.ac.uk

law, law & criminology/politics/sociology/French/German/Welsh, cannon law, European legal studies, governance & devolution, law & governance of the EU, legal & political aspects of international affairs, human rights law, legal aspects of medical practice, international commercial law, social care law, shipping law, intellectual property law, legal practice, bar professional training; LlB, LlM, MPhil, PhD

Cardiff Centre for Lifelong Learning; www.cardiff.ac.uk/learn

languages, business & management, computer studies, science & environment, social studies, humanities, politics & international relations/law

School of Modern Languages; www.cardiff.ac.uk/modern-languages

French, German, Italian, Spanish, Japanese, Portugese, translation studies; Postgraduate; European studies, global area studies, history & ideologies, culture & identity, history & memory, language & translation studies, literature & visual culture; BA, MA, MPhil, PhD

Cardiff School of Music; www.cardiff.ac.uk/music

music, music & English literature/French/German/Italian/Welsh/history/mathematics/physics/religious studies/philosophy; Postgraduate; music studies, composition, ethnomusicology, musicology, music, culture & politics, performance, music studies; BA, BMus, BSc, MMus, MA, PhD

Dept of Politics & International Relations; www.cardiff.ac.uk/politics-international-relations

politics, politics & international relations/economics/French/German/Italian/Spanish/law/modern history/philosophy/religious studies/sociology/Welsh; Postgraduate; European studies, European governance & public policy, international relations, politics & public policy, political theory, social science research (European & international studies/Eurogovernance & public policy), Welsh government & politics; BA, BScEcon, MA, MScEcon, PGDip, PhD

School of Social Sciences; www.cardiff.ac.uk/socsci

criminology, criminology and education/social policy/sociology/, education, education and sociology/social policy/Welsh, social policy and sociology,sociology, sociology and Welsh/politics/law/journalism & media/history/social policy/education/criminology, human and social sciences; Postgraduate; childhood and youth, crime, safety and justice, education, policy and society, social science, social and public policy, science, media and communication, social science research methods, skills and workforce development; BA, BSc, DHS, DSW, MSc,LlB

School of Welsh; www.cardiff.ac.uk/welsh

Welsh, Welsh & ancient history/archaeology/education/English literature/English language/French/ German/ history/ Italian/music/philosophy/politics/religious studies/mathematics/sociology/Spanish, early Celtic studies, medieval British studies, Welsh & Celtic studies, Welsh & law; BA, LlB, MA, PhD

College of Biomedicine & Health Sciences; *www.cardiff.ac.uk/ biomedicine-life-sciences*

School of Biosciences; www.cardiff.ac.uk/ biosciences

biological sciences, biomedical sciences, biochemistry, neuroscience, biological sciences (genetics/zoology), biomedical sciences (anatomy/physiology); Postgraduate; biological sciences, biomedical sciences, biochemistry, neuroscience, tissue engineering,research; BSc(Hons), MRes, MSc, PhD, MBiol, MbBomed, MBiochem, MNuero, PGDip

School of Dentistry; www.cardiff.ac.uk/ dentistry

dental surgery, clinical dentistry, dental therapy & hygiene, implantology, orthodontics, tissue engineering; BDS, BSc(Hons), MClinDent, MD, MPhil, MSc, PhD, PGDip

School of Healthcare Sciences; www.cardiff.ac.uk/healthcare-science

adult/children's nursing, diagnostic radiography and imaging, mental health nursing, midwifery, occupational therapy, operating department practice, physiotherapy, radiotherapy and oncology; Postgraduate; advanced practice, community health studies, advanced clinical practice, clinical photography, image appreciation, managing care in perioperative practice, neuromusculoskeletal physiotherapy, occupational therapy, radiographic reporting, radiography, specialist community public health nursing, sport & exercise physiotherapy, surgical care practice; CertHE, DipHE, MSc, MPhil, PGDip/Cert, PhD

School of Medicine; www.medicine.cf.ac.uk

advanced surgical practice, ageing health and disease, bioinformatics/genetic epidemiology, and bioinformatics, clinical dermatology, critical care, diabetes, genetic counselling, medical research & innovation, medical toxicology, medical ultrasound, neonatal medicine, obstetric and/or gynaecological ultrasound, occupational health, (policy and practice), pain management, pain management,(primary and community care), palliative medicine/palliative care, practical dermatology, psychiatry, public health, therapeutics, wound healing and tissue repair, medicine, surgery, medical pharmacology; MBBCh, MD, MPH, MPhil, MSc/PGCert/Dip, PhD

School of Optometry and Vision Sciences; www.cardiff.ac.uk/optom

clinical optometry, optometry, eye care governance, vision science, glaucoma; BSc, MSc, MPhil, PGCert/Dip, PhD

Cardiff School of Pharmacy and Pharmaceutical Sciences; www.cardiff.ac.uk/pharm

clinical pharmacy, clinical research, pharmacy, independent prescribing, Research; drug delivery and microbiology, medicinal chemistry, pharmacology and physiology, pharmacy, pharmacy practice and clinical pharmacy; PGDipl, MPharm, MPhil, MSc, PhD

School of Psychology; www.cardiff.ac.uk,psych

psychology, psychology with professional placement, clinical/educational psychology, neuroimaging methods & applications, social science research methods; BSc, DEdPsych, DClinPsych, DradDip, PhD

College of Physical Sciences & Engineering; *www.cardiff.ac.uk/pse*

Welsh School of Architecture; www.cardiff.ac.uk/architecture

architecture, architecture/& urban design, architectural professional studies, environmental design of buildings, sustainable energy & environment, vertical studio, sustainable megabuilding/construction, theory & practice of sustainable design; BSc, DipProfStuds, MA, MArch, MPhil, PhD, MSc

Cardiff School of Chemistry; www.cardiff.ac.uk/chemy

chemistry, biomedical science,, medical chemistry, biological chemistry, medical pharmacology, chemical biology, chemistry with physics/industrial experience, catalytic science, inorganic/physical organic chemistry; BSc, MChem, MPhil, PhD

Cardiff School of Computer Science & Informatics; www.cs.cardiff.ac.uk

adv/computer science with high performance computing/security & forensics/visual computing, data science & analytics, applied/software engineering, information security & privacy, visual computing, computing & IT management, computational & data journalism; BSc, MSc, PhD

School of Earth and Ocean Sciences; www.cardiff.ac.uk/earth

applied/environmental geology, environmental geoscience, exploration & resource geology, geology, marine geology, earth & environmental science; BSc, MEnv, MPhil, MSc, PhD

Cardiff School of Engineering; www.cardiff.ac.uk/engin

architectural/civil/environmental/clinical engineering, civil & geoenvironmental/environmental engineering, community engineering & entrepreneurship, electrical & electronic engineering, electrical energy systems, electronic & geoenvironmental/integrated engineering, adv/mechanical engineering, medical/orthopaedic engineering, orthopaedic engineering, structural engineering, sustainable energy & environment, hydroenvironmental engineering, wireless and microwave communications engineering, professional engineering, manufacturing engineering, innovation & management; BEng, EngD, MEng, MPhil, MSc, PhD

Cardiff School of Mathematics; www.cardiff.ac.uk/maths

mathematics, mathematics & its applications, mathematics, operational research & applied statistics, applied statistics & financial risk, data science & statistics, mathematics & computer science/music/physics; BSc, MSc, MMath, MPhil, PhD

School of Physics & Astronomy; www.astro.cardiff.ac.uk

physics, astronomy, astrophysics, biophotonics, physics with mathematics/music/medical physics/astronomy; BSc, MPhil, MPhys, PhD

CARDIFF METROPOLITAN UNIVERSITY
www.cardiffmet.ac.uk

Cardiff School of Art & Design; www.csad.cardiffmet.uwic.ac.uk

animation, architectural design & technology, artist designer: maker, ceramics, fine art, graphic communication, illustration, interior design, international designs, international foundation (art & design), product design, textiles; Postgraduate; product design, art & design, ceramics design, fine art, professional & research skills (art & design); BA(Hons), BSc, FD, MA, MFA, MPhil, MSc, MDes, PGCert/Dip, PhD

Cardiff School of Education; www3.cardiffmet.ac.uk/education

Dept of Humanities; www3.cardiffmet.ac.uk/English/education/humanities

creative writing and media, early childhood studies/and literacy, education, psychology and special educational needs, education studies and drama/early childhood studies/English, literacy/sport & physical activity/ Welsh, drama and creative writing/literacy/media, English and creative writing/drama/media, primary education studies, secondary education: music/Welsh 11-16 (leading to qualified teacher status) TESOL and education studies/English/literacy, youth & community work; Postgraduate; creative writing, English literature, English literature & creative writing, TESOL; BA(Hons), MA, PGCert/Dip, PGCE

Dept of Professional Development; www3.cardiffmet.ac.uk/English/education/profdevelopment

education, youth & community work, managing community practice PGCE PCET, preparing to teach/ in the PCET sector, ECDL; BA, MA, PGD

Dept of Teacher Education & Training

PGCE (primary, secondary), secondary music/Welsh; BA(Hons), PGCE

Cardiff School of Health Sciences; www3.cardiffmet.ac.uk/English/health

Centre for Applied Social Sciences; www3.cardiffmet.ac.uk/English/health/ass

health & social care, housing: policy & practice/supported housing, youth & community, management in the community professions, health & social science res, social science, postqual/social work; BA, BSc, FdSc, GradCert, GradDip, MRes, MSc, PGCert, PGDip

Dept of Biomedical Science; www3.cardiffmet.ac.uk/English/StudyAtUWIC/Courses/Pages/CareerBiomedical

biomedical science, complementary healthcare, dental technology, environmental health, food production management, food science & technology, health sciences, social sciences, health & social care healthcare science, housing: policy & practice/supported housing, human nutrition & dietetics, podiatry, psychology, public health nutrition, social work, speech and language therapy, sports biomedicine & nutrition; Postgrad; advanced dietetic practice, advanced practice, applied public health, biomedical science, clinical research methods, dental technology, dietetics, food safety management, food science & technology, food technology for industry, forensic psychology, health and social science, health psychology, musculoskeletal studies, occupational health, safety & wellbeing; BSc(Hons), MSc, MRes DForenSc, CertHE, DipHE, PGDip/Cert, Dip

Department of Applied Community Sciences; www.cardiffmet.ac.uk/health/Pages/Departments.aspx

Occupational and Environmental Public Health; environmental health, health sciences, applied public health, occupational health, safety & wellbeing
Health and Social Care; social sciences health & social care
Housing Studies; housing: policy & practice, housing: supported housing
Social Work;social work; Dip, BSc(Hons), MSc, FD, PGDip/Cert

Dept of Applied Psychology; www.cardiffmet.ac.uk/health/pages/psycho

Foundation leading to BA/BSc Social Sciences, psychology, Postgraduate; Health Psychology, Forensic Psychology, Forensic Psychology (Practitioner Programme); BSc(Hons) PgD, MSc, DForensPsych

Dept of Healthcare & Food

Dept of Complementary Therapies; www3.cardiffmet.ac.uk/English/health/cct
Complementary Healthcare; complementary healthcare; BSc[Hons], Dip/CertHE
Centre for Dental Technology; www3.cardiffmet.ac.uk/English/health/cdt
dental technology; BSc, FdSc, MSc, PGCert, PGDip

Dept of Nutrition & Dietetics; www3.cardiffmet.ac.uk/English/health/ndfs
human nutrition & dietetics, public health nutrition, advanced dietetic practice, dietetics; BSc(Hons), MSc, PGD
Dept of Food Science
food science & technology, food production management, food technology for industry, food safety management; BSc(Hons), MSc, PGD, PGC
Dept of Applied Psychology; www3.cardiffmet.ac.uk/English/health/cp
forensic/health psychology, psychology, clinical research, health & social science research; BSc, FdSc, MSc, PGDip, MRes, FdSc
Speech & Language Therapy; www3.cardiffmet.ac.uk/English/health/cslt
speech & language therapy; BSc(Hons)
Podiatry; www3.cardiffmet.ac.uk/English/health/wcps
musculoskeletal studies, podiatry, adv/therapeutic footware; BSc, MSc, PGCert, PGDip

Cardiff School of Management; www3.cardiffmet.ac.uk/English/management

accounting, accounting & finance, business & management studies, business & management studies with finance/HRM/information systems management/international business management/law/marketing, business economics, business information systems, computer science, economics, events management, events marketing management, fashion marketing management, games design & development, international hospitality & tourism management, tourism management, international hospitality management, international tourism & events management, international tourism management, international tourism marketing management, marketing management; Postgrad; accounting & finance, banking & finance, computing, data science, executive MBA, economics & finance, financial management, HRM, international business management, information & communication technology management, strategic marketing, Master of Business administration (MBA), mobile technologies, project management, sustainable leadership, technology project management
BSc(Hons), BSc(Econ), BA(Hons), MSc, LlM, PGCert/Dip, MBA, FdA

Cardiff School of Sport; www3.cardiffmet.ac.uk/English/sport

sport & exercise science/& PE, sport coaching, sport conditioning, rehabilitation & massage, sport development/management/performance analysis; Postgraduate; applied sport psychology, performance analysis, physical activity and health, sport & exercise medicine/science, sport coaching, sport management & leadership, sport psychology, sport, body & society, strength & conditioning; BA(Hons), BSc(Hons), MA, MSc, PGDip/Cert

UNIVERSITY OF CENTRAL LANCASHIRE
www.uclan.ac.uk

College of Business, Law and Applied Social Studies; www.uclan.ac.uk/colleges/business-law

School of Business; www.uclan.ac.uk/schools/business

accounting and financial management, business and marketing, marketing management, advertising and marketing communications, international business and management, economics, business administration, international business, accounting, marketing management (digital media), accounting and financial studies, accounting and finance, business administration, business studies, economics, business studies, international business; Postgraduate; marketing management, international applied communication, international business and management, finance and management, marketing and PR, strategic communication, accounting and finance; BA(Hons), BSc(Econ), MA, MSc

School of Management, www.uclan.ac.uk/schools/management

international hospitality management, international tourism management, global business management, business and management, management in tourism, business and management, event management, retail management (buying, fashion, marketing), management in events, management in hospitality; Postgraduate; business administration, HRM/ development (advanced), international hospitality and tourism management, HRM, management (e-learning), international hospitality and event management, leadership in policing, internship in international tourism, hospitality and event management, management studies, business management, international festivals and tourism/event management; BSc(Hons), MSc, MA, MBA, DBA, PGCert, CDip, Cert, Dip

Lancashire Law School; www.uclan.ac.uk/schools/law

criminology and criminal justice/ sociology, law, senior status, law with criminology, law, law with business/international studies/ psychology; Postgraduate; law and international security, law, international business law, financial and commercial law, legal practice, LlM, Mlaw, GDL, PGDip/Cert, LPC, BA(Hons)

School of Social Work, Care and Community; www.uclan.a.uk/social-work-care-community

social pedagogy, advocacy and participation, children schools and families, community leadership, social policy and sociology, social work, community and social care, (integrated)/policy and practice, community leadership, community and social care: policy and practice; Postgraduate; professional development and practice, mental health practice, contemporary practice with children and young people, safeguarding children, specialist child care practice, equality and community leadership, advanced community justice, best interest assessor training, community social care policy and practice, social policy, leadership and management in social work and social care practice, specialist practice with adults community leadership, social work, specialist practice with adults, professional development and practice; BA(Hons), MA, MComSc, PGDip/Cert, DProf

College of Clinical & Biomedical Science; www.uclan.ac.uk/college/clinical-biomedical-science

School of Medicine; www.uclan.ac.uk/schools/medicine

medical education, medical science, medicine, surgery, musculoskeletal practice in primary care, general practice, dermatology in primary care, non-facial aesthetics for healthcare professionals, sports medicine, physician associate; BDS, CertHE, MSc, PGDip/Cert, AdCert, MB, BS, BSc(Hons)

School of Dentistry; www.uclan.ac.uk/schools/dentistry

dentistry, orthodontic therapy, clinical dental technology studies, cosmetic dentistry, clinical periodontology, dental studies (dental care professions), endontology, dental implantology, oral surgery, prosthdontics; BSc(Hons), BDS, MSc, PGCert/Dip

School of Pharmacy and Biomedical Sciences; www.uclan.ac.uk/schools/pharmacy

biomedical sciences, biological sciences, pharmaceutics, biological sciences, healthcare science, pharmacy, physiology & pharmaceutics, cancer biology & therapy, clinical pharmacy practice, industrial pharmacology; BSc(Hons), MPharm, MSc, PGDip/Cert, PhD

College of Culture and the Creative Industries; www.uclan.ac.uk/college/culture-creative-industries;

School of Art, Design & Fashion; www.uclan.ac.uk/schools/art-design-fashion

acting, advertising, animation, antiques, arts health, art & design, fashion brand management/promotion, creative business thinking, dance & somatic wellbeing, performance, & teaching, fine art/studio practice/site & archive, consumer product design, design, digital design for fashion/graphics, Eastern/fashion design, drawing & image making, fashion promotion with styling promotion/design, fashion shaping/design/entrepreneurship, fashion & lifestyle brand studies/brand promotion/with photography/journalism/lifestyle promotion, fine art site & archive interventions, games design, graphics design, children's books/illustration, interior design, journalism, music production & management, music production/theatre/practice, performance, photography, product design, surface pattern & textiles, textiles, toy design, transdisciplinary design; BA(Hons), MA, MBA, MPhil, PGCert/Dip, PhD, UniCert

School of Film, Media and Performance; www.uclan.ac.uk/schools/film-media-performance

web design and development, music, film production, film and media studies, dance performance and teaching, music production, games design, acting, digital visual effects, screenwriting with film, TV and audio, photography, media production, theatre, animation, music theatre, TV production; Postgraduate; dance and somatic wellbeing, scriptwriting, games design, photography, animation, film production, games design, music industry management and promotion, music; BA(Hons), MA, PGCert/Dip

School of Humanities and Social Sciences www.uclan.a.uk/schools/humanities-social-sciences

religion, culture and society, public services, philosophy, English literature, sociology, sociology and psychology, history, history and politics, English literature and creative writing, English and history, politics and social policy, politics and philosophy, politics; Postgraduate; religion, culture and society; BA(Hons), MA

School of Journalism, Language and Communication; www.uclan.ac.uk/schools/journalism-language=communication

journalism, Asia Pacific studies, English with a modern language, business management and Chinese, English language and creative writing/literature, modern languages (Arabic, Chinese, French, German, Japanese, Korean, and Spanish), deaf studies and education, international journalism, English for international corporate communication with a modern foreign language, modern languages (Arabic, French, German, Japanese or Spanish) for international business, English for international corporate communication, sports journalism, international business communication, English language and linguistics; Postgraduate; magazine journalism, publishing, sports journalism, British sign language / English interpreting and translation, interpreting and translation, international journalism, North Korean studies, TESOL with applied linguistics (e-learning), journalism, intercultural business communication, broadcast journalism; BA(Hons), MA

College of Health and Wellbeing; www.uclan.ac.uk/college/health-wellbeing

School of Nursing; www.uclan.ac.uk/schools/nursing

psychosocial mental health care, nursing (children/post-registration/adult), child and adolescent mental health, nursing (mental health, child health; Postgraduate; nursing (adult or mental health), advanced stroke practice, philosophy and mental health, conflict and violence minimisation, personality disorder (practice development), child health, personality disorder, investigating serious incidents, nursing, paediatric critical care, BSc(Hons), MA, PGDip/Cert

School of Health Sciences; www.uclan.ac.uk/schools/health-sciences

enhanced paramedic practice, professional practice, physiotherapy, operating department practice, sports therapy, nurse practitioner; Postgraduate; health informatics, clinical research, health, health informatics, enhanced clinical practice, health informatics, delivering quality cancer services, advanced practice

School of Sport and Wellbeing; www.uclan.ac.uk/schools/sport-wellbeing

sport (studies), outdoor leadership ((blended learning), strength and conditioning army, sports business (management), sports coaching, exercise and fitness management, sports studies, sports coaching and development, strength and conditioning, nutrition and exercise sciences, nutrition and exercise sciences (personal fitness training), outdoor leadership, outdoor leadership, sport and exercise physiology, sport science, sports business management, nutrition and exercise sciences (human nutrition, sports coaching, adventure sports coaching; Postgraduate; physical education and school sport, nutrition and food sciences, elite performance, sport and exercise science, food safety management, hazard analysis critical control point, sports marketing and business management

College of Science and Technology; www.uclan.ac.uk/colleges/college-science-technology

School of engineering; www.uclan.ac.uk/schools/engineering

fire and leadership studies, fire safety management, electronic engineering, fire engineering, robotics engineering, civil engineering, computer aided engineering, construction project management, mechanical engineering, nuclear engineering, motorsports engineering, mechanical engineering, aerospace engineering, facilities management, fire engineering, oil and gas safety engineering, fire safety (engineering), computer aided engineering, electronic engineering, oil and gas safety engineering, building surveying, quantity surveying, robotics engineering, energy engineering, civil engineering, energy engineering, fire safety engineering, motorsports engineering,

building services and sustainable engineering, aerospace engineering, mechanical maintenance engineering; Postgraduate; fire safety engineering, fire investigation, nuclear safety, security and safeguards, project management, nuclear safety, construction project management, fire and rescue service management, maintenance engineering nuclear security and safeguards, fire scene investigation, construction law & dispute resolution, renewable energy engineering (with optional placement), building service; BSc(Hons), PGCert/Dip, BEng(Hons), MEng, FdSc, FdEng

School of Forensic & Applied Sciences; www.uclan.ac.uk/schools/forensic-applied-sciences

policing and criminal investigation, geography, forensic science and anthropology, environmental management, archaeology, forensic science, policing and criminal investigation, policing, geography, archaeology/ and anthropology, forensic science and molecular biology/ chemical analysis/criminal investigation; Postgraduate; document analysis, waste and resource management, counter terrorism, forensic and conservation genetics, urban environmental management, forensic science, criminal investigation, energy and environmental management, cybercrime investigation, DNA profiling, financial investigation, professional practice (early action), forensic anthropology; BA(Hons), MEng, BEng, MChem, BSc(Hons), FdSc, MPhil, PhD, PGDip/Cert, MSc, MSci

School of Physical Sciences and Computing; www.uclan.ac.uk/schools/physical-sciences-computing

computing, astronomy, computer network technology, astrophysics, forensic computing, applied physics, computer games development, astrophysics, physics with astrophysics, multimedia and mobile development, applied physics, chemistry, physics with astrophysics, mathematics, software engineering, mathematics, physics, information systems, computer games development, chemistry; Postgraduate; instrumental analysis, IT security, interaction design computing, database systems, forensic toxicology, agile software projects, child computer interaction, synthetic organic chemistry; BSc(Hons), MSc, MComp, MMaths, MPhys, MRes, GPDip, FdSc

School of Psychology; www.uclan.ac.uk/schools/psychology

neuroscience, social psychology, forensic psychology, neuropsychology, psychology, sport and exercise psychology, psychology and criminology, health psychology, psychology with psychotherapy and counselling; Postgraduate; forensic psychology,

health psychology, psychology, applied clinical psychology, psychology of child development; BSc(Hons), MSc

UNIVERSITY OF CHESTER
www.chester.ac.uk

Faculty of Science & Engineering; www.chester.ac.uk/faculties/science-engineering

Dept of Biological Sciences; www.chester.ac.uk/

animal behaviour/welfare, animal management (welfare & behaviour), biomedical sciences, biology, conservation biology, wildlife conservation, forensic biology, healthcare sciences, applied wildlife forensics; BSc, MSc, PhD

Chester Centre for Research into Sport & Society

sociology of sport & exercise; MSc, PhD
Dept of Research in Clinical Science & Nutrition
cardiovascular health & rehabilitation, exercise & nutrition science, human nutrition, obesity & weight management,nutrition & dietetics, public health nutrition, research; sport & society; MPhil, MSc, PhD
Sport & Community Engagement
Sport & Exercise Science
applied sport & exercise science, sociology of sport & exercise sciences; BA, BSc, MSc, MRes, PhD

Dept of Computer Science; www.chester.ac.uk/csis

computer science, cyber security, games development, software engineering; Postgraduate; computer networks, computer science, project engineering, cybersecurity; FD, BSc(Hons), MPhil, PhD, MRes, PGCert

Dept of Mathematics; www.chester.ac.uk/ maths

mathematics, applied statistics, applied mathematics, computational applied mathematics; BSc, MSc, MRes, PGCert, PhD, MPhil

Dept of Chemical Engineering

chemical engineering, systems biology of ageing & health; BEng, MEng(Hons)

Dept of Electronic & Electrical Engineering

electronic & electrical engineering, power electronics, embedded systems, communication engineering; BEng, MEng(Hons)

Dept of Mechanical Engineering

mechanical engineering, manufacturing engineering; BEng, MEng(Hons)

Dept of Natural Science

natural science; BSc

New Technology Initiatives

programming & project management, risk management; MSci

Faculty of Arts & Media; www.chester.ac.uk/faculties#B

Dept of Art & Design; www.chester.ac.uk/ art & design

animation, fashion design, fashion marketing, and communication, fine art, graphic design, interior design, photography,product design; Postgraduate design; fine art, arts and media; BA(Hons), MSc, MA, MRes

Dept of Media; www.chester.ac.uk/media

advertising, broadcast production and presenting commercial music production, digital photography, film studies, journalism, media/studies, music journalism/production and promotion, radio production, sports journalism, TV production; Postgraduate; broadcast media, media multiplatform production, radio production, TV production; BA(Hons), MA, PGCert/Dip

Dept of Performing Arts; www.chester.ac.uk/departments/ performing-arts

drama and theatre studies, dance, music, pop music performance, performing arts; Postgraduate; dance, drama, pop music; BA(Hons), MA

Chester Centre for Research in Arts & Media

art & design, performing arts, media

University of Chester Business School; www.chester.ac.uk/bell

Business and Finance; accounting and finance, banking/ and business finance, global entrepreneurship and business management, business management, integrated Master's in business, international business management/with a language; integrated Master's in business

Marketing, Tourism, Events Management & HRM; marketing, tourism & events management, events management, marketing management, international tourism management/with a language

Business and Management; business management, business, hospitality management, marketing and advertising management, music events management, sports events management, sport marketing and management;

The following postgraduate degrees are available; Department of Business, Strategy, Entrepreneurship & Finance; management, management with information systems, international business/finance/HRM/ marketing, MBA; Department of Marketing, Tourism, Events Management & HRM; Chester business masters, marketing communications & PR; sustainability for community and business; BA(Hons), BA/ BSc, FdA, MBA, MPhil, PhD, MBA, DProfStuds, MSc, DBA

Centre for Work Related Studies; Professional Development Unit; Work Based Learning Office; www.chester.ac.uk/ pdu

work-based & integrated studies; FD, BA, MA

Faculty of Education & Children's Services; www.chester.ac.uk/education

early years practice, education studies, early childhood studies, childhood and youth professional services, early childhood studies, education studies, QTS, teaching assistant, youth work; Postgraduate; Teacher Training; PGCE primary (5-11 years/ primary/early years (3-7 years)/secondary, primary physical education specialist, school direct initial teacher education, qualified teacher status; Masters and Doctoral Qualifications; creative practices in education, education, dyslexia research and practice, early childhood, educational leadership,,educational practice, inclusion and marginalisation, national award for SEN coordination, special educational needs and disability, school-based continuing professional development; BA(Hons), BEd, EdD, FdA, MA, MEd, PGCE, MATL

Faculty of Health and Social Care; www.chester.ac.uk/health

midwifery,nursing, health and social care (assistant practitioner), health and social care, non-medical prescribing, professional practice, social work, specialist community practice health nursing, specialist practice community; Postgraduate; advanced practice, applied mental health practice, art therapy, cancer care critical care, professional studies, health and social care, public health, endodontology, global health, public health, maternal and women's reproductive health, non-medical prescribing, oncology for health and social care practitioners, palliative and end of life care, professional education, professional nursing (international), professional studies in health and social care, restorative dentistry, return to practice nursing, social work, specialist community practice health nursing, specialist practice community; FdSc, BA, BA(Hons), BSc, BSc(Hons), MA, MSc, PGCert, GradDip, PhD, MPH, DPH, DProf, MPhil, PhD

Faculty of Humanities; www.chester.ac.uk/faculties#F

English; www.chester.ac.uk/english
creative writing, English/ language/literature, 19th-century literature and culture, modern & contemporary fiction, writing & publishing fiction; BA, MA, PhD, MPhil

History and Archaeology; www.chester.ac.uk/departments/history-archaeology
history, American, British, Irish, world history, military history, archaeology, archaeology of death & memory/heritage history; BA(Hons), MA, MPhil, PhD, MRes, PGDip/Cert

Dept of Modern Languages; www.chester.ac.uk/languages
European languages & global cultures, French, German & Spanish, Chinese studies, modern languages; BA(Hons), MA, MRes, PGCert/Dip

Theology & Religious Studies; chester.ac.uk/trs
religious studies, theology, practical & contextual theology, theology, media, & communication; BA(Hons), BTh, DProfDoc, FdA, PhD, MA, MPhil, MTh

Faculty of Social Sciences; www.chester.ac.uk/faculties#G

Geography and Development Studies; www.chester.ac.uk/geography

geography, international development studies, natural hazard/environmental management, regeneration for practitioners, sustainability for community & business, housing; BA(Hons), BSc(Hons), MA, MSc, PhD, PGCert, CertHE, FD, ProfCert

Dept of Psychology; www.chester.ac.uk/psychology

applied/psychology, cognitive & behavioural approaches, cognitive behavioural therapy, family & child psychology, clinical supervision; BA(Hons), BSc(Hons), PGCert, PhD, MPhil, MSc

Dept of Social & Political Science; www.chester.ac.uk/scc

criminology, counselling skills, sociology, politics, economics/business, international relations; BA, BSc, MA, MSc, PGCert

Dept of Social Work

cancer care, health and social care, education for PG medical practice, professional education, professional studies, adv practice critical care; BA(Hons), MA, PGDip, MSc, DProf, MEd, PGCert

Law School; www.chester.ac.uk/law

law, law/business/criminology/politics, contemporary legal studies; LlB, LlM

UNIVERSITY OF CHICHESTER
www.chiuni.ac.uk

dance, musical theatre, event management, fine art, musical theatre, accounting and finance, community sport coaching; Postgraduate; PGCE secondary education, primary teaching, choreography and professional practices, contemporary dance, creative writing, cultural history, early years professional practices, sport and exercise biomechanics/physiology, sports performance analysis; BA(Hons), BSc(Hons), FD, GradDip/Cert, MA, PGCE, MSc, MSW, PhD, MEd, BMus

CITY UNIVERSITY LONDON
www.city.ac.uk

School of of Arts & Social Sciences; www.city.ac.uk/arts-social-sciences

Department of Culture & Creative Industries

cultural & creative industries, creative writing (non-fiction), creative, culture, policy and management, language & translation studies, international publishing, screenwriting, translation

Department of Economics

economics, economics with accounting, financial economics, behavioural economics, business economics, development economics, economic evaluation in healthcare economics, financial economics, financial journalism, health economics, mathematics with finance/economics, international political economics, global politics

Department of International Politics

international political economy, international politics, international politics and sociology, diplomacy and foreign policy, global political economy, international politics, international politics and human rights

Department of Journalism

journalism, broadcast journalism, television/financial/interactive/international/investigative/magazine/newspaper/science journalism, journalism, media and globalisation

Department of Music

music, music, sound & technology

Department of Psychology

politics, psychology, behavioural economics, counselling psychology, clinical, criminal psychology, social and cognitive neuroscience, health psychology/psychology and health, organisational psychology, psychology for health & care

Department of Sociology

criminology, criminology and sociology/social justice, cultural policy management, international politics and sociology, media, communication and sociology, sociology, sociology with psychology, criminology and criminal justice, food policy, international communications and development, media and communications

Centre for Language Studies

BSc(Hons), BA(Hons), BMus(Hons) GradDip/Cert, MA, MSc, PhD, ProfDoc, DPsych,LlB

Cass Business School; www.cass.city.ac.uk

actuarial management, actuarial science, banking & international finance, finance, corporate finance, global finance, investment management, international accounting & finance, real estate investment, finance & investment, mathematical trading & finance, financial mathematics, quantitative finance; BSc(Hons), MSc, Dip, PhD, MPhil

Faculty of Finance; www.cass.city.ac.uk/facfin

accounting/& finance, investment & financial risk management, banking & international finance, business studies, corporate finance, global finance, insurance & risk management, international accounting & finance, finance & investment, investment management, financial mathematics, mathematical trading & finance, quantitative analysis, real estate, shipping, charity marketing & fund-raising, voluntary sector management; BSc, MSc, PGDip, MBA, Exec MBA

Faculty of Management; www.cass.city.ac.uk/facmana

entrepreneurship, innovation & creativity, energy, trade & finance, management, marketing strategy & innovation,, organisational behaviour & HR, international Asian HRM & business, HRM operations & supply chain management, management in the charity sector, management, shipping, trade & finance, strategy, entrepreneurship; BSc(Hons), MBA, MEb, MPhil, MSc, PGDip, PhD

School of Engineering and Mathematical Sciences; www.city.ac.uk/mathematics-computing-science-engineering

Department of Civil Engineering; www.city.ac.uk/department-civil-engineering

civil engineering, cvil engineering with architecture, civil engineering structures/nuclear power plants, construction management, professional engineering; BEng(Hons), MEng(Hons), MSc, FD, MPhil, PhD

Department of Electrical & Electronic Engineering; www.city.ac.uk/department-electrical-electronic-engineering

biomedical engineering/with healthcare technical management, computer systems engineering, electrical & electronic engineering, engineering with management & entrepreneurship, project management, finance & risk, renewable energy & power systems management, systems; BEng(Hons), MEng(Hons), MSc, FD

Department of Mathematics; www.city.ac.uk/department-mathematics

mathematics, mathematical science, mathematical sciences with computer science/finance & economics/statistics/finance, representational theory, mathematical physics/biology, decision sciences; BSc(Hons), MMaths, MSc, MPhil

Department of Mechanical Engineering & Aeronautics; www.city.ac.uk/department-mechanical-engineering-aeronautics

aeronautical engineering, air transport engineering, air safety management, air transport management, aircraft maintenance management, energy & environmental technology & economics, interaction design, mechanical & aeronautic engineering; BEng(Hons), MEng(Hons), MSc, MPhil, PhD, FD

School of Informatics

Department of Computer Science; www.city.ac.uk/department-computer-science

business computing systems, computer science with games technology/cyber security, business systems analysis & design, computer games technology, data science, health informatics, human–computer interaction design, management of information security & risk, information systems & technology, software engineering; BSc(Hons), MSc, MA, MInvo, PhD, MPhil, MSci

Department of Library & Information Science; www.city.ac.uk/library-information-science

information science, library science, library & information science; MSc, MA, MPhil, PhD

School of Health Sciences; www.city.ac.uk/health

speech & language science, nursing (adult/child/ mental health), optometry, radiography (diagnostic imaging/radiotherapy & oncology), speech & language therapy, ophthalmic dispensing)

Postgrad qualifications; midwifery, nursing (adult/ child/mental health), public health (school nursing, health visiting & district nursing), speech & language therapy, advanced practice in health & social care (adult mental health/child & adolescent mental health/health long term conditions & long term care/midwifery/advanced nursing/ophthalmic nursing/clinical optometry/radiotherapy,/language & communication, clinical optometry, clinical research, diagnostic radiography, health management, health policy, health services research, speech, language & communication, health psychology, needs in schools: advanced practice, medical ultrasound, public health, radiography (computed tomography, medical magnetic resonance & radiotherapy), optometry, psychology & health, therapeutic radiography, ophthalmic dispensing; FD, BSc(Hons), MSc, DipHE, PGDip, MPhil, PhD, Grad Dip, MRes, Cert

The City Law School; www.city.ac.uk/law

law,Postgraduate; bar professional training course, civil litigation and dispute resolution, criminal litigation, dispute resolution, European commercial law/ union law, international banking and finance, international business law, international commercial law, international economic law, international energy law and regulation, international human rights legal practice, legal practice, professional advocacy, professional legal skills, public international law
LlB(Hons), LlM, MPhil, PhD, MJur, Grad Dip, MInnov

Degrees validated by City University offered at:

GUILDHALL SCHOOL OF MUSIC & DRAMA
www.gsmd.ac.uk

acting, training actors (voice or movement), music, music composition, music therapy, conducting, performance, singing, electronic music, range of musical instruments, symphony orchestra (composition, leadership), opera making & writing, technical theatre arts, stage management, basic philosophy & the arts, video design for live performance, collaborative performance teaching, collective theatre production design; BA(Hons), BMus, MA, MMA/DMA, MMP, MMus, DMus, MPerf, PGDip, MPhil, PhD

REGENTS UNIVERSITY LONDON
www.regents.ac.uk

Regents University London

European Business School London, Regent's American College London, Regent's Business School London, Regent's Institute of Languages & Culture, Regent's School of Psychotherapy & Psychology, Regent's School of Drama, Film & Media, Regent's School of Fashion & Design

Numerous degree and diploma courses in the following subject areas: management and human resources, economics, accounting and finance, fashion and design, film, drama and acting, media, marketing, communications, PR and events, politics, international relations and social sciences, psychology and psychotherapy; BA(Hons), BSc(Hons), MA, MSc, DCounsPsy, DPsy, PGDip

THE NORDOFF-ROBBINS MUSIC THERAPY CENTRE
www.nordoff-robbins.org.uk

music therapy, music, health, society; MMusTherapy, PGDip, MPhil, PhD, DPsych

TRINITY LABAN CONSERVATOIRE OF MUSIC & DANCE
www.labantrinity.ac.uk

choreography, creative practice: transdisciplinary/ dance professional practice, dance performance, dance science, music, musical theatre performance, jazz composition, music in education & performance, performance science, composition, the teaching musician, musicians in education, piano & organ, strings, vocal studies, wind, brass, percussion, creative practice, dance; PGCE, BA(Hons); BMus, PGCE, BA(Hons); MA, MPhil, MSc, PGDip, PhD

COVENTRY UNIVERSITY
www.coventry.ac.uk

Coventry Business School;
www.coventry.ac.uk/study-at coventry/ faculties-and-schools/coventry-business-school

accountancy, accounting and finance, advertising and marketing, business/administration, business & finance/HRM / marketing, business economics/management, digital marketing, economics, enterprise and entrepreneurship, European business management, event management, finance, finance and investment, financial economics, international business management, international economics and trade, marketing, sport management, sport marketing; Postgraduate; accounting and financial management, advertising and marketing, banking and finance, brand management, international business, international business economics, international HRM, international marketing, investment management, leadership and management, marketing management, sport management, sport marketing, strategic marketing, the MBA in cyber security; BA(Hons), MA, MSc, MBA, PGCert/Dip, PhD

Coventry Law School

commercial law, business law, international corporate governance, international law, international business law, law, international corporate governance, criminality & law; LLB(Hons), LLM

Faculty of Arts & Humanities; www.coventry.ac.uk/study-at-coventry/ faculties-and-schools/arts-and humanities;

Coventry School of Art & Design

architecture, automotive and transport design, fashion, fine art, fine art and illustration, art and design, graphic design, illustration and animation, illustration and graphic design, interior design, product design, architecture, automotive and transport design, fashion, fine art, fine art and illustration, graphic design, illustration and animation/graphic design, interior design, product design; Postgraduate; automotive design, contemporary arts practice, design and transport, graphic design, illustration and animation, industrial product design, interior design, painting; BSc(Hons), BA(Hons), MDes, MSc

School of Media & Performing Arts

dance, digital media. journalism, music technology, photography; Postgraduate; automotive journalism, collaborative theatre making, communication, culture and media, global journalism, health journalism; BA(Hons), MA

School of Humanities

English, English and creative writing/ journalism/ TEFL, French, French and business/international relations/Spanish, history, history and politics, international relations, languages for international business, politics, sociology, sociology and criminology, Spanish, Spanish and business/TEFL; Postgraduate; diplomacy, law and global change, English language teaching and applied linguistics, international relations, teaching English for academic purposes; BA(Hons), MA

Faculty of Engineering, Environment and Computing; www.coventry.ac.uk/study-at-coventry/faculties-and-schools/ engineering-environment

School of Computing, Electronics and Mathematics

business information technology, computing, electrical and electronic engineering, electronic engineering, ethical hacking and network security, games technology, mathematics, mathematics and physics; Postgraduate; advanced computing, computer science, data science and computational intelligence, electrical and electronic engineering, electronic engineering, embedded microelectrics and wireless systems, forensic computing, information technology, management information systems, management of information technology, network computing, software development; BSc(Hons), MSc, MSci, MEng, BEng(Hons), PhD

School of Mechanical, Aerospace and Automotive Engineering
aerospace systems engineering, aerospace technology, automotive engineering, aviation management, engineering, engineering business management, global logistics, manufacturing engineering, mechanical engineering; Postgraduate; aerospace engineering, air transport management, automotive engineering, control engineering, engineering and management, engineering business management, engineering project management, global logistics, human factors in aviation, mechanical engineering, production engineering and operations management, supply chain management, systems and control; BSc(Hons), MSc, MSci, MEng, BEng(Hons), PhD

School of Energy, Construction and Environment
architectural technology, building surveying, civil engineering, construction management, disaster management, disaster management and emergency planning, geography, geography and natural hazards, oil, gas and energy management, quantity surveying and commercial management; Postgraduate; agroecology and food security, civil and structural engineering, civil engineering, construction management, construction project and cost management, disaster management, environmental management, global humanitarian engineering, oil and gas engineering, petroleum and environmental technology; BSc(Hons), MSc, BA(Hons), BEng(Hons)

Faculty of Health and Life Sciences; www.coventry.ac.uk/faculties-and-schools/faculty-of-health-and-life-sciences

School of Life Sciences
analytical chemistry and forensic science, biological and forensic sciences, biomedical science/applied biomedical science, food and nutrition, human biosciences, medical and pharmacological sciences, sport and exercise science; Postgraduate; applied sport and exercise science, biotechnology, sport and exercise nutrition, strength and conditioning; BSc(Hons), MSc

School of Psychological, Social and Behavioural Sciences
childhood and youth studies, criminology and law, criminology and psychology, forensic investigations, psychology, psychology and criminology, social work, sport psychology; Postgraduate; advanced professional practice in social work, applied psychology, business and organisational psychology, career guidance, clinical psychology, forensic psychology, forensic psychology and crime, fraud investigation management, health care management, mindfulness and compassion, occupational psychology, psychology, social work; MBA, DClinPsych, BA(Hons), BSc, BSc(Hons), MA,MSc

School of Nursing, Midwifery and Health
adult nursing, children and young people's nursing, mental health nursing, midwifery, occupational therapy, operating department practice, physiotherapy, paramedic science foundation; Postgraduate; advanced clinical practice, advancing physiotherapy practice, assistive technology, health studies, manual therapy, neurological occupational therapy, neurological rehabilitation, manual therapy, neurological occupational therapy, nursing studies, occupational therapy, public health nutrition, social and therapeutic horticulture, teenage and young adult cancer care; BSc(Hons), MSc, DipHE, PGCert

CRANFIELD UNIVERSITY
www.cranfield.ac.uk

School of Aerospace, Transport Systems and Manufacturing
Aerospace; aerodynamics, aerospace dynamics, aerospace materials/manufacture/propulsion (thermal power), aircraft engineering, airport planning and management, air transport management, vehicle design, computational and software techniques in engineering, computational fluid dynamics, computer aided engineering, digital signal & image processing, flight dynamics, gas turbine technology,

military aerospace and airworthiness, power, propulsion and the environment, rotating machinery, engineering and management, safety and accident investigation – air transport/marine transport/rail transport, safety and human factors in aviation, software engineering for technical computing, through-life system sustainment

Transport Systems; advanced motorsport engineering, airport planning and management (executive), air transport management (executive), airworthiness, automotive engineering/mechatronics, vehicle dynamics and control, safety and accident investigation – air transport/marine transport/ rail transport, safety and human factors in aviation, through-life system sustainment

Manufacturing; advanced materials, aerospace manufacturing, aerospace materials, applied nanotechnology, cost engineering, design, strategy and leadership, engineering and management of manufacturing systems, global product development and management, innovation and creativity in industry, knowledge management for innovation, management and information systems, manufacturing consultancy, manufacturing technology and management, medical technology, regulatory affairs, operations excellence, quality management in scientific research & development,sustainable manufacturing, through-life system sustainment, ultra precision technologies, welding engineering; EngD, MSc, MDes, PhD, PGCert/Dip

School of Energy, Environmental Technology and Agrifood

Environmental Technology; community water and sanitation, design, strategy and leadership, design and innovation for sustainability, economics for natural resource and environmental management, energy from waste, environmental engineering, environmental informatics, environmental management for business, environmental risk management, environmental water management, environment and public policy, food chain systems, geographical information management, innovation and creativity in industry, integrated landscape ecology, land reclamation and restoration, offshore and ocean technology with subsea engineering, renewable

energy technology, waste and resource management, water and wastewater engineering

Energy; advanced mechanical engineering, biofuels process engineering, carbon capture and storage, design of rotating machines, energy from waste, energy systems and thermal processes, flow assurance for oil and gas production, gas energy, materials for energy systems, offshore and ocean technology with offshore materials engineering, offshore and ocean technology with offshore renewable energy/pipeline engineering/risk management/subsea engineering, process systems engineering, renewable energy engineering, renewable energy technology

Agrifood; future food sustainability; MSc, MDes, MPhil, PhD, PGCert/Dip

Cranfield School of Management; www.cranfield.ac.uk/som

executive MBA/ (defence), investment management, management, finance and management, management & corporate sustainability/enterprise, strategic marketing, retail management, logistics and supply chain management, logistics/procurement/and supply chain management,, CPD; DBA, MBA, MSc, PhD, ExecMBA (Defence)

Cranfield Defence & Security www.cranfield.ac.uk/cds

cyber defence & information assurance, cyberspace operations, communication electronic warfare, defence acquisition management, defence leadership, defence simulation & modelling, electronic warfare, explosive ordinance engineering, forensic archaeology & anthropology/ballistics/computing/engineering & science, explosives & explosion investigation, guided weapon systems, military electronic systems, military operational research, gun system design, military electronic systems/OR, information capacity development, international defence & security, military aerospace & airworthiness, program & project management, military vehicle technology, security sector management, systems engineering for defence capacity, vehicle weapon engineering; EngD, MSc, PGDip/Cert, PhD

UNIVERSITY FOR THE CREATIVE ARTS
www.ucreative.ac.uk (at Canterbury, Epsom, Farnham, Maidstone and Rochester)

architecture, art & design, creative media, fine art, graphic design: visual communications, illustration & animation, interior architecture & design, design for theatre, film & performance, digital film marketing, fashion promotion & imaging, graphic design, music journalism/promotion, acting & performance, advertising, computer games arts,/technology digital film & screen arts, film production, glass, ceramics, metalwork, graphic communication, graphic design, vision, illustration & animation, journalism/ & creative writing, media & communications/creative writing, photography, product design, sports journalism, textiles for fashion & interiors, interactive media production, media business management, tv production, computer animation arts, contemporary jewellery, creative arts for theatre & film, fashion accessories/atelier/buying retail management/design/photography/media & promotion/textiles: print, photography, product design, silversmithing, goldsmithing & jewellery

Postgraduate; animation, architecture, curatorial practice, fine art, urban design, creative industries management, design, innovation & brand management, fashion business, fashion promotion & imaging, filmmaking, graphic design, creative arts education, animation, ceramics, documentary practices, glass, illustration, interior design, journalism, jewellery, metalwork, photography, printed textiles for fashion, product design, textiles, crafts; BA(Hons), FD, Grad Dip, MA, MPhil, PGCert, PhD, MRes, FdA

UNIVERSITY OF CUMBRIA
www.cumbria.ac.uk

Creative Arts

performing arts, fine art, art of games design, digital arts, illustration, graphic design acting, illustration, creative practice, ceramics; BA(Hons), MA, FdA

University of Cumbria – Business School; www.cumbria.ac.uk/Courses/SubjectAreas/BusinessComputing/Home.aspx

accounting and finance, business accounting and finance, business management, HRM/marketing, computing and IT, international business management; Postgraduate; business administration, energy and sustainability, events leadership and management, finance and accounting/sustainability,,international business management/business/international management/ marketing management, leadership and sustainability, media leadership, sustainable leadership/ development, sustainable leadership; BSc(Hons), DipHE, PGDip, MA, MSc, MBA

Education

early years education and development, education studies, primary education (3-11) with QTS, primary education with advanced specialism in inclusion/special education needs with QTS (5-11 year olds), secondary education with QTS (numerous subjects), education, professional practice, learning & teaching for HE, national professional qualification for senior/middle leadership, TESOL – with dyslexia; MSc, MBA, BA(Hons), MA, PGDip/Cert, PGCE, FdA, PhD, MPhil, DipHE

Forestry

woodland ecology and conservation, greening outdoor practice, outdoor and experiential learning, outdoor adventure and environment, ecosystem services evaluation, reflective practitioner, outdoor education, outdoor leadership, outdoor education, outdoor leadership, conservation biology, animal conservation science, transcultural European outdoor studies, outdoor adventure and environment, animal conservation science, outdoor and experiential learning (European), conservation biology, outdoor and experiential learning (European); BSc(Hons), MA, FdSc, FdA, PGCert

Humanities

English/& creative writing, English,mass communications, theology, religious studies, journalism; BA(Hons), MA, DipHE

Law & Social Science

applied social science,/psychology criminology & law/social science/policing & investigation,/forensic investigation law, youth & community work, applied psychology, applied forensic psychology, applied social science, interpersonal violence and abuse studies, law, legal and criminological psychology, international business law, policing, psychological research methods, sustainable leadership development, youth & community; BA(Hons), BSc(Hons), LlB, LlM, MSc, PGCert/Dip, FdSc

Outdoor

outdoor education, transcultural European outdoor studies, outdoor leadership, outdoor studies, outdoor adventure and environment, travel and adventure media, outdoor resources, outdoor and experiential learning; BA(Hons), BSc(Hons), PhD, FdA, FaSc, PGDip

Performance

acting, dance, drama and musical theatre, event management, musical theatre, performing arts, production; Postgraduate; directing; MA, BA(Hons)

Policing

policing, investigation & criminology, criminal justice, professional policing, strategic policing, criminology with policing & investigation, policing studies; DipHE, FdSc, BSc(Hons), MSc

Health & Social Care

community specialist practice (community learning disabilities nursing/general practice nursing/district nursing counselling, diagnostic radiography, palliative care, health & social care: dementia practice,,-management and leadership in health and social care, nursing (adult/ chld/international/learning disability/ mental health), practice development (acute and critical care/children and young people's mental health and wellbeing/dementia care/emergency care/enhanced health assessment/ foundations of occupational health/long term conditions/ mental health and wellbeing midwifery/occupational health/paediatric practice/palliative care/respiratory care/stroke and neurorehabilitation, wound care, radiation protection, sexual and reproductive health, social work, specialist community public health nursing (health visiting/ occupational health nursing/school nursing), sexual health advising, working with children and families, working with individuals on the autism spectrum, working with older adults; Postgraduate; medical ultrasound, advanced practice (clinical/cognitive behavioural therapy/social work),

applied public health,(global health, child and adolescent mental health and wellbeing), community specialist practice (community learning disabilities nursing/disabilities nursing (district nursing/general practice nursing), counselling and psychotherapy, evidence based psychological approaches (cognitive behavioural therapy), healthcare science, management and leadership in health and social care, medical imaging, magnetic resonance, medical imaging: ultrasound, mental health practice, non-medical prescribing for allied health professionals – independent prescribing for physiotherapists and podiatrists/ supplementary prescribing for radiographers, non-medical prescribing for nurses/ pharmacists, nuclear security management, nursing (international), nursing practice, occupational therapy, physiotherapy, practice development – developing paramedic practice/acute and critical care/allied health enterprise development/emergency care/enhancing paramedic practice/ long term conditions/midwifery/occupational health/occupational health management/palliative care, respiratory care, safeguarding children and vulnerable adults, social work, specialist community public health nursing (health visiting), specialist community public health nursing (occupational health nursing/school nursing/ sexual health advising, nursing practice, supervision of counselling and therapeutic practice, teaching for health professionals in HE, working with individuals on the autism spectrum
BA, BSc(Hons), GradDip, MA, MSc, PgC/D, UC, UAD, DipHE, FdA, FdSc, MPhil, PhD, MBA, PGDip/ Cert

Science, Technology & Engineering

applied sciences, applied chemistry, biomedical science, conservation biology, forensic science, healthcare science, sustainable energy technology; animal conservation science, biology, forensic/& investigative science, marine & freshwater conservation, zoology; project management; BSc, FdSc, CertHE

Sport

physical activity/exercise & health, PE, sport & exercise science, sports coaching & development, sports rehabilitation/massage therapy, exercise & health, practice development: sport & exercise rehabilitation, outdoor education; BSc(Hons), BA(Hons), DipHE, MSc, PhD

DE MONTFORT UNIVERSITY
www.dmu.ac.uk

Leicester Business School; www.dmu.ac.uk/about-dmu/schools-and-departments/leicester-business-school; also Department of Politics & Public Policy

accounting & business management/economics/finance, advertising & marketing communications, business & globalisation/management/marketing, business entrepreneurship & innovation/economics/finance/HRM, business studies (economics/finance/strategy), economics, economics & finance/politics, finance, global leadership & management, HRM & international business, marketing, politics, public administration & management; Postgrad; accounting & finance, advertising & PR management, business economics & finance/international relations/marketing/risk, diplomacy & world order, finance & investment, forensic accounting, global financial management/banking & finance/investment, housing studies, international business & corporate responsibility/creative enterprise /finance/HRM/management/international relations, HRM, marketing management, politics, project management, risk management, strategic & digital marketing; MBAs, Exec MBA, business administration (global/housing); BA(Hons), BSc(Hons), DipHE, GDL/CPE, FdSc, MA, MPhil, MBA, MSc, PGDip/Cert, PhD, MAccF

Leicester De Montfort School of Law; www.dmu.ac.uk/about-dmu/schools-and-departments/leicester-de-montfort-law-school

law, law & criminal justice, HR & social justice, business law, international business/human right laws law, law & business management, environment/employment/sports law & practice, medical law & ethics, food law, legal practice; LlB(Hons), LlM, LPC, DCCJ, MA, PGDip/Cert

Leicester School of Architecture; www.dmu.ac.uk/about-dmu/schools-and-departments/leicester-school-of-architecture

architecture, architectural design/practice/technology, architecture & sustainability; BA, MArch, PGDip, MA, MSc

School of Arts; www.dmu.ac.uk/about-dmu/schools-and-departments/school-of-arts

arts, art & design, animation, arts & festival management, dance, drama studies, fine art, music, technology & innovation/performance, performing arts, photography/ & video, cultural events management, performance practice; BA(Hons), MA, MSc

School of Design; www.dmu.ac.uk/about-dmu/schools-and-departments/school of design

Product, Craft and Interior Design

design crafts, design products, furniture design, interior design, product design, product and furniture design

Fashion and Textiles

contour fashion, fashion buying with design/marketing, fashion design/and accessories, footwear design, textile design

Postgraduate; bespoke footwear biomechanics, design, design innovation, design management and entrepreneurship, digital design, fashion and textiles, fashion management, with marketing, interior design, product design; BA(Hons), MA, MDes, BSc(Hons)

School of Humanities; www.dmu.ac.uk/about-dmu/schools-and-departments/school-of-humanities

creative writing, English language/with languages, history/with languages, humanities, ELT, photography history, management, law & humanities of sport, sports history & culture, TESOL; BA(Hons), MA, PGDip

Leicester Media School; www.dmu.ac.uk/about-dmu/schools-and-departments/leicester-media-school

animation; communication arts, film studies/with languages, media and communication/with languages, media, media production, game art design; audio and recording technology, music technology/and innovation/performance

Foundation; creative sound technology, graphic design and e-media

Postgraduate; creative technologies, global media, investigative journalism, journalism, TV scriptwriting; BA(Hons), FdA, FdSc, MA, MSc, BSC(Hons), PGDip

Institute of Creative Technologies; www.ioct.ac.uk

creative technologies; Masters, PhD

School of Computer Science & Informatics; www.dmu.ac.uk/about-dmu/schools-and-departments/school-of-computer-science-and informatics

business information systems, computers for business, computer science/security/games programming, computing, cyber security, forensic computing for practitioners, information & communication technology, intelligent systems & robotics, mathematics, professional practice in forensics, software engineering; BSc(Hons), MSc, PGDip/Cert

School of Engineering & Sustainable Development; www.dmu.ac.uk/about-dmu/schools-and-departments/school-of engineering-and sustainable-development

mechanical engineering, mechatronics, electronic engineering, electrical & electronic engineering, engineering management, energy & sustainable building design/development, physics; BSc(Hons), BEng(Hons), MSc

School of Allied Health Sciences; www.dmu.ac.uk/about-dmu/schools-and-departments/school-of-allied-health-sciences

advanced biomedical science, health studies, intercultural business communication, healthcare science (audiology), human communication, speech & language therapy, medical science; BSc(Hons), PGDip/Cert, MSc, FDSc, MA

School of Applied Social Sciences; www.dmu.ac.uk/about-dmu/schools-and-departments/school-of-applied-social-sciences

applied health studies, criminology & criminal justice/with psychology, education studies/ with languages, education with psychology, education practice, health psychology, health & community development studies, policing, psychology/with criminology/education studies, psychology of health studies, psychological wellbeing, sociology, social work, youth work & community development, working with young people & young people's services, youth work, health & communities; BA(Hons), BSc(Hons), FD, MSc, PGDip/Cert

School of Nursing & Midwifery; www.dmu.ac.uk/about-dmu/schools-and-departments/school-of-nursing-and midwifery

palliative care, health and professional practice, higher education/teacher qualification, midwifery, non-medical prescribing, practice education, practice nursing, nursing (specialist practice), specialist community public health nursing; BSc/BSc(Hons), RSHDip, PGCert/Dip, MSc

School of Pharmacy; www.dmu.ac.uk/about-dmu/schools-and-departments/school-of-pharmacy

pharmacy, forensic science, pharmaceutical & cosmetic science, pharmaceutical biotechnology/quality, independent prescribing, clinical pharmacy, prescribing quality by design for pharmaceutical industry, medical leadership & advanced professional skills; BSc(Hons), MPharm, MSc, PGDip/Grad

---

UNIVERSITY OF DERBY
www.derby.ac.uk

College of Art; www.derby.ac.uk/art

Department of Art and Design;

3D animation, animation, fashion/and fashion marketing, fine art, graphic design, illustration, interior design, textile design

Department of Media and Performing Arts

commercial photography, contemporary theatre and performance, costume and set design, dance, drama, film production, film production and production design, film production, visual effects and post production, media production, music, music technology and production, performing arts, photograph, photography/commercial/and film production/media production, pop music with music technology, pop music production, production design, radio production, technical theatre, theatre studies, visual effects and post-production

Postgraduate

fashion and textiles, film and photography, fine art, music production, visual communication, writing for performance; BA(Hons), MDes, MA, MPhil, PhD, Univ Cert/Dip

College of Business; www.derby.ac.uk/business

Derby Business School

accounting and finance, accounting, business, accounting and finance, business studies, business management, business, information technology management for business, international business/and finance, entertainment and leisure marketing, marketing and business intelligence/analytics/consumer psychology/digital media/HRM, marketing, PR and advertising, marketing, banking and finance, leisure & entertainment, economics for business; Postgrad; logistics management, logistics and supply chain management, accounting and finance, financial leadership, supply chain improvement, HRM, international business, international business and finance, business and reward management, marketing management; BA(Hons), BSc(Hons), MSc, DBA, MBA, ProfDoc, MBus, MAAcct

Hotel, Resort and Spa Management

events management, professional culinary arts/ management, corporate hospitality management, international hospitality management, hotel management, international tourism management, tourism destination management, tourism management, international spa management, wellness management, hotel, resort and spa management; FdA, FdSc, BA(Hons), MSc

College of Law, Humanities & Social Sciences; www.derby.ac.uk/lhss

Law & Criminology; www.derby.ac.uk/lhss/law

law, intellectual property & information technology, international & comparative law, international politics of human rights & personal freedom, transnational criminal law, law with criminology/politics, legal practice, medical law, social & public law, corporate & financial law, cyber crime & e-investigation, criminal investigation

Criminology

criminology, criminal psychology, criminal investigation; BA(Hons), BSc(Hons), MSc, LlB, LlM

International Policing, Law & Enforcement; www.derby.ac.uk/lhss/policing

policing, police leadership, strategy and organisation; MSc

Humanities & Media; www.derby.ac.uk/lhss/humanities

American studies, humanities, creative writing, English, history, liberal arts, professional writing, media & communication, media studies/production, writing for performance, journalism; BA(Hons), MA, PGCert/Dip

Social & Political Science; www.derby.ac.uk/lhss/social-political-science

politics, international & global development, sociology; BA(Hons), BSc(Hons)

College of Education; www.derby.ac.uk/education

primary education with QTS, early childhood studies/with early years teacher status (0-5), child and youth studies, education studies, special educational needs and disabilities, children's and young people's services, post-14 education and training; Postgraduate and Professional Education; PGCE primary, primary (school direct) with QTS, secondary (school direct) with qualified teacher status, post-14 (education and training/post-14 with specialism), education, early years/TESOL/leadership coaching and mentoring/leadership and management/lifelong learning/primary mathematics/special educational needs and disabilities, early years with early years teacher status (0-5); BA(Hons), BEd, EdD, PGCE, MPhil, PhD, FdA, PGDip

College of Health & Social Care; www.derby.ac.uk/health-and-social-care

professional development (health and social care), assistant practitioner, applied social work, child and family health and wellbeing, community specialist practice, counselling and psychotherapy principles and practices, creative expressive therapies, dance and movement studies, diagnostic radiography, health and social care, international nursing, nursing (adult/nursing mental health), occupational therapy specialist community public health nursing, systemic thinking and practice, working with young people and communities (youth work or community development)

Postgraduate and Professional Development; advanced occupational therapy/advanced occupational therapy community dip, advanced practice, art therapy, bone densitometry reporting, cognitive behavioural psychotherapy, compassion focused therapy, community specialist practice (district nursing), dance movement psychotherapy, dramatherapy, health and social care practice, hand therapy, health and social care studies, integrative counselling and psychotherapy, interprofessional practice education, leadership for healthcare improvement, management of long term conditions, medical ultrasound, mental health and wellbeing, mentoring in practice, occupational therapy, osteoporosis and falls management, practice certificate in non-medical prescribing, return to practice (nursing), reporting for clinicians, return to practice (diagnostic radiography, occupational therapy), specialist community public health nursing (health visiting or school nursing), social work, systemic psychotherapy, systemic thinking and practice; PGDip/Cert, FdSc, BA(Hons), BSc(Hons), UniAdvDip, MSc, PGCert, MPhil, PhD, ProfDoc, DocHSC

College of Engineering & Technology; www.derby.ac.uk/engineering-technology

Dept of Engineering

architectural studies/technology and practice/design, civil engineering, civil and infrastructure engineering, construction, construction management and property development, electrical and electronic engineering, interior architecture and venue design, manufacturing and production engineering, mechanical engineering, mechanical and manufacturing engineering, motorcycle engineering, motorsport engineering, motorsport and motorcycle manufacturing engineering, professional engineering, property development, quantity surveying, commercial management, product design engineering, sound, light and live event technology, broadcasting & live event technology

Dept of Computing and Mathematics

analytics, programme management, computer networks and security, computer science, information technology, mathematics, mathematics and computer science, mathematics with education

Postgrad; advanced computer networks, audio engineering, big data analytics, building information modelling & project collaboration, civil engineering and construction management, computational mathematics, computing, control and instrumentation, cyber security, data science, digital forensics and computer security, information technology, innovative engineering solutions, mechanical and manufacturing engineering, mobile app development, motorsport engineering, strategic engineering management; BSc(Hons), BA(Hons), MSc, FdSc/Eng, BEng(Hons), MPhil, PhD

College of Life & Natural Science; www.derby.ac.uk/science

human biology, biomedical health, biology, zoology, forensic science, forensic science with criminology/psychology, geography, geology,,environmental hazards, third world development, psychology sport and exercise science, sport management, strength, conditioning and rehabilitation, performance analysis and coaching science, physical activity, nutrition and health, sport and exercise studies, outdoor leadership and management, adventure sport and coaching science, outdoor activity leadership, sport and education, sport therapy and rehabilitation, sport coaching and development, sport coaching; Postgraduate and Professional Science Courses; public health, biological sciences, conservation biology, forensic science, applied petroleum geoscience, applied acoustics, behaviour change health psychology; BSc(Hons), BA(Hons), FdSc, FdA, MPH, MSc, MPhil, PhD, MSci, MRes

UNIVERSITY CENTRE DONCASTER
www.don.ac.uk/university-centre-doncaster

illustration and concept art, fashion and textiles design, fine art and craft, graphic design, illustration and concept art, moving image production, early childhood development and learning in practice, supporting children with special educational needs and disability, early childhood studies, professional studies working with young people and the community, working with children and young people), applied social science, criminal justice, English, social psychology in the community, business management, international football business management, live events production, contemporary performance practice, creative, health & social care, e music technology, dance practice, PE and sports coaching, sports, fitness and exercise science, sports, exercise and health science, art, design and media, creative industries: practice, business and innovation, creative pattern cutting, education & advancing educational

practice, early years, early childhood studies, education studies (primary / secondary), literature and digital culture, leadership and management, business administration, advancing professional practice, HRM; BA(Hons), BSc(Hons), MBA, MSc, PGDip/ Cert, MA, PGCE, FdA, MSc, CertEd

UNIVERSITY OF DUNDEE
www.dundee.ac.uk

College of Art, Sciences and Engineering; www.dundee.ac.uk/case

School of Computing; www.computing.dundee.ac.uk
applied computing (games/human computing interaction), augmentative & alternate computing, computing, computing with international business, computing/science/research, data science engineering, information technology & international business, user experience design; BSc, MSc, PhD

Duncan of Jordanstone College of Art and Design; www.dundee.ac.uk/djcad
animation, art & humanities, art philosophy, art, digital interactive design, society & publics, forensic art & facials, graphic design, interior/environmental/ jewellery & metal/textiles design, fine art, illustration, medical art, product design, textile design, theatre studies, time-based art & digital film; BA, BSc(Hons), BDes, MSc, MFA, PhD, MPhil

School of Science & Engineering; www.dundee.ac.uk/science-engineering
civil engineering/design & materials, concrete engineering & environmental management, electronic studies, earthquake & offshore engineering, geotechnical engineering, mathematics, mathematics & accountancy/financial sector/economics studies/physics, applied/mathematics, mathematical biology, mechanical engineering, physics with renewable energy sciences/mathematics, renewable energy & environmental modelling, structural engineering; BEng, BSc, MEng, MSc, MSci, PhD, PGDE, PGDip

Centre for Anatomy & Human Identification; www.dundee.ac.uk/cahil
anatomical sciences, advanced forensic anthropology, anatomy & advanced forensic anthropology, anthropology for artists, forensic art & facial identification, forensic archaeology & anthropology, human anatomy, medical archaeology; BSc, MBChB, BDS, MSc

College of Arts and Social Sciences; www.dundee.ac.uk/artsoc

School of Business; www.dundee.ac.uk/ business
accountancy, business management, economic studies, finance, international business; Postgraduate: accountancy, accounting, management and strategy, accounting & finance, economics, finance, financial economics, international accounting/business, accounting and finance, international business, marketing and HRM, international business and finance/ banking & finance, HRM/management/marketing, management, management and accounting/finance/ HR; BSc, BAcc, BFin, MA, MRes, PGDip, PhD

Continuing Education; www.dundee.ac.uk/ conted
arts & social sciences; MA

School of Education & Social Work and Community Education; www.dundee.ac.uk/esw
childhood practice/studies community learning & development, education (primary), professional development (community engagement, leadership & management,/innovation tertiary education, volunteer management), volunteering, social work, education/leading learning & teaching/inclusion & learner support/nursery/early education/pupil care & support/adult literacies, international education, primary, policing studies, science (maths/sciences), educational psychology, international education, leadership & innovation, technical qualification FE, teaching in HE, secondary education; chemistry/ physics/home economics), secondary physics with science teaching/(FE)/HE); BA/BA(Hons), PGCert/ Dip, MRes, DSW, PGDE, MSc, MA, PhD, MPhil, ProfDoc, DCLD, DEd, DEdPsych

Interdisciplinary Disability Research Institute (IDRIS)

Institute for Research and Innovation in Social Services (IRISS)

School of the Environment; www.dundee.ac.uk/environment

Architecture: architecture, renewable energy & zero carbon building, adv sustainability of built environment, adv sustainable urbanism, adv sustainability
Environmental Science: environmental science, geography
Geography: geography, catchment hydrology and management, social research methods/population and welfare, water hazards, risk & resilience
Town & Regional Planning: environmental sustainability, geography & planning, town regional planning, sustainable space planning, energy sustainability & international business, urban planning; BSc, MA, BArch, MArch, PhD

School of Humanities; www.dundee.ac.uk/humanities

American Studies
digitalisation & digital preservation, outreach & education, promotion of archive, records management & information rights/digital records, CPD

Gender, Culture & Society; www.dundee.ac.uk/gender-culture-society
gender, society & culture

Languages; www.dundee.ac.uk/languagesstudies
French, German, Spanish, European languages & cultures, European studies, applied languages

English; www.dundee.ac.uk/English
English, English and film studies/modern languages, English literature/studies, philosophy & literature, women, comic & graphic novels, comics studies, theatre studies, writing practice, gender, culture & society, creative writing, science fiction, humanities

European Studies
interdisciplinary courses, practical languages (French, German, Spanish), European studies

History; www.dundee.ac.uk/history
early America, European history, Great Britain in the twentieth century, history, global empires, Scottish history/local studies,, 20th century studies, Scottish historical studies

Philosophy; www.dundee.ac.uk/philosophy;art & humanities
philosophy, philosophy/& literature, continental/recent analytic philosophy, women, culture & society, continental philosophy, art, philosophy

School of Law; www.dundee.ac.uk/law
law, law with language, international commercial law, corporate & commercial law, competition, international & security, international criminal justice & human rights, environmental law & sustainable development, family law, law with language, law of banking & finance, corporate & Euro private law, Scots law, English law, international dispute resolution; LlB, LlM, PhD

Graduate School of Natural Resources Law, Policy and Management; www.dundee.ac.uk/postgradschool
mineral resource management, international oil & gas management, managing in energy industries; MBA, MSc

UNESCO Centre for Water Law, Policy and Science
water law; PGCert, LlM, PhD

Centre for Energy, Petroleum, & Mineral Law & Policy; www.dundee.ac.uk/cepmlp
energy law and policy, energy environment/economics/economics/finance, international mineral resource management,/studies petroleum taxation and finance, water law, mineral law and policy, natural resources law and policy, oil and gas law and policy/economics, international oil & gas management, managing in the energy industries; LlM, PhD, MBA, MSc

School of Psychology; www.dundee.ac.uk/psychology
psychology, psychology of language, psychological research methods, developmental psychology, augmentative & alternative communication, psychology of mental health; BA(Hons), MA(Hons), PhD

College of Life Sciences; www.lifesci.dundee.ac.uk
biochemistry/& drug discovery, biomedical/biological sciences, bioinformatics, drug discovery, cell signalling, cell & developmental biology, immunology, biology, molecular microbiology, neuroscience, pharmacology, physiological sciences, plant science; BSc(Hons), MRes, MSc, PhD

Schools of Research

Biological Chemistry & Drug Discovery (CLS); www.lifesci.dundee.ac.uk/bcdd

Div of Cell and Developmental Biology; www.lifesci.dundee.ac.uk/cdb

Div of Cell Signalling & Immunology; www.lifesci.dundee.ac.uk/csi

Drug Discovery Unit; www.drugdiscovery.ac.uk

Gene Regulation & Expression; www.lifescience.dundee.ac.uk/gre

Molecular Microbiology; www.lifesci.dundee.ac.uk/mmb

Protein Phosphorylating & Ubiquitylation Unit; www.dundee.ac.uk/research

Div of Molecular Medicine; www.lifesci.dundee.ac.uk/mm

Nucleic Acid Structure Research Group; www.dundee.ac.uk/research

Div of Plant Sciences; www.lifesci.dundee.ac.uk/pl

Scottish Institute of Cell signalling

College of Medicine, Dentistry and Nursing; www.dundee.ac.uk/cmdn

School of Medicine; www.medicine.dundee.ac.uk

premedical & medical courses, public health, clinical audit and research for health care professionals, cognitive behavioural psychotherapy,dental public health, forensic medicine, forensics odontology, medical education, motion analysis, cancer biology, oral cancer,health studies, human clinical embryology and assisted conception, global health and wellbeing, midwifery/maternal and infant health, nursing, oral biology, orthodontics, psychological therapy in primary care, quality diabetes care, quality improvement, simulation based education, sports and biomechanical medicine, stratified medicine and pharmacological innovation, orthopaedic and rehabilitation technology, orthopaedic surgery, prosthodontics, public health (palliative care research); MBChB, BMSc, MSc, MChOrth, MRes, MFM, PGDip/Cert, MD, MMSc, MSSc, MDS, MChOrth, MDPH

School of Dentistry; www.dundee.ac.uk/dentalschool

orthodontics, prosthodontics, dental surgery, dental public health, cancer biology, oral cancer, endodontics, oral biology, forensic odontology; BMSc, BSc, MDPH, MRes, MDSc, MFDent

School of Nursing and Midwifery; www.dundee.ac.uk/medden

advanced practice, adult/child/mental health nursing, palliative care, midwifery, global health & well-being, health & social care, infection prevention & control, health studies, community health nursing, mental health, physiotherapeutics, quality improvement, clinical assessment governance, CPD, numerous Master modules, long term conditions, maternal, child & family help, health studies, maternal and infant health, health studies quality improvement; BN, BSc, MNurs, MPhil, MSc

School of Medicine Institutes

Division of Cardiovascular & Diabetes Medicine; Division of Imaging & Technology; Division of Neuroscience; Division of Population Health Sciences; Division of Molecular Medicine

Graduate School; www.graduate.cmdn.dundee.ac.uk

DURHAM UNIVERSITY
www.dur.ac.uk

Faculty of Arts and Humanities; www.dur.ac.uk/arts.humanities

Dept of Classics and Ancient History; www.dur.ac.uk/classics

ancient history & archaeology, ancient history, classics, classical civilisations,, ancient, medieval & modern history, ancient philosophy, Greece, Rome & the Near East

Dept of English Studies; www.dur.ac.uk/english.studies

English literature studies & history/philosophy, medieval & Renaissance literary studies, studies in poetry, 20th/21st-century literary studies, Victorian & romantic literary studies, educational studies

English Language Centre; www.dur.ac.uk/englishlanguage

TESOL English for specific purposes/teaching young learners, English for academic purposes, English language teaching, applied linguistics for/in TESOL

Dept of History; www.dur.ac.uk/history

history, ancient, medieval & early modern/history, modern history, research methods (economic and social history), social & economic history

School of Modern Languages and Cultures; www.dur.ac.uk/mlac

Arabic/English translation & interpreting, arts & social sciences, medieval & early modern studies, French, German, Hispanic studies, Italian, Russian, Chinese/Japanese studies, modern languages & cultural history, translation studies, culture & difference, visual arts & culture

Dept of Music; www.dur.ac.uk/music

music, ethnomusicology, composition, musicology, British music, performance, analytic music technology

Dept of Philosophy; www.dur.ac.uk/philosophy

philosophy (& jt degrees), history & philosophy of science & medicine, metaphysics, ethics, aesthetics

Dept of Theology and Religion; www.dur.ac.uk/theology.religion

Christian theology (Anglican, Catholic studies), historical & systemic theology, Old Testament & related studies, theology, philosophy & theology, theology & religion, biblical studies, spirituality, theology & health, study of religion/film & religion, theology & ethics, theology & science, religion & society; BA(Hons), GDip, MA, MLitt, MMus, MTh, PhD

Faculty of Science; www.dur.ac.uk/science.faculty

School of Biological and Biomedical Sciences; www.dur.ac.uk/biological.sciences

biomedical sciences, biological sciences, biosciences, protein quality control in health & disease, cell biology, molecular cell signalling

Dept of Chemistry; www.dur.ac.uk/chemistry

chemistry (& jt degrees), numerous postgraduate research projects, natural science

Dept of Engineering and Computer Science; www.dur.ac.uk/ecs/computing.science

engineering, civil/electronic/mechanical engineering, communications engineering, computer science, general engineering, internet systems and e-business, new and renewable energy, software development for business, computer science & business/physics/mathematics, natural sciences

Dept of Earth Sciences; www.dur.ac.uk/earth.sciences

earth sciences, climate & environmental change, geohazards, the solid earth, geoenergy, resources & waste, geology, natural sciences, geophysics with geology, geoscience, environmental/geosciences, numerous postgrad projects

Dept of Mathematical Sciences; www.dur.ac.uk/mathematical.sciences

mathematics, mathematical sciences, particles, strings & cosmology, jt degrees including statistics, physics, natural sciences

Dept of Physics; www.dur.ac.uk/physics

physics/& astronomy, particles, strings & cosmology, biophysical science

Dept of Psychology; www.dur.ac.uk/psychology

developmental/cognitive neuroscience, developmental psychopathology, applied/psychology, research methods

BA(Hons), BEng, BSc(Hons), MSc, MA, MChem, MEng, MMath, MPhys, MBiol, MSc, MSci, PhD

Faculty of Social Science and Health; www.dur.ac.uk/science.health

School of Applied Social Sciences; www.dur.ac.uk/sass

criminology & criminal justice/sociology, anthropology & sociology studies, international social work & community development, social policy, social work, society & politics, social research methods (sociology/social policy/criminology/social work), sociology, educational studies – sociology, managing community practice/youth work practice, community and youth work, sport, exercise & physical activity, CPD

Dept of Anthropology; www.dur.ac.uk/anthropology

anthropology/& archaeology, evolutionary anthropology/medicine, health and human sciences, biological/social/medical anthropology, sustainability, culture & development anthropology, energy & society, sociocultural anthropology, research methods (anthropology)

Dept of Archaeology; www.dur.ac.uk/archaeology

archaeology/& ancient civilisations/anthropology/ ancient history, archaeological science, conservation of archaeological & museum objects, international cultural heritage management, paleopathology, museum & artefact studies

Durham Business School; www.dur.ac.uk/dbs

accounting, accounting and finance/accounting and management, business and management, marketing, economics,,economics with management/French/politics, philosophy, politics and economics

Postgraduate; economics, environmental/ and natural resource economics, experimental economics, public economics; finance, finance (accounting and finance / corporate and international finance/economics and finance/finance and investment/international banking and finance/international money, finance and investment), Islamic finance/and management; management, management (business ethics/ entrepreneurship/finance/HRM/international business/supply chain logistics), marketing

BA(Hons), MSc, MBA, executive MBA – Durham & EBS, EMBA

School of Education; www.dur.ac.uk/education

educational assessment, education studies, initial training, PGCE (primary/secondary/partnership/ international) primary education with QTS, secondary education, intercultural education & internationalism, history of art, practice of education, technically enhanced education, research methods (education); BA(Hons), MA, MSc, PGCert, PGCE

Dept of Geography; www.dur.ac.uk/geo

risk & environmental hazards, geography, contemporary human geography, research methods, natural science, risk, health & public policy, risk & security

School of Government and International Affairs; www.dur.ac.uk/sgia

Arab world studies, defence, development, diplomacy, conflict prevention & security/peace-building, global politics, international relations/studies, economics, philosophy/& politics, politics & international relations; BA(Hons), DBA, EdD, MA, MA(Ed), MBA, MAnth, MSc, MScW, PGCE, PGCert/Dip, PhD

Durham Law School; www.dur.ac.uk/law

European trade/international trade & commercial law, law, society & law, legal studies

School of Medicine, Pharmacy; www.dur.ac.uk/school.health

clinical management, global health, health research methods, philosophy of science, interdisciplinary mental health, medical education, pharmacy, public policy and health, spirituality theology & health, medicinal chemistry, pharmacology, pharmacy practice, formulation science, pharmaceutical microbiology

BA(Hons), BA(Ed), BSc(Ed), BSc(Hons), Cert Leg Stud, LlB, LlM, MA, MBBS, MPhil, PGCert, PGCert/ Dip, PGCE, PhD, MA, MPharm, MJur

Degrees validated by Durham University offered at:

CRANMER HALL, ST JOHN'S COLLEGE
www.cranmerhall.com

theology and ministry; BA, MA, diploma/certificate, Doc PhD

NEW COLLEGE DURHAM
www.newdur.ac.uk

applied business computing, applied sport & exercise science, business & management, community studies, children & young people, childhood studies, computing & networks, counselling, design, education/& training, health & wellbeing, graphics/web design, outdoor activity/leadership, podiatry, events/spa/ tourism management, leadership in voluntary & community organisations, public & community service, management & administration in the public sector, supporting learning & teaching, retailing, social work, visual arts, web design, counselling, management, design, education/PGCE, childhood studies & professional practice, community studies, applied health & social care (adults), event management, public health & health promotion, retail management, hospitality management, education; BA(Hons), BSc(Hons), FD

ROYAL ACADEMY OF DANCE
www.rad.org.uk

ballet education, ballet/dance teaching studies, Benesh, dance education, movement notation; BA(Hons), Dip/CertHE, MTeach(Dance), licenciate, PGCE

USHAW COLLEGE
www.ushaw.ac.uk

theology & ministry; BA, Certs, Dipls, MA, PGCert/ Dip

UNIVERSITY OF EAST ANGLIA
www.uea.ac.uk

Faculty of Arts and Humanities; www.uea.ac.uk/hum

Art, Media & American Studies; www.uea.ac.uk/arts-humanities

history of art, archaeology, anthropology and art history, history and history of art, history of art and literature, history of art with gallery and museum studies; Postgraduate; world art studies, museum studies, cultural heritage and museum studies, history of art, the arts of Africa, Oceania and the Americas

Interdisciplinary Institute for the Humanities

American studies, English literature, history, history of art, intercultural communication with business management, philosophy, politics; Postgraduate; creative entrepreneurship.

Centre for Japanese Studies

language and communication studies, art history and world art studies, film, television and media studies; Postgraduate; language and communication studies

School of History; www.uea.ac.uk/history

modern history, history, modern British history, history & politics/landscape/medieval/modern European history, early modern history

School of Literature, Drama & Creative Writing; www.uea.ac.uk/lit

biography & creative non-fiction, creative writing – poetry/prose/fiction/scriptwriting, drama, scriptwriting & performance, English & American literature, English literature & drama, literary translation, literature & history, medieval & early modern textual cultures (1381-1638), theatre directing, text & production, modern & contemporary writing

Politics, Philosophy, Language and Communication Studies; www.uea.ac.uk/ppl

Political, Social and International Studies; politics and media studies, international relations and/modern languages/politics, philosophy and politics, politics, culture, literature and politics, international relations and modern history, society, culture and media; Postgraduate; broadcast journalism: theory and practice, international relations, politics, international security, media and cultural politics, media, culture

Philosophy; philosophy and history, philosophy, English literature and philosophy; Postgraduate; philosophy, philosophy and literature

Language & Communication Studies; intercultural communication with business management, modern language(s) with management studies, modern language, translation and interpreting with modern languages, translation, media and modern languages;

Postgraduate; applied translation studies, communication and language studies, language and intercultural communication
MA, MPhil, PGDip, PhD, MRes, BAH

Norwich Medical School; www.uea.ac.uk/medicine

medicine, surgery, clinical science/research/psychology/education, cognitive behavioural therapy, coloproctology, health economics/research, knee surgery, molecular medicine, onoplastic breast surgery, regional anaesthesia, health economics/research, clinical psychology, physician associate, CPD (numerous topics)

School of Health Sciences; www.uea.ac.uk/health-sciences

adult/ children's/learning disabilities/mental health nursing, midwifery, occupational therapy, operating department practice, paramedic science, physiotherapy, speech and language therapy; Postgraduate; adult nursing,advanced practitioner: emergency care practitioner/midwife/neonatal nurse/nurse/occupational therapy/paramedic/pharmacist/physiotherapist, clinical education, clinical research, occupational therapy, physiotherapy, advanced musculoskeletal research and practice, leadership in dementia care, leading innovation for clinical practitioners
BA(Hons), BSc(Hons), ClinPsyD, DipHE, FD, MBBS, MCE, MD, MHeaRes, MPhil, MSc, PGDip/Cert, PhD, MRes, MA

Faculty of Science; www.uea.ac.uk/sci

School of Actuarial Science; www.uea.ac.uk/actuarial-science

actuarial science, business statistics

School of Biological Sciences; www.uea.ac.uk/biological-sciences

biochemistry, biological sciences, biomedicine, ecology, molecular biology & genetics; Postgraduate; applied ecology & conservation, plant science, molecular medicine, plant genetics & plant improvement

School of Chemistry Science; www.uea.ac.uk/chemistry

chemistry, adv organic chemistry, biological and medicinal chemistry, chemical physics, chemical sciences, forensic & investigative chemistry, physics

School of Computing Science; www.uea.ac.uk/computing

actuarial sciences, applied/advanced computing/science, business information systems, business statistics, computer graphics/systems engineering/science, games development, information systems, knowledge discovery & data mining

School of Engineering; www.uea.ac.uk/engineering

engineering, energy engineering /with environmental management

School of Environmental Sciences; www.uea.ac.uk/env

applied ecology, agriculture, environmental sciences, climate change, environmental assessment & management/chemistry/earth sciences, environmental geography & international development/climate change/geophysics, geography, meteorology & oceanography, international development & the environment, environmental geology

School of Natural Science; www.uea.ac.uk/sci/natsci

natural sciences

School of Mathematics; www.uea.ac.uk/mathematics

mathematics, mathematics with business, energy engineering & environmental management

School of Pharmacy; www.uea.ac.uk/pha

pharmacy practice, pharmacy, manufacture & drug discovery
BSc(Hons), GradDip, MPhil, MSc, MSci, PGDip, PhD, MMath, MChem, MNatSci, MEng, BEng

Faculty of Social Sciences; www.uea.ac.uk/ssf

School of Economics; www.uea.ac.uk/economics

economics/& accountancy, business economics, business/ finance & economics, economics of international finance & trade, economics of money, banking & capital markets, quantitative financial economics, media economics, environmental/experimental/industrial economics, international business finance & economics, philosophy, politics & economics, economics & international relations

School of Education and Lifelong Learning; www.uea.ac.uk/edu

adult literacy, lifelong learning and development: international perspectives, education, PE, counselling, mathematics education, PGCE physics with mathematics, PGCE primary (key stage 2 with primary languages/specialising in key stage 1/ and key stage 2), PGCE secondary numerous secondary subjects, initial teacher education, advanced educational practice/practice, cognitive behavioural therapy, focusing-orientated psychotherapy, learning & development/pedagogy & assessment, person-centred counselling studies, social science research methods

School of International Development; www.uea.ac.uk/international-development

geography and international development, international development/and the environment/with economics/anthropology/social anthropology and politics, media and international development/with overseas experience; Postgraduate; agriculture and rural development, climate change and international development, conflict, governance and international development, development economics, education and development, environment/gender analysis and international development, globalisation business and sustainable development, impact evaluation for international development, international development, international social development, media and international development, water security and international development, social science research methods

Geography; www.uea.ac.uk/geography

geography, environmental geography & climate change/international development, environmental

earth science/geophysics/science, geography & international development, international development & the environment

Law School; www.uea.ac.uk/law

technology & intellectual property law, international commercial & business law/competition law/trade law, law with American law/ French law & language, legal studies, media law, policy and practice

Norwich Business School; www.uea.ac.uk/nbs

accounting and finance, accounting and management, business finance and management, business management, marketing and management; Postgraduate; investment and financial management, enterprise and business creation, brand leadership, business management, finance and management, marketing, marketing and management, HRM, international accounting and financial, operations and logistics management, management MBA, Executive MBA

School of Social Work; www.uea.ac.uk/social work

social work, social science research methods science

School of Psychology; www.uae.ac.uk/psychology

psychology, developmental science, cognitive psychology/neuroscience, social psychology, social science research

BA(Hons), BSc(Hons), CPE/Dip, DEd, GradDip, LlBHons, LLM, MA, MA/DipSW, MBA, MPhil, MRes, MSc, MScEd, PGCert, PGDip, PhD

Degrees validated by University of East Anglia offered by:

CITY COLLEGE NORWICH
www.ccn.ac.uk

applied social work, applied sport health & exercise, arts & wellbeing, business management (finance & accounting/HRM), culinary arts, dementia care, early/childhood studies/years, English/ & cultural studies/psychology, health studies, higher education in social practice, hospitality/tourism & event management, leisure & event management, HRM,

leadership in public services, leadership & management, mental health practice, professional aviation engineering practice, psychology/& sociology, public services, retailing, social work, social care practice, sport, health & exercise, travel & tourism management; BA,BSc(Hons),Cert/DipHE,FdA/Sc

EASTON & OTLEY COLLEGE
www.eastonotleycollege.ac.uk

agriculture, agricultural engineering, countryside management, equine studies, motor vehicles engineering, animal studies, arboriculture, construction, fishery studies, floristry, horticulture, outdoor activities, veterinary nursing

THE UNIVERSITY OF EDINBURGH
www.ed.ac.uk

College of Humanities and Social Sciences; www.hss.ed.ac.uk

The Edinburgh College of Art; www.ed.ac.uk/schools-departments/edinburgh-college-art

School of Art: intermedia art, interdiscipline creative practice, painting, sculpture, photography, contemporary art practice/theory, contemporary art & anthropology, material practice

School of Design: animation, design informatics, fashion, film & TV, glass, graphic design, illustration, interior design, jewellery & silversmithing, performance costume, product design, textiles, film directing, performance costume, film directing, glass, graphic design, interior architectural design, jewellery, textiles

Architecture & Landscape Architecture:
architectural history, architecture, landscape architecture; Postgraduate; advanced sustainable design, architectural & urban design, architectural conservation, architectural history and theory, architectural project management, architecture, art space nature, cultural landscapes, cultural studies, design and digital media, digital media design/studio practice, landscape architecture, material practice, urban strategies & design, architecture by design, cultural studies, interdisciplinary creative practices, landscape architecture, landscape & wellbeing, reflective design practice

Reid School of Music: music, music technology, composition/for screen, composition & performance, digital composition, musical instruments & research, acoustics & music technology, musical composition, musicology, creative music practice, acoustics & music technology

History of Art: history of art, art in the global middle ages, collecting & curating practice, fine art, history of fine art, modern & contemporary art history, curating & criticism, Renaissance & early modern studies, curating & criticism, Scottish art & visual culture, theory & display; BA, MA, MA(Hons), MSc, MArch, MLA, MPhil, PhD, MFA, Dip

The Business School; www.business-school.ed.ac.uk

accounting & finance, business & accounting/economics/finance/geography/law, business management, business with decision science/enterprise & innovation/HRM/marketing/strategic economics, international business with foreign language; Postgraduate; accounting and finance, banking and risk, carbon finance, energy finance and markets, entrepreneurship and innovation, finance and investment, financial management, HRM, international business and emerging markets, international HRM, management, marketing, marketing and business analysis, Edinburgh MBA, Executive MBA; MA, MSc, PhD, MBA

School of Divinity; www.div.ed.ac.uk

divinity/classics, biblical studies, ethics, ministry, philosophy & theology, religious studies/& English literature, science & religion, theology/in history, world Christianity; MA(Hons), MTh, GradDip, MPhil, PhD

School of Economics; www.ed.ac.uk/schools-departments/economics

asset pricing, corporate finance, economics, international money & finance, economics analysis, econometrics/finance, economics, economics (large number of jt degrees), advanced topics in macroeconomics/microeconomics, economics of labour markets, adv time series econometrics, development economics, development of economic thought & methodology, personnel economics, topics in economic history, economic policy, environment & natural resources, health economics, industrial organisation, international trade, MSc in economics, economics (econometrics), economics (finance); MA(Hons), MSc, PhD

School of Health in Social Science; www.ed.ac.uk/schools-departments/health

advancing nursing practice/skills, nursing studies, nursing in clinical research, health science, & society, nursing (adult branch), nursing research, advanced clinical studies, clinical psychology, counselling & psychotherapy/& applied science, counselling studies, health, science & society, including social science in health, integrated service improvement, managing health & social care, nursing in clinical research, clinical psychology, applied psychology for children and young people, dementia: international policy & experience, psychology of mental health, children & young people's mental health and psychological practice, mental health and well-being of children, young people and families, cognitive behavioural therapy for children and young people, psychological interventions for children and young people, CPD courses, psychology of mental health; BNurs(Hons), MA, MSc, CPD, DClinPsych, PhD, MCouns, PGCert/Dip, ProfDoc

School of History, Classics and Archaeology; www.shc.ed.ac.uk

Archaeology; archaeology, environmental archaeology, archaeology & anthropology/social anthropology, ancient Mediterranean civilisations, history & archaeology, archaeological history & archaeology, geography & archaeology, Scottish ethnology & archaeology, Celtic & archaeology

Classics; ancient history, classical studies, classics, Greek studies, Latin studies, ancient & modern history, ancient history & classical archaeology/Greek/Latin, ancient Mediterranean civilisations, classical archaeology & Greek, history & classics, classics & English/languages/Middle East studies

History; economic/ & social history, history, Scottish history, American history, social history, economic history and business, economic and social history and environmental studies, history and archaeology/classics/history of art/politics/Scottish history/sociology,social and architectural history, English literature/language and history, law and history/social studies, languages and history, Celtic & Scottish studies and history, contemporary history, gender history, intellectual history, medieval history, Islamic & Byzantine studies, modern British & Irish history, social & cultural history; MA(Hons), LlB, BSc, MPhil, PhD

School of Law; www.law.ed.ac.uk

Scottish legal system, family law, public law of the UK and Scotland, law, public law and individual rights, evidence and criminal law, property law, commercial law, succession and trust law, optional law or non-law courses, intellectual property law, commercial law, media law, human rights law, commercial law, comparative and European private law, competition law and innovation, corporate law, criminal law/criminology and criminal justice, European law, global crime, justice and security global environment and climate change law, human rights, innovation, technology and the law, intellectual property law, international banking law and finance, legal research, international economic law, international law, law, law and Chinese, history and philosophy of law, medical law and ethics, professional legal practice; LlB, Grad LlB, Dip, LlM/MSc, PhD

School of Literatures, Languages and Cultures; www.ed.ac.uk/schools-departments/literatures-languages-cultures

Asian Studies; Chinese studies, E. Asian relations, Chinese & history/linguistics/history of art/economics/law, Japanese/& linguistics, Japanese society & culture, Chinese society & culture, law & China, Japanese, Japanese & linguistics, Japanese society & culture, Asian relations/religions/studies, Sanskrit, Prakit, & Pali language & literature

Celtic and Scottish Studies; Celtic & Scottish studies Scottish ethnology, Gaelic & primary education, Scottish culture & heritage, Scottish culture, Celtic

English Literature; book history & culture, US literature, creative writing, play writing, creative writing with online learning, book history & material culture, literature & society/enlightenment, romantic & Victorian, literature & modernity, 1900 to the modern day

European Languages and Cultures; French, German, Italian, Russian, Scandinavian, medieval literatures & cultures, comparative literature, film studies, translation studies, theatre & performance

Film; film studies, theatre & performance studies, film exhibition & curating

Islamic and Middle Eastern Studies; Persian studies/civilisation, advanced/Arabic, Middle East studies/with Arabic, Arabic/Islamic studies, European languages & cultures, English literature, European theatre, film studies, Islamic/Arabic & Middle

Eastern studies, Arabic, international relations of Middle East with Arabic, Arabic mentoring
Theatre Studies; theatre and performance studies, European theatre
Translation Studies; translation studies, English and Arabic/Chinese/Danish/French/German/Japanese/Norwegian/Spanish/Swedish/Turkish
MA(Hons), MSc, MPhil, PhD

Moray House School of Education; www.education.ed.ac.uk

primary education, primary education with Gaelic, PE, applied sports science, sport & recreation management, community education, childhood practice, PGDE (primary, secondary), academic practice, additional support for learning, community education, digital education, education, educational research, inclusive education, language teaching, social justice and community action, TESOL, learning for sustainability, language & literacy, creative approaches to literacy in secondary school teaching, creative literacies, art & design
Sport, Physical Education and Health Sciences; dance science and education, performance psychology, physical activity for health, PE (3-14), sport policy, management and international development, sports coaching & performance, strength and conditioning; PGDE (primary/secondary/Canadian); MA(Hons), BA(Hons), BSc(Hons), MSc, PGDip/Cert, MEd, EdD, MPhil, PhD

School of Philosophy, Psychology and Language Science; www.ppls.ed.ac.uk

Philosophy; ancient philosophy, cognition in science & society, epistemology, ethics and mind, mind, language & embodied cognition, philosophy, research philosophy
Psychology; cognition in science & society, human cognitive neuropsychology, individual differences, psychology of language, psychological research, evolution of language & cognition, developmental science, human cognitive neuroscience, parapsychology, psychology of reading, social psychology, visual cognition
Linguistics & English Language(LEL); applied linguistics, cognition in science & society, developmental linguistics, English language, evolution of language & cognition, linguistics, phonetics, speech & language processing, research English language/linguistics, linguistics & English language psychology of language, cognitive science; MA(Hons), BSc(Hons), MSc/Dip, MA, MPhil, PhD

School of Social & Political Science; www.sps.ed.ac.uk

international relations/& law, international relations with quantitative methods; politics with quantitative methods; social anthropology, social anthropology & politics; social anthropology & social policy/development/social history/ south Asian studies; social policy, social policy & law/politics/social & economic history/sociology/social & political studies/economics; social work, social policy with quantitative methods, global & international sociology, sociology, sociology & psychology/politics/social & economic history/social anthropology/South Asian studies/quantitative methods, the internet and society, genetics, nature and society, medical sociology armed force and society, sustainable development, politics, culture & screen in Canada, international relations with quantitative methods, social & political sciences with quantitative methods, social policy, politics, sociology
Postgrad Programmes; African studies, childhood studies, comparative public policy, global crime, justice and security, global environment, politics and society, global health & public policy, health equalities & public policy, health systems and public policy, international and European politics, international development, international political theory, international relations, international relations of the Middle East, Middle East with Arabic, management of bioeconomy, innovation and governance, medical anthropology, nationalism studies, policy studies, science and technology society, social anthropology, social research, sociology and global change, social work, advanced professional studies (mental health officer award), human rights; BSc(Hons), MA, MA(Hons), MPhil/PhD, MSc, PGDip/Cert, MSW, LlM, Dip

College of Medicine and Veterinary Medicine; www.ed.ac.uk/schools-departments/medicine-vet-medicine

medicine, surgery, medical sciences, veterinary medicine, biomedical sciences, child health, infectious diseases, neuroscience, pharmacology physiology, reproductive biology, animal bioscience, cognitive & neural systems, neural science/biology/developmental biology, genetics & genomics, public health, regenerative medicine: sciences biosciences, applied animal behaviour & welfare, cardiovascular biology, dental implantology, human anatomy, integrative neuroscience, oral surgery/health science, orthodontics, paediatric dentistry, prosthodontics, psychiatry, regenerative medicine; clinical & industrial delivery/ science, rehabilitation studies, communication & public health, transfusion, transplantation & tissue banking

School of Clinical Sciences; www.ed.ac.uk/ schools-departments/clinical-sciences

oral surgery, orthodontics, paediatric dentistry, prosthodontics, regenerative medicine: clinical and industrial delivery

School of Biomedical Sciences; www.ed.ac.uk/schools-departments/ biomedical-sciencesci

biomedical sciences, infectious diseases,, medical biology, medical sciences, neuroscience, physiology, reproductive biology, pharmacology, wildlife and ecosystem health, anatomical sciences, clinical microbiology and infectious diseases, global health and infectious diseases, science communication and public engagement

School of Molecular Genetics & Population Health Sciences

The Royal (Dick) School of Veterinary Studies; www.ed.ac.uk/schools- departments/vet

animal biolscience one health, advanced clinical practice, clinical animal behaviour, veterinary anaesthesia & analgesia, conservation medicine, international animal welfare, ethics & law, veterinary medicine & surgery, applied animal behaviour & animal welfare, equine science; BSc(Hons), MBChB, MSC, BVMS, DipCert, MPhil, PhD

College of Science and Engineering; www.scieng.ed.ac.uk

School of Biological Sciences; www.ed.ac.uk/schools-departments/ biology

biochemistry, bioinformatics, biological sciences/& management, biotechnology, cell biology, developmental regeneration & stem cells, ecology, evolutionary biology, genetics, immunology, medical biology, molecular biology, molecular genetics, plant science, zoology, biodiversity & taxonomy of plants, bioinformatics, drug discovery & translational biology, genetics & genome analysis, systems & synthetic biology, synthetic biology & biotechnology, mathematics & biology; BSc(Hons), MSc, MPhil, PhD

School of Chemistry; www.chem.ed.ac.uk

chemical physics, chemistry/with environmental & sustainable chemistry/materials chemistry, medicinal & biological chemistry, materials chemistry, medicinal & biological chemistry, sensor & imaging systems; BSc(Hons), MSc

School of Engineering; www.see.ed.ac.uk

Chemical Engineering with management, materials & processes, energy systems

Civil and Environmental Engineering: civil engineering, structural engineering with architecture/management, structural & fire safety engineering

Electronics and Electrical Engineering: electrical engineering/renewable energy, electronics & computer science/electronic engineering/with management, electronics & software engineering

Mechanical Engineering: advanced materials applications, electrical & mechanical engineering, fluid and particle dynamics, manufacturing & process optimization, mechanical engineering with management/ renewable energy, electrical & mechanical engineering

Institute for Energy Systems: environmental mitigation, energy delivery, renewable energy, restructuring and regulation, energy for sustainable environment

General Engineering; Engineering MSc Programmes adv chemical engineering, bioelectronics and biosensors, electronics, signal processing and communications, structural and fire safety engineering, sustainable energy systems, international master of science in fire safety engineering, structural engineering and mechanics, sensor and imaging systems; BEng(Hons), MEng(Hons), MSc, MPhil, PhD, EngD, PGDip

School of Geosciences; www.geos.ed.ac.uk

Ecological Sciences, Geography, earth science: geography, physical geography, geology, geophysics, meteorology, archaeology, GIS, ecological & environmental science, environmental geoscience, carbon capture & storage/management, carbon innovation, carbon management, earth observation & geoinformation management, environment, food security, culture and society, environment and development, environmental protection & management, environmental sustainability, GIS & archaeology, petroleum geoscience, sustainable resource management/plant health; BSc(Hons), MSc, MEnvSci, PGCert, PhD

School for Informatics; www.inf.ed.ac.uk

informatics, artificial intelligence, cognitive science, computer science, software engineering, adv/ design informatics; BEng(Hons), MEng(Hons), BSc(Hons), MSc, MInf, PhD, MPhil, data science

School of Mathematics; www.maths.ed.ac.uk

mathematics, applied mathematics, mathematics & statistics, mathematics & biology/business/management/music/physics, artificial intelligence & mathematics, operational research & statistics, computer science & mathematics, computational mathematical finance, financial mathematics, financial modelling &

optimisation, financial mathematics & modelling; BSc(Hons), MA, MSc, PhD, MMath

School of Physics and Astronomy; www.ph.ed.ac.uk

astrophysics, physics, chemical physics, computational physics, mathematical physics, theoretical physics, physics and computer sci/mathematics/meteorology/music, high performance computing with data, science; BSc, MChemPhys, MPhil, MPhys, MSc, PGDip, PhD

EDINBURGH NAPIER UNIVERSITY
www.napier.ac.uk

The Business School; www.napier.ac.uk/ business-school

Accounting; accounting, accounting with corporate finance/economics/entrepreneurship/HRM

Business; business and enterprise, business management, banking/entrepreneurship/events/finance/ HRM/ marketing and sales/marketing/sales/engineering with management, festival and event management with entrepreneurship, hospitality management with entrepreneurs, HRM with financial management, international business management/ and language, international business studies

Economics; accounting with economics, economics with management, business management (economics), festival and event and hospitality management/ marketing management/tourism management/festival and event management, festival and event management with entrepreneurship/HRM/language, international event and festival management

Finance; accounting and finance, accounting with corporate finance, banking & financial regulation, business management with finance, business studies with finance,financial services, global investment banking, international banking & finance hospitality

Hospitality; hospitality & marketing management/ service management/tourism management, hospitality management, hospitality management with entrepreneurship/HRM/language, business management/ business studies/festival and event management/ hospitality management with HRM

Human Resource Management; HRM with organisational psychology

Languages; international business management and language;

Management; business management, business management with finance/marketing, economics with

management, engineering with management, entrepreneurial leadership, business management (economics)

Marketing; accounting with marketing management, business management with marketing

Tourism; heritage and cultural tourism management, international marketing with tourism and events, international tourism management, tourism and airline management/hospitality management/ marketing management, tourism management, tourism management with entrepreneurship/HRM/language, MBA; (banking, entrepreneurship, events, executive, finance, health management, tourism and hospitality, HRM, leadership and innovation, leadership practice, marketing and sales); BA, BA(Hons), BSc(Hons) MSc, MBA, MPhil, LlB, LlM, PGCert

Faculty of Engineering, Computing and Creative Industries; www.napier.ac.uk/ fecci

School of Computing; www.napier.ac.uk/ soc/Pages/Home.aspx

advanced networking, adv materials project management/engineering, business information systems/ technology, computer network systems, computing/ science/SWE,computing for educators, creative computing, digital media/global networks, interactive media design, games development/technologies, information technology/systems development, adv security & cybercrime/digital forensics, adv/software engineering, project & programming management, sound design, web technologies/design/development, strategic ITC leadership; BEng/Hons, BSc/ Hons, MPhil, MSc, PhD

Arts & Creative Industries; www.napier.ac.uk/sci/Pages/ SchoolOfArtsCreativeIndustries.aspx

acting for stage & screen/& education, advertising, communication, advertising & PR, creative advertising/writing, digital media global,English/& acting/film, environmental graphics, exhibition design, film, graphic design, interactive media design, interaction/interdisciplinary design, international journalism for media professionals, interior architecture, journalism/for media professionals, lighting design, music, music/(pop), photography, pop music, product design/prototyping, magazine/publishing, motion graphics, publishing, screen screenwriting, spatial design,TV; BA, BA(Hons), BDes, BDes(Hons), BMus(Hons), MDes, MFA, MSc, PGCert/Dip, MA

Engineering & the Built Environment; www.napier.ac.uk/sebe/Pages/ default.aspx

architectural technology & building performance, adv materials engineering, adv structural engineering with management, automation & control, building surveying, biotechnology for environmental systems, civil engineering, civil & timber engineering/transportation, construction/& project/ management, electronic/computer/electrical engineering, energy & environmental engineering, engineering design/with management, environmental sustainability, mechanical engineering, mechatronics, polymer engineering, product design engineering, construction/& project management, project management, property development & valuation/investment/construction management, quantity surveying, adv/structural engineering, real estate surveying, safety & environmental management, renewable energy, timber industry management/engineering, transport management/planning and engineering; BSc, BSc(Hons), BEng, BEng(Hons), MEng, MSc, MSci, PGCert/Dip

Faculty of Health, Life & Social Science; www.napier.ac.uk/fhlss

Life, Sport & Social Sciences; www.napier.ac.uk/FHLSS/SLSSS/Pages/ Home.aspx

animal biology, advanced practice/applied criminology & forensic psychology/disability/child protection, biotechnology for environmental sustainability, career guidance & development, criminology, drug design & biomedical child protection/ healthcare management, psychology, sociology, social science, social research, environmental biology, forensic biology, marine & freshwater, social sciences, careers guidance, human performance, environmental sustainability & sociology, health & well being, business enterprise in sport, medical biotechnology, physical activity & health, psychology & sociology, veterinary psychology, sports & exercise science (coaching/sport performance, enhancement/conditioning/physiology/psychology/injury), wildlife biology & conservation, youth work; BSc(Hons), MSc, BA(Hons), PGCert/Dip, MPhil, MRes, PhD

School of Nursing, Midwifery and Social Care; www.napier.ac.uk/fhlss/NMSC/ Pages/SchoolofNursing.aspx

nursing studies, nursing – child health/adult/mental health/learning disabilities, midwifery, advanced practice (cancer care/child protection/neonatal nursing/diabetes nursing, care of people with epilepsy, nursing & applied education/palliative care/management), healthcare management, clinical research, epilepsy care, health administration, international clinical research & technology; BMid, BN, DipHE, MSc, PGDip/Cert, MRes, MPhil, PhD

UNIVERSITY OF ESSEX
www.essex.ac.uk

Faculty of Humanities and Comparative Studies; www.essex.ac.uk/hcs

History; www.essex.ac.uk/depts/ history.aspx

history (modern, social & cultural, American), film studies, joint honours in range of subjects, cultural & social, local & regional history, public history

Department of Literature, Film, and Theatre Studies; www.essex.ac.uk/depts/lifts.aspx

creative writing &/literature/film, drama/& literature/theatre studies/modern languages, American literature, English literature, English & United States literature, film studies, film & literature, literature & film studies, multimedia journalism, playwriting, wild writing literature, landscape & the environment

Dept of Philosophy & Art History; www.essex.ac.uk/depts/spah

Art History; art history,art history for academic purposes, art history & theory, museum management, philosophy & art history

Philosophy; philosophy, philosophy, religion & ethics, politics, philosophy & economics

Centre for Interdisciplinary Studies in the Humanities; www.essex.ac.uk/depts/centres-and-institutes/cish

Latin American Studies

Latin American studies with human rights/business management/modern languages/Spanish studies

European Studies

European studies/with politics or modern languages, government, law, philosophy & art history, sociology

American studies

American (US) studies with criminology/film, criminology & socio-legal research, organised crime, terrorism research & security, American literature

Liberal Arts

liberal arts with sociology/mathematics

BA(Hons), CertHE, Dip/MA, FdA, MA, MFA, MPhil, PGCert, PhD, LlB

Faculty of Social Sciences; www.essex.ac.uk/ss

Dept of Economics; www.essex.ac.uk/economics

economics, economic analysis for public policy, international economics, financial economics, financial economics and accounting, economics with mathematics, history and economics, economics with modern languages, behavioural economics, economics and econometrics, international economics, management economics; Postgraduate; money and banking, accounting and financial economics, computational economics, financial markets and policy, business economics, financial economics/& econometrics

Dept of Government; www.essex.ac.uk/government

politics, international relations, political economics, elections, public opinions and parties, political theory and public policy, philosophy, politics and economics, economics and politics, politics with human rights, politics/international relations and modern languages, sociology and politics, modern history and international relations/politics, philosophy and politics, law and politics, politics, political science,

multilevel governance in Europe, global and comparative politics, ideology and discourse analysis, international relations, conflict resolution, political economy, political theory, public opinion and political behaviour, international relations, political economy, politics, philosophy, politics and environmental issues, ethics, politics and public policy

Dept of Languages and Linguistics; www.essex.ac.uk/linguistics

modern languages, language studies, French/German/Italian/Portuguese/Spanish and modern languages, modern languages and linguistics, modern languages and English language/TEFL/linguistics, large number of jt degrees with modern languages, Spanish, Portuguese and Brazilian studies, European studies with modern languages, applied linguistics, English language and linguistics/language acquisition/language, TEFL, TESOL, translation, interpreting and subtitling, Chinese-English translation and interpreting, translation, interpreting and subtitling, translation and literature

Dept of Sociology; www.essex.ac.uk/sociology

sociology, communications and digital culture,,sociology and politics, sociology with human rights, sociology and social psychology,,history/philosophy and sociology, English language and sociology, literature and sociology, criminology, sociology and criminology, criminology with social psychology/American studies/social anthropology; Postgraduate; sociology, advertising, marketing and the media, criminology, criminology and socio-legal research, organised crime, terrorism and security, sociological research, survey methods for social research, sociology and management

BA(Hons), BSc(Hons), Diploma, GradDip, MA, MPhil, MRes, MSc, PGDip, PhD, ProcDoc

Faculty of Law and Management; www.essex.ac.uk/lm

Essex Business School; www.essex.ac.uk/ebs

Centre for Global Accountability; Centre for Entrepreneurship Research; Essex Finance Centre; Essex Management Centre

finance/management with Mandarin, accounting with economics/finance/financial management, marketing and management, business & entrepreneurship, banking and finance/with modern languages, finance, financial management, management and marketing, business management and modern languages, marketing, international business/marketing & entrepreneurship, accounting, banking & finance international accounting, international finance, finance and management, banking and finance, finance and investment, financial engineering and risk management/data analytics/global trading, HRM, international business & entrepreneurship, international management, marketing and brand management, entrepreneurship and innovation, global project management, organisation studies and international HRM, accounting and financial economics, computational finance and economics, international marketing & entrepreneurship, advertising, marketing & the media, marketing/and brand management, sociology and management, Essex MBA, MBA topics; BA(Hons), BSc(Hons), BBA, MA, MSc, MBA

Human Rights Centre; www.essex.ac.uk/humanrightscentre

human rights & Latin American studies/law/philosophy/politics/sociology, human rights & cultural diversity/public law, human rights theory & practice, international human rights law, humanitarian law, economics, social & cultural rights, research methods

School of Law; www.essex.ac.uk/law

law/ with philosophy/politics/business/human rights, community business & trade law, EU commercial law, human rights & cultural diversity, international human rights & humanitarian law, international commercial & business law, international trade law, theory & practice of human rights, human rights & public law; BA(Hons), BSc(Hons), DocProg, LlM, LlB, MPhil, MSc, PhD, MBA

Faculty of Science and Engineering; www.essex.ac.uk/se

Dept of Biological Sciences; www.essex.ac.uk/bs

biochemistry, biological sciences, cancer biology, biomedical science, biotechnology, environmental & resource management, genetics, tropical marine biology, molecular medicine, sports & exercise science

School of Computer Science and Electronic Engineering; www.essex.ac.uk/csee

adv/computer science/systems, computer games, computer networks, information and communication technology, computer science, data science and analytics, computer systems engineering, computers with electronics, electronic engineering, telecommunication engineering, electronic engineering, computational finance, advanced computer science, advanced web engineering, artificial intelligence, big data and text analytics, cloud computing, computer engineering, data science, embedded systems, intelligent systems and robotics, computer networks and security, computational financial computing, algorithmic trading, telecommunications engineering

School of Health and Human Sciences; www.essex.ac.uk/hss

adult/mental health nursing, health sciences (care of the adult/mental health), public health, midwifery, clinical psychology, psychological wellbeing practitioner, oral health sciences (hygiene/therapy), speech & language/occupational therapy, physiotherapy, healthcare practice, CPD, social work, sports therapy, health research

Department of Mathematical Sciences; www.essex.ac.uk/maths

mathematics, actuarial science, mathematics & computing/economics/finance/statistics/physics, computing & mathematics, data science/ & analytics, discrete mathematics & its applications, econometrics, financial decision-making with applications, mathematics & economics/physics/modern languages/humanities, operational research & computer science, statistics & data analysis/computer science/econometrics/operational research, mathematics for secondary teaching

Dept of Psychology; www.essex.ac.uk/psychology

advanced/psychology, cognitive neuropsychology/neuroscience, psychology with cognitive neuroscience, research methods in psychology, language & the brain; BA(Hons), BEng, BSc(Hons), GradDip, MA, MPhil, MRes, MSc, PGDip, PhD, ProfDoc

Degrees validated by the University of Essex offered at:

WRITTLE COLLEGE
www.writtle.ac.uk

agriculture, arable crop management/farm, livestock production/sustainable environments, animal science, livestock protection science, animal welfare & conservation, animal management, horticulture, horticultural crop production, post-harvesting technology, garden design, historic designed landscape, landscape architecture, landscape and garden, applied equine science design, garden design, contemporary/art and design, professional floristry, conservation and environment, conservation management, equine behaviour/performance and business management, sports therapy and rehabilitation, veterinary physiology, bioveterinary science, sport & exercise performance, conservation management, energy resources management; BA(Hons), BSc(Hons), CertMS, Certs, DipMS, FdA, Higher Cert, MA, MBA, MSc, PGCert/Dip

UNIVERSITY OF EXETER
www.exeter.ac.uk

University of Exeter Business School; www.business-school.exeter.ac.uk

Accounting & Finance; accounting and finance, business and accounting

Business & Management; business, business and management, management with marketing, business, business and accounting, management and leadership

Economics; economics, business economics, economics with econometrics, economics and finance, economics and politics

Postgraduate; accounting and finance, accounting and tax, financial analysis and fund management, finance and investment, finance and management, marketing and financial services, money and banking, international management, MBA – the one planet MBA, marketing, international tourism management, international tourism and hospitality management, digital economy, management, economics, economics and econometrics, behavioural economics and finance, financial economics, money and banking, engineering business management financial mathematics, international supply chain management, IT management for business

BSc, BA(Hons), MBA, MPhil, MSc, MRes, PGDip/Cert, PhD

College of Engineering, Mathematics & Physical Sciences; www.emps.exeter.ac.uk/ engineering

Computer Science: IT management for business, computer science/& mathematics, artificial intelligence

Engineering: civil engineering, civil and environmental engineering, electronic engineering, electronic engineering and computer science, energy engineering, engineering and management, materials engineering, mechanical engineering (all above degrees available with international study or industrial experience), engineering, engineering business management

Postgrad: engineering business management, international supply chain management, civil engineering, materials engineering, mechanical engineering, structural engineering, water engineering, civil engineering/materials engineering/mechanical engineering/structural engineering/water engineering with management

Geology: applied geology, engineering geology & geotechnics, mining geology, applied geotechnics

Mathematics: adv/mathematics, mathematical biology, mathematics with computer science/accounting/finance/management/economics/physics, financial management, natural science, financial mathematics, fluid dynamics, mathematics (climate science/mathematical biology/geophysical & astrophysical), mathematics with business & finance/computer science, engineering mathematics, computational mathematics

Minerals & Mining Engineering: minerals/mining engineering, mining geology, surveying & land/environmental management, mining life cycle

Natural Sciences: natural sciences

Physics & Astronomy: physics/with astrophysics, biomedical physics, quantum systems, electromagnetic & acoustic materials, nanomaterials, natural science, mathematics & physics; BSc(Hons), BEng, MEng, MSc, MPhil, PhD, MPhys, MMath MPhys, MSci, PGCert/Dip, MGeol

College of Humanities; www.humanities.exeter.ac.uk

Archaeology: archaeology, archaeology and anthropology, archaeology with forensic science, ancient/history and archaeology, bioarchaeology, experimental archaeology

Art History & Visual Culture; art history & visual culture/classics/history/English/modern languages, drama

Classics & Ancient History: ancient history, classical studies, classics, ancient history and archaeology, art history and classical studies, classical studies and English/modern language/ philosophy/theology/French and Latin/history, classics & ancient history

Drama: drama, theatre practice, staging Shakespeare, drama & visual culture/English

English: English, English & history/geography/drama/film studies/modern language/art history/classical studies, English literary studies, American & Atlantic studies, enlightenment to romanticism, Renaissance literature, modern & contemporary, film studies, creative writing, criticism & theory

Film Studies: film studies/with English, modern languages, international film business

History: history & English/philosophy/visual culture/international relations/politics/art history/modern languages/archaeology, ancient history, early modern history, medieval studies, western esotericism, medieval studies, maritime/medical history, war & society, economic & social history

Liberal Arts: liberal arts

Theology & Religion: theology, classical studies, philosophy; BA, BSc, MPhil, PhD

College of Life & Environmental Sciences; www.lifesciences.exeter.ac.uk

Biosciences: animal behaviour, conservation biology and ecology, environmental sciences, evolutionary biology, human sciences/biosciences, marine biology, zoology, biological sciences, biochemistry, biological and medicinal chemistry, applied ecology, conservation and biodiversity, conservation science and policy, evolutionary and behavioural ecology, food security & sustainable agriculture

Geography: geography, environmental science, climate change/& risk management, conservation science & policy, environment energy & resilience, feedback & resilience, critical human geography/science, sustainable development, human/physical geography

Psychology: psychology, animal behaviour, applied psychology (clinical), social & organizational psychology, psychology with sports & exercise science, mindfulness-based cognitive therapy & approaches, psychology research methods

Sport and Health Sciences: paediatric/exercise & health, psychology with sport & exercise science, health & wellbeing, exercise & sport sciences, human biosciences, sport & exercise medical sciences;;MPhil, BA(Hons),DocClinPsy, MSc, PhD, PGCert/Dip, MRes, BClinSci, MSci, BSc(Hons),

College of Social Science & International Studies; www.social sciences.exeter.ac.uk

Arabic & Islamic studies: Arabic & Islamic studies/Middle East studies, politics & international relations in the Middle East, Kurdish/East/Persian/Palestine/Gulf/Iranian studies, ethnopolitics, Middle East history

Graduate School of Education

special educational needs, education, TESOL, educational psychology, childhood & youth studies, English & education, sport science, professional studies, PGCE: primary; English, mathematics, humanities, music, science; 7-11; art, modern languages, main secondary subjects, schools direct, teaching first training, intercultural teaching programme, art/music/science/modern foreign languages, early years, secondary sciences/design & technology/English with media/drama/modern foreign languages/geography/information, post compulsory education; MA topics; creative arts in education, language and literacy, mathematics education, science education, special educational needs, technology, creativity and thinking, creative arts in education, language and literacy, mathematics education, science education, special educational needs, technology, creativity and thinking, EdD generic/educational psychology/SNE/TESOL), educational research

School of Law

law, European (maitrise) law, international commercial/property law, international human rights law, intellectual property law, sociolegal research, legal practice, maritime law

Politics; politics/& international relations, politics, philosophy & economics, number of joint degrees with politics, history/ & politics, conflict, security & development, international relations/studies (& jt degrees), European politics, political thought, public administration, public administration, politics & international relations of the Middle East, applied security strategy,, security, conflict & justice

Sociology, Philosophy & Archaeology: sociology/& anthropology/criminology, philosophy, archaeology & anthropology, sociology & anthropology/criminology, politics, philosophy & economics, philosophy & sociology of science, sociology & politics, philosophy, science & technology studies

Strategy & Security Institute; applied security studies; BA(Hons), MA, PhD, MPhil, MA, PhD, LlB, LlM, MRes, DEdPsych, EdD, MEd, MPubAdmin, MArabic

University of Exeter Medical School; www.exeter.ac.uk/medicine

clinical sciences, environmental & human health, medicine, surgery, medical sciences, applied health services research, surgery, medical imaging diagnostic radiography, sport and exercise, environment and human health, genomic medicine, clinical education, health services improvement; BClinSci, BMBS, MSc, MS, MPhil, PhD, MD, PhD, MSc, PGDip/Cert, PGCE

Degrees validated by University of Exeter offered at:

UNIVERSITY OF ST MARK & ST JOHN
www.marjon.ac.uk

accounting, acting, business management for the armed forces, armed forces, sport, fitness and health science, business law, business management, children and families, clinical exercise physiology,early childhood education, early childhood studies, early years, education studies, English and creative writing, English language & linguistics, football coaching and development, global education, health and social care, journalism, learning support, education – professional development, business administration, music production, nutrition, osteopath, osteopathic medicine, outdoor adventure education, performing arts education, early years with initial teacher training, PGCE; primary; secondary education with drama/ geography/media studies/ modern foreign languages/PE/RE/ physical education – secondary education (with QTS)/ coaching and mentoring, primary education/with QTS/early years/, add professional studies (English literature/leadership & management)/ sport and health sciences/sport development, outdoor education, outdoor learning, psychology, public health, rehabilitation in sport and exercise, school direct, social policy, social sciences, sociology, special educational needs & disability studies, speech and language sciences/therapy, sport and exercise science, sport coaching, sport development (sport management), sport development, sport rehabilitation, sport, physical activity and health, sport journalism, sports therapy, strength and conditioning, TESOL, youth and community work; BA(Hons), BA/BSc, BEd, FdA/Sc, MTL, BEd(Hons), MA, MEd, MSc, MOst,MBA, PGDip/Cert,MPH

FALMOUTH UNIVERSITY
www.falmouth.ac.uk

Falmouth School of Art
drawing, fine art, illustration, authorial practice

School of Architecture & Interior Design
business enterprise, interior design, sustainable product design

School of Communication Design
creative advertising, graphic design

Fashion & Textiles Institute
fashion design/marketing/photography, performance sportswear design, textile design

Academy of Innovation & Research
business enterprise

School of Film & TV
animation & visual effects, film, TV

Academy of Music & Theatre Arts
creative events management, music theatre & entertainment management, acting, music, dance & choreography, creative music technology, music, pop

School of Writing & Journalism
creative writing/& journalism, English, journalism & communication/creative writing, English & journalism/creative writing, sports journalism

Games Academy
computing for games, digital games
BA(Hons), Foundation Dip, MPhil, PhD, FdA, PGDip, MA, MFA

College of Arts; www.gla.ac.uk/colleges/arts

School of Critical Studies
English language/literature/English linguistics, Scottish literature, theology & religious studies, political Islam, creative writing, fantasy, medieval & Renaissance studies, literature, theory & culture, religion, literature & culture, Victorian literature, value based practice (faith communities/health & social care/peace-building), spiritual & religious care in health & social care

School of Culture & Creative Arts
electronics & music, film & TV studies, history of art/art world practice, music, theatre studies; Postgrad; art history, art, politics, transgression, 20th century avant-gardes/collecting and provenance in an international context/dress and textile histories/technical art history, making & meaning/the Renaissance in northern Europe and Italy, art in Germany kunst in Deutschland, creative industries and cultural policy creative practice, curatorial practice (contemporary art),film & TV studies, film curation, filmmaking and media arts, historically informed performance practice, media management, museum studies, music industries, playwriting & dramaturgy, sonic arts, textile conservation, theatre practices, theatre studies

School of Humanities
archaeology, Celtic civilisation/studies, classics, classical civilisations, digital media & information studies, Gaelic, Greek, history, Latin, philosophy, Scottish history, American studies, ancient cultures, Celtic & Viking archaeology, Celtic studies, classics, conflict archaeology & heritage, early modern history, history, information management & preservation (digital)/(archives & records management), material culture & artefact studies, medieval history, museum studies, music studies, philosophy, Scottish history, war studies

School of Modern Languages & Cultures
comparative literature, French, German, Hispanic studies, Italian, Portuguese, Russian, Spanish, comparative literature, cultures, societies & language, modern languages & cultures, translation studies, translation & professional practice, TESOL; BD(Min), BMus, DLitt, MA, MA(Hons), MLitt, MPhil, MTh, PhD, MFA, PGCert/Dip, MSc, MMus

College of Medical Veterinary & Life Sciences; www.gla.ac.uk/colleges/mvls
Institutes: Biodiversity, Animal Health & Comparative Medicine; Cancer Sciences, Cardiovascular & Medical Science, Health & Wellbeing, Infection, Immunity & Inflammation, Molecular, Cell & Systems Biology, Neuroscience & Psychology;
Postgrad: Biomedical Science, biotechnology, infection biology, cancer sciences, bioinformatics, polyomics & systems biology

School of Life Sciences
anatomy, biochemistry, genetics, human biology, human biology & nutrition, immunology, marine & freshwater biology, microbiology, molecular & cellular biology, molecular & cellular biology (with biotechnology/ plant science), neuroscience, parasitology, pharmacology, physiology, physiology & sports science, physiology, sports science & nutrition, virology, zoology; Postgraduate; bioinformatics, polyomics and systems biology, biomedical sciences, biomedical sciences, human anatomy, medical visualisation & human anatomy
Medical & Clinical Sciences; clinical sciences, translational medical sciences, forensic toxicology, clinical trials & stratified medicine, human nutrition, medical physics, health professions education, medical

genetics, oral & maxillofacial surgery, endodontics, fixed & removable prosthodontics

Animal & Plant Sciences; veterinary public health, animal welfare, science, ethics and law, quantitative methods in biodiversity, conservation & epidemiology, ecology and environmental biology, food security

Cardiovascular & Pharmacology; cardiovascular science; diabetes, clinical pharmacology, sport and exercise science & medicine, forensic toxicology

Health and Wellbeing; global mental health, health technology assessment, primary care, advanced practice in health care

Neuroscience & Psychology; brain sciences: from molecules to mind, applied neuropsychology

School of Medicine; www.gla.ac.uk/medicine

dentistry, medicine, nursing (community, adult, surgical, children, public health), advanced lymphoedema management, advanced practice in health care, child health, clinical nutrition, endodontics, fixed & removable prosthodontics, forensic toxicology, health-professions education, healthcare chaplaincy, human nutrition, medical genetics, medical physics, translational medical sciences, genetic and genomic counselling, leading, improving and transforming care, medical genetics and genomics, nursing: see advanced practice in health care, oral & maxillofacial surgery, orthodontics, spiritual and religious care in health and social care, sports nutrition

School of Veterinary Medicine; www.gla.ac.uk/schools/vet

animal welfare science, ethics & law, quantitative methods in diversity, conservation & epidemiology, veterinary biosciences, animal reproduction, veterinary medicine & surgery, biomedical sciences, veterinary public health, global veterinary medicine, zoonoses and infectious disease, veterinary epidemiology: quantitative methods, hygienic production of food, veterinary epidemiology: methods in surveillance and filed investigation

BSc, BSc(Vet Sci), BVMS, MVPH, PhD, B(MedSci), MSc(MedSci/DentSci), MBChB, MD, MML, MMLE, MPC, MPH, PhD, BDS, BSc(Dent Sc), DDS, MSc, PGDip/Cert, MRes

College of Science & Engineering; www.gla.ac.uk/colleges/scienceengineering

School of Chemistry; www.gla.ac.uk/schools/chemistry

chemistry, chemical physics, medical chemistry

School of Engineering; www.gla.ac.uk/schools/engineering

aeronautical engineering, aerospace systems, biomedical engineering, civil engineering, civil engineering with architecture, electronic & software engineering, electronics & electrical engineering, electronics with music, mechanical design engineering, mechanical engineering, mechanical engineering with aeronautics, mechatronics, product design engineering

Postgrad; aeronautical engineering, aerospace engineering & management, aerospace systems, biomedical engineering, civil engineering/& management, computer systems engineering, electronics & electrical engineering/& management, mechanical engineering/ & management, mechatronics nanoscience and nanotechnology, product design engineering, structural engineering & mechanics, sustainable energy

School of Computing Science; www.gla.ac.uk/schools/computing

computing science (numerous jt degrees incl physics/mathematics), informatics, data science, electronic & software engineering/development, mobile/software engineering, software engineering, information/security/technology

School of Geographical & Earth Sciences; www.gla.ac.uk/schools/ges

archaeology/geography, earth sciences, geography, business economics/geography, numerous jt degrees, central & east European studies/geographaquatic system science, coastal system management, freshwater system science, geoinformation technology and cartography, geomatics & management, geospatial and mapping sciences, human geography: spaces, politics & ecologies, marine system science

School of Mathematics & Statistics; www.gla.ac.uk/schools/mathematicsstatistics

mathematics, applied/pure mathematics, finance/accounting & mathematics/statistics, biostatistics, adv/statistics, environmental/social statistics, financial modelling/finance, statistics

School of Physics & Astronomy; www.gla.ac.uk/schools/physics

astronomy, physics, chemical/theoretical physics, astrophysics, physics: advanced materials/energy & the environment/global security/life sciences/nuclear technology, sensor & imaging systems

School of Psychology; www.gla.ac.uk/schools/psychology

psychology, brain imaging/sciences psychological studies/science, research methods
BEng, BSc, EngD, MEng, MSc, PGDip, PhD, EngD, PGDip, MRes

College of Social Sciences; www.gla.ac.uk/schools/social sciences

Adam Smith Business School; www.gla.ac.uk/schools/business

Business & Management; business & management with archaeology/Celtic civilisation/music/philosophy/Russian/Scottish history/Scottish literature/Spanish/Celtic studies/classics/comparative literature/digital media & information studies/English literature/French/Gaelic/German/history of art/history/Italian/Latin/Portuguese/theology & religious studies/mathematics/social & public policy/computing science/economic & social history/geography/sociology/law

Business Economics; business economics with computing science/ law/archaeology/business & management/economic & social history/geography/mathematics/philosophy/politics/psychology/Scottish history/social & public policy/sociology/central & east European studies/business economics

Economics; economics with accountancy/mathematics/statistics/law/comparative literature/English language/English literature/French/Greek/history/music/philosophy/Russian/Scottish history/theatre studies/theology & religious studies/German/Spanish/archaeology/central & east European studies, economic & social history/business & management/Celtic civilisation/geography/politics/psychology/social & public policy/sociology

Postgraduate; asset pricing & investment, banking & financial services, biotechnology & management, corporate governance & accountability, development studies, economic development, economics, banking & finance, environment & sustainable development, finance & economic development, finance & management, financial economics, financial forecasting & investment, financial modelling, financial risk management, international accounting & financial management, international banking & finance/business & entrepreneurship/corporate finance & banking/development/finance/finance & economic policy/financial analysis/management & design innovation/management & leadership/real estate & management/strategic marketing/trade & finance, investment banking & finance/investment fund management, management, management with enterprise & business growth/HR/international finance, business administration, quantitative; LlB, finance; BA, BSc, MA, MAQ(SocSci), MAcc, MBA, MFin, MSc, PhD, MPA, MBA

School of Education; www.gla.ac.uk/schools/education

childhood practice, community development, education with teaching qualification (primary), music, primary education with teaching qualification, religious & philosophical education, technological education

Postgraduate; academic practice, adult & continuing education, adult education for social change, childhood practice, children's literature & literacies, community learning & development, education, education (primary/secondary), education, public policy & equity, educational studies, inclusive education: research, policy & practice, learning & teaching in HE, learning and teaching of modern languages in the primary school, middle leadership and management in schools, museum education, professional learning & enquiry, professional practice with PGDE, teacher leadership and learning, teaching adults, TESOL: teaching of English to speakers of other languages, youth studies; BA(Hons), BTechEd, BEd, BTechS, EdD, MA, MA(Hons), MEd, MLitt, MSc, MusicBEd, PhD, IM, MEd, PGDE

School of Interdisciplinary Studies; www.gla.ac.uk/schools/interdisciplinary

environmental science & sustainability, health & social policy, primary education with teaching qualification, enhanced practice in education, environment, culture & communication, environmental science, technology & society, tourism, heritage & development, tourism, heritage & sustainability
BSc, MA, MLitt, PGCert/Dip, MSc, TQ

School of Law; www.gla.ac.uk/schools/law

law with/business & management/business economics/economic & social history/economics/English literature/Gaelic language/history/philosophy/politics/social & public policy; Postgraduate; corporate & financial law, professional legal practice, intellectual property & the digital economy, intellectual property, innovation and the creative economy, international commercial law, international competition law & policy, international law, international law & security, law, socio-legal studies; MRes, LlB, LlM, MRes, PGDip/Cert, PhD

School of Social & Political Science; www.ac.uk/schools/socialpolitical

Central & East European Studies, Economic & Social History, Politics, Social & Public Policy, Sociology; in combination with one of the following: Celtic civilisation/Celtic studies/classics, digital media & information/English literature/German/history of art/ Italian/Latin/Scottish history/Scottish literature/comparative literature/Gaelic/philosophy/Portuguese/ Russian/Spanish/business economics/economics/geography/history/mathematics, politics/psychology/ public policy/law/economic & social history & archaeology/Celtic studies/French/history/music/ Scottish history/computing science/business & management/politics /public policy/Scottish history/politics & law/archaeology/English language/film & television studies/French/ Greek/history/music/

philosophy/theatre studies/ theology & religious studies; Postgraduate; antiquities trafficking & art crime, Chinese studies, city & regional planning, city planning & real estate development, city planning & regeneration, criminology/ & criminal justice, equality & human rights, global economy, global markets, local creativities, global security, history/ history of medicine, housing studies, human rights & international politics, international planning studies, international real estate/& management, international relations, international security, intelligence & strategic studies, media, communications & international journalism, political communication, public and urban policy, public policy & management, public policy research, real estate, real estate & regeneration, Russian for social scientists, Russian language, Russian, central & east European studies, Russian, east European & Eurasian studies, sociology, sociology & research methods, spatial planning, transnational crime, justice & security, urban research, urban transport; MA, MA(SocSci), MSc, MRes, CPD, MLitt, EdD, PhD, PGCert/Dip, IM

GLASGOW CALEDONIAN UNIVERSITY
www.gcu.ac.uk/ebe

School of Engineering & the Built Environment; www.caledonian.ac.uk/ebe

animation & visualisation, audio systems engineering technology, building services engineering, computer aided mechanical engineering, computer games (art & animation/design/software development/indie development), computing, computer aided material, construction management, cyber security ethical, electrical & electronic engineering/energy engineering, power engineering, energy & environmental management/oil & gas, environmental civil engineering/management & planning, fire risk engineering, forensic investigation, graphic design for digital media, engineering, health & safety & environmental management, interior design, mechanical & power plant systems, mechanical electronic systems engineering, mechanical engineering design/manufacture, management & valuation, networked systems security, quantity surveying, real estate management, software development for business, sustainable energy technology/management

Postgraduate; applied instrumentation and control, applied instrumentation and control (oil & gas), big

data technologies, big data technologies, building services engineering, applied instrumentation and control, applied instrumentation and control (oil & gas), big data technologies, building services engineering, climate justice, computer science, construction management, electrical and electronic engineering, energy & environmental management, international project management (oil and gas), maintenance, management (oil & gas), mechanical engineering with options in design or manufacture, quantity surveying, sustainable urban environments, telecommunications engineering; BA/BA(Hons), BEng/BEng(Hons), BSc/BSc(Hons), DipHE, MA/ PGD, MSc/PGDip, PhD, FD, Dips

Glasgow School for Business & Society; www.caledonian.ac.uk/cbs

accountancy, business/& management, economics & finance/law/risk, finance, investment & risk, law with risk, international business & hospitality management/marketing/tourism management/finance/international fashion/language, international business & economics/finance/business/sports management/

event management/fashion branding, international development/business management/fashion marketing/marketing/retail management/supply chain management, international sports management/tourist management, law, media communication,multimedia journalism, risk & law/management, risk & law, social science & media, social enterprise, social sciences, risk management, international banking, finance and risk management, international business management, international economics and finance, international HRM, international marketing, international operations and supply chain management, international tourism management, management, multimedia journalism, risk management, risk management (oil & gas), social business and microfinance, TV fiction writing
BA(Hons), MRes, PhD, LlB, LlM, MSc, PGD/C, PhD, MBA

School of Health & Life Sciences; www.caledonian.ac.uk/hls
adv nursing practice, adv practice in district nursing, applied psychology, applied/biomedical science, biomolecular & biomedical science, cellular molecular biology, clinical microbiology, clinical nutrition & health/physiology, diagnostic imaging studies, clinical ophthalmology & vision, counselling & psychology, diabetes care & management, dietetics, digital health, education in /health & social care/adv professional practice, food bioscience, forensic psychology, human nutrition & dietetics, human bioscience, life sciences, medical ultrasound, microbiology, nursing (adult/child/mental health/learning disabilities), nursing studies, occupational therapy, optometry, orthoptics, ophthalmic dispensing, oral health science, pharmacology, podiatry, professional studies in nursing, physiotherapy, public health, radiography, radiotherapy & oncology, specialist community public health nursing (health visiting), social work, theory of podiatric surgery, pharmacology, psychology; BSc, BSc(Hons), DipHE, DPsych, MSc, Ophth-Disp, PGCert/Dip, PhD, MRes, BSc(Hons), BA(Hons), GradCert, MPhil, MSc, PGCert/Dip, PhD, ProfDoc, BMidwifery, BN

THE GLASGOW SCHOOL OF ART
www.gsa.ac.uk

architecture/studies, communication design, cultural practice(contemporary art, design innovation & citizenship/environment, engineering with architecture, fashion design, fine art photography, interactive design, interior/silversmithing & jewellery/fashion & textiles/product design engineering, fine art practice, graphics, graphic illustrative photography, interior design, international management & design/ innovation, international teaching & learning, medical visualisation & human anatomy, painting & printmaking, product design engineering, sculpture & environmental art, serious games design & virtual technology, sound for the moving media; BA(Hons), BEng, BArch, DipArch, MA, MArch, MDes, MEng, MPhil, MRes, PhD, MFA, PGCert

UNIVERSITY OF GLOUCESTERSHIRE
www.glos.ac.uk

School of Art & Design; insight.glos.ac.uk/ academicschools/art-and-design.aspx
advertising, fashion/interior/graphic design, fine art, illustration, photojournalism & documentary philosophy, photography/editorial & advertising, illustration, landscape architecture, visual communication

The Business School; School of Business & Management; insight.glos.ac.uk/ academicschools/business.aspx
accounting & business management/financial management/finance, business administration (MBA), business & marketing management, business management & strategy, business/information technology, economics, international business studies, marketing, advertising & branding, strategy, law, marketing management & branding/advertising, management

studies, hospitality management, HRM/strategy, marketing, retail management, tourism management

School of Media; insight.glos.ac.uk/academicschools/media.aspx

animation,creative music technology, film/production/studies, sport/journalism, mass communication, media production, music business, pop music, radio/TV production, magazine publishing & production, music & media management

School of Computing & Technology; insight.glos.ac.uk/academicschools/computing-and-technology.aspx

business information computing, computing, computer & cyber forensics computing, information technology, computer games design, multimedia web design, product design, dependable software, integrated engineering, IT management, information security, digital media & web technology

School of Humanities; insight.glos.ac.uk/academicschools/humanities.aspx

creative writing, English literature/language, history, languages, religion, philosophy & ethics, theology & religious studies, creative & critical writing, philosophical & religious thought

School of Leisure; insight.glos.ac.uk/academicschools/leisure.aspx

drama, events management, critical & creative writing, events tourism/hotel and resort/ hotel resort and events/ hotel resort and tourism management, performing arts, sports management and development, strategic events/hospitality/sports/tourism management, tourism management, hospitality and tourism management, professional studies/in children's play, philosophy & religious thought

School of Natural & Social Sciences; insight.glos.ac.uk/academicschools/natural-and-social-sciences.aspx

applied ecology, animal biology, biology, counselling, criminology, ecology & environmental science, geography, psychology/& criminology/sociology, sociology, sustainable environment, applied social sciences, applied/business/criminal/forensic/occupational psychology

School of Sport & Exercise; insight.glos.ac.uk/academicschools/sport-and-exercise.aspx

sports management & conditioning, applied sport and exercise studies, professional practice in sport coaching/therapy, exercise, fitness & health, PE & coaching, sport and exercise sciences, sports coaching and development/education, sports fitness and physical activity, sports leadership/strength and conditioning/therapy, physical activity, exercise and health practice, psychology of sport & exercise, sport and exercise psychology, sports therapy

School of Health & Social Care; glos.ac.uk/academicschools/health-and-social-care-aspx

children and young people's practice, community and district nursing specialist practice, community and health management, health and social care practice, health community and social care, mental health practice, social work, advancing practice (health), community and district nursing specialist practice, community and primary care practice, youth work

School of Education; insight.glos.ac.uk/academicschools/education

early years, education and learning, early childhood studies with early years initial teacher training, early childhood studies, education & learning, education studies/leadership, health, teacher training, youth studies, QTS (primary and secondary), educational leadership, inclusive education, mentoring & coaching, professional studies in childrens' play/education, PGCE (primary/secondary), practice teacher, post-compulsory education & training, teaching studies; BA/BA(Hons), BSc/BSc(Hons), DipSW, BEd, LlB, MA, MPhil, MRes, MSc, PGCert/Dip, MBA, CMS, DMS, FD, GradDip/Cert, CertHE

GLYNDWR UNIVERSITY
www.glyndwr.ac.uk

Undergraduate Subjects

Animal & Plant Biology

Animal Studies and Equine Science

animal studies, equine science and welfare management, wildlife and plant biology

Art and Design

Applied Art, Design Communication & Digital Art; design/animation, visual effects and game art, design/film and photography, design/graphic design and multimedia, design/illustration, graphic novels and children, publishing, fine art

Building Studies

architectural design technology, construction management, real estate; housing; housing and sustainable communities, housing studies

Business

accounting and finance, applied business, business entrepreneurship, global business, marketing and consumer psychology, hospitality tourism and event management, sports management

Complementary Medicine

acupuncture, complementary therapies for healthcare, rehabilitation and injury management

Computing

computing, computer science, computer game development, computer network and security, computing philosophy, creative computing, immersive technology, intelligent computing, library and information management/information practice, telecommunications

Creative Media Technology

music technology, sound technology, television production and technology

Criminal Justice

criminology and criminal justice

Education, Family & Childhood Studies

Childhood Studies

education and childhood studies, families and childhood studies, childhood studies: families and young children/education/special educational needs, childhood studies

Education

education (ALN/SEN), education (counselling skills and psychology), education studies, person-centred and experiential counselling and psychotherapy

Engineering and Applied Physics

aeronautical and mechanical engineering/manufacturing; electrical and electronic engineering, industrial engineering, performance car technology, motorsport design and management, renewable energy and sustainable technologies

Health, Psychology & Social Care

person-centred and experiential counselling and psychotherapy, health and social care, health, wellbeing and community, community specialist practice (district nursing), healthcare leadership and management, specialist community public health nursing (health visiting/school nursing), occupational therapy, psychology

Humanities

broadcasting, journalism and media communications, journalism, history and creative writing, English and creative writing, English, English and history, history, information management, library and information practice/management, theatre, TV and performance

Science and Environment

chemistry with green nanotechnology, forensic science, geography, ecology and environment

Social Care

social work, therapeutic child care, health and social care

Sport & Exercise Sciences

sport & exercise sciences, sport coaching, sports management; FdSc, BSc(Hons), BA(Hons), MA, MDes, MComp, MEng, BEng, DipHE, FdA

Youth and Community

youth and community work

Postgraduate Degrees

Aeronautical and Mechanical Engineering

aeronautical engineering, aircraft design, aircraft structure, engineering, mechanical manufacturing

Art and Design

art practice, design practice

Built Environment

Business and Management

HRM, business administration, management

Complementary Therapies; Humanities; Mechatronics

Computing

computer networking, learning and technology, computer science, media technology

Creative Media Technology

Education;

education, professional development in HE, learning and technology, professional development (education)

Electrical Engineering;

electrical power engineering, electronic engineering, mechatronics, renewable engineering and sustainable energy

Health and Medical Sciences

advanced clinical practice, health sciences, specialist community public health nursing; Postgraduate; diplo specialist community public health nursing (school nursing), specialist community public health nursing (health visiting)

Psychology

psychology of religion

Science and Environment

formulation science, polymer & biopolymer science

Society and Community

social care, social work, education (youth and community work), education (counselling children and young people), education (counselling skills for education)

CriminalJustice

criminology and criminal justice

Sport and Exercise Sciences

MA, MSc, MPhil, PhD, MRes, PGCert/Dip, ProfDoc, MBA, EdD, GradDip, LlM

accounting, acupuncture,aeronautical and mechanical engineering/manufacturing, animal studies, applied arts, applied business, architectural design technology, broadcasting and journalism, business, chemistry with green nanotechnology, childhood studies, community specialist practice (district nursing), complementary therapies for healthcare, computer game development, computer networks and security computer science, computing, computing

philosophy, construction management, counselling and psychotherapy, creative computing criminology and criminal justice, design: animation, visual effects and game art, design: film and photography, design: graphic design and multimedia, design: illustration, graphic novels and children, publishing, district nursing (community specialist practice), education and childhood studies, education (ALN/SEN), education (counselling skills and psychology), education studies, electrical and electronic engineering, English, English and history/creative writing, entrepreneurship, families and childhood studies, film and photography, fine art, forensic science, geography, ecology and environment, graphic design and multimedia, global business, health and social care, health visiting/wellbeing and community, healthcare leadership and management, history/ and creative writing, housing and sustainable communities, housing studies, hospitality, tourism and event management, illustration, graphic novels & children's publishing, industrial engineering industrial engineering, intelligent computing, immersive technology, journalism, library and information management, marketing and consumer psychology, motorsport design and management, music technology, occupational therapy, performance car technology, psychology, real estate, renewable energy and sustainable technologies, rehabilitation and injury management, social work, sound technology, specialist community public health nursing (health visiting/school nursing), sport and exercise sciences, sport coaching, sports management, TV production and technology, telecommunications, theatre TV and performance, therapeutic child care, wildlife and plant biology, youth and community work

Postgraduate and Professional

advanced clinical nursing practice, aeronautical engineering, aircraft design, aircraft structure, art practice, business administration clinical practice, computer networking, computer science, criminology and criminal justice, design practice, district nursing (community specialist practice), education, electrical power engineering, formulation science, HRM, health sciences, learning and technology, management, marketing, business administration (MBA), mechanical manufacturing, mechatronics, polymer & biopolymer science, professional development in HE, psychology of religion, psychology, renewable engineering and sustainable energy, return to practice in nursing, specialist community public health nursing

BEng(Hons), MComp, BA(Hons), FdA, FEng, PhD, MPhil, MA, MBA, MSc, ProfDoc, MBA, BSc(Hons), FdSc, MRes, BA(Hons), Dip/CertHE, EdD, PGCert/Dip, DipHE,

UNIVERSITY OF GREENWICH
www.gre.ac.uk

Faculty of Architecture, Computing & Humanities; www2.gre.ac.uk/about/faculty/ach

Dept of Architecture & Landscape
architecture & landscape architecture, garden design, landscape architecture, landscape management (land use), advanced landscape and urbanism, architectural design, architectural practice, architecture and construction, architecture, landscape architecture, landscape design

Dept of Built Environment
design and construction management, building studies/surveying, occupational safety, health and environment, property development and management, architecture and construction – research, construction management and economics, facilities management, occupational hygiene, project management – international, real estate/ development and investment, sustainable building engineering

Dept of Computing & Information Systems
business information system/technology, business computing, computer science, computer security and forensics, computer systems and networking, computing with digital media/games development, computing, software engineering, creative digital media, digital media technologies, games design and development, web technologies, big data & business intelligence, computer science, computing and information systems, software engineering, enterprise systems and database administration, information security and audit, information systems management, management of business information technology, computer forensics and cyber security, computer systems and network engineering, network and computer systems security

Dept of Creative Professions & Digital Arts
3D digital design and animation, graphic and digital design, digital film production, film and TV production, film studies, digital arts practice, media and communication, web design and content planning, film production, sound design

Dept of Literature, Language & Theatre
drama/and English literature, professional dance and musical theatre, creative writing/and English literature, English language and literature, English literature/with creative writing, English language and ELT, international languages and international relations, English: literary London, language learning and Japanese language teaching, second language learning and teaching, humanities and social sciences – research

Dept of Law
criminology and criminal psychology, criminology, commercial law, law, law senior status, international and commercial law, law – research

Dept of Mathematical Sciences
financial mathematics, mathematics and computing, mathematics with business, mathematics with economics, mathematics, statistics, applicable mathematics, computational finance, computing and mathematical sciences

Dept of History, Politics & Social Sciences
history and English/ politics/ sociology, counselling, history, politics and international relations, sociology/ and psychology/criminology, history, international maritime policy, maritime studies, international relations, humanities and social sciences – research, public policy and practice, sociology & criminology; BA(Hons), BSc(Hons), MSc, MA, PGDip/Cert, LlB, LlM, MPhil, PhD

Business School
accounting and finance, accounting and financial information systems, finance and investment banking; business economics, business with law/economics with banking/economics with language, international business/ with language, business management, business psychology, HRM advertising and marketing communications with language, advertising and marketing communications, events management, events management, hospitality management, marketing, marketing with language, PR and communications, tourism management, tourism management with language; business, business

131

entrepreneurship and innovation, business purchasing and supply chain management, business studies, business with finance/finance/HRM/marketing; Postgraduate; accounting and finance, business – research, business, finance and investment, financial management, financial management and risk, international banking and finance; business, business and financial economics, business, computational trading, international business; business, HRM, international HRM, business, events management, international tourism management, PR and corporate communications, strategic marketing communications, business, e-logistics and supply chain management, business administration, project management for logistics, transport and logistics management; FD, BA(Hons), BSc(Hons), certs, MBA, DBA, MA, MSc, MPhil, PhD

Faculty of Education & Health; www2.gre.ac.uk/about/faculty/eduhea

Dept of Adult Nursing & Paramedic Science

assistant health and social care practitioner, health and social care: care, health and social care: early years care, acupuncture, nursing (pre-registration) – adult nursing, paramedic science, advanced practice in health and social care, nursing, specialist practitioner (district nursing)

Dept of Education & Community Studies

childhood and youth studies, early childhood studies, early years, education studies, education, early years teacher status/ (professional), early years, education & training, education, youth and community

Dept of Family Care & Mental Health

mental health work, midwifery (pre-registration), nursing (pre-registration) – child nursing/learning disability/mental health nursing/sexual health, specialist community public health (health visiting and school nursing), health and social care – research, specialist community public health nursing (health visiting and school nursing), speech & language therapy

Dept of Primary Education

primary education, primary education with QTS, primary education with mathematics specialism, school direct training programme (primary)

Psychology, Social Work & Counselling

counselling, health and social care, health and well-being, psychology with counselling, psychology, public health, social work; child and adolescent psychology, health and social care – research, psychology, social work, therapeutic counselling, sport & exercise psychology

Secondary, LLTE & PE & Sport

language and literacy education, teaching English (ESOL/literacy/and ESOL), teaching mathematics (numeracy), mathematics education, PE and sport, qualified teacher status (secondary school level), HE, teaching literacy & ESOL in the lifelong learning sector (ESOL, literacy, numeracy), school direct training programme (secondary), secondary education computer science and information/ design and technology/mathematics/modern languages (French)/ PE, physics with mathematics, secondary education science with biology/chemistry/ physics, secondary musicians in education; FD, BSc(Hons), BA(Hons), MA, MSc, PGCert/Dip, PGCE, EdD, MPhil, PhD, CertHE, LlB

Faculty of Engineering & Science; www2.gre.ac.uk/about/faculty/engsci

Applied Engineering and Management; applied professional studies, business administration, business administration with accounting and finance/ marketing, design, innovation and entrepreneurship, design, industrial engineering, information technology, management for business, mechanical engineering, Engineering Science; civil engineering,computer engineering, electrical and electronic engineering,engineering for intelligent systems, engineering technology, Life and Sports Sciences; applied biomedical science, biological sciences, biology, biomedical science, human nutrition, natural sciences, science sports science with coaching, sports science with professional football coaching, sports science, Pharmaceutical; Chemical & Environmental Sciences; chemistry, forensic science with criminology, forensic science, pharmaceutical sciences, Natural Resources Institute; biology, environmental science, geography, Royal School of Military Engineering; building services engineering, construction management, electrical engineering, highway engineering and plant management; Postgraduate; Applied Engineering and Management; engineering, global oil and gas management, global shipping management, mechanical and manufacturing engineering, Engineering Science; civil engineering, electrical and electronic engineering, electrical power engineering, Life & Sports Sciences; applied plant science, biomedical sciences, strength and conditioning, Pharmaceutical, Chemical & Environmental Sciences; biotechnology, environmental conservation, formulation science, landscape ecology with GIS, pharmaceutical biotechnology, pharmaceutical sciences, science – research, Natural Resources Institute; agricultural and food sciences,agriculture for sustainable development,

development studies, food innovation, food safety and quality management, natural resources, sustainable environmental management; BEng(Hons), BSc(Hons), MEng, MSc, MPhil, PhD, MBiol, MOst, MChem, BA(Hons), FD

GRIMSBY INSTITUTE/UNIVERSITY CENTRE
www.grimsby.ac.uk

games design & development, computer technologies, business management/with management/marketing, structural business environment, criminological studies with social science, children, young people & families, creative music, special effects make-up design for TV, film & theatre, early childhood studies, education/technology in the lifelong learning sector, counselling studies, applied

psychology, health & social care, mental health studies, hospital & healthcare(adult), tourism & business management, events management, sport & recreation management, industrial management & food marketing, media writing, commercial photography, professional writing; BA(Hons), BSc(Hons), FdA, FdEd, FdSc, HEdDip, MA, MBA, MSc, PGCE

HARPER ADAMS UNIVERSITY
www.harper-adams.ac.uk

advanced veterinary nursing, agri-business, agricultural engineering, agricultural engineering with marketing and management, agriculture, agriculture with animal science/crop management/farm business/management, mechanisation, agri-food marketing with business, animal behaviour and welfare (clinical animal behaviour), animal health and welfare, animal management and welfare, animal production science, automotive engineering (off highway), bioveterinary science, business management with marketing, countryside and environmental management, countryside management, food and public health nutrition, food business innovation and entrepreneurship, food manufacture with marketing, food sustainability management, food technology and product development, food technology with nutrition, geography and environmental management, mechanical engineering, rural enterprise and land management (realm), rural property management, veterinary nursing,veterinary nursing with companion animal behaviour rehabilitation therapy, veterinary physiotherapy, wildlife conservation

Postgraduate; advanced veterinary practice sciences, agricultural engineering (mobile machinery), agricultural law, agriculture, agro-ecology, applied mechatronic engineering, aquaculture, automotive engineering (off highway), conservation and forest protection, ecological applications, entomology, exotic animal studies, farm and agri-business management, feline veterinary studies, food industry management, forestry management, integrated pest management, international agri-business and food chain management, pig production, plant pathology, poultry production, ruminant nutrition, rural estate and land management, small animal cardiology studies, small animal diagnostic imaging, small animal emergency medicine and surgery, small animal medicine, small animal ophthalmology, small animal surgery, veterinary nurse practitioner,- veterinary nursing, veterinary oncology nursing, veterinary pharmacy, veterinary physiotherapy, veterinary rehabilitation nursing, western veterinary acupuncture and chronic pain management
BSc(Hons), FdSc, MBA, MSc, PGDip/Cert, MRes, PhD

Degrees validated by Harper Adams University offered at:

ASKHAM BRYAN COLLEGE
www.askham-bryan.ac.uk

public service, agriculture/ & land management/ urban forestry, animal management & science/conservation, applied horticulture,, arboriculture, canine & feline training welfare, countryside management/ collection & conservation, enterprise (land-based), equine science/& management, equine business/ & event management, equine sports management, sport surface management/coaching & fitness, arboriculture, applied/horticulture, landscaping & garden management, sport (outdoor & adventure education), veterinary health studies/nursing, zoo management; BSc, BSc(Hons), Nat Dips, FD

HERIOT-WATT UNIVERSITY
www.hw.ac.uk

Energy, Geoscience, Infrastructure and Society

Architectural Engineering; architectural engineering/ with international studies, (interior) design

Civil and Structural Engineering; civil engineering / with international studies, structural engineering, structural engineering with architectural design/ international studies

Construction Management and Surveying; construction project management, quantity surveying

Civil/Safety/Water Engineering, building planning & design

Urban Studies; urban planning and property development, geography, society and environment

Postgrad Taught Programmes

Centre of Excellence in Sustainable Building Design; architectural engineering, architectural project management, building conservation (technology and management), carbon and energy management, construction project management, quantity surveying, sustainable urban management, urban and regional planning, urban strategies, design

Institute for Infrastructure & Environment; civil engineering, civil engineering and construction management, safety and risk management, safety, risk and reliability engineering, structural and foundation engineering, water and environmental management, water technology and desalination, ergonomics, engineering, psychology, high speed train & track systems, human factors

Geography, Society & Environment; urban planning & development

Institute of Petroleum Engineering; petroleum engineering/reservoir evaluation, geoscience

Institute for Social Policy, Housing, Environment and Real Estate; real estate and planning, real estate investment and finance, real estate management and development; BSc(Hons, Ord), BEng, MEng, MRes, MSc, PGDip/Cert, PhD, Diploma

School of Mathematical and Computer Sciences; www.macs.hw.ac.uk

actuarial science/mathematics, computer science (artificial intelligence/games programming/software engineering), computer systems (games programming), computational mathematics, financial mathematics/quantitative finance, financial risk management/engineering, information systems/interaction design/internet systems/management), information technology, mathematics, mathematics with computer science/finance/French/German/physics/Spanish/ statistics, mathematical statistics & actuarial science, network security, statistics, software engineering, statistical modelling; BSc(Hons), MEng, MMath, MRes, MSc, PGDip/Cert, PhD

School of Engineering and Physical Sciences; www.eps.hw.ac.uk

Chemical Engineering: chemical engineering with energy engineering/pharmaceutical chemistry, industrial engineering (chemical), sustainable engineering, oil & gas technology

Chemistry: chemistry with materials/ biochemistry/ computational chemistry/pharmaceutical chemistry/ European language/nanotechnology, numerous research topics

Electrical, Electronic & Computer Engineering; electrical and electronic engineering, electrical power and energy, robotics, autonomous and interactive systems, computing and electronics, engineering, industrial engineering; Postgraduate; embedded systems, mobile communications, robotics, autonomous and interactive systems, smart systems integration, vision image & robotics

Mechanical Engineering: mechanical engineering and energy, engineering/advanced energy, oil and gas technology, renewable energy and distributed generation, renewable energy engineering, smart grid demand management, sustainability engineering; Postgraduate; advanced mechanical engineering, energy, oil and gas technology, renewable energy and distributed generation, renewable energy engineering, smart grid demand management, sustainability engineering

Physics; physics, chemical physics physics with energy science and technology, engineering physics, mathematical physics, nanoscience optics, photonics, and nanotechnology; Postgraduate; photonics and optoelectronic devices; BEng, BSc(Ord, Hons), EngD, MChem, MEng, MPhil, MPhys, PhD

School of Life Sciences; www.hw.ac.uk/sls

Psychology; psychology, psychology (applied/forensic science), psychology with management, applied psychology, business psychology, human factors,

Biological Sciences; biological sciences, biological sciences (cell and molecular biology/food science/human health)

Brewing & Distilling; brewing & distilling

Food Science; food science technology & management, food technology, food & beverage science, food science & nutrition, food science, safety & health

Marine Science; climate change: impacts & mitigation/marine biodiversity & biotechnology, marine renewable energy, marine resource development & protection, marine resource management, marine science, marine planning for sustainable development, renewable energy development

Energy and Renewables; renewable energy development, marine renewable energy, environmental interactions of marine renewable energy,marine resource management; BSc(Hons), MSc/Cert/Dip, PGDip, PhD

School of Management and Languages; www.hw.ac.uk/sml

Accountancy & Finance; accountancy and business law/finance, business and finance, finance, finance and business; Postgraduate; finance, finance and management, international accounting and environmental economics/finance/ management, international banking and finance, international finance and corporate accountability, international finance and environmental economics, investment

management, strategy and international management accounting

Business Management; business management; business management with business law/enterprise/HRM, business management with marketing, international business management, business administration; Postgraduate; international business management, international marketing management, leadership and organisational performance, logistics and supply chain management

Economics; economics; economics and accountancy/business law/business management/finance; Postgraduate; economics, banking and finance, international finance and economic development

Languages and Intercultural Studies; applied languages and translating (French/German)/ (French/Spanish)/(German/Spanish)/(French/British sign language)/(German/British sign language)/(Spanish/British sign language), British sign language (interpreting, translating and applied language studies), languages (interpreting and translating) (French/German)/(French/Spanish)/(French/British sign language)/(German/British sign language)/(Spanish/British sign language), French/German/Spanish and applied language studies, international business management and languages: Chinese/French/German/Spanish as main language; Postgraduate; cultural resource management, international management and business communication; BA(Hons, Ord), GradDip, MA(Hons), MSc

Heriot-Watt Institute of Petroleum Engineering; www.pet.hw.ac.uk

marine resource management, marine renewable energy, petroleum engineering/geoscience, renewable energy development, reservoir evaluation & management; MPhil, MSc, PhD

School of Textiles and Design; www.tex.hw.ac.uk

design for textiles (fashion, interior, art), fashion, fashion communication/marketing and retailing/menswear/technology/womenswear, interior design; Postgrad; ethics in fashion (communication, consumerism and sustainability), fashion & textiles design/management, knitwear (design, heritage & production), interior architecture & design; BA, BSc(Hons, Ord), MA, MSc, MPhil, PhD, Diploma

Edinburgh Business School; www.ebsglobal.net

financial management, HRM, marketing, strategic planning; DBA, MBA, MSc

Degrees validated by Heriot-Watt University offered at:

EDINBURGH COLLEGE OF ART
www.eca.ac.uk

Architecture & Landscape Architecture; architectural history, architecture, architectural & urban design, architectural conservation, architectural history and theory, architectural project management, art space nature, cultural landscapes, cultural studies, design and digital media, landscape architecture, sustainable design, School of Art; painting, photography, sculpture, contemporary art practice/theory, interdisciplinary creative practices, contemporary art & anthropology, History of Art; fine art, history of art, art in the global middle ages, history of art, theory and display, modern and contemporary art, history, curating and criticism, Renaissance and early modern studies, School of Design; animation, fashion, film & TV, graphic design, illustration, interior design, jewellery & silversmithing, performance costume, product design, textiles, design informatics, fashion, film directing, glass, material practice, performance costume, Reid School of Music; music, music technology, acoustics and music technology, composition/for screen, digital composition and performance, musical instrument research, musicology, sound design; BArch, MArch, MLA, MFA, BA(Comb), BSc(Hons, Ord), MA(Hons), MPhil, MSc, PhD, BMus(Hons), MMus

UNIVERSITY OF HERTFORDSHIRE
www.herts.ac.uk

Hertfordshire Business School; www.herts.ac.uk/apply/schools-of-study/courses/bs

accounting with finance, business administration/economics/analysis & consultancy, accounting & financial management, business, business analytics & consultancy, business with accounting/HRM/information systems/law/marketing, business administration with /marketing/sports management, business & economics/event management/finance/HR/information systems, tourism, economics, business economics, delivering organisational change, event management with marketing/tourism, finance economics/investment management, financial management, HRM, information systems/ & marketing, information technology management, HRM, information systems, IT for business, international business/management, leadership & management in public services, management/studies, managing major projects, managing organisational change, marketing, marketing with digital communication, tourism management, professional studies, project management/practice; BA/BSc, BA(Hons), BSc, DBA, DMan, MA, MBA, MPhil, MSc, PGCert/Dip, PhD, FD

School of Computer Science; www.herts.ac.uk/courses/schools-of-study/computer-science

advanced computer science, computer science (artificial intelligence/networks/software engineering), artificial intelligence with robotics, computer technologies (media systems/networks/software development), software development for business, computer networking principles & practices, distribution systems & networks, elearning systems, information technology, software engineering; BSc(Hons), MEng, MPhil, MSc, PGCert/Dip, PhD, FD

School of Creative Arts; www.herts.ac.uk/courses/schools-of-study/creative-arts

animation and character for digital media, 3D computer animation and modelling, 3D games art & design, audio recording and production, contemporary design crafts (ceramics and glass/jewellery/digital media arts, fashion and fashion business, fashion, film and tv (production), fine art, graphic design, illustration, industrial design, interactive media design, interior architecture and design, model design (character and creative effects/model effects); Postgraduate; animation, applied arts, contemporary textiles, digital media arts, fashion, film and television, fine art, games art and design, graphic design, illustration, interior architecture and design, music and sound technology (audio engineering/ audio programming), music composition for film and media, photography, product design; BA(Hons), MA, PGCert/Dip, MSc, MPhil, PhD, FdA, DipHE

School of Education; www.herts.ac.uk/ courses/schools-of-study/applyeducation

early years/leadership, early childhood education, education studies/with learning & teaching/special education & disabilities, working with young people, education studies, PGCE/ProfPGCE (primary, education: secondary: biology, chemistry, physics, mathematics, business education, art & design), practice based teaching, primary education, teaching & learning, CPD, primary/secondary education; BA(Hons), BEd, EdD, FdA, MA, MPhil, PGCert/ Dip, PGCE, PhD, MSc, MLT

School of Engineering & Technology; www.herts.ac.uk/courses/schools-of-study/engineering-and-technology

aerospace engineering/systems/management/space technology with pilot studies/with space technology, aerospace systems engineering, with pilot studies, aerospace technology with pilot studies/management, automotive engineering/with motorsport technology/management, biomedical engineering, broadcast media technology, computer & network technology, computer engineering construction management, digital communication & electronics, electronics, adv digital systems, digital systems, electronics & communications/computer engineering, embedded intelligent systems, mechanical engineering/& mechatronics, motorsport technology, multimedia & internet technology, multimedia systems technology, digital systems & computer engineering, electronics/electrical engineering, adv digital systems, interactive technology with animatronics manufacturing management, mobile & smart systems, operations & supply chain management, professional engineering radio & mobile communication systems; BSc(Hons), BEng, MEng, MSc, PGDip/Cert, MPhil, PhD

School of Health and Social Work; www.herts.ac.uk/courses/schools-of-study/health-and-social-work

clinical imaging, midwifery and women's health, nursing (adult/child/learning disabilities/specialist community nursing (community district nursing/ public health nursing (school nursing),advanced physiotherapy (neuromusculoskeletal), cognitive behavioural therapy, contemporary nursing, dietetics (advanced practice), intellectual and developmental disability, midwifery, medical imaging and radiation sciences – diagnostic imaging/ diagnostic ultrasound/ image interpretation, radiation sciences – radiotherapy and oncology, heathcare (adults), paramedic science;BSc(Hons), DHRes, FDSc, MPhil, MSc, PGCert/Dip, PhD

School of Humanities; www.herts.ac.uk/ courses/schools-of-study/humanities

creative writing and English language and communication, creative writing and English literature/ history/philosophy, English language & communication and journalism/media/American studies/creative writing/philosophy/public history/religious studies/ Spanish, English literature and American studies, English literature and English language & communication, history/English literature and history/journalism/media/philosophy/American studies/creative writing/English language, teaching/film/French/German/history/Italian/Japanese/journalism/Mandarin/ media cultures/new media publishing/public history/ religious studies/Spanish, new media culture, Numerous additional joint degrees including journalism, creative writing, media, philosophy, publishing, English language teaching, film French, German, Italian, journalism, Japanese, Mandarin, new media publishing, Spanish; BA(Hons), MA, MPhil, PGCert/ Dip, PhD

School of Law; www.herts.ac.uk/courses/ schools-of-study/law

law, commercial law, international law, legal practice, maritime law, commercial & workplace mediation, government & politics; BSc(Hons), Diploma, LlB(Hons), LlM, MPhil, PGDip, PhD, GradCert

School of Life & Medical Sciences; www.herts.ac.uk/courses/schools-of-study/life-and-medical-sciences

animal/equine management, adv clinical pharmaceutics, biochemistry, biological/biomedical/science, biotechnology, business psychology, cardiology & stroke, contemporary therapeutic counselling, counselling, dermatological skills & treatment, medical healthcare simulation, health & medical education, psychiatric/mental health practice, public health, nutrition, therapeutic counselling, environmental management for agriculture/business, human/physical geography, molecular biology, pharmaceutical/& health science/analysis, pharmacology, pharmacovigilance, advancing/pharmacy practice, mental health & practice, molecular biology, optometry, pharmacy, pharmaceutical practice, research in clinical psychology, psychology clinical/business/health/occupational/personal/organisational, physiology, public health, sports studies/therapy, sport & exercise science, sustainable agriculture & food security, sustainable planning & environmental management/& transport, water & environmental management; BSc/BSc(Hons), MSc, PGCert/Dip, FdSc, CertHE, MHMEd

School of Physics, Astronomy and Mathematics; www.herts.ac.uk/courses/schools-of-study/physics-astronomy-and-mathematics

astrophysics, financial mathematics, mathematics, physics; BSc(Hons), MPhil, MSc, PhD, MPhys

Degrees validated by the University of Hertfordshire offered at:

HERTFORDSHIRE REGIONAL COLLEGE
www.hrc.ac.uk

3D dimensional design, art & design, business with HRM/accounting/information systems/marketing computing technologies, fine art practice, graphic design, visual merchandising; FD

NORTH HERTFORDSHIRE COLLEGE
www.nhc.ac.uk

accounting/information systems/ computing technology, business/with HRM, creative enterprises-fashion & textile, early years, marketing, sports studies, business with HRM/accounting/information systems/marketing; FD, extended degrees

OAKLANDS COLLEGE
www.oaklands.ac.uk

animal/equine management, business/with management/information, construction management, early years, engineering & technology, fine arts practice, sports studies; FD, extended degrees

WEST HERTS COLLEGE
www.westherts.ac.uk

accounting with HRM/information systems/law/marketing, engineering, fashion & textiles, graphic design, illustration, business/ & management, media & photography, sports studies, teaching; FD, Dip teaching

THE UNIVERSITY OF HUDDERSFIELD
www.hud.ac.uk

School of Applied Sciences; www.hud.ac.uk/sas

Chemical & Biological Sciences: analytical chemistry/bioscience, chemistry/with chemical engineering/forensic science, biochemistry, biological sciences, chemical engineering/science, biology (molecular & cellular), food nutrition & health, forensic & analytical science, forensic anthropology/entomology, forensic science (body fluids/DNA/toxicology), medical biochemistry/biology/genetics, pharmaceutical & analytical science, food science, pharmaceutical chemistry/science, pharmacy, professional pharmaceutical studies, nutrition & public health/food science, accelerator applications; BA(Hons), BSc(Hons), MA, MChem, MPharm, MSc, MSci, PhD

School of Art, Design and Architecture; www.hud.ac.uk/ada

animation, architecture, adv architectural design, adv project management in construction, sustainable architecture construction/& project management, contemporary art, & illustration, costume/with textiles, creative pattern cutting, design integration & building information modelling, digital media, fashion communication & promotion/design with marketing & production/textiles, fashion and textiles buying management, fashion textile practices/communication, graphic design/& animation, illustration, interior design, international fashion management, photography, product design, textile design/surface design/textile crafts & design, textile practice (surface design/textile crafts & art/textile design), building/quantity surveying, urban design; BA(Hons), BSc(Hons), CertHE, DipHE, FdA, FdSc, MA, MArch, MSc

University of Huddersfield Business School; www.hud.ac.uk/uhbs

Undergraduate; accountancy with financial services, advertising and marketing communications, air transport and logistics management, business administration and management, business and HRM/marketing, business information management/management and leadership/management, business management with finance/accountancy, business studies with environmental management financial services, business with financial services supply chain management/management studies, economics and politics, economics, economics with financial services, entrepreneurship and business, European business, events management, global business management, global marketing, hospitality business management/with a modern language, HRM, international accountancy/international business/with a modern language, law,law and business, logistics and supply chain management, marketing, marketing with PR, supply chain management, transport and logistics management/tourism management; Postgraduate; accounting and finance, accounting, banking and finance, business, business economics, commercial law, management studies, business administration, finance, financial economics, hospitality management, HRM/HRD,international business management, international business with financial services, international finance with law, international hospitality/and tourism management, international HRM, international law, international marketing, law with finance, legal practice management, logistics and supply chain management, marketing, management with marketing, marketing communications, risk disaster and environmental management, strategic HRM

BA(Hons), FdA, DPubAdmin, GradDipLaw, LlB(Hons), LlM, MBA, DBA, MSc, PGCE, PGDip, PGDip/Cert, GradDip, CPE, MHRM, DMS, MLP

School of Computing and Engineering; www.hud.ac.uk/ce

Undergraduate; applied computing, computer games design, computing, computing science, computing science with games programming, computing in business, information and communication technology, software engineering, web design/technologies, automotive and motorsport engineering, chemical engineering and chemistry, chemical engineering, computer systems engineering, electronic and communication engineering, electronic and electrical engineering, electronic engineering and computer systems, electronic engineering, energy engineering, engineering, mechanical engineering, product design Postgraduate; advanced computer science, applied computing, information systems management, digital media, advanced metrology, automotive engineering, electronic and communication engineering, embedded systems engineering, engineering control systems & instrumentation, engineering management, mechanical engineering design, mechanical engineering

oil and gas engineering with management
BEng(Hons), MEng, MSc, PhD, UniFdCert, MChem. MSci

School of Education & Professional Development; www.hud.ac.uk/edu

childhood studies, early years, religion and education, learning support, education, HRD and training, education and professional development, TESOL, early childhood education with early years teacher status, Postgrad; EYTS, TESOL QTS; secondary music education/religious education with QTS; Postgraduate; secondary business education/ computer science/ mathematics/music/ science with biology/ science with chemistry/science with physics with QTS, school direct; lifelong learning/service, lifelong learning PGCE pre-service/in-service education; PGCE, youth and community work; BA/BA(Hons), CertEd, FdA, MA, PGradDip/Cert, PGCE, EdD

Human and Health Sciences;
www.hud.ac.uk/hhs

Health Sciences: health professions, midwifery, nursing (adult, child, mental health, learning disabilities), occupational therapy, operating dept practice, physiotherapy, podiatry, community nursing practice (district nursing), health studies, advanced diabetes care/advanced practice in acute and critical care/advancing midwifery practice/health professional education: teaching/healthy lifestyles/long-term conditions, health studies/ & community development, healthcare management, forensic podiatry, podiatry, nutrition, public health nursing practice: health visiting/school nursing, hospital management, theory of podiatric surgery

Social Sciences: behavioural sciences, counselling studies/with mentoring, criminology, criminology & criminal justice, forensic science, health and social care, international/politics, politics/& criminology/sociology, psychology, psychology/with counselling/criminology, social work/& social policy, sociology and criminology, sociology, social research and evaluation, exercise science, sport science, sport, exercise & nutrition; DipHE, MA, MSc, PGDip/Cert, PhD, ProfDoc, MBA, BA(Hons), BSc(Hons)

Music, Humanities and Media;
www.hud.ac.uk/mhm

English language/& literature/modern language/creative writing/applied linguistics, drama, dance & performance, English language & English literature with a modern language/creative writing, English literatuye & history/language/politics,English and history/politics, history with a modern language, business English &/ intercultural communication/creative writing, broadcast journalism, film studies & drama/English literature/ history, journalism, cultural & media studies, media and popular culture, music journalism, sports journalism, music and sound for image, music, music technology – creative music technology/& popular music/audio systems, music technology/production; BA(Hons), FdA, MA, PdF, PhDs, MMus, PGDip, MEnt, EntD

Degrees validated by The University of Huddersfield offered at:

HERTFORD REGIONAL COLLEGE
www.hrc.ac.uk

3dimensional design, business, engineering, fine art practice, computing, graphic design, visual merchandising, early years

NORTH HERTFORDSHIRE COLLEGE
www.nhc.ac.uk

engineering, science,, business management, computing technologies, early years, sports studies, business administration; Extended Degrees, FD, BA(Hons)

OAKLANDS COLLEGE
www.oaklands.ac.uk

animal management, business early years, media production, engineering, sports studies, sustainable agriculture and food security; FD, Extended Degree, BSc(Hons)

UNIVERSITY OF HULL
www.hull.ac.uk

Faculty of Arts and Social Sciences;
www.hull.ac.uk/fass

Drama, Music & Screen

drama & theatre/history, theatre practice, music/& theatre/ practice, pop music, performance, composition, creative writing, English, creative writing & film studies, early modern literature, 18th & 19th century literature, creative music technology, digital design/media studies, applied digital media, film studies & drama, game & entertainment design, digital design, media & screen studies, media, musicology

English

English & American literature & culture, English language & literature, English language research, creative writing/ with American studies/English/philosophy/religion, English literature, modern & contemporary literature, literary & visual cultures studies, English in jt degrees, media, literature & creative writing

History

history (20th century/social/economic/archaeological), history with maritime history/history of art, archaeological & medieval history, historical research, history & religion, Chinese & history/American studies/English language & literature, history & anthropology/economics

School of Law

law, international law, senior status, law with business/criminology/foundation English/French/German/Spanish, law & legislative studies/history/politics, philosophy, international business law, restorative justice

Languages, Linguistics & Culture

Chinese/French/German/Italian Spanish studies, Chinese with American studies/English/film studies/history/religion/politics & international studies/business/management/marketing, applied English studies, English language studies, EFL, translation studies, TESOL, American studies with creative writing/history/English/film studies, modern language studies, combined language degrees

Politics, Philosophy & International Studies

politics, British politics & legislative studies, politics & international relations/history/war & security studies, philosophy, politics & economics, war & security studies, EU governance, global political economy, global communication & international politics, international politics/political economy, international law & politics, strategy & international security

Social Sciences

anthropology & economics/sociology/criminology/philosophy/religion, criminology & sociology/law/forensic science/sociology & anthropology & gender studies, sociology, social anthropology & sociology, social work, community & youthwork studies, media studies, applied social research, restorative justice, theology, religion & social class/philosophy/film studies/politics/sociology/creative writing/education/English/history, Europe & gender studies; BA(Hons), BMus, BSc(Hons), LlB, LlM, MA, MEd, MMus, MPhil, MR/MRes, PGDip/Cert, PhD

The Hull University Business School;
www.hull.ac.uk/hubs

accounting, business, business economics, economics with mathematics, financial management, management, marketing, supply chain management, business management, international business, accounting and finance

MSc degrees; advertising and marketing, business management, economics and business, energy markets, finance and investment, financial management, financial mathematics, HRM, international business, logistics and supply chain management, management consulting, marketing management,money, banking and finance, strategic brand management, MBA degrees

BA(Hons), BSc(Hons), MBA, MPhil, MRes, MSc, PhD, MBA, BSc(Econ), MSc(Econ)

Faculty of Health and Social Care;
www.hull.ac.uk/fhsc

adv practice (neonatal), nursing (adult/mental health/children's/learning disability nursing, community nursing, critical care, colonoscopy, gastroenterology, health/professional studies, leadership in health & social care, operating department practice, practice teacher, educator in practice, return to practice, midwifery, the associate practitioner/health and social care, practice skills for health and social care, clinical psychology, cognitive behavioural therapy, practice skills for health and social care, working with children, young people and families, health and social care of adults, the theory and practice of counselling; Adv Diploma, BSc(Hons), FD, MPhil, MRes, PhD, Univ Cert, PGDip/Cert, DClinPsy, MSc

The Hull York Medical School;
www.hyms.ac.uk

anatomical science, biomedical science, cancer, cardiovascular medicine, child health, clinical sciences, clinical techniques & skills, cognitive behavioural therapy, dermatology, evidence-based decision making, gastrointestinal medicine, health professions education, human anatomy & evolution/science, immunology, medicine, medical education/science, medical & human science, mental health, metabolic & renal medicine, pathology, person-centred care, population health & medicine, public health, reproduction, respiration, sport, health & exercise science, surgery, interacted degrees, health professions education, physician associate, clinical anatomy; BSc(Hons), MBBS, MPhil, MA, MRes, MSc/Dip/Cert, PGCert/Dip, PhD, MPH

Faculty of Education; www2.hull.ac.uk/ifl

learning support3 childhood studies, education and early years, early childhood education & care, education and learning, education studies, learning & teaching primary, primary teaching, education and early years, education studies, social inclusion and special needs, education studies with TESOL, early childhood studies, children's inter-professional studies, primary teaching, learning and teaching – (primary education), education and early years, education and learning, early childhood education and care;; Postgraduate; education, education and early childhood, education, inclusion and special needs, education and digital technologies, education and leadership, pedagogy and practice, education by research, PGCE primary: early years (3 to 7 years) 5 to 11, PGCE secondary (numerous subjects); BAHons), EdD, FD, GradCert, MA, MEd, MPhil, MSc, PGCE, PhD, PGCert(HE), CertEd, MTL, FD, BEd, Prof Doc

Postgraduate Medical Institute; www2.hull.ac.uk/pgmi

post-graduate medical education; PGCME, MD, MPhil, PhD

Faculty of Science & Engineering; www.hull.ac.uk/science

Biological, Biomedical & Environmental Sciences: biology/with ecology, ecology & the environment, biomedical science, cancer imaging, human biology, marine and freshwater biology, environmental management & change, zoology, translational oncology

Chemistry: biological chemistry, biochemistry, chemistry, forensic analytical science, analytical & forensic chemistry

Computer Science: adv/computer science, computing, games development/programming, software engineering, information systems, computer graphics/games programming, NET distribution systems/development, computer systems engineering, control & instrumentation, embedded systems, computer science for games development/software engineering/embedded systems, software engineering/security & distributed computing

Engineering: chemical/& energy engineering, biomedical engineering, mechanical & medical engineering, energy engineering, computer aided engineering, electrical/& electronic engineering/& energy engineering, mechanical/ & energy/manufacturing/medical/automotive engineering, product innovation, embedded systems, wireless systems engineering, plant & process/process engineering management, logistics/technology, petroleum, oil & gas chemical engineering management/technology

Geography, Environment & Earth Sciences: human/physical geography, geology/with physical geography, renewable energy, geography & history/business/management, archaeology & human geography/environments

Physics & Mathematics, Astrophysics: physics/with astrophysics/mathematics, nanotechnology, philosophy, mathematics, financial mathematics, theoretical physics

Sports Science, Health & Exercise Science: applied exercise for health, applied sport science for performance, sports coaching & performance science, sport & exercise nutrition, sports rehabilitation, cardiovascular rehabilitation

Psychology: psychology, clinical applications of psychology, clinical psychology, psychology with criminology, health psychology, psychology & health, clinical psychology; BA, BEng, BSc, BSc/MEng, MPhil, MPhys, MPhysGeog, MRes, MSc, PhD, FdEng, MPharmSci

Degrees validated by the University of Hull offered at:

BISHOP BURTON COLLEGE
www.bishopburton.ac.uk

agriculture, animal management and veterinary, applied science, art, design and fashion, business and management, construction, countryside and environmental studies, engineering, equine, floristry, food, health and social care and childcare, horticulture, public services, sport, teacher training, tourism; BA(Hons), BSc(Hons), FdA/Sc, MSc, PGCE

DONCASTER COLLEGE
www.don.ac.uk

illustration and concept art, fine art and crafts, graphic design, moving image production; early childhood development and learning in practice, supporting children with special educational needs and disability, early childhood studies, professional studies working with young people/and the community, applied social science, criminal justice, English, psychology in the community; business management, international football business management; live events production, contemporary performance practice, creative music technology, dance practice; physical education and sports coaching, sports, fitness and exercise science/health science; Postgraduate; creative industries: practice, business and innovation, creative pattern cutting; early childhood studies; education studies (primary/secondary, literature and digital culture ; business administration, HRM, creative music technology; advancing professional practice, PGCE, education; BA(Hons), BSc, BSc(Hons), FD, MA, MSc, PGCE, PGCert/Dip, MBA, CertHE, MMus

UNIVERSITY CENTRE GRIMSBY
www.grimsby.ac.uk

applied psychology; business management; business management with accounting/marketing; counselling studies; early childhood years top-up; health and social care top-up; hospital and healthcare (adult); mental health studies (nursing pathway); strategic business environment; tourism and business management top-up; BA, BSc, FdSc, MBus

IMPERIAL COLLEGE, LONDON
www.imperial.ac.uk

Faculty of Engineering;
www.imperial.ac.uk/engineering

Aeronautics: adv composites, adv aeronautical engineering, adv computational methods for aeronautics/flow management and fluid-structure interaction, composites: the science, technology and engineering application of advanced composites, aeronautics & spacecraft engineering

Bioengineering: bioengineering, biomedical engineering, medical device design & entrepreneurship, nanotechnology, molecular engineering

Chemical Engineering: chemical engineering/with nuclear engineering, adv chemical engineering with biotechnology, process automation, instrumentation and control

Civil & Environmental Engineering: adv structures, civil/structural engineering, civil & environmental engineering, earthquake engineering, engineering geology, general structural engineering, geotechnics, concrete structures/and business management sustainable development, environmental engineering and business management/ sustainable development, hydrology, soil mechanics/and business management/engineering seismology/environmental geotechnics/sustainable development, structural steel design/and business management/sustainable development, transport/ and business management/ sustainable development

Computing: computing, computing – computation in biology and medicine/software engineering/artificial intelligence/games, vision and interaction/computational management, mathematics and computer science; advanced computing, computing (machine learning/ secure software systems/visual computing and robotics/robotics and image guided intervention, computing (machine learning/secure software systems/visual computing and robotics/robotics and image guided intervention

Design Engineering: design engineering, global innovation design, innovation design engineering

Earth Science & Engineering: geology, geophysics, environmental/petroleum geoscience/ & geophysics, metals & energy finance, petroleum engineering/ geophysics, remote sensing

Electrical & Electronic Engineering: electronic & electrical engineering/information engineering, analogue & digital integrated circuit design, information engineering, communications & signal processing, control systems, future power networks

Materials: adv/material science & engineering/management, aerospace materials, biomaterials & tissue engineering, materials & nuclear engineering, advanced materials, composites, adv nuclear engineering, materials with management, sustainable energy

Mechanical Engineering: adv/mechanical engineering, nuclear engineering, innovation design engineering, global engineering design, sustainable energy; BEng, MA, MEng, MSc, MSci, PhD, MRes

Faculty of Medicine; www.imperial.ac.uk/medicine

medicine, surgery, cardiovascular sciences, endocrinology, gastroenterology and hepatology, global health, haematology, immunity and infection, neuroscience and mental health, pharmacology, reproductive and developmental sciences, respiratory science, surgery and anaesthesia, anaesthetics, pain medicine and intensive care, bacterial pathogenesis and infection, biomedical research, data science, epidemiology, evolution and control of infectious diseases, microbiome in health and disease, molecular basis of human disease, personalised healthcare, respiratory and cardiovascular science, cancer biology,experimental neuroscience, genes, drugs and stem cells, novel therapies, human molecular genetics, immunology, molecular biology and pathology of viruses, molecular medicine, reproductive and

developmental biology, translational neuroscience, medical robotics and image guided intervention, health policy, healthcare and design, patient safety, public health, allergy, cardiorespiratory nursing, genomic medicine, medical ultrasound, paediatrics and child health, preventive cardiology, surgical innovation, diabetes and obesity, human nutrition, translational medicine

BSc, CAS, MB BS, MEd, MPH, MRes, MSc, MSci, PhD, PGDip/Cert

Imperial College Business School; www.imperial.ac.uk/business-school

accounting, business strategy, organisational behaviour, marketing, sustainable business, entrepreneurship business economics, global business, innovation management, finance & financial management, managerial economics, corporate finance, finance and financial management, managing organisations, project management, strategic management; Postgraduate; management, finance, finance & accounting, investment & wealth management, risk management & financial engineering, business analytics, climate change, management & finance, economics & strategy for business, innovation, entrepreneurship & management, international health management, strategic marketing; BSc(Hons), MA, MSc, MBA, PhD

Faculty of Natural Sciences; www.imperial.ac.uk/naturalsciences

Chemistry: chemistry, chemical biology/health & design, bioimaging sciences, chemistry and management/medicinal chemistry/molecular physics/French, German, Spanish for science, green chemistry, nanomaterials, plant chemical biology, drug discovery & development, theory & simulation of materials, catalysis: chemistry and engineering, green chemistry, energy and the environment, nanomaterials, plant chemical biology

Life Sciences: biology, theoretical systems biology, bioinformatics & theoretical systems biology, biomedical science, biosystematics, biochemical & biotechnology, biology, ecology & environmental biology, microbiology, plant science & biodiversity, taxonomy & biomedicine, zoology, biodiversity informatics and genomics, chemical biology of crop sustainability and protection, conservation science, ecology, molecular & cellular biosciences, molecular plant and microbial sciences quantitative biology, structural molecular biology, systems and synthetic biology, applied biosciences and biotechnology, computational methods in ecology and evolution, ecological applications, ecology, evolution and conservation/ research, ecosystem and environmental change, plant chemical biology, taxonomy and biodiversity, tropical forest ecology

Mathematics: applied/pure mathematics, computational statistics/logistics, mathematical sciences/ & finance, mathematical physics, statistical financial management, statistics, numerical analysis, stochastic analysis & mathematical finance

Physics: physics, optics and photonics, controlled quantum dynamics, nanophysics, photonics, physics with shock physics, physics with music performance/

science education, plastic electronics materials, quantum fields and fundamental forces, theoretical physics, theory and simulation of materials; BSc, MRes, MSci, PhD

Materials: aerospace materials, biomaterials and tissue engineering, biomedical engineering, materials science and engineering, materials with management/nuclear engineering, advanced materials science and engineering, adv nuclear engineering

Dyson School of Design Engineering; design engineering

KEELE UNIVERSITY
www.keele.ac.uk

Faculty of Health; www.keele.ac.uk/facs/health

School of Medicine; www.keele.ac.uk/depts/schoolofmedicine

biomedical science/engineering, cell and tissue engineering, clinical audit, end of life care, health professionals education, healthcare leadership & management, biomedical blood science, biomedical science/engineering, foundation medical practice: medical education, medical ethics & law/palliative care, medical humanities, medical science (anatomical sciences/clinical audit), end of care in non-specialist settings/leadership & management continuing professional development, individual health, primary care, parasitology, natural sciences with neuroscience/ psychology/ biochemistry/ biomedical science, anatomy, vector biology, foundation medical practice/ethics, geriatric medicine, leadership & management, medical science/practice, medicine, obstetrics & gynaecology, stroke treatment, surgery, medical science (obstetrics & gynaecology/stroke/surgery)

School of Pharmacy; www.keele.ac.uk/schools/pharm

adv professional practice (pharmacy), clinical (hospital) pharmacy, pharmacist, community pharmacy, independent prescribing, medicines, research evaluation, prescribing studies, pharmaceutical science, technology & business, research and evaluation, community pharmacy, pharmacy, clinical pharmacy for general practice, professional Masters

School of Nursing and Midwifery; www.keele.ac.uk/depts/ns

acute care, adult/children's nursing/mental health/learning disabilities, adv professional practice, applied clinical anatomy, adv clinical practice, critical care, end of life care, independent practice development, midwifery, operating department practice, pain science & management, physiotherapy (neurology/rheumatology/cardiorespiratory nursing), advancing professional practice (AHPS, nursing and midwifery), neurological rehabilitation, neuromusculoskeletal healthcare, pain studies management, specialist community nursing – district nursing, specialist community public health nursing – health visiting/specialist school nursing

School of Health and Rehabilitation; www.keele.ac.uk/healthandrehabilitation

applied clinical anatomy, health science/social care, individual health, neurological rehabilitation, neuromusculoskeletal healthcare, neurology, osteopathy, pain science management, physiotherapy, rehabilitation science; MBChB, BSc, MSc, MSci, MPharm, PGCert/Dip, MMedSci, MPhil, PhD, MD

Faculty of Humanities and Social Sciences; www.keele.ac.uk/facs/humass

Keele Management School; www.keele.ac.uk/schools/ems

accounting/& finance/financial management, business management/economics/administration, economics, industrial relations & employment law, European industrial relations & HR, finance & IT/management/risk management, HRM, international business & law, leadership & management, management & IT, marketing; MA, MBA, MSc, PGCert, PGDip, UnivCert

School of Humanities; www.keele.ac.uk/schools/hums
American studies, English, English literature, English and American literatures/creative writing, film studies with creative wring, humanities, media communication, global media & culture, history, philosophy, medical humanities, creative music technology, music & music technology, human & social science research

Keele Law School; www.keele.ac.uk/depts/law
child care law & practice, gender, human rights, globalization & justice, medical ethics & law/palliative care, law, law with politics/criminology, law & society, safeguarding adults, law policy & practice, international business & law

School of Politics, International Relations and Philosophy; www.keele.ac.uk/spire
diplomatic studies, environmental politics, environment, European politics & culture, global security, international relations, parties & elections, philosophy, politics

School of Social Science & Public Policy; www.keele.ac.uk/sspp
education, criminology & social justice/criminal justice liberal arts, social work, sociology, social science research methods;bGradDip Law, EdD, LlB,

LlM, MA, MBA, MRes, MSc, PGCE, PGDip/Cert, PhD, ProfDoc

Faculty of Natural Sciences; www.keele.ac.uk/facs/sci/

School of Computing and Mathematics; www.scm.keele.ac.uk
actuarial science, adv/computer science, creative computing, finance/ management and IT, information systems, mathematics (pure, applied, statistics), project management, web & internet technologies, analytics for business and research

School of Life Sciences; www. keele.ac.uk/depts/bi
biomedical blood science, molecular parasitology and vector biology, neuroscience, scientific research training

School of Physical and Geographical Sciences; www.keele.ac.uk/schools/dps
chemistry, medicinal chemistry, forensic science, geography, geology & environment, astrophysics, physics, geoscience research, geology and earth sciences, mathematics

School of Psychology; www.keele.ac.uk/depts/ps
psychology, child development, clinical psychology research, cognitive psychology, social & community psychology, counselling psychology, health & wellbeing; BA, BSc, DClinPsy, DSc, MGeoscience, MRes, MSc, PGCert, PGDip, PhD, MMath, MComp

UNIVERSITY OF KENT
www.kent.ac.uk

Faculty of Humanities; www.kent.ac.uk/humanities

Kent School of Architecture; www.kent.ac.uk/architecture
architecture, architectural visualisation, architecture & urban design/sustainable development, architectural conservation

School of Arts; www.kent.ac.uk/arts
art history, art history and classical & archaeological studies/English and American literature/film/French/German/History/Italian,classical and archaeological studies and film, drama and English and American literature/theatre, film, film and drama/religious studies, media arts; Postgraduate; applied theatre,

contemporary performance practice, creative producing, curating, drama by practice as research, drama by research, European theatre,,film, film with practice, film: practice by research, history & philosophy of art, history of art, physical acting, Shakespeare, stand up comedy, theatre direction

School of English; www.kent.ac.uk/english
English/American literature/creative writing, postcolonial studies, creative writing, critical theory, Dickens & Victorian culture, 18th century studies, jt degrees, the contemporary

School of European Culture & Languages; www.kent.ac.uk/secl

ancient history, archaeology, Asian studies, classical & archaeological studies/history, comparative literature, European studies (Humanities), European language & linguistics, heritage management, linguistics, applied linguistics for TESOL, history, medical humanities, modern French/German/Hispanic/Italian studies & comparative literature, Italian theory, world literature, modern European literature, philosophy, medical humanities, reasoning, religious studies, Roman history & archaeology

School of History; www.kent.ac.uk/history

American studies, history, European history, imperial history, modern history, medieval & early modern studies, military history, 1st world war studies, war, media & society, science, communication & society, science technology, environment & medicine & society; BA(Hons), BSc(Hons), MA, MArch, MDram, MPhil, PhD

Faculty of Science; www.kent.ac.uk/stms

School of Biosciences; www.kent.ac.uk/bio

biology, biomedical sciences, biochemistry, biotechnology & bioengineering, drug design, infectious diseases, reproductive medicine, cancer biology, science, communication & society

School of Computing; www.cs.kent.ac.uk

adv/computer science – artificial intelligence/consultancy/networks, computing/ & entrepreneurship, computational intelligence, computer animation, computing security, IT consultancy, adv software development, networks & security, information & biometrics

School of Engineering and Digital Arts; www.eda.kent.ac.uk

advanced/electronic/computer systems engineering, architectural visualisation, bioengineering, broadband & mobile communications networks, computer animation, digital visual effects/arts, electronic & communications engineering/computer systems, embedded systems & instrumentation, engineering with finance, information security/biometrics, mobile applications design, multimedia technology & design, wireless communication & signal processing

School of Mathematics, Statistics & Actuarial Science; www.kent.ac.uk/Ismsas

applied/actuarial science, statistics, mathematics, statistics & finance, mathematics & statistics, financial investment & management, mathematics & its applications, statistics with finance

Medway School of Pharmacy; www.msp.kent.ac.uk

medicines management, pharmacy/& physiology, general pharmacy practice, independent supplementary prescribing, applied drug discovery, applied bioscience technology

School of Physical Sciences; www.kent.ac.uk/physical-sciences

astrophysics, astronomy, space science & astrophysics, forensic chemistry, chemistry, physics, applied optics, astrophysics, astronomy & planetary science, forensic imaging/science, functional materials; BA(Hons), BEng, BSc(Hons), DClinPsych, MD, MRes, MPhil, MSc, MSurg, PGCert, PGDip, PhD

School of Sport & Exercise Science; www.kent.ac.uk/sportscience;

sport & exercise science/management, sports therapy/science/management, sports therapy, sport for exercise & health science, sport science for optimal performance; BSc(Hons), MSc, ProfDoc, MPhil, PhD

Faculty of Social Sciences; www.kent.ac.uk/socsci

School of Anthropology and Conservation; www.kent.ac.uk/sac

anthropology (social/biological/medical), human ecology, social anthropology & economics/philosophy/politics/social policy, environmental anthropology, social anthropology, social anthropology and computing/conflict, social anthropology with visual ethnography, social anthropology of Europe, ethnobotany, evolution and human behaviour, conservation biology, conservation and international wildlife trade/primate behaviour/conservation and rural development/conservation and tourism, conservation project management; BA(Hons), BSc(Hons), MA, MSc, PhD

Kent Business School; www.kent.ac.uk/kbs

accounting & finance/management, business administration, business & management (retail), business, business analytics, finance & management,, international accounting & finance, international business & economic development, international business/management, logistics & supply chain management, HRM, management, marketing; BA(Hons), BBA, BSc(Hons), MBA, MEBA, MPhil, MSc

School of Economics; www.kent.ac.uk/economics

accounting and finance and economics, economics, economics and politics/Spanish/computing/econometrics, European economics, European economics (French/German/Spanish), financial economics/with econometrics, law and economics, social anthropology and economics, sociology and economics, economics and econometrics, economics and finance, finance and econometrics, international finance and economic development, agri-environmental economics and policy, international business and economic development, applied economics and international development; BSc(Hons), MPhil, PhD, MSc

Centre for Journalism; www.kent.ac.uk/journalism

journalism, international multimedia journalism, journalism & the news industry; BA(Hons), MA

Kent Law School; www.kent.ac.uk/law

law, law (French/German/Spanish), European law, international communication law, criminal justice, international criminal justice, international environmental law, European law, international law with international relations, international commercial law, international law, medical law and ethics, human rights law, law and the humanities; BA(Hons), LlB, LlM, MPhil, PhD, GradDip

School of Politics and International Relations; www.kent.ac.uk/politics

economics and politics, history and politics, philosophy and politics, politics, politics and English language and linguistics, politics and international relations/law, social anthropology/politics/sociology and politics, war and conflict – European and global governance, international conflict analysis, international relations, international relations with international law, peace and conflict studies, political psychology, political theory and practices of resistance, terrorism and society; BA(Hons), MA, MPhil, PhD, PGDip

Dept of Psychology; www.kent.ac.uk/psychology

applied psychology/with clinical psychology, psychology, psychology with clinical psychology/forensic psychology, social psychology, psychology and law/social anthropology/sociology; developmental psychology, forensic psychology, group processes and intergroup relations, organisational psychology, research methods in psychology, social and applied psychology; BSc(Hons), MPhil, MSc, PhD

School of Social Policy, Sociology and Social Research; www.kent.ac.uk/sspssr

autism studies, criminal justice and criminology, criminology/& cultural studies/social policy/sociology, cultural studies and comparative literature/film/media/social anthropology, health and social care, intellectual and developmental disabilities, social policy and politics/sociology, quantitative research, social sciences, social work, sociology and economics/politics/social anthropology, statistical social research Postgrad; advanced child protection, autism studies, social work – research, analysis and intervention in intellectual and developmental disabilities, applied behaviour analysis, applied health research, civil society, NGO and non-profit studies, environmental social science, international social policy, methods of social research, philanthropic studies, political sociology,, sociology, social work, sociological research; BA(Hons), BSc(Hons), GradDip/Cert Diplomas, MA, MPhil, MSc, PhD

KINGSTON UNIVERSITY
www.kingston.ac.uk

Faculty of Art, Design and Architecture; www.kingston.ac.uk/faculties/#design
UG; art & design: architecture, history and practice, fashion, filmmaking, fine art and art history, fine art, graphic design, historic building conservation, illustration animation, interior design, photography, product and furniture design, film studies
PG; architecture, applied architectural stonework, space, communication design & the creative economy/ illustration/graphic design, creative practice, curating contemporary design, design: product and space/ & the creative economy, experimental film, fashion, fashion: knit, fashion & the creative economy, film (experimental), fine art, historic building conservation, landscape architecture, landscape and urbanism, museums and galleries/ & the creative economy, photography, professional practice architecture, sustainable building design and performance, sustainable design, urban design and

planning; BA(Hons), FdA, FdSc, MA, MSc, PGCert/ Dip, FDip, BSc(Hons), MFA, MArch, MLA

Faculty of Arts and Social Sciences; www.fass.kingston.ac.uk

UG; Economics, History & Politics; applied economics, business, business economics, economics, financial economics, history, human rights, politics/ and international relations, politics/& international relations, humanities

Humanities; creative writing, English language and linguistics, English literature, French, journalism, Spanish, screen studies

Performance & Screen Studies; dance, drama, film studies, music, creative music technologies, TV and new broadcasting media, media and communication

Criminology, Psychology & Sociology; criminology, psychology, sociology

economics, history and politics

PG; Economics; applied econometrics, development and international economics, economics, economic policy, financial economics, international politics and economics, philosophy/ and political economy

History: Politics; human rights, international conflict, international relations, terrorism and political violence, humanities

Creative Writing: creative writing, creative writing and publishing, English literature, applied linguistics for language teaching

Journalism; journalism, magazine journalism, journalism & the creative economy

Philosophy; aesthetics and art theory, contemporary European philosophy, modern European philosophy, philosophy and contemporary critical theory, philosophy, history & philosophy

Publishing; Performance & Screen Studies; film making, film studies, media and communication, publishing & the creative economy

Music: composing for film and TV, music education, music, music performance, production of popular music, music & the creative economy

Criminology and Sociology; criminological psychology, criminology/with forensic psychology

Psychology: behavioural decision science, child psychology, clinical applications of psychology, psychology, forensic psychology

The Media/Performing Arts and the Creative Economy; creative writing and the creative economy, film making/journalism/publishing/the creative economy, music and the creative economy

BA(Hons), BMus, MA, PGCert/Dip, LlM, EdD, MMus, MSc, MFA

Faculty of Law & Business; www.business.kingston.ac.uk

Kingston Business School

accounting and finance, business management, international business, marketing & advertising (with business experience) business, business management practice; Postgraduate; business administration, business & management, Kingston MBA, accounting, banking & finance, logistics and supply chain management, creative industries, general management, leadership & HRM, marketing & communications, occupational and business psychology

Kingston School of Law

international law, law, law with business, real estate management, corporate and financial law, dispute resolution, employment law, environmental law and sustainability, general law, international commercial law

BA(Hons), BSc(Hons), DBA, FdA, PGGradDip, LlM, MA, MBA, MSc, PhD

Faculty of Science, Engineering & Computing; www.kingston.ac.uk/sec

actuarial mathematics & statistics, actuarial science, aerospace engineering, astronautics & space technology aerospace engineering (maintenance, repair & overhaul),aircraft engineering, automotive engineering, automotive engineering (motorsport), aviation operations with commercial pilot training, biochemistry, biological sciences, biological sciences (environmental biology/genetics and molecular biology/ human biology, biomedical science, building surveying; chemistry, civil engineering, computer graphics technology, computer science, computer science (games programming/network communications), computing and mathematics, computing with business, construction management, creative technology, cyber security & computer forensics with business, aerospace, civil, mechanical engineering, environmental hazards & disaster management, environmental management, environmental management with business, environmental science, financial mathematics with business, criminology, games technology, geography, geology, human geography, information systems, information systems (internet business), mathematics, mathematics with business/ statistics, mechanical engineering, medical biochemistry, motorsport engineering/motorsport engineering (motorcycle), nutrition (exercise and health/human nutrition), pharmaceutical science, pharmaceutical & chemical sciences, pharmacology, quantity surveying consultancy, science, software engineering, sport science, sport science (coaching)

Postgraduate; advanced industrial & manufacturing systems, advanced product design engineering, aerospace engineering, analytical chemistry, analytical chemistry with management studies,automotive engineering, biomedical science with management studies, biomedical science (haematology/medical microbiology), building surveying, cancer biology, computer animation, embedded systems, embedded systems with management studies, embedded systems (computer vision) with management studies, engineering projects & systems management, environmental management, environmental management (energy/water resources), environmental & earth resource management, forensic analysis, game development (design/programming), geographical information systems & science, hazards & disaster management, information systems, information systems (e-commerce/health information management), IT & strategic innovation, management in construction, management in construction with law, civil engineering), mechanical engineering, mechatronic systems, network & information security, network &,information security with management studies, networking & data communications, networking & data communications with management studies, pharmaceutical analysis, pharmaceutical analysis with management studies, pharmaceutical science, pharmaceutical science with management studies, pharmaceutical technology, pharmacy practice (overseas pharmacists assessment programme), professional engineering, quantity surveying, renewable energy engineering, software engineering, software engineering with management studies, structural design & construction management/ with sustainability, sustainability & environmental change, sustainable environmental development with management studies, user experience design; BSc(Hons), BEng, FdSc, FdEng, MComp, MPh, MPharmSci, MPhil, MSc, PhD, PGCert/Dip, MEng

Faculty of Health, Social Care Sciences & Education;
www.healthcare.kingston.ac.uk

adult nursing, breast imaging, child centred interprofessional practice/children's nursing, early years, early years: education & leadership in practice, early years: leadership & management, early years: teaching & learning, healthcare practice, learning disability nursing, mental health nursing,midwifery/registered midwife, paramedic practice, paramedic science, physiotherapy, primary teaching leading to QTS, radiography(diagnostic/therapeutic), social work, special educational needs & inclusive practice,working with children & young people; Postgraduate; adult nursing, advanced social work, applied exercise for health), child centred interprofessional practice, children's nursing, clinical leadership, clinical research, education, early years teacher initial teacher training, professional studies in education, mental health nursing, midwifery, physiotherapy, practice education, primary teaching leading to (QTS) professional education and training, radiography: breast evaluation/medical imaging/medical imaging (mammography/ oncology practice, rehabilitation, secondary teaching leading to qualified teacher status (QTS), social work; BSc(Hons), DipHE, FdSc,EdD, MRes, MPhil, MSc, MA, MSW, PGCert/Dip, PhD, PGDip, FdA, FdSc, PGCE, GradCert

LANCASTER UNIVERSITY
www.lancs.ac.uk

Faculty of Arts and Social Sciences;
www.lancs.ac.uk/fass/faculty

European Languages and Cultures;
www.lancs.ac.uk/fass/eurolang

dance/English language & French studies/German studies/Spanish studies, French studies/German studies/Spanish studies – large number of jt degrees, management studies and European languages, modern languages, modern languages and cultures, languages & culture

Sociology; www.lancs.ac.uk/fass/sociology

criminology and sociology, film and sociology, film, media and cultural studies, management and sociology, media and cultural studies, politics and sociology, religious studies and sociology, social work, social work, ethics and religion, sociology; Postgraduate; advanced social work, child welfare, environment, culture and society, gender and women's studies, gender and women's studies and English/

sociology, media and cultural studies, social research, social work, sociology

Educational Research; www.lancs.ac.uk/fass/edres
educational research, education & social justice, HE research, evaluation & enhancement, e-research & technology enhanced learning (PhD)

English and Creative Writing; www.lancs.ac.uk/fass/english
English literature, English literature and history/literature/linguistics/ philosophy religious studies/creative writing, English literature, creative writing and practice, film/French studies/German studies/Spanish studies/theatre and English literature; Postgraduate; English literary studies, creative writing

History; www.lancs.ac.uk/fass/history
history, English literature/French studies/German studies and history, history and international relations/philosophy/politics/religious studies, history, philosophy and politics, medieval and Renaissance studies, Spanish studies and history; Postgraduate; pathways in medieval and early modern, modern, heritage history

Lancaster Institute for the Contemporary Arts; www.lancs.ac.uk/fass/licr
design, film studies, film and creative writing/English literature/philosophy, theatre, film, media and cultural studies, fine art, fine art and creative writing/film/theatre, French/German studies and film/theatre, IT for creative industries, Spanish studies and film/theatre, theatre, theatre and creative writing/English literature; Postgraduate; art by research, arts management, contemporary arts consultancy, design management, design by research, film studies by research, international innovation (computer science/design), sound by research, theatre and performance by research

School of Law; www.lancs.ac.uk/fass/law
law, international business & corporate law, international human rights/law, law & criminology/politics; Postgraduate; international business and corporate law, international human rights/ and terrorism law, international law, bioethics and medical law, diplomacy and international law, international law and international relations, environment and law, human rights and the environment

Linguistics & English Language; www.ling.lancs.ac.uk
English language, English language & creative writing/Chinese/French/German/Spanish/the media/linguistics, linguistics, linguistics and philosophy/psychology/ Chinese; Postgraduate; Spanish studies and linguistics, applied linguistics and TESOL, discourse studies, English language, English language and literary studies, language testing, language and linguistics, TESOL

Politics, Philosophy & Religion; www.lancs.ac.uk/fass/ppr
economics and international relations/politics, English literature and philosophy, religious studies, ethics, philosophy and religion, film and philosophy, French/German studies and philosophy/politics, history and international relations/philosophy/politics/religious studies, history, philosophy and politics, international relations and religious diversity, law and politics, linguistics and philosophy, management, politics and international relations (industry), mathematics and philosophy, peace studies and international relations, philosophy, philosophy and politics/religious studies/Chinese, philosophy, politics and economics, politics, politics and international relations/religious studies/sociology/Chinese, religious studies, religious studies and sociology/Chinese, social work, ethics and religion, Spanish studies and philosophy/politics
Postgraduate; conflict, development and security, conflict resolution and peace studies, diplomacy and foreign policy, diplomacy and international law/international relations/ religion, international law/ and international relations, politics, philosophy and religion, politics and philosophy, religion and conflict, international relations, philosophy and management, philosophy; philosophy, philosophy and religion, politics, philosophy and religion, politics and philosophy, religious studies, diplomacy/philosophy and religion, politics, philosophy and religion, Quakerism in the modern world, religion and conflict, religious studies, Quaker studies
BA(Hons), BSc(Hons), MA, MSc, LlB(Hons), LlM, MSci, MSocialWork, PhD, PGCert/Dip, MRes

School of Health and Medicine; www.lancs.ac.uk/shm/faculties

Biomedical & Life Sciences; www.lancs.ac.uk/shm/bls
biochemistry/with biomedicine or genetics, biomedical sciences, applied bioscience & business

management, biological sciences, biomedical & life sciences, premedical studies, biology/with psychology

Lancaster Medical School;
www.lancs.ac.uk/shm/med

medicine & surgery, biochemistry, biochemistry with biomedicine/ genetic, biological sciences, biological sciences with biomedicine, biology, biology with psychology, biomedical science, biomedicine, bioscience with entrepreneurship, medicine and surgery, clinical research, innovation and improvement science, leadership and management/ health care, medical education/leadership, organisation development, professional development, professional practice, advanced social work, clinical research, biomedicine, biomedical sciences, medical sciences, biomedical and life sciences, health research, statistics and epidemiology, medical statistics, biomedical, clinical psychology, health research, environmental and biochemical toxicology, quantitative methods for science,, epidemiology, cellular responses to DNA damage, premedical studies, science & technology in clinical practice, reproductive immunology, toxicology, parasitology, quantitative methods in health research; BSc(Hons), CertHE, DClinPsych, MBChB, MBiomed, MD, MHospice leadership, MPhil, MRes, MSc, PGDip/Cert, PhD

Lancaster University Management School; www.lums.lancs.ac.uk

accounting and finance, business analytics and consultancy, business studies, economics, entrepreneurship, international business management, management, management, politics and international relations, organisation, work & technology, management studies and European languages, marketing and advertising, management and information technology
Postgraduate; accounting, finance and banking, economics, marketing, project management, the Lancaster executive MBA, leadership practice and responsibility, hospice leadership, practising management; MRes, BA(Hons), BSc(Hons), BBA, MEcon(-Hons), MRes, PGDip, MBA, LlM, MPhil, PhD, MA

Faculty of Science and Technology; www.lancs.ac.uk/shm/sci-tech/faculties

Chemistry; www.chemistry.lancs.ac.uk

chemistry, environmental chemistry, analytical chemistry & spectroscopy, chemical theory & computation, chemical synthesis

Computing & Communication;
www.lancs.ac.uk/scc

accounting, finance and computer science, computer science, computer science and mathematics, French/German studies and computing, IT for creative industries, management and information technology, software engineering, Spanish studies and computing; Postgraduate; communication systems (by research), computer science, cyber security, data science, international innovation (computer science/telecommunications), wireless communication systems

Engineering; www.engineering.lancs.ac.uk

chemical engineering, electronics engineering, electronic & electrical engineering, mechatronics, mechanical engineering, nuclear engineering
Postgraduate; electronic engineering, energy and the environment, engineering (by research), engineering project management, international innovation (engineering) mechanical engineering, mechanical engineering with project management

Lancaster Environment Centre;
www.lec.lancs.ac.uk

biological sciences, biology, earth and environmental science, ecology and conservation, economics and geography, environmental chemistry, environmental science, environmental science and technology, French/German/Spanish studies and geography, geography; Postgraduate; physical geography, biological science, contamination, risk assessment and remediation, data science for the environment, ecology (by research), ecology and conservation, energy and the environment, environment and development, environment and law, environment, culture and society environmental management and consultancy, environmental science, environmental science and technology, food challenges for the 21st century, geography, human rights and the environment, international innovation (computer science/ design/ engineering/ entrepreneurship/ environmental science/telecommunications), plant sciences, resource and environmental management, sustainable agriculture and food security, sustainable water management, volcanology and geological hazards

Mathematics Statistics;
www.maths.lancs.ac.uk

mathematics, computer science and mathematics, financial mathematics, mathematics & philosophy/statistics/psychology/theoretical physics/economics, quantitative methods for science/social science/

medicine, statistics & operational research, accountancy, finance & mathematics, French/Spanish studies & mathematics, management mathematics, statistics, data science, quantitative finance

Natural Sciences; www.naturalsci.lancs.ac.uk

combined science, combined technology, natural sciences

Physics; www.lancs.ac.uk/depts/physics

physics, physics with particle physics/astrophysics & cosmology, astrophysics, cosmology, physics, theoretical physics/with mathematics, particle physics

Psychology; www.psych.lancs.ac.uk

development psychology/disorders, language, organisational studies & psychology, linguistics & psychology/French/German/Spanish/management, psychology, psychology of advertising, social psychology, psychological research methods, language, speech & hearing

Biological sciences

biological sciences
BEng(Hons), BSc(Hons), MChem, MEng(Hons), MPhil, MPhys(Hons), MRes, MSc, MSci(Hons), PGDip, PhD

Degrees validated by Lancaster University offered at:

BLACKPOOL AND THE FYLDE COLLEGE
www.blackpool.ac.uk

automotive engineering and technology (automotive/ motorsport), aerospace engineering, business and financial management, criminology and criminal justice, early childhood studies, English: communication at work, English: language, literature and writing, family support and wellbeing, fashion design/contemporary costume, fine art & professional practice, graphic design and visual communication, health and social care (adults/children), history and heritage/heritage, hospitality and event management, interactive media development, tourism management, management, management in the workplace, mechanical and production engineering, mechatronics, network engineering security and systems administration, photography, professional certificate in education, professional practice health and social care (children and families/combined health/learning disability/ mental health), professional practice in early years, project management, public services and the community, software engineering and game development, working with young people; FD, BEng(Hons), BA(Hons), BSc(Hons), PGCE

EDGE HILL UNIVERSITY
www.edgehill.ac.uk

Undergraduate
advertising, marketing and public relations, advertising, business and management with marketing, marketing, marketing with advertising, marketing with digital communications, marketing with PR, PR; business and management with marketing, marketing, marketing with advertising, digital communications, PR
animation, biology, biotechnology, ecology and conservation, genetics, human biology
accountancy, business and economics, business and management, business and management with accounting and finance/HRM/leisure and tourism/ marketing, business innovation and enterprise, international business

child health and wellbeing, childhood and youth studies, early childhood studies, education, education & English/mathematics/religion/education & science, children and young people, learning and development, early years education, teaching, learning and child development/ mentoring practice
computer science, computer science and mathematics, computing, computing (application development/games programming/information systems/networking, security and forensics) computing, information technology management for business, web design and development, business information systems, computer security and networks, software application development, web design and development

creative writing, English, English language, English literature, film and TV production, film studies/ with film production, media, film and TV, TV production management

environmental science, geography, geology with physical geography, human geography, physical geography and geology, history; criminology, criminology and law/psychology, law, law with criminology/politics, policing, psychology and criminology, psychosocial analysis of offending behaviour

media, film and television, media, music and sound, music, music production, musical theatre, pop

child health and wellbeing, counselling and psychotherapy, family and community studies, health and social wellbeing, nutrition and health, psychosocial analysis of offending behaviour, midwifery, nursing (adult)/children/)learning disabilities/mental health), operating department practice, paramedic practice.;

dance, dance and drama, drama, musical theatre, performing arts;

criminology and psychology, educational psychology, psychology, psychology and criminology, psychosocial analysis of offending behaviour, sport and exercise psychology

physical education and school sport, sport and exercise psychology, sport and exercise science, sports coaching and development, sports development and management, sports management and coaching, sports therapy, sports coaching and development

primary and early years initial teacher training; early years education with QTS, primary education with QTS, secondary initial teacher training; secondary computer science and information technology education with QTS /mathematics education with QTS/ science (biology) education with QTS, science (chemistry) education with /science (physics) education with QTS further education and training; education, education & English/mathematics/religion/science; professional education; children and young people, learning and development, early years education, teaching, learning and child development, teaching, learning and mentoring practice, childhood and youth studies, early childhood studies, sociology

Postgraduate

marketing communications and branding, MBA master of business administration marketing

biology, conservation management, physical geography

accounting, finance and management, critical management research, leadership and management

development, management and entrepreneurship, MBA Master of Business Administration; HRM/ information technology/marketing), computing, cyber security, information security and IT management, MBA IT

creative writing, English, English language, English literature, humanities, popular culture, critical screen practice, film and media, film studies

advanced fertility practice, advanced practice, applied clinical nutrition, clinical and health research, clinical education, clinical reproductive medicine, cognitive behavioural psychotherapy, dental implantology, international midwifery studies, leadership development, medical,leadership, medicine, mental health law and ethics, professional clinical practice, public health nutrition, simulation and clinical learning, surgery, surgical care practice, teaching and learning in clinical practice, workplace-based medical education courses

history, history and culture, humanities, popular culture,criminology, research

film and media, media, media management, creative and cultural education, making performance

psychology childhood and youth, sociology, social work

coach education, football rehabilitation, physical education and school sport, sport and exercise science, sports development, sport, physical activity and mental health, sports studies, sports therapy

Early Years and Primary Initial Teacher Training; PGCE/ primary education with QTS/ primary mathematics specialist primary physical education (PE) specialist with QTS PGCE secondary business education (age phase 14-19) with QTS(secondary computer science and information technology education (age phase 11-16) with QTS, secondary design and technology (age phase 11-16) with QTS,secondary English (age phase 11-16) with QTS, secondary geography (age phase 11-16) with QTS, secondary history (age phase 11-16) with QTS, secondary mathematics (age phase 11-16) with QTS, secondary modern languages (age phase 11-16) with QTS, secondary music (age phase 11-16) with QTS, secondary physical education (age phase 11-16) with QTS, secondary religious education (age phase 11-16) with QTS, secondary science (biology) (age phase 11-16) with QTS, secondary science (chemistry) (age phase 11-16) with QTS, secondary science (physics) (age phase 11-16) with QTS; PGCE further education and training, early years initial teacher training (early years teacher status, subject knowledge enhancement biology/computer science/

geography/mathematics/physics; professional development; early mathematics intervention, education, special educational needs coordination, specialist primary mathematics practice (dyslexia),TESOL;

BA(Hons), BSc(Hons), FDA, FDSc, LlB(Hons), LlM, MA, MSc, MSci, PhD, MBA, MRes, PGDip, MSocial-Work, PGDip/Cert, CertHE, FD, MTL, MComp, MMed

UNIVERSITY OF LEEDS
www.leeds.ac.uk

Faculty of Arts; www.leeds.ac.uk/arts

School of English; www.leeds.ac.uk/english
American literature & culture, critical & cultural research, English language/literature, modern & contemporary/Renaissance literature, post-colonial literary & cultural studies, romantic literature & culture, theatre & global development, English literature & linguistics/theatre studies, English & film studies, Victorian literature, jt degrees

School of History; www.leeds.ac.uk/history
history, international history & politics, modern history, race & resistance, social & cultural history, jt hons courses

School of Philosophy, Religion & History of Science; www.leeds.ac.uk/religion_philosophy_and_history_of_science
philosophy, philosophy, ethics and religion, philosophy, politics and economics, philosophy, psychology and scientific thought, religion, politics and society, theology and religious studies, religion and public life, religious studies and global development, theology and religious studies, history & philosophy of science, philosophy of science, history of science, technology & medicine

Institute for Colonial and Post-colonial Studies; www.leeds.ac.uk/icps
post-colonial literary & cultural studies, race & resistance, world cinema, modern languages & cultures

School of Modern Languages and Cultures; www.leeds.ac.uk/smlc
Arabic & Middle Eastern/Islamic studies, Asia-Pacific studies, Chinese, Japanese, South/East Asian studies, Thai studies, French, German, Italian, linguistics & phonetics, Russian & Slavonic studies, Spanish, Portuguese and Latin, applied translation studies, diplo applied translation studies, audiovisual translation studies, conference interpreting and translation studies, diplo conference interpreting, professional language and intercultural studies, Arabic/English translation, linguistics, linguistics and English language teaching, middle eastern and Islamic studies, Chinese studies, Chinese business/and the Asia pacific, East Asian regional development, Japanese business/studies, world cinemas, numerous jt honours

Classics
classical civilisation, liberal arts, liberal arts (international language), ancient history and English/history/ history and philosophy of science/philosophy, theology and religious studies, Arabic and classical literature, classical civilisation and English/ history/ history and philosophy of science/ philosophy, theology and religious studies, classical literature and English, classical literature and French/history/ Italian/philosophy/Russian/Russian/Spanish; Postgrad; Classics; BA(Hons), MA, MPhil, PGDip, PhD, MRes

Faculty of Biological Studies; www.fbs.leeds.ac.uk
biochemistry, biology/with enterprise, biological science, bioscience, biotechnology, biodiversity & conservation, infection, immunology & human disease, medical sciences, plant science & biotechnology, ecology & environmental biology, biodiversity & conservation, genetics, human physiology, medical biochemistry/sciences, microbiology, neuroscience, pharmacology, virology, sport & exercise sciences, sport science & physiology, zoology; BSc(Hons), MRes, MSc, PhD, MBiol

Faculty of Business; www.fbs.leeds.ac.uk

Leeds University Business School; www.leeds.ac.uk/lbs
accounting and finance, actuarial mathematics, aviation technology & management, business analytics, business economics, economics, economics and finance, economics and management, environment, HRM, international business, international business and economics/finance/marketing, management,

management and the human resource, management with marketing, mathematics & finance, economics (numerous jt degrees), management, management (numerous jt degrees), philosophy, politics & economics

Postgrad; accounting and finance, actuarial finance, advertising and design, advertising and marketing, banking and international finance, business analytics and decision sciences, business psychology, consumer analytics & marketing strategy, corporate communications, marketing and PR, economics, economics and finance, engineering, technology and business management, enterprise, executive MBA, finance and investment, financial mathematics, financial risk management, full time MBA, global innovation management, global supply chain management, HRM, information systems & information management, international business, international marketing management, management, organizational behaviour, organizational psychology, strategic management in the global environment; BSc(Hons), BA(Hons), ExecMBA, MA, MBA, MPhil, MSc, PhD

Faculty of Education, Social Sciences & Law; www.essl.leeds.ac.uk

School of Education; www.education.leeds.ac.uk

childhood studies, English, language and education, (degree courses are offered by The Lifelong Learning Centre)

Postgraduate; teaching, education, technology, education and learning, international educational management, education and professional enquiry, special educational needs, provision for children with developmental disorders, deaf education (teacher of the deaf qualification), TESOL/studies, information and communications technology, TESOL for young learners/teacher education, teaching English for academic purposes, educational research methods, clinical education, PGCE; Primary; 3-7 and 7-11; secondary; biology, chemistry, English, mathematics, modern foreign languages, physics, School Direct PGCE primary; 3-7 and 7-11; secondary; various subjects, SCITT PGCE; BA(Hons), MA, MSc, PGCert, MEd, PGCE, PhD

School of Law; www.law.leeds.ac.uk

law, criminal justice & criminology/criminal law, law & French law, European & international business law/corporate law/trade/banking & finance law, intellectual property law, international law, international corporate law, international & European human rights law, law & finance, security & justice, LlB, LlM, MSc, MA, PhD

School of Politics and International Studies; www.leeds.ac.uk/polis

economics & politics, international development/relations, politics, politics & parliamentary studies, theatre & religious studies/global development, international relations & politics of the Middle East, conflict, development & security, security, terrorism & insurgency; BA, MA, MPhil, PhD

School of Sociology and Social Policy; www.sociology.leeds.ac.uk

sociology, social policy, social policy and crime, interdisciplinary social policy and sociology/social and public policy, social policy with enterprise, politics and sociology, politics and social policy, geography and sociology, sociology and international relations, social scxience

Postgrad; social & public policy, social research, international social transformation, social and political thought, global racism studies, disability studies, disability and global development/special education/social policy, gender studies, gender, sexuality and the body; BA(Hons), MA, MPhil, PGCert, PhD

Faculty of Engineering; www.engineering.leeds.ac.uk

School of Civil Engineering; www.engineering.leeds.ac.uk/civil

architectural engineering, civil & environmental engineering/structural engineering, civil engineering with project management/transport, adv concrete engineering, international construction management & engineering, engineering project management, water, sanitation & health engineering, structural engineering, environmental engineering & project management

School of Computing; www.engineering.leeds.ac.uk/comp

applied computer science, computer science, computer science with artificial intelligence/distributed systems/ mathematics, electronics and computer engineering, high performance graphics & games engineering; Postgrad; advanced computer science, advanced computer science (cloud computing/data analytics/intelligent systems), mathematics and computer science, mobile computing and communications networks

School of Electronic and Electrical Engineering;
www.engineering.leeds.ac.uk/elec

electronic engineering, electronic and electrical engineering/communications engineering, electronics and computer engineering/renewable energy systems, mechatronics and robotics, music, multimedia and electronics; Postgrad; communications & signal processing, digital communications networks, electrical engineering and renewable energy systems, electronic and electrical engineering, embedded systems engineering, engineering, technology and business management, mechatronics and robotics, mobile computing and communications networks

Mechanical Engineering;
www.engineering.leeds.ac.uk/mech

aeronautical/& aerospace engineering, automotive engineering, adv/mechanical engineering, mechatronics & robotics, medical engineering, oilfield corrosion engineering, product design, tribology of surfaces & interfaces

School of Chemical & Process Engineering;
www.engineering.leeds.ac.uk/chemical

aviation technology with/management/pilot studies, chemical & energy/materials/minerals/nuclear engineering, chemical engineering, energy & environment, fire & explosion engineering, food processing engineering, materials science & engineering, sustainable energy systems, petroleum production engineering; BEng, MEng, MSc, MSc(Eng), MPhil, PhD

Faculty of the Environment; www.leeds.ac.uk/foe

School of Earth & Environment;
www.see.leeds.ac.uk

geological sciences, geophysical sciences, environmental science, meteorology and climate science, environment and business, sustainability and environmental management; Postgrad; exploration geophysics, structural geology with geophysics, engineering geology petroleum exploration, climate change and environmental policy, environment and development, sustainability and business, sustainability and consultancy, ecological economics

School of Geography;
www.geog.leeds.ac.uk

geography, geography/with transport studies/mathematics/management/economics, geography, geology, GIS, river basin dynamics & management with GIS,

environmental water conservation, consumer analytics & marketing strategy, global urban justice

Institute for Transport Studies;
www.its.leeds.ac.uk

civil engineering with transport, transport planning with environment/mathematical modelling, geography with transport planning, transport economics, sustainability in transport

Earth & Biosphere Institute;
www.earth.leeds.ac.uk/ebi

global change & the biosphere; BA(Hons), BSc(Hons), MA, MGeol, MGeophys, MRes, MSc, PGCert/Dip, PhD, MEnv, MGeol

Faculty of Mathematics and Physical Science; www.maps.leeds.ac.uk

School of Chemistry;
www.chem.leeds.ac.uk

chemistry, chemical process research & development, medicinal chemistry, polymers, colorants & fine chemicals, chemical biology & drug design, natural sciences, chemistry & mathematics

School of Food Science and Nutrition;
www.food.leeds.ac.uk

food quality & innovation, nutrition, food science/& nutrition, food studies

School of Mathematics;
www.maths.leeds.ac.uk

actuarial/financial mathematics, mathematics with statistics, mathematics with biology/economics/management/music, data science & analytics; BSc(Hons), MChem, MMath, MNatSci, MPhil, MPhys, MSc, PhD, GradDip

School of Physics and Astronomy;
www.physics.leeds.ac.uk

physics/with astrophysics, theoretical physics, physics with business management

Faculty of Medicine & Health; www.leeds.ac.uk/medhealth

Leeds Dental Institute; www.leeds.ac.uk/dental

dental hygiene & dental therapy, clinical dentistry, restorative/implant dentistry, dental nursing/surgery/technology, dental public health, paediatric dentistry, oral science

School of Healthcare;
www.healthcare.leeds.ac.uk

adult/child/adult nursing, adv practice, midwifery, social work, advanced practice, clinical assessment, clinical research methods, leadership and management in health and social care, pharmacy practice, psychotherapy and counselling, social work, palliative care, independent and supplementary prescribing

Leeds School of Medicine;
www.leeds.ac.uk/medicine

applied health (medical education/primary care/public health), healthcare science (audiology/cardiac physiology/clinical leadership), clinical sciences (cardiovascular medicine/medical imaging/molecular medicine), international health, medicine and surgery, radiography

Postgraduate; child health, clinical embryology, clinical embryology and assisted reproduction technology, diagnostic imaging, education in primary care, epidemiology and biostatistics, family therapy, health economics, health informatics, health management, planning and policy, health research, international health, international hospital management, medical imaging, medicine, molecular medicine, physician associate studies, international hospital management, public health (international), systemic practice

School of Psychology;
www.psych.leeds.ac.uk

adv/psychology, psychological approach to health, psychology, psychological sciences
BSc, BSc(Hons), CPD, DClinPsych, GradDip, MA, MBChB, MD, MMedSci, MPH, MPsycObs, MSc, PGDip/Cert, PhD

Faculty of Performance, Visual Arts and Communication; www.leeds.ac.uk/pvac

School of Design; www.design.leeds.ac.uk

adv/textile design, advertising & design, art & design, design, fashion design/marketing/technology, fashion, enterprise & society, graphic and communication design, textiles, textile innovation & branding/industry

School of Fine Art, History of Art and Cultural Studies; www.leeds.ac.uk/fine_art

cultural and media studies, fine art, fine art with contemporary cultural theory/ history of art/museum and gallery studies, history of art, history of art with cultural studies/museum studies; Postgraduate; arts management and heritage studies, critical and cultural theory, art gallery and museum studies, fine art, history of art

School of Media & Communication; www.media.leeds.ac.uk

broadcast journalism, communication & media, digital media,, international/political communications, film, photography & media, journalism, new media, media industries, PR & society

School of Music; www.leeds.ac.uk/music

app psychology of music, critical & applied musicology, critical & experimental composition, music, music (performance), music & management, electronic & computer music, musicology, music & management/enterprise, music psychology

School of Performance & Cultural Industries; www.pci.leeds.ac.uk

culture, creativity & entrepreneurship, dance, managing performance, performance design/culture & context, theatre & performance (numerous jt degrees), writing for performance and publication, app theatre & intervention
BA(Hons), GradDip, MFA, BMus, BSc(Hons), MA, MMus, MSc, PhD, PGCert/Dip

Degrees validated by University of Leeds offered at:

COLLEGE OF THE RESURRECTION
college.mirfieldcollege.org.uk

theological studies, ministry & theology, liturgy;
BA(Hons), DipHE, MA, MPhil, PGDip, PhD

LEEDS COLLEGE OF ART
www.leeds-art.ac.uk

creative advertising, creative practice, animation, fashion, fine art, graphic design, illustration, fashion/photography, printed textiles & surface pattern design, visual communication; BA(Hons), FD, MA

LEEDS COLLEGE OF MUSIC
www.lcm.ac.uk

music (classical/folk/pop/production/business), jazz, musicology, new music, songwriting, film music, creative musician; BA(Hons), FD, MA, PGDip, MMus

LEEDS TRINITY UNIVERSITY
www.leedstrinity.ac.uk

Undergraduate & Foundation

accounting and business, broadcast journalism, business and management, business and marketing, counselling psychology, creative and professional writing, criminology, early childhood studies, economics, education and religious studies, education studies, English and creative writing/film studies/media, English language and linguistics, English literature, exercise, health and fitness, exercise, health and nutrition, film, forensic psychology, history, history and philosophy, history and politics, international business, journalism, journalism and politics, magazine journalism, media, media and marketing, nutrition, philosophy, ethics and religion, politics and international relations, primary education – early years (QTS)/ later years (QTS), primary physical education and sports coaching/psychology, psychology and child development, public health and individual wellbeing, secondary education, physical education and sport, secondary physical education and sports coaching/sports development, sociology, sociology and criminology, sport and exercise sciences, sport and exercise sciences (sports nutrition), sport management, sport psychology, sports coaching, sports journalism, strength and conditioning, television production, theology and religious studies, working with children, young people and families

Postgraduate; film, forensic psychology, history, history and philosophy, history and politics, international business, journalism, journalism and politics BA(Hons), BSc(Hons),FD, PGCert/Dip, PGCE, MA, MSc, MPhil, PhD, MBA

NORTHERN SCHOOL OF CONTEMPORARY DANCE
www.nscd.ac.uk

contemporary dance; BPA(Hons), PGDip, MA, FD

YORK ST JOHN UNIVERSITY
www.yorksj.ac.uk

Faculty of Arts; www.yorksj.ac.uk/arts/faculty.of.arts

applied theatre, music composition, computer science/aided design, dance, education & community, English literature, film studies, fine arts, graphics/interior design, history, human geography, illustration,mass communication, media/production/journalism/theatre, theatre & performance; FD, BA(Hons), PGCert/Dip, MA

Faculty of Education & Theology; www.yorksj.ac.uk/education-theology

PGCE, primary/secondary education, education studies, early childhood studies, academic practice, religious studies, initial teacher education, contemporary religion,, supporting learning, theology & ministry/religious studies, chaplaincy studies, military chaplaincy, religion, philosophy & ethics, religion & education/public life, Christian theology, Catholic studies, theology & ministry, primary education with QTS, teacher education, children, school leadership, schools direct (primary/secondary), children, sociology, working with children & young people, youth & community work; MFL, BA(Hons), GradDip, PGDip, PGCE, PhD

Faculty of Health & Life Sciences; www.yorksj.ac.uk/health-and-life-sciences

applied cognitive psychology, biomedical sciences, counselling/supervision, coaching & /psychotherapy studies, occupational therapy, physiotherapy, psychology, community & clinical social psychology, psychology/of child & adolescent development, applied sport & exercise science, nutrition & exercise for health, PE/& sport coaching/youth sport, sports development & coaching, sports science & injury rehabilitation, strength & conditioning; BA(Hons), MA, MSc, PGDip/Cert, PhD

York St John Business School; www.yorksj.ac.uk/business

accounting & finance, business management/& HRM/languages/finance, business administration with finance/design management/media management, business information technology, coaching & mentoring, applied linguistics TESOL, English language & linguistics, design & creativity, languages, British sign language & English language/literature, French/German/Spanish/Japanese and English literature/language, strategic/HRM, international business management, marketing management/ web technology, global marketing, languages, leadership & management, leading innovation & change, international business, international tourism management/& hospitality management, tourism management/& marketing, MBA (finance/design/marketing); BA(Hons), FD, MA, PGDip/Cert, MBA

LEEDS BECKETT UNIVERSITY
www.leedsbeckett.ac.uk

Faculty of Arts, Environment & Technology; www.leedsbeckett.ac.uk/aet

The Leeds School of Art, Architecture & Design; www.leedsbeckett.ac.uk/aet/#art-architecture-design

architecture, architectural professional practice, art & design, artist teacher in art & design, design practice, fashion, fine art, interior architecture & design, urban design, graphic art & design, professional studies, landscape architecture & design, urban design

School of Built Environment & Engineering; www.leedsbeckett.ac.uk/aet/#built-environment-engineering

adv engineering management, building/engineering studies/services engineering, civil engineering/& construction, construction/commercial/management, strategic/project management, facilities management, architectural technology, building/quantity surveying, environmental engineering & construction, health & neighbourhood planning, housing/strategy, housing, regeneration & urban management, planning law & practice, strategic project management, project management/construction, town & regional planning, UK planning law & dispute practice, sustainable urban planning

School of Computing, Creative Technology & Engineering; www.leedsbeckett.ac.uk/aet/#computing-creative-technology

advanced engineering management, business information technology/intelligence, computer forensics/& security, computer science computing/systems engineering, computer sustainable engineering, creative media/technology, digital forensics & security/journalism/photography, electrical & electronic engineering, engineering robotics & automation, food engineering, games design, information management/systems, web applications development, mathematics & computer science, mobile device applications, information & technology/management, broadcast media technologies, computer animation/& special effects & visual effects, sustainable computing/technology, creative technology, 3D visualisation & interactive environments, networking systems engineering

School of Cultural Studies & Humanities; www.leedsbeckett.ac.uk/as/cs

English/& history/media/creative writinf, English literature, history, media, communication & cultures, English contemporary literature, social history; BA(Hons), BSc(Hons), DipHE, FdAA, GradCert, MPhil, MRes, MSc, PGDip

School of Film, Music & Performing Arts; www.leedsbeckett.ac.uk/aet/#film-music-performingarts

music performance/production/technology, dance, audio engineering, performance, music for moving image, sound & music for interactive games, sound design, pop music & culture, documentary film making

Northern Film School

animation, film making, film & TV

Faculty of Business and Law; www.leedsbeckett.ac.uk/fbl

Leeds Business School; www.leedsbeckett.ac.uk/fbl/leeds_business_school

business analytics/finance/marketing, business management development, business studies/administration/economics, business & management/HRM/management studies, action by facilitation, corporate governance/communications, executive leadership/business coaching, entrepreneurship & business, HRM, international HRM, international business/communications/business law/trade & finance/banking & investment/leadership/marketing, journalism, leadership & change, management, marketing, marketing & advertising management, PR & communication/journalism/strategic communication, retail marketing management, strategic & digital marketing, supply chain management & logistics, MBA (Executive/Graduate)

Leeds Law School; www.leedsbeckett.ac.uk/lbs/law

law, legal practice, international business law, law & finance/international business/management; BA(Hons), HND, LlB(Hons), LlM, MA, MSc, PGDip/Cert, MBA, DBA

Faculty of Health & Social Sciences; www.leedsbeckett.ac.uk/hss

Social Sciences & Psychology

playwork, youth work & community development, young people, communities and society, criminology, criminology & psychology, psychology, psychology & society, social psychology, social work, sociology, therapeutic counselling, young people, communities and society, youth work & community development,- Postgraduate; advanced social work practice, art psychotherapy practice, criminology, interdisciplinary psychology, interpersonal & counselling skills, mental health practice, psychological therapies, psychology, psychotherapy, youth work & community development, community & youth studies

Health

environmental health, toxicological sciences, nutrition adult nursing, biomedical sciences (human biology/microbiology/molecular biology), dietetics, environmental health, health and community care, mental health nursing, nutrition, nutritional health, physiotherapy, safety, health & environmental management, speech & language therapy, sports and exercise therapy, support work; Postgraduate; acoustics, advanced practice, advanced social work practice, applied biomedical sciences research, chaplaincy in health & social care, community & youth studies, community specialist practitioner – district nursing, dietetics, eating disorders, environmental health, health and community care, health and safety, mental health practice, microbiology and biotechnology, nutrition in practice, occupational therapy, physiotherapy, play therapy, practice based play therapy, public health, health promotion, social work, specialist community public health nursing – health visiting/occupational health nursing/school nursing, therapeutic play skills, toxicological sciences

Short Courses and CP; BA(Hons), BSc(Hons), CertHE, MA, MSc, PGDip/Cert, Prof Dip, DipHE, FdAA, GradCert, MPhil, MRes, PGDip, MBioms

Carnegie Faculty; www.leedsbeckett.ac.uk/carnegie

childhood and early years, higher and further education, childhood studies, education studies, internationalisation inclusion training in intellectual disability for educators in Europe, partnerships with schools playwork researchers, childhood outdoor & adventurous activities, psychology, strength & coordination, PE, leisure, sport & culture, PE with outdoor education, sport & exercise science, sport & business management/development/management/coaching/studies, sport physical activity & health, sport & exercise medication, psychology of sport & exercise, international/event management, sport event management, sport & exercise/biomedicine/

nutrition/physiology/health/psychology/science/therapy, sport, law & society, conference & exhibition management, entertainment management, managing cultural & major events, event sponsorship and fundraising; BA(Hons), BSc(Hons), FdSc, PGCE, PGCert/Dip, MA, PhD, Prof DocEd

UNIVERSITY OF LEICESTER
www.le.ac.uk

College of Arts, Humanities and Law; www2.le.ac.uk/colleges/artshumlaw

School of Archaeology & Ancient History; www.le.ac.uk/ar
American studies, ancient history and archaeology/classical archaeology/history, archaeology, contemporary history, English and American studies/ history, history and American studies/archaeology/politics, humanities and arts, international relations and history; Postgraduate; archaeology, archaeology and heritage, archaeology of the Roman world, country house (art, history and literature), English local history and family history, heritage and interpretation, history, the classical Mediterranean, urn conservation/ Victorian studies

School of English; www.le.ac.uk/ee
English studies, English, English & American studies/history/French/Spanish/Italian/film studies/history of art, history & literature, modern literature & creative writing/linguistics, Victorian studies

Dept of History of Art and Film; www.le.ac.uk/ha
the country house in art, history & culture, film studies and visual arts/English/media studies, history of art/& English, film & film cultures

School of History; www.le.ac.uk/hi
contemporary history, English local history & family history, history, history and politics/international relations/ancient history/archaeology/English/American studies, urban history/conservation,

School of Law; www.le.ac.uk/law
law, international/human rights/commercial law/law, public international law, general law, law with French law, law & criminology/politics/languages

School of Modern Languages; www.le.ac.uk/ml
European studies, French/German/Italian/Spanish & English, modern language studies, modern languages with management/EFL/film studies/translation, translation & interpreting/ international communication & culture, translation studies

Museum Studies; www.le.ac.uk /ms
art museum/& gallery studies, heritage & interpretation, museum studies, security engaged practice

Education
primary PGCE,/School Direct, Secondary PGCE/School Direct; Masters; applied linguistics and TESOL, education: learning and teaching, International education, TESO)L

Economics
economics and accounting, economics, business economics, financial economics, banking and finance; Postgraduate; banking and finance, business analysis and finance, economics, financial economics, financial risk management

Criminology
criminology, clinical criminology, applied criminology, terrorism, security & policing
BA(Hons), BSc(Hons), LlB, LlM, MSc, MA/GradDip, MPhil, PhD

College of Science and Engineering; www2.le.ac.uk/colleges/science

Dept of Chemistry; www.le.ac.uk/ch
biomedical engineering,chemistry, cancer chemistry, chemistry with forensic science, pharmaceutical chemistry, chemical research (biological/green/physical chemistry), forensic science & criminal justice

Dept of Computer Science; www.cs.le.ac.uk
advanced computational methods/distributed systems/software engineering, agile software engineering technologies, adv/computer science, computing, computing with management, software engineering for financial services, web applications & services, cloud computing

Dept of Engineering; www2.le.ac.uk/departments/engineering
advanced control & dynamics, advanced engineering, advanced materials engineering, aerospace engineering, communications & electronic engineering, high reliability embedded systems, engineering management, adv/electrical & electronic engineering,

embedded systems & control engineering, general engineering, information & communication engineering, adv/mechanical engineering, software & electronic engineering

Dept of Geography; www.le.ac.uk/geography

environmental informatics, geography, geology, GIS with industry, human/physical geography, sustainable management of natural resources

Dept of Geology; www2.le.ac.uk/departments/geology

applied & environmental geology, crustal processes, geology, geology with geophysics/palaeobiology, geography, rock physics & boreholes, palaeobiology, palaeoenvironments, palaeoclimates

Dept of Mathematics; www2.le.ac.uk/departments/mathematics

mathematics, actuarial science, data analysis, financial mathematics/& computation, mathematical modelling in biology, mathematics with management/economics/actuarial science

Dept of Physics and Astronomy; www2.le.ac.uk/departments/physics

astronomy, physics, physics with nanotechnology/astrophysics/space science & technology/planetary science, space exploration systems, natural sciences, applied computation & human modelling, BA(Hons), BSc(Hons), BEng/MEng, MA, MChem, MComp, MGeol, MMath, MPhil, MPhys, MSc, MSci, PGDip, PhD

College of Medicine, Biological Sciences and Psychology; www2.le.ac.uk/colleges/medbiopsych

School of Biological Sciences; www2.le.ac.uk/departments/biologicalscience

bioinformatics, biological sciences (biochemistry/genetics/microbiology/physiology with pharmacology/zoology), medical genetics, microbiology/physiology, molecular genetics, cell physiology & pharmacology

Dept of Medical & Social Care Education Medicine; www2.le.ac.uk/departments/msce

medicine, operating department practice, physiotherapy, social work
medicine, cancer cell studies & molecular medicine/biology, bioinformatics, cardiovascular sciences,

chronic disease & immunity, clinical science, health sciences, infection & immunisation, medical statistics, medical & social care education, molecular pathology/toxicology, mountain medicine, occupational psychology, operating department practice, pain management, physiotherapy, primary care research, social science applied to health, child & adolescent mental health, integrated provision for children & families, social work

School of Psychology; www2.le.ac.uk/departments/psychology

psychology/with sociology/cognitive neuroscience/media, applied psychology,clinical/forensic psychology, applied forensic psychology, forensic legal psychology, psychological research methods
Dept of Health & Social Care
applied health nursing, diabetes
DocClinPsych, BSc, MBChB, MBioSci, MD, MSc, PostgradDip/Cert, PhD

College of the Social Sciences; www.le.ac.uk/colleges/socsci

Dept of Criminology; www2.le.ac.uk/departments/criminology

applied/clinical/criminology, terrorism, security & policing, criminology

Dept of Economics; www2.le.ac.uk/departments/economics

banking & finance, business/financial economics, economics, business analysis & finance, financial risk management

School of Education; www2.le.ac.uk/departments/education

action research, educational studies, education, educational leadership, learning & teaching, understanding and managing children/mental health problems and children with social, learning/emotional and behavioural difficulties, specialist assessment and teaching of pupils with specific learning difficulties, promoting language development in the early years, issues in mathematics/science/English education, mentoring and coaching, developing leadership in education, teaching mathematics, teaching English for academic purposes, education and sustainable development, PGCE primary/secondary education, teachfirst, TESOL & applied linguistics

Institute of Lifelong Learning; www2.le.ac.uk/departments/lifelong-learning

global ecology and wildlife conservation, leadership and business management, psychology, social science, social welfare, advice and guidance, humanities and arts, counselling, integrative counselling, drug and alcohol counselling and treatment, psychodynamic counselling and psychotherapy, popular culture and spirituality/religion

School of Management; www2.le.ac.uk/departments/management

accounting economics, management studies (finance/organisation studies), finance, markets & organisational management, marketing, finance, economics, politics, business administration, global financial markets, HRM/ & training, management & economics/politics

Dept of Media & Communication; www.le.ac.uk/mc

mass communication, global media & communication, mass communication, media & PR/advertising, film & media, new media & society, media & communication/society, media, culture & society, journalism studies

Dept of Politics and International Relations; www2.le.ac.uk/departments/politics

diplomatic studies, politics/ & international relations/history, politics & sociology/history/management studies/economics, human rights & global ethics, international relations & history, politics of the EU, law with politics, international relations & world order, intelligence & security, politics, conflict & violence

Dept of Sociology; www2.le.ac.uk/departments/sociology

politics & sociology, psychology with sociology, media, culture & society, migration studies, sociology, contemporary sociology, social research; BA(Hons), DocSocSci, EdD, FD, MA, MBA, MPhil, MSc, PGCE, PGDip/Cert, PhD, CertHE

Degrees validated by the University of Leicester offered at:

NEWMAN UNIVERSITY
www.newman.ac.uk

accounting and finance; counselling studies and working with children, young people and families / international social work/and education studies, social sciences, safeguarding; art and design, art and education; business management, marketing, master of business administration (MBA); PGCE secondary computer science and ICT (QTS); counselling, counselling studies and working with children, young people and families, education and counselling studies, integrative counselling, professional integrative psychotherapy (child and adolescent or adult), social sciences; drama, theatre and applied performance, drama and education/English, humanities; community & applied drama, early childhood education and care, early years early childhood education and care, EYITT (GE/GET); economics, economics practice, art/drama/counselling studies/English/history/philosophy/religion & education, professional practice, sport and education, studies in primary education, theology and education, working with children, young people & families and education studies, teaching and learning support, catholic school leadership, education, higher education practice; English literature, creative writing/drama/creative writing//education & English, PGCE secondary English (QTS) applied health and social care, history, history and education/theology, heritage and public history, humanities, Victorian studies; mathematics; sport and education, sport and exercise science, sport and exercise studies, sport coaching science, sport coaching science and tournament golf; psychology and childhood studies, psychology, psychology and counselling studies, sport and exercise psychology, applications of psychology, clinical applications of psychology; subjects with QTS, classroom musical skills, school direct (QTS), education, theology, English and theology, history and theology, philosophy, religion & education theology and education, contemporary Christian theology, humanities, Catholic social teaching, Catholic certificate in religious studies, people and families, applied social science, counselling studies and working with children, young people and families, working with children, young people and families /international social work/education studies, youth and community work, social sciences,youth studies, chaplaincy with young people, chaplaincy studies; BA/BSc(Hons), FD, MA, MPhil, PGCE, PhD, MBA

UNIVERSITY OF LINCOLN
www.lincoln.ac.uk

School of Architecture & Design;
www.lincoln.ac.uk/home/ad
architecture, creative advertising, design for exhibition and museums, interactive design, interior architecture and design; Postgraduate; architecture-research opportunities, design for exhibition and museums, graphic design, interior architecture and design, international design enterprise, professional practice and management in architecture

School of English & Journalism;
www.lincoln.ac.uk/home/ej
English, English and creative writing/ history/ journalism, journalism, PR, journalism and PR; Postgraduate; 21st century literature, arts journalism, creative writing, digital journalism, English – by research, English studies, journalism/ by research, journalism war and international human rights, nineteenth century studies, PR, science and environmental journalism, sports journalism

Lincoln School of Film & Media;
www.lincoln.ac.uk/home/fm
animation, audio production, film and television, media production, photography; Postgraduate; digital media, media & cultural studies, media, media, film and TV production, photography

School of Fine & Performing Arts;
www.lincoln.ac.uk/home/fpa
dance, drama, drama and English, fashion, fine art, music; Postgraduate; art, art and design research, choreography, drama, fine art, performing arts research

School of History & Heritage;
www.lincoln.ac.uk/home/hh
conservation of cultural heritage, history; Postgraduate; historical studies, history research, medieval studies; BA(Hons), BArch, GradDip, MA, MArch, MPhil, PhD, MRes

College of Social Science;
www.lincoln.ac.uk/home/ collegeofsocialscience

School of Education; www.lincoln.ac.uk/ home/ed

educational research & development, PGCE secondary, social research

School of Health & Social Care
adv professional practice in social work, nursing, nursing (mental health), health & social care, professional practice, interprofessional practice (mental health professional), non-medical/independent prescribing, social research, social work

Lincoln Law School
law, law & criminology, international business law, international law, social research

School of Psychology
psychology, psychology with clinical forensic psychology, developmental psychology, social research, healthcare in secure environment, psychological research methods

School of Social & Political Science
politics, sociology, politics & social policy, criminology, criminology & politics/social policy/society, global justice, social research, social science, international relations/& politics/social policy, social policy & society, gender studies

School of Sport & Exercise Science
physical activity & health development, sports & exercise science, sports development & coaching, sport & PE, sports coaching/development/science, strength & conditioning in sport
BA(Hons), BSc(Hons), CertHE, DClinPsy, MA, MClinRes, MPhil, PGCert, PhD, LlB(Hons), LlM, MBA, MPhil, MRes, MSc, EdD

Lincoln International Business School;
www.lincoln.ac.uk/home/lbs
accountancy & finance, accounting, advertising & marketing, banking & finance, business & finance/management/marketing/entrepreneurship

development, business studies, crisis global operations, management & industrial relations, marketing/with luxury brands, project management, tourism & marketing; BA(Hons), BSc(Hons), MA, MSc, MFin, MEcon, PGCert/Dip, MBA

College of Science; www.lincoln.ac.uk/science

Lincoln School of Chemistry
chemistry, forensic chemistry/science, research in chemistry, conservation science

Lincoln School of Computer Science
computer science, games computing, intelligence systems

Lincoln School of Engineering
automation engineering/building control, electrical engineering (control systems/electronics/power & energy), mechanical engineering/control systems, engineering management

School of Life Science
animal behaviour & welfare/science, clinical animal behaviour, biochemistry/molecular biology, biology,

biomedical science, bioveterinary science, biotechnology, evolution & ecology, life sciences, microbiology, biomedical & medical science, forensic science, zoology

School of Mathematics & Physics
mathematics, physics, mathematics & physics/computer science, pure/applied mathematics, computational physics

Lincoln School of Pharmacy; www.lincoln.ac.uk/home/lsp
pharmacy/& pharmaceutical science

National Centre for Food Manufacturing
food manufacture (operations management/quality assessment & technology management), food manufacture & technology

Centre for Educational Research & Development
educational research, social research, PGCE secondary; BA(Hons), BSc(Hons), BEng(Hons), MEng(Hons), FdSc, MA, MComp, MPhil, MRes, MSc, PhD, EdD, PhD, MPharm, MBio, MMath, MPhys

Degrees validated by the University of Lincoln offered at:

EAST RIDING COLLEGE
www.eastridingcollege.ac.uk

contemporary media, design and production, education and professional development, early childhood policy and practice, learning support, leisure management, early childhood policy and practice, sport, exercise and health sciences; BA(Hons), FdA, FdEd, FdSc, PGCE

HULL COLLEGE
www.hull-college.ac.uk

Faculty of Arts

Hull School of Art & Design; www.hull-college.ac.uk/hull-school-of-art-and-design
technical and theatre production, acting with theatre practice, animation, architecture, broadcast media, creative practice, dance, design (interior, product, designer maker), fashion, film-making & creative media, production, fine art, games design, graphic design, illustration, journalism & digital media, music production/theatre, performance arts, photography, textiles, web design, visual culture: theory and practice; BA(Hons), FdA, MA, MArch

Faculty of Business & Science
applied social sciences, business leadership, business management, computing, construction management, travel & tourism management, criminology, engineering technology, express logistics, management, sport, young children's learning and development, health, exercise and lifestyle and health and social care, engineering, sport & health science, sport studies, sustainable construction, digital; FdA, FdSc, BSc(Hons), BA(Hons), PGCE, BEng(Hons)

NORTH LINDSEY COLLEGE
www.northlindsey.ac.uk

applied studies, business studies, business & HRM, biochemistry, bioscience, counselling, leadership & management, applied studies, children learning & development, learning support, integrated engineering (electrical/mechanical), English, history, social science, sport development & coaching, PGCE, sport & exercise science (personal training/coaching); BA(Hons), Dips, FdA/Sc/Ed/Eng, Grad Cert Ed, PGCE

UNIVERSITY OF LIVERPOOL
www.liv.ac.uk

Faculty of Health & Life Sciences; www.liv.ac.uk/health_and_life_sciences

Dentistry; www.liverpool.ac.uk/dentistry
dental hygiene/therapy/surgery, orthodontics, endodontics

Health Sciences; www.liverpool.ac.uk/health-sciences
adv practice in healthcare, diagnostic radiography, health & veterinary studies, nursing, occupational therapy, orthoptics, physiotherapy, radiotherapy, CPD

Life Sciences; www.liverpool.ac.uk/life-sciences
anatomy & human biology, biochemistry, biological/ & medical sciences, bioveterinary science, genetics, microbiology, molecular biology & biotechnology, pharmacology, physiology, tropical disease biology, zoology, advanced biological science (numerous subjects)

Medicine; www.liverpool.ac.uk/medicine
medicine, surgery, medical science, public health, CPD

Psychology; www.liverpool.ac.uk/psychology
psychology, investigative & forensic psychology, mental health psychology, organisational & business psychology, research methods

Veterinary Science; www.liverpool.ac.uk/veterinary-science
veterinary science, health & veterinary science, veterinary physiology/professional studies/business management, adv veterinary practice, bovine reproduction

Institute of Ageing & Chronic Disease; www.liv.ac.uk/ageing-and-chronic-diseases
anatomy & human biology, clinical sciences, musculoskeletal ageing

Institute of Infection & Global Health; www.liv.ac.uk/infection-and-global-health
clinical science, critical care, dental microbiology, epidemiology/ & population health, food security, gastrointestinal diseases, global health, immunology, infectious diseases, infection & global health (medical/veterinary), infection & immunity, medical parasitology, neurological science, one health medical/veterinary), respiratory diseases, veterinary epidemiology/ immunology/ microbiology/ parasitology/ pathology/ virology), virology

Institute of Integrative Biology; www.liv.ac.uk/integrative-biology
advanced biological sciences, biochemistry, evolution, ecology & behaviour, functional & comparative genomes

Institute of Psychology, Health & Society; www.liv.ac.uk/psychology-health-and-society
medicine and surgery, psychology, dental surgery, medical education, mental health psychology, organisational and business psychology, psychology, primary care, public health, reading for life

Institute of Translational Medicine; www.liv.ac.uk/translational-medicine
physiology, pharmacology, anatomy & human biology, biomedical science & translational medicine, biostatistics, cancer biology, cancer medicine, cellular and molecular physiology, child health, gastroenterology, haematology and leukaemia, medical imaging, ocular oncology, orthopaedic biology, pancreatology, pathology, pharmacology, radiotherapy, surgery and oncology, women's health

BSc(Hons), BN, BVSc, BDS, MBChB, FD, PGCert/Dip, MRes, MSc, MPhil, PhD, MD, MChOrth, MCommH,

D/MClinPsychol, MDS, MPH, MRCPsych, MTCH&CP, MTropMed, MTropPaed

Faculty of Humanities & Social Sciences; www.liv.ac.uk/ humanities_and_social_sciences/hss

School of the Arts; www.liv.ac.uk/arts

Architecture; www.liv.ac.uk/lsa/index.htm

architecture, digital integrated design, sustainable architectural design, design studies, building information modelling, arts

Communications & Media; www.liv.ac.uk/ communication-and-media/index.htm

communications & media, politics & mass media, arts (communication), media & communication (digital culture & communication)

English; www.liv.ac.uk/english/index.htm

applied linguistics, English language/literature, arts, directed studies/modern & contemporary literature/ Renaissance & 18th century literature, Victorian literature, reading in practice, TESOL

Music; www.liv.ac.uk/music/index.htm

music, pop music, music industry,arts (music), music & technology

Philosophy; www.liv.ac.uk/philosophy/index.htm

philosophy, philosophy & mathematics/law, art aesthetics & cultural institutions

Combined Honours

combined honours, science programme, two/three subject, first/second year

School of History, Language & Cultures

Archaeology, Classics & Egyptology; www.liv.ac.uk/ sace/index.htm

archaeology, classics/ & ancient history, classics, palaeanthropology Egyptology, ancient history & archaeology

History; www.liv.ac.uk/history/index.htm

history, 18th century worlds, 20th century history, cultural history, medieval & Renaissance studies

Irish Studies; www.liv.ac.uk/irish/index.htm

Irish studies, peace & conflict studies

Modern Language & Cultures; www.liv.ac.uk/soclas/ index.htm

French, German, Basque, Catalan, Portuguese, Italian, Spanish, Latin American studies, Chinese, modern languages & cultures, film studies; BA(Hons), MA, MArch, MPhil, PhD, MAML, LAML

Politics; www.liv.ac.uk/politics/index.htm

politics, international politics & policy, politics & international business, international relations & security

School of Law & Social Justice; www.liv.ac.uk/law-and-social-justice/index.htm

Liverpool Law School; www.liv.ac.uk/law/index.htm

law, law & business & accounting/accountancy & finance/business studies/criminology/philosophy/ French/German/Italian/Spanish, international human rights/business law, European law, law, medicine & healthcare

Dept of Sociology, Social Policy & Criminology; www. liv.ac.uk/sociology-social-policy-and-criminology

sociology, sociology, criminology & security/psychology/politics, law with criminology, sociology & history/philosophy, criminology research, social policy/criminology/history/philosophy, research methodology (sociology & social policy), social research

School of Management; www.liv.ac.uk/ management

University of Liverpool Management School: accounting & finance, big data management, business economics/management, digital business enterprise management, economics, finance, finance & investment management, international business, marketing, finance risk management,, law with accounting/business, operations & supply chain management, programme & project management, management & entrepreneurship/finance, management, managing international development, marketing, business law & HRM; BA(Hons), MA, MMus, MPhil, MBA, PhD, MRes, PGDip/Cert

Faculty of Science & Engineering; www.liv.ac.uk/science_and_engineering

School of Engineering; www.liv.ac.uk/ engineering

adv/aerospace engineering/pilot studies, adv engineering management, adv manufacturing systems & technology,architectural engineering, biomedical engineering, civil engineering, civil & structural/ environmental engineering, adv/mechanical engineering/with business, industrial design, mechanical engineering, materials, mechanical & materials engineering, nuclear power engineering, product design & management, risk & uncertainty, sustainable structural engineering

Electrical Engineering & Electronics; www.liv.ac.uk/eee

avionic systems, computer science & electronic engineering, electrical & electronic engineering, engineering, mechatronics & robotic systems, microelectronic systems & telecommunications, energy & power systems, telecommunications & wireless systems

Dept of Computer Science; www.csc.liv.ac.uk systems/engineering

adv/computer science, computing, electronic commerce computing, computer information systems, internet computing, software development, artificial intelligence, e-finance, mathematics and computer science, computer science and electronic engineering, advanced computer science/with internet economics, big data and high performance computing

School of Environmental Sciences; www.liv.ac.uk/environmental-sciences

earth sciences, geology (North America), geology and geophysics, geology and physical geography, geology, geophysics (geology/physics), geology & geophysics, ocean sciences, geography and oceanography, marine biology with oceanography, sea level: from coast to global ocean, ecology and environment, marine biology, marine biology with oceanography, conservation & resource management, marine planning & management environment, geography, mathematics with ocean & climate science, geology & physical geography, oceans, climate and physical geography, contemporary human geography (research methods), environment and climate change, environmental science, geographic data science, geography & planning, petroleum reservoir science, population and health, geography and planning, environment and planning, urban regeneration and

planning, town and regional planning, environmental assessment and management, marine planning and management, town and regional planning, urban regeneration and management, urban design and property development, environmental sciences, conservation and resource management

School of Physical Sciences

Chemistry; www.liv.ac.uk/chemistry/index.htm

chemistry, medicinal chemistry with pharmacology, adv chemical science (organic with catalysis/chemical synthesis/biomolecular chemistry/nanoscale with materials interfacial chemistry), chemistry with nanotechnology

Mathematical Sciences; www.liv.ac.uk/mathematical-sciences/

mathematics, actuarial mathematics, pure/applied mathematics, mathematical sciences, financial mathematics, mathematical/theoretical physics, statistics & probability, mathematics with economics/computer science/education/physics/European languages/statistics

Physics; www.liv.ac.uk/physics

physics, astronomy, astrophysics, mathematical/theoretical physics, nuclear science/& technology, physics with medical applications/astronomy/radiation protection/nuclear science/business studies, finance, physics for new technology, medical physics & clinical engineering, radiometrics: instrumentation & modelling; BSc(Hons), MChem, BEng, MEng, DEng, MPhil, MMath, MPhys, MSci, MRes, MSc, PhD, MSc(Eng), MMarBiol, MEcol

Degrees validated at the University of Liverpool offered by:

LIVERPOOL HOPE UNIVERSITY
www.hope.ac.uk

Faculty of Arts & Humanities; www.hope.ac.uk/artsand humanities

Business School; accounting, business management, law, marketing, business & management, HRM/D, Int MBA, marketing management, tourism management
Drama, Dance & Performance Studies; creative & performing arts, dance, contemporary pop theatre, drama & theatre studies
English; English language/literature
Fine & Applied Art; art & design history, design, fine art, art history & curating, creative practice, museum & heritage studies

History & Politics; history, international relations/& politics, peace studies
Law; law
Media & Communications; media & communications, creative writing, film, media & society
Music; music, creative practice, the Beatles,pop music & society
Social Work, Care & Justice; childhood & youth, social policy/work, health & wellbeing, youth & community work
Social Science; criminology, sociology
Theology, Philosophy & Religion; biblical studies, Christian theology, philosophy & ethics/religion,

theology, world religions, biblical & pastoral theology, theology & religious studies
BA(Hons), BSc(Hons), MA, PGCert, BMin, MMin, FdA, MSc, BDes, LlB

Faculty of Education; www.hope.ac.uk/ education

disability studies in education, primary education (QTS), special educational needs, early childhood, education
Postgraduate; disability studies, special educational needs, developmental psychology and early childhood, interdisciplinary studies in education, PGCE primary (QTS), PGCE early Years (QTS)
PGCE secondary (QTS), PGDE, MEd professional practice, School Direct, education, international education, education (subject specialisms), education & biology/English language/ English literature/geography/music; BA(Hons), MA, EdD, PGCE

Faculty of Science; www.hope.ac.uk/ science

Geography & Environmental Science: environmental science/management, tourism, geography
Health Sciences: biology, applied exercise physiology, biological sciences, skills acquisition and human movement, human biology, exercise and ageing, nutrition, sports nutrition, sport and exercise science, international sports management, sport and physical education, bioinformatics and systems biology, sport psychology
Mathematics & Computer Science: computing, computer science, information technology, mathematical informatics, mathematics, electronic engineering
Psychology: psychology, sports psychology, cognitive neuroscience & neuroimaging
Social Work, Care & Justice: social work, criminology, criminal justice, social policy; BA(Hons), BSc(Hons), MA, MBA, MPhil, MSc, PhD

LIVERPOOL JOHN MOORES UNIVERSITY
www.ljmu.ac.uk

Faculty of Arts, Professional & Social Studies; www.ljmu.ac.uk/APS

Liverpool Business School; www.ljmu.ac.uk/lbs

accounting & finance, business administration (M/DBA) studies/management, business & PR/HRM, digital/financial/marketing, executive/financial management, finance, international business & management, entrepreneurship, HRM/D, management & digital humanities, marketing, management

School of Law; www.ljmu.ac.uk/LAW

law, law & /criminal justice, forensic psychology, global crime, justice & security, international business, corporate & finance law, legal practice; BA(Hons), BSc(Hons), DBA, MBA, LlB, LlM, MA, MBA, MPhil, MRes, MSc, PGDip/Cert, PhD

Liverpool School of Art & Design; www.ljmu.ac.uk/addies

architecture, art & design, art in science, contemporary art, fashion/innovation & realisation, graphic design & illustration, fine art, history of art, exhibition studies, urban design

Liverpool Screen School; www.ljmu.ac.uk/ LSS

creative writing, English, drama, media production, international news journalism, journalism, writing, screenwriting, film studies

School of Humanities & Social Science; www.ljmu.ac.uk/HSS

critical social science, criminology & psychology/sociology, English/& creative writing, international policing policy, media & cultural studies, modern/history, history & English, mass communications, media/& cultural studies, policing studies & computer forensics/cyber crime/evidence-based policing/forensic psychology/forensics, cities, culture & creativity, sociology; BA, BA(Hons), BDes, DipArch, DipHE, MA, MPhil, MRes, PG, PGCE, PhD

Faculty of Education, Health & Community; www.ljmu.ac.uk/ECL

Centre for Public Health

public health, international public health, public health (addictions), public health: policy and practice, environmental health, epidemiology, public health intelligence, research methods, health improvement, health protection, violence, alcohol and tobacco control, work based learning, understanding addictions, addictions: interventions and policies, epidemiology, public health intelligence, research methods, health improvement, health protection, violence, alcohol and tobacco control, work based learning, understanding addictions, addictions: interventions and policies

School of Sports Studies, Leisure & Nutrition

dance practices, disability sport coaching and development, events management, food development and nutrition, nutrition, outdoor education, physical education, sport and nutrition for health, sport business, sport coaching, sport development, tourism and leisure management, dance practices, Postgraduate; international events management, international tourism management, public health nutrition, sport studies, leisure and nutrition, sport coaching

School of Education

early childhood studies, education studies and early years, education studies and special and inclusive needs, learning, development and support, mathematics and education studies, primary education with recommendation for qualified teacher status (QTS); Postgraduate; advanced educational practice: dyslexia, advanced educational practice: leadership and management, advanced educational practice: special educational needs, PGDE; biology/chemistry/QTS, digital literacies and learning, education and society, education, globalisation and social change, education practice, English: international approaches to early childhood education, PGDE, PGDE primary key stage 1/2 (5-11 years)/physics/physics with mathematics: primary foundation stage/key stage 1 (3-7 years) with QTS PGDE, PGDE, QTS, special educational needs

School of Nursing & Allied Health

nursing with registered nurse status (adult/child/mental health), midwifery with registered midwife status, health and social care for individuals, families and communities, special community practitioner children's nursing/district nursing/health visiting/school nursing/general practice, paramedic practice, advanced healthcare practice(clinical), counselling and psychotherapeutic practice, social work, improving access to psychological therapies in primary care, continuous professional development; BA(Hons), BSc(Hons), EdD, FD, MA, MPhil, MRes, PGCert, PGDip, PhD

Faculty of Science; www.ljmu.ac.uk/faculties/scs

School of Sports & Exercise Science; www.ljmu.ac.uk/sps

sport & exercise science/physiology, clinical biomechanics/exercise psychology, science & football, app/sports psychology, clinical exercise physiology, sport nutrition

School of Pharmacy & Biomolecular Sciences; www.ljmu.ac.uk/PBS

applied chemistry, biomedical sciences, biochemistry, industrial biotechnology, forensic science/bioscience, analytical forensic science, pharmaceutical science, clinical/pharmacy, drug discovery & design, virology, pharmaceutical manufacture & quality control

School of Natural Sciences & Psychology; www.ljmu.ac.uk/NSP

animal behaviour, analytical forensic science, applied psychology, bioarchaeology, biology, forensic anthropology, human/forensic/applied psychology, health psychology, geography, zoology, wildlife conservation & UAV technology, natural sciences, primate behaviour & conservation; BSc(Hons), MPhil, MPhys, MRes, MSc, PGCE, PhD

Astrophysics Research Institute www.ljmu.ac.uk/astro

physics, astronomy, observational/ astrophysics; BSc(Hons), PhD

Faculty of Technology & the Environment; www.ljmu.ac.uk/faculties/TAE

Dept of Computer Sciences; www.ljmu.ac.uk/cmp

adv/computer studies/forensics, multimedia computing, computer games development, computer network security, computing & information systems, software engineering, computer science/studies/forensics

Dept of Maritime & Mechanical Engineering; www.ljmu.ac.uk/eng

transport and logistics, marine operations, maritime business and management, maritime studies, mechanical and manufacturing systems engineering/marine engineering, mechanical engineering/with management, nautical science, product design engineering

Postgraduate; international transport, logistics & supply chain management, trade and logistics, manufacturing engineering, marine and offshore engineering, maritime management, mechanical engineering, port management

Dept of Applied Mathematics
mathematics

Dept of Civil Engineering
civil engineering, civil & environmental engineering/ offshore engineering/transportation engineering/ structural engineering, civil engineering & architecture, construction planning

Dept of the Built Environment; www.ljmu.ac.uk/BLT
architectural technology, building services engineering/ project management, building surveying, civil and environmental engineering, construction management, construction management, quantity surveying, real estate management/ and business

Postgrad; applied facilities management, architectural engineering, commercial building surveying, commercial property management, construction project management, construction & property, facilities management, integrated building information management, project management, quantity surveying and commercial management, real estate, water, energy and the environment

Dept of Electronics & Electrical Engineering
audio & music production, control & automation engineering, electrical & electronic engineering,electrica; power engineering, electronic engineering, product design engineering, electrical power and control engineering, microelectronic systems design, telecommunication engineering; BA(Hons), BSc(Hons), BEng(Hons), MEng, FdSc, MPhil, MSc, PGCert, PGCE, PGDip, PhD

UNIVERSITY OF THE ARTS LONDON
www.arts.ac.uk

Camberwell College of Art & Design; www.camberwell.arts.ac.uk
3D design, art & design, conservation, drawing, graphic design, visual arts (book arts/design maker/ illustration/fine arts digital/printmaking), illustration, painting, photography, sculpture; BA(Hons), Dip, FdA, MA, MPhil, PGDip, PhD, MFA

Central Saint Martins College of Art & Design; www.csm.arts.ac.uk
acting, applied imagination in creative industries, architecture: arts & cultural enterprise, spaces and objects/cities & innovation, art: exhibition studies, art theory & philosophy, art & design/science, art, exhibition studies, ceramic design, character animation, culture, communication design, criticism & curation, art & design (ceramics/furniture/jewellery), directing, dramatic writing, fashion design/knitwear/ marketing/menswear/womenswear/fashion production/journalism/ promotion/ communication/print, fashion & theory, fashion, communication: fashion history & theory/communication & promotion, fashion journalism, fine art, graphic/communication design, industrial design, innovation management, jewellery design, journalism design, screen acting/ directing/writing, material futures, narrative environments, performance design & practice, photography,

product design, textile design; BA(Hons), FdA, FD, GradDip, MA, MPhil, PGCert/Dip, MRes, PhD

Chelsea College of Art & Design; www.chelsea.arts.ac.uk
art & design, curating & collections, fine art, graphic design communication, interior & spatial design, textile design; BA(Hons), FdA, Foundation Dip, GradDip, MA, MPhil, PGCert/Dip, PhD, MRes

London College of Communication; www.lcc.arts.ac.uk
advertising, animation, applied branding & identity, arts & lifestyle journalism, book arts, design for art direction, design management & cultures, design for visual communication, film, graphic communication for interactive & moving image, contemporary graphic media, documentary film, film practice, film & TV, games design, graphic design, graphic branding & moving image/identity, graphic & media design, graphic branding, information & interface design, illustration & visual media, interactive design culture, international design communication, international journalism (online) journalism (print/online/ TV/magazine/sports), live events & TV, photojournalism & documentary, magazine publishing & publishing, marketing, media & cultural studies, media communication/critical practice, photography,

photojournalism & documentary photography, photographic portfolio development, PR, publishing, production for live events & TV, magazine publishing, screenwriting, service design experience innovation, sound arts/& design, spatial design, TV; BA(Hons), FdA, ABCDip, MA, MDes, MRes, MSc, PGDip

London College of Fashion;
www.fashion.arts.ac.uk

international preparation for fashion, 3D effects for performance and fashion, bespoke tailoring, Cordwainers fashion bags and accessories: product design and innovation/footwear: product design and innovation, costume for performance, creative direction for fashion, fashion (business/buying and merchandising/contour design/design and development/design technology: menswear/ womenswear/ illustration/jewellery/ journalism/ management/ marketing/ media/ pattern cutting/ photography/ PR and communication/ sportswear/s tyling and production, textiles: embroidery/ knitwear/print fashion: retail management), retail branding and visual merchandising, marketing and promotion, hair and make-up, design and technology, design and marketing, buying and merchandising, visual merchandising and branding, beauty and spa management, hair and make-up for film and TV/ fashion: styling and photography

Postgraduate; international fashion production management, cosmetic science, international fashion management, fashion; management, fashion design management, fashion enterprise creation, fashion entrepreneurship and innovation, fashion media practice & criteria,fashion retail management/production & management, strategic fashion marketing, fashion: buying and merchandising, costume design for performance, fashion cultures, fashion curation, fashion futures, psychology for fashion professionals, applied psychology in fashion, footwear, fashion design technology women's/menswear, pattern and garment technology, footwear: production and manufacture, fashion media styling, fashion journalism, fashion media production, fashion photography, fashion & professional styling journalism; BA(Hons), BSc(Hons), diplomas; FD, MA, PGDip/Cert, MDes

Wimbledon College of Art;
www.wimbledon.arts.ac.uk

art & design, digital theatre, drawing, fine art (painting/sculpture/print & time-based media), painting, print & time-based media, theatre & screen (costume design/interpretation/set design for screen/ technical arts & special effects, theatre design); BA(Hons), FdA, MA, MFA

LONDON CONTEMPORARY DANCE SCHOOL
www.theplace.org.uk

contemporary dance, dance training & education, developing artistic practice, performance EDge; BA(Hons), PGDip, MA

LONDON METROPOLITAN UNIVERSITY
www.londonmet.ac.uk

Faculty of Social Sciences & Humanities;
www.londonmet.ac.uk/faculties/
faculty-of-social-sciences-and-
humanities

community development and leadership, creative writing/and English literature, criminology and law/policing/ psychology/sociology/youth studies, dance, digital media design, digital media, diplomacy and international relations/law, early childhood studies, education and social policy, education studies/and English literature, fashion marketing and journalism, film and TV studies, health and social care/social policy, international relations and law/politics, international relations, peace and conflict, international relations, journalism, film and TV studies – journalism and digital media, journalism, media and communications, media, communications and journalism, Montessori early childhood practice, police studies, procedure and investigation, politics, public health and health promotion/social care, public service management, social science, social sciences and humanities, sociology and social policy – social work, sociology, theatre and film, translation, well-being in later life, working with older people, youth studies, youth work

Postgraduate; child abuse, conference interpreting, counter-terrorism studies, creative writing, crime, violence and prevention, criminology, early childhood studies, education, filmmaking, health and social care, management and policy, intelligence and security studies, international human rights and social justice, international relations, international security studies, interpreting, journalism, learning and teaching in HE, public administration, media and communications, PGCE (early years, primary (5-11), school direct early years, school direct secondary citizenship/English with media/ mathematics/modern languages/music/PE/science with biology/physics/biology/chemistry/physics), policing, security and community safety, public health, screenwriting, security studies, social policy and evaluation, social policy, social work, specialised translation, supporting older children and young people with dyslexia /SplDs, teaching Arabic, TESOL and applied linguistics, translation/and technology, violence against women, women and child abuse; BA(Hons), BSc(Hons), EdD, MPA, MA, MPhil, MRes, MSc, PGCert/Dip, PhD, FdA, PGCE, ProfDoc

Sir John Cass Faculty of Art, Architecture and Design; www.thecass.com

architectural interior design, architecture & interior design, architecture, art & design, art design media, energy & sustainability, art, media & design, curating the contemporary, fashion, fashion & textiles, film & broadcasting, film photography & media, drawing, film & broadcast production, fine art, furniture & product design, graphic design, illustration, interior design/& decoration, photography, spatial planning & urban design, theatre design, textile design; BA(Hons), PGCert, FdA, MA, MPhil, MSc, PhD, ProfDip

Faculty of Life Sciences & Computing; www.londonmet.ac.uk/depts/flsc

Electronics, Networking & Communications Engineering

computer networking/systems engineering, computing, electronic communications engineering, computer networking & cyber & methods

Applied Computing

business computing systems, business IT, computer forensics & IT security, computer networking & IT security, computing & business IT, data analytics, IT, software engineering, computing technology & mathematics

Mathematics

mathematics & computer science/statistical modelling, mathematical sciences, mathematics, data analytics, computing, technology & mathematics, games modelling, animation & effects

Computer Science & Creative Technologies

computer science, computer games programming, games modelling, animation & effects, computing/information systems, computing, technology & mathematics, software engineering; BSc(Hons), FdSc, MEng, MRes, MSc, PhD

School of Human Sciences; www.londonmet.ac.uk/depts/fls/hhs

biochemistry, bioethics, biological sciences, applied/biology, biotechnology, appl/biomedical science, blood science, chemistry, diet, food & nutrition, dietetics & nutrition, food science, football & community sport, forensic science, crime science & forensic investigation, health, herbal medicinal science, human nutrition (public health/sport), medical bioscience, molecular & pharmaceutical science, obesity & weight management, PE & coaching, personal training with strength & conditioning, PE & football coaching, fitness consultancy, pharmaceutical science, pharmacology, sports science & sports dance therapy, sports psychology & coaching, sport science & PE, sport nutrition, sports rehabilitation & therapy, sports science & therapy

School of Psychology; www.londonmet.ac.uk/depts/flsdops

applied/psychology, addiction & mental health, child & family mental health, psychology & sociology, psychology of counselling/health/psychology, business/consumer/criminal/forensic, occupational/organisational & consumer psychology, psychology of mental health, sport psychology & coaching; BSc(Hons), DipHE, FdSc, GradDip/Cert, MOst, MOstMed, MSc, Prof Doc, PGDip/Cert

Faculty of Business & Law; www.londonmet.ac.uk/faculties/ faculty-of-business-and-law

accounting & finance, airline, airport & aviation management, advertising, marketing communications & PR, banking & finance/compliance, business management & marketing/law/administration, business, innovation & creative enterprise, business economics, economics/& finance, events management, fashion marketing & business management, fashion retail management, finance, finance (accounting), international financial strategy, intelligence & security studies, international banking, financial & company law, international business, international family & child law, financial service law, regulation & compliance, HRM, marketing management, international business management, international common law/family law, international law, international oil, gas & energy law, legal practice, media & entertainment law, international trade, transport & maritime law, international marketing communications, legal practice, law/with international relations, management & strategic leadership, maritime law, marketing & communications, music industry management/& enterprise, music business & live entertainment, sports/business/management, tourism & travel management, transport & logistics management, executive & professional courses; DPS, FdSc, GradConv, MA, MBA, DBA, MSc, PGDip, ProfDoc, LlB, LlM, PGDip, GDL

THE LONDON SCHOOL OF OSTEOPATHY
www.lso.ac.uk

osteopathy; BOst, MOst

LONDON SOUTH BANK UNIVERSITY
www.lsbu.ac.uk

School of Applied Sciences; www.lsbu.ac.uk/schools/applied-sciences

Food Science; food and nutrition, food science, human nutrition, baking technology management, culinary arts, food safety and control, food sciences, baking technology management

Human Sciences; bioscience, forensic science, sport and exercise science, sports coaching and analysis, human sciences; Psychology; psychology, psychology (addiction psychology/ child development/clinical psychology/forensic psychology), choice and control in addictive behaviour; cognitive behaviour therapy for problem drinking, insights into social identity in addiction treatment, addiction psychology and counselling, investigative forensic psychology, mental health and clinical psychology, psychology; BSc(Hons), MSc, PGCert/Dip, PhD

School of Arts and Creative Industries

arts and festival management, digital design, drama and performance, English with creative writing, film practice, film studies, game design and development, journalism, photography, theatre technologies, visual effects, web production and social media, sound design, creative media industries: cultural management, creative writing, critical arts management, cultural and media studies, development journalism, digital film, digital photography, media writing, new media, theatre practice, arts and creative industries; BA(Hons), MA, MRes, PhD

School of Built Environment and architecture; www.lsbu.ac.uk/schools/built-environment-and architecture

architecture, architectural engineering, architectural technology, building services engineering, civil engineering, environmental and architectural acoustics, structural engineering, sustainable energy systems, transport engineering and planning, engineering and the built environment, building surveying, commercial management (quantity surveying), construction management, property management (building surveying), quantity surveying, real estate, built environment, construction project management, international planning buildings for health, building surveying, property development and planning, construction management and economics; BSc(Hons), BEng(Hons), PGDip, MArch, MSc

School of Business; www.lsbu.ac.uk/schools/business

accounting and finance, accounting, applied accounting, international accounting and finance, international finance, accounting and finance, accounting and entrepreneurship, corporate governance, business management, business management with accounting/analytics/corporate sustainability/e-business/economics/enterprise and entrepreneurship/finance/human resources/ law/marketing/project management/retail, business studies, international business management, economics, economics with accounting/business analytics/business management/e-business/econometrics/enterprise and entrepreneurship/finance/human resources/law/marketing/project management/retail management, business administration, business, business project management, international business management, international business management with finance/HRM / marketing/project management, business and enterprise, marketing, management studies, business administration, public administration, digital marketing, international health services and hospital management, HRM, international marketing, marketing, marketing communications/management, international marketing, human resource development, management, marketing and people, marketing communications; BSc(Hons), FdA, DBA, DMS, MBA, DBA, PhD, PGDip/Cert, MPH

School of Engineering; www.lsbu.ac.uk/schools/engineering

chemical/ and process engineering, general engineering, chemical process and energy engineering, general engineering, business information technology, business intelligence, computer science, computer systems management, computing, digital business, information technology, engineering project management, internet and database systems, IT management for business, social and digital media, computing science and informatics, business information technology, business intelligence, computer systems management, digital business,information technology, computer engineering, computer systems and networks, electrical and electronic engineering, electrical engineering and power electronics, telecommunications engineering, engineering management, computer engineering, general engineering, research in electrical and electronic engineering, advanced telecommunication and wireless engineering, biomedical engineering and instrumentation, mechatronics, robotics and embedded systems, production and manufacturing; BSc(Hons), BEng(Hons), MEng, MSc, MRes, MEM, PhD

School of Health and Social Care; www.lsbu.ac.uk/schools/health-and-social-care

adult nursing, midwifery, health and social care (acute hospital care/maternity support), midwifery and excellence in practice, adult nursing, continuous personal and professional development; health and social care, Chinese medicine: acupuncture, diagnostic radiography, occupational therapy, operating department practice, radiographic studies, therapeutic radiography, perioperative practice, diagnostic imaging, breast imaging, radiographic reporting, therapeutic radiography, occupational therapy, allied health professions, health studies, children's nursing, advanced neonatal nurse practitioner, children's advanced nurse practitioner, professional practice: children's nursing, nursing, learning disability nursing, mental health nursing, advanced CBT practice (resilience and positive development; treatment of anxiety and depression), resilience and positive development), mental health nursing, social work, health and social care: administration and management, health visiting/ occupational health nursing/ school nursing (specialist community public health nursing), health and social care (primary care), workplace health management, public health and health promotion, careers education, leadership and service improvement, practice education, health visiting/occupational health nursing (specialist community public health nursing), primary care district nursing, school nursing (specialist community health nursing), advanced nurse practitioner; BSc(Hons), BA(Hons), MSc, GradDip/Cert, PhD, FdSc, ProfDoc, GradCert, CertHE, DipHE, MCMAcc

School of Law and Social Sciences; www.lsbu.ac.uk/schools/law-and-social-sciences

Common Professional Exam, legal studies, business law, criminal law, entertainment and media law, family law, human rights, law, law with criminology, civil litigation and dispute resolution, crime and litigation, international commercial law, international criminal law and procedure, international human rights and development; politics, criminology, criminology with law/psychology, sociology, sociology with criminology, development journalism, criminology and social research methods, development and urbanisation, development studies, housing studies, tourism, hospitality and leisure management, urban and environmental planning, urban regeneration international tourism and hospitality management,housing studies, town planning, planning studies and tourism, hospitality and events; BA(Hons), BSc(Hons), LlB, LlM, MSc, CPE, PGDip/Cert, PhD

UNIVERSITY OF EAST LONDON
www.uel.ac.uk/

School of Arts and Digital Industries; www.uel.ac.uk/school/adl
acting, advertising, animation, computer games design/development, creative & professional writing, cultural studies, dance, digital media design, drama, applied theatre & performance, English literature, film-making, fine art, graphic design, fashion, film, heritage studies, history, international fashion management, illustration, sports/journalism, magazines, media & communication, music technology/performance & production, photography, print design, theatre directing, writing imaginative practice; BA(Hons), BSc/BA, FdA, GradCert, MA, MPhil, MSc, PGC, PhD, ProfDoc

School of Combined Honours; www.uel.ac.uk/combined
range of subjects for which combined honours courses are conducted

School of Architecture, Computing and Engineering; www.uel.ac.uk/ace
architecture, architectural design technology, interior design, product design, architecture: computing and design/design/interpretation and theories/sustainability and design/urban design, landscape architecture
civil engineering, civil engineering and surveying/construction management, engineering, business information systems, civil engineering, structural engineering, surveying & mapping science
computing for business, computing, computer science; postgraduate; business information technology, data science, information security/and computer forensics, software engineering, electrical & electronic engineering, product design, construction management, mechanical engineering; BA/BEng(Hons), BA/BSc, BSc(Hons), MPhil, MSc, PhD, ProfDoc

Royal Docks Business School; www.uel.ac.uk/school/Cass

School of Business & Law
accounting & finance, business management (finance/HR/marketing) investment/risk management, economics, entrepreneurship, event management, finance & risk, hospitality & international tourist management, HRM, international business/& leadership/HR/marketing management, international accounting/banking & finance, international tourism management, Islamic finance, luxury brand management, music industry management, marketing, sports management; BA(Hons), DBA, HND, LlB, MA, MBA, MPhil, MSc, PGDip, PhD

Cass School of Education & Communities; www.uel.ac.uk/school/education
early years, early childhood education and care, early childhood with health promotion/psychology/special education, early childhood studies, early years ITT, education with psychology, education studies, special education/& additional learning needs, autism spectrum & education, social work, child care and education, creative leadership in education, education, English language teaching, post-qualifying professional practice, social work, special educational needs/coordination, teaching in HE, youth and community work, secondary teacher training, school direct, subject knowledge enhancement, post compulsory teacher training, teacher training, primary (core), primary with early years (3-7)/, English/English as an additional language, English/humanities and RE/ICT and computing/ early years (3-7)/modern languages/music, PGCE secondary education (numerous subjects), PGCE (primary education), mathematics with education & QTS, Madrassah teaching/teacher, early years/primary teacher training, post compulsory teacher training, youth & community work, social work/with adults/children & families, post qualifying professional practising/teacher, mentoring & supporting behaviour, CPD; BA(Hons), EdD, FdA, MA, PGCE, PGDip, ProfDoc, UnivCert

School of Health, Sport and Bioscience; www.uel.ac.uk/school/Health-Sport-and=Bioscience
biotechnology, contemporary nursing practice, early childhood with health promotion, health science, human biology, medical physiology, podiatry, public health/and health promotion/ health services

management, adv practice for health professions, applied/health science, biochemistry, bioinformatics/ promotion, bioscience, biomedical science, biotechnology/management, musculoskeletal ultrasonogram/practice for podiatrists, pharmacology, phyto/ pharmaceutical science, applied/sport and exercise science, sport, PE and development, sports coaching, sport management, sports therapy, physiotherapy, podiatric medicine, sports science/psychology, strength & conditioning, applied community sport; BA(Hons), BSc(Hons), FdSc, MPhil, MSc, PGCert, PhD, ProfDoc, MRes

School of Social Sciences; www.uel.ac.uk/ school/socialsciences

anthropology, criminology & social justice/law/psychosocial studies; conflict, displacement & human security, human rights, international humanitarianism, consultation & the organisation: consultation & the organisation (psychoanalytical approaches), emotional features in learning & teaching, infant mental health, international development, international development & anthropology/NGO management/ international politics, international relations; narrative research, NGO & development management, psychodynamic approach to working with adolescents/people with learning disabilities/personality disorders, psychosocial studies/with professional practice/art/criminology, psychosocial approaches to working with adolescents/with people with learning disabilities, psychosocial perspectives on working

with people with personality disorders, refugee studies/with community development, therapeutic communication with children, sociology/(professional development), sociology with anthropology/ criminology/international politics, sociology with law, terrorism studies, sustainability & society, working with groups, working with people with eating disorders/youth & community work; BA(Hons), BSc(Hons), LlB, LlM, MSc, PostGDip, DChPsych, MSystPsych, MPsych, DConsOrg, ClinPsyD, Prof-Doc, DEdChPsy

School of Psychology; www.uel.ac.uk/ school/psychology

child psychology, clinical and community psychology, counselling, educational & child psychology, forensic psychology, psychology, psychology and sociology, psychology, applied positive psychology and coaching psychology, business psychology, clinical and community psychology, criminal and investigative psychology, international humanitarian psychosocial intervention, forensic psychology, occupational and organisational psychology, clinical psychology, counselling/ psychology, counselling/ and psychotherapy, counselling psychology, medical psychology, psychological & social studies with professional practice, integrative counselling and coaching, career coaching, career coaching, coaching, integrative counselling and coaching; BA(Hons), BSc(Hons), ClinPsyD, FdA, GradDip/Cert, MA, MSc, ProfDoc, DAppEdChPsych, MPsych, UnivCert

UNIVERSITY OF WEST LONDON
www.uwl.ac.uk

London College of Music; www.uwl.ac.uk/ academic-schools/music

acting; film music composition; live sound production; music composition and recording; music composition with music management/music technology; music management; music performance; music performance and music management/recording; music performance with music technology; music technology audio post production/electronic music production/mixing and mastering/recording and production/specialist/top-up; music technology and radio broadcasting/video production; music technology with music composition/music performance/popular music performance; musical theatre; theatre production – design and management; voice in performance. Postgrad: advanced music technology;

composition; composition concert music/electronic music/for film & TV; electro-acoustic composition; music; music industry management and artist development; music production; music technology; performance; popular music performance; record production; BA(Hons), BMus(Hons), DMus, FdA, MA, MMus, MPhil, PGDip, PhD

London School of Film, Media and Design; www.uwl.ac.uk/academic-schools/film-media-design

advertising and PR, broadcast journalism; commercial photography; English and creative writing/film/ media & communications; fashion branding and marketing; fashion buying and management; fashion and textiles; film production; graphic design (visual communication and illustration); media and communications; photography; radio and multimedia audio production; visual effects. Postgrad: advertising, branding and communication; film production; luxury design innovation and brand management; media; BA(Hons), FdA, MA, MPhil, PhD

School of Human & Social Sciences; www.uwl.ac.uk/academic-schools/psychology

forensic science; nutritional therapeutics; nutritional therapy/top-up; psychology, psychology with applied forensic investigation/counselling theory/criminology/substance use and misuse studies. Postgrad: clinical hypnotherapy; communicable diseases; health psychology; psychology BSc(Hons), GradDip, DipHE, FdSc, MSc, MPhil, PhD

School of Nursing, Midwifery & Healthcare; www.uwl.ac.uk/academic-schools/nursing-midwifery

health promotion and public health; health and social care assistant practitioner; healthcare top-up; healthcare play specialism; midwifery; nursing adult/children/learning disabilities/mental health; nursing and healthcare top-up; operating department practice; professional practice; psycho-social interventions for psychosis; working in integrated services for children and young people; working with children and young people. Postgrad: advanced practice healthcare education/infection prevention and control/leadership/mental health/midwifery/substance misuse; healthcare; health science; midwifery; improvement science; management studies – health and social care; nursing; nursing – adult/mental health/top-up; professional practice; psychosocial interventions for psychosis, public health and wellbeing; strategic workplace planning; BA(Hons), BSc(Hons), DHSc, DMid, DNurs, FdA, FdSc, MPhil, MSc, PGCert, PGDip, PhD

The Claude Littner Business School; www.uwl.ac.uk/academic-schools/business

accounting & finance/with internship; business studies/top-up; business studies with entrepreneurship/finance/HRM/internship/marketing; credit management top-up; international business management; procurement and supply. Postgrad: finance and accounting/risk management; human resource management; international business management/marketing; management; managing HR; MBA/with internship; BA(Hons), Grad Cert, Grad Dip, MA, MBA, MPhil, MSc, PGDip, PhD

Ealing Law School; www.uwl.ac.uk/academic_schools/law

criminology/with criminal justice/law/psychology/sociology; criminology, policing & forensics; law; sociology/with criminology. Postgrad: criminology/& criminal justice, international banking & finance/business & commercial law; international studies in intellectual property law; legal practice; BA(Hons), LLB(Hons), LLM, MA, PGDip, PGCert, PhD

London School of Hospitality & Tourism; www.uwl.ac.uk/academic-schools/hospitality-tourism

airline & airport management; culinary arts management; event management/with hospitality/tourism; food and professional cookery; hospitality management/and food studies; international culinary arts/hotel management; international travel and tourism management. Postgrad: food business management; food management with internship; hospitality; international tourism & aviation management/with internship; luxury hospitality management/with internship; BA, BA(Hons), BSc(Hons), FdA, FdSc, MA, MPhil, PhD

School of Computing & Technology; www.uwl.ac.uk/academic-schools/computing

applied sound engineering; architectural design and technology; building surveying; civil and environmental engineering; computer game technology; computer science; computing and information systems; construction project management; creative computing; cyber security; digital and technology solutions apprenticeship; electrical and electronic engineering; information technology; information technology for business; mobile computing. Postgrad: applied project management; civil engineering, civil and environmental engineering; cyber security; engineering; information systems; software engineering; structural engineering; sustainable and built environments; BSc(Hons), BEng(Hons), FdSc, FdEng, MSc, MPhil, PhD

UNIVERSITY OF LONDON; BIRKBECK
www.bbk.ac.uk

School of Arts; www.bbk.ac.uk/arts

creative writing and English, English film and media, French studies, German, global cinemas and screen arts, history of art, history of art with curating, Iberian and Latin American studies (Spanish or Portuguese), Japanese and/with film and media/ history/journalism/management, journalism and media, language and film/media (French, German, Portuguese, Spanish), language and global politics (French, German, Japanese, Portuguese, Spanish, language and history (French, German, Portuguese, Spanish), language and management (French, German, Portuguese, Spanish, language and politics (French, German, Japanese, Portuguese, Spanish), language and/with English (French, German, Japanese, Portuguese, Spanish) language and/with international law (French, German, Japanese, Portuguese, Spanish), media and culture, theatre and drama studies/English; Postgraduate; arts management, arts policy and management, contemporary literature/ and culture, creative producing (for theatre and live performance), creative writing, cultural and critical studies, digital media management, film curating, film, television and screen media, French studies, German studies, history of art, history of art and architecture, photography, Iberian and Latin American studies, journalism, medical humanities, medieval literature and culture, modern and contemporary literature, museum cultures, romantic studies, screenwriting, Spanish, Portuguese and Latin American cultural studies, text and performance, theatre directing, Victorian studies, world cinema; BA, CertHE, MA, MPhil, PhD, PGDip/Cert, MRes

School of Business, Economics and Informatics; www.bbk.ac.uk/business

Economics, Mathematics & Statistics; Management: Computer Science & Information Systems; Organisational Psychology

accounting, accounting and management, accounting and management with finance, accounting with finance, applied accounting and business, management and accounting,,business, funeral management, management, business psychology, management for personal assistants, marketing, professional studies; Postgraduate; accounting and finance, accounting and financial management), investment management, business innovation with e-business, business

innovation with entrepreneurship and innovation management, business innovation with international technology management, business innovation, corporate governance and business ethics, corporate responsibility & sustainability, creative industries (management), international business, international business and development, international management, international marketing, marketing, marketing communications, sport management and marketing, sport governance, sport management, sport management and marketing, sport management and the business of football, sport management, governance and policy, sport marketing, career management and coaching, coaching, HRD and consultancy, HRM, management consultancy and organisational change, occupational psychology, organizational behaviour, organizational psychology; BSc(Econ), BSc, CertHE, MPhil, PhD, MSc, MRes, FD

School of Law; www.bbk.ac.uk/law

law, criminal law & criminal justice, language & international law,criminal law and criminal justice, global criminology, human rights, international economic law (finance or justice and development/ justice and development, law general, law, democracy, and human welfare: global perspectives, qualifying law degree; MA, LlB, MPhil, PhD, LlM, BSc

School of Science; www.bbk.ac.uk

Biological Sciences: biomedicine, life sciences for subjects allied to medicine, analytical bioscience, bio-business, bioinformatics with systems biology, microbiology, principles of protein structure, protein crystallography, structural biology, structural molecular biology, techniques in structural molecular biology

Earth & Planetary Sciences: geology, earth sciences, environmental geology, planetary science with astronomy, geochemistry

Psychological Sciences: psychology, psychology for education professionals, cognition & computation, cognitive neuroscience & neuropsychology, developmental science, educational neuroscience, psychological research methods; MRes, PGDip/Cert, BSc, MPhil, PhD, FD, CertHE

School of Social Sciences, History and Philosophy; *www.bbk.ac.uk/sshp*

Applied Linguistics & Communication: communication for business & the professions, intercultural communication/for business & professions, linguistics & language (Italian, German, Japanese, Portuguese, Spanish), linguistics studies, applied linguistics, & communication, intercultural, language teaching, TESOL

Geography, Environmental & Development Studies: community leadership, development studies, development & globalisation, social anthropology, sociology, community development and public policy, development studies with environment, environmental management, environmental science, social science(s), children, youth and international development, climate change environment and sustainability, environmental management (countryside management/protected area management), GIS, international development & social anthropology, social and cultural geography, community, youth and voluntary sector, international childhood studies

History, Classics & Archaeology: history, archaeology, archaeological practice, classical archaeology, classical studies/civilisations, classics, contemporary history & politics, early modern history, European history, gender, sexuality & sociology/culture, psychoanalytic studies, global history, history & culture/international relations/archaeological studies, history of British Isles, history of ideas, medieval history, public history, historical research

Philosophy: philosophy, politics, philosophy, history

Politics: politics, history & philosophy, global politics & international relations,,global environmental politics and policy, European politics and policy, global governance and emerging powers, global politics, government, policy and politics, international security and global governance, Middle East in global politics: Islam, conflict and development, nationalism and ethnic conflict, politics, politics of population, migration and ecology, public policy and management, social and political theory, social research

Psychosocial Studies: psychosocial studies, social science, culture, diaspora, ethnicity, psychoanalysis, history & culture, psychoanalytical studies, education, power & social change, psychodynamics of human development, psychosocial studies; BA, BSc, MA, MRes, MPhil, PhD, MPhilSt, CertHE, FDSc

UNIVERSITY OF LONDON; COURTAULD INSTITUTE OF ART
www.courtauld.ac.uk

conservation of easel paintings, curating the art museum, history of art, Buddhist art, conservation of wall painting, curating the art museum; BA(Hons), GradDip, MA, PGDip, MPhil, PhD

UNIVERSITY OF LONDON; GOLDSMITHS
www.goldsmiths.ac.uk

Dept of Anthropology; www.gold.ac.uk/anthropology

anthropology, anthropology & media/sociology/history/visual practice, cultural politics, applied anthropology & cultural politics, applied anthropology & community development/community & youth work, development & rights, visual arts, politics, philosophy & economics; BA(Hons), MPhil, PhD, MRes

Dept of Art; www.gold.ac.uk/art

fine art/& history of art, art writing, creative/curating, digital arts computing, artists' film; BA(Hons), MFA, MPhil, PhD

Dept of Computing; www.gold.ac.uk/computing

computing, digital arts computing, music computing, business computing & entrepreneurship, computer science, games programming, creative computing, digital arts computing; Postgraduate; computational arts, computer games & entertainment., data science, computer games art & design, creative & cultural entrepreneurship, digital journalism, computer science, arts & computational technology, intelligent games & game intelligence; BSc(Hons), BA(Hons), BMus, MA, MSc, MPhil, PhD, MFA

Centre for Cultural Studies; www.gold.ac.uk/cultural-studies

cultural studies/industry, post-colonial culture & global policy, digital culture; MA, MPhil, PhD

Dept of Design; www.gold.ac.uk/design

design, design education, creative & cultural entrepreneurship, design futures/& metadesign, design/fashion, interaction design, design & innovation/critical practice, design & environment; BA(Hons), BSc(Hons), BEng/MEng, MPhil, MRes, PhD, Grad-Dip/Cert, PGCE

Dept of Educational studies; www.gold.ac.uk/educational-studies

computing & Chinese, business computing, computer science, digital journalism/sociology/arts/music computing, games programming, journalism; education studies & Chinese, education, culture & society, education, culture and society, teacher training; PGCE (primary with mathematics, primary, secondary (art & design, standard programme, design and technology, drama, English, mathematics, media studies with English, science education: biology, chemistry, physics, modern languages; Postgraduate; artist teachers & contemporary practices, children's literature, education: culture, language & identity, multilingualism, linguistics & education, writer/teacher, art practice & learning, education; BA(Hons), DPS, MA, MPhil, PhD, PGCE

Dept of English & Comparative Literature; www.gold.ac.uk/ecl

English, English and American literature/comparative literature/drama/history, English language and literature, English with creative writing, media and English; Postgraduate, black British writing, children's literature, American literature & culture, comparative literature & criticism, modern literary theory, modern literature, romantic & Victorian literature & culture, Shakespeare, :early & modern, creative & life writing, multilingualism, linguistics & education, sociocultural linguistics, translation, writer/teacher, creative writing, English, comparative literature or linguistics, English; BA(Hons), MA, MPhil, MRes, PhD

Centre for English Language & Academic Writing; www.gold.ac.uk/eap

art, English language, humanities & social science, media, communication, counselling & therapy, creative & cultural industries, design, music; GradDip, IntCert

Dept of History; www.gold.ac.uk/history

history, history & anthropology/history of ideas/politics/journalism, English & history; BA(Hons), MA, MPhil, MRes, PhD

Institute for Creative and Cultural Entrepreneurship; www.gold.ac.uk/icce

arts management, creative & cultural industries Postgraduate; arts administration & cultural policy (music), creative & cultural entrepreneurship, computing/design/fashion/ leadership/media & communications/music/theatre & performance, cultural policy, relations & diplomacy, social entrepreneurship, tourism & cultural policy, translation, museums & galleries entrepreneurship; BA(Hons), GradDip, PGCert, MA, MPhil, PhD

Institute of Management Studies; www.gold.ac.uk/institute-management-studies

economics, economics with econometrics, management & entrepreneurship, management with economics/marketing, marketing, economics with econometrics, management and entrepreneurship; Postgraduate; management of innovation, psychology, consumer behaviour, occupational psychology; BA(Hons), BSc/Hons, MPhil, PhD, MSc

Dept of Media and Communications; www.gold.ac.uk/media-communications

anthropology & media, journalism, media & communications/English/sociology, history and journalism

Postgraduate; brands, communication & culture, digital media: technology & cultural form, film & screen studies, filmmaking, filmmaking (cinematography/directing fiction/editing/filmmaking/producing/screen documentary/ filmmaking/sound recording & design), gender, media & culture, global media & transnational communications, journalism, media & communications, political communications, promotional media: public relations, advertising & marketing, radio, script writing, TV journalism, digital journalism, media & communications, filmmaking, photography & electronic arts; BA(Hons), MA, MPhil, PhD, MRes, MA/MSc

Dept of Music; www.gold.ac.uk/music

arts administration & cultural policy, composition, contemporary music studies, pop music, creative practice, creative & cultural entrepreneurship, ethnomusicology, historical musicology, music, music computing/performance & related studies, composition, sonic arts; BMus(Hons), BMus/BSc(Hons), MA, MMus, MPhil, PGCert, PhD, GradDip

Dept of Politics; www.gold.ac.uk/politics

economics, politics & public policy, international studies, international studies & Chinese, politics, politics & international relations, philosophy & economics, history & politics, sociology & politics; Postgraduate; art & politics, international relations, politics, development & the global south; BA(Hons), DPS, MA, MPhil, MRes, PhD

Dept of Psychology; www.gold.ac.uk/psychology

psychology, psychology with clinical psychology cognitive neuroscience/ forensic psychology; Postgraduate; psychology, research methods in psychology, cognitive & clinical neuroscience, forensic psychology, foundations in clinical psychology & health services, music, mind & brain, psychology of social relations, translational behavioural science; BSc(Hons), BSc,MPhil, MSc, PhD, MRes

Dept of Sociology; www.gold.ac.uk/sociology

sociology, anthropology/media & sociology, politics, criminology, sociology/& politics/criminology/

Chinese, cities & society, brands, communication & culture, critical & creative analysis, gender, media & culture, human rights, culture & social justice, photography & urban cultures, social research, visual sociology, digital sociology; BA(Hons), MA, MSc, MPhil, PhD

Dept of Theatre & Performance; www.gold.ac.uk/theatre-performance

drama, drama and theatre arts/English, applied theatre: drama in educational community and social contexts, black British writing, creative and cultural entrepreneurship, drama/comedy, musical theatre, performance making, performance & culture/interdisciplinary perspective, writing for performance, world theatres; BA(Hons), MA, MPhil, PhD

Dept of Visual Cultures; www.gold.ac.uk/visual-cultures

contemporary art theory/history, fine art/ & history of art, research architecture, contemporary art theory, research architecture, curatorial/knowledge, visual cultures; BA(Hons), MA, MPhil, PGDip, PhD

UNIVERSITY OF LONDON; HEYTHROP COLLEGE
www.heythrop.ac.uk

Abrahamic religions, biblical studies, canon law, Christian spirituality/theology, Christianity & inter-religious relations, contemporary ethics, Ignatious spirituality, pastoral/ministry/theology, philosophy/& religion, philosophy in/of education, philosophy of religion & ethics in religion, psychology of religion, theology; BA, Certs, BD, GradDip, MA, MRes, MPhil, PhD

UNIVERSITY OF LONDON; INSTITUTE IN PARIS
www.ulip.lon.ac.uk

French studies/with history, Paris studies – history & culture, international relations; BA, MA, MPhil, PhD, LlM

UNIVERSITY OF LONDON; INSTITUTE OF EDUCATION
www.ioe.ac.uk

education studies, psychology with education, social sciences, social sciences with quantitative methods, working with children: education and wellbeing; Postgraduate; applied educational leadership and management, applied linguistics, art and design in education, child development, citizenship, history or religious education (humanities), clinical education, comparative education, curriculum, pedagogy and assessment, development education and global learning, developmental and educational psychology, digital media, culture and education, early years education, education, education (psychology), education and international development, education and technology, education, gender and international development, education, health promotion and international development, educational assessment, educational leadership (international), educational neuroscience, educational planning, economics and international development, effective learning and teaching, English education, evaluation, inspection and educational improvement, geography education, rehabilitation and disabilities of sight (children and young people), higher and professional education, higher education management, history of education, leadership, lifelong learning, literacy learning and literacy difficulties, mathematics education,

museums and galleries in education, music education, special educational needs co-ordination, philosophy of education, policy studies in education, primary education (policy and practice), primary mathematics specialist teaching, professional education and training, psychology, psychology of education, quantitative research methods, science education, social justice and education, social policy and social research, social science research methods, sociology of childhood and children's rights, sociology of education, special and inclusive education, specific learning difficulties (dyslexia), speech, language and communication needs in schools: advanced practice, systematic reviews for public policy and practice, teaching, TESOL, Teacher Training; Early Years (initial teacher training), Primary PGCE, Secondary PGCE numerous secondary taught subjects, Post Compulsory, PGCE inservice, preservice, literacy & ESOL, mathematics; BEd, Certs, DedPsy, EdD, GradDip, MA, MBA, MPhil, MRes, MSc, MTg, PGCE, PhD, MTL, BA/BSc, FD, MTeach

UNIVERSITY OF LONDON; KING'S COLLEGE LONDON
www.kcl.ac.uk

The School of Arts & Humanities; www.kcl.ac.uk/humanities

Classics; classical archaeology, the classical world and its reception, classical studies, classical art & archaeology, ancient history (Latin with Film Studies classics)

Comparative Literature; American studies, Byzantine & modern Greek studies, digital humanities, classics, English and modern languages (French, German, Spanish and Portuguese), theorising literature across cultures: contemporary debates

Culture, Media & Creative Industries; cultural and creative industries,digital culture and society, and arts and cultural management

Digital Hunanities; digital humanities, big data in culture & society, digital culture, digital asset & media management, digital curation, digital culture & society

English; English material, visual and textual and digital cultures, literature, medicine and science, life writing, performance and creative writing, sexuality and gender studies, colonial, postcolonial, and transnational cultures

European & International Studies; European politics, international political economy, European studies, European political economy, Asian & European affairs, European studies (Spanish/German/French pathway)

Film Studies; film studies (film & philosophy pathway), film studies, Spanish/English with film studies, comparative literature with film studies, liberal arts, French; French & history/Spanish, English law & French law, French & management/film studies, French research, French with English,

German; German & history, German & comparative literature, German, German & philosophy/Portuguese/management/English/music/Spanish, German & music

History; history and international relations, history, world history & cultures, politics & contemporary history, liberal arts

Modern Language Centre

Music; advanced musical studies, music

Philosophy; mathematics & philosophy, philosophy of medicine, history of philosophy, philosophy, philosophy of psychology, philosophy & Spanish, physics & philosophy, philosophy research

Spanish, Portuguese & Latin American Studies; Spanish, Portuguese & Latin American studies, Spanish & Latin American studies, Spanish & Portuguese, Spanish with film studies/English/management, Spanish, Portuguese & Latin American studies research, philosophy & Spanish, German and Spanish, European studies (Spanish pathway)

Theology & Religious Studies; theology & religious studies, theology & religious studies research, theology, religion, politics & society, systematic theology, religion in contemporary society, Christianity & the arts, Jewish studies, religion, philosophy & ethics, biblical studies, with pathways (language and literature; theology); BA(Hons), LlB, BSc, MA, BMus, MMus, MRes, MSc, PGCE, GradDip, MPhil, PhD, MPhilSt, PGCE

Faculty of Life Science & Medicine; *www.kcl.ac.uk/lsm*

This Faculty comprises the institutions listed below. Each provides education and research in their appropriate specialist area, offering degrees at undergraduate, postgraduate and research level

School of Bioscience Education, GKT School of Medical Education, Analytical & Environmental Sciences Division, Asthma, Allergy & Lung Biology, Bioscience Education, Cancer Studies, Cardiovascular, Centre for Global Health, Centre of Human & Aerospace Physiological Sciences, Cicely Saunders Institute of Palliative Care and Rehabilitation, Diabetes & Nutritional Sciences, Genetics & Molecular Medicine, Imaging Sciences & Biomedical Engineering, Immunology, Infection & Inflammatory, Life Science & Medicine, Pharmaceutical Science, Health & Social Care Research, Medical Education, Randall Division of Cell & Molecular Biophysics, Transplantation Immunology & Mucosal Biology, Women's Health, Department of Anatomy, Department of Biochemistry, Department of Genetics, Centre of Immunology, Department of Neuroscience, Department of Nutrition & Dietetics, Department of Pharmacology & Therapeutics, Department of Pharmacy & Forensic Science, Department of Physiology, Department of Physiotherapy, Institute of Psychiatry, Psychology, Physiotherapy

GKT School of Medical Education; www.kcl.ac.uk/lsm/education/meded

medicine (standard five-year programme), medicine graduate & professional entry (four-year fast-track programme), extended medical degree programme (six-year widening access programme), MaxFax (four-year programme for qualified dentists)

School of Bioscience Education; www.kcl.ac.uk/lsm/education/ bioscibiomedical & life sciences

healthcare leadership & management, imaging sciences & biomedical engineering, pharmacy, pharmacology & forensic science, training for healthcare professionals, anatomy, developmental & human biology, biochemistry, biomedical science, medical physiology, molecular genetics, neuroscience, nutrition, pharmacology, pharmacology & molecular genetics, human physiology, neuroscience, pharmacology, nutrition & dietetics, physiotherapy

Postgraduate; Medicine, advanced (neuromusculoskeletal) physiotherapy, advanced paediatrics, cardiovascular research, clinical dermatology, genomic medicine, medical immunology, research biobanking, rheumatology, translational cancer medicine

Dietetics and Physiotherapy; dietetics, physiotherapy

Ultrasound & Imaging for health professionals; medical ultrasound, nuclear medicine: science and practice, specialist ultrasound practice, vascular ultrasound

Biomedical & Life Sciences; global air quality: management & science, biomedical & molecular sciences research, cardiovascular research, cellular therapy from bench to market, genomic medicine, immunology, molecular biophysics for medical sciences, nutrition, research biobanking, human & applied physiology, space physiology & health, translational cancer medicine

Healthcare Management & Leadership; global health, global surgery, health professions education, disasters adaptation, conflict & security, palliative care, public health, primary care

Imaging Sciences & Biomedical Engineering; medical engineering & physics, medical imaging sciences, radiopharmaceutics and PET radiochemistry,

Ultrasound & Imaging for health professionals, medical ultrasound, nuclear medicine: science and practice, specialist ultrasound practice, vascular ultrasound

Pharmacy, Pharmacology & Forensic Science; (drug discovery & development) clinical pharmacology, drug development science, drug discovery skills, pharmacology, biopharmaceuticals, pharmaceutical analysis & quality control, pharmaceutical technology, translational medicine (forensic & analytical science), analytical science for industry, analytical

toxicology, forensic science (pharmacy practice); independent prescribing, pharmacy practice
Training for Healthcare Professionals; (medicine); advanced (neuromusculoskeletal) physiotherapy, advanced paediatrics, cardiovascular research, clinical dermatology, genomic medicine, medical immunology, research biobanking, rheumatology, translational cancer medicine (dietetics and physiotherapy), dietetics, physiotherapy,(ultrasound & imaging); medical ultrasound, nuclear medicine: science and practice, specialist ultrasound practice, vascular ultrasound; GradCert/Dip, MRes, MSc, PGDip, MPhil, PhD, MD

Dental Institute; www.kcl.ac.uk/dentistry

dentistry, digital culture, conscious sedation for dentistry, dental public health, endodontology, maxillofacial & craniofacial technology, orthodontics, paediatric dentistry, periodontology, prosthodontics, regenerative dentistry, special care dentistry; BDS, MClinDent, MOrth, MSc, PGDip, BA

Institute of Psychiatry, Psychology & Neuroscience; www.iop.kcl.ac.uk

psychology, neuroscience & neuropsychology/clinical applications, cognitive behavioural therapies for children & adolescents/psychosis, health psychology, mindfulness, neuroscience, addictions, basic & clinical neuroscience,,biostatistics, child and adolescent psychiatry, forensic & neurodevelopment science, health service & population research, neuroimaging, old age psychiatry, psychological medicine, psychology, psychosis studies, social, genetic & development; BSc, BA, DClinPsy, GradCert, MSc, PGDip, MPhil, PhD, MD

School of Law; www.kcl.ac.uk/law

law, English & French/German/American/Hong Kong/Australian law, politics, philosophy & law, medical ethics & law, medical law, international corporate and commercial law, global justice, transnational law, construction law & dispute resolution, UK, EU, & US copyright law, medical ethics & law, international financial law, international business law; LlB, LLM, MA, MPhil, MSc, PhD, JD

Florence Nightingale School of Nursing & Midwifery; www.kcl.ac.uk/nursing

midwifery studies with registration, nursing practice, nursing studies with registration (adult nursing, children's nursing, mental health nursing), nutrition & dietetics, advanced practice (district midwife with registration, nursing/leadership/midwifery/specialist community public health nursing/health visiting/

school nursing/district nursing, clinical nursing/research/practice, education for healthcare professionals, health studies; BSc(Hons), DipHE, DHC, DPhil, MRes, MSc, PGCert/Dip

School of Natural & Mathematical Sciences; www.kcl.ac.uk/nms

Chemistry; chemistry, chemistry with bioscience, analytical science for industry, biopharmaceuticals, medical imaging sciences, pharmaceutical analysis & quality control, pharmaceutical technology, education (chemistry), radiopharmaceutics & pet radiochemistry, science education
Informatics; adv computing with management, computer science, computer science with intelligent systems/management, robotics with management, computer systems engineering with management, electronic & information engineering, electronic engineering, electronic engineering with management, mathematics & computer science, robotics & intelligent systems, adv computing, adv software engineering, computing & internet systems, computing & security, computing, IT, law & management, electronic engineering with management, intelligent systems, mobile & personal communications, telecommunications & internet technology, web intelligence
Mathematics; mathematics & philosophy/physics/computer science/complex modelling systems, mathematics, complex systems modelling – from biomedical and natural to economic and social sciences, financial mathematics, PGCE (mathematics/physics with mathematics), mathematics education
Physics; physics & mathematics/philosophy/medical applications/theoretical physics, robotics & intelligent systems; BEng, BSc, MSc, MPhil, MSci, GradDip, PhD

School of Social Science and Public Policy; www.kcl.ac.uk/sspp

Management & Business: business management, accounting, accountability & financial management, economics/ & management/French/German/Spanish, HRM & organizational analysis, international management/marketing, mathematics with management & finance, computer science with/electronic engineering with management, public service & management, risk analysis, healthcare management
Education & Professional Studies: English language & linguistics, education, PGCE, Latin with classics, biology, chemistry, English, IT and computer, science, computer science, mathematics, modern foreign languages, physics/ with mathematics, religious education, schools direct, applied linguistics and

ELT, international/ child studies, education in arts & cultural setting, education programmes, language & cultural diversity, TESOL

Political Economy: politics of international economy, international politics/studies/conflict studies, public policy, political economy, politics, philosophy & economics, politics

War Studies: international relations, war studies & history, conflict, security & development, history of war, intelligence & international security, international conflict studies, international peace & security, military & security studies, non-proliferation & international security, science & security, South Asia & global security, terrorism, security & society, war studies, air power in the modern world, international relations & contemporary war, war in the modern world

Defence Studies: defence studies, international security & strategy, war studies, history of warfare, international conflict studies, international peace & security, terrorism, security & defence studies, war studies & history/philosophy, South Asia & global security, conflict security & development, intelligence & international security, non-proliferation & international security

Geography: geography, aquatic resource management, climate change: environment, science and policy/history, culture, society, disasters, adaptation and development, environment and development, environment, politics and globalisation, environmental monitoring, modelling and management, geopolitics, territory and security, risk analysis, sustainable cities, tourism, environment and development, water: science and governance

Social Science, Health & Medicine: ageing & society, bioethics & society, gerontology, concept in social media, global health & social justice, medicine, health & public policy, health & society/promotion, medicine, science & society, ageing & public policy, foundations in social science/social theory research methods

School of Global Affairs; emerging economies and inclusive development, emerging international development, Brazil in global perspective, China & globalisation, conflict resolution in divided societies economies and international development, Eurasian political economy & energy, Latin American development, leadership & development, middle eastern studies, political economy of emerging markets, political economy of the middle east, Russia in global systems, Russian policy & society, security, leadership & society (South Asia & global security);

BA, MA, MSc, MRes, GradDip, PGDip/Cert, FD, DThMin, DrPS, MPhil, PhD, EdD

UNIVERSITY OF LONDON; LONDON SCHOOL OF ECONOMICS & POLITICAL SCIENCE
www.lse.ac.uk

Departments at LSE:

Accounting, Anthropology, Economics, Finance, Geography & Environment, Government, International History, International Relations, Law, Management, Mathematics, Media and Communications, Philosophy, Logic and Scientific Method, Social Policy, Sociology, Statistics

UG

accountancy & finance, anthropology & law, social anthropology, actuarial science, business mathematics and statistics, statistics with finance, actuarial science, economic history, economic history with economics, economics and economic history, economics, econometrics and mathematical economics, economics with economic history, environmental policy with economics, environment and development finance, finance, geography, geography & economics, history, international relations/ and history, international relations, language studies, law, management, mathematics & economics, philosophy, politics and economics, philosophy and economics, philosophy, logic and scientific method, social policy, social policy and economics, social policy and sociology, social policy with government, sociology, societal psychology: theory and applications

PG

accounting & finance, accounting, organisations & institutions, anthropology & development, African development, applicable mathematics, behavioural science, China in comparative perspective, city design & social science, comparative politics, conflict studies, criminal justice policy, culture & society, development management/studies, econometrics & mathematical economics, economic history, economics, economics & management/philosophy,

187

economics, risk & society, empires, colonisation & globalisation, environmental economics & climate change, environment & development/policy & regulation, environmental policy & regulation, European politics, European studies/ideas, human resources & organisations (international employment relations & HRM), ideologies & identities, finance & private equity, financial mathematics, gender, gender development & globalisation/media & culture/policy & inequalities, global health/history/politics, health policy, planning & financing, health, population & science,communication & development, history of international relations, human geography & international studies, human resources & organisations, human resource management, human rights, inequalities & social science, international development & humanitarian emergencies, international health policy, international management, international management & public policy, international political economy, international relations/theory, law & accounting, law, anthropology & sociology, local economic development, management & strategy, management science, management information systems & digital innovation, management (organisation & governance)/management science (decision sci/OR) media & communication (data & society/media & communications governance), media, communication & development, organisational & social psychology, organisational behaviour, philosophy & public policy, philosophy of science/social science, political economy of Europe/late development, political science & political economy, political sociology/theory, politics & communication, population & development, psychology of economics, public management & governance, public policy & administration, quantitative economic history, real estate economics & finance, regional & urban planning, regulation, religion in the contemporary world, risk & finance/stochastics, social anthropology, social & cultural psychology, society & public communication, social policy (European & comparative social policy), social policy & planning/development/research, social research methods, sociology (contemporary social thought/research), statistics, financial statistics, theory & history of international relations, urbanisation & development

BA(Hons), BSc(Hons), Dips, EMBA, LlM, ELLM, MBA, MPA, MPhil, MRes, MSc, MA, PhD

UNIVERSITY OF LONDON; LONDON SCHOOL OF JEWISH STUDIES
www.lsjs.ac.uk

Jewish education, Jewish studies, school direct; MA

UNIVERSITY OF LONDON; QUEEN MARY
www.qmul.ac.uk

Humanities & Social Sciences
School of Business & Management; www.busman.qmul.ac.uk

Undergraduate; business management, marketing and management, accounting and management
Postgrad; public administration, marketing, management, management and organisational innovation, international HRM, international financial management, international business, international business and politics, business and management, accounting and management, accounting and finance; BSc, MSc, MPA, MRes, PhD

School of Economics & Finance; www.econ.qmul.ac.uk

accounting & finance, banking/ & finance, behavioural finance, business finance, economics, economics/& finance/politics/finance & management/statistics & mathematics, economics, economics & international finance, statistics & mathematics, finance & econometrics, finance, investment & finance, law & economics/finance, mathematical finance, wealth management; BSc, MPhil, MSc(Econ), PhD

School of English and Drama; www.sed.qmul.ac.uk

Dept of Drama

creative arts & mental health, drama, drama & English/French/German/Hispanic studies/Russian/film studies, theatre & performance

Dept of English

English studies, English/& drama/film studies/history/modern language/French/German/English literature/Hispanic studies/Russian, English literature & linguistics, English literature, poetry, early modern studies, 1300-1700, 18th century literature and romanticism, Victorian literature, writing in the modern age, contemporary writing, post colonial & global writing; BA(Hons), MA, MRes, PhD

Dept of Geography; www.geog.qmul.ac.uk

geography, cities & cultures, development & global health, environmental geography/science/with business management, human geography, environmental science: integrated management of freshwater environment, global development futures, London studies; BA(Hons), BSc(Econ), BSc(Hons), MA, MSc, PhD

Dept of History; www.history.qmul.ac.uk

history,modern & contemporaryBritish/medieval/history, history & politics/film studies/English/German/French/comparative literature, European Jewish history, global imperial history, medieval & Renaissance/American/cultural history, Middle Eastern studies, global & imperial history, history of political thought & intellectual history; BA(Hons), MA, PhD

School of Languages, Linguistics & Film; www.sllf.qmul.ac.uk

honours combinations of French, German, Hispanic studies, Russian, Catalan languages, Portuguese, with English language/literature, business management, film studies, linguistics, politics, history, drama, Anglo-German cultural relations, comparative literature with language/film/linguistics, applied linguistics for English literature, documentary practice, linguistics, language teaching, Anglo-German relations; BA(Hons), MA, PhD

School of Law; www.law.qmul.ac.uk

law, English & European law/Chinese law, law & politics, banking and finance law, commercial and corporate law, comparative and international dispute resolution, competition law, computer and communications law, criminal justice, energy and natural resources law, environmental law, European law, global law, human rights law, immigration law, insurance law, intellectual property law, international business law, international dispute resolution (arbitration/mediation), international economic law, international finance law, international shipping law, law and economics/finance, law by research, laws, legal theory, management of intellectual property, media law, medical law, public international law, trade marks law and practice; Dips, LlB, LlM, MPhil, MSc, PGDip/Cert, PhD

Dept of Philosophy; www.philosophy.qmul.ac.uk

philosophy; MPhil, PhD

School of Politics & International Relations; www.politics.qmul.ac.uk

international relations, British politics, theory & practice, international/public policy, European public policy, politics/& economics/law/history/business management/French/German/Russian/Hispanic studies, international business & politics, numerous postgrad modules available; BA(Hons), MA, MPhil, MRes, PhD

School of Medicine & Dentistry; www.smd.qmul.ac.uk

Barts and The London School of Medicine and Dentistry; www.smd-edu.qmul.ac.uk/medicine

medicine, surgery, dentistry, aesthetic medicine, biomedical science (medical microbiology), burn care, clinical dermatology, clinical drug development, aesthetic medicine, cancer and therapeutics, cancer and clinical oncology, clinical dermatology,clinical drug development, clinical endocrinology, clinical microbiology, clinical research, creative arts and mental health, critical care, diabetes, endocrinology and diabetes, forensic medical sciences, gastroenterology, genomic medicine, global health, law and governance, global public health and policy, healthcare research method, health systems and global policy, inflammation: cellular and vascular aspects, international primary health care, mental health and law, mental health: psychological therapies, mental health: transcultural mental healthcare, migration, culture and global health, cancer molecular pathology and genomics, neuroscience and translational medicine, orthopaedic trauma science, reconstructive microsurgery, regenerative medicine: science and application, sport and exercise medicine, surgical skills and sciences, trauma sciences, trauma sciences (military and humanitarian), dental clinical sciences, dental materials, dental public health, dental technology, endodontic practice, experimental oral pathology (oral sciences), oral biology, oral medicine, orthodontics, paediatric dentistry, periodontology, prosthodontics

Research Institutions
Barts Cancer Institute
Bizard Institute of Cell and Molecular Science
Institute of Dentistry
Institute of Health Science and Education
William Harvey Research Institute
Wolfson Institute of Preventative Medicine
BDS, BMedSci, FD, MBBS, BDental Science, MBBS, MClinDent, MD, MRes, MPhil, BSc, MSc, NVQ, PGDip, PhD, MPrth, PG Cert/Dip, MRes

Department of Science & Engineering

School of Biological and Chemical Sciences; www.sbcs.qmul.ac.uk
aquatic biology, biochemistry, bioinformatics, biology, biomedical sciences, chemistry, chemical research, ecology & evolutionary genomics, ecological & environmental biology, freshwater & marine ecology, immunology, medical/genetics, neuroscience, pharmaceutical chemistry, pharmacological & innovative therapies, plant & fungal taxonomy; diversity & conservation, psychology, zoology; BSc(Hons), FD, MPhil, MSci, PhD

School of Electronic Engineering & Computer Science; www.eecs.qmul.ac.uk
computer systems engineering, electrical and electronic engineering, electronic engineering, information and communications technologies, information technology management for business, multimedia and arts technology, computer science, computer science and mathematics/multimedia/business management/ and accounting, computer systems engineering, electronic engineering & telecommunications, electronics with music and audio systems, big data science, computer vision, computing and information systems, digital signal processing, electronic engineering by research, financial computing, internet of things (engineering/intelligent sensing/data), media and arts technology by research, network science, software engineering for business, sound and music computing, telecommunications & wireless systems/ management, software engineering; BEng, BSc(Eng), MEng, MSc, PhD, MSci

School of Engineering and Materials Science; www.sems.qmul.ac.uk
aerospace engineering, biomedical engineering & clinical materials/biomaterials & tissue engineering/ imaging & instrumentation, design, innovation & creative engineering, materials & design, materials science & engineering, dental materials, biomaterials/ for biomedical science, adv/mechanical engineering, materials research, medical materials/electronics & physics/science, polymer science & nanotechnology, regenerative medicine, robotics engineering, sustainable energy systems/engineering/materials; BEng, BSc, MEng, MPhil, MRes, PhD

School of Mathematical Sciences; www.maths.qmul.ac.uk
mathematics, actuarial science, chemical engineering, statistics & mathematics, pure mathematics, mathematics with statistics/finance & accounting, financial economics, finance & accounting, mathematical finance, maths with business management/ & finance, financial mathematics, networks science, mathematical/financial computing; BSc(Hons), MPhil, MSc, MSci, PGDip/Cert, PhD

School of Physics & Astronomy; www.ph.qmul.ac.uk
astrophysics, astronomy, physics, theoretical physics, physics with particle physics, condensed matter physics; BSc(Hons), MSc, MSci, PGDip, PhD

UNIVERSITY OF LONDON; ROYAL HOLLOWAY
www.rhul.ac.uk

Faculty of Arts; www.rhul.ac.uk/ departments/arts

Dept for Classics; www.rhul.ac.uk/classics
ancient history/with philosophy, archaeology, classical studies, classics, classical studies & drama/Italian, English & classical studies/Latin, Greek/Latin, adv Latin, German & classical studies/Greek, ancient & medieval history, classical art & archaeology, classical studies & comparative literature & culture/philosophy/modern languages, classics, reception, rhetoric, history, Helenic studies; BA(Hons), MA, MRes, MPhil, PhD

Dept of Drama & Theatre; www.rhul.ac.uk/drama

applied & participative theatre, drama & creative writing/dance/English literature/theatre studies, English & creative writing, contemporary performance practices, playwriting, courses in the archive; BA(Hons), MA, MPhil, PhD

Dept of English; www.rhul.ac.uk/english

English, English & philosophy/classics/modern languages/film studies/drama/creative writing/history/music/American literature/comparative literature, creative writing, English literature, modern & contemporary literature, medieval studies, poetic practice, Shakespeare, Victorian literature, art, culture; BA, MA, PhD

Dept of Media Arts; www.rhul.ac.uk/media-arts

documentary by practice, international TV industries, production, film studies/& philosophy, screenwriting/producing TV & film, film, TV & digital production, international TV industries; BA(Hons), BSc, MA, MPhil, PhD

Dept of Modern Languages, Literature & Culture; www.rhul.ac.uk/mllc

French, German, Italian, Spanish, Hispanic studies, comparative literature & culture, visual arts, visual cultures & international film, liberal arts, linguistics, multilingual studies; BA, BSc, MA, MA by Research, PhD

Dept of Music; www.rhul.ac.uk/Music

music, composition, music performance, music & drama/economics/modern foreign language/history/mathematics/philosophy/political studies/physics, advanced musical studies; BA(Hons), BMus, MMus, MPhil, PhD, PGDip

Faculty of History & Social Sciences; www.rhul.ac.uk/departments/hss

School of Law; www.rhul.ac.uk/criminologyandsociology

law, criminology & sociology/psychology, consumption, culture & marketing, forensic psychology; BSc, MA, PhD

Dept of Economics; www.rhul.ac.uk/economics

economics, economics & management/mathematics, economics, policy & international relations, accounting, finance & economics, financial & business economics, policy economics, finance, computational finance, economics with business; BSc, MSc, PhD

Dept of European Studies; www.rhul.ac.uk/EuropeanStudies

European studies (French/Spanish/Italian/German), European research, international relations, social science, European integration, contemporary Europe; BA

Dept of History; www.rhul.ac.uk/history

history, public history, late antique & Byzantine studies, crusader studies, Helenic studies, Holocaust studies, medieval studies, modern history & politics, history & international relations/music/philosophy/French/German/Spanish; BA, MA, PhD

School of Management; www.rhul.ac.uk/management

accounting & finance, business & management, management with accounting/entrepreneurship/human resources/ information technology/ international business/marketing/sustainability, integrating management, entrepreneurship, business information systems, consumption, culture & marketing, marketing, international accounting/HRM, management, business leadership; BSc, MA, MBA, MSc, PhD

Dept of Politics & International Relations; www.rhul.ac.uk/politicandir

politics, international relations, politics and international relations, politics with philosophy, politics, philosophy and economics (PPE), economics/geography, politics and international relations, politics and international relations and philosophy

PG; contemporary political theory, elections, public opinion and parties, media, power and public affairs, politics, international relations, transnational security studies; BA(Hons), BSc(Hons), MA, MBA, MSc, MPhil, PhD, PGCert, Grad Dip, PGDip

Dept of Social Work; www.rhul.ac.uk/socialwork

social work, Advanced practice; BA(Hons), MA, MSc

Faculty of Science; www.rhul.ac.uk/departments/science

School of Biological Sciences; www.rhul.ac.uk/biological-sciences

biochemistry, biology, ecology & evolution & behaviour/the environment, molecular biology, biomedical sciences, medical biochemistry, plant molecular sciences, psychology, zoology; BA(Hons), BSc(Hons), MSc, PhD

Dept of Computer Science; www.cs.rhul.ac.uk

computer science/& mathematics, computing & business, artificial intelligence, computational finance, big data, data science & analytics, digital media communication, information security, machine learning, software engineering; BSc(Hons), MPhil, MSc, PhD

Dept of Earth Sciences; www.rhul.ac.uk/earthscience

environmental geology/geoscience, geoscience, geology, petroleum geology, physical geography & geology, petroleum geoscience, quaternary science & security; BSc, MSc, MSci, PhD

Dept of Geography; www.rhul.ac.uk/geography

geography, cultural/human/physical practising sustainable development, geopolitics & security; BA, BSc, MA, MSc, PhD

Dept of Mathematics; www.ma.rhul.ac.uk

mathematics, maths of cryptology & communication, computer science & mathematics, /finance/French/management, mathematical studies, economics with statistics, finance & mathematics, mathematics for applications, mathematics with physics/philosophy/management/foreign language/music/statistics, information security, joint degrees; BSc(Hons), MSc, MSci, PhD

Dept of Physics; www.rhul.ac.uk/physics

physics/with mathematics/philosophy/music, astrophysics, experimental physics, particle physics, theoretical physics, Masters by research; BSc(Hons), MPhil, MPhys, MSc, PhD

Dept of Psychology; www.rhul.ac.uk/psychology

psychology, applied/social psychology, forensic psychology, psychological development & developmental disorders, clinical psychology & mental health, clinical & cognitive neuroscience; BSc(Hons), DClinPsych, MSc, PhD

UNIVERSITY OF LONDON; ROYAL VETERINARY COLLEGE
www.rvc.ac.uk

applied biological/veterinary research, bioveterinary sciences, biological science (animal behaviour & welfare & ethics), intensive/livestock health & production, veterinary nursing/medicine, wild animal health/biology, veterinary/education/epidemiology & public health, sustainable agriculture in health & food safety, one health (infectious diseases), veterinary clinical studies; BSc(Hons), BVetMed, FdSc, MPhil, PhD, MVMed, MRes, MSc, PGDip/Cert

UNIVERSITY OF LONDON; SCHOOL OF ORIENTAL AND AFRICAN STUDIES
www.soas.ac.uk

Faculty of Languages & Cultures; www.soas.ac.uk/languagecultures

Undergraduate Degrees; African language and culture, African studies, ancient Near Eastern studies, Arabic/and Islamic studies, Chinese (modern and classical), Chinese studies, English, Hebrew and Israeli studies, international management and South East Asian Studies, Islamic studies, Japanese/studies, Korean, linguistics, Middle Eastern studies, Persian, South Asian studies, South Asian studies (Bengali/Hindi/Nepali/Sanskri/Urdu pathways), South East Asian studies, Turkish

Numerous Undergraduate (Combined) Degrees

Postgraduate Degrees; postcolonial studies, cinema, nation and the transcultural, global cinemas and the transcultural, Japanese post-war film genres and the avant-garde, Japanese transnational cinema, theory and practice of translation (Asian and African languages), intensive language (Arabic/Japanese/Korean), advanced Chinese studies, African literature, ancient Near Eastern languages, anthropological research methods and Nepali, applied linguistics and language pedagogy, Arabic literature, Chinese literature/studies, Islamic societies and cultures, Islamic studies, Israeli studies, Japanese literature/studies, Korean literature/studies, language documentation and description, languages and cultures of

South Asia, linguistics, Near and Middle Eastern studies, Pacific Asian studies, sinology, South Asian area studies, South East Asian Studies, Taiwan studies, theory and practice of translation (Asian and African languages), Turkish studies, Iranian studies

Research Degrees; African studies, Chinese and Inner Asian Studies, interdisciplinary programmes (comparative literature, cultural studies and postcolonial studies), Japanese and Korean studies, linguistics, Near and Middle Eastern studies, South Asian studies, South East Asian studies

Diplomas & Certificates; Sanskrit, ancient Near Eastern studies, Arabic studies, modern Hebrew, Persian, South Asian studies, Turkish studies

Faculty of Law & Social Sciences; www.soas.ac.uk/lawsocialsciences

Undergraduate Degrees; development studies, international management and south east Asian studies, international relations, politics, development economics, economics, international management (China/Japan and Korea/Japan/international management, Korea/Middle East and North Africa/Middle East and North Africa, management, senior status (law), development studies and economics, law, politics

Taught Masters Degrees; law, banking law, environmental law, international economic law, law and gender, law in the Middle East and North Africa, South Asian law, gender studies and law, gender and sexuality, politics (with language), African politics, Asian politics, comparative political thought, development economics, development studies (special reference to Central Asia/economics with reference to Africa/environment and development/South Asia/the middle east), environment, politics and development, finance and development, globalisation and development, labour, social movements and development, Middle East politics, migration mobility and development, political economy of development, politics of China, research for international development, violence, conflict & development, global diplomacy

Research Degrees: economics, Certificate in political studies

Faculty of Arts & the Humanities; www.soas.ac.uk/artshumanities

Undergraduate Degrees; development studies, international management and South East Asian studies,

international relations, politics, development economics, economics, international management (China/Japan and Korea/Middle East and North Africa), management, senior status (law), economics, law

Masters Degrees; Chinese law, dispute and conflict resolution, environmental law, human rights, conflict and justice, international economic law, international law, international and comparative commercial law, international & comparative law, Islamic law, law and gender, law, law, culture & society, law, development & globalisation, the Middle East and North Africa/culture and society/development and globalisation, gender studies/and law, gender and sexuality, legal studies, Chinese law, dispute and conflict resolution environmental law and sustainable development, human rights law, law, development and globalisation, politics with (language), finance and management, African politics, Asian politics, comparative political thought, development economics/studies, development studies (Central Asia/contemporary India/Palestine), economics with reference to Africa/environment and development/South Asia/Asia Pacific region/Middle East, environment, politics and development, finance and development/financial law, global economic governance and policy, globalisation and development, international management (China/Japan/Middle East and North Africa) international politics, labour, social movements and development, Middle East politics, migration mobility and development, political economy of development, politics of China, politics of conflict, rights & justice, public financial management, public policy and management, research for international development, state, society and development, violence, conflict & development (Palestine), global diplomacy, finance

Research Degrees; music, anthropology & sociology, art & archaeology, history, media studies, economics of religions

Diplomas; postgraduate Asian art course, diploma or certificate

Certificates; political studies, economics

BA(Hons), LlB, LlM, MMus, MRes, MPhil, MSc, PGDip, PhD, Certs, Dips

UNIVERSITY OF LONDON; THE SCHOOL OF PHARMACY
www.pharmacy.ac.uk

pharmacy, clinical pharmacy, international practice and policy, pharmaceutics, pharmaceutical formulation and entrepreneurship, drug delivery, drug discovery and development/pharmacy management, medicinal natural products and phytochemistry, experimental pharmacology and therapeutics, drug sciences; Certs, MPharm, MSc, PGDip, PhD, MRes

UNIVERSITY OF LONDON; UNIVERSITY COLLEGE LONDON (UCL)
www.ucl.ac.uk

UCL School of Life and Medical Science (including UCL Medical School); www.ucl.ac.uk/slms

Faculty of Brain Sciences; www.ucl.ac.uk/brain-sciences

brain sciences, translational neurology, brain and mind sciences, advanced neuroimaging, translational and regenerative neuroscience, translational, imunobiology, vision research, biology of vision, mental health

sciences research, applied research in human communication disorders, cognitive and decision sciences, stroke medicine, neuromuscular disease

Audiology and Hearing Research; advanced audiology, audiological science, audiological science with clinical practice, medical otology and audiology (audiovestibular medicine/medical ENT practice)

Ophthalmology and Vision Research; clinical ophthalmic practice, clinical ophthalmology, ophthalmology with clinical practice

Psychiatry and Mental Health Sciences; clinical/mental health sciences

Neurology and Neuroscience; clinical neurology, clinical neurology, clinical neuroscience, neurology for clinical trainees

Speech and Language Therapy; speech and language sciences

Clinical Psychology; cognitive behavioural therapy for children and young people, low intensity cognitive behavioural interventions

Neuroscience; cognitive neuroscience, dementia/neuroscience, developmental neuroscience and psychopathology, language sciences (linguistics with neuroscience/neuroscience and communication), translational and regenerative neuroscience, advanced neuroimaging, dual masters in brain and mind science, clinical neurology, clinical neuroscience, neurology for clinical trainees, diploma in

clinical neurology via distance learning, translational neurology, brain science

Psychology; clinical psychology and psychotherapy; cognitive behavioural therapy for children and young people, developmental neuroscience and psychopathology, developmental psychology and clinical practice, low intensity cognitive behavioural interventions, psychoanalytic developmental psychology, theoretical psychoanalytical studies, cognition and research skills; cognitive and decision sciences, cognitive neuroscience, research methods in psychology, social cognition, speech, language and cognition, developmental psychology; cognitive behavioural therapy for children and young people, developmental neuroscience and psychopathology, developmental psychology and clinical practice, psychoanalytic developmental psychology, organisational psychology; industrial/organisational and business psychology, human-computer interaction with ergonomics

Language; applied research in human communication disorders, language sciences with specialisation in language development/linguistics with neuroscience/neuroscience and communication/sign language studies/speech and hearing sciences, linguistics, linguistics with specialisation in phonology/pragmatics/semantics/syntax, speech and language sciences, speech, language and cognition; BSc(Hons), BA(Hons), MSc, MA, MPhil, PhD, GradDip/Cert, MRes

Faculty of Life Sciences; www.ucl.ac.uk/life-sciences

UG; Biosciences: biochemistry, biological sciences (including genetics, human genetics, biodiversity and conservation and zoology), biomedical science, biotechnology, human sciences & evolution, immunology, molecular biology, neuroscience, genetics/human genetics, pharmacology, physiology anatomy, cell & developmental biology,genetics/ human genetics, neuroscience, pharmacology, physiology/ and pharmacology

PG; advanced pharmacy practice, biosciences, biomedical sciences, clinical pharmacy, international practice and policy, drug discovery and development/ pharma management, experimental pharmacology and therapeutics, genetics of human disease, drug sciences, neuroscience, pharmaceutics, pharmacogenetics and stratified medicine,medicinal natural products and phytochemistry, pharmaceutical formulation and entrepreneurship

Institute of Child Health

advanced physiotherapy (cardiovascular and paediatric) or physiotherapy studies (cardiovascular and paediatric), cell and gene therapy, child and adolescent mental health, paediatrics and child health (advanced paediatrics, community child health, gastroenterology and global child health) paediatric neuropsychology (applied and clinical), biomedicine, paediatrics and child health

Faculty of Medical Sciences; www.ucl.ac.uk/medical-sciences

UG; applied medical sciences, clinical science, orthopaedic science, surgical science, immunology, infection & cell pathology, medicine

UCL Medical School; medicine surgery, clinical & professional development

Division of Medicine; applied medical sciences, advanced biomedical imaging, clinical and public health nutrition, eating disorders and clinical nutrition, clinical drug development, drug design

UCL Cancer Institute

cancer

UCL Eastman Dental Institute

advanced aesthetic dentistry, conservative dentistry, dental sedation and pain management, endodontic practice, endodontics, endodontology, implant dentistry, oral medicine, oral surgery, oral and maxillofacial surgery, orthodontics, paediatric dentistry, periodontology, prosthodontics, restorative dental practice, special care dentistry

Division of Infection & Immunology; immunology, infection & cell pathology, immunology & infection, healthcare associated infection control, infection and immunity, mycology

Division of Surgery & Interventional Science; burns, plastic & reconstructive surgery, evidence-based healthcare, musculoskeletal science, nanotechnology & regenerative medicine, performing arts medicine, perioperative medicine, sports medicine, exercise &

health, surgical & interventional sciences, trauma & orthopaedics, rehabilitation and assistive technologies, physical therapy in musculoskeletal healthcare and rehabilitation, orthopaedics, orthopaedic science, surgical sciences, introduction to systematic reviews, perioperative fluid therapy

Division of Medical Science

clinical & medical education, medical education

Wolfson Institute for Biomedical Research

drug discovery

BSc(Hons), iBSc, MBBS, MSc, PGDip, Cert, PhD, MRes, MSci, MPharm

Faculty of Population Health Sciences; www.ucl.ac.uk/populationhealth-sciences

Institute of Epidemiology and Health Care; population health

Institute of Cardiovascular Science; cardiovascular science

Institute of Child Health; advanced physiotherapy (cardiovascular and paediatric pathways), biomedicine, cell and gene therapy, child and adolescent mental health, child health, paediatric neuropsychology (applied and clinical pathways), paediatrics and child health (advanced paediatrics, community child health, gastroenterology, molecular and genomic and global child health pathways), physiotherapy studies (cardiorespiratory and paediatric pathways

Institute of Epidemiology and Health Care; dental public health, health and society: social epidemiology, health psychology, population health

Institute for Global Health; global health and development

Institute of Health Informatics; data science for research in health and biomedicine, heath and medical sciences; health and medical sciences (quality, information and safety), health informatics

Institute for Women's Health; prenatal genetics and fetal medicine, reproductive science and women's health

BSc(Hons), DipCDSc, IbSc, MBBS, MClinDent, MD(Res), MPhil, MRes, MSc, MSci, PGCert/Dip, PhD, MOrth, MRD

The Bartlett, Faculty of the Built Environment

Built Environment; www.bartlett.ucl.ac.uk

Centre for Advanced Spatial Analysis; smart cities and urban analytics, spatial data science and visualisation

School of Architecture: UG; architecture, project management for construction, urban planning,

design & management, architectural & interdisciplinary studies, project management for construction, planning & real estate, urban studies
PG; architecture, architectural design, urban design, architectural history, architectural computation, spatial design: architecture and cities, architecture and digital theory,architecture and historic urban environments
School of Construction & Project Management: project management for construction, PG; construction economics & management, project enterprise & management, strategic management of projects, infrastructure investment and finance
Development Planning Unit: building and urban design in development, development administration & planning, environment and sustainable development, social development practice, urban development planning, urban economic development
Advanced Spatial Analysis: smart cities & urban analytics, smart cities, spatial data science & visualisation
School of Planning: urban planning, design & management, urban studies, PG; planning and real estate, inter-disciplinary urban design, dip spatial planning, international planning, international real estate & planning, urban regeneration, sustainable urbanism, planning, design & development, mega infrastructure planning appraisal & delivery, housing development & urban analytics, smart cities, transport and city planning, urban design & city planning, housing & city planning
Energy Institute: energy demand studies, economics & policy of energy & the environment, energy
Sustainable Resources: economics & policy of energy & the environment, sustainable use of resources & the environment, sustainable resources
Sustainable Heritage; sustainable heritage, science & engineering in arts
Institute for Environmental Design and Engineering; environmental design and engineering, facility and environment management, light and lighting
BSc(Hons), BA(Hons) Diplomas, EngD, MA, MArch, MPhil, MSc, PhD, PGDip, MRes

Faculty of Engineering Sciences; www.ucl.ac.uk/engineering

Biochemical Engineering; www.ucl.ac.uk/biochemeng

biochemical engineering, bioprocessing of new medicines, synthetic biology, emerging bioprocess sectors & applications, adv life sciences, bioscience engineering principles, adv bioprocessing, adv biochemical engineering

Chemical Engineering; www.ucl.ac.uk/chemeng

chemical engineering/with biochemical engineering, chemical process engineering

Civil, Environmental & Geomatic Engineering; www.cege.ucl.ac.uk

civil engineering, earthquake engineering with disaster management, environmental systems engineering, geomatics for building information analytics, GIS, hydrographic surveying, rail integrated design, transport, transport health & policy, spatio-temporal analytics & big data mining, engineering for international development, geoinformatics for building information modelling, surveying, integrated design management

Computer Science; www.cs.ucl.ac.uk

computer science, mathematical computation, business analytics, computational finance, computational statistics and machine learning computer graphics, vision and imaging, financial systems engineering, financial risk management, human-computer interaction with ergonomics, logic, semantics & verification of programs, information security, machine learning, networked computer systems, software systems engineering, web science and big data analytics, robotics & computation

Electronic and Electrical Engineering; www.cs.ucl.ac.uk

electronics engineering with communications engineering/computer science/nanotechnology, electrical & electronic engineering, internet engineering, nanotechnology, integrated photonic & electronic systems, space science & engineering, satellite communications development, telecommunications/with business, wireless & optical communications

School of Management; www.mgt.ucl.ac.uk

management science, business analytics, information management for business, management, technology entrepreneurship, healthcare management

Mechanical Engineering; www.ucl.ac.uk/mecheng

engineering (mechanical) with business/finance, marine engineering, mechanical engineering, naval architecture, power systems engineering, biomaterials & tissue engineering, engineering with innovation & enterprise

Medical Physics & Bioengineering; www.ucl.ac.uk/medphys

biomedical; engineering, medical imaging/computing, physics & engineering in medicine, medical physics, radiation physics; MEng, BSc, Certs, MEng, MPhil, MRes, MSc, PGDip, PhD

Faculty of Mathematical and Physical Sciences; www.ucl.ac.uk/maps-faculty

Chemistry; www.ucl.ac.uk/chemistry

chemistry, chemical physics, organic chemistry, drug discovery, chemical research, materials for energy & the environment, medicinal chemistry, molecular modelling/& materials science, chemistry with mathematics/Euro lamguage/management studies

Earth Sciences; www.ucl.ac.uk/es

earth science, environmental geoscience, geology, geophysical hazards, geophysics, geosciences, natural hazards, natural sciences, risk & disaster reduction, global management of natural resources

Mathematics; www.ucl.ac.uk/mathematics

mathematics with economics/modern languages/management studies/physics/statistics, mathematical modelling, financial mathematics

Physics and Astronomy; www.phys.ucl.ac.uk

astronomy, astrophysics, physics, theoretical physics, planetary science, nanotechnology, scientific computing, quantum technologies, biological physics

Science and Technology Studies; www.ucl.ac.uk/sts

science, technology & society, natural sciences, history & philosophy of science, philosophy, medicine & society

Space and Climate Physics; www.mssl.ucl.ac.uk

space science & engineering, technology management, systems engineering management, management of complex projects

Statistical Science; www.ucl.ac.uk/stats

statistics, economics & finance/languages/statistics, mathematics & statistical science, statistics/& management for business, medical statistics, data science; BSc, BSc(Econ), EngD, MRes, MSc, MSci, PhD

Faculty of Arts & Humanities; www.ucl.ac.uk/ah

English Language & Literature: English, English and a modern language, English; issues in modern culture, English linguistics, medieval and Renaissance studies, early modern studies, English & Latin/Greek

European Social & Political Studies, Dutch, French, German, Italian, Russian, Spanish, Scandinavian studies, Spanish & Latin American studies, East European language & culture, Hebrew & Jewish studies, anthropology, economics, geography, planning, political science, philosophy, international relations, history, law

Greek & Latin: classics: languages & literature, ancient world studies, reception of classical world, archaeology

Hebrew & Jewish studies: Jewish history, language & culture, history (central & E Europe)/ & Jewish studies, ancient languages

Information Studies: library & information studies, archive & information studies/records management, digital humanities, publishing, information science/systems, publishing

Philosophy: philosophy, philosophy and economics/Greek/history of art, philosophy, politics and economics of health

European Languages, Culture & Society: French, Dutch, German, Italian, Spanish, Portuguese & Latin American studies, comparative literature, translation studies, language, history & culture, Scandinavian studies, language & culture

Slade School of Fine Art

fine art, sculpture, history & theory of art, critical studies;
BA(Hons), BFA, MA, MPhil, MRes, PhD, MFA

Faculty of Law; www.ucl.ac.uk/laws

law, law & adv studies/another legal system (Australia, Singapore), French/German/Hispanic law, competition/comparative/corporate law, criminal justice, family & social welfare, dispute resolution, environmental law & policy, human rights/intellectual property law, international banking & finance/commercial law, international law, jurisprudence & legal theory, legal history, litigation & dispute resolution, maritime law, public law, law with another legal subject, law & economics, EU law; LlB and Baccalaureus Legum, LlBHons, LlM, MPhil, PhD

Faculty of Historical and Social Sciences; www.ucl.ac.uk/shs

Anthropology; www.ucl.ac.uk/anthropology

anthropology/& anthropology, digital anthropology, environment & development, ethnographic & documentary film, social & cultural anthropology, materials, anthropological design, human evolution & behaviour, human sciences, medical anthropology, materials & visual culture, anthropology with modern European studies; BA(Hons), BSc(Hons), MA, MPhil, MRes, MSc, PhD

Archaeology; www.ucl.ac.uk/archaeology

archaeology & anthropology, archaeology, ancient history & Egyptology, classical archaeology & classical civilization; PG; archaeology, archaeology and heritage of Asia, archaeology of Egypt and the near east, artefact studies, comparative art and archaeology, cultural heritage studies, managing archaeological sites, materials anthropology design, Mediterranean archaeology, museum studies, principles of conservation, public archaeology, research methods for archaeology, urban archaeology, bioarchaeology and forensic anthropology, computational archaeology: GIS, data science and complexit, conservation for archaeology and museums, environmental archaeology, palaeoanthropology and palaeolithic archaeology, the technology and analysis of archaeological materials; BA(Hons), BSc(Hons), MA, MPhil, MSc, PhD

Economics; www.ucl.ac.uk/economics

economics, economics & geography/statistics/philosophy/mathematics, microeconomics, economic policy,economics and business with East European studies, economics and geography, European social and political studies, philosophy and economics, mathematics with economics, statistics, economics and finance, statistics, economics and language; BSc(Hons), MSc, PhD

Geography; www.geog.ucl.ac.uk

geography, economics and geography, environmental geography, aquatic science, climate change, conservation, environmental mapping/modelling, environment, science, politics and society, GIS geospatial analysis, global migration, remote sensing, urban studies; BA(Hons), BSc(Hons), MSc, PhD

History; www.ucl.ac.uk/history

history, history with a European language, ancient history/and Egyptology, ancient history, Chinese health and humanity, Dutch golden age, European history, history of political thought and intellectual history, late antique and Byzantine studies, medieval & Renaissance; BA(Hons), MA, MPhil, PhD

History of Art; www.ucl.ac.uk/art-history

history of art/with material studies, methods, debates and sources in history of art, human and non-human in medieval art, cannibalism and the early modern image, vision, tourism, imperialism, American media: publicity and the logics of surveillance, politics of the image: Germany 1890–1945, art as theory: the writing of art, contemporary art and globalisation
BA(Hons), MA, MPhil, PhD

Political Science; www.ucl.ac.uk/spp

philosophy, politics and economics, political studies (political science and international relations), European social and political studies; PG; democracy and comparative politics, international public policy, European public policy, legal and political theory, global governance and ethics, public policy, human rights, security studies, global public policy and management, public administration and management; MA, MPhil, MSc, PhD, MPA

School of Slavonic and Eastern European Studies; www.ssees.ucl.ac.uk

languages/literature & culture, politics & sociology, economics & business, history; BA(Hons), MA, MPhil, MRes, PhD

UNIVERSITY OF LOUGHBOROUGH
www.lboro.ac.uk

Faculty of Engineering; www.lboro.ac.uk/eng

Aeronautical and Automotive Engineering; www.lboro.ac.uk/departments/tt/

aeronautical engineering, automotive engineering/ systems engineering

Chemical Engineering; www.lboro.ac.uk/departments/cg

chemical engineering, advanced/chemical engineering/IT & management, advanced process engineering, chemical engineering with management

Civil and Building Engineering; www.lboro.ac.uk/departments/cv

air transport management, architectural engineering & design management, civil engineering, commercial management & quantity surveying, construction engineering management/project management, construction business management, demand studies, energy demand studies, low energy building services engineering, low carbon building design & modelling, transport, building, infrastructure in emergencies, transport & business management, water & waste engineering/environmental management

Electronic, Electrical & Systems Engineering; www.lboro.ac.uk/departments/el

digital communication systems, electronic & electrical engineering, mobile communications, networked communications, renewable energy systems technology, systems engineering, electronic & computer systems engineering

Dept of Materials Engineering

automotive materials, biomaterials engineering, design with engineering materials, materials engineering, materials science and technology, polymer science and technology; BEng(Hons), MEng(Hons), MSc

Mechanical and Manufacturing Engineering; www.lboro.ac.uk/departments/mm

adv engineering, adv manufacturing engineering & management, engineering design & manufacture, innovative manufacturing engineering, mechanical engineering, product design engineering, sports technology, sustainable engineering; BEng, BSc(Hons), MDes, MRes, MSc, PhD, Cert, Dip

Faculty of Science; www.lboro.ac.uk/sci

Faculty of Chemistry; www.lboro.ac.uk/departments/cm

chemistry, analytical & pharmaceutical science, analytical chemistry, chemistry/& analytical science/sport science, environmental studies, pharmaceutical science & medicinal chemistry, medicinal & pharmaceutical chemistry; BSc(Hons), MChem, MSc, PhD

Dept of Computer Science; www.lboro.ac.uk/departments/co

adv/computer science, computer science/& mathematics/AI/management, IT management for business, information management, computing & management, internet computing & network security; BSc(Hons), MSc, PhD, PGDip/Cert

Dept of Materials; www.lboro.ac.uk/departments/materials

automotive materials, design with engineering materials, materials engineering/science & technology, polymer science & technology, biomaterials engineering; BEng/MEng, BSc(Hons), Dip Industrial Studies, MSc, PGDip/Cert, PhD

School of Mathematical Sciences; www.lboro.ac.uk/departments/maths

industrial mathematical modelling, mathematical finance, mathematics, financial mathematics, mathematics & accounting & financial management/sports science/economics/management/statistics; BSc(Hons), MSc, PhD

Dept of Physics; www.lboro.ac.uk/departments/ph

adv physics, astrophysics & cosmology, engineering physics, physics, physics & maths/management/ sports science/cosmology, physics with astrophysics & cosmology/mathematics, physics of materials; BSc(Hons), MSc, PhD

Faculty of Social Sciences and Humanities; www.lboro.ac.uk/ssh

School of the Arts, English & Drama; www.lboro.ac.uk/departments/sota

fine art, graphic communication & illustration, textiles, innovation & design, art & design (studio practice), drama, English & drama/business studies/ American studies/sports science, graphic design & visualisation, creative writing, publishing, animation for health and wellbeing, art(studio practice) BA(Hons), MA, MSc, MPhil, PhD

School of Business & Economics; www.lboro.ac.uk/departments/sbe

Business; accounting and financial management; banking, finance and management, information management and business, international business, management sciences, retailing, marketing and management

Economics; economics, economics and management, business economics and finance, international economics, economics with accounting, economics with geography, economics with politics postgraduate taught programmes

Postgraduate; banking and finance, business analysis and management, business analytics consulting, business psychology, corporate finance, economics and finance, employment relations and HRM, finance, finance and investment, finance and management, human resource management, information management and business technology, international crisis management, international management, management, marketing, work psychology

Accredited programmes

Leadership and Management; the Loughborough MBA; Organisational Resilience; health, safety; occupational health and safety management, occupational health and safety management, healthcare management and governance, healthcare and societal resilience;Crisis and Emergency; international crisis management, crisis and emergency resilience; Security and Diplomacy; Security Risk Management (Intelligence and International Security; Automotive Management; automotive retail management, strategic automotive dealership management, automotive dealership management;Tailored programmes; leadership and management, management and leadership, wealth management

Executive Education: management & leadership, automotive management, occupational health & safety management, healthcare management;

BSc(Hons), MA, MSc, MRes, MPhil, PhD, Cert, Dip,MBA

Loughborough Design School; www.lboro/departments/lds

design/ergonomics, ergonomics (human factors in design/in health & community care), ergonomics & human factors, product/industrial design & technology, design & innovation for sustainability, human factors in transport/for inclusive design, interaction design; BA, MA, MSc, MDes, PGCE with QTS

Dept of Geography; www.lboro.ac.uk/departments/gy

geography, geography & management/economics/ sports management/sports science, globalization & society/sport science, human geography research, international financial & political relations, environmental monitoring for management, history & geography; BSc, MPhil, MSc, PhD

Dept of Politics, History & International Relations; www.lboro.ac.uk/departments/phis

history & geography/English/international relations/ politics, politics & international relations, international financial & political relations, politics, history & international relations; BSc(Hons), MPhil, MSc, PhD

Dept of Social Sciences; www.lboro.ac.uk/departments/socialsciences

communications and media studies, criminology & social policy, digital media & society, global media & cultural industries, global political communication, global media & cultural analysis, media, culture & society, social psychology/with criminology, sociology; BSc(Hons), MPhil, MSc, PhD

School of Sport, Exercise and Health Sciences; www.lboro.ac.uk/departments/ssehs

human biology, psychology, sport and exercise science, exercise physiology/psychology, human biology, musculoskeletal medicine, musculoskeletal sport science and health, PE with QTS, psychology of sport and exercise, sociology of sport, sport and exercise nutrition, sport coaching, sport management, sports biomechanics, sports science with management; BSc(Hons), MPhil, MSc, PhD

Teacher Education Unit;
www.lboro.ac.uk/departments/teu
initial teacher training (mathematics/PE); MSc, PGCE, QTS

UNIVERSITY OF MANCHESTER
www.manchester.ac.uk

Faculty of Engineering and Physical Sciences; www.eps.manchester.ac.uk

School of Chemical Engineering and Analytical Science; www.ceas.manchester.ac.uk
adv/chemical engineering, adv process integration & design, chemical engineering/energy & the environment/year abroad; BEng, MEng, MSc, PhD

School of Chemistry; www.chemistry.manchester.ac.uk
chemistry/medicinal chemistry/industrial experience, polymer & materials science & engineering; BSc(Hons), EngD, MChem, MEnt, MPhil, MSc, PhD

School of Computer Science; www.cs.manchester.ac.uk
artificial intelligence, computer science, computer systems engineering, computer science with business and management/mathematics, computer science (human computer interaction), software engineering, advanced computer science, advanced web technologies, artificial intelligence, computer systems engineering, computer security, data and knowledge management, digital biology, multi-core computing, semantic technologies, advanced computer science and IT management, information management, computer science foundation; BSc(Hons), MEng, MEnt, MPhil, MSc, PhD

School of Earth, Atmospheric & Environmental Sciences; www.seaes.manchester.ac.uk
earth sciences, applications in/environmental sciences, policy & management, geochemistry, geography/& geology, environmental & resource geology, geology with planetary science, petroleum engineering, geoscience, pollution & environmental control; BSc(Hons), MEarthSci, MEng, MSc, PhD

School of Electrical and Electronic Engineering; www.eee.manchester.ac.uk
communication engineering, advanced control & systems engineering, digital signal processing, electrical & electronic engineering/industrial experience, adv/electrical power systems engineering, mechatronic engineering, power electronics, machines & drives, renewable & clean technology; BEng(Hons), Dip, BSc(Hons), EngD, MEng(Hons), MPhil, MSc, PhD

School of Materials; www.materials.manchester.ac.uk
materials science and engineering, materials science and engineering with biomaterials/polymers/ metallurgy corrosion/textile technology, textiles, textile science and technology, fashion management/marketing/buying and merchandising; Postgrad; advanced engineering materials, biomaterials, corrosion control engineering, international fashion marketing/retailing, polymer materials science and engineering, textile technology (technical textiles); BSc, MEng, MPhil, PhD

School of Mathematics; www.maths.manchester.ac.uk
actuarial science and mathematics, mathematics, mathematics and philosophy/ statistics/modern language/business & management/finance/financial mathematics, computer science and mathematics, mathematics and physics; Postgrad; actuarial science, applied mathematics, mathematical finance, pure mathematics & mathematical logic, statistics; BSc, MMath, MPhil, MSc, PhD

School of Mechanical, Aerospace and Civil Engineering; www.mace.manchester.ac.uk
adv manufacturing technology & systems management, aerospace engineering with industrial experience/ management, civil engineering /(enterprise)/ with industrial experience, civil and structural engineering, mechanical engineering with industrial experience/management, management of projects, advanced manufacturing technology and systems management, reliability engineering and asset management, mechanical engineering design, thermal power and fluid engineering, renewable energy and

clean technology, structural erngineering; BEng, EngD, MEng, MEnt, MPhil, MSc, PhD

School of Physics & Astronomy;
www.physics.manchester.ac.uk

physics, physics & astrophysics/mathematics/theoretical physics/philosophy, astronomy and astrophysics, nonlinear dynamics, nuclear physics, nuclear science and technology, particle physics, soft matter and liquid crystals, theoretical physics, astronomy and astrophysics, biological physics, condensed matter physics, nonlinear dynamics, photon physics, soft matter and liquid crystals, applications of graphine and related nanomatter; BSc, EngD, MMath & Phys, MPhys, MSc, PhD

Faculty of Humanities;
www.humanities.manchester.ac.uk

School of Arts, Languages and Cultures;
www.arts.manchester.ac.uk

American studies, Arabic and Middle Eastern studies, archaeology, art history and visual studies, Chinese studies, classics and ancient history, drama, English literature and creative writing, French studies, German studies, history, Italian studies, Japanese studies, linguistics and English language, music, religions and theology, Russian and East European studies, Spanish, Portuguese and Latin American studies, translation and intercultural studies

Postgraduate; Arabic and Middle Eastern Studies; conference interpreting, translation and interpreting studies,

Archaeology; archaeology,

Art History and Visual Studies; art gallery and museum studies, arts management, policy and practice

Chinese Studies; conference interpreting, intercultural communication, translation and interpreting studies

Classics and Ancient History; classics and ancient history

Drama; arts management, policy and practice, film studies

English Literature and Creative Writing; English studies, English studies with pathway in modernism and after, English studies (postcolonial literatures/ contemporary literature and culture), gender sexuality and culture, creative writing, medieval and early modern studies, screenwriting

French Studies; conference interpreting, intercultural communication, translation and interpreting studies

German Studies, conference interpreting, intercultural communication, translation and interpreting studies

History; history, history of science, technology and medicine (including medical humanities and science communication), medieval and early modern studies

Humanitarian and Conflict Response Institute; global health, humanitarianism and conflict response, peace and conflict studies, international disaster management

Institute for Cultural Practices; art gallery and museum studies, arts management, policy and practice

Italian Studies; intercultural communication, translation and interpreting studies

Japanese Studies; conference interpreting, intercultural communication, translation and interpreting studies

Linguistics and English Language; intercultural communication, linguistics

Music; arts management, policy and practice, composition (electroacoustic music and interactive media/instrumental and vocal), music (ethnomusicology/ musicology)

Religions and Theology; religions and theology

Russian and East European Studies; intercultural communication, translation and interpreting studies

Spanish, Portuguese and Latin American Studies; intercultural communication, translation and interpreting studies

Translation and Intercultural Studies conference interpreting, intercultural communication, translation and interpreting studies; BA(Hons), MA, MMus, MSc, PML, PhD

Manchester Institute of Education;
www.seed.manchester.ac.uk/subject education

digital technologies, communication and education, education (international), educational leadership, psychology of education, TESOL, PGCE primary, secondary (numerous subjects), PGCE primary school direct 5-11, PGCE secondary school direct (numerous subjects), English language & education, management & leisure

School of Environment, Education & Development; www.seed.manchester.ac.uk
Planning and Environmental Management

planning, urban and regional planning, urban studies, environmental impact assessment & management, geography with planning, urban regeneration and development, global urban development and planning, urban design and international planning, planning with real estate, real estate development, real estate asset management

architecture, architecture & urbanism

Geography

geography, geography & geology/international studies/planning, environmental governance, environmental monitoring, modelling & reconstruction, GIS, international development

Global Development Institute

development economics and policy, development finance, global health, global urban development and planning, human resource development (international development), HRM and development (international development), ICTs for development, international development, international development: development management/environment, climate change and development/globalisation, trade and industry/politics, governance and development policy/poverty, inequality and development/poverty, conflict and reconstruction/public policy and management, management and implementation of development projects, management and information systems: change and development, organisational change and development

BA(Hons), DCons, DEd, EdD, MA, MEd, MPhil, MSc, PGCE, PGCert/Dip, PhD, UGCert/Dip, BArch, MArch, MGeog, MPlan, IMPRE

School of Law; www.law.manchester.ac.uk

criminology, law with criminology, criminology and quantitative methods, philosophy/politics/social statistics, social anthropology and criminology, law, law with criminology/politics; corporate governance, healthcare ethics and law, healthcare ethics/law, intellectual property law, international business and commercial law, international financial law, international trade transactions, public international law, security and international law, transnational dispute resolution; BA, LlB, LlM, MA, MPhil, MSc, MRes, PGDip/Cert, PhD, BASS, MDiplo

Manchester Business School; www.mbs.manchester.ac.uk

accounting, information technology management for business, information technology management for business (strategy and economics), information technology management for business (marketing), international business, finance and economics, international management/with American business studies, management, experience, management, management (accounting and finance), HRM, management (innovation, sustainability and entrepreneurship),

management (international business economics), management (international studies), management (marketing), sustainable & ethical business

The above courses provide the opportunity for professional or industrial experience; management with compliance, management with trusts and estates

Masters Courses: analytics: operational research & risk analysis, business psychology, corporate communications & reputation management, finance & business economics, HRM & industrial relations, international HRM & comparative industrial relations, innovation management & entrepreneurship, international business & management (management/research), management, marketing, operations, project & supply chain management, organisational psychology, quantitative finance, MBA, Kelley-Manchester Global MBA, Executive Education, MBA; BA, BSc, MBA, MBus, MDA, MEnt, MPA, MRes, MSc, PhD, DBA, PGCert

School of Social Sciences; www.socialsciences.manchester.ac.uk

accounting and finance, business studies, business studies and economics/politics/sociology, development studies, economics, economics and philosophy/finance/politics/sociology, finance, criminology and quantitative methods, philosophy and criminology/politics/quantitative methods, politics and criminology/social anthropology/sociology/ quantitative methods, social anthropology and criminology/philosophy/sociology quantitative methods, international relations, sociology and criminology/philosophy/quantitative methods, economics, philosophy, politics and international relations, politics, philosophy and economics, sociology, social anthropology; Postgrad; anthropology, econometrics, economics (economics of health/environmental economics), economics and econometrics, economics, financial economics, philosophy, politics, human rights, political science, international politics, international political economy, political economy, theoretical political economy, finance, business & employment, political, political science, democracy and elections, European politics & policy, governance and public policy, political theory, ethics and political philosophy, politics, research, social anthropology, social anthropology – cities and migration/culture, ethnography and development/Latin American studies/visual and sensory media, visual anthropology, social statistics, social research methods and statistics, sociology, sociological research; BAEcon, BSc, MA, MRes, MSc, PGDip, PhD, BASS, BEconSc

Faculty of Life Sciences; www.ls.manchester.ac.uk

anatomical sciences, biochemistry, biology with science & society, biological sciences, biology, biology with science & society, biomedical sciences, biotechnology/& enterprise, cell biology, cognitive neuroscience and psychology, developmental biology, genetics, biology, life sciences, medical biochemistry, microbiology, molecular biology, neuroscience, optometry, pharmacology, physiology, plant sciences, zoology

Postgraduate; biochemistry, bioinformatics and systems biology, biological sciences, biotechnology and enterprise, cancer research and molecular biomedicine, cell biology, developmental biology, history of science, technology and medicine, neuroscience, plant sciences, science communication; BSc, MNeuroSci, MRes, MSc, PhD

Faculty of Medical & Human Sciences; www.mhs.manchester.ac.uk

School of Dentistry; www.dentistry.manchester.ac.uk

dental implantology, dental public health, dentistry, endodontics, fixed & removable prosthodontics, oral & maxillofacial surgery, oral health science, orthodontics, periodontology, restorative & aesthetic dentistry; BDS, BSc, MDen, MDPH, MSc, MSc(Clin), PGDip/Cert, PhD, MRes

School of Medicine; www.medicine.manchester.ac.uk

medicine, surgery, pathology, advanced audiology studies, advanced practice in forensic mental health, advanced practice and leadership, nursing, midwifery, social work, allied healthcare, advanced professional practice and leadership, allied healthcare, speech and language therapy, audiology, physiotherapy, paramedics, occupational therapy, dieticians, advanced nursing practice, advanced midwifery practice and leadership, advanced social work practice and leadership/social work, advanced specialist training in emergency medicine, approved mental health professional practice, audiology, cardiovascular health and disease, clinical and health psychology, clinical and health services pharmacy, clinical immunology, clinical pharmacy, clinical research, clinical rheumatology, clinical trials, dementia care, dental implantology, dental public health,

dental public health/dentistry, digital biology, evidence-based health care, experimental cancer, fixed and removable prosthodontics, forensic psychology and mental health, genetic counselling, genomic medicine genomics, genetics, health and social care, health care ethics and law, health psychology, industrial pharmacy, investigative ophthalmology and vision sciences, medical education, medical microbiology, medical mycology, medical sciences, medical virology, modelling and simulation in pharmacokinetics and pharmacodynamics, molecular pathology, neuroimaging for clinical and cognitive neuroscience, occupational hygiene industrial, environment, occupational medicine, oncology, oral and maxillofacial surgery, orthodontics, periodontology, pharmaceutical business development and licensing, pharmaceutical industrial advanced training, pharmaceutical microbiology, pharmaceutical technology and quality assurance, physician associate studies, primary mental health care, psychology, psychosocial interventions for psychosis, public health and primary care, public health, primary care, public health, reproduction and pregnancy, restorative and aesthetic dentistry, skin ageing and aesthetic medicine, social work, tissue engineering for regenerative medicine, translational medicine (interdisciplinary molecular medicine)

ChB, MB, MD/ChM, MPH, MPhil, MRes, MSc, PGCert, PGDip, PhD, BSc(Hons), APIMH, Ad Dip, CPD Dip, MScClin

School of Nursing and Midwifery & Social Work; www.nursing.manchester.ac.uk

advanced nursing/midwifery studies, midwifery, adult/child/mental health nursing, advanced practice interventions in mental health psychosocial interventions for psychosis (primary mental health care, dementia care, advanced practice and leadership, advanced nursing practice and leadership, advanced midwifery practice and leadership, advanced social work practice and leadership, advanced professional practice and leadership, clinical research, health and social care, social work, continuing professional development; BMidwif, BNurs, MA, MClinRes, MPhil, MRes, MSc, PGCert, PGD, PGDip, PhD, MResHSC

School of Pharmacy & Pharmaceutical Sciences; www.pharmacy.manchester.ac.uk

pharmacy, clinical & health services pharmacy, clinical pharmacy, independent prescribing, pharmaceutical industrial advanced training, pharmacological technology and qualitative assessment, pharmacy, modelling & simulation in pharmacokinetics/dynamics; MPharm, MPhil, MSc, PGCert/Dip, PhD

School of Psychological Sciences; www.psych-sci.manchester.ac.uk

approved mental health professional practice, adv professional practice leadership, cognitive neuroscience & psychology, psychology, healthcare science (audiology), health psychology, speech & language therapy, advanced audiology studies, advanced practice in forensic mental health, audiology, clinical and health psychology, deaf education, forensic psychology and mental health, neuroimaging for clinical and cognitive neurosciences, psychology; BSc, MPhil, MRes, MSc, PGDip, PhD, ClinPsyD

MANCHESTER METROPOLITAN UNIVERSITY
www.mmu.ac.uk

Manchester School of Art; www.artdes.mmu.ac.uk

acting, animation, architecture/& urbanism, art history, collaborative practice, contemporary art history/curating, contemporary visual culture, design (ceramics/furniture/glass/jewellery/lab), design cultures, drawing, embroidery, fashion (knitwear/menswear/womenswear/fashion graphics/art direction), film & media studies, filmmaking, fine art/& history of art, graphic design & art direction, illustration/& animation, interactive arts, interior design, graphic art & design, interior/3D design, landscape architecture/design, media arts, photography, product design, textiles for fashion, textiles in practice, theatre design; BA(Hons), BArch, BL and Arch, MA, MEnterprise, MPhil, PGDip/Cert, PhD, MFA, MSc

Faculty of Health, Psychology & Social Care; www.hpsc.mmu.ac.uk

Health Professions; Nursing; Social Work & Social Change

Department of Health Professions; physiotherapy, physiotherapy, speech pathology and therapy PG; advanced physiotherapy; physiotherapy, professional practice development, speech and language therapy Department of Nursing Adult Nursing; community health, contemporary health practice, specialist community public health nursing (health; Post Reg, continuing professional development (CPD), emergency medicine, international nursing studies Department of Psychology; forensic psychology, psychology, psychology with counselling and psychotherapy, philosophy/psychology, psychology/sociology; PG; clinical skills in integrative practice, forensic psychology, psychological wellbeing in clinical practice, psychology and criminology, psychology and psychology by research

Dept of Social Care; social care, social work, PG; advanced social work practice, health and social care, social work; BA(Hons), BSc(Hons), BA/BSc, MA, FdA, DipHE, PGCert/Dip, PhD, MPhil

Faculty of Humanities, Languages & Social Sciences; www2.hlss.mmu.ac.uk

English; English, English and American literature/creative writing/film/Arabic/Chinese/Japanese/Urdu, English

French/history/linguistics/philosophy/politics/social history/Spanish/German/multimedia/psychology Italian/TESOL/sociology, education studies, creative writing, English studies

history, politics & philosophy, history (international politics/philosophy/social history/sociology), American history, ancient history, ancient and medieval history, medieval and early modern history, modern history, war and society; philosophy, environment, technology & philosophy, ethics, religion & philosophy, history (politics, international politics, public services (governance/social policy/uniformed services), international relations, European philosophy, European philosophy (aesthetics), international relations and global communications, public administration

Language, Linguistics & TESOL: Arabic, French, German, Italian, Japanese; linguistics, Spanish, TESOL, Urdu, applied linguistics, Mandarin Chinese Journalism, Information & Communication; information and communications, multimedia journalism, web development, digital media and communications, science communication, information management, library & information management, multimedia journalism with English/ Arabic/ Chinese/ French/ German/ Italian/ French/ Japanese/ Spanish/ Urdu international fashion journalism

Sociology; criminology, criminology and sociology, criminology and sociology/with quantitative methods, forensic science, applied criminology, communication, behavioural creditability analysis, criminology with quantitative methods, sociology, sociology with quantitative methods, criminology/psychology, education studies/sociology, English/sociology, philosophy/sociology, applied quantitative methods, sociology and global change, probation officer qualifications, British studies for foreign teachers, community engagement training, history/sociology; BA(Hons), BSc(Hons), PGDip/Cert, MA, MPhil, PhD, LlB, LlM, MSc, MFA

Faculty of Science & Engineering; www.sci-eng.ac.uk

School of Computing, Mathematics & Digital Technology; www.scmdt.mmu.ac.uk

adv/computer science, computing, computer animation & visual effects, computer forensics & security, computer games technology, computer science, cyber security, data analytics/science, engineering with management, games design & development, computer science/& information systems, media technology, multimedia & web computing, software engineering, web technologies, mathematics, financial mathematics, economics/mathematics, computing, mathematics & digital science; FdSc, BSc(Hons), MSc, PGDip/Cert, PhD, BA/BSc(Hons)

School of Engineering; www.soe.mmu.ac.uk

automotive engineering, computer & network technology, electrical & /electronic engineering, engineering with management, design engineering, industrial communications & automation, mechanical engineering, product/design & technology, computer networks, apprenticeship; BSc(Hons), BEng(Hons), MSc, PGDip/Cert, MPhil, PhD

School of Healthcare Science

biomedical science, biology & healthcare, dental technology, physiology (physical activity & health), healthcare science (physiological sciences/life sciences), human biology, cellular pathology, clinical biochemistry, haematological transfusion science, medical microbiology, sport science & human biology/physiology; BSc(Hons), MSc

School of Science & the Environment; www.ssty.mmu.ac.uk

Biology & Conservation Ecology

animal behaviour, biology/& chemistry/psychology, biological recording/& species identification, bird conservation, conservation biology/genetics, ecology & conservation, environmental management & business, forensic biology, wildlife biology, GIS, microbiology & molecular biology, countryside/environmental management, sustainable aviation zoo conservation biology; BSc(Hons), MSc, PGDip/Cert, MPhil, PhD

Chemistry & Environmental Science

chemistry, chemical/& pharmaceutical science, biology & chemistry, environmental science, forensic science & applied criminology/medicinal & biochemical/pharmaceutical chemistry, medicinal & biological chemistry, forensic biochemistry; MChem, BSc(Hons)

Geography & Environmental Management

geography, environmental management & business/sustainability, human/physical geography, GIS studies, sustainable aviation; BSc(Hons), PGCert/Dip, MSc, MPhil, PhD, MGeog

Faculty of Business & Law; www.business.mmu.ac.uk

Accounting and Finance; accountancy & finance, banking and finance, economics and finance, finance/& business, financial studies, international financial management, professional accounting, economic and financial analysis, financial planning and business management, taxation and fiscal policy, sustainable performance management

Business Management & Leadership; business, business administration, business administration with information technology, business/economics, business management with law, HRM, international business/management, business management, international business management, business technology and analytics, finance and business, financial planning and business management, international business management, international HRM, with leadership, leadership in health and social care, logistics and supply chain management, management, management and leadership, business administration (MBA), place management, project management, strategic business management

Digital Business and Communications; business technology and analytics, digital communications management, PR and digital communications, digital marketing

Economics; economics, business/economics, economics & international business/politics/mathematics/banking/finance, applied economics, economic & financial analysis, taxation/fiscal policy

Law; law, legal practice, Bar professional training

Marketing, Advertising and Public Relations; business/marketing, digital media/marketing, advertising and brand management, marketing management, place management, PR/and marketing/digital communications/media management, marketing (communications/creative advertising), place management, retail management & marketing

Sports Management; sports management, sports marketing management

Human Resources; human resources, HRM

Retail; retailing, logistics and supply chain management, retail management & marketing

Business Technology; business technology

BA(Hons), BSc(Hons), MA, MSc, MBA, DBA, PhD, FD, PGCert/Dip

Manchester Law School; www.law.mmu.ac.uk

law, legal practice, legal management; LlB(Hons), LlM, MPhil, PhD, Grad Dip, PGCert, GDl

Faculty of Education; www.ioe.mmu.ac.uk

childhood and family studies, early years and childhood studies, education studies, education studies (early years specialism), education, global and citizenship studies, education, theatre and performance, inclusive education and disability studies, primary education with mathematics, primary education with QTS, religion, education and community, secondary mathematics with QTS, youth and community

Postgraduate; autism spectrum conditions, bilingualism, education and society, childhood and youth studies, coaching and mentoring, community development and youth work:, leadership and practice, education, early childhood studies, education and society, education studies, educational leadership, educational leadership and management, inclusive education and disability, inclusive education and special educational needs and disability, language education, leadership in early years, PGCE; primary education with QTS, PGCE primary education with QTS (early years), professional development and enquiry, technology, engineering and mathematics,

PGCE; numerous secondary subjects, specific learning difficulties, teaching and learning, childhood and youth studies, doctor of education, education and society, education studies, educational leadership and management, inclusive education and disability; BA(Hons), BA/BSc, Certs, EdD, FD, MA, MPhil, MSc, PGDip/Cert, PhD

Hollings Faculty; www.hollings.mmu.ac.uk

Department Apparel

fashion buying & merchandising, fashion design & technology (womenswear/sportswear/menswear), int fashion/practice/promotion, fashion business & management; fashion futures; BA(Hons)

Department of Food, Nutrition & Hospitality

events management, events, hospitality and tourism, food business entrepreneurship, hospitality business management, nutritional sciences, tourism management, food innovation, food safety, responsible food, nutrition and health, occupational safety, health and environment, sport & exercise science; BA(Hons), BSc(Hons), FdA, FdSc, MA, MPhil, PhD, BTech

MMU Cheshire; www.cheshire.mmu.ac.uk

Dept of Business & Management Studies; www.cheshire.mmu.ac.uk/bms

business, business management with logistics/financial management/marketing, events management (creative industries), global business management, marketing/management, sports development, strategic leadership & change, sustainable management; BA/BSc, BA(Hons), FD, MBA, MSc, MPhil, PhD

Dept of Contemporary Arts; www.cheshire.mmu.ac.uk/dcu

contemporary arts, contemporary theatre & performance, creative music production, creative writing, dance, drama, music, popular music, communal practice; BA(Hons), MA, MPhil, PhD

Dept of Exercise & Sports Science; www.cheshire.mmu.ac.uk/exspsci

coaching and sport development, coaching studies, science, PE & sports pedagogy/science, sport development, sport & exercise science; BA, BSc, FD, MA, MSc

MIDDLESEX UNIVERSITY
www.mdx.ac.uk

School of Arts and Design; www.mdx.ac.uk/aboutus/Schools/art-and-design

animation, art & design, art & social practice, children's book illustration & graphic novel, 3D animation & games, illustration, jewellery futures, photography, fine art, graphic design, design crafts, fashion textiles/design, fashion communication & styling, fashion textiles, product design, fashion, printmaking, visual culture, practice & action; BA(Hons), MA, FdA, MSc, PhD, BSc, MRes

Middlesex University Business School; www.mdx.ac.uk/aboutus/Schools/business-school

Accounting & Finance; business, banking and finance, business management (finance), financial services/management, accounting and finance; Postgrad; banking and finance, accounting, finance/accounting practice management, investment & finance, private equity, financial management

Business and Management; international business, business management (marketing/finance/Spanish/innovation/Mandarin/human resources/innovation/supply chain management/ project managemet), business & trade, int international business admin, business and management (HR); Postgrad;ship superintendency, global energy management, media management, management, international business management, marine surveying, arts management, business administration, professional practice, global supply chain management, innovation management and entrepreneurship, shipping and logistics, administration of oil and gas

Economics; economics, business, business economics; Postgraduate; behavioural economics in action

Human Resource Management; business, business management (HR), international HRM; Postgrad; HRM/development/practice, globalisation and work, stakeholder communications, international HR practice

International Tourism & Hospitality Management, tourism management, professional studies, management, international tourism management (Spanish); Postgrad; international hospitality & tourism management, tourism, professional studies

Marketing; marketing, business management (marketing), advertising, PR and media; Postgrad; marketing communications/management, e-marketing and social media

MBAs; innovation management and entrepreneurship, shipping and logistics, oil and gas, strategic management and leadership; BA(Hons), BSc(Hons), MA, MSc, PhD, MBA, MProf, PGCert/Dip

School of Health and Education; www.mdx.ac.uk/aboutus/Schools/health-and-education

Education; early childhood studies/ with early years teacher status, early years initial teacher training, learning and teaching, education studies; Postgrad; leading inclusive education, higher education, education

Teacher Training; learning and teaching, primary education (with QTS), early childhood studies with early years teacher status, psychology with education; Postgraduate; pre-teaching and training, school direct, QTS, PGCE secondary education (numerous subjects), PGCE primary education with QTS, early years initial teacher training, qualified teacher status – assessment only (primary and secondary), early years initial teacher training

Healthcare Science; audiology, healthcare science (medical engineering/rehabilitation engineering/cardiac physiology/neurophysiology)

Integrative Medicine; Chinese medicine

Mental Health; professional practice in mental health nursing, care leadership and management, nursing (mental health); Postgrad; mental health and substance use (dual diagnosis), mental health studies, promoting mental health in adolescents and young people, child, adolescent and family mental health work, dementia care and practice, child and family mental health work, professional practice (health, social care, public and community sectors)

Midwifery; midwifery; Postgrad; midwifery studies, neonatal care

Nursing; professional practice in practice nursing/mental health nursing, care leadership and management, European nursing (adult), nursing (adult/child/mental health) veterinary nursing; Postgrad; nursing studies, leading and developing public and community services, mental health studies nursing, professional practice (health, social care, public and community sectors)

Social Work; care leadership and management, social work; Postgrad; comparative drug and alcohol studies, advanced professional practice in social work (adults), promoting mental health in adolescents and young people, leading and developing public and community services, evidence based parenting; supervision theory, child, adolescent and family mental health work, advanced professional practice in social work (practice education), evidence based parenting: supervision & leadership, advanced professional practice in social work (children and families), child and family mental health work, social work, professional practice (health, public and community sectors)

Veterinary Nursing; veterinary nursing
CertHE, DipHE, BSc, MSc, PGDip, PGCE

School of Law; www.mdx.ac.uk/aboutus/ Schools/law

law, law with international relations/human rights/ criminology, European law and politics, commercial law, law (general); Postgrad; human rights, law, international relations, migration law and policy, European law, commercial law, international law, environmental law and justice,employment law, international business law, global governance and sustainable development, international minority rights; BA(Hons),Grad Dip, LlB, LlM, PGDip/Cert, D/MProf, FdA, MPhil, PhD

School of Media and Performing Arts; www.mdx.ac.uk/aboutus/Schools/ performing-arts

Film, Media & English; audiovisual literary translation, business & legal translation, digital media, media & culture studies, advertising and PR & media, creative writing/technology/& journalism, English literature and language, film/& TV, games design, journalism/publishing/English language & media, media technology, novel writing, TV production, legal/media interpreting, professional practice in visual effects, publishing & digital culture, PGCE secondary English/education, drama with English, 3D animation with games; BA(Hons), MA, MSc, PhD

School of Science & Technology; www.mdx.aboutus/Schools/science-and-technology

Computer Science, Engineering and Maths

Computer and Communications Engineering; computer forensics, computer networks, computer systems engineering, computing and engineering, robotics, mobile systems and communication engineering, computer communication and networks; Postgraduate; engineering and computing, computer networks and network design, ambient assisted living, data science, security, network management and cloud computing, telecommunications engineering, network security and pen testing, building information modelling management

Computer Science and Informatics

sports informatics and data analytic, business informatics and data analytics, computer science, information technology, business information systems, computing and engineering, information technology and business information systems; Postgraduate; robotics, engineering and computing ambient assisted living, computer science, data science, PGCE secondary education computer science with ICT, security, visual analytics, creative technology, business information systems management, electronic security and digital forensics

Design Engineering; architectural technology, design engineering, computing and engineering, robotics, mechatronics, electronic engineering, product design, Postgraduate; robotics, mechatronic systems engineering, project management, engineering management, creative technology, building information modelling management, engineering project management; Postgraduate; project management, engineering management, building information modelling management

Mathematics; mathematics; Postgraduate; operational research, financial mathematics, applied statistics, PGCE secondary education mathematics

Natural Sciences

Biology & Biomedical Sciences; neuroscience, medical physiology (cardiovascular science), medical physiology (neuroscience), biomedical engineering, biology (biotechnology), biomedical science, biology (molecular biology) biology, biomedical sciences, environmental and public health, psychology with neuroscience, biology (environmental biology); Postgraduate; clinical physiology (cardiology),evolutionary behavioural science, PGCE secondary education science with biology,clinical physiology (neurophysiology), biomedical science (medical microbiology, masters or doctorate professional studies, biomedical science (cellular pathology) biomedical science (clinical biochemistry)

Environmental, Occupational and Public Health; environmental health, public and environmental health, environmental health, occupational safety, health and environment; Postgraduate; environmental science, environmental health, applied public health, sustainability and environmental management, environmental pollution control, global governance and sustainable development, professional studies, occupational safety, health and environmental management, medical science (haematology and transfusion science); BSc(Hons), BEng, MEng, MA, MSc, PGCert/Dip, MPhil, PhD

Psychology

psychology, sociology with psychology, psychology with education/ neuroscience/counselling skills/criminology; Postgraduate; psychology, psychoanalysis, applied clinical health psychology, applied psychology, health psychology, forensic psychology; BA(Hons), BSc(Hons), MA, MSc, DocProf, MPhil, PhD

Sport and Exercise Science and Rehabilitation

sports informatics and data analytics, sport and community development, sport and exercise science, sport and exercise science (performance analysis), sport and exercise rehabilitation, sport and exercise science (strength and conditioning), sport and exercise science (teaching and coaching sport); Postgraduate; strength and conditioning, sport and exercise nutrition, sport and exercise science, sport performance analysis, sport rehabilitation, sport physiotherapy and exercise medicine; BSc(Hons), MSc, PhD, DocProf

---

UNIVERSITY OF NEWCASTLE UPON TYNE
www.ncl.ac.uk

Faculty of Humanities and Social Sciences; www.ncl.ac.uk/hass

School of Architectural Planning and Landscape; www.ncl.ac.uk/apl

architecture, architecture & practice/and management/urban planning, architectural planning & landscape/design, geography & planning, architectural planning/landscape, planning for sustainability & climate change, landscape architectural studies, planning & environmental research/sustainability & climate change, international spatial planning, regional development & spatial planning, sustainable building & environment, town planning, urban design/planning, urban & landscape planning, urban energy technology; BA, BArch, Cert, Dip, MA, MPhil, MSc, PGCert, PhD, MPlan, MRes

School of Arts and Cultures; www.ncl.ac.uk/sacs

Music; www.ncl.ac.uk/sacs/music
folk & traditional music, analysis, musicology, music, musical history, popular & contemporary music, composition, performance, ethnomusicology, mixed media; BA, BMus, Diploma, MA, MLitt, MMus, MPhil, PhD

Fine Art; www.ncl.ac.uk/sacs/fineart
fine art; BA(Hons), MFA, MPhil, PhD
Media, Culture, Heritage; film & media, film practice, journalism, media & culture, media, communication & cultural studies; Postgraduate; art museum and gallery studies, heritage, gallery and museum studies, heritage studies, international multi media journalism, media and journalism, PR, museum studies, art museum and gallery practice, heritage practice, museum practice
BA(Hons) MA, MPhil, MPrac, PGCert, PGDip, PhD, MRes, MPrac

Business School; www.ncl.ac.uk/nubs

accounting and finance, business accounting and finance, business management, international business management, marketing/ & management, economics, economics and finance/business management, accounting/mathematics/politics and economics
Postgrad; banking and finance, finance, finance, accounting and business, international economics and finance, international financial analysis, quantitative finance and risk management, accounting, finance and strategic investment, advanced international business management,international business management, advanced international business management and marketing, operations management, e-business, e-business (e-marketing/information systems), HRM, international HRM, arts, business and creativity, innovation, creativity and entrepreneurship, advanced international business management and marketing, international marketing, operations, logistics and supply chain management, operations management, operations management, logistics and accounting, computing science, medical technology innovation, cross-cultural communication and international management, international development

and education, transport planning and business management, rail, freight and logistics; MBAs (full-time, global), BA(Hons), BSc(Hons), MA, MSc, MPhil, PhD

School of Education, Communication and Language Sciences; www.ncl.ac.uk/ecls
speech and language sciences, education: PGCE primary/secondary, coaching and mentoring, innova-tive pedagogy and curriculum, education: interna-tional perspectives, international development and education with cross-cultural communication, educa-tion research, education and communication/& inno-vation, education and applied linguistics, applied linguistics research, applied linguistics and TESOL/education, evidence based practice, language pathol-ogy, speech and language sciences, speech and language therapy, clinical linguistics and evidence based practice (research) and applied linguistics/international marketing/international relations/media culture/education, applied educational psychology
BA(Hons), BSc(Hons), DAppEdPsych, EdD, MA, MEd, MSc, PGCE, PhD, QTS

School of English Literature, Language, Linguistics; www.ncl.ac.uk/elll
English literature/with creative writing, English language/literature, linguistics, classical studies and English, English literature and history, linguistics with Chinese or Japanese/French/German/Spanish, literature, linguistics & English language; Postgrad-uate; English literature, writing poetry, linguistics, sociolinguistics (research), film: theory and practice, creative writing, literature, linguistics and/or English language, creative writing; BA(Hons), MA, MLitt, MPhil, PGCert, PhD

Geography, Politics and Sociology; www.ncl.ac.uk/gps
geography, physical/human geography (research), local & regional development, regional development & spatial planning, government/& European Union studies, international political economy, international studies, international politics (global justice & ethics/critical geopolitics/globalization, politics/& econom-ics/sociology/history), sociology, world politics & popular culture; BA(Hons), BSc(Hons), MA, MSc, PhD

Global Urban Research Unit; www.ncl.ac.uk/guru
cities and international development, power, place & materiality, planning & environmental dynamics, cities, security & vulnerability; MPhil, PhD

Institute of Health and Society; www.ncl.ac.uk/ihs/
public health & health services research, epidemiol-ogy, epidemiology & health service research, social sciences & health research, medicine; MSc, PGDip/Cert, MRes, MD, PhD

School of History, Classics & Archaeology Studies; www.ncl.ac.uk/historical
history, ancient history/& archaeology/politics, archaeology, British history, classical studies/& Eng-lish, classics/& ancient history, English literature & History, European history, Greek & Roman/Byzan-tine archaeology, heritage, history & archaeology, history, politics/& history, history of medicine, Roman frontier studies; BA(Hons), MA, MLitt, MPhil, PhD

Newcastle Law School; www.ncl.ac.uk/nuls
law, environmental regulation & sustainable devel-opment, criminology, European legal studies, inter-national law, international business law, law (com-plete range of legal areas taught at UG level); LlB, LlM, MPhil, PhD

Centre for Learning and Teaching; www.ncl.ac.uk/cflat
innovative pedagogy & curriculum, coaching and mentoring for teacher development, teaching and learning in HE, educational research in practice, educational leadership, educational leadership and management, information, communication and entertainment technology, international development and education, pedagogy and learning, inclusive education, educational leadership and management, information, communication and entertainment tech-nology, international development and education, pedagogy and learning, education & communication, applied educational psychology, PGCE primary & secondary education, educational research; EdD, MA, MEd, PGCE, DEdPsy, DAppEdPsy, IPhD

Newcastle Centre for the Literary arts; www.ncl.ac.uk/ncla
creative writing; MA, PhD, PGCert

School of Modern Languages; www.ncl.ac.uk/sml

modern languages, translation and interpreting, modern languages (French, German, French and German, French and Spanish, German and Spanish or French, German and Spanish) Portuguese, Dutch, Catalan or Quechua, Chinese studies, Japanese studies, translating/& interpreting, Latin American, film: theory and practice, modern languages and business studies, modern languages and linguistics, professional translation,European translation studies, Spanish, Portuguese and Latin American studies; BA(Hons), MA, MLitt, PhD

Policy, Ethics and Life Sciences Research Centre; www.ncl.ac.uk/peals

reproduction & genetic medicine, families, kinship & childhood, embodiment & identity; PhD

Centre for Research in Linguistics and Language Science; www.ncl.ac.uk/linguistics

linguistics, European or Asian language, English language/& literature, applied linguistics and TESOL, clinical linguistics research, evidence based practice in communication disorders, language pathology, linguistics (with English language/language acquisition/European languages), applied linguistics research; BA(Hons), MA, MEd, MSc, PhD

Centre for Urban and Regional Development Studies; www.ncl.ac.uk/curds

local & regional development, regional development & spatial planning; MA, PhD

Faculty of Medical Sciences; www.ncl.ac.uk/aboutpeoplestudies academic/biosciences

Newcastle Biomedicine; www.ncl.ac.uk/biomedicine

Biomedical and Biomolecular Science; biomedical sciences, biochemistry, biomedical genetics, exercise biomedicine, pharmacology, physiological sciences, medical science
Medicine; medicine, surgery
Psychology; psychology, biology/mathematics/nutrition and psychology
Postgraduate; Biomedicine; clinical and health sciences, clinical research/clinical research (ageing)/leadership), clinical leadership, medical education, clinical psychology, cognitive behavioural therapy, genomic medicine, health services research, low intensity psychological therapies, medical sciences, clinical sciences (physiological sciences with specialisms in: cardiac, vascular, respiratory and sleep science, gastrointestinal physiology and urodynamic science), clinical sciences (medical physics with specialisms in: radiotherapy physics, radiation safety, imaging with ionising radiation, imaging with non-ionising radiation), oncology and palliative care, cancer studies, praxis cognitive behavioural therapy studies, psychology (clinical and health psychology/clinical and forensic psychology), public health, public health and health services research, social science and health research, clinical and health sciences, transplantation
BA, BSc(Hons), DClinPsychol, MB, MClinEd, MClinRes, MD, MRes, MSc, MSci, PGCert/Dip, PhD, MBBS

School of Dental Sciences; www.ncl.ac.uk/dental

clinical implants surgery, conscious sedation in dentistry, dental surgery, dentistry & dental science, orthodontics, restorative dentistry, oral & dental health sciences; BDS, DDS, MSc, PGDip/Cert, PhD, MPhil

Faculty of Science, Agriculture & Engineering; www.ncl.ac.uk/aboutpeoplestudies/academic/sage

School of Agriculture, Food and Rural Development; www.ncl.ac.uk/afrd

agri-business management, animal science agriculture, agriculture with agronomy, agriculture with animal production science, agriculture with management, countryside management, environmental science, rural studies, food & human nutrition, food marketing & nutrition, field work
Postgrad; food and rural development research, applied animal behaviour & welfare, agricultural & environmental science, environment & conservation medicinal plant & functional foods, food & rural development, organic & ecological farming, sustainable agricultural & food security, agricultural and environmental science; BSc(Hons), MPhil, MSc, PhD

School of Biology; www.ncl.ac.uk/biology

biology, cellular & molecular biology, ecology & conservation, ecological consultancy, industrial & commercial biotechnology, zoology, wildlife management; BSc(Hons), MSc, MRes, PhD

School of Chemical Engineering and Advanced Materials; www.ncl.ac.uk/ceam

applied/process control, bioprocessing engineering, chemical engineering, clean technology, industry, materials, design & engineering, process automation/control, sustainable/chemical engineering, renewable energy flexible training/enterprise and management; BEng(Hons), MEng(Hons), MSc, PGDip

School of Chemistry; www.ncl.ac.uk/chemistry

chemistry, drug chemistry, medicinal & synthetic product, chemistry with medicinal chemistry, structural chemistry & spectroscopy, synthetic & medicinal chemistry; BSc(Hons), MChem(Hons), MPhil, MSc, PhD

Civil Engineering and Geosciences; www.ncl.ac.uk/ceg

civil engineering, civil and structural engineering, civil and surveying engineering, earth science, surveying and mapping science, GIS, physical geography, civil and surveying engineering; Postgrad; environmental engineering, environmental consultancy, environmental/and petroleum geochemistry, structural engineering, geotechnical engineering, engineering geology, transport planning and ITS/engineering/business management/environment, hydrogeology and water management, flood risk management, hydroinformatics, hydrology and climate change, hydroinformatics and water management, renewable energy, enterprise and management; BEng, PostgradCert/Dip, BSc(Hons), MEng, MPhil, MSc, PhD

Computing Science; www.cs.ncl.ac.uk

computer science (bioinformatics, computational systems biology, mobile & distributed systems, games engineering, biocomputing, security & resilience, human-computer interaction, software engineering); Postgrad; computer science, advanced computer science, synthetic biology, computational neuroscience and neuroinformatics, computational systems biology, bioinformatics, computer security and resilience, computer game engineering, cloud computing, e-business and information systems; BSc(Hons), MPhil, MSc, MComp, PhD

Electrical & Electronic Engineering; www.ncl.ac.uk/eee

automation and control, communications & signal processing, digital electronics, electrical & electronics engineering, electronics & computer engineering, adv/electrical power, electrical power engineering, electronic communications, computer engineering, power distribution, wireless embedded systems, electrical power, microelectronics engineering, power distribution, wireless embedded systems; BEng, EngD, MEng, MPhil, PhD

Newcastle Institute for Research on Sustainability; www.ncl.ac.uk/sustainability

research projects; MPhil, MRes, PhD

Digital Institute; www.ncl.ac.uk/digitalinstitute

research projects; PhD

Newcastle Centre for Railway Research; www.ncl.ac.uk/newrail

rail freight & logistics; MSc, PhD

School of Marine Science and Technology; www.ncl.ac.uk/marine

marine biology and oceanography/zoology, engineering and science in the marine environment integrated, international marine environmental consultancy, marine engineering, marine transport & management, naval architecture, offshore and environmental technology, offshore engineering, pipeline engineering, renewable energy enterprise and management, subsea engineering and management, technology in the marine environment, marine technology; BSc(Hons), MEng, MRes, MSc, PGDip/Cert, PhD

Mathematics and Statistics; www.ncl.ac.uk/maths

mathematics, financial mathematics/with management, mathematics & statistics/accounting/economics/psychology/management/finance, mathematical sciences, pure mathematics, applied mathematics, statistics; BSc(Hons), MMath, MMathStat, MPhil, PhD

School of Mechanical & Systems Engineering; www.ncl.ac.uk/mech

mechanical engineering, mechanical design and manufacturing engineering, mechanical and low carbon transport engineering, mechanical engineering with mechatronics/bioengineering, biomedical engineering, design and manufacturing engineering, low carbon transport engineering, mechatronics, rail & logistics, rail freight and logistics, biomedical engineering, MEMS, design, manufacture and materials, fluid dynamics and thermal systems; BEng, MEng, MSc, PhD

Centre for Rural Economy; www.ncl.ac.uk/ cre

food & rural development; MPhil, MSc, PhD, MRes

Sir Joseph Swan Institute for Energy Research; www.ncl.ac.uk/energy

renewable energy, enterprise & management; MRes, MSc, PhD

UNIVERSITY OF NORTHAMPTON
www.northampton.ac.uk

School of Science & Technology; www.northampton.ac.uk/science-technology

Division of Computing; www.northampton.ac.uk/about-us/ academic-schools/school-of-science-and-technology/subject-areas/computing

business computing (systems/web design), computer games development, computing, computing (computer networks engineering/computer systems engineering/graphics and visualisation/internet technology and security/mobile computing/software engineering/serious games), computing (internet technology and security/computer networks engineering/software engineering/immersive technologies/ environmental informatics, web technology & security; BA/BSc, BSc(Hons), MSc, PhD

Division of Engineering; www.northampton.ac.uk/about-us/ academic-schools/school-of-science-and-technology/subject-areas/engineering

civil engineering, construction management, electro-mechanical engineering, electrical and electronic engineering, engineering, lift/& escalator engineering/technology, mechanical/production engineering, non-destructive testing; BSc(Hons), BTEC, FdSc, BEng(Hons), MEng, MSc, ProfCert

Environmental Sciences; www.northampton.ac.uk/about-us/ academic-schools/school-of-science-and-technology/subject-areas/environmental-and-geographical-sciences

country & wildlife management, cleaning studies, environmental management, environmental science (climate change/landscape ecology/waste,geography (human/physical), international environmental management, wildlife conservation, infection control, waste management; BA/BSc, BSc(Hons), FdSc, HND, MBA, MSc, UnivCerts

Leather Technologies; www.northampton.ac.uk/about-us/ academic-schools/school-of-science-and-technology/subject-areas/leather-technology

leather technology/development (professional), leather technology

The School of The Arts; www.northampton.ac.uk/about-us/ academic-schools/school-of-the-arts

Division of Design; www2.northampton.ac.uk/arts/home/ Design

architectural technology, art design, design, fashion (textiles for fashion), graphic design, interior design, product design, design (textiles/footwear/graphic communication/photographic communication/product & spatial innovation/illustration/fashion & textiles), web design games art; BA(Hons), BSc(Hons), MA

Division of Fashion; www2.northampton.ac.uk/arts/home/ Division-of-Fashion

fashion, footware & accessories, interior design, printed textile fashion, surface design & printed textiles, international fashion marketing, textiles for fashion; BA(Hons), MA

Division of Media; www2.northampton.ac.uk/arts/home/ Media

creative writing, commercial & creative photography, digital film production, English/contemporary literature, English & drama/education, film & screen studies, multimedia journalism/ & English/media production, production & moving image, music production, sports studies, photography, pop; BA(Hons), MA

**Division of Performing Arts Studies;
www2.northampton.ac.uk/arts/home/
performing arts**

acting (creative theatre), English & drama, music
production, psychology & drama, dance, drama,
theatre practice, performing arts, pop music, music
practice & production; BA(Hons), MA, PhD, BA/BSc

School of Education;
www.northampton.ac.uk/about-us/
academic-schools/school-of-education

early years education, early childhood studies,
education (primary), early years (primary/early
years/secondary/PGCE)/teacher status (0-5), education, education studies, childhood & youth, developmental & educational psychology, early young
people teacher status (0-5), education management
& leadership, English/history & education, (GTP),
learning & teaching, practice education, primary
English/computing/mathematics, special education
needs & inclusion (autism), post-compulsory education & training, primary mathematics, OCR Level 5
and Level 7, specific learning difficulties/dyslexia,
psychology & educational studies,primary education
(3-7/5-11) QTS, PGCE (primary/early years/second-
ary), Schools Direct; SEN coordination, PGCE; QTS,
GTI, BA(Hons), GTP, PGCE, BSc(Hons), BA/BSc, FD,
CertHE, FD, PhD

School of Health;
www.northampton.ac.uk/about-us/
academic-schools/school-of-health

adv professional practice, dental nursing, autonomous, cancer care, community practice, applied/
cancer studies, counselling, health studies, health &
social care (community care), leadership or health &
social care, mental health non-medical prescribing,
midwifery, nursing (adult/children's/learning disabil-
ities/mental health), learning disability nursing, adv
occupational therapy, palliative & supportive care,
paramedic science, adv podiatry, practice education,
public health, social & community development,
social care/& health studies, social work, specialist
community public health nursing, sport studies/&
education studies/therapy; BSc(Hons), MPhil,
PGCert, PhD, FD

Northampton Business School;
www.northampton.ac.uk/about-us/
academic-schools/northampton-
business-school

accounting/& finance, advertising & digital marketing, banking & financial planning, business/& man-
agement/accounting/entrepreneurship/management,
business computing/entrepreneurship/studies/sys-
tems/web design, business administration (MBA),
corporate governance & leadership, economics/&
business/management, events management/& business entrepreneurship, fashion marketing, international marketing strategy, ELT, HRM/& business,
international accounting/banking & finance/business/
business communications/development/logistics &
trade financing/leadership/marketing studies, international hospitality management, international
development & human geography/economics, international marketing strategy(logistics/marketing/
events management/business entrepreneurship),
international tourism management/development, IT
service management, management & business entre-
preneurship/tourism management, marketing &
advertising/business/events management/manage-
ment, marketing management, psychology & busi-
ness/marketing, sports studies & business/marketing,
supply chain management, travel & tourism management, web design; BA(Hons), BA/Bsc(Hons), CMS,
DBA, DMS, FdA, HND, MA, MBA, MSc, PGDip
(marketing), MBL, ProfDip

School of Social Sciences;
www.northampton.ac.uk/about-us/
academic-schools/school-of-social-
sciences

**History; www.northampton.ac.uk/about-
us/academic-schools/school-of-social-
sciences/subject-areas/history**

history, social & cultural history, history & English/
educational studies, heritage

**Law; www.northampton.ac.uk/about-us/
academic-schools/school-of-social-
sciences/subject-areas/law**

law criminal legal practice, international business
law/criminal law & security/commercial law, law,
appl criminal justice, offender management, police &
criminal justice, law & criminology/business/psychol-
ogy, public service interpreting law

Psychology; www.northampton.ac.uk/about-us/academic-schools/school-of-social-sciences/subject-areas/psychology

child & adolescent mental health, counselling children & young people, development & educational/sport & exercise psychology, counselling, psychology, psychology & law/marketing/drama/English/educational studies/business/criminology, transpersonal psychology & consciousness

Social Science/Sociology; www.northampton.ac.uk/about-us/academic-schools/school-of-social-sciences/subject-areas/sociology

international relations, sociology, police & criminal justice service, probation & policing, urban affairs, community practice, social work, sociology, youth & community work, social psychology, social innovation, sociology & criminology/psychology, social care & educational studies

Politics; www.northampton.ac.uk/about-us/academic-schools/school-of-social-sciences/subject-areas/politics

media studies, philosophy, media, politics, international relations, politics, international relations

Criminology; www.northampton.ac.uk/about-us/academic-schools/school-of-social-sciences/subject-areas/criminology

criminology

Human Geography; www.northampton.ac.uk/about-us/academic-schools/school-of-social-sciences/subject-areas/human-geography

geography (human/physical)

Police and Criminal Justice; www.northampton.ac.uk/about-us/academic-schools/school-of-social-sciences/subject-areas/police-and-criminal-justice

police & criminal justice studies, offender management

Urban Affairs; www.northampton.ac.uk/about-us/academic-schools/school-of-social-sciences/subject-areas/urban-affairs

sustainable communities
FdA, BA(Hons), BSc(Hons), BA/BSc, MA, LlB, LlM, PhD

Youth and Community Work

youth and community work; MA

Sport

sport strength & conditioning, sport therapy/studies, performance & coaching, sport development & PE, sport marketing management, sport & exercise science, sports studies & education studies/business/marketing/multimedia/psychology; BA(Hons), BSc(Hons), MSc

UNIVERSITY OF NORTHUMBRIA AT NEWCASTLE
www.northumbria.ac.uk

Faculty of Business & Law

Newcastle Business School; www.northumbria.ac.uk/sd/academic/bs

accounting/& finance, business studies, business leadership & corporate management, business with accounting/ economics/financial management/law/business management/international management/logistics & supply chain management/hospitality & tourism management, business with financial entrepreneurship/ management/ law/ finance/ marketing/ marketing management, entrepreneurial business management, finance & investment management, global finance management, HRM, international management with logistics & supply chain management/marketing management/public administration/business management/banking & finance/hospitality & tourism management, business & law (MBA), HRM/ & development, international business management with business with French/Spanish, marketing management

Postgraduate; business with business analytics/ with advanced practice, business with entrepreneurship with advanced practice, business with financial management/with advanced practice, business with hospitality and tourism management, business with HRM, business with international management, business with international management and finance advanced practice, business with logistics and supply chain management/management/ management and finance/marketing management, coaching, digital marketing/ with advanced practice, forensic accounting, global logistics, operations and supply chain management, HRM & development, international business management/finance and investment/international finance/ and investment with advanced practice, international financial management with advanced practice, international HRM, leadership and management, MBA, business with entrepreneurship; BA, DBA, MA, MBA, MSc, PhD

Northumbria School of Law; northumbria.ac.uk/sd/academic/law

advanced legal practice, law, bar practice/professional training, business/commercial/employment law, CPE conversion, data protection law, & information governance, employment law in practice, information rights law and practice, international commercial/trade/environmental law/HRM, law with business/international business, legal practice, medical law, professional practice in law,mental health law & practice; GradCert, LlM, LlB, LPC, PGCert, MLaw, MSc, MBA

Faculty of Arts, Design & Social Sciences; www.northumbria.ac.uk/sd/academic/sass

Dept of Arts; www.northumbria.ac.uk/sd/academic/sass/about/arts

arts, arts & media management, cultural heritage management, contemporary photographic practice, music management & promotion, conservation of fine art, cultural/events management, performance, fine art, music management, museum & heritage management, preventive conservation, theatre & performance; MA, MRes, BA(Hons), FD

Dept of Humanities; www.northumbria.ac.uk/sd/academic/sass/about/humanities

American studies, applied linguistics for TESOL, creative writing, English literature/& creative writing/history, history/& politics, English literature, history/& politics, linguistics; BA(Hons), MA, PGCert, MRes, PhD, PGCert

Dept of Media & Communication Design; www.northumbria.ac.uk/sd/academic/sass/about/media

animation, film & TV studies, graphic design, interactive media design, mass communication with management/PR/business/advertising, media, media & journalism, media production, performance production; BA(Hons), MA

Dept of Social Sciences & Languages; www.northumbria.ac.uk/sd/academic/sass/about/socscience

criminology & sociology/criminal justice, modern foreign languages (French, Spanish), health & social care quality programme, international public health programme, integrated health & social care, international development, international relations & politics, public administration, social sciences, social work, social sciences, politics, sociology; BA(Hons), BSc, MSc, MPA, MRes, MA, PhD, MPA

Northumbria Design

3D design, design for industry, design/management/ & marketing, fashion communication/marketing/graphic design, interior design,, multidisciplinary design innovation, performance production design, service design; BA(Hons), BSc(Hons), MA, MSc, MRes, MPA, PhD, PGCert/Dip

Faculty of Engineering & Environment; www.northumbria.ac.uk/sd/academic/ee

Architecture & the Built Environment

architectural technology/engineering/studies, architecture, building design management/project management/services engineering, building surveying, built/& natural environment, quantity surveying, civil engineering, future cities, interior architecture, real estate (international)/with adv practice, renewable & sustainable energy technology, sustainable development in the built environment; BA(Hons), BSc(Hons), MArch, BEng(Hons)

Computer Science & Business Technology

computer & network technology/IT/science, applied computing, computing networks/ & cyber security, computer science with animation/graphic/vision/AI/ games development/web development, computer & digital forensics, mathematics & computer science, web & mobile data technologies; BSc, BEng, MEng MSc, MComp

Mechanical & Construction Engineering

automotive engineering with adv practice, building services engineering, civil engineering, construction project management/with information modelling,, engineering management, mechanical design/engineering, mechanical & automotive technology/architectural engineering, microelectronic & communications engineering, pipeline integrity management, professional engineering, renewable sustainable energy technologies, surveying/construction/housing; BSc, BEng, MEng

Mathematics & Information Science
computing and information technology, information technology management for business, information technology and data science, mathematics, mathematics and computer science/physics, information science (data analytics) with advanced practice information science, information science (data analytics/ library management/ records management/ with advanced practice, project management; BSc(Hons), MSc, MMath

Physics & Electrical Engineering
physics, mathematics & physics,, mobile communications engineering, astrophysics, electronic design engineering, electric power engineering, microelectronic & communication engineering, electrical & electronic engineering; BEng, MEng MPhys, BSc(Hons), MSc

Geography
geography, physical/human geography, geography & the environment, disaster management & sustainable development, environmental geography/science, environmental health, safety, health & environmental management; BSc(Hons), BA(Hons), FdSc, MA, MSc, PGDip/Cert, PhD, ProfDip

Faculty of Health & Life Sciences

School of Health, Community & Education Studies; www.northumbria.ac.uk/sd/academic/shes
Health: clinical practice (adv critical care practice), clinical exercise psychology, emergency care practice, health science, health in contemporary society, midwifery studies, healthcare/nursing leadership, nursing studies/registered nurse/child/mental health/ adult/learning disabilities, occupational therapy, operating dept practice, physiotherapy, public health; AdvDipHE, BSc, MSc, PGDip, MClinPract, MNurs
Education: academic practice, childhood studies & early years, creative writing in the classroom, autism, early primary education, education with teaching & learning, education, education & training, guidance, counselling & early years, PGCE early years & primary/secondary, early years education/& disability studies, education studies/leadership, professional practice, post-compulsory education & training

(literacy/numeracy), education with curriculum development/learning disabilities, adult learners with learning difficulties/disablement, leadership & management in integrated children's services, psychoanalytical observational studies, systematic teacher training, teaching lifelong learning (English literacy/(CPD)/mathematics/numeracy), teaching dyslexic children, secondary education (art, craft & design/PE), special education needs & inclusion, schools direct, TESOL; BA(Hons), MSc, MA, MTL, Cert/DipHE, PGDipCert
Social Work: social work/with children, young people & their families/in mental health services; BSc(Hons), PGDip/Cert, ProfDoc, PhD, Prof Doc

School of Life Sciences; www.northumbria.ac.uk/sd/academic/lifesciences
Biology, Food & Nutrition Science
applied biology, applied sciences, biology with forensic biology, biotechnology, food science/ & nutrition, human nutrition, nutritional science, microbiology; BSc(Hons), MSc
Chemical & Forensic Science
applied sciences, biomedical sciences, human biosciences, forensic science, drug design with pharmacological analysis, pharmaceutical chemistry, medical science; BSc(Hons), MSc
Biomedical Sciences; www.northumbria.ac.uk/sd/academic/lifesciences/ad/biomed/bmsug
applied science, biomedical sciences, human biosciences, medical science; BSc(Hons)
Psychology
psychology with criminology/sport science, psychology, health psychology, occupational psychology, organisational psychology, psychology of health & wellbeing, psychology of sport & exercise behaviour; BSc(Hons), MSc, MRes
Sport & Exercise Science
applied sport science with coaching/exercise science, psychology & sport science, sport exercise & nutrition, clinical exercise psychology, psychology of sport & exercise behaviour, sport & exercise physiology, strength & conditioning; BSc(Hons), MSc, MRes
Sport Development
sport, sport coaching, sport development/management/with coaching, international sport management, professional practice in sport coaching, sport marketing; BA(Hons), BSc(Hons), MSc

UNIVERSITY OF NOTTINGHAM
www.nottingham.ac.uk

Faculty of Arts; www.nottingham.ac.uk/ arts

School of American and Canadian Studies; www.nottingham.ac.uk/american

American and Canadian literature, history and culture, film and television studies and American studies, American studies and English/history, Latin American studies, politics and American studies; Postgraduate; American literature, history, foreign policy, politics, intellectual and cultural history, film studies, visual and cultural studies, and Canadian literature and culture
BA(Hons), MA, MRes, PhD

Dept of Archaeology; www.nottingham.ac.uk/archaeology/ index.aspx

archaeology, archaeology, historical archaeology, archaeology and history of art/geography/classical civilisation/ history, natural sciences, Viking studies, archaeology, archaeological science, Mediterranean archaeology; BA(Hons), BSc(Hons), MA, MPhil

Art History; www.nottingham.ac.uk/ classics

history of art, history of art & English/archaeology/ history, art history, visual culture; BA(Hons), MA

Dept of Classics; www.nottingham.ac.uk/ classics

classical civilisation with art history/archaeology/ English/philosophy, ancient history, classical literature, classics, Latin, visual culture of classical antiquity, ancient history with archaeology/history, classics & English/history; BA(Hons), MPhil/PhD

Dept of Culture, Film & Media; www.nottingham.ac.uk/cfm

cultural industries & entrepreneurship, international media & communications studies, critical theory & politics/cultural studies, modern languages & critical theory, film & TV studies, French/German/Portuguese & communications studies, international media, numerous jt degrees; BA(Hons), MA, MPhil

School of Culture, Languages & Area Studies; www.nottingham.ac.uk/clas

Refer to American and Canadian, Culture, Film and Media, Modern Languages Depts; BA(Hons), MA, MPhil, PhD

School of English; www.nottingham.ac.uk/ english

English, English language & literature, applied linguistics/English language, contemporary literature, English studies, creative writing, communication & international entrepreneurship, English literature, literary linguistics, Viking & Anglo Saxon studies, American studies/history of art/classics/Hispanics/French/German/history/philosophy and English; BA(Hons), MA, MPhil, MSc, PGDip, PhD

Dept of French & Francophone Studies; www.nottingham.ac.uk/french

French studies, modern languages, French and contemporary Chinese studies, French/history/ international media communications studies/ politics/ philosophy, modern European studies/economics, modern language studies, modern languages with business/ translation, management studies with French, comparative literature, translation studies, modern languages and critical theory; BA(Hons), MA, MPhil, PhD

Dept of German Studies; www.nottingham.ac.uk/german

English and German, German and contemporary Chinese studies/philosophy/politics, German, modern languages, modern language studies, modern European studies, modern languages/with business, economics with German, law with German and German law, management with German, modern and contemporary German studies, modern languages and critical theory, comparative literature studies, literatures in translation; BA(Hons), MA, MPhil, PhD

School of History; www.nottingham.ac.uk/ history

history, ancient history, archaeology, British history, church history, gender history, women's studies & global gender history, environmental/international history, contemporary Chinese studies, art history, politics, local & regional history, medieval studies, modern history, Viking studies, warrior societies; BA(Hons), MA, MPhil, PhD

School of Humanities; www.nottingham.ac.uk/humanities

Refer fo Depts of Archaeology, Classics, History, History of Art, Music, Philosophy, Theology &

Religious Studies; BA(Hons), BSc(Hons), MA, MSci, MSc, MPhil, PhD

Music; www.nottingham.ac.uk/music

music, early music, music on stage & screen, music theory & analysis, musicology, history & culture, music & philosophy; BA(Hons), MPhil, PhD

Dept of Philosophy; www.nottingham.ac.uk/philosophy

philosophy, music/classical civilisation/English/French/economics/physics/psychology and philosophy, philosophy, politics and economics, religion, philosophy and ethics; BA(Hons), BSc(Hons) MA, MPhil, PhD

Russian & Slavonic Studies; www.nottingham.ac.uk/slavonic

Russian studies, Russian and contemporary Chinese studies, Russian and history, economics with Russian, modern European studies, history and East European cultural studies, modern languages, modern languages with business, modern language studies, modern languages with translation Russian, Serbian/Croatian, and Slovene studies, literatures in English translation, translation studies, comparative literature, modern languages and critical theory; BA(Hons), MA, MPhil

Spanish, Portuguese and Latin American Studies; www.nottingham.ac.uk/splas

American studies and Latin American studies, Portuguese and international media and communications studies, modern European studies, modern languages, economics with Hispanic studies, English and Hispanic studies, modern languages with translation, Hispanic studies and history, Hispanic studies, law with Spanish and Spanish law, management with Spanish, modern language studies, modern languages with business, Spanish and contemporary Chinese studies, Spanish and international media and communications studies, modern languages and critical theory, comparative literature, translation studies; BA(Hons), MA, MPhil, PhD

Faculty of Science; www.nottingham.ac.uk/science

School of Biosciences; www.nottingham.ac.uk/biosciences

agriculture, agricultural and crop science/environmental science, livestock science, animal science, biotechnology, environmental science/biology, food science, microbiology, nutrition/and dietetics/food science, advanced dietetic practice, advanced genomic and proteomic sciences, agrifood, animal nutrition, plant science, applied bioinformatics, applied biomolecular technology, applied biopharmaceutical biotechnology and entrepreneurship, behaviour change, brewing science/and practice, brewing and packaging, brewing/principles and practice, clinical nutrition, crop biotechnology and entrepreneurship, crop improvement, dietetics, food production management, food production management, food science and engineering, global food security, industrial physical biochemistry, nutritional sciences, plant genetic manipulation, sensory science, sustainable bioenergy/and industrial biotechnology, techniques in cell and development biology; BSc(Hons), Cert, Grad Dip, MRes, MSc, MNutrition, MPhil, PhD

School of Chemistry; www.nottingham.ac.uk/chemistry

chemistry, biochemistry, medical/& biological chemistry, chemistry, nanoscience, chemistry & molecular physics, biochemistry & biological chemistry, natural sciences, green & sustainable chemistry; BSc(Hons), MChem, MPhil, MSc, MSci, PhD

School of Computer Science; www.nottingham.ac.uk/computerscience

computer science, computer science and artificial intelligence, software engineering, data science, management & information technology, human-computer interaction; BSc(Hons), MPhil, MSc

School of Mathematical Sciences; www.maths.nottingham.ac.uk/

mathematics, financial mathematics, data science, mathematics and economics/management studies, physics and astronomy, mathematical physics, natural sciences, financial and computational mathematics, gravity, particles and fields, mathematical medicine and biology, pure mathematics, scientific computation/with industrial mathematics/mathematical medicine and biology, statistics/and applied probability; BSc(Hons), MSc, MMath, PhD

School of Pharmacy; www.nottingham.ac.uk/pharmacy

medicinal & biological chemistry, pharmacy, drug discovery & pharmacological science; MPharm, MRes, MSc, MSci, PhD

School of Physics & Astronomy; www.nottingham.ac.uk/physics

astronomy, mathematical physics, medical physics, nanoscience, physics, physics & philosophy/

astronomy/medical physics/nanoscience/theoretical astrophysics/European language, chemistry & molecular physics, experimental/condensed matter & nanoscience theory, particle theory, ultracold atoms, magnetic resonance & spectroscopy; BSc(Hons), MSc, MSci, PhD, MRes, MPhil

School of Psychology; www.nottingham.ac.uk/psychology

psychology/& cognitive neuroscience, brain imaging, psychology/& philosophy, psychology research-methods; BSc(Hons), MSc, PhD, DAppPsych, DEdPsych

Faculty of Engineering; www.nottingham.ac.uk/engineering

Dept of Architecture & Built Environment; www.nottingham.ac.uk/abe

architectural environment engineering, architecture, architecture & environmental design/tectonics, design, energy conversion & management, environmental design/engineering/management, professional practice in architecture, renewable energy & architecture, sustainable built environment/energy & entrepreneurship, sustainable tall buildings/building technology, theory & design, sustainable urban design, sustainable digital architecture & tectonics; BA(Hons), BArch(Hons), BEng(Hons), Dip Arch, MEng, MPhil, PhD

Dept of Chemical and Environmental Engineering; www.nottingham.ac.uk/scheme

chemical engineering/with environmental engineering, efficient fossil energy techniques; BEng(Hons), MEng(Hons), MPhil, MRes, MSc, PhD

Dept of Civil Engineering; www.nottingham.ac.uk/civil

civil engineering, civil engineering (engineering surveying/highways and transportation/structural engineering), risk and reliability methods, environmental management and earth observation, engineering surveying with GIS, positioning and navigation technologies; BEng(Hons), MEng(Hons), MPhil, MSc, PhD

Dept of Electrical & Electronic Engineering; www.nottingham.ac.uk/eee

electronic and computer engineering, electrical engineering and renewable energy systems, electrical engineering, electronic engineering, electronic and computer engineering/communications engineering, electronic and communications engineering, electrical and electronic engineering, electrical transportation systems and infrastructure, electrical and electronic engineering and entrepreneurship, electrical engineering for sustainable and renewable energy, electronic communications and computer engineering, photonic and optical engineering, power electronics, machines & drives,, sustainable transportation and electrical power systems, sustainable energy engineering, biophotonics, communications and computer engineering, power electronics and drives; BEng, MEng, MPhil, MRes, MSc, PGDip, PhD

Dept of Mechanical, Materials and Manufacturing Engineering; www.nottingham.ac.uk/schoolm3

advanced materials, aerospace technologies/engineering, applied ergonomics & the human factor, biomedical materials science, bioengineering, biomaterials & biomechanics/imaging & sensing, human factors & ergonomics, manufacturing engineering/& management, materials engineering & design, mechanical engineering, product design & manufacture, usability & human-computer interaction; BEng, MEng, MSc, PGCert, PhD

Faculty of Medicine & Health Science; www.nottingham.ac.uk/mhs/index.aspx

School of Life Sciences; www.nottingham.ac.uk/life-sciences

biochemistry, biology, genetics, neuroscience and zoology (biochemistry and molecular medicine, human genetics and tropical sciences), medicine, pharmacy; Postgraduate; biological photography and imaging, clinical microbiology, drug discovery and pharmaceutical sciences, immunology and allergy, integrated physiology in health and disease, microbiology and immunology, molecular genetics and diagnostics, molecular medical microbiology, sports and exercise medicine, clinical science; BSc, MSc, MSci, PhD, MRes, MPharm, BMMS

School of Medicine; www.nottingham.ac.uk/scs

medical physiology and therapeutics, applied psychology, biomedical sciences, medicine, molecular medical sciences, nursing, midwifery and physiotherapy, veterinary medicine and science, cancer and stem cells, child health, obstetrics and gynaecology, clinical neurosciences, digestive diseases, epidemiology and public health, mental health, musculoskeletal and dermatology, primary care, rehabilitation and ageing, respiratory medicine, vascular and renal medicine, assisted reproduction technology, cancer immunology and biotechnology, clinical psychology, forensic and criminological psychology, forensic psychology, health psychology, management psychology, medical physiology and therapeutics,medical education, medicine, mental health research, musculoskeletal sport science and health, occupational psychology, oncology, public health, public health (international health, rehabilitation psychology, sports and exercise medicine, stem cell technology, translational neuroimaging, work and organisational psychology, workplace health and wellbeing; FRCS(Orth), MMedSci, DM, MSc, PhD, BM, BS, MPH, DForensPsych

Faculty of Social Sciences, Law & Education; www.nottingham.ac.uk/ social-sciences/index.aspx

School of Contemporary Chinese Studies; www.nottingham.ac.uk/chinese

business and economy of contemporary China, contemporary Chinese studies/ with international relations, accounting and finance for contemporary China, business and economy of contemporary China, contemporary Chinese studies, global issues and contemporary Chinese studies; Postgraduate; accounting and finance for contemporary China, banking and financial markets in contemporary China, business and economy of contemporary China, contemporary Chinese studies, management in contemporary China and emerging markets; BA, MSc, MSci, PhD

Economics; www.nottingham.ac.uk/ economics

economics, economics and econometrics/international economics, economics with Chinese studies/ French/German/Hispanic studies/Russian, economics and philosophy, mathematics and economics, politics and economics, philosophy, politics and economics, applied economics, economic development and policy analysis, applied economics and financial economics, economics, economics and development economics, economics and financial economics, behavioural economics; BA(Hons), BSc(Hons), MPhil, PGDip, PhD

School of Education; www.nottingham.ac.uk/education

Teacher Training; PGCE, QTS; primary school teaching; School Direct, Teach First, secondary school teaching; Teach First, School Direct, PGCE; several secondary subjects, humanistic counselling practice, fine art; creativity, arts, literacies and learning, education, mentoring and coaching beginning teachers, educational leadership and management, special and inclusive education, learning, technology and education, teaching Chinese to speakers of other languages, international student advice and support, person-centred experiential counselling and psychotherapy, trauma studies; education – international (PGCE), adv counselling practice, counselling/children & young people/& psychotherapy, educational leadership & management, special needs, trauma studies, learning technology & education, special needs, TESOL, TCOL; BA(Hons), MA, MPhil, MRes, PGCE, PGCert/Dip, PhD, SCITT, EdD

School of Geography; www.nottingham.ac.uk/geography

geography/with Chinese/business, environmental management,, environmental geoscience, human geography, landscape & culture; BA(Hons), BSc(Hons), MArts, PhD, MRes

School of Law; www.nottingham.ac.uk/law

law, law with French & French law/German and German law/Spanish & Spanish law, senior status law, American/Australian/European/Chinese/New Zealand/South East Asia law, environmental law, human rights law, international law/& development, international commercial law, criminal justice & armed conflict, international criminal law, European law, international law, international law/and development, law & environmental science, maritime law, public international law, public procurement law, security & terrorism, sociolegal & criminal research; BA(Hons), LlB, LlM, MA, MSc, PhD

Nottingham University Business School; www.nottingham.ac.uk/business

accountancy, finance, accounting and management, international management, industrial economics/ with insurance, management, management with French/German/Spanish/Chinese studies; Postgraduate; accounting and finance, banking and finance/ risk/managerial economics, business and management, corporate strategy & governance, entrepreneurship, innovation and management, finance and investment, HRM and organisation, industrial engineering/information systems and operations management, international business, logistics and supply chain management, management, management, science and operations management, marketing, risk management supply chain and operations management, sustainability, studies; applied biopharmaceutical biotechnology and entrepreneurship, communication/crop biotechnology/cultural industries/electrical and electronic engineering and entrepreneurship/energy

MBAs; finance, entrepreneurship, corporate social responsibility, executive, healthcare; BA(Hons), MBA, MA, MSc

Politics & International Relations; www.nottingham.ac.uk/politics

Asian & international studies, diplomacy, international relations/ & global issues, international

security & terrorism, politics/& economics/contemporary history/history/American studies/German/French/international relations, social, politics, philosophy & economics; BA(Hons), MA, MPhil, MRes, PhD

School of Sociology and Social Policy; www.nottingham.ac.uk/sociology

criminology, global citizenship, identities & human rights, public administration/policy, international/social policy, social work, sociology/& social policy, criminology & social policy/sociology; BA(Hons), MA, MPA, MPhil, MSWS, PhD, PGCert, MPA

NOTTINGHAM TRENT UNIVERSITY
www.ntu.ac.uk

School of Animal, Rural and Environmental Sciences; www.ntu.ac.uk/ares

animal science, environmental conservation and countryside management, horticulture/garden design, sport horse management and coaching, wildlife conservation/countryside management, food science and technology, animal biology, zoo biology, environmental conservation/science, equine sports science, equestrian psychology and sports science, geography (physical), geography, wildlife conservation, international horticulture, veterinary nursing science, food science and technology, zoo biology

Postgrad; animal health and welfare, applied anthrozoology, biodiversity conservation, endangered species recovery and conservation, equine health and welfare, equine performance, equine performance, health and welfare, food industry management, global food security and development; BSc(Hons), MSc/MRes/PGCert/PGDip, FdSc

School of Architecture, Design and Built Environment; www.ntu.ac.uk/adbe

adv property design engineering, architecture, architectural technology & design, built environment studies, civil engineering design & construction, commercial management, construction/management, interior architecture & design, international real estate investment & finance, civil engineering, furniture & product design, building/quantity surveying, planning & development, real estate, construction management, medical product design, planning/& design, urban design & residential development,

product design (business/finance), project management (construction), property finance & investment, innovation & management, quantity surveying & construction, smart design, structural engineering/with management/materials, smart design; BSc(Hons), MA, MSc, MArch, PGDip/Cert, PhD

School of Art & Design; www.ntu.ac.uk/art

fashion design, fashion knitwear design and knitted textiles, fashion communication and promotion, fashion management, fashion marketing and branding, international fashion business, textile design innovation, fashion and textile design, creative pattern cutting, international fashion management, fashion marketing, fashion communications, luxury fashion brand management, art & design media practice, graphic design, photography, media creatives, costume design and king, decorative arts, design for film and television, fine art, theatre design, branding and identity, illustration, graphic design theory and practice, film practice, puppetry and digital animation, fine art; BA(Hons), GradDip, MA, MPhil, PhD,FdA, MFA

School of Arts & Humanities; www.ntu.ac.uk/hum

broadcast journalism, journalism, media, English, history, international relations, communication and society, TV, European studies, global studies, linguistics, philosophy, TESOL, modern languages

Postgraduate; broadcast/digital and newspaper/magazine/documentary journalism, media and globalisation, creative writing, English literary research, international development, history, museum and heritage development, English language teaching; Research; philosophy, Holocaust and genocide, linguistics; BA(Hons), MA, PGDip/Cert, MPhil, PhD

Nottingham Business School; www.ntu.ac.uk/nbs

business, business management and accounting and finance/economics/ entrepreneurship/ human resources, marketing, economics, economics with business/international finance and banking/trade and development/accounting and finance/marketing, international business, international business (with French/German/Spanish)

Postgraduate; management and global supply chain management/innovation and enterprise/international business/finance/marketing/international publishing, marketing, branding and advertising, digital marketing, management and marketing, HRM, economics, economics and investment banking/international business, management and global supply chain management, finance, finance and accounting/investment banking, management and finance, economics and investment banking, entrepreneurship, management and leadership, executive master of business administration (EMBA), HRM; BA(Hons), DBA, MBA, MSc, BIntBan, MBA, BSc(Hons)

School of Education; www.ntu.ac.uk/edu

PGCE early years initial teacher training, primary education; PGCE primary, English, schools direct, childhood studies, education studies, early years and psychology, early years and special and inclusive education, education studies and early years/ psychology/special and inclusive education/ sports education, psychology and special and inclusive education, sports education and psychology/special and inclusive education, early years teacher status, educational support, education, computing in education, PGCE secondary science/design and technology, secondary science education, Schools Direct training, post compulsory education & training, school centred initial teacher training, mathematics and secondary education, childhood, early years and digital learning, secondary design and technology education, science, engineering and mathematics education, education, early years initial teaching training, primary and secondary teaching, primary, secondary and post-compulsory teaching; BA(Hons), BSc(Hons), MA, MSc, FdA, PGDE, PGCE, PGCert, ProfCert, ProfDoc

Nottingham Law School; www.ntu.ac.uk/nls

law, international law, European law, business law, law with criminology/ psychology/business/journalism; senior status, corporate and insolvency law, health law and ethics, human rights and justice, intellectual property law, international trade and commercial law, oil, gas and mining law, sports law, corporate and insolvency law/European and insolvency law, legal practice Bar professional training; GDL, GradDip, LlB, LlM, LPC, PhD

School of Science & Technology; www.ntu.ac.uk/sat

Engineering; biomedical engineering, electronic engineering, sport engineering

Biosciences; biological sciences, biomedical science, biochemistry, pharmacology, biomedical science, biotechnology, environmental management,,molecular cell biology, pharmacology, neuropharmacology, cancer biology, molecular biology, molecular microbiology, neuropharmacology

Chemistry; chemistry, pharmaceutical and medicinal chemistry, analytical chemistry, pharmaceutical analysis, pharmaceutical and medicinal science

Computing and Technology; computer science, computer science (games technology), software engineering, computer systems engineering, computer systems (networks/forensic and security), computing, digital media technology, information systems, information and communications technology, computer science, computing systems, computer games systems, IT security, cloud and enterprise computing, interactive media engineering, engineering (cybernetics and communications), engineering (electronics), engineering management, data analytics for business, electronic systems

Forensics; forensic science

Mathematics; mathematics, financial mathematics, computer science and mathematics, sport science and mathematics, mathematical sciences, data analytics for business

Physics; physics, physics with nuclear technology, physics with forensic applications, physics with astrophysics, medical and materials imaging

Sport Science; sport science and management, sport and exercise science, coaching and sport science, exercise, nutrition and health, sport science, exercise physiology, performance nutrition, performance analysis, biomechanics, sport and exercise psychology; BSc(Hons), MSc, MRes, MSci, PhD, FdSc, MComp(Hons), MMath(Hons), MBiol, MChem

School of Social Sciences; www.nlu.ac.uk/soc

criminology, health and social care, international relations, politics, politics and international relations, psychology, psychology with criminology/sociology, sociology,social work, youth justice, youth studies, applied child psychology, psychological research methods, forensic mental health, forensic psychology, psychology in clinical practice,,psychological well-being and mental health, criminology, sociology, politics, international relations, public health; BA(Hons), MA, MRes, MSc, PGDip/Cert, PhD, ProfDoc

Degrees validated by Nottingham Trent University offered at:

SOUTHAMPTON SOLENT UNIVERSITY
www.solent.ac.uk

www.solent.ac.uk/courses

Art, Design & Fashion

Fashion

beauty management, fashion, fashion buying & merchandising, fashion graphics,/journalism/film fashion marketing with management, fashion photography, fashion promotion & communication, fashion styling, visual merchandising & retail design

Photography

photography, fashion photography, photojournalism

Visual Arts & Design

animation, computer & video games, computer generated images, digital animation, fine art, graphic design/web & mobile devices, illustration, interior design/decoration, product design, special effects, visual arts, fashion, web design & development, digital graphics for web; BA(Hons), BSc(Hons), FdA, MA

Built Environment

architectural technology, construction management, interior design/decoration, civil engineering, quantity surveying, international construction, design & managemenr; BA(Hons), BSc(Hons)

Business, Management and Economics

accounting & finance, business economics, business enterprise & entrepreneurship, creative enterprise, advertising/& PR, international/business management, business (professional development), business administration, international management, business, business & management/marketing, law, promotional media, business information technology, information technology management, information technology for business, festival/& events management, fashion buying & merchandising, fashion promotion & communication, fashion with PR, international tourism management, international air travel & tourism management, maritime business,, ship & port management, marketing/with advertising/management, PR & communication, advertising & PR, media communication & culture, music management/promotion, creative advertising, sports marketing, visual marketing & retail distribution,, marketing, advertising & outdoor marketing, fitness management & personal training, football studies & business, PR; BA(Hons), BSc(Hons), LlB, LlM, FdA, MBA, PGD, MSc

Computing, Games and Networking

animation, digital animation, computing & video games, computer games, software development, computer generation imagery, computer networks & web design, computer systems & networks, network security management, web design & management/development, computing, software engineering, information technology for business; BA(Hons), BSc(Hons)

Engineering and Yacht Design

electronic engineering, engineering design & manufacture, production design, manufacturing & mechanical engineering, applied acoustics, yacht & power craft design, yacht design, & production, BEng(Hons), BA(Hons), BSc(Hons), MSc

Maritime & Geography

geography with environmental studies/marine studies, maritime, business, shipping & port management, marine engineering & management, marine electrical & electronic engineering, marine engineering; BEng(Hons), BSc(Hons), FdEng, MSc

Media and Media Technology

audio & acoustics, audio engineering, broadcasting systems, computer generated imagery, digital music pop journalism/performance/production, performance & promotion, songwriting, film, film & TV studies, film production, live sound, technology, music systems, outside broadcasting (production operations), screenwriting, sound engineering, sound for film, TV special effects/production, TV & video production, TV postproduction/studio production, marketing with advertising management, music management/promotion, media culture & production, media production/writing, audio engineering/technology, digital music, live sound technology, media technology, music studio technology, outside broadcast/production operations, social media, sound engineering, sound for film, TV & games, TV production technology; BSc(Hons), BA(Hons)

Music and Performance

pop music journalism/production, TV & games, music management & promotion; BSc(Hons), BA(Hons)

Health and Social Sciences

criminal investigation with psychology, criminology/psychology, psychology (criminal behaviour/counselling), fitness/management & personal training, health, exercise & physical activity, psychology (counselling/criminal behaviour/education/health), criminology & counselling, social work, criminology & criminal justice; BA(Hons), BSc(Hons), MSc

Sport and Fitness

applied sport science, fitness & personal training, training, fitness management & sport training, health, exercise & physical activity, sports coaching & development, adventure & extreme sport management; BA(Hons), BSc(Hons), MA, MSc

Writing and Communication

advertising & PR, creative enterprise, English & creative writing/film/magazine journalism/PR/advertising/media, fashion & events management,, fashion journalism, journalism, magazine journalism, multimedia journalism, photojournalism, pop music/sports journalism, advertising/& PR, event management, fashion buying & merchandising, fashion promotion & communication, fashion with PR, PR & communications, promotional media, marketing with advertising management, media communication & culture, promotional media, music/production/promotion/management, sports marketing; BA(Hons)

Postgraduate; international accounting and finance, HRM, personnel and development, Master of Business Administration, international business management, management, project management, applied computing, computer engineering, cyber security engineering, data analytics engineering, digital design, applied acoustics, biography and life writing, creative direction for fashion and beauty, fashion merchandise management, film production, athletic development and peak performance, sports broadcast journalism, international trade regulation, criminology and criminal justice, creative advertising, creative enterprise, marketing, management, PR and multimedia communications, visual communication, MBA international maritime management, international maritime business, international shipping and logistics, shipping operations; MA, MSc, MBA, LlM

THE OPEN UNIVERSITY
www.open.ac.uk

Faculties of the University and Qualifications conferred

Faculty of Arts; www.open.ac.uk/Arts
BA(Hons), MA, PGDip, PhD

Open University Business School; www.open.ac.uk/business-school
BA/BSc, Diplomas, Dip/CertHE, FD, MA, MSc, PGDip/Cert, MBA

Faculty of Education & Language Sciences; www.open.ac/uk/education-and-language-studies
BA(Hons), BSc(Hons), Diplomas, Cert/DipHE, Certificated, PGCE, PGDE, QTS, MEd, DEd

Faculty of Health & Social Care; www.open.ac.uk/health-and-social-care
BA/BSc(Hons), FD, MA, CertHE, Dip/CertHE

Open University Law School; www.open.ac.uk/law
LlB(Hons), PGDip, LlM

Faculty of Mathematics, Computing & Technology; www.open.ac.uk/mathematics-computing-and-technology
BSc(Hons), BA/BSc(Hons), BEng(Hons), MEng, FD, Dip/CertHE, DipHE, MSc

Faculty of Science; www.open.ac.uk/science
BSc(Hons), DipHE, FD, MSc

**Faculty of Social Sciences;
www.open.ac.uk/social-sciences**
BSc(Hons), BA(Hons), FD, DipHE, Dip/CertHE, MA,
PGDip

**Institute of Educational Technology;
www.open.ac.uk/iet**
MAODE, EdD,PhD

Courses Offered

Arts & Humanities
arts & humanities, humanities, philosophy and
psychological studies, politics, philosophy and eco-
nomics/psychological studies, psychology/and law,
classical studies, English language and literature,
English literature/and creative writing, history, language studies

Business & Management
business management, business management (sport
and football), computing & IT and a second subject,
business administration, finance, HRM, technology
management, management, accounting

Computing & IT
computing and IT, computing and IT practice,
computing & IT and a second subject

Design
design and innovation

Education, Childhood & Youth
childhood and youth studies, childhood education
studies, children & families, youth work, early years,
youth justice studies, sport, fitness and coaching,
mathematics and its learning, working with young
people, primary teaching and learning, working with
young people, childhood practice, primary teaching
and learning, sport and fitness, professional practice,
supporting teaching and learning in primary schools,
sport, fitness and management, mathematics education, working together for children, effective practice
(youth justice)

Engineering
engineering, environmental management and technology, engineering, design & innovation

Environment & Development
environment, environmental management and technology, environmental science, natural sciences,
design and innovation, environmental studies

Health & Social Care
health and social care, health sciences, healthcare and
health science, nursing practice, adult nursing,

psychology with counselling, childhood and youth
studies, social work, youth work, youth justice
studies, mental health nursing, healthcare practice,
counselling, working with young people, childhood
practice, social care, adult health and social care,
children and families, health and social care, promoting public health

Health & Wellbeing
sport, fitness and coaching, adult health & science,
healthcare and health science, health sciences, mental
health nursing, sport and fitness, healthcare practice,
sport, fitness and management, health sciences, end-
of-life care, promoting public health

Languages
arts with humanities, humanities, language studies,
English language and literature, English literature,
English literature and creative writing, classical
studies

Law
criminology and law, psychology and law, laws,
youth justice studies, counselling with law

Mathematics & Statistics
mathematics and statistics, computing & IT and a
second subject, economics and mathematical
sciences, mathematics, mathematics and physics,
mathematics and its learning, mathematics education

Medical Sciences
health sciences,

Nursing & Healthcare Practice
nursing practice, health and social care, healthcare &
health sciences, children and families, healthcare with
health science, healthcare practice, promoting public
health adult/mental health nursing

Psychology & Counselling
combined social sciences, counselling, philosophy
and psychological studies, computing & IT and a
second subject, criminology and psychological studies, psychology, psychology and law, psychology
with counselling, forensic psychology, social psychology, childhood and youth studies, counselling,
healthcare practice, children and families

Science
health sciences, natural sciences, mathematics and
physics, environmental science, environmental studies, environmental management and technology,
environment, paramedic science, physics, astronomy
and planetary science

Social Sciences

combined social sciences, history & politics, philosophy and economics, economics and mathematical sciences, environmental studies, philosophy and psychological studies, social policy and criminology, international studies, criminology and psychological studies, forensic psychology, psychology, psychology and law, psychology with counselling, criminology and law, international studies, youth justice studies, social psychology, childhood and youth studies, counselling, combined social sciences, environmental management and technology, social policy and criminology, criminology and law, healthcare practice, children and families, youth justice studies

Technology

environmental management and technology

UNIVERSITY OF OXFORD
www.ox.ac.uk

Division of Humanities; www.ox.ac.uk/ divisions/humanities

Rothermere American Institute; www.rai.ox.ac.uk

American studies/history/politics/literature; MSt

Faculty of Classics; www.classics.ox.ac.uk

classics, classics and English/ modern languages/ oriental studies, classical archaeology and ancient history, ancient and modern history, Greek and/or Roman history, Greek and/or Latin languages and literature, ancient history, classical languages and literature, classical archaeology, late antique & Byzantine; BA(Hons), MPhil, MSt, DPhil

Ruskin School of Drawing and Fine Art; www.ruskin-sc.ox.ac.uk

art history & theory, contemporary art, drawing, fine art, theoretical & practice-led research, history of art & visual culture; BFA, MLitt, DPhil

Faculty of English, Language & Literature; www.english.ox.ac.uk

English language and literature (650-1550; 1550-1700; 1600-1830; 1800-1914; 1900-present day), English & modern languages/classics/history, literature in English, English language, English & American studies, English studies/medieval studies, history & English, Shakespeare, women's studies: film aesthetics, studio world literatures in English; BA(Hons), DPhil, MLitt, MPhil, MSt

History of Art Department; www.hoa.ox.ac.uk

history of art, topics include art and culture in Renaissance Florence and Venice, The Dutch Golden Age: 1618-72, painting and culture in Ming China,English architecture,art and its public in France, 1815-67, authenticity and replication in art and visual culture, French painting, 1880-1912, gothic: artistic originality and the transmission of style in medieval art, image and thought, media and modernity: art and mass culture, 1880–2000, portraiture as genre, the apparatus of art history, theories of vision: the eye and the gaze, women, art and culture in early modern Europe

BA(Hons), DPhil, MLitt, MSt

Faculty of History; www.history.ox.ac.uk

history of the British Isles, general history,,historical methods, British history, general history, ancient and modern history, history and economics, history and English, history and modern languages, history and politics; Postgraduate studies include; British and European history, from 1500 to the present, economic and social history, global and imperial history, history of art and visual culture, history of science, medicine and technology, late antique and Byzantine studies, medieval history, medieval studies, modern south Asian studies, US history; BA(Hons), DPhil, MPhil, MSc, MSt, MLetters

Faculty of Linguistics, Philology and Phonetics; www.ling-phil.ox.ac.uk

modern languages and linguistics, psychology, philosophy and linguistics, Graduate Courses; general linguistics and comparative philology, general linguistics and comparative philology, comparative philology and general linguistics; BA, MPhil, PhD, MSt

Faculty of Medieval & Modern Languages; www.mod-langs.ox.ac.uk

Arabic, Czech (with Slovak, modern Greek, classics, French, German, Hebrew, history, Italian, linguistics, Persian, philosophy, Polish, Portuguese, Russian, Spanish, Turkish; Graduate Taught Courses; modern languages, Celtic studies, Slavonic studies, Yiddish studies, women's studies, film aesthetics, medieval studies; BA(Hons), DPhil, MPhil, MSt

Faculty of Music; www.music.ox.ac.uk
chamber music, choral studies/conducting performance, composition & analysis, dance music, musicology, ethnomusicology, historical musicology, jazz, musical history/theory, the motet in the 14/15th centuries, orchestration, music analysis & criticism, performance & interpretation, psychology of music, theory & analysis, source studies, technology of composition, south Western music theory; Masters;- composition, ethnomusicology, musicology, performance, psychology of music; BMus, DPhil, MA(Hons), MPhil, MSt, MLitt

Faculty of Oriental Studies; www.orinst.ox.ac.uk
Arabic, Aramaic with Syriac, Armenian, Asia & Near Asian studies, bible interpretation, Buddhist studies, Chinese studies, classic & oriental studies, Classical Armenian studies, Classical Hebrew studies, Classical Indian religion, Coptic, Cuneiform studies, Eastern Christian studies, eastern Christianity, Egyptology, Egyptology & ancient Near East, European & Middle East languages, Hebrew & Jewish studies, Hindi & Urdu, Hindi and Urdu, Islamic art and archaeology, Islamic studies and history, Islamic world, Japanese studies, Jewish studies, Jewish studies in the Graeco-Roman period, Judaism and Christianity in the Graeco-Roman World, Korean, Korean studies, Medieval Arabic thought, Modern Chinese studies, Modern Jewish studies, Modern Middle Eastern studies, Modern South Asian studies, Old Iranian, Oriental studies, Ottoman Turkish studies, Pali, Pali and Prakrit, Persian, Sanskrit, Syriac studies, theology & oriental studies, Tibetan and Himalayan studies, Traditional East Asia, Turkish; BA(Hons), DPhil, MPhil,MSt

Faculty of Philosophy; www.philosophy.ox.ac.uk
philosophy and modern languages; philosophy and theology; physics and philosophy; mathematics and philosophy; psychology, philosophy and linguistics; computer science and philosophy
early modern philosophy, knowledge and reality, ethics: philosophy of mind, philosophy of science and social science, philosophy of religion, the philosophy of logic and language, aesthetics, medieval philosophy: Aquinas/Duns Scotus and Ockham, the philosophy of Kant, post-Kantian philosophy, theory of politics, Plato, Republic, Aristotle, Frege, Russell and Wittgenstein, formal logic, philosophy of physics, philosophy of mathematics, philosophy of science, philosophy of cognitive science, the philosophy and economics of the environment, philosophical logic, Plato, Latin philosophy, jurisprudence; BA(Hons), BPhil, MPhil, PhD

Faculty of Theology; www.theology.ox.ac.uk
theology & religion/oriental studies, philosophy & theology, applied theology, theology in applied theology, sociology of religion, pastoral psychology, science and faith in the modern world, the use of the bible, Christian spirituality, liturgy and worship, Christian ethics, mission in the modern world, inter-faith dialogue, ecclesiology in an ecumenical context, Old Testament, New Testament, biblical interpretation, Christian ethics, philosophical theology, science & religion, modern/Reformation/scholastic/patristic theology, ecclesiastical history, the study of religions, issues in theology, Judaism and Christianity in the Graeco-Roman world; BA(Hons), BTh, MTh, MSt, MLitt, MPhil, DPhil, PGDip/Cert

Division of Mathematical, Physical and Life Sciences; www.ox.ac.uk/divisions/mpls

Dept of Chemistry; www.chem.ox.ac.uk
chemical biology, inorganic chemistry, organic chemistry, physical chemistry, mathematical techniques, molecular biochemistry/& chemical biology, organic chemistry/reactions/synthesis, organometallic chemistry, physical & theoretical chemistry, quantum mechanics, reaction mechanisms, solid state chemistry, spectroscopy, theoretical chemistry, thermodynamics; DPhil, MChem, MSc

Dept of Computer Science; www.cs.ox.ac.uk
computer science, mathematics/ & computer science, modelling & scientific computing, mathematics & foundations of computer science & philosophy, software engineering, software & systems security; BA(Hons), MSc, DPhil, PhD

Dept of Engineering Science; www.eng.ox.ac.uk
engineering science, autonomous intelligent machines and systems, gas turbines aerodynamics, synthetic biology, renewable energy marine structures; research in engineering science, automotive engineering, aerothermal engineering, micromechanics and materials modelling, mechanical

performance and integrity, advanced structures, biotechnics, hydraulics, sustainable energy, environmental engineering, bioprocesses, process systems, chemical engineering, production engineering, optoelectronics, microelectronics, communications, power electronics, machine vision and robotics, machine learning, multivariable control, nonlinear and predictive control, medical imaging and informatics, cellular engineering and therapy, dynamic systems, chaos, optimization and mathematical models, autonomous intelligent machines and systems CDT, gas turbines aerodynamics CDT; DPhil, MEng, MSc, EngD

Life Science Interface; Doctoral Training Centre; www.lsi.ox.ac.uk

biological systems, biological experimental techniques, biological physics, organic chemistry, molecular genetics & cell biology, mathematical biology, medicinal chemistry, programming, bioinformatics, statistical data systems, structural biology; DPhil

Division of Materials; www.materials.ox.ac.uk

materials science, materials structures & mechanical properties of metals, electrical/mechanical properties, nanoelectronics, materials economics, non-metallic materials, composites, polymers, packaging/superconducting/semiconducting materials, structural & nuclear materials, device materials, nanomaterials, process & manufacturing, characterisation, computational nuclear modelling; DPhil, MEng, MSc, MS, MEm

Mathematical Institute; www.maths.ox.ac.uk

mathematics, mathematics and statistics/philosophy/computer science/theoretical physics; Research Areas; algebra, combinatorics, functional analysis, geometry, history of mathematics, logic, mathematical and computational finance, mathematical physics, number theory, numerical analysis, industrial and applied mathematics, nonlinear partial differential equations, stochastic analysis, topology, mathematical biology; BA(Hons), DPhil, MCF, MFoCS, MS, MSc, MMath

Dept of Physics; www.physics.ox.ac.uk

physics, atmospheric oceanic & planetary physics, astrophysics, condensed matter physics, cosmology, general relativity, quantum theory, sub-atomic physics, particle physics, physics, atomic & laser/theoretical physics, physics & philosophy; BA(Hons), DPhil, MPhys, MPhysPhil

Dept of Plant Science; www.plants.ox.ac.uk/plants

biochemistry & systems biology, biological science, cell biology/physiology, cell & development biology, comparative developmental genetics, ecology, evolution & systematics, plant science; DPhil, MRes, MSc

Dept of Statistics; www.stats.ox.ac.uk

applied statistics, mathematics & statistics, applied probability & research in statistics; BA(Hons), DPhil, MMath, MSc, PGDip

Dept of Zoology; www.zoo.ox.ac.uk

animal behaviour/welfare, ageing biology, biological science, infectious disease, ecology & conservation, evolution & development, food science, molecular biology & bioinformatics, indigenous biology, ornithology, integrative bioscience, wildlife conservation; DPhil, MRes, MSc

Biological Science; www.biologyy.ox.ac.uk

organisms, cells & genes, ecology, qualitative methods, evolution, adaptation to the environment, cell & developmental biology, animal behaviour, disease, plants

Division of Medical Sciences; www.ox.ac.uk/divisions/medical_science

Dept of Biochemistry; www.bioch.ox.ac.uk

biochemistry, molecular & cellular biology, structural chromosome and developmental biology, infection, immunity and translational medicine, neuroscience, integrative systems biology, life sciences interface systems approaches to biomedical science e biochemistry, biomedical imaging, synthetic biology, iological chemistry and biophysical chemistry, organic chemistry and maths & statistics, macromolecular structure and function, bioenergetics and metabolism, genetics and molecular biology, cell biology, molecular immunology, plant molecular biology, neuropharmacology, membrane transport, glycobiology, human disease, bionanotechnology, systems biology and signalling to the nucleus, biochemistry, medical sciences, chromosome & developmental biology, structural biology, infection, immunity and translational medicine; DPhil, MBiochem, MSc, PhD

Nuffield Dept of Clinical Medicine; www.ndm.ox.ac.uk

cancer biology, genetic medicine, immunology & infectious diseases, protein science & structural biology, physiology, cellular & molecular biology, tropical medicine & global health; PhD, MSc

Dept of Clinical Neurosciences; www.ndcn.ox.ac.uk

medicine, medical sciences, sleep medicine, MRT physics/analysis, biomedical sciences, experimental psychology, clinical neurology, functional MRI of the brain, anaesthesia; DPhil, MSc

Dept of Experimental Psychology; www.psy.ox.ac.uk

experimental psychology, psychology, philosophy & linguistics, psychological research; BA(Hons), DPhil, MSc

Radcliffe Department of Medicine

Division of Cardiovascular Medicine, Oxford Centre for Diabetes, Endocrinology and Metabolism, MRC Weatherall Institute of Molecular Medicine, Nuffield Division of Clinical Laboratory Sciences, The Oxford Acute Vascular Imaging Centre, Centre for the Advancement of Sustainable Medical Innovation Investigative Medicine Division

Nuffield Dept of Obstetrics & Gynaecology; www.obs-gyn.ox.ac.uk

obstetrics & gynaecology, clinical embryology; MSc, DPhil

Dept of Oncology; www.oncology.ox.ac.uk

oncology, radiation biology, experimental therapeutics, medical oncology, radiation oncology & radiobiology; DPhil, MRes, MSc

Department of Orthopaedics, Rheumatology and Musculoskeletal Sciences; www.ndorms.ox.ac.uk

orthopaedics, rheumatology, musculoskeletal sciences, translational medicine & medical technology, immunology; MSc, DPhil

Dept of Paediatrics; www.paediatrics.ox.ac.uk

medicine, paediatric infection and immunity, paediatric infectious diseases, international child health, paediatric endocrinology and diabetes, paediatric haematology, neonatology, paediatric gastroenterology and nutrition, HIV infection and immune control, molecular infectious diseases, developmental immunology, paediatric neuroimaging and pain, vaccinology; PhD, MSc, DPhil

Sir William Dunn School of Pathology; www.path.ox.ac.uk

bacteriology and virology, cell biology, infection,immunology & molecular medicine, microbiology and molecular biology; DPhil

Dept of Pharmacology; www.pharm.ox.ac.uk

pharmacology, cardiovascular/autonomic in vivo/systems neuroscience, drug discovery/medicinal chemistry, cell signalling, molecular neuroscience and disease, cellular neuroscience, experimental therapeutics, practical drug therapy, medical chemistry for cancer; MSc, DPhil

Dept of Physiology, Anatomy and Genetics; www.dpag.ox.ac.uk

functional genomics, cell physiology, development cell biology,neuroscience, cardiac science; BA, MPhil, MSc, DPhil

Nuffield Department of Population Health; www.ndph.ox.ac.uk

global health science, population technology, population health, ethics & law, medical sociology, population pathology, integrated population health, global health, preventive medicine; DPhil, MSc

Nuffield Dept of Primary Health Sciences; www.phc.ox.ac.uk

evidence-based health care, health research, primary healthcare, behavioural medicine, evidence-based medicine, health service economics and organisation, chronic kidney disease, clinical trials, tobacco addiction, diabetes and long-term conditions, health, heart failure research, hypertension, infectious diseases research; DPhil, MSc

Dept of Psychiatry; www.psychiatry.ox.ac.uk

experimental psychology, eating disorders, suicide, child & adolescent psychiatry, clinical psychopharmacology, bipolar research, experimental psychopathology & cognitive therapies, forensic psychiatry, neural correlates of gene function, neurobiology and experimental therapeutics, neurobiology of ageing, autism, eating disorders, human brain activity, cognitive approaches to psychosis, cognitive health and neuroscience clinical trials, mindfulness, perinatal psychopathology and offspring development, psychological medicine, psychopharmacology and emotion, social psychiatry, translational neurobiology of psychosis, translational neuroimaging, translational neuroscience & dementia MSc, DPhil, MRCPsych

Nuffield Dept of Surgical Science; www.surgery.ox.ac.uk

surgical science, endovascular neurosurgery, integrated immunology, surgical science and practice; DPhil, MCh, MS, MSc

Division of Social Sciences; www.socsci.ox.ac.uk

School of Anthropology and Museum Ethnography; www.anthro.ox.ac.uk

anthropology, archaeology & anthropology, human science, medical anthropology, cognitive & evolutionary anthropology, visual material & museum anthropology, migration studies; BA, BSc, DPhil, MPhil, MSc

Pitt Rivers Museum; www.prm.ox.ac.uk

visual, material & museum anthropology, material culture, visual anthropology, art and aesthetics, sensory anthropology, ethnographic photography and film, and museum anthropology; DPhil, MPhil, MSc

School of Archaeology; www.arch.ox.ac.uk

archaeology & anthropology, bioarchaeology, Eurasian prehistory, classical archaeology & ancient history, historical & classical chronology, materials & technology, chronology, Eurasian prehistory, Palaeolithic archaeological science; BA(Hons), DPhil, MLitt, MSc, MSt

SAID Business School; www.sbs.ox.ac.uk

law and finance, major programme management, MBA economics and management, management studies, executive MBA, financial economics, strategic management, financial strategy, global business, organisational leadership, strategy and innovation, cyber risk for managers, finance, high performance leadership, performing leaders, private equity, real estate, women transforming leadership; BA, Dip, MBA, Exec MBA, MSc

Dept of Economics; www.economics.ox.ac.uk

economics, macroeconomics, microeconomics, quantitative economics, British economic history since 1870, command & transitional economies, comparative demographic systems, econometrics, economics of developing countries, economics of industry, finance, game theory, international economics, labour economics & industrial relations, mathematical methods, microeconomic theory, money & banking, philosophy & economics of the environment, public economics, advanced econometrics, advanced macroeconomics, advanced microeconomics, behavioural economics, development economics, economic history, financial economics, industrial organisation, international trade, labour economics, public economics,

theory based empirical analysis; BA(Hons), DPhil, MEng, MSc, MPhil

Dept of Education; www.education.ox.ac.uk

applied linguistics, education (comparative & international education/higher education/learning & technology/children & education/research), learning and teaching/in HE, PGCE (numerous secondary subjects, Schools Direct), teaching English in university setting; DPhil, MSc, PGCE, PGDip

School of Geography & the Environment; www.geog.ox.ac.uk

geographical research, space, place and society, earth system dynamics, biogeography, biodiversity and conservation, climate change and variability, climate change impacts and adaptation, complexity, contemporary urban life, island life, cultural spaces: geographies of affective experience, desert landscapes and dynamics, environmental change & management, environmental geography, European integration, forensic geography, geographies of finance, geographies of nature, geopolitics in the margin, heritage science & conservation, post-Soviet Russia in transition, quaternary period: natural & human systems, transport & mobilities, geography & the environment, conservation/environmental change & management, nature, society & environmental governance, water science, policy & management; BA(Hons), BCL, Dip, DPhil, MJur, MLitt, MPhil, MSc, MSt, PGDip

School of Interdisciplinary Area Studies; www.area-studies.ox.ac.uk

African studies, Latin American studies, contemporary Chinese studies, contemporary India, modern Japanese studies, Middle East studies, Russian and East European studies, MBA, MSc, MPhil, DPhil

Dept of International Development; www.qeh.ox.ac.

international development, development studies, economics for development, global governance and diplomacy, migration studies; MPhil, MSc, DPhil

Oxford Internet Institute; www.oii.ox.ac.uk

social science of the internet, information, communication & the social sciences; DPhil, MSc

Faculty of Law; www.law.ox.ac.uk

law, jurisprudence, jurisprudence with senior status, law with law studies in Europe, legal studies, Postgraduate; civil law, magister juris, criminology and criminal justice, law and finance, taxation, international human rights law, intellectual property law and practice

BA(Hons), BCL, Dip. DPhil, MJur, MLitt, MPhil, MSc, MSt, PGDip, MJur

Oxford Martin School; www.oxfordmartin.ox.ac.uk

research in health & medicine, energy & environment, technology & society, ethics & governance

Oxford-Man Institute of Quantitative Finance; www.oxford-man.ox.ac.uk

data analysis and patterns in data, decision making under uncertainty and asset allocation, efficient markets, risk premia and market anomalies, electronic trading, numerical methods and high performance computing in finance, pensions, investments and hedge fund industry, stability of financial systems

Dept of Politics & International Relations; www.politics.ox.ac.uk

history and politics, international relations, politics (political theory/European politics & society), political/political theory research, philosophy, politics and economics; BA(Hons), DPhil, MLitt, MPhil, MSc

Dept of Social Policy & Intervention; www.spi.ox.ac.uk

comparative social policy, evidence-based social intervention and policy evaluation, social policy or social intervention, social policy, social intervention
BA, MPhil, MSc

Dept of Sociology; www.sociology.ox.ac.uk

sociology, history & politics, human sciences, philosophy, politics & economics, sociology and demography; BA(Hons), DPhil, MPhil, MSc

OXFORD BROOKES UNIVERSITY
www.brookes.ac.uk

Faculty of Business; www.brookes.ac.uk/ about/faculties/business

Business School; www.business.brookes.ac.uk

accounting and finance, applied accounting, automotive management, business and management, business management, business & management, business management, enterprise and entrepreneurship, economics, economics, finance and international business/politics and international relations, events management, internatio HRM, international business management, marketing(and business), marketing management
Postgrad; accounting, accounting and finance, business management(corporate social responsibility/ economics/HRM/marketing/entrepreneurship), digital management, HRM, international business economics, international management, international management and international relations, international trade and logistics, strategic management and leadership, management, marketing, mentoring and coaching/practice/& brand marketing, strategic management and leadership, tourism and hotel management; BA(Hons), BSc(Hons), Certs, DCM, DBA, Dips, FdA, MA, MBA, MRes, MSc, PhD

Oxford International Centre for Publishing; www.publishing.brookes.ac.uk

publishing media, publishing, publishing studies, digital publishing, Cert, BA(Hons), European Master's in Publishing, MA

Oxford School of Hospitality; www.hospitality.brookes.ac.uk

international hospitality management, international hospitality, events & tourism management, international hospitality, hotel & tourism management, food, tourism futures; BSc(Hons), MSc

Faculty of Human & Life Sciences; www.hls.brookes.ac.uk

Dept of Biological & Medical Sciences; www.bms.brookes.ac.uk

animal behaviour & welfare/biology & conservation, applied animal management, biological sciences, biology, biomedical science, conservation ecology evolution & development, countryside management, environmental science, human biology, infection, prevention & control, biosciences, medical genetics & genomics, medical science, equine science/& management/thoroughbred management, life sciences; BA(Hons)/BSc(Hons), MSc, PGDip, PhD, BMedSci

Dept of Clinical Health Care; www.chc.brookes.ac.uk

adult & mental health nursing, adult nursing, adv practice (clinical), cancer studies, childrens/& mental health nursing, health and social care, nursing studies, leadership in clinical practice, non-medical prescribing, operating department practice, palliative care, paramedic emergency care,

Postgraduate;adult intensive care practice, adult nursing, advanced communication and supportive relationships, advanced practice (clinical),

cancer studies, cardiorespiratory practice, children's high dependency practice,

children's nursing, community practitioner nurse prescriber,dementia in context for health and social care, emergency nursing practice,

independent and supplementary prescribing/conversion course for ahps,

managing patients receiving systemic anti-cancer treatments, mental health nursing, minor illness and injury management, neonatal practice, non-medical prescribing, nursing studies (leadership in clinical practice), orthopaedic practice, planning and managing clinical trials, renal and urology practice; BSc(Hons), FdSc, FdA, MA, MSc, PgDip/Cert, MPhil, PhD

Dept of Psychology; www.psychology.brookes.ac.uk

psychology, developmental psychology; BSc(Hons), BA(Hons), MPhil, PhD, MSc, PGDip/Cert

Dept of Social Work & Public Health; www.swph.brookes.ac.uk

community children's nursing/in the home, district nursing, midwifery, public health, specialist community public health, social work; BSc(Hons), BA(Hons), PGDip/Cert, Cert HE, MA, MSc, MPhil

Dept of Sport & Health Science; www.shs.brookes.ac.uk

supervision in health & social care, nutrition, physiotherapy, sport & exercise science, sports coaching & PE, sports science, applied human nutrition, applied sports & exercise nutrition, contemporary/ occupational therapy, rehabilitation; BSc(Hons), BA(Hons), Cert/DipHE, MSc, PGDip/Cert, MOst, MSc, MPhil, PhD

Faculty of Humanities & Social Sciences; *www.brookes.ac.uk/about faculties/hss*

School of Education; www.education.brookes.ac.uk

early/childhood studies, early years, education/studies, adv educational practice, CPD, education & lifelong learning, English language & communication, education (leadership & management/TESOL), PGCE primary/secondary/post-compulsory education, primary teacher education, school direct, special educational needs support for learning,challenging behaviour, childrens literature, primary mathematics, science education, 5-13 years, teaching English as an additional language (EAL), artist teacher scheme, early childhood, SENCO, working with children with literacy difficulties, PGCE without QTS; BA(Hons), BSc(Hons), CertEd, FdA, MA, MPhil, PGCE, PGDip, PhD, QTS, DEd

Dept of English & Modern Languages; www.english-language.brookes.ac.uk

English, English literature, creative writing, drama, international business, culture & language, French, Spanish, Japanese studies, app langs; BA(Hons), MA

Dept of History, Philosophy & Religion; www.history.brookes.ac.uk

history, history of medicine, history of art, philosophy, communication, media & culture, ministry; BA(Hons), MA, FdA

School of Law; www.law.brookes.ac.uk

law, international/economic/human rights/trade & commercial law, international law, globalisation & development, legal practice; BA/BSc, LlB, PGDip, GradDip, LlM

Dept of Social Sciences; www.social-sciences.brookes.ac.uk

anthropology, geography, international relations, politics, primate conservation, international studies, international studies, sociology, policing; BA/BSc, MA, MSc, GradDip, FdA

Faculty of Technology, Design & Environment; www.brookes.ac.uk/tde

School of Architecture; www.architecture.brookes.ac.uk

architecture, interior architecture, built environment, development & emergency practice, humanitarian action & conflict, shelter after disaster, international architectural regeneration & development, applied design in architecture, sustainable building:

performance & design; BA(Hons), MArch, MArchD, PhD, FdA, PGDip

School of Arts; www.arts.brookes.ac.uk

fine art, composition & sonic art, art & design, contemporary arts/& music, creative arts & design practice, creative music production, digital media production, music, film studies & digital media, fine art, graphic design, illustration narrative & sequential, composition & sonic arts, contemporary arts/& music, social sculpture, film studies/popular cinema, publishing/media/& language, book history & popular culture, digital international publishing; BA(Hons), BA/BSc, MA, MPhil, PhD, FdA

Dept of Planning; www.planning.brookes.ac.uk

built environment, environmental assessment & management, spatial planning, historic conservation, city & regional planning, planning/& property development, quantity surveying & commercial management, urban design/planning development & transitional regions ; BA(Hons), MPlan, MSc, PhD, MPhil, PGDip/Cert, FBE

Dept of Real Estate & Construction; www.rec.brookes.ac.uk

built environment, building information modelling & management, construction project management, investment finance, quantity surveying & commercial management, real estate/management, spatial planning, project management in the built environment; BSc(Hons), MSc, PhD

Dept of Computing & Communication Technologies; www.cct.brookes.ac.uk

computer science, computer science for cyber security, computing, computing for robotic systems, computing & informatics, ebusiness, information technology management for business/systems & management, mobile computing, computer vision, IT systems, administration & management, mobile wireless & communications, network computing, software engineering, multimedia production, software development for business, sound mobile & high-speed telecommunications networks, wireless communication systems, digital media production; BSc(Hons), MSc, PhD

Dept of Mechanical Engineering & Mathematical Science; www.mems.brookes.ac.uk

mathematics, mathematical sciences, mechanical engineering, motorsport engineering/technology, automotive engineering, racing engine design, electronic engineering; BSc(Hons), BA(Hons), B/MEng, MSc, MRes, MPhil, PhD

UNIVERSITY OF PLYMOUTH
www.plymouth.ac.uk

Faculty of Arts; www.plymouth.ac.uk/faculties/arts

School of Architecture, Design and Environment; www1.plymouth.ac.uk/schools/ade

architecture, architectural technology & the environment, architectural engineering, brand & design management, design thinking, 3D design, English & culture, environment conservation/science, building surveying & the environment, high performance buildings, mechanical design & manufacture, sustainable construction/cost management/project management, construction management & the environment, PGCE; primary creative design/secondary art & design/design & technology; BA(Hons), MA, MRes, MArch, MSc

School of Art & Media; www.plymouth.ac.uk/schools/artmedia

digital art & technology, graphic communication with typography, film & video, fine art, illustration, media arts, contemporary art/film practice, film & video, photography/& the book/land, TV art, photographic arts; BA(Hons), MA, MArch, GradDip, MRes, PhD, MSc, BSc

School of Humanities & Performing Arts; www.plymouth.ac.uk/schools/hpa

art history, fine art & art history, choreography, computer music, dance/theatre performance, creative arts management, English & creative writing/history/French/Spanish/culture/publishing, events management, fine art & art history, history with international relations/politics/English, modern/music, music & sound production, primary music/English/

humanities, politics with history, theatre & performance; BA(Hons), MA, PGDip/Cert, MRes, PhD

Faculty of Health & Human Science;
www.plymouth.ac.uk/faculties/hhc

School of Nursing & Midwifery; www.plymouth.ac.uk/schools/school-of-nursing-and midwifery

adult/child/health/mental health nursing, adv critical care practice, midwifery, professional developmental nursing, contemporary healthcare (advancing practice/children & young people/community nursing), dental therapy & hygiene, healthcare management, leadership & innovation, paramedic practice, urgent & emergency care, clinical research; BSc(Hons), MSc, PGDip

School of Health Professions; www.plymouth.ac.uk/schools/hp

dietetics, adv/occupational therapy, adv professional practice (dietetics/neurological rehabilitation/occupational therapy/paediatric dietetics/physiotherapy/ social work with children & families), human nutrition, optometry, paramedic practitioner physiotherapy, podiatry, pre-hospital critical care/retrieval & transfer, social work, clinical research; BSc(Hons), DipHE, MSc, PGCert, PGDip

School of Psychology; www.plymouth.ac.uk/ school_of_psychology

psychology, psychological studies, adv psychology, clinical psychology, psychology with human biology/ bioscience, sociology/criminology & criminal justice/ international relations, clinical research/ methods; BSc(Hons), MSc, PGDip

School of Education; www.plymouth.ac.uk/ schools/education

education (incorporating education and training), early childhood studies, education studies, primary (art and design/computing and ICT/early childhood studies/English/humanities/mathematics/music/physical education/science), primary (special educational needs); Postgraduate; early childhood, education, learning for sustainability,PGCE (incorporating the diploma in education and training), PGCE primary, (early years), PGCE secondary; numerous secondary subjects, special educational needs coordination, PGCE (primary and early years, secondary and further education, school direct), education & training; BEd, CertEd, MA, MSc, Masters in Teaching & Learning, PGCE, Dip, PGCert, ProfDoc, FdA

Faculty of Business;
www.plymouth.ac.uk/faculties/business

Plymouth Business School; www.plymouth.ac.uk/schools/plymouth-business-school

accounting and finance, business, business administration, business economics, business enterprise & entrepreneurship, business management/with business English, business studies, economics, economics with international relations/law/politics, financial economics, HRM, international business economics/ French/Spanish, international finance, international management, international supply chain and shipping management, international supply chain management, international trade and operations, management, management, government and law, management practice, maritime business and logistics, maritime business and maritime law; Postgrad; accounting & finance, finance & investment, international finance; BA(Hons), BSc(Hons)

Plymouth Graduate School of Management; www.plymouth.ac.uk/ schools/pgsm

accounting and finance, brand and design management, business administration, business and management, digital and social media marketing, entrepreneurship/ and international development, finance/ and investment, HRM, international business, international finance, international logistics/procurement and supply chain management, international shipping, management, marketing management, operations and supply chain management, public administration, marketing & innovation; MBA, DPA, DPubAdmin, PGDip, MPhil, ResM, PhD, MSc, MA

Plymouth Law School; www.plymouth.ac.uk/schools/law

law, law and business, law with criminology and criminal justice studies, marine environmental law and sustainability, criminology and criminal justice studies with law, criminology and criminal justice studies with international relations/politics/ psychology/ sociology, police and criminal justice studies, criminology; BA(Hons), BSc(Hons), LlB, LlM, MSc, PGDip

School of Tourism & Hospitality; www.plymouth.ac.uk/schools/th

business and tourism, cruise management, events management, hospitality management, hospitality, tourism and events management, international tourism management, tourism and hospitality management, tourism management, international hospitality management, tourism and hospitality management; BSc(Hons), BA(Hons), MSc, PGDip

School of Government; www.plymouth.ac.uk/schools/school-of-government

international relations, international relations with French /law/ politics/Spanish/psychology, politics with criminology and criminal justice studies, French/politics/history, international relations with law/Spanish/psychology/public services; Postgraduate; applied strategy (international security/maritime security), international relations: global security and development, social research methods; BSc(Hons), MSc, DPA

Faculty of Science & the Environment; www.plymouth.ac.uk/faculties/science

School of Biological Sciences; www.plymouth.ac.uk/schools/school-of-biological-science

animal behaviour & welfare, animal conservation science, biological sciences, biomedical science, biosciences, conservation biology/science, environmental biology, sustainable aquaculture systems, zoo conservation biology; BSc(Hons), PGDip, MSc

School of Computing & Mathematics; www.plymouth.ac.uk/schools/compmath

computer science, computer & information security, computer systems & networks, computing & games development, data modelling & analytics, electrical & electronic engineering, mathematics/with statistics/education/finance/high performance computing, network systems engineering, robotics, robotics technology/engineering, signal processing; BSc, MSc, MRes

School of Geography, Earth & Environmental Sciences; www.plymouth.ac.uk/schools/sogees

chemistry, biology, applied/geology, environmental science/conservation, earth sciences, extended science, geography, geology with ocean science, human/marine biology,marine science, physical geography & geology, planning; BA(Hons), BSc(Hons), MGeol, MSc, MRes, PGCert

School of Marine Science & Engineering; www.plymouth.ac.uk/schools/mse

civil and coastal engineering, applied marine science, civil engineering, hydrography, oceanography, ocean science, marine/ and composites technology, marine biology, marine biology and coastal ecology/oceanography, marine technology, mechanical design and manufacture, mechanical engineering, mechanical engineering with composites, navigation and maritime science, ocean exploration and surveying, ocean science, ocean science and marine conservation, oceanography and coastal processes; Postgrad; advanced hydrography for professionals, applied marine science, civil engineering, coastal engineering, hydrography, marine biology, marine renewable energy; BSc(Hons), MEng, MRes, MSc, BEng, FdSc, PGDip

School of Psychology; www.plymouth.ac.uk/school_of_psychology

psychology, psychological studies, adv psychology, psychology with human biology/sociology/criminology & criminal justice studies/international relations, clinical psychology, psychology research methods; BSc(Hons), MSc, PGDip, MPsych

Plymouth University Peninsular School of Medicine and Dentistry; www.plymouth.ac.uk/peninsular

Plymouth University Peninsular School of Dentistry

Plymouth University Peninsular School of Medicine

The School of Biomedical & Healthcare Sciences

medicine, surgery, clinical education, adv critical care practitioner, healthcare management, leadership and innovation, physician associate, remote and global healthcare, remote healthcare, simulation and patient safety, dental surgery/therapy, restorative dentistry, biomedical science, health and fitness, healthcare science (life sciences/physiological sciences), human biosciences, nutrition, exercise and health, urgent & emergency care; MBBS, BDS, MD, MS, MPhil, PhD, PGDip/Cert, MSc, MClinEd

Degrees validated by the University of Plymouth offered at:

SOUTH DEVON COLLEGE
www.southdevon.ac.uk

applied/animal science, adventure leadership, child development & education, coaching, digital management, drama, performance & arts management, early year care & education, healthcare practice, biosciences, business, civil and coastal engineering, computing, criminology and psychology, extended science, fashion with textiles, film and photography, game and interactive design, healthcare practice, professional practice in construction, operations management, history with English, illustration arts, law, leadership & management, marine science/technology, psychology with sociology, sport and exercise science, sustainable construction and the built environment, teaching & learning, three dimensional design, tourism, hospitality and events management, yacht operations, PGCE (Education & training); FdSc, FdA, BSc(Hons), CertHE

TRURO & PENWITH COLLEGE
www.trurocollege.ac.uk

action photography, archaeology, applied media, applied social science, applied computing technologies, applied psychology, archaeology, biomedical science/studies, bioscience, business, childhood education, children & young people's workforce, commercial music performance & production, applied/computer technology, computer games design & production, community studies (development & youth work), counselling studies, early childhood education (3-8 yrs), education/and training, education in lifelong learning sector, English studies, exercise, health & fitness/nutrition, health & social care, geography & sociology/environment, history & heritage, human behaviour studies, illustration (digital), illustration, interior design practice, law, managing business resources, media advertising/moving images, photography & moving image,, music performance, outdoor education, photography & digital imaging, public services, PGCE, silversmithing & jewellery, sports coaching & performance/rehabilitation, web technology; BA(Hons), BSc(Hons), FdA, FdSc, PCET, PGCE, UnivCert/Dip, CertHE

UNIVERSITY OF PORTSMOUTH
www.port.ac.uk

Portsmouth Business School;
www.port.ac.uk/departments/faculties/
portsmouthbusinessschool

Accounting & Finance, Economics, Human Resource & Marketing Management, Law, Strategy & Business Systems

accountancy and financial management, accounting and business, accounting with finance, business and management/supply change management, business economics, business with business communication, digital marketing, economics and management, economics, finance and banking, finance with business communication, financial management for business, hospitality management, hospitality management with tourism, HRM with psychology, international business, law, law with business/business/communication/criminology/international relations, leadership & marketing, business and management, marketing, marketing with psychology

Postgraduate; accounting and finance, business administration (DBA), business and management, business economics, finance and banking, coaching and development, corporate finance, corporate governance and law, digital marketing, economics, finance & banking, finance, forensic accounting, HRD, HRM, innovation management and entrepreneurship, international finance and banking, international HRM, law, leadership and management, marketing, MBA (executive), project management, risk, crisis and resilience management, sales management, strategic quality management, strategic quality management; BA(Hons), BSc(Hons), MSc, BSc(Econ)(Hons), PGDip/Cert, MPhil, PhD, LlB, LlM, MBA, DBA, Exec MBA

Faculty of Creative and Cultural Industries; www.port.ac.uk/ departments/faculties/facultyofcreative artsandindustries

Portsmouth School of Architecture; www.port.ac.uk/departments/academic/ architecture/

architecture, interior architecture/ & design, sustainable architecture, urban design, historic building conservation; BA(Hons), MA, MArch, MSc

School of Art & Design; www.port.ac.uk/ school-of art-and-design

creative visualisation design, fashion & textile design, fine art, graphic design, illustration, photography; BA(Hons), MA

School of Media & Performing Arts; www.port.ac.uk/school-of-media-and-performing-arts

creative & media writing, drama/& performance, English/film studies & creative writing, media & communication, creative writing, media studies/& entertainment technology, music theatre; BA(Hons), MA, MRes

School of Creative Technologies; www.port.ac.uk/departments/academic/ct

animation/with business communication, computer animation/with business communication, computer games/enterprise/technology/with business communication, digital media, film production, entertainment technology with business communication, music and sound technology, TV and broadcasting/ with business communication, film & TV, mobile media applications, creative professional practice; BA(Hons), BSc(Hons), FdSc, MSc

Faculty of Humanities and Social Sciences; www.port.ac.uk/ departments/faculties/ facultyofhumanities

Institute of Criminal Justice Studies; www.port.ac.uk/departments/academic/ icjs

counter fraud and criminal justice studies, crime and criminology/criminal justice/forensic studies, criminology with psychology, law with criminology, policing and investigation, risk and security management

Postgrad; counter fraud and counter corruption studies, crime science, criminology & criminal justice/forensic studies/psychology, forensic studies, investigation and intelligence, criminology and criminal justice/criminal psychology, international criminal justice, policing, policy and leadership, criminal justice, security risk management, security management; BSc(Hons), FdA, LlB, MSc, DCrim Studs, DCrim, ProfDoc

School of Education and Continuing Studies; www.port.ac.uk/school-of-education-and-continuing-studies

childhood & youth studies/with psychology, early childhood studies/with psychology, early years care & education, education & training studies, education studies, education leadership & management, further education & training, humanities & social science, PGCE in numerous subject courses/post-compulsory education/schools direct/teacher training, learning support, learning & teaching; BA(Hons), CertEd, FdA, MA, MSc, PGCE, PGCert, EYPS

School of Languages & Area Studies; www.port.ac.uk/school-of-languages-and-area-studies

American studies & history, applied languages, combined modern languages, English & American studies, English language, European studies/ & international relations, French/German studies, humanities & social science, international development studies/business communication/& languages, international relations & language, international trade & business communication, logistics & business communications, languages & business communication/European studies/law, logistics, Spanish studies, communication & applied linguistics, Spanish & Latin American studies, international transport & business, applied linguistics & TESOL, translation studies; BA(Hons), MA

School of Social, Historical and Literary Studies; www.port.ac.uk/school-of-social-historical-and-literary-studies

English & history/media studies/languages & literature, English with psychology, government, history/ & politics, history of war, culture & society, international relations & history/politics, journalism/with English literature/language, politics, sociology/& criminology/psychology; Postgraduate; literature, history, history of war, international relations, European politics, literature, culture & identity/society, humanities & social science, public administration; BA(Hons), BSc(Hons), MPA, Sciences & Social WorkSc

Faculty of Science; www.port.ac.uk/departments/faculties/facultyofscience

School of Biological Sciences; www.port.ac.uk/school-of-biological-sciences

applied aquatic biology, biology, biochemistry, marine biology, science; BSc(Hons), MSc, MPhil, PhD, MRes

School of Earth & Environmental Sciences; www.port.ac.uk/school-of earth-and-environmental sciences

engineering geology/& geotechnics, environmental geology/& contamination, crisis & disaster management, environmental science, geological & environmental hazards, geology, marine environmental science, palaeontology, applied physics, physics, astronomy & cosmology, science; BScHons), MEng(Hons), MSc, MRes, MPhys

Dept of Geography; www.port.ac.uk/geography

geography, coastal marine resources management, GIS, human geography, physical geography, science; BA(Hons), BSc(Hons), MSc, MRes

The Dental Academy; www.port.ac.uk/dentalacademy

dental hygiene/therapy/nursing, professional courses; BSc(Hons), CertHE

School of Health Sciences & Social Work; www.port.ac.uk/shssw

health & social care, human communication science, speech, language & communication, operating dept practice, paramedic science, social work, radiography (diagnostic/therapeutic), science, optometry, systemic reviews in health; DipHE; GradDip, PGCert, BSc(Hons), MSc, ProfDoc, MOptom

Pharmacy & Biomedical Sciences; www.port.ac.uk/pharmacy

biomedical science, pharmacy/practice, pharmacology, biomedicine, science; FdSc, BSc(Hons), MSc, MRes, MPharm(Hons)

Psychology; www.port.ac.uk/psychology

psychology, forensic psychology, psychology of learning disabilities, psychological health law, science; BSc(Hons), MSc, PGCert, MPhil, PhD, MRes, ProfDoc

Sport & Exercise Science; www.port.ac.uk/sportscience

sport & exercise science/psychology, exercise & fitness management, sport management with business communication, sports development/business management/performance, sports science & management, clinical exercise science, science; BSc(Hons), MSc, MRes

Faculty of Technology; www.port.ac.uk/departments/faculties/facultyoftechnology

Civil Engineering & Surveying; www.port.ac.uk/sces

civil engineering, construction engineering management, property development, civil engineering with environmental/geotechnical/structural engineering, construction project management, building/quantity surveying, technology; BSc(Hons), BEng(Hons), MEng, MSc, MRes

Computing; www.port.ac.uk/comp

business information systems, computer science, computing & information systems/security, computing security, forensic computing/information technology, technology, software engineering, web technologies; BSc(Hons), MSc, MRes

Engineering; www.port.ac.uk/eng

computer-aided product design, computer engineering/networks, electronic engineering, electronic systems engineering, engineering & technology, innovation engineering, mechanical & manufacturing engineering, mechanical engineering, petroleum engineering, product design innovation; Postgraduate; adv manufacturing technology, communication network planning/administration & management/systems engineering, energy & power systems management, technology management, medical technology, petroleum & gas engineering; BSc(Hons), BEng(Hons), MEng, MSc, MRes

Learning at Work; www.port.ac.uk/learningatwork

occupational health & safety at work, partnership technology; PGCert, MA, MSc

Mathematics; www.port.ac.uk/maths

mathematics, mathematics for finance & management/with statistics, logistics & transportation/

supply chain management, technology; BSc(Hons),MSc, PGCert/Dip, MPhil, PhD, MRes

QUEEN MARGARET UNIVERSITY COLLEGE
www.qmu.ac.uk

nutrition, nutrition and food science, physical activity, health and wellbeing, applied pharmacology, human biology, applied nursing, podiatry, radiography, occupational therapy, physiotherapy, diagnostic radiography, dietetics, hearing aid audiology, nursing, occupational therapy, physiotherapy, podiatry, speech and language therapy,therapeutic radiography, international hospitality and tourism management, business management, acting for stage and screen, costume design and construction, drama and performance, psychology, psychology and sociology, public sociology, events management, PR & media, PR, marketing & events, film and media, media, theatre and film

Postgraduate Courses; international management and leadership, MBA, international management and leadership with tourism/events/family and smaller enterprises, MBA; family and smaller enterprises/tourism, arts, festival and cultural management, culture and creative enterprise, stage management,

dietetics, public health nutrition, collaborative working: education and therapy, professional and higher education, dispute resolution, public administration/governance, gastronomy, international management and leadership with hospitality, hospitality, applied social development, global health, health in fragile and conflict-affected states, sexual and reproductive health, social development and health, social justice, development and health, cognitive behavioural therapy, palliative care, person centred practice (district nursing/health visiting/school nursing), music/occupational/art/occupational/play therapy, physiotherapy, diabetes, podiatry, theory of podiatric surgery,strategic communication and PR, health and social sciences, diagnostic radiography, mammography, medical imaging ((ultrasound)/(clinical reporting), radiotherapy/and oncology, rehabilitative audiology; BA/BA(Hons), BSc/BSc(Hons), MA, MBA, PGDipCert, MSc, PhD, ProfDoc, HECert/Dip, MRes, MPA

UNIVERSITY OF READING
www.reading.ac.uk

Faculty of Arts & Humanities; www.reading.ac.uk/fah

School of Arts & Communication Design; www.reading.ac.uk/sacd

art, film, film & theatre, graphic communication, fine art, history of art, theatre, art and theatre/history of art/philosophy/psychology, film, theatre & TV, Samuel Beckett, book design, creative enterprise (communication design/art/film), typeface design, typography & graphic communication; BA(Hons), MA, MA(Res), MFA, MPhil, PhD

School of Humanities; www.reading.ac.uk/humanities

Classics: ancient history, classics, classical studies, ancient history and archaeology, archaeology and classical studies, ancient history and history, classical and medieval studies/English/history of art, museum and classical studies, classics and ancient history, the

classical tradition, the city of Rome, ancient maritime trade and navigation

History: history, archaeology/ancient history and history, history and economics/English/French/German/international relations/Italian/philosophy, history and politics

Philosophy: philosophy, ethics value and philosophy, PPE philosophy politics and economics, philosophy and classical studies/English literature/international relations/politics, art and philosophy, history of art/psychology/history and philosophy, ethics and political theory

BA(Hons), MA, MPhil, PhD

School of Literature & Languages

Dept of Modern Languages & European Studies; www. reading.ac.uk/modern-languages-and-european-studies/mles-home

European Studies: European studies, European studies with a major European language

French Studies: French studies, European studies with French, French and German/Italian/Spanish/economics/English language/English literature/history/international relations/management, international management and business administration with French

German Studies: German studies, European studies with German, German and French/ Italian/Spanish/economics/English language/English literature/history/international relations/management, international management and business administration with German

Italian Studies: Italian studies, European studies with Italian, Italian and German/Spanish/economics/English language/English literature/history/international relations/management, international management and business administration with Italian

Spanish Studies: European studies with Spanish, Spanish and French/Italian/German/English language/English literature/history/management, international management & business

Postgrad: Franco-British history, Modern Italian history, French studies, German studies, Italian Studies; BA(Hons), MA, MA(Res), PhD

Dept of English Language & Applied Linguistics; www. reading.ac.uk/english-language-and-applied-linguistics/elel/home.aspx

English language/literature, applied linguistics, TESOL, French/German/Italian/Spanish & English language; BA(Hons), MA, MA(Res), PhD

Dept of English Literature; www.reading.ac.uk/english-literature

English literature, English literature and Italian/politics/German/French/ international relations/classical studies/French/history/philosophy and English literature/art, English literature and film and theatre, English literature and film/theatre, English language and literature, Spanish and English literature; Postgrad; English, children's literature, early modern studies, Samuel Beckett, children's literature and writing and publishing history; BA(Hons), MA, MA(Res), PhD

Faculty of Social Sciences; www.reading.ac.uk/internal/fss

Institute of Education; www.reading.ac.uk/education

education, theatre arts, education and deaf studies, childrens development and learning, education studies, QTS primary education with art/English/maths/music specialism, secondary ITT, postgraduate initial teacher education and training, PGCE, school direct, subject knowledge enhancement courses(chemistry, computer science, mathematics,physics), language and literacy in education: first and second language research, equity, inclusion and improvement, values in practice, education, early years teacher status, professional development, special educational needs coordinators; BA(Hons), FdA, PGCE, PhD, EdD

School of Law; www.reading.ac.uk/law

law, advanced legal studies, legal studies in Europe, completion in global crisis, conflict and disaster management, advanced legal studies, international law, human rights, international commercial law, law and economics, international corporate finance, international financial regulation, oil and gas, intellectual property law and management, international corporate law, law and economics law and society, legal history;DPhil, LlB, LLM, MARes, MRes, MSc, PhD

School of Politics & International Relations; www.reading.ac.uk/spirs

politics and international relations/economics, war, peace and international relations, English literature and international relations/politics, economics/French/Italian/philosophy/history and international relations, history/economics and politics, philosophy, politics and economics; Postgrad; international relations, diplomacy, international security studies, strategic studies, military history and strategic studies, public policy, politics and international relations; BA(Hons), MA, MPhil, MRes, PhD

The School of Economics; www.reading.ac.uk/economics

economics, economics and finance/econometrics, business economics, accounting/politics/international relations/history/French/German/Italian/ geography/mathematics & economics, economics of climate change, European studies/with optional language, philosophy, politics, economics; Postgrad; public policy, business economics, business economics in emerging economies, economics of international business, economics & finance, labour economics, urban & regional economics, political economics of development; BA(Hons), BSc(Hons), MSc, PhD

Henley Business School; www.henley.ac.uk

accounting and business/finance/management, business and management, economics & finance, entrepreneurship, entrepreneurship and management, international business and management, international management and business administration with French/German/Spanish, international business and finance, management with information technology, finance and investment banking/psychology/management, mathematics with finance & investment banking, real estate, investment and finance in property, rural property management, real estate with urban planning & development; Postgrad; accounting and financial management/international management, entrepreneurship and financing/management, international business, international business and finance, international HRM, marketing(digital marketing), international marketing, international management, health and social care management, leadership, applied management, international securities, investment and banking, capital markets, creative enterprise, regulation and compliance, corporate finance, financial engineering, financial risk management, international shipping and finance, information systems, informatics, investment management, behavioural finance, business information management, economics & finance leadership, information management (big data in business/business analytics & service design/systems analysis & design) & systems, business technology consulting, management, spatial planning and development, spatial planning and research, rural land and business management, real estate, real estate finance, corporate real estate, real estate investment and finance, conservation of the historic environment; MBA, DBA, BA(Hons), BSc(Hons), MA, MSc, PhD

Faculty of Life Sciences; www.reading.ac.uk/internal/lifesci

School of Agriculture, Policy & Development; www.reading.ac.uk/apd

agriculture, agricultural business management, animal science, consumer behaviour & marketing, development environmental & countryside management, food marketing/& business economics; Postgraduate; agriculture and development, applied international development climate change and development, communication for development, development finance, environment and development, food

security and development, agricultural economics, food economics and marketing, research agricultural and food economics;BA(Hons), BSc(Hons), MPhil, PhD

School of Biological Sciences; www.reading.ac.uk/biologicalsciences

biochemistry, biological sciences, biomedical sciences, biomedicine, ecology & wildlife conservation, microbiology, molecular medicine, plant diversity, species identification & survey skills, wildlife management & conservation, zoology; BSc(Hons), MPhil, MSc, PhD

School of Chemistry; www.reading.ac.uk/chemistry

chemistry, chemistry with forensic analytics, chemistry for life and the environment, materials chemistry, molecular chemistry, chemical research; BSc(Hons), MSc, MChem, PhD, Dip

School of Chemistry, Food & Pharmacy; www.reading.ac.uk/fcfp

chemistry, food science/technology, forensic analysis, medical chemistry, nutrition & food science, pharmacy, quality assurance; BSc(Hons), MPharm, MSc, PhD, MChem

School of Psychology & Clinical Language Sciences; www.reading.ac.uk/pcls

psychology, psychology and philosophy/neuroscience, psychological theory and practice, speech and language therapy, language sciences research methods in psychology, cognitive neuroscience, development and psychopathology, clinical aspects of psychology, evidence-based psychological treatment, speech & language therapy; PGDip/Cert, BSc(Hons), MSc, PhD, MSci

Faculty of Science; www.reading.ac.uk/internal/facsci

School of Systems Engineering; www.reading.ac.uk/sse

artificial intelligence, adv computer science/and informatics/communication, digital signal processing & communications, electronic engineering, IT, robotics; BEng, BSc(Hons), FdSc, MEng, MPhil, MRes, MSc, PhD

School of Construction Management and Engineering; www.reading.ac.uk/CME

building/quantity surveying, construction management & surveying, construction in emerging economies, construction cost management, design & management of sustainable built environment, project management, renewable energy, technology & sustainability; BSc(Hons), MPhil, MSc, PGDip, PhD

School of Mathematical & Physical Sciences; www.smps.reading.ac.uk/

mathematics, statistics, meteorology, mathematics with finance and investment banking, computational mathematics, mathematics and economics/meteorology/meteorology/ psychology/statistics, data assimilation and inverse methods in geoscience, financial engineering; BSc(Hons), MMath, MPhil, MSc, PhD

School of Human & Environmental Science; www.reading.ac.uk/shes

archaeology ancient history and archaeology, archaeology and classical studies/ history, museum studies and archaeology, environmental science, geography and economics, human geography, human and physical geography, physical geography environmental science; Postgraduate; archaeology, archaeology (medieval Europe/bioarchaeology/Middle East), environmental archaeology, environmental pollution, environmental management, human geography; BSc(Hons), MSc, MA, MPhil, PhD

ROBERT GORDON UNIVERSITY
www.rgu.ac.uk

Faculty of Health and Social Care

School of Applied Social Studies; www.rgu.ac.uk/social

applied social sciences, applied psychology, corporate social responsibility, social care/work; BA(Hons), GradCert, MSW, MSc, PGDip, PhD

School of Health Sciences; www.rgu.ac.uk/health

Health Professions; Health & Exercise Professions; Laboratory, Biomedical & Sport Sciences;

applied biomedical science, nursing, adult/ children and young people/mental health, midwifery, clinical pharmacy practice, advanced district nursing, health promotion & public health, learning, teaching and assessment (nursing and midwifery, physiotherapy, study food science and health, occupational therapy, diagnostic radiotherapy, pharmacy, physiotherapy, diagnostic radiography. applied biomedical science, sports and exercise science, biomedical science, bioscience with biomedical sciences, forensic and analytical science, nutrition and dietetics, nutrition, advanced nursing practice, clinical pharmacy practice, learning, teaching and assessment (nursing and midwifery), instrumental analytical science DNA analysis, proteomics and metabolomics, instrumental analytical science drug analysis and toxicology, instrumental analytical science oilfield chemicals, environmental science, instrumental analytical science environmental analysis, instrumental analytical science oilfield chemicals, clinical biomechanics, applied sports performance analysis; BSc(Hons), CertHE, MPhil, MSc, PhD, MNursing, BNursing, BMidW, MPhysiotherapy, PGCert, MRes, MPharm

School of Nursing & Midwifery; www.rgu.ac.uk/nursing

midwifery, occupational health practice, public health nursing, advanced nursing practice, advanced district nursing, acute/adult/children & young people/mental health; BNurs, DipHE, MPhil, MSc, PhD, MNurs, MRes, BMidW

School of Pharmacy & Life Sciences; www.rgu.ac.uk/pharmacy-life

applied/biomedical science, bioscience with biomedical sciences, forensic and analytical science, pharmacy, nutrition, nutrition and dietetics, clinical pharmacy practice, environmental science, instrumental analytical science environmental analysis/ drug analysis and toxicology/oilfield chemicals/ DNA analysis, proteomics and metabolomics, clinical pharmacy service development; MPharm, MSc, PGDip, PhD, DocProfPract

Aberdeen Business School; www.rgu.ac.uk/abs

Accounting & Finance: accounting/& finance, strategic accounting, financial management, oil & gas accounting/finance

Management: business management; international business management, management, management studies, management with HRM, project management; Postgraduate; business administration (MBA DBA, AMBA), energy management, HRM, international business, management, oil and gas management, project management, purchasing and supply chain management, quality management

Law: law, law & management, online law, construction law & arbitration, employment law & practice, international commercial law/trade, oil & gas law, Communication, Marketing & Media: fashion management, international hospitality management, journalism, management with marketing, media, PR, digital marketing, fashion management, corporate communication and public affairs, international marketing management, international tourism, journalism, events management

Information Management: information management, information & library studies, digital curation, organisational learning; BA/BA(Hons), DBA, LlB, LlM, MBA, MPA,MPhil, PhD, MSc, DInfSci, Grad Cert, PGDip/Cert

Faculty of Design & Technology

School of Computing, Science & Digital Media; www.rgu.ac.uk/computing

computer science, computer network management & design, cyber security, information & network security, data science, digital media, software engineering/development, IT for oil & gas industry; BSc(Hons), MSc, PGCert/Dip, PhD

School of Engineering; www.rgu.ac.uk/eng

electrical & electronic engineering, engineering management, mechanical engineering, offshore engineering, oil & gas/drilling & well engineering, energy & sustainability, offshore renewables/oil & gas engineering, professional engineering, renewable energy, subsea engineering, petroleum engineering; BSc(Hons), BEng, MEng, MPhil, MSc, PhD

Grays School of Art, Design & Craft; www.rgu.ac.uk/grays

art & design, commercial photography/design, contemporary art practice, fashion design, painting, 3D design contextualised practice; BA/BA(Hons), BDes/BDes(Hons), MDes, MRes, PGDip/MA, MFA

The Scott Sunderland School of Architecture and Built Environment; www.rgu.ac.uk/sss

architectural studies/technology, architecture, architectural/construction technology, construction/project management, design management, quantity/building surveying, commercial practice for the energy sectors, visualisation in architecture and the built environment; GradDip, MArch, MSc, PhD, BSc(Hons)

ROEHAMPTON UNIVERSITY
www.roehampton.ac.uk

Dept of Dance; www.roehampton.ac.uk/dance

dance studies, dance anthropology/choreography, choreography/& performance, dance politics & sociology/philosophy & history; BA, MA, PGDip/Cert, MRes, MFA

Dept of Drama, Theatre & Performance; www.roehampton.ac.uk/drama-theatre-and-performance

drama, drama studies, dance, London's theatre & professional viewing, making, writing, theatre & performance studies, performance & creative research; BA(Hons), MPhil, MRes, MA, PhD

Department of Education; www.roehampton.ac.uk/education

dyslexia – identification, assessment, provision, education policy/practice, inclusive special education, education, education leadership & early childhood studies, education policy, learning & teaching, PGCE (primary education/secondary education/

schools direct (primary/secondary), special/& inclusive needs education, sounds of intent, sports coaching/practice, technology & learning design; BA(Hons), BA/BSc, EdD, FdA, Froebel Cert and Grad Cert, MA, MPhil, PhD

Dept of English & Creative Writing; www.roehampton.ac.uk/English-and-creative-writing

creative writing, English literature, children's literature; BA, MA, MPhil, PhD

Dept of Humanities; www.roehampton.ac.uk/humanities

classical civilization, classical research, history, philosophy, Christian ministry, historical research, practical theology, studies in contemporary Catholicism, theology & religious studies/leadership, ministerial theology; BA, MTh, PGDip, MPhil, PhD

Dept of Life Sciences;
www.roehampton.ac.uk/life

anthropology/of health, social anthropology, biological sciences, biomedical sciences, biomechanics, health sciences, nutrition & health, clinical neuroscience/nutrition, obesity: risks & prevention, behaviour & conservation, stress & health, social anthropology, sport psychology, psychology of sport & exercise physiology/science/psychology, zoology; BA, BSc, MSc, MPhil, PGDip, PhD

Dept of Media, Culture & Language;
www.roehampton.ac.uk/media-culture-and-language

English language and linguistics, film, French/and Spanish, journalism, mass communications, media, culture and identity, photography, Spanish, translation; Postgrad; accessibility and filmmaking, applied linguistics and TESOL, audiovisual translation, film and screen cultures, international communication in creative industries, media communication and culture, specialised translation; BSc, BA, MA, MRes, MPhil, PGDip, PhD

Dept of Psychology;
www.roehampton.ac.uk/psychology

psychology, psychology and counselling, therapeutic psychology; Postgrad; art psychotherapy, attachment studies, counselling psychology, dance movement psychotherapy, dramatherapy, integrative/counselling and psychotherapy, music therapy, play therapy, psychological science; BSc, PsychD, MA, MPhil, PhD, ProfDoc, MSc

Dept of Social Sciences;
www.roehampton.ac.uk/social-sciences

criminology, law/ & criminology, human rights/ international relations/policy & practice, sociology; BA/BSc, MA, PGDip/Cert, PhD

Roehampton Business School;
www.roehampton.ac.uk/business

accounting, business management, business management and economics/entrepreneurship, HRM, international business, marketing; Postgrad; international management, international management with finance/HRM; MBA, PGDip/Cert, BA/BSc, BSc(Hons), MSc, MPhil, PhD

THE ROYAL ACADEMY OF DANCE
www.rad.org.uk

ballet education, dance education, professional dancers' teaching, PGCE education (dance teaching); BA(Hons), CertHE, DipHE,MA

ROYAL ACADEMY OF DRAMATIC ART
www.rada.org

acting, technical theatre & stage management, theatre lab, text & performance, theatre costume; BA(Hons), MA, FdA, PGDip

ROYAL AGRICULTURAL UNIVERSITY
www.rau.ac.uk

agricultural management, agriculture, agriculture and farm management, applied equine science and business, archaeology and historic landscape conservation, bloodstock and performance horse management, British wildlife conservation, countryside management

Postgraduate; advanced farm management, agricultural technology and innovation, applied equine science, business management, food safety and quality management, agriculture, international food and agribusiness, international real estate, international rural development, research programme, real estate, real estate (aviation), real estate and land management, real estate (London), rural estate management, rural tourism management, sustainable agriculture and food security; FdSc, BSc(Hons), BSc(Hons), GradDip, MSc, MA, MBA

Degrees validated by Royal Agricultural University offered at:

ASKHAM BRYAN COLLEGE
www.askham-bryan.ac.uk

applied/agriculture, agriculture & urban forestry, animal management/& science/conservation, applied ecology & conservation, canine & feline training & behaviour, countryside management/animal collection & conservation, equine management/& science, equine business management, sport surface management, applied/horticulture, sport (outdoor & adventure education), sport training & fitness, uniformed public services, veterinary health studies/nursing; BSc, BSc(Hons), Nat Dip, FD, MSc

ROYAL BALLET SCHOOL
www.royalballetschool.org.uk

classical ballet training, performing dancing/arts, professional dance; BTEC, NatDip

ROYAL COLLEGE OF ART
www.rca.ac.uk

School of Architecture; www.rca.ac.uk/ Default.aspx?ContentID=160131
architecture, interior design, critical & historical studies, architecture research

School of Communication; www.rca.ac.uk/ Default.aspx?ContentID=160132
animation, information experience design, visual communication, communication design

School of Design; www.rca.ac.uk/ Default.aspx?ContentID=501976
design interactions/products, global innovation design/engineering, service design, vehicle design, design research

School of Fine Art; www.rca.ac.uk/ Default.aspx?ContentID=160134
critical writing & art & design, painting, photography, print, sculpture, moving image, curating art practice, fine art/research

School of Humanities; www.rca.ac.uk/ Default.aspx?ContentID=160135
critical writing in art & design, curating contemporary art, critical and historical studies, history of design, humanities research

School of Material; www.rca.ac.uk/ Default.aspx?ContentID=160133
ceramics & glass, fashion menswear/womenswear/footwear/accessories & millinery, goldsmithing, metalwork & jewellery, silversmithing, textiles, materials design; MA, MPhil, PGCert, PhD

ROYAL COLLEGE OF MUSIC
www.rcm.ac.uk

vocal performance, composition, composition for screen, conducting, contemporary culture, ensemble performance, opera, performance, historical/orchestral performance, music/in context, performance science, physics & musical performance, vocal studies; DipRCM, BMus, BSc, PGDip, MMus, DMus, GradDip, MPerf, MSc, ArtDip, MMusicEd, MComp, MPerf

THE ROYAL COLLEGE OF ORGANISTS
www.rco.org.uk

teaching, choral directing; CertRCO, ARCO, FRCO, LTRCO, DipCHD

ROYAL CONSERVATOIRE OF SCOTLAND
www.rcs.ac.uk

Music
keyboard, vocal studies, opera, strings, guitar & harp, woodwind, brass, timpani & percussion, Scottish music, composition, traditional music, conducting, jazz, Scots music/pipe music; BA(Hons), BMus(Hons), MA, MMus, MOpera, MPhil, PGDip, PhD

Drama
acting, classical & contemporary text (acting/directing), contemporary performance practice, technical & production arts & design, musical theatre/directing/performance, choreography

Dance
modern ballet

Production
production arts & design, production technology & management

Screen
filmmaking

Learning & Teaching
learning support & administration, higher art education, learning & teaching in art education/higher arts education/Gaelic arts/performance; BA(Hons), BMus(Hons), MA, MMus, MOpera, MPhil, PGDip, PhD, BEd, MEd

ROYAL NORTHERN COLLEGE OF MUSIC
www.rncm.ac.uk

advanced studies, composition, conducting & repetiteurship studies, chamber music, keyboard studies, strings, jazz, vocal studies, wind, brass & percussion, music, musicology, music psychology, performance, orchestral studies, performing arts leadership, piano for ballet, popular music practice/performance, solo performance, specialist instrument techniques; BA(Hons), MusB, MMus, MPhil, PhD, GradDip, MPerf

UNIVERSITY OF ST ANDREWS
www.st-andrews.ac.uk

Faculty of Arts

School of Art History; www-ah.st-andrews.ac.uk
art history (with numerous joint degrees), ancient history, gallery studies; GradCert, GradDip, MA, MLitt, MPhil, PhD

School of Classics; www.st-andrews.ac.uk/classics
ancient history, classics, classical studies, Greek, Latin, Greek and Latin literature, ancient history, art, archaeology, ancient philosophy and classical reception.; MA, MLitt, MPhil, PGDip, PhD

School of Economics & Finance; www.st-andrews.ac.uk/economics

analytical finance, finance, applied economics, economics, international strategy & economics, microeconomics, macroeconomics, sustainable development; Postgrad; economics, financial economics, money, banking & finance; BSc, MA, MSc, MPhil, PhD, MA/BSc

School of English; www.st-andrews.ac.uk/english

English, Postgraduate creative writing, creative writing (poetry, prose or writing for performance), medieval English, modern and contemporary literature and culture, romantic/Victorian studies, Shakespeare and Renaissance literary culture, women, writing and gender; GradDip, MA, MLitt, MPhil, PhD

School of History; www.st-andrews.ac.uk/history

history, mediaeval history, mediaeval history and archaeology, mediaeval studies, middle eastern history; Postgraduate; the book, history and techniques of analysis, Central and Eastern European studies, early modern history, environmental history, intellectual history, Iranian studies, legal and constitutional studies, mediaeval history, mediaeval studies, Middle Eastern history, modern history, Reformation studies, Scottish historical studies; GradDip, MA, DLitt, MPhil, PhD

School of International Relations; www.st-andrews.ac.uk/intrel

international relations (numerous jt hons degrees), international security studies, international political theory, Middle East & Central Asian security studies, peace & conflict, terrorism studies; MA, MLitt, MPhil, MRes, PhD

School of Management; www.st-andrews.ac.uk/management

organisations and society/analysis, management and society, analysis, organisational studies, contemporary issues in management, enterprise and creativity, corporate finance and control, international marketing, human resource management, management of change, international banking, corporate social responsibility, accountability and reporting, sustainable development and management, philanthropy and philanthropreneurs, behavioural decision making, leadership development, financial markets and investments, international business, consuming culture, public sector management, sociology of finance,

knowledge work: practice and context, advertising and marketing communications, entrepreneurship and small business development, scenario thinking, non-governmental organisations (ngos): contexts, contributions and challenges

Postgraduate; banking and finance, finance and management, HRM, international business, management, management and information technology, marketing; BSc, DipRes, MA, MLitt, MSc, MRes, PhD

School of Modern Languages; www.st-andrews.ac.uk/modlangs

Arabic, French/German/Italian studies, Russian, Central & Eastern European studies, Persian, Spanish, Spanish & Latin American studies, medieval studies; Postgraduate; comparative literature, cultural identity studies, French studies, German and comparative literature, Italian studies,Middle Eastern literary and cultural studies; DLang, MA, MLitt, MPhil, PGDip, PhD

School of Philosophical, Anthropological & Film Studies; www.st-andrews.ac.uk/philosophy

Philosophy; philosophy and ancient history/Arabic/art history/biblical studies/classical studies/classics/economics/English/French/German/ Greek/international relations/Italian/Latin/management/mathematics/mediaeval history/ modern history/ psychology/Russian/Scottish history/social anthropology/Spanish/statistics/ theological studies, logic and philosophy of science and computational science, internet computing, mathematics, physics, statistic; Postgrad; epistemology, mind and language, history of philosophy, logic and metaphysics, moral, political and legal philosophy

Social Anthropology; social anthropology, social anthropology and Arabic, ancient history, art history, classical studies, economics, English, French, geography, international relations, Italian, mediaeval history, Middle East Studies, modern history, philosophy, psychology, Russian, Scottish history, Spanish, theological studies, social anthropology with geography/economics/geography; Postgraduate; social anthropology, social anthropology and Amerindian studies, social anthropology with Pacific studies, anthropology, art and perception

Film Studies; film studies, theory & practice of research on film; Postgraduate optional modules

Music; understanding music, making music, reading opera, advanced performance, concert performance, Scottish music, electronic music

BSc, MA, MLitt, MPhil, MRes, PhD, PGDip

Faculty of Divinity

School of Divinity; www.st-andrews.ac.uk/divinity

bible & the contemporary world, biblical studies, divinity, Hebrew, New Testament, Old Testament, theological studies, analytic & exegetical theology, biblical language & literature, scripture & theology, systematic & historical theology, theology, theological studies, imagination & the arts, numerous jt honours degrees; BD, MA, MLitt, MPhil, MTheol, PGDip, PhD

Faculty of Medicine

Bute Medical School; www.medicine.st-andrews.ac.uk

health psychology, medicine, surgery, community health, molecular medicine, global health implementation; BSc, MD, MPhil, MSc, PhD, MRes

Faculty of Science

School of Biology; www.biology.st-andrews.ac.uk

behavioural biology, biochemistry, biology, biology and economics/geography/ geology/ logic and philosophy of science/ mathematics or statistics/ psychology, cell biology, ecology & conservation, evolutionary biology, marine biology, molecular biology, psychology with biology, zoology; Postgrad; marine mammal science, ecosystem-based management of marine systems, sustainable aquaculture/development; BSc, MPhil, MRes, PhD, PGDip/Cert, MSc

School of Chemistry; www.st-andrews.ac.uk/chemistry

biomolecular/chemical sciences, biological chemistry, chemical science, inorganic/physical/organic chemistry, materials chemistry, medicinal chemistry, chemistry & physics, molecular synthetic and structural chemistry, catalysis, chemical biology, surface science, theoretical chemical physics; BSc, MChem, MSci, PGDip, PhD, PGDip/MSc

School of Computer Science; www.cs.st-andrews.ac.uk

advanced/computer science, AI, human-computer interaction, information technology, computing/management & IT, networks & distributed systems, software engineering, dependable software systems, jt degrees; BSc, MPhil, MSc, PhD, MSci(Hons)

School of Geography & Geosciences; www.st-andrews.ac.uk/gg

geology, environmental earth sciences, geography & sustainable development, sustainable development & environmental economics; BSc, MA, MLitt, MPhil, MRes, MSc, PGCert, PGDip, PhD, MGeol

School of Mathematics & Statistics; www.maths.mcs.st-andrews.ac.uk

applied mathematics, applied statistics & data mining, mathematics, pure mathematics, statistics; BSc, GradDip, MA, MLitt, MMath, MPhil, MSc, PhD

School of Physics & Astronomy; www.st-andrews.ac.uk/physics

astrophysics, physics, theoretical physics & mathematics, photonics & optoelectronic devices, physics & mathematics/computer science/logic & philosophy of science/chemistry, physics & astronomy; BSc, EngDoc, MPhys, MSc, PhD, MSci

School of Psychology & Neuroscience; www.psy.st-andrews.ac.uk

evolutionary & comparative psychology, adults with learning disabilities, neuroscience, perception, psychology, psychology of dementia care, health psychology, adult support, protection & safeguarding, social psychology, perception, cognitive psychology and emotional disorders, behavioural neuroscience, evolutionary and comparative psychology, and the psychology of music; BSc, MA, MPhil, MRes, MSc, PhD

UNIVERSITY OF SALFORD
www.salford.ac.uk

College of Arts & Social Sciences;
www.famss.salford.ac.uk

School of Arts & Media;
www.salford.ac.uk/arts-media

Art and Design; design, fashion design, fashion image making and styling, film and TV set design, graphic design, graphic design, interior design, media make-up for fashion, photography, visual arts; Postgraduate; art and design: communication design/contemporary fine art /creative education

English; drama, English and creative writing/ drama, English language, English language and creative writing, English literature, English literature with English language

Journalism; journalism (broadcast/multimedia), journalism and English; Postgraduate; international journalism for digital media

Media; animation, computer and video games, English and film, film production, film studies, media production, media technology, professional broadcast techniques, television and radio, digital media; Postgraduate; media production: animation/ children's TV production/post-production for TV/TV documentary production/TVdrama production, wildlife documentary production

Music; creative music, music: creative music technology/ music: musical arts/ popular music and recording; Postgraduate; music

Performance; dance

Performing Arts; comedy writing & performance, media and performance, theatre and performance practice; Postgraduate; TV and radio scriptwriting

Politics and Contemporary History; contemporary history and politics, contemporary military and international history, international politics and security, international relations and politics, politics; Postgraduate; intelligence and security studies, terrorism and security

English and Creative Writing; Postgraduate creative writing: innovation and experiment, literature, culture and modernity

TESOL and Linguistics; Postgraduate; TESOL and Applied Linguistics

BA(Hons), BSc(Hons), PGDip, MA, PGDip/Cert, PhD, MRes

College of Business & Law;
www.salford.ac.uk/cbl

Salford Business School;
www.salford.ac.uk/business-school

accounting and finance, business and economics, business and events management, business and financial management/ management/hospitality management/marketing/tourism management, business information technology, business management with law, business management with sport, corporate law, international events management, law, law (media and digital industries), law with criminology, law with management, marketing

Postgraduate; accounting and finance, digital marketing, MBA executive education leadership, financial services management, global management, HRM and development, information systems management, international banking and finance, international business, international business with law, international commercial law, international corporate finance, international events management, international management, Islamic banking and finance, management, marketing, executive education leadership, procurement, logistics and supply chain management, project management, risk and crisis management (food safety assurance), social business and sustainable marketing; Salford MBA; BA(Hons), BSc(Hons), CertHE, DipHE, FD, GradCert/Dip, LlM, MA, MSc, MBA, MPhil, ProfDip, ProfPGDip, PhD

Salford Law School; www.salford.ac.uk/law

construction law & practice, environmental/health case law, international business law & regulation, international social justice, law/& criminality/finance/ Spanish, law, law (media & digital industries), corporate law, law with criminology/management; LlB, LlM, MA, MSc, PGCert/Dip

College of Health & Social Care;
www.fhsc.salford.ac.uk

School of Health Sciences;
www.salford.ac.uk/health-sciences

diagnostic radiography, exercise, physical activity and health, occupational therapy, physiotherapy, podiatry, prosthetics and orthotics, psychology, psychology and counselling, psychology and criminology, sport rehabilitation, sport science (human performance, performance analysis, strength & conditioning), public health

Postgrad; advanced medical imaging, advanced occupational therapy, advanced physiotherapy, applied psychology (addictions), cancer survivorship, clinical gait analysis, geriatric medicine, media psychology, nuclear medicine imaging, occupational and vocational rehabilitation, public health, service transformation and integration in health and social care, sports injury rehabilitation, strength and conditioning, trauma and orthopaedics (lower limb/spinal/upper limb), ultrasound imaging; BSc(Hons), MSc, PGDip/PGCert, MPhil, PhD

School of Nursing, Midwifery & Social Work; www.salford.ac.uk/nmsw

counselling and psychotherapy: professional practice, criminology/and sociology, enhancing professional health care practice, integrated practice in learning disabilities nursing and social work, midwifery, nursing (adult/children and young people's/mental health), social policy, social work, sociology

Postgrad; advanced counselling & psychotherapy studies, advanced practice (health and social care), applied social work practice, cognitive behavioural therapy/psychotherapy, counselling and psychotherapy studies, dementia: care and the enabling environment, diabetes care, leadership and management for healthcare practice, leading education for health and social care reform, leading education in practice: midwifery, nursing/ (adult, mental health or children & young people), nursing: research, practice, neuroscience, international, palliative and end of life care, social policy, social work, the criminal justice process, health & social care; BSc(Hons), MA, ProfDoc, MSc, PGDip/PGCert

College of Science & Technology; www.fsee.salford.ac.uk

School of the Built Environment; www.sobe.salford.ac.uk

architecture, architectural design & technology, BIM & integrated design, building/quantity surveying,

construction, construction project management, construction law & practice/management, project management in construction, real estate & property management; BSc(Hons), DBEnv, DConstMangt, DRealEst, MSc, MPhil, PGDip/Cert, PhD, ProfDoc

School of Computing, Science & Engineering; www.cse.salford.ac.uk

audio acoustics, adv control systems, aeronautical engineering, aircraft engineering/technology with pilot studies, audio production, civil/& architectural engineering, computer networks/science, mathematics, mechanical engineering, petroleum & mechanical engineering/gas engineering, professional sound & video technology, pure & applied/physics, robotics & embedded systems/automation, software engineering; Postgraduate; aerospace engineering, structural engineering, transport engineering and planning, data telecommunications networks, advanced computer science, databases and web-based systems, software engineering, gas engineering and management, industrial and commercial combustion engineering, advanced control systems, robotics and automation; BEng, BSc(Hons), HND, MEng, MEnt(Tech), MPhys, MSc, PGDip, PG(Tech)

School of Environmental & Life Sciences; www.els.salford.ac.uk

environmental health, environmental management, environmental studies, geography, human biology and infectious diseases, wildlife and practical conservation, wildlife conservation with zoo biology

Postgrad; environmental and public health, environmental assessment and management, environmental modelling, GIS, molecular, occupational safety, health and the environment, safety, health and environment, wildlife documentary production; BSc(Hons), BA(Hons), MSc, MA, FD, PGDip

Degrees validated by University of Salford offered at:

RIVERSIDE COLLEGE, HALTON
www.riversidecollege.ac.uk

sport coaching and sport development, sport coaching, counselling, education, health & social care; Dip, FD, FdSc, BSc(Hons), PCET

UNIVERSITY OF SHEFFIELD
www.sheffield.ac.uk

Faculty of Arts & Humanities; www.sheffield.ac.uk/faculty/arts-and-humanities

Dept of Archaeology; www.sheffield.ac.uk/archaeology

archaeology, classical and historical archaeology, prehistoric archaeology, archaeology and history/languages/religion, archaeology, religion, theology and the Bible; Postgrad; Aegean archaeology, archaeology of the classical Mediterranean, medieval archaeology, landscape archaeology, cultural material studies, osteoarchaeology, environmental archaeology and palaeoeconomy, human osteology and funerary archaeology, palaeoanthropology; BA(Hons), BSc(Hons), MA, MPhil, MSc, PhD, MSt

School of English Literature, Language and Linguistics; www.sheffield.ac.uk/english

18th/19th-century studies, applied linguistics with TESOL, creative writing, English literature, English language & linguistics,/literature language acquisition, language & literature/linguistics, English & theatre, theatre & performance. triple/double honours, English Lit with numerous range of subjects; BA(Hons), MA, MPhil, PhD

Dept of French; www.sheffield.ac.uk/french

French studies, French & archaeology/business management/economics/English/German/Hispanic studies /history/linguistics/music/philosophy/politics/religion/Russian, modern languages, French & Dutch, Czech, Japanese & Luxembourg, Chinese studies, Polish; BA(Hons), MA, MPhil, PhD

Dept of Germanic Studies; www.sheffield.ac.uk/german

German studies, German & archaeology/business management/ economics/English/French/Hispanic studies/history/linguistics/music/philosophy/politics/religion/Russian/Luxembourg studies, modern languages, 19th century German literary studies, 20th century German literary writing, modern German thought, post-war German politics, modern German political culture, Dutch literature since 1945, linguistics of Dutch, linguistics of German; comparative Germanic linguistics; BA(Hons), MPhil, PhD

Dept of Hispanic Studies; www.sheffield.ac.uk/hispanic

Hispanic studies & archaeology/business management/economics/ English/ French/history/linguistics/music/philosophy/politics/religion/Russian, applied Hispanic studies, Catalan studies, Japanese, Polish, Chinese studies, Czech, Latin American studies, Portuguese studies, modern language studies; BA(Hons), MA, MPhil, PhD

Dept of History; www.sheffield.ac.uk/history

history, American history, early/modern history, historical research, international/medieval history, numerous dual honours degrees; BA(Hons), MA, MPhil, PhD

School of Languages & Cultures; www.sheffield.ac.uk/slc

Catalan, Czech, Dutch, French, Germanic studies, Hispanic studies, cultural history, crossways in cultural narratives, intercultural communication/& international development, modern languages, multilingual information & management Polish, Russian, Russian and Slavonic studies, Spanish, Latin American, Luxembourgish, Japanese, screen translation, translation studies, numerous jt degrees; BA(Hons), MA, MPhil, PhD

Department of Music; www.sheffield.ac.uk/music

music, performance, composition, musicology, ethnomusicology, music psychology, music technology, music performance studies, musicology & composition, traditional music of the British Isles, sonic arts, world music, numerous jt degrees, music psychology in education, psychology of music; BA(Hons), BMus(Hons), DPhil, MA, MMus, PhD

Dept of Philosophy; www.sheffield.ac.uk/philosophy

philosophy, metaphysics, epistemology, logic, philosophy of language & the mind, ethics, political theory, cognitive studies, philosophy religion, religion theology the Bible, numerous joint degrees; BA(Hons), MA, MPhil, PhD, PGDip

Dept of Religion, Theology & the Bible; www.sheffield.ac.uk/theology

archaeology, religion, theology & the bible, philosophy/French/German & religion, biblical literature and English, archaeology, religion theology & the bible, religion, theology, the bible & linguistics & religion, religion, theology & music;]Postgrad; biblical studies research, theology, ministry and theology, ministry and biblical studies, leadership, inclusion & support, theological studies, liturgy; BA(Hons), MA, PGDip/Cert

Russian & Slavonic Studies; www.sheffield.ac.uk/russian

Russian studies, Polish studies, Czech studies, translation studies, screen translation, intercultural communication, multilingual information management, modern languages, numerous jt degree courses; BA(Hons), MA, MPhil, PhD

Faculty of Engineering; www.sheffield.ac.uk/faculties/engineering

Dept of Aerospace Engineering; www.sheffield.ac.uk/aerospace

adv aerospace materials, aerospace engineering/with private pilot instruction, aerostructures & aerodynamics, adv manufacturing technologies, adv control systems & systems engineering; BEng, MEng, MPhil, MSc, PhD, PGDip, MSc(Res), MSc, MSc(Eng)

Dept of Automatic Control & Systems Engineering; www.sheffield.ac.uk/acse

adv control & systems, computer systems engineering, computational intelligence & robotics, mechatronic & robotic engineering, systems & control engineering, engineering management; BEng, MEng, MPhil, MSc, PhD

Dept of Bioengineering; www.sheffield.ac.uk/bioengineering

bioengineering, biomedical engineering, biomanufacture, biomaterials with tissue engineering, biomaterials & regenerative medicine, dental materials science, medical devices & systems; BEng, MEng, MSc

Dept of Chemical & Biological Engineering; www.sheffield.ac.uk/cbe

biological and bioprocessing engineering, biochemical engineering & industrial management, chemical engineering, chemical engineering with energy/chemistry/biotechnology/nuclear technology/modern language, environmental & energy engineering, energy engineering with industrial management, process safety & loss prevention; BEng, MEng, MPhil, MSc, MSc(Eng), PhD

Dept of Civil & Structural Engineering; www.sheffield.ac.uk/civil

civil engineering, civil and structural engineering, structural engineering and architecture, architectural engineering design, civil engineering with a modern language, architectural engineering design, earthquake and civil engineering dynamics, steel construction, structural engineering, structural and concrete engineering, water engineering; BEng, MEng, MPhil, MSc, PGDip/Cert, PhD

Dept of Computer Science; www.sheffield.ac.uk/dcs

computer science, computer science and mathematics, artificial intelligence and computer science, software engineering, information technology management for business, software development for business, physics with computer science, advanced software engineering, advanced computer science, advanced computer science (enterprise computing/verification and testing), computer science & management/with speech and language processing, data science, IT management for business, software systems and internet technology, software engineering, data communications, information systems; BEng, BSc, MComp, MEng, MPhil, MSc, MSc(Eng), PhD

Dept of Electronic & Electrical Engineering; www.sheffield.ac.uk/eee

electrical engineering, electronic engineering, electrical and electronic engineering, electronic and communications engineering, digital electronics, microelectronics, electronic & electrical engineering, advanced electrical machines, power electronics and drives, data communications, electronic and electrical engineering, semiconductor photonics and electronics,wireless communication systems; BEng, MEng, MPhil, MSc, PhD

Dept of Materials Science & Engineering; www.sheffield.ac.uk/materials

aerospace materials, nuclear materials manufacturing, adv metallurgy, materials science & engineering (biomaterials), polymers & polymer composites science & engineering, nanomaterials & materials science,, nuclear materials/engineering & science, biomaterials & regenerative medicine, material science & nanomaterials; BEng, EngD, MEng, MPhil, MSc, MRes, PhD, MMet

Dept of Mechanical Engineering; www.sheffield.ac.uk/mecheng

advanced/mechanical engineering, advanced manufacturing technologies, aerodynamics & aerostructures, mechanical engineering with Spanish/French/Italian/German/industrial management/biomechanics, nuclear technology; BEng, MEng, MPhil, MSc, MSc(Res), PhD

Faculty of Medicine, Dentistry & Health; www.sheffield.ac.uk/faculties/medicine-dentistry-health

The Medical School; www.sheffield.ac.uk/medicine

human metabolism/nutrition, infection & immunity, medicine, medical education, molecular/& genetic medicine, musculoskeletal ageing, reproductive & developmental medicine, translational oncology, orthoptics, surgery, vision & strabismus; medical education, physician's associate, medical science, clinical neurology, genomic medicine, translational neuroscience, translational pathology (neuroscience); BMedSci, MBChB, MD, PhD, PGCert/Dip

School of Clinical Dentistry; www.sheffield.ac.uk/dentalschool

clinical dentistry, dental hygiene and therapy, dental implantology, dental materials science, dental public health, dental surgery, dentistry, endodontics, diagnostic oral pathology, orthodontics, paediatric dentistry, periodontics, prosthodontics, dental public health, dental technology, restorative dentistry; BDS, ClinDent, Diploma, MSc, MClinD, MDPH, MMedSci, MPhil, PhD

Health & Related Research; www.sheffield.ac.uk/scharr

adv emergency care, clinical research, health services, public health (management & leadership), health economics & decision making, European public health (health service research/management & leadership), international health technical assessment/management & leadership; MSc, PGDip/Cert, MPH, MEuro PubHealth

Dept of Human Communication Sciences; www.sheffield.ac.uk/hcs

acquired communication disorders, cleft & speech, cleft palate studies, clinical communication studies, language & communication impairment in children, language & literacy, speech difficulties, speech & language sciences;

Dept of Infection & Immunity & cardiovascular disease; www.sheffield.ac.uk/infectionandimmunity

molecular medicine (cancer, cardiovascular, experimental medicine, genetic mechanisms,microbes & infection, translational neuroscience; BMedSci, MSc, MRCPsych

Dept of Neuroscience; www.sheffield.ac.uk/neuroscience

translational pathology (neuroscience) genomic medicine; BMedSci, MSc, MRCPsych

School of Nursing & Midwifery; www.sheffield.ac.uk/snm

acute care, cancer care, adult nursing studies, advanced practice, adv neonatal nurse practitioner, dementia care, health & social care studies/human sciences, high dependency & critical care, infection control, long term conditions, maternity care, midwifery, neonatal intensive care, nursing studies, nurse practitioner, occupational health nursing, palliative care, public health, primary/critical/cancer/neonatal intensive care, advanced paediatric nurse practitioner, dementia studies, specialist practice, advanced nursing studies, primary care and community nursing, general practice advanced nurse practitioner; BMedSci, MMedSci, MMid, MPhil, PGCert, PhD

Dept of Oncology; www.sheffield.ac.uk/oncology

clinical oncology, molecular oncology, human nutrition, ophthalmology and orthoptics, supportive care, surgical oncology,urology, inflammation and tumour targeting; MSc, MSD, PhD

The Faculty of Science; www.sheffield.ac.uk/faculties/science

Dept of Animal & Plant Sciences; www.sheffield.ac.uk/aps

biology, ecology & conservation biology, plant sciences, ecology & environment, evolution & behaviour, environmental science, plant & microbial biology, zoology; MBiolSci, PhD, MPhil, MEnvSci

Dept of Biomedical Science; www.sheffield.ac.uk/bms

biomedical science, genomic approaches to drug discovery, integrative physiology and pharmacology, sensory neuroscience, stem cell and regenerative medicine; BSc(Hons), MSc, PhD

Dept of Chemistry; www.sheffield.ac.uk/chemistry

chemistry, polymers for advanced technologies, science communication, chemical physics, chemistry with biological & medicinal chemistry; BSc, MChem, MPhil, MPhys, PhD

School of Mathematics & Statistics; www.sheffield.ac.uk/maths

mathematics, statistics, financial maths, statistics with medical applications, maths with language, science communication studies; BSc, MSc, PhD, MMath, MComp

Dept of Molecular Biology & Biotechnology; www.sheffield.ac.uk/mbb

biochemistry, biochemistry & genetics/microbiology, chemistry with biological & medical chemistry, molecular cell biology, genetics/& molecular cell biology, human & molecular biosciences, medical genetics/biochemistry, microbiology/molecular cell biology, biochemistry, microbiology, molecular biology/& biotechnology, biology, medical microbiology, science communication; BSc(Hons), MBiolSci, PhD

Dept of Physics & Astronomy; www.sheffield.ac.uk/physics

astronomy & astrophysics, physics with astrophysics/computer science/philosophy, biophysics, chemical physics, inorganic semiconductors, medical physics, particle physics & particle astrophysics, soft matter, physics, theoretical physics; BSc(Hons), MPhys, MSc, PhD

Dept of Psychology; www.sheffield.ac.uk/psychology

cognitive studies, cognitive & computational neuroscience, cognitive neuroscience & human neuroimaging, science communication, psychology, psychological research methods; BA(Hons), BSc(Hons), DClinPsych, MA, MPhil, MSc, PhD

Faculty of Social Science; www.sheffield.ac.uk/faculty/social-science

School of Architecture; www.sheffield.ac.uk/architecture

architecture, architecture and landscape, engineering and architecture, architectural and interdisciplinary studies, architecture and TRP, architecture and landscape architecture, architecture: collaborative practice; Postgraduate; digital design and interactive built environments, sustainable architecture studies, urban design, architectural design; BA(Hons), MArch, MPhil, MSc, PhD, MEng

School of East Asian Studies; www.sheffield.ac.uk/seas

Chinese studies, East Asian studies, Japanese studies, /Korean studies, jt honours degrees; Postgraduate; contemporary China, Teaching Chinese as a foreign language, contemporary Japan, East Asian business, media in East Asia; BA(Hons), MA, PhD

Dept of Economics; www.sheffield.ac.uk/economics

economics, accounting & financial management & economics, business management & economics, economics & mathematics/politics/philosophy/finance, economics & public policy, business finance & economics, finance, financial economics, economics & health economics, international finance and economics, money, banking & finance, French/German/Hispanic studies/Russian & economics; Adv Cert, BA(Hons), BSc(Hons), MSc, PhD

Sheffield School of Law; www.sheffield.ac.uk/law

law, corporate & commercial law, European law, law with French/German/Spanish law, criminology, law & criminology, international law & global justice, international criminology, international/& European law, legal practice; LlB, LlM, MAPhil, PhD, GradDip

Sheffield Management School; www.sheffield.ac.uk/management

accounting and financial management, business management, international business management, business management with Japanese studies/Chinese studies/French/German/Hispanic studies/Korean studies/Russian, accounting and financial management and economics/mathematics, business management & economics/mathematics, business management and economics/mathematics/social policy/sociology; Postgrad; accounting, governance, & financial management, creative and cultural industries management, entrepreneurship and management, finance and accounting, global marketing management, HRM, information systems management, international management, international management and marketing, leadership and management, logistics and supply chain management, management, management (international business), marketing, marketing management practice, occupational psychology, work psychology; MSc, MPhil, PhD, Sheffield MBA, Exec MBA, adv manufacturing management, MBA with engineering

Dept of Politics; www.sheffield.ac.uk/politics

politics, European law/& governance & politics, European & global affairs, international relations/political economy, global politics and law/security/justice, globalisation & development, global justice/security, governance & public policy, international relations & politics, international politics & security studies/public policy, political theory, politics with research methods, sociology with public policy, politics/& history/sociology/economics/philosophy/French/German/Russian/Hispanic studies; BA, MA, MPhil, PhD

Dept of Sociological Studies; www.sheffield.ac.uk/socstudies

business management & social policy/sociology, dementia studies, sociology/& English language/history/politics/criminology, digital media & society, integrated practice with children & families, international social change & policy, social policy/politics & sociology, sociology with public policy, social research, sociology, social work; BA(Hons), MA, MPhil, PhD

Dept of Urban Studies & Planning; www.sheffield.ac.uk/usp

cities & global development, commercial real estate, geography & planning, commercial real estate planning/& development, town & regional planning, urban studies/design & planning & planning, planning research, applied GIS, TR; BA(Hons), MA, MPlan, PhD

The School of Education; www.sheffield.ac.uk/education

applied professional studies in education, children, schools & families, education, culture & childhood, education, policy & practice, education: early childhood, globalising education: policy and practice, psychology and education, educational research, education: language and education, applied professional studies in education, teaching and learning in higher education, higher education learning, applied professional studies in education, education: early childhood education/early childhood/language & education, educational child psychology, globalising education, higher education, language, learning & teaching, literacy & learning, policy & practice, PGDE (11-18 age range in English, geography, history, mathematics, modern languages & science), school direct, psychology & education, educational research; EdD, MA, MEd, MPhil, MSc, PGDE, PGCE, PhD, PCHE, DEdPsy

Dept of Geography; www.sheffield.ac.uk/geography

geography, applied GIS, environmental change & international development, environmental science, food security & food justice, geography & planning, international development, polar & alpine change; BA(Hons), BSc(Hons), MEnvSci, PhD, MPH, MGeogSci

School of Information; www.sheffield.ac.uk/is

data science, digital library management, health informatics, information management, information systems/management, librarianship, library & information service management, multilingual information management; MA, MChem, MSc, MSc(Res), PhD/MPhil

Dept of Journalism Studies; www.sheffield.ac.uk/journalism

global/magazine journalism, journalism studies, international political communication, broadcast journalism, print journalism, science communication; BA, MPhil, PhD

Dept of Landscape; www.sheffield.ac.uk/landscape

landscape architecture, landscape management, architecture & landscape, landscape studies, landscape research; BA(Hons), BSc(Hons), MA, PGDip, PhD, MLA, BA/BSc

---

SHEFFIELD HALLAM UNIVERSITY
www.shu.ac.uk

Faculty of Arts, Computing, Engineering & Science; www.shu.ac.uk/art/faculties.aces

Art & Design; www.shu.ac.uk/prospectus/subject/art-design

art & design, arts & cultural management, fashion design/management & communication, fine art, graphic design, illustration, interior design, design (packaging/ graphics/product/interiors/illustration/fashion/jewellery & metalwork), product design: jewellery & metalwork/furniture, product design, PGCE secondary design technology/illustration; BA(Hons), MA, MArt, MDes

Computing; www.shu.ac.uk/prospectus/subject/computing

advanced computer networks, big data analytics, business information systems, computing, computer & information security, computer science, computer security with forensics, computing management/networks, data science, games/software design/development, IT with business technologies/digital media/networks, IT with business studies, IT management, information systems/security, networking professional, software engineering; BEng, BSc(Hons), FdSc, GradDip, MComp, MSc, MPhil, PhD

Engineering; www.shu.ac.uk/prospectus/subject/engineering

advanced engineering/management, aeronautical/aerospace/electronic engineering, advanced design/aeronautical materials engineering/engineering metals, automation & control engineering/control & robotics, automotive engineering, chemical engineering, computer systems engineering, electrical/ & electronic engineering, food engineering, industrial management, integrated engineering (manufacturing/materials/electrical), materials engineering, manufacturing engineering, adv/mechanical engineering, product design, railway engineering, sports technology/engineering, telecommunication & electronic engineering; BSc(Hons), BEng, FdSc, MBA, MSc, PhD, MBA

Mathematics; www.shu.ac.uk/mathematics

mathematics physics; BSc(Hons), MSc, PhD, CertHE, MA/PGDip

Media Arts; www.shu.ac.uk/prospectus/subject/media-arts

animation/& digital effects, digital media production, games design, journalism, film & media production, photography, filmmaking; BA(Hons), MA, MComp, MArt, MSc

Media, PR & Journalism; www.shu.ac.uk/prospectus/subject/media-pr-journalism

journalism, digital media production, international broadcast journalism, PR, media, sports journalism, cultural communication & computer, photography, PR/ & media, games design; BA(Hons), MA, MPhil, PhD, PGCert/Dip

Faculty of Development & Society; www.shu.ac.uk/faculties/ds/nbe

Natural & Built Environment

architectural technology, architecture, building/quantity surveying, construction, project management, built environment, environmental science/management, human/geography, GIS, planning & geography, urban regeneration planning, real estate, project management in the built environment, transport planning, urban planning/regeneration; BSc(Hons), MPhil, MSc, PGDip/Cert, PhD, MBA

Criminology & Community Justice; www.shu.ac.uk/prospectus/subject/law

law, law & criminology, applied human rights, forensic criminology/science/law/psychology/accounting, international commercial law; BEng, BSc(Hons), FdSc, MA/PGDip/PGCert, MSc

Education; www.shu.ac.uk/prospectus/subject/education-studies

Asperger syndrome, autism spectrum, design 7 technology education & QTS, early/childhood studies, early years/education with QTS/teaching, design & technology, education, educational studies with psychology & counselling, education & learning support, education: early years teaching for academic purposes, English & educational studies, knowledge enhancement in mathematics, languages & TESOL (French/Spanish/German), learning & teaching in HE/in primary education with QTS, mathematics/ science with education & QTS, mathematics with education & QTS, PE & school sport, post-16 education & training, teaching & learning in early years & the primary sector/with QTS/early years/HE, special needs coordination, education studies, primary ed with QTS, science with education & QTS, PGCE (early years education, learning & skills, mathematics education, primary, secondary,broad range of taught subjects, secondary citizenship), youth work

Teacher Education: post-16 education & FE, teach first, school direct, special educational needs coordination, teaching English for academic purposes; BA(Hons), CertE, EdD, FdA, MA, MPhil, MSc, PGCert/Dip, PhD, PGCE

English; www.shu.ac.uk/prospectus/subject/english

creative writing, writing, English & history, English/ language/literature, TESOL, English language teaching, ESOL, secondary English, English by research; BA(Hons), PGCE, MA, PGDip, MPhil, PhD

Environment; www.shu.ac.uk/prospectus/subject/environment

environmental management/science; BSc(Hons), MPlan, MSc/PGDip/PGCert

Geography; www.shu.ac.uk/prospectus/subject/geography

geography/and planning, GIS, human geography; BA(Hons), BSc(Hons), MSc, PGDip/Cert, PGCE

History; www.shu.ac.uk/prospectus/subject/history

history, English & history, criminology, politics, local & global history, imperialism & culture, history by research; PGCE, BA(Hons), MA, PGDip, MPhil, PhD

Law; www.shu.ac.uk/prospectus/subject/law

law applied human rights, international sport law in practice, global communication law, law with criminology; LlB, LLM, MSc, PGCert/Dip

Planning, Regeneration & Housing; www.shu.ac.uk/planning

geography & planning, built environment, business property management, urban planning, urban regeneration; BA(Hons), BSc(Hons), MPlanning and Transport, MSc/PGDip, DipHE, MBA

Psychology; www.shu.ac.uk/psychology

psychology, applied cognitive neuroscience, cognitive analytic therapy, criminology & psychology, developmental/health psychology, clinical cognitive neuroscience, education with psychology & counselling, psychology & sociology, sport & exercise psychology; BSc(Hons), MRes/PGDip/PGCert, MSc, ExecMBA

Sociology & Politics; www.shu.ac.uk/prospectus/subject/sociology-politics

applied social science, applied human rights, criminology/& sociology,, politics, psychology/& sociology, public health, social sciences, sociology, planning and policy; BA(Hons), GradDip, MA, MPhil/PhD, MRes/PGDip/PGCert

Stage & Screen; www.shu.ac.uk/prospectus/subject/stage-screen

animation & visual effects, film studies, film and media/production, international documentary production, performance & professional practice/for stage & screen, film studies & screenwriting; BA(Hons), FdA, MA, MArt, MA/PGDip/PGCert

Faculty of Health & Wellbeing; www.shu.ac.uk/faculties/hwb

Sport and Active Lifestyles; www.shu.ac.uk/prospectus/subject/sport-active-lifestyles

adv sport coaching practice, PE & school sport, sports development/with coaching, sport engineering/studies/coaching, sport & physical activity, physical activity, sport & health, sports studies, app/sport & exercise science, sport & exercise technology, sport business management; BA(Hons), BSc(Hons), MA, MSc, PGDip/Cert, ProfDoc, PGCE

Biosciences & Chemistry; www.shu.ac.uk/bio

analytical chemistry, biochemistry, biology, biomedical/laboratory sciences, biosciences, biotechnology, chemistry, forensic science, human biology, molecular & cell biology, pharmaceutical analysis, pharmacology and biotechnology, professional studies, secondary science; BSc(Hons), MSc/PGDip/PGCert, ProfDocBiomedSc, PGCE

Centre for Medical & Dental Education; www.shu.ac.uk/faculties/hwb/medical

MSc, PGCert/Dip

Diagnostic Radiography; www.shu.ac.uk/prospectus/subject/diagnostic-radiography

advanced diagnostic imaging practice, advancing professional practice, diagnostic radiography, medical ultrasound, radiological studies; DocProf Studies (Health and Social Care), BA(Hons), BSc(Hons), MSc/PGDip/PGCert

Nursing & Midwifery; www.shu.ac.uk/faculties/lwb/departments/nursing-midwifery

applied nursing (learning disability) and generic social work, perinatal and maternal mental health, specialist practice district nursing, specialist community public health nursing, health visiting/school nursing, acute and critical care of the child, child, adolescent and family mental health, nursing, nursing (adult/child/mental health), specialist practice district nursing, midwifery, advancing professional practice (paediatrics), approved mental health professional nursing, public health/primary & community care, health and social care leadership & management, healthcare education, maternal health care, midwifery, medical ultrasound, supportive and palliative care, primary care nursing/district nursing, professional practice (nursing/midwifery), prostate cancer care, health visiting and school nursing; AdvDip, AdvProfDev, BA(Hons), BSc(Hons), DocProfStud, FD, MSc/PGDip/PGCert

Occupational Therapy; www.shu.ac.uk/occupational

applying/occupational therapy, advancing (paediatric) practice, vocational rehabilitation; BSc(Hons), DocProf, MSc/PGDip/PGCert

Operating Department Practice; www.shu.ac.uk/odp

operating dept practice, advancing professional practice; DipHE, DocProfStud, MSc/PGDip/Cert

Paramedic Studies; www.shu.ac.uk/paramedic

paramedic practice; DipHE, MSc, PGDip/Cert, ProfDoc

Physiotherapy; www.shu.ac.uk/physio

advancing/applying physiotherapy practice, physiotherapy (practice based), adv professional practice (paediatrics), vocational rehabilitation, medical ultrasound therapy, manual therapy; BA(Hons), BSc(Hons), MSc, PGCert, PGDip, ProfDoc

Radiotherapy and Oncology; www.shu.ac.uk/radiotherapy

adv practice radiotherapy & oncology, prostrate cancer care, radiotherapy planning, radiotherapy & oncology in practice, supportive and palliative care,, radiological studies; BA(Hons), BSc(Hons), DipHE, MSc/PGDip/PGCert, ProfDoc

Social Work; www.shu.ac.uk/socialwork

applied nursing (learning disabilities) & generic social work, social work, specialist mental health practice/practitioner, working with children, young people & families, youth & community work, youth work, health and social care leadership & management; BA(Hons), GradDip, MSc, PGDip, MSW, PGCert, DocSocWork, FD

Sheffield Business School; www.shu.ac.uk/sbs

Accounting, Banking & Finance; www.shu.ac.uk/prospectus/subject/accounting-banking-finance

accounting & finance/economics, banking & finance, economics, financial management, forensic accounting, risk management, wealth management; BA(Hons), MA, MSc, PGDip/Cert

Business & Management; www.shu.ac.uk/prospectus/subject/business-management

business and management/finance/HRM/English, business administration, business administration (facilities management), business analytics/ economics/ management/finance/financial management/ HRM/marketing/ studies, business and enterprise, coaching and mentoring, economics, executive MBA (psychology/facilities management/built environment), international business with Spanish/French/German, international HRM, international business management, international business, international marketing, logistics and supply chain management, oil and gas management, managing global business, total/ quality management and organisational excellence, marketing, communications and advertising, business information systems, charity research management, coaching & mentoring, facilities management, financial management, food marketing management, global supply chain management, HRM/D, IT with business studies, HRM/HR development, leadership & management, logistics & supply chain management, organisational development & consultancy, industrial management,languages with business/tourism, sales leadership, total, strategic operations management, Exec MBAs (psychology/ facility management/built environment); BSc(Hons), DBA, FD, GradDip, Exec MBA, PGCE, MBA, MPhil, MSc, PGCert, PGDip, PhD, MRes, MBusiness

Languages; www.shu.ac.uk/prospectus/ subject/languages/

business & English, English language teaching, languages with TESOL/international business/tourism/marketing, international business studies & languages (French/German/Spanish), teaching English for academic purposes; GradDip/Cert, MPhil, PGCert, PhD

Tourism, Hospitality & Events Management; www.shu.ac.uk/prospectus/subject/ tourism-hospitality-events

tourism management, international tourism management, event management, tourism management or event management with accounting, business, economics, European studies, finance, human resources, information systems, marketing or a language; either French, German, Spanish, Italian or mandarin Chinese; Postgraduate; international tourism and hospitality management

BSc(Hons), FdSc, MA, MPhil, MSc, PGCert, PGDip, PhD

UNIVERSITY OF SOUTH WALES
www.southwales.ac.uk

Faculty of Creative Industries; www.southwales.ac.uk

School of Drama & Music; www.southwales.ac.uk/drama-music

Dance & Performance

dance, performance & media, scriptwriting, theatre & drama, performing arts, scriptwriting; Postgrad; drama

Music & Sound

music business, contemporary music performance, pop & commercial music, creative industries (popular music technology), music technology, sound engineering; Postgrad; music therapy, songwriting and production, music engineering and production

School of Media; www.southwales.ac.uk/ school/media

Journalism & Media

film studies, journalism, sports journalism, media production, media, culture and journalism, performance and media, photojournalism, scriptwriting; Postgrad; drama, research media

Film

film, creative industries (film and video), documentary film and TV, film studies; Postgrad; film producing

Animation, Games & Visual Effects

animation (2D and stop motion), computer animation, computer games design, computer games enterprise, game art, visual effects and motion graphics, art & design; Postgrad; animation, computer animation, games enterprise, visual effects

School of Art & Design; www.southwales.ac.uk/art-design

Art

creative & therapeutic art, art practice, art & design, art psychotherapy, arts practice, art health & wellbeing

Design

illustration, advertising design, computer games design, fashion design, fashion promotion, graphic communication, interior design, TV and film set design, fashion marketing and retail design; Postgrad; graphic communication,

Photography

photography, creative industries (photography, photojournalism, documentary photography; Postgrad; documentary photography

Fashion

fashion design/promotion/marketing/retail design, fashion retailing; BA(Hons), FdA, MFA, MA, MPhil, DDes, BMus(Hons), MSc, PhD

Faculty of Computing, Engineering & Science; www.southwales.ac.uk/ computing-maths

Computing & Mathematics

Computing

computer science, computer systems engineering/ applications development, computer forensics, computer games development, computer security, computing, computing mathematics, information communication technology, information technology management for business; Postgrad; computer forensics, computer science, computer systems security, computing and information systems, cyber security

Mathematics

mathematics, computing mathematics

Engineering; www.southwales.ac.uk/school-engineering

Aerospace Engineering

aeronautical engineering, aircraft maintenance engineering

Civil Engineering

civil engineering; Postgrad; civil engineering and environmental management, civil and structural engineering

Electrical & Electronic Engineering

electrical and electronic engineering; Postgrad; electronics and information technology, embedded systems design, mobile and satellite communications, optoelectronics

Mechanical Engineering

mechanical engineering, professional engineering

Renewable Energy

renewable energy & resource management,

Lighting & Live Event Technology

live event technology, lighting design & technology

Property, Construction & Surveying

project management (surveying) quantity surveying & commercial management, surveying Postgrad; construction project management, safety, health & environmental management

BSc(Hons), BA(Hons), BEng(Hons), MEng, MSc, UnivHCert, MComp(Hons), MMus

Faculty of Business & Society; www.southwales.ac.uk/faculty-business-society

Business School; www.southwales.ac.uk/bus-school

business management, business, business studies, business and accounting/finance/HRM/management/marketing/supply chain management, event management, HRM, international business, logistics and supply chain management, marketing, retail management, finance and investment, business studies; Postgrad; procurement and supply, business administration, engineering management, fashion marketing, HRM, international business and enterprise, international logistics and supply chain management, leadership and management, management, marketing, project management, PR, strategic digital marketing, strategic procurement management, (MBA)

School of Humanities & Social Sciences; www.southwales.ac.uk/hass

History

history, history with English, history by research

English & Creative Writing

English, English & history, English by research, writing, English & creative writing, TESOL

Religious Studies

religious studies, Buddhist studies

Public Services & Emergency Services

public services, global/governance, governance, health & public services management

Criminology

criminology & criminal justice/& youth justice, forensic science & criminology, criminology & law/psychology/sociology, criminology & social justice criminal justice, crime & justice, major crime investigation management, working with adult & youth offenders

Sociology

sociology with criminology & social justice/education/psychology

Combined studies

combined studies

Welsh

Welsh in the workplace

Youth & Community

childhood studies, working for/with children & young people, youth & community work/youth justice, social sciences

School of Law, Accounting & Finance; www.southwales.ac.uk

Accounting & Finance

accounting and finance, forensic accounting, finance and investment, financial planning, investment and risk; Postgrad; accounting and finance/financial management, finance/and investment, forensic audit and accounting, management and development of international financial systems, trading and risk

Law

law, legal practice, law and business, criminology and criminal justice and law, law with criminology and criminal justice, law with Welsh in the workplace; Postgrad; international commercial law, law, legal practice

BA(Hons), BA/BSc, BSc(Hons), DocPublServ, FCert, FdA, GradDip Law, LlB(Hons), LlM/PhD, MA/PDip/Cert, MSc, CertHE, PGDip, MBA, DBA

Faculty of Life Science & Education

School of Psychology, Early Years & Therapeutic Studies/pet; fbs.glam.ac.uk/psychology
Psychology
criminology and criminal justice with psychology, psychology, psychology with behaviour analysis/cognitive behavioural therapy/counselling/criminology & criminal justice/developmental disorders/education, sociology with psychology
Postgrad; behaviour analysis and therapy, business psychology, clinical and abnormal psychology, consultative supervision, counselling skills developmental disorders, health psychology, play therapy, play and therapeutic play, psychology by research, systemic/psychotherapy, behaviour analysis supervised practice, consultative supervision
Psychotherapy & Counselling
creative and therapeutic arts; Postgrad; systemic counselling, art psychotherapy, consultative supervision, counselling children and young people, integrative counselling and psychotherapy, music therapy, cognitive behavioural psychotherapy, systemic counselling/psychotherapy

School of Education; www.southwales.ac.uk/school-education
Welsh in the workplace with education, early years education and practice, history with education, childhood development, childhood studies, psychology/sociology with education, childhood; Postgrad; child and adolescent mental health, developing professional practice in higher education, early years, ICT & education, leadership & management (education/ post compulsory education and training/FE/PCET), professional practice in higher education, special educational needs (SEN / autistic spectrum), teaching English (TEAL/ TESOL/TEYL), teaching, primary studies with QTS, secondary design and technology/mathematics with ICT/with science, secondary science with ICT, mathematics with QTS, introduction to secondary teaching
Postgraduate and Professional; Advanced Certificate in Teaching Adult Literacy and Communication/teaching adult numeracy and maths, ESOL, PGCE post compulsory education and training/secondary design and technology with QTS, adult literacy and communication/adult numeracy and maths/ESOL), professional graduate certificate in education (ESOL), education (PCET), returning and supply teachers

Health, Sport & Professional Practice
Sport
sports leadership and development, football coaching and performance, football coaching, development and administration, rugby coaching and performance, sport psychology, sport and exercise science, sports coaching, sports coaching and performance, sports studies, strength and conditioning, community football coaching and development, football coaching and development, rugby coaching and development
Postgraduate; sport, health and exercise science, sports coaching and performance, sports and exercise medicine,
Chiropractic
chiropractic
Social Work & Social Care Management
social work, health & social care, sociology
Policing & Security
police sciences; Postgrad; community and partnerships, international policing

Care Science; www.southwales.ac.uk/care
Nursing & Health Science
nursing (adult/child health/learning disabilities/mental health), health care nursing support worker education, community health and wellbeing, acute and critical care, community health studies (specialist practitioner community children's nursing/district nursing), community health studies (specialist practitioner general practice nursing), community mental health practice, professional practice (health care studies/ nursing/violence reduction), specialist community public health nursing (health visiting/occupational health nursing/school nursing), occupational health (nursing/technician); Postgraduate; professional practice, advanced clinical practitioner, clinical practice for nurses and midwives, community health studies (children's community nursing/ district nursing/ practice nursing), diabetes, disaster healthcare, education for health and social care professionals, endocrinology, obesity and weight management, preventative cardiovascular medicine, professional practice (cancer and palliative care/learning disability/mental health/vulnerable person), public health, respiratory medicine, rheumatology, specialist community public health nursing health visiting/school nursing), clinical endodontics, public health and social care professionals, palliative care, genomic medicine and healthcare, obesity and weight management, preventative cardiovascular medicine, respiratory medicine, rheumatology, return to practice

Midwifery

midwifery, professional practice (midwifery); BA(Hons), BSc(Hons), BN, FoundCerts, CertHE, MSc, BMid, PGCert/Dip, FD

UNIVERSITY OF SOUTHAMPTON
www.soton.ac.uk

Faculty of Business and Law; www.southampton.ac.uk/faculties/faculty_business_law.html

School of Law; www.soton.ac.uk/law

law, law/ & psychology, commercial & corporate law, crime analysis, European law/legal studies, general law, insurance law, IT & commerce, international law/business law/legal studies, maritime law; LlB, LlM, MPhil, PhD

Southampton Business School; www.sbs.ac.uk/business-school

accounting and finance business history, business analytics, business innovation, business management, business philosophy, business entrepreneurship, international marketing, marketing, management, accounting and management/finance, business analytics & management science, corporate business risk & security management, cyber risk management, digital marketing, finance, global enterprise and entrepreneurship, HRM, business administration, corporate social responsibility, international banking & financial studies/marketing, international financial markets, international management, knowledge and information systems management, leadership and management in health and social care, management science & finance, marketing analytics, marketing management, project management, risk and finance, risk management, strategy and innovation, supply chain management and logistics; BSc(Hons), MSc, PhD, MBA, DBA, PGCert, MPhil

Winchester School of Art; www.soton.ac.uk/wsa

advertising design/management, communication/fashion/textiles design, design/fashion management, contemporary curation, fashion & textile design, fashion design (knitwear for fashion/textiles/woven textiles/printed textiles), games design & art, graphic arts (design/illustration/photography/motion graphics), luxury brand management, photography, fine art, fashion marketing/management/& branding, global media management, textile design; BA(Hons), MA, MPhil, PhD

Faculty of Engineering & the Environment; www.southampton.ac.uk/engineering

Acoustical Engineering

acoustical engineering, acoustics & music, engineering

Aeronautics and Astronautics

aeronautics & astronautics, aeronautics & astronautics (aerodynamics/air vehicle systems design/computational engineering design/engineering management/materials and structures/spacecraft engineering

Mechanical Engineering

mechanical engineering (acoustical engineering/advanced materials/aerospace/automotive/biomedical engineering), computational engineering and design, engineering management, mechatronics, naval engineering, sustainable energy systems

Computer Science and Software Engineering

electrical and electronic engineering (EEE), electrical engineering, electromechanical engineering, electronic engineering, information technology in organisations, aerospace electronics, biomedical electronics, web science

Environmental Science

environmental management with business, environmental monitoring and modelling, environmental sciences

Audiology

healthcare science (audiology)

Civil Engineering

civil engineering/& architecture, civil & environmental engineering

Ship Science

ship science, ship science/advanced materials/engineering management/naval architecture/naval engineering/yacht & small craft, offshore engineering

Postgrad

Audiology; audiology, clinical and health research, clinical practice

Engineering; acoustical engineering, adv mechanical engineering science, aerodynamics and computation, biomedical engineering, civil engineering, coastal and marine engineering and management, computational engineering design, electronics & computer science, energy and sustainability(engineering, environment & buildings/energy resources & climate change) engineering in the coastal environment, engineering materials, marine technology, maritime engineering science (advanced materials/marine engineering/maritime computational fluid dynamics/naval architecture/offshore engineering/ maritime engineering science /yacht and small craft), mechatronics, propulsion and engine systems engineering, race car aerodynamics, sound and vibration studies, space systems engineering, surface engineering and coatings, sustainable energy technologies, transportation planning and engineering Environmental Science; biodiversity and conservation, environmental monitoring and assessment, environmental pollution control, integrated environmental studies, water resources management, unmanned aircraft systems design; BEng, MEng, BSc(Hons), MEnvSci(Hons), DClinPract, MRes, MSc, MPhil, PhD, EngD

Faculty of Health Sciences; *www.soton.ac.uk/healthsciences*

midwifery, nursing (adult and child/adult and mental health/adult/child/mental health), clinical practice, healthcare science (cardiovascular, respiratory and sleep science), healthcare: management, policy and research, occupational therapy, physiotherapy, podiatry, public health practice: specialist community public health nursing (schools nursing/occupational technology), advanced clinical practice (advanced nurse practitioner)

Postgrad; advanced clinical practice (children and young people/critical care/(district nursing/children's community nursing), advanced practice, adv neonatal practice, advanced rehabilitation technologies, clinical and health research, clinical leadership in cancer, complex care in older people, palliative and end of life care, health and rehabilitation, health sciences (standard, mental health and neonatal), nursing (adult, child, mental health), leadership and management in health and social care, low intensity cognitive behaviour therapy,midwifery, physiotherapy, trauma care, specialist community public health/ public health nursing, integrated preparatary skills; Medicine; allergy, diabetes best practice, genomic medicine, public health

BSc(Hons), BN(Hons), BMid(Hons) MSc, PGDip, MPhil, PhD, MRes, DocClinPract, PGDip

Faculty of Humanities; *www.soton.ac.uk/about/faculties/ faculty_humanities*

Archaeology; www.southampton.ac.uk/ archaeology/

archaeology, archaeology and anthropology/geography/history; Postgrad; archaeological computing (GIS and survey), archaeological computing (virtual pasts), business and heritage management, ceramic and lithic analysis for archaeologists, maritime archaeology, osteoarchaeology, palaeolithic archaeology and human origins, Rome and the Mediterranean, social archaeology

English; www.southampton.ac.uk/english

English, English and French/German/Spanish,English and history/music, English literature, language & linguistic, film/philosophy and English; Postgraduate; 20th and 21st century literature, creative writing, eighteenth-century studies, English literary studies, global Englishes, medieval and Renaissance culture

Film; www.southampton.ac.uk/film

film, film studies, film & cultural management, film and French/German/Spanish/ history/music

History; www.southampton.ac.uk/history

history, modern history, jt hons incl archaeology, English, foreign language, philosophy, modern history & politics, Jewish history & culture, 18th century studies, medieval & Renaissance culture

Modern Languages; www.southampton.ac.uk/ml/

applied English language studies, English and French/German/ Spanish, film and French/ German/ Spanish, French, French and German/ linguistic studies, French and German (linguistic studies)/ history/music/philosophy, German, German and Spanish linguistic studies, history/ music/ philosophy, German (linguistic studies) (integrated masters in languages) language and society, language learning, languages and contemporary European studies(English), management sciences/mathematics with French/ German/Spanish, modern languages management sciences/mathematics with French/ German/ Spanish, modern languages, language acquisition research, transnational studies, ELT/TESOL studies

Music; www.southampton.ac.uk/music

acoustics/English/French/German/philosophy/mathematics and music, music and management sciences; Postgrad; 18th-century studies, medieval and Renaissance culture, music (performance, composition, musicology)

Philosophy; www.southampton.ac.uk/philosophy

philosophy: jt hons degrees incl sociology, politics, mathematics, foreign language, philosophy, politics, economics, aesthetics; BA(Hons), MA, MRes, MPhil, PhD, CertHE, MMus, MA/MSc, MLang

Faculty of Medicine; www.southampton.ac.uk/faculties/ faculty_medicine.html

Medicine; www.southampton.ac.uk/medicine

allergy, public health, diabetes best practice, genomic medicine, biomedical sciences/cell biology & immunology of cancer, immunity & infection, medicine, surgery, stem cell science, nutrition, health sciences, numerous postgraduate modules; BM, MSc, BMedSci, PGDip/Cert, PhD, DM

Faculty of Natural and Environmental Sciences; www.soton.ac.uk/about/ faculties/faculty_ natural_environmental-sciences

Biological Sciences; www.soton.ac.uk/biosc

biochemistry, adv biological science, wildlife conservation, biochemistry/biomedical science, pharmacology, biology/and marine biology, neuroscience, zoology,, chemistry and biochemistry, ecology; BSc(Hons), Cert/DipHE, MPhil, PhD, BNatSci, MBiSci, MEcol, MSci, MBioSci

Chemistry; www.soton.ac.uk/chemistry

chemistry, chemistry and biochemistry/maths/medicinal sciences, electrochemistry, chemistry by research, instrumental analytical chemistry; BSc(Hons), MPhil, PhD, MSci, MChem

National Oceanography Centre, Southampton; www.noc.soton.ac.uk

marine biology, oceanography, geology, geophysics, engineering in coastal environment, marine environment & research; BSc, MSc, MSci

School of Ocean and Earth Science; www.soton.ac.uk/soes

marine biology with oceanography, oceanography, oceanography with French/physical geography, geology, geophysics, marine biology, Postgrad; ocean science, geology and geophysics, vertebrate palaeontology, engineering in the coastal environment, marine environment and resources; BSc(Hons), MSci, BNatSci, MRes, MPhil, PhD

Faculty of Physical and Applied Sciences; www.soton.ac.uk/about/faculties/ faculty_ physical-applied _sciences

Electronics and Computer Science; www.ecs.soton.ac.uk

computer science and software engineering, electrical and electronic engineering, electrical engineering, electromechanical engineering, electronic engineering, information technology in organisations, web science, biomedical electronic engineering; Postgrad; embedded computing systems, artificial intelligence, biodevices, computer science & software engineering, computer & web science, cyber security, data science, embedded systems, energy microelectronics systems design, nanoelectronics and nanotechnology, software engineering, system on chip, systems, control and signal processing, web science, web technology, wireless communications, optical fibre technologies, photonic technologies; BEng, MEng, MSc, MComp, PhD

Optoelectronics Research Centre; www.orc.soton.ac.uk

optical fibre/photonic technologies; MSc, PhD

Physics & Astronomy; www.phy.soton.ac.uk

astronomy/& space environment physics, theoretical high energy physics, space environment physics, quantum, light & matter, particle physics, physics/with astronomy/nanotechnology/space science/photonics/mathematics; BSc(Hons), European Masters, MPhy, PhD

Faculty of Social and Human Sciences; www.soton.ac.uk/about/faculties/ facultysocial_human-sciences

School of Education; www.southampton.ac.uk/education

education, education & training (primary), educational studies with psychology/training, education (management & leadership/practice & innovation/specific learning difficulties (dyslexia)/mathematics &

science), PGCE (primary, numerous secondary subjects/FE learning & skills), school direct, PCET, PGCE sciences, SKE computer sciences, subject knowledge enhancement (mathematics/computer science/biology/ physics), teacher specialism training; BSc(Hons), BA(Hons), MSc, MA(Ed), CertEd, MPhil, PhD, EdD

Geography & Environment; www.soton.ac.uk/geography

geography, geography with geology/oceanography, geology/oceanography with physical geography, population and geography; Postgrad; applied GIS and remote sensing/earth observation, GIS, sustainability, sustainability (consultancy/GIS/population/ research; BSc(Hons), BA(Hons), MA, MSc, MPhil, PhD

School of Mathematics; www.soton.ac.uk/ maths

actuarial science, mathematical studies, mathematical physics, mathematics with actuarial science/astronomy/biology/computer science/finance/music/OR/ physics/statistics/French/German, operational research & finance/statistics, mathematics, philosophy with mathematics, statistics with applications in medicine; BSc(Hons), MMath, MSc, PGDip, PhD

School of Psychology; www.southampton.ac.uk/psychology

psychology/& education/criminology/law, CBT for anxiety & depression, foundations of clinical psychology, psychology, research methods, CBT/ theory, health psychology, low intensity CBT; BSc(Hons), MSc, MPhil, PhD, PGDip

School of Social Sciences; www.southampton.ac.uk/socsci

accounting and economics, criminology, criminology and psychology, economics, economics and actuarial science/finance/management sciences/philosophy/ international relations, modern history and politics, mathematics, operational research, statistics and economics, philosophy and politics/sociology, politics, politics and economics/French/German/international relations, politics and Spanish (or Portuguese) and Latin American studies, population and geography, social policy and criminology, sociology, sociology and criminology/social policy/anthropology
Postgrad; economics, politics & international relations, social statistics & demography, sociology & social policy, gerontology, international social policy, global ageing & policy, global health; BSc(Hons), BA(Hons), MEcon, MSc, MPhil, PGDip, PhD

Southampton Statistical Sciences Research Institute; www.southampton.ac.uk/s3ri

demography, actuarial science, statistics, statistics with applications in medicine, official statistics, public health, public health, nutrition/intelligence/ global health, social statistics (research methods/ social statistics); MSc, PGDip/Cert, PhD

STAFFORDSHIRE UNIVERSITY
www.staffs.ac.uk

Faculty of Business, Education & Law; www.staffs.ac.uk/academic _depts/fbel

Staffordshire University Business School; www.staffs.ac.uk/business

Accounting & Finance: accounting & business/ finance, business administration (finance), international accounting & financial management, Islamic finance & accounting
Business, Management & Enterprise: business, business and HRM/marketing management, business management/ and enterprise, international business management, business administration (finance/international), economics for business analysis, economics of globalisation and European integration, leadership & management

Economics: economics for business analysis, economics of globalisation & European integration, business & economics
Human Resource Management: HRM, business & HRM, HR practice
Marketing: marketing management, business & marketing management, digital marketing management, professional marketing, digital strategy
Tourism & Events: tourism management, events management, visitor attraction & resort management
Professional Courses; MBA (finance/international)
BA, BSc, MA, MBA, MPhil, MSc, PGCert/Dip, PhD, PGCE, FD

School of Education; www.staffs.ac.uk/ depts_education

early childhood studies with early years teaching status (EYTS), education, PGCE; post compulsory education and training, international education, early years teacher status (EYTS), qualified teacher status (QTS), primary; PGCE (art and design/computer science/design and technology/economics and business/mathematics), qualified teacher learning and status (QLTS); Postgrad; early childhood, education, higher and professional education
BA(Hons), MA, MPhil, PhD, EdD, FD, PGCert/Dip

School of Law; www.staffs.ac.uk/ academic_depts/law

law, international business law, criminology, family law & society, HRM & employment law, legal practice; LlB, LlM, MPhil, PhD, GradDip, CPE, LPC

Faculty of Arts & CreativeTechnologies; www.staffs.ac.uk/academic_depts/fact

School of Art & Design; www.staffs.ac.uk/ academic _ depts/artanddesign

3D design: ceramics/contemporary jewellery and fashion accessories/crafts, advertising and brand management, animation, art cartoon and comic arts, art/design foundation year, design for outdoor living, fine art, graphic design, heritage interior design, illustration, interior design, photography, photo-journalism, product design, retail design, stop motion animation and puppet making, surface pattern design, textile surfaces, transport design, VFX: visual effects and concept design, computer games design, computer games design and programming, games art, computer gameplay design and production; Postgrad; 3D computer games design, arts and creative technologies, ceramic design, creative futures: 3D design/advertising and brand management/animation/applied theatre/contemporary art practice/design/graphic design/heritage and culture/ illustration/photography/product design/surface pattern design/textile design/VFX, design management, graphics & digital design, writing; BA(Hons), BSc(Hons), BEng, FD, MA, MSc, PGDip/Cert

School of Film, Sound and Vision; www.staffs.ac.uk/academic_depts/fsv

acting and screen performance/theatre arts, advertising, film and music video production, experimental film production, film, TV and radio studies, media (film) production, radio production

Film; digital film and post production technology, film production/ technology, film and television production technology
FX; CQI and digital effects, digital film and 3D animation technology, games concept design
Music; creative music technology, music technology/ with management, sound design, musical theatre, electronic music(composition & performance), music business & practice, music production/technology, sound design
Postgrad; arts and creative technologies, digital feature film production, film by negotiated learning (raindance), music technology, theatre practice by negotiated learning; BA(Hons), BSc(Hons), MA, MSc, PGDip/Cert

School of Journalism, Humanities & Social Sciences; www.staffs.ac.uk/ academic_depts/jhss

Journalism; broadcast journalism, English literature,and journalism, games photojournalism, journalism, PR,, professional sports writing and broadcasting, sports journalism, sports PR and journalism
Humanities and Social Sciences; creative writing, English/ literature, English and creative writing, history (modern/and international),history & politics, sociology, sociology, crime and deviance
Postgrad; arts and creative technologies, broadcast journalism, journalism, sports broadcast journalism, continental philosophy, international history, international policy and diplomacy, international relations, social and cultural theory, sociology, terrorism, crime and global security, transnational organised crime; BA(Hons), MA, MSc, BA, FdA, MFA, MPhil, MSc, PhD

Faculty of Computing, Engineering & Science; www.staffs.ac.uk/ academic_depts/fecs

School of Computing; www.staffs.ac.uk/ academic_depts/computing

applied computing, business information systems/ technology, computing, cloud computing (virtual reality), computer systems for business, computing/ computer science, computer games development, cyber rsecurity, forensic computing, information systems; software engineering, network computing, web development/design; Postgraduate; cloud computing, computer networks & security, computer science, computing, cyber security, digital forensics & cyber crime, information systems, mobile device applications, professional computing, software engineering, web development

School of Engineering; www.staffs.ac.uk/academic_depts/engineering

automotive engineering/technology/sport, motorsport engineering, motorsport technology, aeronautical technology, electronic engineering/& electrical engineering, engineering, telecommunications engineering, mathematics & statistics, PGCE in mathematics, mechanical engineering, mechatronics, product design engineering, mechanical/manufacturing technology, advanced technology, professional education, aeronautic engineering, automotive & autosport engineering

School of Sciences; www.staffs.ac.uk/academic_depts/sciences

animal biology & conservation, biology, biomedical science, forensic biology, human biology, ecology & conservation, healthcare science management, forensic/investigative science, policing & criminal investigation, crime scene investigation, fire investigation, firearm examination, geography, environment & sustainability, geography & mountain leadership, governance & sustainable development, invertebrate biology & conservation, sustainability & environmental management; BA, BEng, BSc, FdSc, MEng, MSc, MPhil, MRes, PGCE, PGCert, PGDip, PhD

Faculty of Health Sciences; www.staffs.ac.uk/academic_depts/ health

School of Nursing & Midwifery; www.staffs.ac.uk/academic_depts/ nursingandmidwifery

adult/children's/mental health nursing, integrated care practice, midwifery, mental health; Postgrad;

advanced clinical practice, advanced forensic practice (custody health/sexual assault/sexual assault and custody health professional), health care practice (ageing/contraception and sexual health/mental health/nursing), specialist community public health nursing (health visiting or school nursing), specialist practice – district nursing, health studies, health and welfare studies; DAHP, DM, DN, MPhil, MRes, MSc, PGDip/Cert, PhD, DipHE, FD

School of Psychology, Sport & Exercise; www.staffs.ac.uk/academic-depts/pse

psychology, forensic psychology, sport development & coaching, PE & youth coaching, counselling/therapy & practice, psychotherapeutic counselling, psychology & child development/counselling/criminology, applied sport & exercise psychology/science, sport studies/therapy, sport & exercise psychology, sports coaching with PE, clinical biomechanics, clinical psychology, cognitive behavioural therapy, health psychology, mechanics of diabetes foot, sport strength & conditioning, gait analysis

School of Social Work, Allied & Public Health; www.staffs.ac.uk/academic-depts/ swaph

paramedic science, health and social care, paramedic science, operating department practice, social welfare law, policy and advice practice, social work, anaesthetic care, osteopathy, ageing, mental health and dementia, medical education, physical activity and public health, public health (health informatics), social welfare law, policy and advice practice, public health

BSc, MA, MPhil, MSc, PGCert, PGDip, PhD, MOst, Adv Univ Dip, FD

UNIVERSITY OF STIRLING
www.stir.ac.uk

Faculty of Social Sciences; www.stir.ac.uk/social-sciences

criminology, criminology and sociology, social work, sociology and social policy, education (primary, secondary), teaching qualification in FE
Postgraduate; applied professional studies, applied social research, applied social research, applied social research (social statistics and social research/criminology), criminological research, dementia studies,

education, education studies and TESOL, educational leadership (with specialist qualification for headship), educational research, housing studies, management and English language teaching, TESOL research, social enterprise, social work studies, teaching English to speakers of other languages (TESOL), teaching qualification in further education (TQFE),

BA, GradCert, MSc, PGCert, PGDip, PhD, EdD

Faculty of Arts & Humanities; www.stir.ac.uk/schools/arts-humanities

Communications, Media & Culture; History & Politics, Law & Philosophy, Literature & Language

digital media, education (primary), professional education (primary) with specialism in modern languages/the environment/early years, European film and media, film and media, French, global cinema and culture, heritage and tourism, history, journalism studies, law, literature & cinema, international management studies & international studies, modern languages, politics, politics (international politics), politics, philosophy and economics: PPE, religion, Scottish history

Postgrad; Atlantic studies, corporate social responsibility, creative writing, diplomatic studies, diplomacy, English language and linguistics, environment, heritage and policy, environmental policy and governance, film studies: theory and practice, gender studies (applied), historical research, humanities, international conflict and cooperation, international energy law and policy, law, media and communications management, media management, media research, modern Scottish writing, business, international trade and diplomatic studies, diplomacy and security studies, philosophy, public policy, publishing studies, Renaissance studies, Spanish & Latin American studies, strategic communication & public relations, strategic public relations/& communication management, the Gothic imagination, translation studies, translation studies with TESOL; MPP, DDip, BA, LLB, LLM, MSc, MLitt, MRes, MPhil, PhD

School of Education; www.ioe.stir.ac.uk

education (primary/secondary), professional education with specialism in modern languages/environment/early years, tertiary education (TQFE/TQAE), EFL, educational leadership, professional learning & leadership, enquiry, teaching qualifications in adult education/FE, TESOL teaching qualification in adult education/FE, tertiary education, educational research; BA, BSc, EdD, MEd, MPhil, MRes, MSc, PGCert/Dip, PhD, UnivCert

School of Natural Sciences; www.stir/schools/natural-sciences

Institute of Aquaculture; www.aqua.stir.ac.uk

aquaculture, aquaculture: sustainable aquaculture, aquaculture: sustainable aquaculture, aquatic food security, aquatic pathobiology, aquatic veterinary studies, marine biotechnology, marine biology, sustainable aquaculture; BSc, MPhil, MSc, PGCert, PGDip, PhD

School of Biological & Environmental Sciences; www.sbes.stir.ac.uk

applied biological science, biology, cell biology, conservation biology & management, conservation & sustainability, ecology, environmental geography/management/science/outdoor education, environmental management (conservation/energy); BSc, MPhil, MRes, MSc, PGCert, PGDip, PhD

Dept of Computing Science & Mathematics; www.cs.stir.ac.uk

applied/computing, big data, business computing, computing science, computing for financial markets/business, IT, mathematics/& its applications, information technology, software engineering; BSc, MSc, PhD, MBA

Dept of Psychology; www.psychology.stir.ac.uk

psychology, health psychology, psychological research methods, autism research, child development, human/animal interaction, perception & action, psychology of faces, evolutionary psychology, psychology applied to health, psychological therapy in primary care; BA, BSc, MSc, PGDip, PhD

School of Health Sciences; www.nm.stir.ac.uk/health-sciences

advanced/professional practice, early year practice health visiting, health & wellbeing of the older person, paramedical practice, midwifery, nursing (adult, mental health), return to practice nursing, welfare & benefits advice; BM, BN, BSc, DAHP, DM, DN, MPhil, MRes, MSc, PGDip, PhD, DipHE, DClin, Grad Cert

School of Sport; www.sports.stir.ac.uk

health & exercise sciences, performance coaching, psychology of sport, sport & exercise science, sport coaching/management/nutrition, sports studies; BA, BSc, MPhil, MSc, PGDip, PhD

Stirling Management School; www.stir.ac.uk/management

accountancy/& finance, banking & finance, data science for business, investment analysis, business administration, business studies, finance, business & management, HRM, international business, international management studies/European languages &

society management/& intercultural studies, international accounting & finance/HRM, management, marketing, retailing, retail marketing, behavioural science for management, economics, energy management, sport business management, sport events management, management & ELT; BA, BSc, MBA, MSc, PhD, BAcc, MPhil, PGDip, MBA, MRes, MBM

Institute for People-Centred Healthcare Management
PhD

Institute for Retail Studies
retail studies; PhD

Institute for Social Marketing
PhD

Institute for Socio-Management
PhD

STOCKPORT COLLEGE
www.stockport.ac.uk

childcare: early years practice/working with children and young people, childhood studies, computing: enterprise computing, design: graphic arts and design/illustration/motion design/interior design with sustainability, forensic science, health and social care, contemporary photography, television production; various HND/Cs in engineering; BA, FdA, FdSc

UNIVERSITY OF STRATHCLYDE
www.strath.ac.uk

Strathclyde Business School;
www.strath.ac.uk/business
accounting, business/administration/enterprise, business analysis & technology, economics, finance, hospitality & tourism management, HRM, management, marketing, business law, international business & modern languages
Postgrad: economics & finance, finance, finance & law, finance & management, international accounting & finance, international banking & finance, investment & finance, global energy management, global sustainable cities, HRM, human resources & international management, international HRM, managing human resources, entrepreneurship, innovation & technology, business analysis & consulting, operational research, international marketing, marketing, tourism marketing management, human resources & international management, finance & management, international management, international management & law, business & management, project management & innovation, business administration (MBA), Strathclyde executive MBA international, business administration (MBA) (leadership studies); BA, MSc, MBA, DBA, MPhil, PhD, MRes, PGCert/Dip, MBM

Faculty of Engineering;
www.strath.ac.uk/engineering

Dept of Architecture; www.strath.ac.uk/architecture
architecture, architectural studies, adv architectural design/international, urban design, architectural design for conservation of built heritage, sustainable engineering: architecture & ecology; BSc, MArch, MRes, MSc, PGCert, PGDip

Biomedical Engineering; www.strath.ac.uk/biomedeng
medical devices, biomedical engineering, prosthetics & orthotics, rehabilitation studies; EngD, MPhil, MRes, MSc, PGCert, PGDip, PhD, BEng, MEng

Dept of Chemical & Process Engineering; www.strath.ac.uk/chemeng
adv chemical & processing engineering, chemical engineering, process technology & management, sustainable engineering: chemical processing; BEng, MEng, MSc, PGCert, PGDip, PhD

Dept of Civil & Environmental Engineering; www.strath.ac.uk/civeng
civil & environmental engineering, civil engineering, environmental engineering/health sciences, entrepreneurship, hydrogeology, sustainability &

environmental studies, geo environmental engineering, integrated pollution prevention & control; BEng, BSc, MEng, MPhil, MRes, MSc, PhD

Dept of Design, Manufacture & Engineering Management; www.strath.ac.uk/dmen

adv engineering technology & systems, design engineering,, global innovation management, lean six sigma for process, mechatronics & automation, operations management in engineering, product design engineering/design & innovation, production engineering design, production engineering & management, sports engineering, supply chain & logistics/operations/procurement management, sustainable engineering/product development; BEng, BSc, MEng, MSc, PGCert, PGDip

Dept of Electronic & Electrical Engineering; www.strath.ac.uk/eee

electronic & electrical engineering, electronic & electrical engineering with business studies, electrical energy systems, electronic & digital systems, electrical & mechanical engineering, computer & electronic systems; Postgrad; wind energy systems, communications, control & digital signal processing, signal processing, electronic & electrical engineering, electrical power engineering with business, advanced electrical power engineering
BEng, MEng, MSc, PGCert, PGDip

Dept of Mechanical & Aerospace Engineering; www.strath.ac.uk/mecheng

aero-mechanical engineering, mechanical engineering, mechanical engineering with aeronautics/financial management/materials engineering; Postgrad; sustainable engineering: renewable energy systems and the environment, advanced mechanical engineering, advanced mechanical engineering with aerospace/energy systems/materials/power plant technologies; BEng, MEng, MPhil, PGCert, PGDip, PhD

Dept of Naval Architectural & Marine Engineering; www.strath.ac.uk/na-me

naval architecture and marine engineering/ocean engineering, high performance; Postgrad; marine engineering, offshore floating systems, sustainable engineering: offshore renewable energy, naval architecture, ocean & marine engineering, subsea engineering & pipelines, ship & offshore structures, ship & offshore technology, marine technology
BEng, MEng, MPhil, MSc, PGCert, PGDip, PhD

Faculty of Humanities & Social Sciences; www.strath.ac.uk/humanities

Undergraduate; Arts & Social Studies: English studies, French, history, Italian, journalism & creative writing, psychology, politics, Spanish
Education: education & economics/HRM/social policy/social services/English/French/history, Italian/law/politics/psychology/Spanish/journalism & creative writing/social policy, childhood practice, education & social services, primary education, teaching with chemistry/mathematics/physics, primary education
Law: law, law with a modern language
Social Work: social work
Speech and Language: speech & language pathology
Sports Science: sport & physical activity
BA(Hons), BSc(Hons), BEd, LlB
Postgrad: Social Work & Social Policy; advanced residential childcare, autism, child and youth care studies by distance learning, social services management, social policy, social policy & economics/HRM/sport/social work/law/Italian/history/French/English
Education: applied education and social research, autism, children & young people, literacy, language, early years pedagogy, educational studies, education learning/psychology, Gaelic immersion for teachers, genealogical, palaegraphic & heraldic studies, inclusive education, philosophy with children, primary education, social work, immersion for teachers studies, educational support, Gaelic immersion for teachers, management & leadership in education, education, philosophy with children, primary education, supporting bilingual learners in the mainstream classroom, supporting teacher learning
Government & Public Policy: public policy, international public policy, European public policy, political research, international politics and organisations
Humanities: historical studies, health history, investigative journalism, digital journalism, literature, culture & place, north Atlantic world c900 c1800, creative writing
Law: advocacy, construction law, climate change law and policy, criminal justice & penal change, professional legal practice, human rights, internet law & policy, international economic law, international law & sustainable development, mediation & conflict resolution, employment and labour law
Psychological Sciences & Health: educational psychology, counselling, counselling skills, research methods in psychology, clinical health psychology

MSc, PGDip/Cert, PGCE, PGDE, BEd, MEd, MLitt, LlM, DEdPsy, PGCert/Dip, MCounselling, MPhil, EdD, MRes

Faculty of Science; www.strath.ac.uk/ science

Dept of Pure & Applied Chemistry; www.chem.strath.ac.uk

chemistry, chemistry with analytical chemistry, chemistry with drug discovery, forensic science, forensic and analytical chemistry, applied chemistry and chemical engineering, chemistry with teaching, forensic science, medicinal chemistry; BSc, MChem, MSc, PGDip, PhD

Dept of Computer & Information Sciences; www.strath.ac.uk/cis

enterprise/business information systems, computer & electronic systems, adv/computer science, adv/software engineering, data analytics, information & library studies, information management, mathematics & computer science; BEng, BSc, MEng, MPhil, MRes, MSc, PGCert, PGDip

Dept of Mathematics & Statistics; www.mathstat.strath.ac.uk

mathematics, mathematics, statistics & accounting/ economics/finance, mathematics & physics, mathematics with teaching, mathematics & computer science, quantitative finance, applied statistics in health sciences; BSc, MSc, PhD, MMath

Dept of Physics; www.strath.ac.uk/physics

physics, applied physics, nanoscience, optical technologies, photonics & device fabrication, mathematics with physics, physics with teaching, industrial photonics; BSc, MPhys, MSc, PhD

Strathclyde Institute of Pharmacy & Biomedical Sciences; www.strath.ac.uk/ sipbs

advanced pharmaceutical manufacturing, biomedical sciences, adv clinical pharmacy practice, pharmacy practice, pharmacy, industrial biotechnology, pharmaceutical analysis, pharmaceutical quality and good manufacturing practice; BSc, MPharm, MPhil, MSc, PGCert, PGDip, PhD, MRes

UNIVERSITY CAMPUS SUFFOLK
www.ucs.ac.uk

Faculty of Arts, Business and Applied Social Science; www.ucs.ac.uk/ Faculties-and-Centres/Faculty-of-Arts,- Business-and-Applied-Social-Science/ Faculty-of-Arts,-Business-and-Applied- Social-Science.aspx

Department of Arts and Humanities

computer games design, dance, English, film, fine art, graphic design/graphic illustration, history, interior architecture and design, photography, arts practice, digital film production, screenwriting & film studies

Department of Children, Young People and Education

early years practice, early childhood studies, early learning, special educational needs and disability studies, childhood and youth studies

Department of Psychology, Sociology and Social Work

criminology, criminology and youth studies, psychology and criminology, psychology and sociology, psychology and youth studies, law with community/ethics/sociology, crime & community safety/

evidence based practice, sociology and youth studies, social work

Suffolk Business School

accounting and financial management, business & management, HRM, event management, event management and tourism management, business management, business administration (MBA), HRM, enterprise, leadership & tourism; FdA, BA(Hons), MA, PGDip/Cert, FdSc, MSc, MBA

Faculty of Health and Science; www.ucs.ac.uk/faculty-of-health-and- science

Department of Health Studies

public health, operating department practice, diagnostic radiography, midwifery, public health, radiotherapy and oncology, specialist community public health nursing (school nurse or health visiting), healthcare education

Department of Nursing Studies

adult nursing, child's health nursing, mental health nursing, acute health care practice, nurse practitioner, advanced health care practice, health care practice (acute care/end of life/long term care/mental health/dementia care), end of life care, long term care, mental health

Department of Science and Technology

applied computing, bioscience, coaching, communication technology: network engineering/software engineering, sport coaching & development, computer games design/programming, nutrition and human health, sport and exercise science, performance analysis for football/physiology for football, psychology/strength & conditioning for football; Postgrad; regenerative medicine; BSc(Hons), MSc, DipHE, MA, FdSc, PGDip/Cert

---

UNIVERSITY OF SUNDERLAND
www.sunderland.ac.uk

Faculty of Applied Sciences;
www.sunderland.ac.uk/faculties/apsc

Dept of Computing, Engineering & Technology; www.sunderland.ac.uk/faculties/apsc/ourdepartments/cet

mechanical engineering, engineering management, power engineering, engineering management, automotive engineering, information computing, extended computing, manufacturing engineering, computer systems engineering, engineering, network systems, electronic and electrical engineering, computer forensics, telecommunications engineering, project management, network computing, health information management, games software development, computing, information technology management, applied business computing, computer science, network systems; BA, BEng, BSc, FdSc, MSc

Dept of Pharmacy, Health & Wellbeing; www.sunderland.ac.uk/faculties/apsc/ourdepartments/phw

nursing, medicines management, biopharmaceutical science, pharmacy, clinical pharmacy, pharmaceutical science, drug discovery and development, independent prescribing for pharmacists, biomedical science, biopharmaceutical science, pharmaceutical and biopharmaceutical formulations, healthcare science: physiological/life sciences, healthcare science: physiological/life sciences, environmental management and assessment, sports coaching, practice development in chronic heart failure, cosmetic science
BA, BSc, FdA, MPharm, MSc, PGCE, Univ Dip, PGDip, Adv Dip

Dept of Psychology;
www.sunderland.ac.uk/faculties/apsc/ourfaculty/ourdepartments/psychology

counselling, psychology, psychology with counselling, psychological research, extended psychology; BA, FdA, MA, MSc

Dept of Sport & Exercise Sciences; www.sunderland.ac.uk/faculties/apsc/ourdepartments/sport/

sport & exercise sciences, sports coaching/development, exercise, health & fitness, sport, exercise & fitness; BA, BSc, FdA, MSc

Faculty of Arts, Design & Media;
www.sunderland.ac.uk/faculties/adm/

Dept of Arts & Design;
www.sunderland.ac.uk/faculties/adm/ourfaculty/ourdepartments/departmentofartsdesign

Numerous qualifications grouped under following subject headings;
animation, broadcast & digital media, dance, drama music, fashion, film, media and cultural studies, fine art, foundation art and design, glass and ceramics, graphics & advertising, illustration, PR, photography, Postgraduate; art and design, media; BA, BSc, FdA, MA

Faculty of Business & Law;
www.sunderland.ac.uk/faculties/bl

Sunderland Business School;
www.sunderland.ac.uk/faculties/bl/departments/business

accounting & finance/financial management, accountancy & management, applied management/investment, banking & finance, business administration, business & financial management, business management/enterprise management/HRM/marketing, finance & management, marketing management, HRM, innovation & enterprise, investigative management, international management, marketing/management, MBA (HRM/hospitality management/innovation & enterprise/supply chain management/transformation/global business/finance/general management/marketing/finance); BA(Hons), FD, CertHE, MBM, MBA, MA, MSc, PGDip

Dept of Law; www.sunderland.ac.uk/faculties/bl/departments/law

law, criminal law & procedure, international, international law, legal practice, human rights, business law; LlB, LlM, LPC, BA(Hons)

Dept of Tourism, Hospitality & Events; www.sunderland.ac.uk/faculties/bl/departments/tourism

international hospitality & tourism management, tourism management, events management, travel & tourism, tourism & events/hospitality (jt degrees); BA(Hons), BA/BSc, FD, BSc(Hons)

Faculty of Education & Society

Dept of Education; www.sunderland.ac.uk/faculties/es/ourfaculty/ourdepartments/departmentofeducation

childhood studies, community and youth work studies, early years teaching, history, English education with QTS, education and care, education and training, education studies – combined subjects, social sciences, criminology, health and social care, social work, English and creative writing, combined subjects, education and curriculum studies secondary, English education, mathematics education ostgrad; post compulsory education, education, PGCE; business/design and technology/English/geography/computer science education/mathematics/primary education/science with biology/science with chemistry/science with physics education, School Direct, international education, special educational needs coordination, social work, teaching and learning in HE, TESOL, education overseas; BA, BSc, MA, PGCE, FD, PGDip/Cert, MSc

Dept of Culture; www.sunderland.ac.uk/faculties/es/ourfaculty/ourdepartments/departmentofculture

English, creative writing, history, modern foreign languages, politics, TESOL; BA, BSc, MA, PGCE

Dept of Social Sciences; www.sunderland.ac.uk/faculties/es/ourfaculty/ourdepartments/departmentofsocialsciences

childhood studies, community & youth studies, community engagement, criminology, education & care, health & social care, practice development, social work, sociology, supporting career learning & development, working with young people, social sciences; BA, FdA, MA, BA(Hons), BEng(Hons), BSc(Hons), EdEng, FdSc, LLM, MBA, MSc, PGCE, PGCert

Degrees validated by University of Sunderland offered at:

SUNDERLAND COLLEGE
www.sunderlandcollege.ac.uk

applied music practice, biomedical science, biopharmaceutical science,, psychology, counselling, health & social care, practice dance, drama, exercise health & fitness, health & safety management, leadership & management, post compulsory education & training; FdA, FdSc, BSc

UNIVERSITY OF SURREY
www.surrey.ac.uk

Faculty of Arts & Human Sciences;
www.surrey.ac.uk/fahs/

School of Arts; www.surrey.ac.uk/schoolofarts

Dance; dance; Postgrad; dance cultures, creative practices and direction

Media, Digital Arts & Film; digital media arts, film, film and video production engineering, media, culture and society; Postgrad; film, digital arts

Music; creative music technology, actor musician, music and sound recording; Postgrad; sound recording/psychoacoustic engineering, musical theatre, practice of voice and singing, creative practices and leadership, music

Theatre; theatre and performance, theatre, acting, actor musician, musical theatre, professional production skills; Postgrad; theatre, acting, musical theatre, contemporary theatre making, creative practices and direction

Sound Recording; music and sound recording; Postgrad; sound recording/psychoacoustic engineering; BA(Hons), BSc(Hons), BMus, MA, PhD, MPhil, MMus, PGDip

School of English & Languages; www.surrey.ac.uk/englishandlanguages

Communication, Languages & Translation Studies; applied languages (French and Spanish/German and French/Spanish), business management and French business management and German/Spanish, English literature and French/German/Spanish, liberal arts and sciences; Postgrad; business interpreting in Chinese and English, business translation with interpreting, communication and international marketing, intercultural communication with international business, interpreting, TESOL, translation studies, translation studies with intercultural communication

English Literature & Creative Writing; creative writing, English literature, English literature and French/German/Spanish, English literature with creative writing, liberal arts and sciences; Postgrad; creative writing, English literature, higher education, English (literature, creative writing or linguistics), intercultural communication

Liberal Arts & Sciences; liberal arts and sciences; BA(Hons), BSc(Hons), MA, PhD

School of Politics; www.surrey.ac.uk/politics

politics, international politics, politics & sociology/economics, politics with policy studies, international relations, European politics & policy; BA(Hons), BSc(Hons), MSc, MPhil, PhD

School of Sociology; www.surrey.ac.uk/sociology

sociology/& criminology, criminology, criminal justice, computational model making, social research methods, media studies, politics wiih sociology; BA(Hons), BSc(Hons), MA, MSc, PsychD, PGDip, LlB

Dept of Economics; www.econ.surrey.ac.uk

business economics, economics, economics and finance/mathematics, politics and economics; Postgraduate; business economics and finance, economics, economics and finance, economics for public policy, energy economics and policy, health economics, international economics, finance and development; BSc, MSc, PhD

Faculty of Engineering & Physical Sciences; www.surrey.ac.uk/feps

Dept of Computing; www.surrey.ac.uk/computing

computer science, computing & information technology, information systems, information security; BSc, MSc, PhD

Dept of Electronic & Electronic Engineering; www.ee.surrey.ac.uk

biomedicine with electronic engineering, communication systems,computer and internet engineering, electronic engineering, electronic engineering for medicine and healthcare, electronic engineering with computer systems/nanotechnology/space systems

Postgraduate; communications networks and software, computer vision, robotics and machine learning, electronic engineering, medical imaging, mobile and satellite communications, mobile communications systems, mobile media communications, nanotechnology and renewable energy, RF and microwave engineering, satellite communications engineering; BEng(Hons), MEng(Hons) BSc(Hons), MMath, MSc, PhD

Dept of Mathematics; www.surrey.ac.uk/maths

mathematics, financial mathematics, mathematics with statistics/music/physics, biosystems, dynamical systems & partial differential equations, strings & geometry, and fluid mechanics & meteorology; BSc(Hons), MPhys MSc, MMath, MSc, PhD

Dept of Physics; www.surrey.ac.uk/physics

mathematics and physics, physics, physics with astronomy/nuclear/astrophysics; Postgraduate; medical physics, physics, radiation and environmental protection, nuclear physics; BSc, MSc, MPhys(Hons), MMath(Hons), EngD

Division of Chemistry; www.surrey.ac.uk/chemistry

chemistry/with forensic investigation, medicinal chemistry, drug discovery; BSc, MSc, MChem, MRes, PhD

Division of Civil, Chemical & Environmental Engineering; www.surrey.ac.uk/cce

Dept of Civil & Environmental Engineering

civil engineering, bridge engineering, structural engineering, water & environmental engineering, infrastructure engineering & management, advanced geotechnical engineering

Dept of Chemical & Process Engineering

chemical engineering, chemical & biosystems engineering, petroleum engineering; Postgraduate; information/& processing systems engineering, process & environmental systems engineering, renewable energy petroleum refining

Centre for Environmental Strategy

environmental strategy, sustainable development, corporate environmental management; BEng, MEng, MSc, PGCert, PGDip, PhD

Division of Mechanical Engineering Science; www.surrey.ac.uk/mma

advanced materials, aerospace/mechanical/automotive engineering, biomedical/medical engineering; BEng, MEng, MSc, PGCert, PGDip, PhD, MPhil

School of Health Sciences; www.surrey.ac.uk/school-health-sciences

Health Sciences, Nursing and Midwifery; www.surrey.ac.uk/subjects/health-sciences-nursing-and-midwifery

electronic engineering for medicine and healthcare, midwifery, registered midwife, nursing studies (registered nurse adult/children/mental health), operating department practice, paramedic practice; Postgraduate; delivering quality healthcare, education for professional practice, health care management,nursing studies (adult nursing/mental health nursing), physician associate, primary and community care (community children nursing/ district nursing/general practice nursing), public health practice with health visiting/health sciences

Continuing Professional Development

primary and community care (district nursing/general practice nursing, public health practice (health visiting/school nursing), education for professional practice, delivering quality healthcare, primary and community care (community children nursing/ district nursing/ general practice nursing), public health practice health visiting

School of Biosciences and Medicine; www.surrey.ac.uk/biosciences-and-medicine

biochemistry, biological sciences, biomedical science, biomedicine with data science/electronic engineering, biotechnology, food science and microbiology, microbiology, microbiology (medical), nutrition, nutrition and food science, nutrition/dietetics, sport and exercise science, veterinary biosciences; Postgraduate; human nutrition, medical microbiology, nutritional medicine, physician associate, veterinary microbiology,biochemistry and physiology, microbial and cellular sciences

Continuing Professional Development; applied systems biology, applied toxicology, integrative interpretation of large-scale data, medical microbiology, nutritional medicine, pharmaceutical medicine and clinical pharmacology, systems modelling and network analysis, veterinary microbiology; BSc(Hons), MSc, PhD, MD, DipHE, PGCert/Dip, PhD, DClin-Pract, BVi, DipHE

School of Psychology; www.surrey.ac.uk/psychology

psychology, environmental/health/social psychology, occupational & organisational psychology, supervision & consultation: psychotherapeutic & organisational approaches, psychological intervention, research methods in psychology; BSc(Hons), MSc, PsychD, PhD, PGCert/Dip

Faculty of Business, Economics & Law; www.surrey.ac.uk/fbel

Surrey Business School; www.surrey.ac.uk/sbs

Accounting & Finance

accounting and finance, economics and finance; Postgraduate; accounting and finance, banking and finance, international financial management, investment management, business and retail management, business management, business management (entrepreneurship/HRM/marketing), business management and French/German/Spanish, international business management, sustainable enterprise management, business analytics, entrepreneurship, health care management, HRM, intercultural communication with international business, international business management/financial management/marketing management/international retail marketing, investment management, marketing management, MBA business administration, occupational and organizational psychology, operations and logistics management, business and management, health care management and policy, management

Economics

business economics, economics, economics and finance/mathematics, politics and economics; Postgraduate; business economics and finance, economics, energy economics and policy, international economics, finance and development

Environment and Sustainability

sustainable enterprise management

Postgraduate; corporate environmental management, environmental psychology, sustainable development, water and environmental engineering, environment and sustainability, corporate environmental management, environmental strategy; BSc(Hons), DBA, MBA, MA, MD, MSc, PhD

School of Law; www.surrey.ac.uk/law

law, international/international commercial law, law & international studies/criminology, senior status; LLB, LLM, MA, PhD, MRes

School of Hospitality & Tourism Management; www.surrey.ac.uk/shtm

international event management, international hospitality and tourism management, international hospitality management, international tourism management; Postgraduate; air transport management, international events management, international hospitality management, international hotel management, international tourism development, international tourism management, international tourism marketing, strategic hotel management
BSc(Hons), MSc, PhD, MBus(Hons)

Department of Health Care Management and Policy; www.surrey.ac.uk/hcmp

health care management, health economics; MSc, PhD

Degrees validated by the University of Surrey offered at:

FARNBOROUGH COLLEGE OF TECHNOLOGY
www.farn-ct.ac.uk

business management/& computing, early childhood studies/early years practice/learning, criminology & sociology, documentary film/radio/TV, early years education and practice, early years care and education, electronic engineering, English literature & criminology/sociology, graphic design, health care practice, hospitality management, HR management, photography, media production, psychology & criminology, sports science/human performance, sports coaching,, software engineering; BA(Hons), BSc(Hons), FdA, FdSc, FdEng, PGEd

---

NESCOT (NORTH EAST SURREY COLLEGE OF TECHNOLOGY)
www.nescot.ac.uk

applied biological and healthcare science, computing, business accounting & technology management, osteopathic medicine, perfusion science, sports therapy, education and training, educational support, PGCE education & training, education studies; Additional Nongraduate Courses;acoustics, biomedical science, business management, health & social care, computing/& IT, early years, educational support, music technology, orthopaedic medicine, osteopathic medicine, photography, photo-imaging, perfusion science, psychodynamic counselling, sports

therapy, teacher training, teaching & learning in lifelong learning sector, travel & tourism management; BA(Hons), BSc(Hons), DipHE, FdA, FdSc,MSc, PGDip, Masters, MOst, BOst

---

ST MARYS UNIVERSITY
www.smuc.ac.uk

acting, business law/management, business & finance/management & entrepreneurship, creative writing/first novel, criminology & society, drama, drama and applied/physical theatre/theatre arts, education and social science/drama, English/ & drama, film & screen media, geography, health & exercise science, history, international business management, law/with criminology, media arts, nutrition, philosophy, psychology, sociology, sport rehabilitation, science sport science, sports coaching science, tourism/management; Postgraduate; applied linguistics and ELT, applied sport and exercise, physiology, applied sport psychology, applied sports nutrition, bioethics and medical law, catholic school leadership,

charity management, creative writing: first novel, education, culture and society,education: leading innovation and change, education: pedagogical leadership in physical education and sport, education: pedagogy, education: pedagogy, Gothic: culture, subculture, counterculture, human nutrition, Irish studies, international business practice, international tourism development, PGCE primary/secondary, physical theatre, public history, sport, health and applied science, sport rehabilitation, sports journalism, strength and conditioning,theatre directing, theology; BA, BSc, FdA, LlB, LLM, MA, MPhil, MSc, MRes, PGCE, PGCert, PGDip, PhD

UNIVERSITY OF SUSSEX
www.sussex.ac.uk

Brighton & Sussex Medical School; www.bsms.sussex.ac.uk

medicine, surgery, anaesthesia and perioperative medicine, cardiology, clinical radiology, dementia studies, diabetes in primary care, global health, healthcare leadership and commissioning, medical education, medical research, paediatrics and child health,,physician associate studies, psychiatry, public health, simulation in clinical practice
MoMEd, MA, MSc, MRes, MD, MPhil, PGCert, PGDip, PhD

School of Business, Management & Economics; www.sussex.ac.uk/aboutus/schoolsdepartments/bmec

Dept of Business & Management; www.sussex.ac.uk/bams

accounting and finance, business and management studies, finance, international business, marketing and management, law with business & management, entrepreneurship & innovation

Postgrad; banking and finance, financial risk and investment analysis, global supply chain and logistics management, HRM, international accounting and corporate governance, international management, international marketing, management, management and entrepreneurship/finance, mathematics with finance, Masters in business administration MBA; BA, BSc, MSc, PGDip, LlB, MPhil, DPhil

Dept of Economics; www.sussex.ac.uk/economics

economics, economics & international development/international relations/management studies/politics/finance/business, business & management studies, development economics, finance & business, mathematics with economics, international business economics, PPE, psychology with economics, international economics, international finance & economics; BA, BSc, GradDip, MSc, MPhil, MMath, DPhil

Dept of Science Policy Research (SPRU); www.sussex.ac.uk/spru

science & technology policy, energy policy for sustainability, innovation for sustainable international development, project management, strategic innovation management, sustainability development; DPhil, MPhil, MSc

School of Education & Social Work; www.sussex.ac.uk/aboutus/schoolsdepartments/esw

Dept of Education; www.sussex.ac.uk/education

childhood & youth: theory & practice, early years education, education, pedagogy & practice, education studies, psychology & education, working with children & young people, initial teacher education, international education & development, overseas teacher education, PGCE: primary, 11-18/7-14 maths/modern foreign languages/secondary (numerous subjects)/international, school direct, subject knowledge enhancement; BA, BSc(Hons), MA, PGCE, PGCert/Dip, EdD, MPhil, PhD, MSc, QTS

Dept of Social Work & Social Care; www.sussex.ac.uk/socialwork

childhood & youth studies, leadership & management in integrated children's services/& supervision in children's services, supervision of children's services, effective practice in children's services, practice education, social work, social work & social care, wellbeing, social research methods; BA, DPhil, MA, MPhil, MSc, PGCert, DSW

School of Engineering & Informatics; www.sussex.ac.uk/ei

Engineering & Design: advanced mechanical engineering, automotive/mechanical engineering, electrical/& electronic engineering, computer engineering, digital communications & business management, engineering, product design, computer science & AI, computing for/with digital media/business & management, evolutionary & adaptive systems, games & multimedia environments, intelligent systems, Postgrad; advanced mechanical engineering, digital communication systems, embedded digital systems, engineering business management, robotics and autonomous systems, robotics and autonomous systems

advanced computer science, human-computer interaction, information technology with business and management, intelligent systems, management of information technology, web development

BA, BSc, BEng, MEng, DPhil, MA, MComp, MPhil, MSc, PGCert

School of English; www.sussex.ac.uk/aboutus/schoolsdepartments/english

drama: theatre and performance, drama studies and English/film studies/a language; American studies and English, English, English and art history/film studies/history/media studies, English language and literature, philosophy and English, English language and linguistics/literature

Postgrad; English language and literature, applied linguistics, creative and critical writing, English: literature, culture and theory, literature and philosophy, modern and contemporary literature, culture and thought, sexual dissidence; BA, DPhil, MA, MPhil

School of Global Studies; www.sussex.ac.uk/aboutus/schoolsdepartments/global

Dept of Anthropology; www.sussex.ac.uk/anthropology

anthropology, anthropology & cultural studies/history/a language, anthropology & international development/geography/international relations, anthropology of development/social transformation, social anthropology of global economy; BA, DPhil, MA, MSc

Dept of Geography; www.sussex.ac.uk/geography

geography, geography & international relations/development/anthropology/a language, climate change & policy/development, migration studies; BA, BSc, DPhil, MA, MPhil, MSc

International Development; www.sussex.ac.uk/development

international relations & development, sociology & international development, international development & anthropology/economics/geography/French/Italian/Spanish, anthropology & international development, environment, development & policy; BA, MA, MPhil, DPhil

Dept of International Relations; www.sussex.ac.uk/ir

conflict, security & development, geopolitics & grand strategy, global political economy/governance, international security, international relations, international relations and anthropology/ development/French/Italian/sociology/Spanish/a language, economics/geography/law/politics and international relations; BA, LlB, DPhil, MA

School of History, Art History & Philosophy; *www.sussex.ac.uk/aboutus/ schoolsdepartments/hahp*

Dept of American Studies; www.sussex.ac.uk/americanstudies

American studies, American studies with history/ English/film studies/politics/law; BA, MA, MPhil, DPhil, LlB

Dept of Art History; www.sussex.ac.uk/ arthistory

art history, art history & museum curating/with photography/film studies/English; BA, MA, MPhil, DPhil

Dept of History; www.sussex.ac.uk/history

contemporary history, history/& American studies/ English/philosophy/sociology/anthropology/film studies, intellectual history/politics, intellectual history; BA, MPhil, DPhil, MA

Dept of Philosophy; www.sussex.ac.uk/ philosophy

philosophy, philosophy and English/sociology, philosophy, politics and economics, history/politics and philosophy; Postgrad; literature and philosophy, philosophy, social and political thought; BA, MA, MPhil, DPhil

School of Law, Politics & Sociology; *www.sussex.ac.uk/aboutus/ schoolsdepartments/lps*

Dept of Politics; www.sussex.ac.uk/politics

history and politics, politics, politics and economics/ law with politics, philosophy, politics and economics; Postgrad; corruption and governance, European governance and policy, international politics; BA, DPhil, MPhil

Sussex Law School; www.sussex.ac.uk/law

law, criminal law & criminal justice, international criminal law/trade law/financial law/commercial law, law & business/American studies/international relations/politics/criminology/a language/climate change/media, information technology & intellectual property law; CPE, DPhil, GradDip, LLB, LLM, MPhil, MSc

Dept of Sociology; www.sussex.ac.uk/ sociology

sociology, criminology/& sociology, sociology/with cultural studies/politics/media studies/international relations/philosophy/a language, international

development, gender studies, psychology with criminology; BA, DPhil, MA, MPhil, MSc

School of Mathematical & Physical Sciences; *www.sussex.ac.uk/aboutus/ schoolsdepartments/mps*

Dept of Mathematics; www.sussex.ac.uk/ maths

mathematics, computational mathematics, corporate & financial risk management, financial mathematics, mathematics with finance, economics, mathematical physics, data science; BSc, DPhil, MMath, MPhil, MSc, PGDip

Dept of Physics & Astronomy; www.sussex.ac.uk/physics

astronomy, astrophysics, cosmology, physics with astrophysics, particle physics, theoretical physics, frontiers of quantum technology, mathematics with physics; BSc, DPhil, MPhil, MPhys

School of Life Sciences; *www.sussex.ac.uk/aboutus/ schoolsdepartments/lifesci*

Biochemistry & Biomedicine; www.sussex.ac.uk/lifesci/biochemistry

biochemistry, biomedical science, genetic manipulation & molecular cell biology, biosciences

Evolution, Behaviour & Environment; www.sussex.ac.uk/lifesci/ebe

biology, biosciences, ecology, conservation & environment, genetics, zoology, evolution, global biodiversity conservation, conservation biology, animal behaviour, evolutionary biology

Genome Danger & Stability; www.sussex.ac.uk/gdsc

various research topics

Neuroscience; www.sussex.ac.uk/lifesci/ neuroscience

neuroscience, biosciences, medical neuroscience, neuroscience with cognition science/psychology; BSc, DPhil, MPhil, MChem, MSc, MSci, MRes

School of Media, Film & Music; *www.sussex.ac.uk/aboutus/ schoolsdepartments/mfm*

Dept of Media & Film; www.sussex.ac.uk/ mediaandfilm/

English and film studies, film studies, journalism, media practice, media and communications/cultural studies, American studies and film studies, anthropology and cultural studies, art history/drama studies and film studies, English and media studies, history and film studies, law & media, sociology and cultural studies/media studies; Postgrad; digital documentary, digital media, film studies, filmmaking, gender and media, international journalism, journalism, journalism and documentary practice/ media studies, media practice for development and social change, media and cultural studies; BA(Hons), LlB, MA, PhD, MPhil

Dept of Music; www.sussex.ac.uk/music

music, music technology, music & sonic media; BA, BSc, DPhil, MA, MPhil, PhD, PGDip

School of Psychology; *www.sussex.ac.uk/psychology*

psychology, psychology with business and management, psychology with clinical approaches, psychology with cognitive science, psychology with criminology, psychology with economics, psychology with education

Postgraduate; psychology with neuroscience, applied social psychology, cognitive neuroscience, experimental psychology, foundations of clinical psychology and mental health, low-intensity psychological interventions for children and young people, mental health practice, psychological methods; BSc(Hons), MRes, MSc, PGDip/Cert

SWANSEA UNIVERSITY
www.swansea.ac.uk

College of Arts & Humanities; *www.swansea.ac.uk/artandhumanities*

American studies, ancient and medieval history, classics, ancient history and Egyptology, Welsh, English – Chinese translation and interpreting, English language, TESOL and English language, English literature/with creative writing, French, German, history, Italian, media and PR, medieval studies, modern languages, translation and interpreting, politics and international relations, Spanish, war and society; numerous jt degrees involving combinations of the above subjects

Postgrad; ancient Egyptian culture, ancient history and classical culture, ancient narrative literature, Chinese-English translation and language teaching, classics, communication, media practice & PR, creative writing, development and human rights, digital media, early modern history, English literature, journalism, media and globalisation, gender and culture, history, international journalism, international relations, international security and development, medieval studies, modern history, politics, public policy, TEFL, translation and interpreting, professional translation, war and society, Welsh writing in English, translation technology; BA, MA, MPhil, MSc, MScEcon, PhD, GradDip

College of Business & Economics & the Law; *www.swansea.ac.uk/business*

School of Law; www.swansea.ac.uk/law

law, law (crime and criminal justice), human rights, criminology, criminology and criminal justice/social policy/psychology, law & American studies/criminology/French/ German/history/Italian/media/politics/ Spanish/Welsh; Postgraduate; legal practice and advanced drafting, intellectual property and commercial practice, international commercial and maritime law, international commercial law, international maritime law, international trade law, oil and gas law, criminology, applied criminal justice and criminology; LlB, LlM, GDL, MPhil, PhD, MLaw

School of Management; www.swansea.ac.uk/som

accounting, accounting & finance, business management (marketing/operations & supply management/ business analytics/HRM)/finance/ebusiness/management consulting/operations & supply management, economics, economics & business/finance, finance/& business analytics, international banking and finance/ management financial management, financial forecasting & investment, investment management, management; BA, BSc, MBA, MPhil, MSc, MScEcon, PhD

College of Engineering; www.swansea.ac.uk/engineering

aerospace engineering, chemical engineering, desalination and water re-use, fuel technology, membrane technology, civil engineering, computational mechanics, computer modelling and finite elements in engineering mechanics, computer modelling in engineering, research in civil engineering, electronic and electrical engineering, communication systems/engineering, power engineering and sustainable energy, nanoscience to nanotechnology, research in electronic and electrical engineering, environmental engineering, materials science and engineering, sports materials, materials engineering, steel technology, research in materials engineering, steel process and product development, steel engineering, mechanical engineering, research in mechanical engineering, medical engineering, research in tissue engineering and regenerative medicine, nanoscience to nanotechnology, nanotechnology, sports science, sports materials; BEng, EngD, MEng, MPhil, MRes, MS

College of Human & Health Sciences; www.swansea.ac.uk/HumanandhealthSciences

adult/child/mental health nursing, education, health and social care, healthcare science (audiology/cardiac physiology/nuclear medicine/respiratory and sleep physiology), maternity care, medical sciences and humanities, midwifery, osteopathy, paramedic science, psychology, social work, social policy, criminology & social policy, criminology & psychology, politics & social policy

Postgraduate; international/gerontology and ageing studies, childhood studies, developmental and therapeutic play, enhanced neonatal care, child public health, education for health professions, advanced critical care practice, advanced practice in health care, advanced specialist, blood transfusion practice, enhanced professional practice, approved mental health professional, long term and chronic conditions management, community and primary health care practice, health care law & ethics, non-medical prescribing, public health & health promotion, social work, health care management, abnormal and clinical psychology, research methods in psychology and cognitive neuroscience, research methods in psychology, social research methods; BA, BSc, BMid, BN, DipHE, HND, LLB, MA, MPhil, MSc, MScEcon, PGCert/Dip, PhD, DipHE, MOst, BScEcon

College of Medicine; www.swansea.ac.uk/medicine

medicine, surgery, genetics, biochemistry, medical genetics, medical biochemistry, rural & remote health, applied analytical science, applied liquid chromatography and mass spectrometry, autism and related conditions, clinical sciences (medical physics), health data science, health informatics, leadership for the health professions, life science and healthcare enterprise, medical radiation physics, nanomedicine, trauma surgery, trauma surgery (military), education for the health professions (human and health sciences), health informatics, life science and health care enterprise, medicine and life sciences, medical and health care studies, chemistry, education for the health professions, biomarkers and genes, devices, microbes and immunity, patients and population health and informatics, research in health professions education, medical and health care studies, chemistry; BSc, MBBCh, MD, MPhil, MSc, PhD, MRes, DProf, PGCert

College of Science; www.swansea.ac.uk/science

Dept of Biosciences; www.swansea.ac.uk/biosci

biology, biological sciences, biosciences, marine biology, zoology, environmental biology, conservation & resource management, high performance & scientific computing

Dept of Computer Science; www.swansea.ac.uk/compsci

computer science, software engineering, computing & software engineering, adv software technology; Postgraduate; advanced/computer science, advanced software technology, high performance and scientific computing, human computer interaction, theoretical computer science, visual and interactive computing, computing and future interaction technologies, visual computing, logic and computation

Dept of Geography; www.swansea.ac.uk/geography

geography, human geography, physical geography, physical earth science, geography & geoinformatics/European studies, environmental dynamics & climate change, geographical information & climate change, high performance & scientific computing, earth observation, environmental dynamics, glaciology, global environmental modelling, global migration, media geographies, social theory and space, urban studies

Dept of Mathematics; www.swansea.ac.uk/maths

mathematics, pure/applied mathematics, mathematics for finance, mathematics & physics/geoinformatics/computing for finance, high performance & science computing, stochastic processes, theory & application; BSc, MEng, MMath, MPhil, MPhys, MRes, MSc, PhD, FSc

Dept of Physics; www.swansea.ac.uk/physics

physics, theoretical physics, physics & nanotechnology, particle physics & cosmology, antimatter physics, cold atoms and quantum optics, laser physics, lattice gauge theory, nanotechnology, quantum fields & strings, theoretical particle physics, high performance & scientific computing

UNIVERSITY OF TEESSIDE
www.tees.ac.uk

School of Arts & Media; www.tees.ac.uk/schools/sam

Art: digital arts & design, fine art

Design: comics, graphic novels and sequential design, contemporary fashion, design for the creative industries, fashion enterprise, graphic design, interior architecture, interior design, textile design, digital arts and design, future design

English: English studies, creative writing

History: history, cultural history, European history, local & regional history

Media & Journalism: broadcast media production, journalism, journalism (magazine/sport), journalism and news practice, media studies, multimedia journalism/PR, TV & film production, mass communication

Performing Arts & Music: music technology, performing arts, dance, performance and events production, performance for live and recorded media; BA(Hons), BSc(Hons), FdA, MA, MPhil, MSc, PhD

School of Computing; www.tees.ac.uk/schools/scm

computer/character/animation/games/science, computer animation & visual effects, computing, computing (networks), computing, games AI/development/systems, conception by games & animation, digital story telling, games & animation, games development, creative digital media, concept art form, computer science, computer games design/programming/art, computer & digital forensics, computing networking, digital strategic development, web & multimedia, web design, computing security & networks, data science, indie games development, information visualisation, IT project management, mobile application development, software engineering, technical direction for visual effects, technical games development; BA, BSc, DProf, FdSc, MA, MPhil, MProf, MSc, PGDip, PhD

School of Health & Social Care; www.tees.ac.uk/schools/soh

adult social care, social care, dental hygiene and dental therapy, dental nurse practice, diagnostic radiography, midwifery, nursing studies (adult/learning disabilities/mental health), occupational therapy, operating department practice, paramedic practice, physiotherapy, social work, nursing in the home/district nursing, integrated care studies, operating department practice

Postgraduate; advancing quality improvement in health and social care, nursing (advanced cardiac care/advanced nurse practitioner, nursing (specialist field), surgical care practitioner (cardiothoracic/general/orthopaedic surgery), surgical gastroenterology and minimally invasive surgery, health education, specialist community public health nursing (health visiting/occupational health/school nursing), food and nutrition, advanced clinical practice, advanced clinical practice (cardiac care/management of long-term health conditions/neurological rehabilitation), advanced social work studies, advancing human factors in health and social care, advancing practice, advancing quality improvement in health and social care/ safety and governance in health and social care, autism practice, clinical psychology, clinical research, clinical research and evidence-based medicine, cognitive behaviour therapy, diagnostic radiography, evidence-based medicine, evidence-based medicine (anaesthesia, orthopaedic/perioperative medicine and pain), evidence-based practice, forensic radiography, health and social care, health and social care sciences (generic pathway), leadership in health and social care, manipulative therapy, medical ultrasound, midwifery studies, neurological rehabilitation, nursing (advanced cardiac care/advanced nurse practitioner/specialist field), occupational therapy, orthopaedics, physiotherapy, primary mental health care, public health,, specialist community public health nursing (health visiting), specialist community public health nursing (occupational health nursing/school nursing), surgical care practitioner (cardiothoracic surgery/general surgery/orthopaedic surgery), surgical gastroenterology and minimally invasive surgery, the management of long-term health conditions, transformational leadership in health and social care, research degrees

BA, BSc, Cert/DipHE, FdSc, MCh, MA, MPhil, MSc, PGCert/Dip, MRes, DClinPsy, Doc Health & Social Care

Science & Engineering; www.tees.ac.uk/schools/sse

crime scene & forensic science, computer and digital forensics, computer and digital forensic, crime scene science, forensic and investigative sciences, forensic biology, forensic science, crime and investigation, criminology, aeronautical engineering, chemical engineering, civil engineering, civil engineering with disaster management, civil engineering with industry, electrical and electronic engineering, electrical and electronic engineering, instrumentation and control engineering, mechanical engineering, biological sciences, biomedical science, chemistry, environmental science, food and nutrition, food science and engineering, biological sciences,chemistry, environmental science, food and nutrition, food science and engineering, human biology

Postgraduate; forensic science, criminal investigation, civil & structural engineering, electrical power and energy systems, food processing engineering, instrumentation and control engineering (oil and gas), mechanical engineering, oil and gas management, petroleum engineering, project management, energy and environmental management, food science and biotechnology

BEng, BSc, FdEng, MPhil, MRes, MSc, PGDip, PhD, MSci

School of Social Sciences, Business & Law; www.tees.ac.uk/schools/sssbl

Business, Accounting & Marketing; applied accounting and business finance, business with law, business and computing, airport and airline management, culinary arts and management, digital marketing, economics, hospitality management, sports management and marketing, travel and tourism, business finance and accounting, tourism management, law with business management, marketing, public services, tourism and aviation, tourism and events management, business finance and accounting

Criminology & Sociology; criminology, criminology and sociology/law/psychology/youth studies, social and public sector evolution, sociology, crime and investigation, crime scene science; Postgraduate; criminology, criminology (contemporary drug issues), global development and social research, research degrees, criminal investigation, education, early childhood & youth; education, education (early childhood studies), education (educational leadership), education and training, research degrees

Law, Policing & Investigation; crime and investigation, law, law with business management, police studies, policing; Postgraduate; criminal investigation, criminal law, medical law, research degrees, forensic science

Psychology; counselling, forensic psychology, psychology, psychology and counselling, psychology and criminology, psychology with business, therapeutic counselling Postgraduate; forensic psychology, health psychology and clinical skills, psychology doctorate; counselling psychology, research degrees, clinical psychology

Sport & Exercise; applied sport and exercise, fitness instruction and exercise therapies, physical activity, exercise and health, sport and exercise (applied sport science/coaching science/personal training/sport studies), sport and fitness, sports coaching and exercise, sports development, sports therapy and rehabilitation, sports management and marketing, applied sports rehabilitation, movement science and multimodal rehabilitation, sport and exercise, sports therapy, strength and conditioning, research degrees;

BA, BSc, DProf, FdA, FdSc, FdSocSc, GradCert, CertEd, LLB, LLM, MA, MPhil, MProf, MSc, PhD, DBA PGDip, DClinPsych

Degrees validated by University of Teesside offered at:

ASKHAM BRYAN COLLEGE
www.askham-bryan.ac.uk

agriculture & land management, animal management & science, animal conservation, applied horticulture/agriculture, arboriculture & urban forestry, canine & feline behaviour & welfare, countryside management/collection & conservation, equine science/management, enterprise (land-based), equine business & event management, equine sports management, sport surface management, arboriculture, applied/horticulture, landscaping & garden management, public services,sport (outdoor & adventure education/coaching & fitness), veterinary health studies/nursing/medicine, zoo management; BSc, BSc(Hons), Nat Dips, FDSC

UNIVERSITY CENTRE GRIMSBY
www.grimsby.ac.uk

computing technologies; commercial photography; design; games design and development; music; professional writing; special effects make-up design for TV, film and theatre; BA(Hons), BSc(Hons), FdSc

TRINITY COLLEGE LONDON
www.trinitycollege.co.uk

dance, drama & speech, music, performing & teaching, rock & pop, DaDa, English language, teaching English; PGDip, Music Diplomas, Teaching Diplomas

UNIVERSITY OF ULSTER
www.ulster.ac.uk

Faculty of Arts, Design & the Built Environment; www.adbe.ulster.ac.uk

Belfast School of Architecture
architectural technology and management; architecture; interior design; product and furniture design; Postgrad; architecture; BSc(Hons), BDes(Hons), MArch

Belfast School of Art
animation; art & design; contemporary applied arts; graphic design and illustration; fine art; interaction design; multidisciplinary design; photography; textile art design and fashion. Postgrad: fine art; multidisciplinary design; photography; BA(Hons), BDes(Hons), MFA

School of the Built Environment
architectural engineering; architectural technology and management; building surveying; civil engineering; civil engineering (geoinformatics); construction engineering and management; energy; energy and building services engineering; environmental health; planning and property development; quantity surveying and commercial management; real estate. Postgrad: commercial planning in construction; community planning and governance; construction business and project management; fire safety engineering; housing studies; infrastructure engineering; real estate; renewable energy and energy management; BEng(Hons), BSc(Hons), MEng, MPhil, MSc, MSci, PGCert, PGDip, PhD

Faculty of Arts; www.arts.ulster.ac.uk

School of Creative Arts and Technologies
Creative Technologies; cinematic arts; design; drama; drama with advertising/Irish/marketing; music; music with advertising/drama/Irish/marketing. Postgrad: contemporary performance practice; creative

technologies; drama; music; BA(Hons), BSc(Hons), MMus, MA, PhD

School of English and History

English; English with/and education/history/media studies; history; history with/and education/English/media studies; journalism with English/history. Postgrad: English; English literature; Irish history and politics; history; BA(Hons), MA, MRes, PhD

School of Irish Language and Literature

Irish language and literature; Irish with computing/drama/music/marketing/management studies. Postgrad: Irish language; Irish language translation interpreting and professional language skills; modern Irish; Irish studies; BA(Hons), Cert/Dip, MA

School of Media, Film and Journalism

English/history and media studies; interactive media; journalism with education/English/history; media and production; media studies with education/English/history. Postgrad: documentary practice; journalism; media management; media studies; BA(Hons), BSc(Hons), MA, PhD

Faculty of Computing & Engineering; www.compeng.ulster.ac.uk

School of Computing & Information Engineering

computing; computing (game development/internet systems); computing with business/Chinese/education. Postgrad: professional software development; BSc(Hons), MSc

School of Computing & Intelligent Systems at Magee

computational intelligence; computer science; computer science (software systems development); computer games development; computer engineering, computer games, modelling and animation; creative computing (design/games); electrical and electronic engineering; electronics & computer systems; information and communication technologies; information technologies; mechanical manufacturing engineering; renewable energy engineering. Postgrad: computational intelligence; BEng(Hons), BSc(Hons), PGDip

School of Computing & Mathematics

computing science; computing systems; computing technologies; interactive multimedia design; software engineering. Postgrad: professional software development; BSc(Hons), BEng(Hons) MSc, PhD

School of Engineering

biomedical engineering; clean technology; electronic engineering/and German masters; engineering management; mechanical/mechatronics engineering; mechatronics engineering and German masters; sports technology; technology with design. Postgrad: advanced composites & polymers; biomedical engineering; manufacturing management, nanotechnology; BSc(Hons), BEng(Hons), MEng, MSc, PGDip, PhD

Faculty of Life & Health Sciences; www.science.ulster.ac.uk

School of Biomedical Sciences

applied biosciences; biology; biomedical and healthcare sciences; biomedical and bio-industrial sciences; biomedical sciences; biomedical science (pathology); biotechnology; dietetics; food and nutrition; human nutrition; optometry; stratified medicine. Postgrad: medical professional practice; biomedical science; cataract and refractive surgery; clinical visual science; diabetes; dietetics; food and nutrition; food regulatory affairs; human nutrition; medical and healthcare biotechnology; nutraceuticals, functional foods and supplements; sports and exercise nutrition; stem cell biology; stratified medicine; veterinary public health; BSc(Hons), MRes, MSc, PGCert, PhD

School of Environmental Sciences

environmental science; environmental science with education/psychology; geography; geography with education/psychology. Postgrad: coastal zone management; geographic information systems; marine spatial planning; environmental management; environmental management with/and geographic information systems; environmental toxicology and pollution monitoring; BSc(Hons), PGDip, MRes, MSc, PhD

School of Health Sciences

diagnostic radiography & imaging; healthcare science; health physiology; occupational therapy; physiotherapy; podiatry; radiology & oncology; speech & language therapy. Postgrad: advancing practice in an AHP specialism; lower limb preservation in diabetes; medicines management; sensory integration; BSc(Hons), MSc, PGCert/Dip

School of Nursing

applied health studies; education for nurses and midwives; health and wellbeing; nursing (adult/mental health); specialist community public health nursing; specialist nursing with pathways. Postgrad: applied health studies; health and wellbeing; health promotion and public health; nursing; specialist community public health nursing; specialist nursing with pathways; BSc(Hons), MRes, MSc, PGCert, PGDip, PhD

School of Pharmacy and Pharmaceutical Sciences

pharmaceutical bioscience; pharmacy. Postgrad: pharmacy management; MPharm(Hons), MSci(Hons), PGDip

School of Psychology

psychology; social psychology. Postgrad: applied behavioural analysis; applied psychology (mental health and psychological therapies); family therapy and systemic practice; health psychology; BSc(Hons), MRes, MSc, PGCert, PhD

School of Sports

sport, physical activity and health; sports coaching; sport & exercise sciences; sports studies (sport: theory and practice). Postgrad: physical activity and public health; sport and exercise medicine/nutrition/psychology; sports development and coaching; BSc(Hons), MRes, MSc, PhD

Faculty of Social Sciences; www.ulster.ac.uk/socialsciences

School of Communication

advertising and marketing; communication, advertising and marketing; communication management and PR; counselling; professional development in counselling; language and linguistics (with optional specialism in counselling studies); therapeutic communication and counselling studies; Postgrad: communications and PR (advertising, political lobbying, healthcare); counselling and therapeutic communication; digital media communication; English language and linguistics; BSc(Hons), MSc, PGCert, PGDip

School of Education

certificate in teaching; education with English/environmental science/history; headship; library and information management; master of education; middle leadership; PGCE (post-primary, primary, in numerous school subjects, FE), teaching English to speakers of other languages (TESOL); BA(Hons), BSc(Hons), MA, MEd, MSc, PGCE, PGCert, PGDip

School of Law

law; law and/with criminology/politics/accountancy/HRM/marketing/Irish. Postgrad: clinical legal education; commercial law; gender, conflict and human

rights; human rights law and transitional justice; LLB(Hons), LLM, PhD

School of Criminology, Politics & Social Policy

criminology and criminal justice; law/politics/social politics/sociology with criminology; health and social care policy; politics; politics with criminology; law with politics; sociology with politics; social policy; social policy with criminology/sociology. Postgrad: public administration; social research skills with specialisms; social policy, criminology, public policy and social work; BSc(Hons), LLB(Hons) MPA, PGCert, PGDip, MPhil, PhD

School of Sociology & Applied Social Studies

community development/youth work, social work; sociology; sociology with criminology/politics; social policy with sociology. Postgrad: community youth work; professional development in social work; restorative practices; social policy, criminology, public policy and social work; BSc(Hons), MPhil, MSc, PGCert, PGDip, PhD

Ulster Business School; www.ulster.ac.uk/faculties/ulster-university-business-school

Department of Hospitality and Tourism Management

consumer management and food innovation; culinary arts management; event management; international event/hospitality/tourism/travel and tourism management; leisure and events management. Postgrad: International event/hospitality/tourism management; BSc(Hons), MSc, PhD

Department of International Business

accounting and advertising/HRM/marketing; accounting with specialisms; advertising; advertising and HRM; advertising with computing/drama; business administration, business information systems; business studies; business studies with advertising/computing/drama/Irish; HRM and marketing. Postgrad: international business; BSc(Hons), MSc, PhD

Department of Management and Leadership

HRM; management and leadership development. Postgrad: business administration; business improvement; HRM; management; management and corporate governance; sport management; BSc(Hons), eMBA, MBA, MSc, PhD

Department of Marketing, Entrepreneurship and Strategy

business studies; marketing. Postgrad: business development and innovation; marketing; BSc(Hons), MSc, PhD

Department of Accounting Finance and Economics

accounting (pathways); accounting and law/management; business economics; business economics with accounting/marketing; business technology; economics; economics with finance; finance and investment management. Postgrad: accounting; advanced accounting; applied finance; BSc(Hons), GradDip, MSc, PhD

Business Institute

civic leadership and community planning; management practice. Postgrad: executive leadership; BSc(Hons), GradDip, MSc

---

UNIVERSITY OF WALES TRINITY SAINT DAVID
www.uwtsd.ac.uk

Faculty of Architecture, Computing & Engineering; www.uwtsd.ac.uk/face

School of Applied Computing

applied computing; business information technology; computer games development; computer graphics and visualisation; computer networks; computer systems and electronics; computing and information systems; electrical and electronic engineering; mobile computing and application development; software engineering; web development. Postgrad: applied computing; business information technology; computer games development; computer games and VFX programming; computer networks/and security; computing and information systems; ecommerce; software engineering; web development; BSc(Hons), BEng(Hons), MComp, MSc, PhD

School of Architecture, Built & Natural Environment

architecture; architectural technology; building surveying; civil engineering and environmental management; project and construction management; quantity surveying and commercial management. Postgrad: properties and facilities management; sustainable construction; BSc(Hons), MSc

School of Automotive Engineering

automotive engineering; motorcycle engineering; motorsport engineering (all offered as undergraduate and postgraduate courses); BEng(Hons), BSc(Hons), MEng

Logistics and Transport

logistics and supply chain management; logistics and transport; motorsport management. Postgrad: engineering project management; lean and agile manufacturing; logistics; BSc(Hons), ProfDip, MSc

School of Mechanical and Manufacturing Engineering

mechanical and manufacturing engineering; mechanical engineering; energy and environmental engineering; extreme sports engineering. Postgrad: engineering project management; lean and agile manufacturing; logistics; non-destructive testing and evaluation; BSc(Hons), BEng(Hons), MSc

Natural Environments

environmental conservation; environmental sciences; marine and coastal geography. Postgrad: environmental conservation and management; BSc(Hons), MSc

Swansea College of Art; www.uwtsd.ac.uk/art-design

Automotive, Transport and Product Design

product design; product design & technology; automotive design; transport design. Postgrad: industrial design; product design; transport design; transportation design; BA(Hons), MA, MDes(Hons), MPhil, MSc, PhD

Film & Digital Media

creative computer games design; digital arts digital film and TV production; film and video culture; music technology; new media production; 3D computer animation. Postgrad: creative sound production; 3D computer animation; BA(Hons), MA, MArts, MMus Tech, MPhil, PhD

School of Fine Art & Photography

fine art, studio, site and context; photography in the arts; photojournalism and documentary photography. Postgrad: fine art (contemporary dialogues; photography (contemporary dialogues); BA, BA(Hons), MA fine art, MArt, MPhil, PhD

School of Visual Communication

graphic design; illustration; advertising and brand design. Postgrad: visual communication (contemporary dialogues); BA(Hons), MPhil, PhD

Surface Pattern Design and Glass

surface pattern design (fashion object/maker/textiles for fashion/textiles for interior). Postgrad: textiles (contemporary dialogues); surface pattern design (contemporary dialogues); BA, BA(Hons), MA, MDes

Faculty of Humanities & Performing Arts; www.uwtsd.ac.uk/faculty-of-humanities-performingarts

School of Archaeology, History and Anthropology

ancient history, ancient and mediaeval history; ancient civilisations; ancient history and anthropology/archaeology; ancient history with education studies/ancient Egyptian culture; anthropology; applied anthropology; anthropology and Chinese studies/English/Heritage studies/history/mediaeval studies/philosophy/religious studies; anthropology, education studies & ancient history/archaeology/classical studies/English/history/philosophy/religious studies; history with heritage management/digital humanities; anthropology with applied psychology/digital humanities/heritage management; archaeology; archaeology and anthropology/classical studies/education studies/heritage studies/history/mediaeval studies; archaeology and education studies; archaeology of Egypt and the near east; archaeology professional practice; archaeology with forensic studies/education studies/ancient Egyptian culture/heritage management/ digital humanities; Chinese civilisation/studies and mediaeval studies; conflict and war; environmental archaeology; environmental studies; history; history and ancient history/anthropology/archaeology/English/heritage studies/mediaeval studies/philosophy/theology; history, education studies & ancient history/anthropology/archaeology/classical studies/English/philosophy/religious studies; history with heritage management/digital humanities; mediaeval studies; mediaeval studies and anthropology/archaeology/classical studies/English/heritage studies/modern historical studies/philosophy; medieval studies with heritage management; modern historical studies; nautical archaeology; nautical archaeology and heritage studies. Postgrad: cultural astronomy and astrology; engaged anthropology; landscape management and environmental archaeology; local history; heritage practice; medieval studies; BA(Hons), MA, MRes

School of Classics

ancient history and related courses (see School of Archaeology above); classical studies, classical civilisation, classics, combinations of classical studies and/with ancient Egyptian culture/archaeology/creative writing/digital humanities/education studies/ English/Greek/heritage management/Latin/mediaeval studies/philosophy/religious studies/theology. Postgrad: ancient history; ancient religions; classical studies, classics; Greek; Latin; BA(Hons), MA, MRes, PGCert, PGDip

School of Cultural Studies

Chinese Studies: Chinese civilisation; Chinese studies; combinations of Chinese civilisation/studies and/with anthropology/education studies/ English/heritage management/heritage studies/mediaeval studies/philosophy/religious studies

Creative Writing: creative writing; creative writing and digital humanities/education studies/English/heritage management/heritage studies/philosophy/publishing

English: English; English and/with combinations of ancient history/anthropology/Chinese civilisation/Chinese studies/classical studies/digital humanities/education studies/heritage management/heritage studies/history/mediaeval studies/philosophy/religious studies/TEFL

Philosophy: philosophy; ethical and political studies; philosophy and/with combinations of ancient history/anthropology/Chinese civilisation/Chinese studies/classical studies/creative writing/digital humanities/education studies/English/ethics/heritage management/heritage studies/history/mediaeval studies/religious studies/theology

School of Cultural Studies postgraduate options: applied philosophy; creative writing; creative and script writing; English with TEFL; European philosophy; medieval and early modern literature; modern literature; ethics; literary studies; medieval literature; MA, MPhil, MRes, PhD

School of Theology, Religious Studies and Islamic Studies

astudiaethau crefyddol; bible and theology; religious studies; Islamic studies; combinations of ancient history/anthropology/applied psychology/archaeology/Chinese studies/classical studies/education studies/heritage management/heritage studies/history/ Islamic studies/ mediaeval studies/religious studies/

theology. Postgrad: biblical interpretation; Christian theology; church history; Islamic studies; religious experience; study of religions; BA(Hons), GradDip, MA, MRes, MTh

The School of Performing Arts
acting; applied drama; dance; theatre design and production; perfformio; performing arts (contemporary performance); technical theatre top-up; BA(Hons)

Welsh International Academy of Voice
Postgrad: advanced pianoforte studies; advanced vocal studies; MA, PGDip

Faculty of Business & Management; www.uwtsd.ac.uk/business-management

Swansea Business School
accounting; business; business and finance; business management; e-business; finance; HRM, international business; management; management and leadership; marketing; marketing management; law and business. Postgrad: financial management, marketing; digital marketing; e-MBA; HRM; MBA, MBA educational management; professional programmes in human resource management/practice; learning and development; marketing; BA, MA, MBA, MBus, MSc, DBA, DipM, MPhil, PGDip, PGCert, PhD

School of Sport, Health & Outdoor Education
children and young people; health; health and social care; health management; law & public services; international sports management; stadium and sports facility management; nutrition and lifestyle; outdoor adventure education; outdoor fitness; personal training (health & exercise); physical education; public health; public services; sport and health; sport therapy; sports management. Postgrad: outdoor education, physical education; BA, BSc, FDA, MA

The School of Tourism and Hospitality
events management; international hotel management; international travel and tourism management; leisure management; tourism management. Postgrad: international tourism management, sports management, events management, international tourism, sports management; BA

Wales Institute for Work-Based learning
Postgrad: professional practice; DProf

Faculty of Education & Community; www.uwtsd.ac.uk/education-and-communities

School of Early Childhood
early childhood. Postgrad: early literacy; BA, FdA, MA, MEaCH, PGDip

School of Social Justice and Inclusion
advocacy; counselling skill and interdisciplinary studies; counselling studies and psychology; education studies; inclusive studies for teaching assistants; learning support; primary education studies; social inclusion (inclusive education); social studies (additional needs/communities, families and individuals/ health and social care); supporting learning and teaching; youth and community work. Postgrad: equality and diversity in society; psychotherapeutic practice (emotion-focused therapy); youth work; BA, FdA, GradCert, MA, MScoStud

School of Welsh and Bilingual Studies
applied bilingualism (Welsh with English). Postgrad: bilingualism & multilingualism; Celtic studies; BA, MA

School of Psychology
adolescent psychology; anthropology with applied psychology; applied psychology; counselling studies/ education studies and psychology; philosophy with applied psychology; psychology; religion ethics and applied psychology; religious studies with applied psychology. Postgrad: applied social and health psychology; BA, BSc, GradCert, MA, MPhil, MSc, PhD

South West Wales Centre of Teacher Education
BA primary education with QTS. Postgrad: PGCE primary/secondary with QTS, PGCE secondary with QTS: art & design/computing and ICT/ business studies/maths 11-18/maths 11-16 with ICT/biology/ design and technology/geography/physics/science 11-16/English/history/modern foreign languages/religious education/Welsh/chemistry

UNIVERSITY OF WARWICK
www.warwick.ac.uk

Faculty of Arts; www2.warwick.ac.uk/fac/arts

Dept of Classics and Ancient History; www2.warwick.ac.uk/fac/arts/classics

ancient history & classical archaeology/with study in Europe; classical civilization/with philosophy; classics; classics (Latin/ancient Greek); English & Latin literature; Italian & classics; philosophy with classical civilisation. Postgrad: ancient visual & material culture; visual & material culture in ancient Rome/Greece; BA(Hons), MA, MPhil, PhD

Dept of English and Comparative Literary Studies; www2.warwick.ac.uk/fac/arts/english

English literature; English literature & creative writing/theatre studies; English & French/German literature/Hispanic studies/Italian literature/Latin literature; film/philosophy & literature. Postgrad: English literature; global Shakespeare; world literature; writing, translation & transcultural studies; BA(Hons), MA, MPhil, PGDip, PhD

Dept of Film and Television Studies; www2.warwick.ac.uk/fac/arts/film

film & literature; film studies; French/German/Italian with film studies. Postgrad: film & TV studies; research in film and TV studies; BA(Hons), MA, MPhil, PhD

Dept of History (now including Comparative American Studies); www2.warwick.ac.uk/fac/arts/history

history; history, literature and cultures of the Americas; history and philosophy/politics/sociology/French/German/global sustainable development/Italian; liberal arts history pathway. Postgrad: early modern history; eighteenth century studies; global history; modern history; history of medicine; BA(Hons), MA, MPhil, PhD

Dept of History of Art; www2.warwick.ac.uk/fac/arts/arthistory

history of art; art history with Italian/French, Italian and history of art. Postgrad: history of art; history of art – Venice & its legacies; BA(Hons), MA, MPhil, PGDip, PhD

School of Theatre; www2.warwick.ac.uk/fac/arts/theatre_s

English/French/German/Italian/Hispanic studies &/with theatre studies; theatre and performance studies/with global sustainable development. Postgrad: theatre and performance research; theatre consultancy; BA(Hons), MA, MPhil, PhD

Schools of Modern Languages and Cultures:

French Studies; www2.warwick.ac.uk/fac/arts/French-studies

French studies; French studies and/with German/Italian/Hispanic studies; modern languages; modern languages and economics; modern languages and/with linguistics. Postgrad: French studies; pan-romanticisms; research in French/French and Francophone studies; translation, writing and cultural difference; BA, MA, MPhil, PhD

Dept of German Studies; www2.warwick.ac.uk/fac/arts/german-studies

German studies; German studies and/with French/Italian/Hispanic studies; modern languages; modern languages and economics; modern languages and/with linguistics. Postgrad: German studies; pan-romanticisms; research in German studies; translation, writing and cultural difference; BA, MA, MPhil, PhD

Dept of Hispanic Studies; www2.warwick.ac.uk/fac/arts/Hispanic-studies

Hispanic studies; Hispanic studies and/with French/German/Italian studies; modern languages; modern languages and economics; modern languages and/with linguistics. Postgrad: Hispanic studies; pan-romanticisms; research in Hispanic studies; translation, writing and cultural difference; BA, MA, MPhil, PhD

Dept of Italian; www2.warwick.ac.uk/fac/arts/Italian-studies

Italian studies; Italian studies and/with French/German/Hispanic studies; modern languages; modern languages and economics; modern languages and/with linguistics. Postgrad: Italian studies; pan-romanticisms; research in Italian studies; translation, writing and cultural difference; BA, MA, MPhil, PhD

Centre for the Study of the Renaissance; www2.warwick.ac.uk/fac/arts/ren

Postgrad: culture of the European Renaissance, including Venice programme; Renaissance studies; MA, MPhil, PhD

Yesu Persaud Centre for Caribbean Studies; www2.warwick.ac.uk/fac/arts/ccs

Postgrad: history, literature, culture or societies of the Caribbean; PhD

Faculty of Medicine; www2.warwick.ac.uk/fac/med

Warwick Medical School

Postgrad: advanced clinical practice/for health care professionals; advanced critical care practice; diabetes; diabetes (paediatrics); doctor of medicine; endodontics; health research, interdisciplinary biomedical research; leadership for health care; medical education; medical sciences; medicine and surgery; metabolic medicine; molecular analytical science; nursing; psychiatry; orthodontic theory; orthodontics; pre-hospital critical care; public health; reproductive health; restorative and aesthetic dentistry; trauma and orthopaedics/musculoskeletal; MBChB, MD, MMedEd, MPhil, MPH, MSc, PGDip, PGCert, PhD

Faculty of Sciences; www2.warwick.ac.uk/fac/sci

Dept of Life Sciences; www2.warwick.ac.uk/fac/sci/lifesci

biochemistry, biomedical science, biological sciences, biotechnology, bioprocessing & business management, environmental bioscience in changing climate, food security, integrative medical microbiology & virology, medical bioscience & business management, sustainable crop production, agronomy for the 21st century; BSc, MD, MPhil, MSc, PhD

Dept of Chemistry; www2.warwick.ac.uk/fac/sci/chemistry

chemistry/with medicinal chemistry. Postgrad: analytical science and instrumentation; analytical and polymer science; chemistry with scientific writing; diamond science & technology; molecular analytical science; polymer chemistry; polymer science; scientific research and communications; Warwick-Monash polymer science; BSc(Hons)/Chem/ChMC, MChem, MSc, PhD, ChM

Dept of Computer Science; www2.warwick.ac.uk/fac/sci/dcs

computer and management sciences; computer science; computer systems engineering; data science; discrete mathematics. Postgrad: computer science; data analytics; BSc(Hons), MEng, MPhil, MSc, PhD

School of Engineering; www2.warwick.ac.uk/fac/sci/eng

automotive engineering; civil engineering; computer systems engineering; electronic engineering; engineering and business studies; engineering business management; general engineering; manufacturing and mechanical engineering; mechanical engineering. Postgrad: advanced mechanical engineering, biomedical engineering, communications and information engineering, energy and power engineering, sustainable energy technologies, tunnelling and underground space; BEng, BSc, EngD, MPhil, MSc, PhD

School of Life Sciences; www2.warwick.ac.uk/fac/sci/lifesci

biochemistry; biological sciences; biomedical science; life sciences and global sustainable development. Postgrad: biotechnology, bioprocessing and business management; environmental bioscience in a changing climate; food security; medical biotechnology and business management; sustainable crop production – agronomy for the 21st century; BSc(Hons), BASc, MBio, MSc, PhD

Dept of Mathematics/Warwick Mathematics Institute; www2.warwick.ac.uk/fac/sci/maths

mathematics: mathematics & business studies/economics/philosophy. Postgrad; advanced study in mathematical sciences; financial mathematics: interdisciplinary mathematics; mathematics; mathematics for real world systems; BSc(Hons), MMath, MSc, PhD

Dept of Physics; www2.warwick.ac.uk/fac/sci/physics

mathematics & physics, physics/& business studies. Postgrad: Master project options; BSc, MMathPhys, MPhys, MSc, PhD

Dept of Psychology; www2.warwick.ac.uk/fac/sci/psych

psychology. Postgrad: behavioural & economic science; clinical applications of psychology; clinical psychology; psychological research; psychology; BSc(Hons), MPhil, MSc, PhD, Doc ClinPsych

Dept of Statistics; www2.warwick.ac.uk/fac/sci/statistics

data science; mathematics, operational research, statistics and economics (MORSE); mathematics and statistics. Postgrad: statistics; financial mathematics; BScMathStat(Hons), BScMORSE(Hons), MMathStat; MPhil, MSc, PhD

Warwick Manufacturing Group; www2.warwick.ac.uk/fac/sci/wmg

Postgrad: cyber security; e-business; engineering business management; innovation and entrepreneurship; international technology management; international trade, strategy and operations; management for business excellence; manufacturing systems engineering and management; programme and project management; service management and design; sustainable automotive engineering; supply chain and logistics management; MSc, EngD, EngD International, PhD

Faculty of Social Sciences; www2.warwick.ac.uk/fac/soc

Centre for Applied Linguistics; www2.warwick.ac.uk/fac/soc/al

English language and logistics; language, culture & communication; linguistics with a modern language (Arabic/Chinese/ French/German/Italian/ Japanese/Portuguese/Russian/Spanish). Postgrad: English Language teaching; intercultural communication for business and the professions; BA(Hons), MA, MSc, MPhil, PhD

Centre for Education Studies; www2.warwick.ac.uk/fac/soc/ces

Postgrad: drama and theatre education; drama education and ELT; educational leadership and management; educational studies; educational innovation; global education and international development; psychology and education; religions and education; EdD, MA, MSc, MRes, MPhil, PhD

Centre for Professional Education; www2.warwick.ac.uk/fac/soc/cps

Postgrad: PGCE early years/international/primary/secondary; professional education school groups/individuals; teaching advanced mathematics; MA, PGCert

Dept of Economics; www2.warwick.ac.uk/fac/soc/economics

economic studies and global sustainable development; economics; economics, politics and international studies; economics and industrial organisation; French/German/Italian/Hispanic studies and economics; liberal arts; mathematics and economics; mathematics, operational research, statistics and economics (MORSE); modern languages and economics; philosophy, politics and economics. Postgrad: behavioural and economic science; economics; economics and international financial economics; finance and economics; BA(Hons), BSc(Hons), BASc(Hons), MRes, PGDip, PhD

Warwick Institute for Employment Research; www2.warwick.ac.uk/fac/soc/ier

Research; PhD

Dept of Philosophy; www2.warwick.ac.uk/fac/soc/philosophy

philosophy; philosophy & global sustainable development/history/literature/maths/psychology/classical civilisation; philosophy of mind, philosophy, politics & economics. Postgrad: continental philosophy; philosophy; philosophy and literature/ the arts; BA(Hons), BSc(Hons), MA, MPhil, PhD

Dept of Politics & International Studies; www2.warwick.ac.uk/fac/soc/pais

politics; politics and international studies/sociology; politics, international studies and global sustainable development/quantitative methods/modern languages. Postgrad: PAIS – big data & quantitative methods; political & legal theory; research in PAIS; US foreign policy; international development; public policy; international politics & Europe/East Asia; international security; international political economy; international relations; BA(Hons), MA, MPhil, PhD

Dept of Sociology; www2.warwick.ac.uk/fac/soc/sociology

sociology; sociology & quantitative methods; sociology with specialisms in social and political thought/research methods/gender studies/race and global politics/social inequalities and public policy/technologies and markets; sociology and French/global sustainable development/history/law/politics. Postgrad; sociology; social research; social and political thought; gender and international development; women's and gender studies; BA(Hons), MA, MPhil, PhD

Warwick School of Law;
www2.warwick.ac.uk/fac/soc/law

European law with French or German law; law; law and business studies/humanities/social sciences/ sociology; law with study abroad in English. Postgrad: advanced legal studies; international commercial law; international corporate governance and financial regulation; international development law and human rights; international economic law; BA(Hons), LLB(Hons), LLM, MPhil, PhD

Warwick Business School;
www2.wbs.warwick.ac.uk/fac/soc/

accounting & finance; international business; international management; management; information systems management & innovation. Postgrad; accounting & finance; applied management; business (consulting/accounting & finance/financial management/marketing; business analytics; doctor of business administration; finance; finance & economics; financial mathematics; HRM & employment relations; information systems management & innovation; international business; management; marketing and strategy; MBA/Exec MBA; service excellence; BSc(Hons), DBA, MBA, MSc, MPA, MPhil, PGDip, PhD

UNIVERSITY OF WEST OF SCOTLAND
www.uws.ac.uk

School of Business & Enterprise;
www.uws.ac.uk/schools/business-school

accounting; applied enterprise; business; business (London); business/& English language; events management; HRM; law & business; marketing; tourism management. Postgrad: accounting; creative branding; digital marketing; doctor of business administration; finance and accounting with CIMA; financial accounting; HRM; international events management; international financial management; international HRM; international management; international marketing management; logistics and supply chain management, management accounting; master of business administration; BA/BA(Hons), BAcc(Hons), DBA, MSc, MBA, EMBA, PGDip/Cert

School of Education; www.uws.ac.uk/ schools/school-of-education

childhood practice; childhood studies; community education, education; ESL. Postgrad: artist teacher; childhood practice; coaching and mentoring; education (primary); education (secondary); enhanced educational practice; inclusive education; leadership for learning; mental health and education; teaching and learning in HE; primary physical education; TESOL; BA/BA(Hons), BEd, MEd, PGCert, PGDip, PGDE

School of Engineering & Computing;
www.uws.ac.uk/schools/school-of- engineering-and-computing

aircraft engineering; business technology; chemical engineering; civil engineering; computer animation; computer games development/technology; computer networking; computer-aided design; computing; computing science; engineering management; information technology; mechanical engineering; mechatronics; music technology; physics; physics with nuclear technology; product design & development; web and mobile development. Postgrad; advanced computer systems development; advanced computing; advanced thin film technologies; big data; chemical engineering; civil engineering; engineering management; information and network security; information technology; internet of things; mechanical engineering; mobile web development; smart networks; BEng,/BEng(Hons), BSc/BSc(Hons), PGCert, PGDip, MSc

School of Health, Nursing & Midwifery;
www.uws.ac.uk/schools/school-of health- nursing-and-midwifery

adult nursing; integrated health and social care; integrated health and social care with administration; mental health nursing; midwifery. Postgrad: acute mental health care; adult nursing; advancing practice; child protection; cognitive behavioural therapy, gerontology and later life studies; global primary health care management; health studies, health studies (family health/maternal and child health); healthcare associated infection improvement; mental health nursing; mental health practice; midwifery; neonatal nursing; nursing studies; personality disorder; professional health studies; public health nursing; sexual and reproductive health; specialist community public health nursing (health visiting/ occupational health); specialist practitioner (district nurse); vulnerability; working with older people; BA/ BA(Hons), BSc/BSc(Hons); MSc, PGCert, PGDip

School of Media, Culture and Society; www.uws.ac.uk/schools/school-of-media-culture-and-society

broadcast production; commercial music; commercial sound production; criminal justice; digital art and design; filmmaking and screen-writing; journalism; performance; psychology; society, politics and policy; technical theatre. Postgrad: applied social science; broadcast journalism; careers guidance and development, contemporary drug and alcohol studies; creative media practice; cultural diplomacy and international events/music/sports; filmmaking;

music: policy analysis and global governance; psychology; social work; BA, BA(Hons), BAcc, DProf, MA, MSc, PGCert, PGDip

School of Science & Sport; www.uws.ac.uk/school-of-science

applied bioscience; applied bioscience and zoology/ forensic science; biomedical science; applied biomedical science; chemistry; environmental health; forensic science; occupational safety and health; pharmacy science and health; sport & exercise science; sport coaching/development. Postgrad: advanced biomedical science; biotechnology; drug design & discovery; exercise and health science; project management; sports coaching; waste & clean technologies; BA, BSc/BSc(Hons), DProf, PGCert, PGDip, MSc

THE UNIVERSITY OF WESTMINSTER
www.wmin.ac.uk

Faculty of Architecture and the Built Environment; www.westminster.ac.uk/about-us/faculties/architecture-and-the-built-environment

Architecture and Interiors

architectural technology; architecture; architecture and environmental design; designing cities, planning and architecture; interior architecture; Postgrad: architecture; architecture and environmental design; interior design; master of architecture; urban design; BA(Hons), BSc(Hons), MA, MArch, MSc, PGDip

Planning, Housing and Urban Design

designing cities, planning and architecture; property and planning; Postgrad: energy and environmental change; international planning and sustainable development; urban and regional planning; urban design; housing practice; BA(Hons); BSc(Hons), MA, PGDip

Property and Construction

architectural technology; building engineering; building surveying; construction management; property and planning; quantity surveying and commercial management; real estate; Postgrad: building information management; construction commercial management; construction project management; facilities and property management; property finance; real estate development; BSc(Hons), MSc, PGCert, PGDip

Tourism and Events

tourism and events management; tourism management (top-up); tourism planning and management; tourism with business; Postgrad: events and conference management; tourism management; BA(Hons), MA

Westminster School of Media Arts and Design; www.westminster.ac.uk/about-us/faculties/westminster-school-of-media-arts-and-design

Art and Design

animation; fine art mixed media; graphic communication design; illustration and visual communication; Postgrad: design for communication; interactive media practice; BA(Hons), DProf, MA, MPhil, MRes, PhD

Fashion

fashion buying management; fashion design; fashion marketing and promotion; fashion merchandise management; Postgrad: fashion business management; menswear; BA(Hons), MA

Journalism and Mass Communication

digital media and communications; journalism; medical journalism; public relations and advertising; radio and digital production; television production; Postgrad: communication; communications policy; diversity and the media; global media; global media business; media and development; media management; media campaigning and social change; multimedia journalism (broadcast/print and online); public relations; social media culture and society; BA(Hons), DProf, MA, MPhil, MRes, PGCert, PGDip, PhD

Music

commercial music; commercial music performance; Postgrad: audio production; music business management; BA(Hons), BMus(Hons), DProf, MA, MPhil, MRes, PhD

Photography

contemporary media practice; imaging art and science; photography; Postgrad: documentary photography and social journalism; photography arts; BA(Hons), DProf, MA, MPhil, MRes, PhD

Television, Film and Moving Image

contemporary media practice; film; television production; Postgrad: film and television theory culture and industry; BA(Hons), DProf, MA, MPhil, MRes, PhD

Faculty of Science and Technology; www.westminster.ac.uk/about-us/ faculties/science-and-technology

Biomedical Sciences

applied biomedical science; biomedical and physiological sciences; biomedical sciences; human and medical science; pharmacology and physiology; Postgrad: applied biomedical science; biomedical sciences; biomedical sciences (cancer biology/cellular pathology/clinical biochemistry/haematology/medical microbiology); medical molecular biology; medical molecular biology bioinformatics; BSc(Hons), DProf, MSc, MPhil, MRes, PhD

Biosciences

biochemistry; biological sciences; pharmacology and physiology; Postgrad: applied biotechnology; pharmacology; BSc(Hons), DProf, MSc, MPhil, MRes, PhD

Business Information Systems

business information systems; Postgrad: business information systems; business intelligence and analytics; database systems; BSc(Hons), DProf, MSc, MPhil, MRes, PhD

Complementary Medicine

Chinese medicine acupuncture/with foundation; herbal medicine/with foundation; Postgrad: Chinese herbal medicine; Chinese medicine acupuncture; herbal medicine; medicinal plant science; BSc(Hons), DProf, MSc, MPhil, MRes, PhD

Computer and Network Engineering

computer network security/with foundation; computer networks and communications/with foundation; computer systems and robotics/with foundation; computer systems engineering/with foundation; Postgrad: computer networks and communications; computer networks with cloud technologies/with security; BSc(Hons), DProf, MSc, MPhil, MRes, PhD

Computer Science and Software Engineering

computer science; software engineering; Postgrad: advanced software engineering; cyber security and forensics; interactive media practice; BSc(Hons), DProf, MEng(Hons), MA, MSc, MPhil, MRes, PhD

Electronic Engineering

biomedical electronic and instrumentation engineering/with foundation; electronic and electrical engineering/with foundation; electronic engineering/with foundation; Postgrad: electronics with embedded systems/medical instrumentation/robotic and control systems/system-on-chip technologies; telecommunications with digital systems processing/satellite and broadband technologies/wireless technologies; BSc(Hons), DProf, MEng(Hons), MSc, MPhil, MRes, PhD

Multimedia and Games Computing

computer games development; multimedia computing; Postgrad: interaction design and computing; interactive media practice; BSc(Hons), DProf, MA, MSc, MPhil, MRes, PhD

Nutrition

human nutrition/with foundation; Postgrad: international public health nutrition; public health nutrition; sport and exercise nutrition/advanced standing; BSc(Hons), DProf, MSc, MPhil, MRes, PhD

Psychology

cognitive and clinical psychology; psychology; Postgrad: business psychology; cognitive rehabilitation; health psychology; psychology; BSc(Hons), DProf, MSc, MPhil, MRes, PhD

Faculty of Social Sciences and Humanities; www.westminster.ac.uk/ about-us/faculties/social-sciences-and-humanities

Criminology/Sociology

criminology; sociology; sociology and criminology; BA(Hons)

English

Arabic and English language/literature; Chinese and English language/literature; creative writing and English language/literature; English language and French/linguistics/Spanish; English literature and French/history/language/Spanish; English literature; Postgrad: creative writing; writing the city; cultural and critical studies; English language and creative writing/linguistics/literature; English literature; modern contemporary fictions; teaching English to speakers of other languages (TESOL); TESOL and creative writing; BA(Hons), MA, MPhil, PhD

History

English literature and history; history; history and politics; BA(Hons)

Languages

Arabic and English language/linguistics/ literature; Chinese and English language/linguistics/literature; creative writing and English language/literature; English language and French/Spanish; English literature and French /Spanish; French and linguistics/Spanish; international relations and Arabic/Chinese/French/Spanish; linguistics and Spanish; modern languages (Arabic/Chinese/French/Spanish) and global communications; translation studies French/Spanish; Postgrad: international liaison and communication; specialised translation; translating cultures; translation and interpreting; BA(Hons), MA, MPhil, PhD

Linguistics

Arabic/Chinese English language/French/Spanish and linguistics; Postgrad: teaching English to speakers of other languages (TESOL); BA(Hons), MA, MPhil, PhD

Politics and International Relations

history and politics; international relations and Arabic/Chinese/development/French/Spanish; international relations; politics; politics and international relations; Postgrad: energy and environmental change; international relations; international relations and democratic politics/security; BA(Hons), MA, MPhil, PhD

Westminster Business School; www.westminster.ac.uk/about-us/ faculties/westminster-business-school

Accounting, Finance and Economics

accounting; business economics; business management (finance); business management accounting/economics; finance; Postgrad: finance and accounting; finance banking and insurance; global finance; international economic policy and analysis; investment and risk finance; BA(Hons), BSc(Hons); MA, MSc, MPhil, PhD

Business and Management; HR Management; Marketing

business finance (management/legal regulation); business management; business management accounting/economics/entrepreneurship/HR management/marketing; business management; entrepreneurship; HR management; international business; international business (Chinese); international business with Arabic/French/Spanish; international marketing; marketing communications; marketing management; Postgrad: HR management; international business and management; international HR management; management; marketing communications; marketing management; MBA; project management; purchasing and supply chain management; BA(Hons), MA, MBA, MSc, MPhil, PGCert, PGDip, PhD

Education

higher education; special study in supporting learning; MA, MPhil, PGCert, PhD

Westminster Law School; www.westminster.ac.uk/about-us/ faculties/law

Law

European legal studies; law; law with French law; MLaw (integrated masters in law); Postgrad: conflict prevention dispute resolution; corporate finance law; energy and environmental change; entertainment law; graduate diploma in law; international commercial and dispute resolution law; international commercial law; international law; legal practice; GradDip, LLB(Hons), LLM, MLaw; MA, MPhil, PhD

THE UNIVERSITY OF WINCHESTER
www.winchester.ac.uk

Faculty of Arts; www.winchester.ac.uk/ aboutus/Universitystructure/arts/Pages/ faculty_of_arts.aspx

English, Creative Writing and American Studies
American studies; American studies and history/ politics; creative writing/creative professional writing; English literature; English language studies; English with American literature; Postgrad: creative and critical writing; writing for children; BA(Hons), MA

Performing Arts
choreography and dance; comedy performance and production; drama; musical theatre; performing arts; street arts, performance and production; theatre for children and young people; theatre production (arts and stage management); vocal and choral studies; Postgrad: cultural and arts management; creative arts; BA(Hons), MA, PhD

School of Media and Film
broadcast television and media production; digital media design; film production; film studies; mass communication; media and audio communication; media and communication; media, communication and advertising/journalism/social media; Postgrad: digital media practice; BA(Hons), MA

Faculty of Business, Law and Sport; www.winchester.ac.uk/aboutus/ Universitystructure/BLS/Pages/ FacultyofBusiness,LawandSport.aspx

Winchester Business School
accounting and finance; accounting and management; business management/(top-up)/with enterprise and innovation; events management; fashion, media and marketing; marketing; Postgrad: accounting and finance; applied global practice (management); insight management; international business; marketing and innovation; project management; executive MBA; doctor of business administration; BA(Hons), MA, MSc, ExecMBA, DBA, PhD

Law
law; law and ethics; BA(Hons), LLB(Hons), LLM

Sport and Exercise
sport and exercise science; sport psychology and coaching; sports business and marketing; sports coaching; sports studies; strength conditioning and fitness; Postgrad: applied sport and exercise science; sport and exercise psychology; sport and exercise; BA, BSc, MPhil, MSci, MRes, MSc, PhD

Faculty of Education, Health and Social Care; www.winchester.ac.uk/aboutus/ Universitystructure/BLS/Pages/ FacultyofEducation/ HealthandSocialCare.aspx

Education Studies and Liberal Arts
education studies/(early childhood)/(special and inclusive education); modern liberal arts; Postgrad: education studies/(early childhood)/(special and inclusive education); philosophy of education; modern liberal arts; BA(Hons), MA, Med Stud(Hons),

Interprofessional Studies
childhood studies; childhood, youth and community studies; health, community and social care studies; social work; Postgrad: delivery of primary health care; health and social care; medical education; GP education; social work; BA(Hons), BSc(Hons), FdA, MA, MSc, PGCert, PGDip

Teacher Development
primary education with recommendation of qualified teacher status (QTS); Postgrad: education; doctor of education; PGCE primary education; PGCE secondary religious education; postgraduate early years ITT; school leadership; BEd(Hons), EdD, MA, MEd(-Hons), PGCE

Faculty of Humanities and Social Sciences; www.winchester.ac.uk/ aboutus/Universitystructure/BLS/Pages/ FacultyofHumanitiesandSocial Sciences.aspx

Animal Welfare Centre
animal welfare and society; Postgrad: animal welfare science, ethics and law; BA(Hons), MA

Applied Social Sciences
criminology; forensic studies; sociology; geography; Postgrad: applied criminology; BA(Hons), MSc

Archaeology

ancient, classical and mediaeval studies; archaeology; archaeological practice/with professional placement; classical studies; history, civilisations and beliefs; Postgrad: archaeology; human bioarchaeology; cultural heritage and resource management; human osteology and funerary studies; BA(Hons), BSc(Hons), MA, MRes

History

American studies and history/politics; ancient, classical and mediaeval studies; classical studies; history; history and the mediaeval/modern world; history, civilisations and beliefs; global history and politics; politics and global studies; Postgrad: history; BA(Hons), MA, MPhil, PhD

Psychology

psychology; psychology and child development; psychology and cognition; psychological science; social psychology; Postgrad: forensic psychology; BSc(Hons), MSc, MPhil, PhD

Theology, Religion and Philosophy

philosophy, politics and economics; philosophy, religion and ethics; theology, religion and ethics; Postgrad: Christian approaches to leadership; Christian liturgy/spirituality; death, religion and culture; orthodox studies; reconciliation; reconciliation and peacebuilding; theology, theology and practice; imagination and culture; BA(Hons), MA, MPhil, PhD, ProfDoc

---

UNIVERSITY OF WOLVERHAMPTON
www.wlv.ac.uk

Faculty of Arts; www.wlv.ac.uk/about-us/our-schools-and-institutions/faculty of arts

Wolverhampton School of Art

applied arts; fashion and textiles; fine art; interior design; photography; product design; visual communication; visual communication (graphic design/illustration); Postgrad: design and applied arts; fine art; digital and visual communications; BA(Hons), BDes(Hons), MA, PhD

School of Humanities

English; English & deaf studies/education studies/film studies/history/philosophy; Postgrad: English; BA(Hons), MA

Creative and Professional Writing; creative and professional writing and English/film studies/media and communication studies/philosophy; BA(Hons)

English Language; English language and creative and professional writing/ linguistics/media and communication studies/media and cultural studies; BA(Hons)

Linguistics; linguistics and English language/deaf studies, linguistics and TESOL; Postgrad: language and information processing; BA(Hons), MA

Philosophy; philosophy and creative professional writing/English/film studies/law/politics/religious studies/sociology/war studies; Postgrad: human sciences; BA(Hons), MRes

Religious Studies; religious studies and education studies/history/philosophy/sociology; BA(Hons)

Cultural Heritage; cultural heritage; Postgrad: popular culture; BA(Hons), MA

School of Media

Animation, Games & Film Production; animation, computer games design, video and film production, art and design, commercial video production; BA(Hons), FdA

Broadcasting, Film & Media Studies; broadcasting and journalism, film studies, media and communication studies, media and cultural studies, film studies and philosophy, film, media and cultural studies, English and film studies, creative and professional writing and film studies, media and cultural studies and English language, media and cultural studies and sociology, film, media and communication studies, broadcast journalism, public relations; Postgrad: contemporary media; film studies; PR & corporate communication; BA(Hons), FdA, MA

School of Performing Arts

dance; dance and drama; drama; drama and musical theatre; music; music technology, musical theatre, music technology and popular music, popular music, sound production; Postgrad: dance; dance science; music; audio technology; BA(Hons), BMus(Hons), MA, MMus, MSc

Faculty of Education, Health and Wellbeing; *www.wlv.ac.uk/about-us/our-schools-and-institutes/faculty-of-education-health-and-wellbeing*

Institute of Education
chemistry or computer science or mathematics with education; childhood studies; family and community studies; childhood and family studies and education studies/social policy/sociology/special educational needs, disability, inclusion; childhood studies with early years teacher status; education; education (learning education with progression); education studies; education studies and English; early years primary; early years services; primary education; special educational needs, disability, inclusion studies; special educational needs, disability, inclusion studies and education studies; supporting children in primary education; Postgrad: education; higher education and professional practice; PGCE; professional graduate certificate post-compulsory education; professional practice and lifelong education; BA(Hons), BA (PCE), BEd(Hons), BSc(Hons), CertED, PGCert, DEd, EDD, PGCE, PhD, FdA

Institute of Health Professions
developing palliative and end of life care practice; emergency practitioner (top-up); nursing (adult/children's/mental health/community health/learning disabilities); health and social care practice/top-up/restraint reduction; health and wellbeing (learning, education and progression); health studies (top-up); lymphoedema care; nursing studies fast track/top-up/subject-specific pathways (acute care/care of the older person/critical care/mental health and psychological interventions/orthopaedic care/renal care); midwifery; palliative and end-of-life care/for adults with life-limiting illness/for adults with progressive life-limiting illness; paramedic science; podiatry; special educational needs, inclusion and childhood and family studies; Postgrad: adult nursing; advanced clinical practice; advanced practice for allied health professionals (diabetology/musculoskeletal disorders); commissioning for health and social care; education for health social care and allied professionals; emergency planning, resilience and response; health and social care; health and wellbeing; health and wellbeing top-up; healthcare leadership; medical education; mental health; mental health nursing; midwifery studies; nursing; physician associate studies; return to nursing; service improvement; specialist clinical nursing; specialist community public health nursing (health visiting);

BA(Hons), BNurs(Hons), BSc, BSc(Hons), MNurs, MAN, MMHN, MSc, PGCert, PGDip, ProfDoc

Institute of Psychology
psychology; psychology (counselling psychology/criminal behaviour); Postgrad: counselling psychology; forensic and investigative psychology; psychology; psychology (forensic/occupational); BSc(Hons), PGCert, MSci(Hons), PhD, ProfDoc

Institute of Public Health, Social Work & Care
health studies; health studies (top-up); health and social care; public health; social care; social care and criminology and criminal justice/deaf studies/health studies/sociology/social policy; social care (learning, education and progression); social work; social work studies; specialist social work studies; Postgrad: health and social care; health and wellbeing; master of public health; mental health practice for approved mental health professions; BSc(Hons), FD, MA/MSc, MPH, PGCert, PGDip

Institute of Sport
exercise and health; physical education; sport and exercise science; sport, culture, media and development; sport and exercise; sports coaching practice; sports coaching practice (football/martial arts); strength and conditioning; youth sport; Postgrad: sport and exercise science; BA(Hons); BSc(Hons); MRes; MSci(Hons); PhD

Faculty of Science & Engineering; *www.wlv.ac.uk/about-us/our-schools-and-institutes/faculty-of-science-and-engineering*

School of Architecture & Built Environment
architecture; architectural design technology; building surveying; civil engineering; civil and environmental engineering; constructional management; environmental health; geography, urban environments and climate change; infrastructure engineering management; interior architecture and property development; quantity surveying; Postgrad: building information modelling; civil engineering; civil engineering management; computer aided design for construction; construction law dispute and resolution; climate change management; construction project management; environmental management; environmental technology; BSc(Hons), BEng(Hons), MSc, PGCert

School of Biology, Chemistry & Forensic Science

Biology: animal behaviour and wildlife conservation; biochemistry; biological sciences; biotechnology; genetics and molecular biology; microbiology; molecular bioscience

Chemistry: chemistry, chemistry with secondary education (QTS)

Forensic Science: forensic science; forensic science and criminology

Postgrad: animal behaviour and wildlife conservation; molecular biology with bioinformatics, computational bioinformatics, forensic genetics and human identification, forensic mark comparison, fire scene investigation, medical biotechnology, applied microbiology and biotechnology; wildlife conservation; BSc(Hons), MSc, MSci

School of Biomedical Science & Physiology

biomedical science; healthcare science (biomedical science/physiological sciences); human biology; medical physiology and diagnostics; medical science; Postgrad: biomedical science; biomedical science (cellular pathology/clinical biochemistry/haematology)/medical microbiology); BSc(Hons), BMedSci(-Hons), MSc, DMedSci

School of Engineering

aerospace engineering; automotive engineering; chemical engineering; electronic and telecommunications engineering; mechanical engineering; mechatronics engineering; motorsport engineering; Postgrad: advanced technology management; advanced technology management – engineering analysis/manufacturing/sustainability; manufacturing engineering; BEng(Hons), MEng(Hons), MSc, PGCert

School of Mathematics & Computer Science

business intelligence; cloud computing; computer networks (top-up); computer science; computer science (games development/software engineering); computer science with secondary education (QTS); computer science (smart technologies); computer security (top-up); computing; computing games development (top-up); computing software development (top-up); cyber security; data science; industrial mathematics; mathematics; mathematics with secondary education (QTS); mathematical sciences; Postgrad: computer science; information technology; information technology management; mathematics; web and mobile application development; BSc(Hons), MSc, PGCert

School of Pharmacy

pharmaceutical science; pharmacology; pharmacy; Postgrad: pharmaceutical science (drug discovery & design/pharmacological sciences), independent prescribing; BSc(Hons), MPharm, MSc

Faculty of Social Sciences; www.wlv.ac.uk/about-us/our-schools-and-institutions/faculty-of-social-sciences

The Wolverhampton Business School

accounting & finance; business and accounting/economics/finance/HR management/marketing management; business management; business management with foundation year; event and venue management; economics; economics and politics/social policy/sociology; human resource management; international business management; international hospitality management; marketing management; tourism management; Postgrad: coaching and mentoring, finance and accounting, healthcare leadership, HR development and organisational change, HR management, innovation and entrepreneurship, international banking and finance, international business management, management, marketing, event and venue management, international hospitality management/managing PR for events and venues; Postgrad Certs, Dips: coaching and mentoring; event and venue management; healthcare leadership; HRD and organisational change; HRM; international hospitality management; leadership; management studies; marketing (CIM); medical education; MBA, BA(Hons), BSc(Hons), FdA, MA, MBA, PGCert/Dip, MSc

Wolverhampton Law School; law, accounting and law, business and law

accounting and law; business and law; HR management and law; law; law and philosophy, law and social sciences with foundation year; social policy and law; Postgrad: Chartered Institute of Legal Executives certification; common professional examination; international commercial and financial law; international corporate and financial law; law; professional practice top-up; legal practice; BA(Hons), LLB(Hons), PGDip/Cert, LLM

School of Sociology, History & Political Studies

criminal justice and sociology/social policy; criminology; criminology and criminal justice; criminology and criminal justice and law/social care/social policy/

sociology; deaf studies and English/linguistics/social policy/special educational needs, disability and inclusion studies; English and history; history; history and religious/war studies; politics and history/media and communication studies/philosophy/social policy/war studies; childhood and family studies/media cultural studies/philosophy/religious studies/social care and sociology; childhood and family studies/social care

and social policy; social policy and law; interpreting; interpreting with foundation year; sociology; sociology and history/politics/social policy; war studies; war studies and philosophy; Postgrad: conflict studies; military history by distance learning; history of the first world war; second world war studies, conflict, society, holocaust; BA(Hons), MA

UNIVERSITY COLLEGE WORCESTER
www.worc.ac.uk

Institute of Education; www.worc.ac.uk/discover/institute-of-education

collaborative working with children, young people and families; early childhood (professional practice); education and training; education studies; integrated working with children and families; learning support; music education; primary and outdoor education; primary initial teacher education; professional practice; religion, philosophy and values in education; special educational needs, disability and inclusion; teaching and learning; teaching English (literacy and ESOL); university diploma in private tutoring; Postgrad: education; education (church school leadership/early childhood/leadership and management/leading, learning and teaching/mentoring and coaching/religions and values education/special and inclusive education); higher education; leading early years practice; mentoring in early childhood; national awards SENCo (Special Educational Needs Coordination); PGCE (primary/secondary); teaching and learning in higher education; QTS, BA, CertHE, EdD, FdA, MA, MMus, PGCE, PGCert, PGDip

Institute of Health & Society; www.worc.ac.uk/discover/institute-of-health-and-society

applied criminology; applied health and social science; business psychology; child and adolescent mental health; clinical psychology; counselling; counselling psychology; criminology; crisis workers for sexual violence; developmental psychology; forensic psychology; fundamentals of general practice nursing; health and social care; health sciences; integrative counselling; learning disabilities; mental health; midwifery; nursing (adult, children, mental health); nursing studies (for overseas nurses); occupational therapy; physiotherapy; paramedic science; psychology; social work; sport and exercise psychology; youth and community work; youth justice;

Postgrad: advancing practice; business/occupational psychology; clinical education; counselling; diet, nutrition and health; dynamics of domestic violence; EMDR therapy; health science; independent sexual violence advisers; law and ethics for health and social care; nursing studies; nutritional therapy; physician associate; professional development eye witness; psychology; public health; social work; supervision; transformative practice; urgent and acute clinical care; BA, BSc, DHSc, FdA, FdSc, MA, MRes, MSc, PGCert, PGDip

Institute of Humanities & Creative Arts; www.worc.ac.uk/discover/institute-of-humanities-and-creative-arts

animation; archaeology & heritage studies and art & design; art and design; creative & professional writing; creative digital media; drama and performance; English language; English literature; film production; film studies; fine art; game art design; graphic design and multimedia; history; illustration; journalism; law; media and culture; politics, people and power; screenwriting; sociology; touring theatre; Postgrad: creative digital media; design; early modern studies; drama; fine art; green media; history; theatre and performance; BA, BSc, LLB, MA, MRes, MTheatre

Institute of Science & the Environment; www.worc.ac.uk/discover/institute-of-science-and-the-environment

animal biology; arboriculture; archaeology and heritage studies; biochemistry; biology; ecology; environmental science; forensic and applied biology; geography; horticulture; human biology; human geography; human nutrition; mathematics; physical geography; plant science; Postgrad: archaeological landscapes; sustainable development advocacy; research in biology/river science/ ecology and environmental management; evaluation for a sustainable future; BA, BSc, FdSc, MA, MRes, MSc, PGCert

Institute of Sport & Exercise Science; www.worc.ac.uk/discover/institute-of-sport-and-exercise-science

cricket coaching & management; dance and community practice; football business management and coaching; outdoor adventure leadership & management; physical education (PE); PE and dance/ outdoor education; sport and exercise science; sport business management; sports coaching science; sports coaching science with disability sport; sports development and coaching; sports performance and coaching; sports studies; sports therapy; Postgrad: applied sport science; applied sports performance analysis; European basketball coaching science; outdoor education; socio-cultural studies of sport and exercise; sports coaching; sports management; BA, BSc, FdSc, MSc, MPhil, PhD, MRes

Worcester Business School; www.worc.ac.uk/discover/worcester-busines-school

accounting; accounting and finance; advertising; business administration; business information technology; business, business management; combination degrees in accountancy/advertising/economics/entrepreneurship/finance/HR management/law/leadership/management/marketing/public relations; computer games design and development; computing; entrepreneurship; finance; international business management; leadership and management; marketing; marketing, advertising and public relations; web development; Postgrad: business administration; finance; HR management; leadership and management; international management; marketing; master of business administration/MBA leadership and management; BA, BSc, DBA, FdA, MA, MBA, MComp, MPhil, MSc, PGCert, PhD

UNIVERSITY OF YORK
www.york.ac.uk

Dept of Archaeology; www.york.ac.uk/archaeology

archaeology; archaeology and heritage; historical archaeology; bioarchaeology; Postgrad: archaeological information systems; bioarchaeology; digital heritage; early prehistory; funerary archaeology; human anatomy and evolution; zooarchaeology; the archaeology of buildings; conservation studies; cultural heritage management; field archaeology; historical archaeology; medieval archaeology; landscape archaeology; mesolithic studies; BA, BSc, MA, MPhil, MSc, PhD

Dept of Biology; www.york.ac.uk/biology

biology; biochemistry; biomedical sciences; biotechnology & microbiology; ecology; genetics; molecular cell biology; industrial biotechnology (MSc only); BSc, MPhil, MRes, MSc, PhD, MBiol

Dept of Chemistry; www.york.ac.uk/chemistry

chemistry; chemistry, management & industry; chemistry, resources & the environment; chemistry, biological and medicinal chemistry; green chemistry and sustainable industrial technology; BSc, MChem, MPhil, MSc, PhD

Dept of Computer Science; www.cs.york.ac.uk

advanced computer science; computer science; computer science with artificial intelligence; computer science with embedded systems; computer science and mathematics; computing; cyber security; doctorate in intelligent games and game intelligence; human-centred interactive technologies; information technology; safety critical systems engineering; safety critical systems engineering with automotive applications; social media & interactive technology; software engineering; systems safety engineering; BEng, BSc, MEng, MMath, MPhil, MSc, PGCert, PGDip

Dept of Economics & Related Studies; www.york.ac.uk/economics

economics; economics and finance; economics and econometrics; economics, econometrics and finance; economics and mathematics; economics and philosophy; economics and politics; history and economics; mathematics and finance; philosophy, politics and economics; Postgrad: development economics and emerging markets; econometrics and economics; economics; economics and finance; economics and public policy; finance and econometrics; financial engineering; health economics; project analysis, finance and investment; BA, BSc, MPhil, MSc, PGCert, PGDip, PhD

Dept of Education; www.york.ac.uk/education

education; English in education; sociology and education; psychology in education, PGCE (English, history, maths, economics, geography, foreign languages, sciences, teaching & learning, teacher training); Postgrad: applied linguistics; applied linguistics for ELT; applied linguistics for language teaching; global & international citizenship education; science education; social justice and education; teaching English to speakers of other languages; teaching English to young learners; BA, MA, MPhil, PhD, PGCE

Dept of Electronics; www.york.ac.uk/electronics

electronic engineering; electronic and communication engineering; electronic and computer engineering; electronic engineering with nanotechnology; electronic engineering with business management; music technology systems; Postgrad: audio and music technology; communications engineering; digital systems engineering; electronic engineering; embedded wireless systems; engineering management; intelligent robotics; music technology; nanoscale VLSI design; BEng, MEng, MSc, MPhil, PhD

Centre for Eighteenth Century Studies; www.york.ac.uk/eighteenth-century-studies

MA in eighteenth century studies; MA

Dept of English & Related Literature; www.york.ac.uk/english

English; English/history; English/history of art; English/linguistics; English/philosophy; English/politics; Postgrad: culture & thought after 1945, eighteenth century studies; English literary studies; film and literature; global literature and cultures; literature of the Romantic period, 1775-1832; medical history and humanities; medieval literatures & languages, modern and contemporary literature and culture; poetry and poetics, Renaissance literature, 1500-1700; Victorian literature and culture; BA, MA, MPhil, PhD

Dept of Environment; www.york.ac.uk/environment

environment, economics and ecology; environmental geography; environmental science; human geography and environment; Natural Sciences specialising in Environment; Postgrad: environmental economics & environmental management; environmental science and management; marine environmental management; corporate social responsibility and environmental management; BSc, MPhil, MSc, MEnv, PhD

Centre for Health Economics; www.york.ac.uk/che

economic evaluation of health technologies; economic evaluation for health technology assessment, health econometrics & data; health economics; health economics for healthcare professionals; health policy, mental health policy; MSc, PhD

Dept of Health Sciences; www.york.ac.uk/healthsciences

biomedical sciences; nursing (adult); nursing (child); nursing (learning disability); nursing (mental health); midwifery practice; applied health research, health research and statistics; health sciences; health & social care; international humanitarian affairs; public health; BA, BSc, DipHE, MPhil, MSc, PGCert, PGDip, PhD, MPH, FD, MNursing, Dip

Dept of History; www.york.ac.uk/history

history; English history; French history; history/economics; history/philosophy; history/politics; history of art; Postgrad: contemporary history and international politics; culture and thought after 1945; early modern history; eighteenth century studies; heritage, history and the parish church; medical history and humanities; medieval history; medieval studies; modern history; public history; Renaissance and early modern studies, women's studies; BA, MA, MPhil, PhD, PGDip

Dept of History of Art; www.york.ac.uk/history-of-art

history of art, English/history of Art; history/history of Art; Postgrad: history of art; history of art (architectural history and theory); history of art (British art); history of art (medieval art and medievalisms); history of art (modern and contemporary art); history of art (sculpture studies); stained glass conservation & heritage management; BA, MA, MPhil, PhD

Hull York Medical School; www.hyms.ac.uk

undergraduate qualifying medical courses; biomedical sciences; clinical anatomy; clinical anatomy and education; human sciences, medical sciences; medicine; public health; health professions education; human anatomy and evolution; physicians associate studies; MBBS, MSc, PGCert, MD, PhD, MPhil, BSc

Centre for Applied Human Rights; www.york.ac.uk/cahr

applied human rights, international human rights law & practice; LLM, MA, PhD, PGCert

Dept of Language & Linguistic Science; www.york.ac.uk/language

studying two languages: French and German/Italian/Spanish; German and Italian/Spanish; Italian and Spanish; studying one language and linguistics: French/German/Italian/Spanish; linguistics with French/German/Italian/Spanish; history/French; French/philosophy; German/philosophy; studying English, English language & linguistics; English/linguistics; studying linguistics: linguistics; linguistics/mathematics; philosophy/linguistics; Postgrad: linguistics; comparative syntax and semantics; forensic speech science; language and communication; language variation and change; linguistics by research; phonetics and phonology; phonological development, psycholinguistics; sociolinguistics; BA, MA, MPhil, MSc, PhD

York Law School; www.york.ac.uk/law

law, international corporate governance & commercial law, international human rights law & practice; legal & political theory; LLB, LLM, MPhil, PhD

York Management School; www.york.ac.uk/management

business and management; accounting, business finance and management; actuarial science; marketing; Postgrad: accounting and financial management; global marketing; human resource management; international business and strategic management; management; management with business finance; BA, BSc, MA, MPhil, MRes, MSc, PhD

Dept of Mathematics; maths.york.ac.uk/www/Home

mathematics; actuarial science; mathematics with computer science/economics/physics/statistics/finance/philosophy; Postgrad: advanced mathematical biology; financial engineering, mathematical finance (distance learning also available); statistics & computational finance; BA, BSc, MMath, MPhil, MRes, MSc, PGCert, PGDip, PhD

Centre for Modern Studies; www.york.ac.uk/modernstudies

culture & thought after 1945; MA

Dept of Music; www.york.ac.uk/music

music; music and sound recording; Postgrad: music; community music; music education; music production, music technology; BA, MA, MPhil, PhD, PGDip/Cert

Dept of Philosophy; www.york.ac.uk/philosophy

philosophy, philosophy with economics/politics/politics & economics/mathematics & physics/neuroscience/social & political sciences/English/French/German/ History/ mathematics/linguistics/sociology/physics; BA, BSc, GradDip, MA, MPhil, MPhys, PhD

Dept of Physics; www.york.ac.uk/physics

physics; physics with astrophysics/mathematics/philosophy; theoretical physics, fusion energy; BA, BSc, MMath, MPhil, MPhys, MSc, PhD

Dept of Politics; www.york.ac.uk/politics

politics; politics with international relations/English/history/economics/philosophy (including PPE); social and political sciences; Postgrad: conflict, governance & development; environment and politics; international political economy; international relations; political research, political theory; political philosophy, public administration; public administration & public policy/international development; postwar recovery studies; BA, MA, MSc, PhD

Dept of Psychology; www.york.ac.uk/psychology

psychology; Postgrad: applied forensic psychology; cognitive neuroscience; forensic psychology studies; development, disorders and clinical practice; developmental cognitive neuroscience; research in psychology; BSc, MPsych, MPhil, MRes, MSc, PhD

Dept of Social Policy & Social Work; www.york.ac.uk/spsw

applied social science (children & young people/crime & criminal justice); applied social science & social policy; criminology; social and political sciences; social policy; social work; Postgrad: comparative and international social policy; comparative applied social and public policy; global crime and justice; global social policy; master of public administration; master of public administration, international development; public policy and management; public policy and management (online); social and public policy (online); social policy; BA, MA, MPA, MPhil, MRes, PhD

Dept of Sociology; www.york.ac.uk/sociology

sociology, sociology with criminology/ social psychology, sociology/education, philosophy/sociology, social and political sciences/ with philosophy;

Postgrad; criminology/ and social research, culture, society and globalization, social media and social research, social media and management, social media and interactive technologies; BA, MA, MPhil, MSc, PhD

Dept of Theatre, Film & Television; www.york.ac.uk/tft

interactive media; theatre writing, directing & performance; film & TV production; Postgrad: digital film & TV production; post-production with visual effects/sound design; theatre – writing direction and performance; theatre, film, TV and interactive media by research; BA, BSc, MA, MPhil, MSc, PhD

YORKSHIRE COAST COLLEGE
www.yorkshirecoastcollege.ac.uk

www.yorkshirecoastcollege.ac.uk/higher-education-course-areas.php

fine art; historical and performance costume for stage & screen; education (teaching in lifelong learning sector); events management; social care; sport and recreation management; tourism management; BA, CertEd, FdA, GradCert, PGCE

Part 5

Qualifications Awarded by Professional and Trade Associations

THE FUNCTIONS OF PROFESSIONAL ASSOCIATIONS

Qualifications

Some associations qualify individuals to act in a certain professional capacity. They also try to safeguard high standards of professional conduct. Few associations have complete control over the profession with which they are concerned. Some professions are regulated by the law, and their associations act as the central registration authority. Entry to others is directly controlled by associations that alone award the requisite qualifications. If a profession is required to be registered by the law and is controlled by the representative council, a practitioner found guilty by his or her council of misconduct may be suspended from practice or completely debarred by the removal of his or her name from the register of qualified practitioners. In other professions the consequence of misdemeanour may not be so serious, because the profession does not exercise the same degree of control.

The professions registered by statute, and therefore subject to restrictions on entry and loss of either privileges or the right to practise on erasure, are listed in Table 5.1. Certain other professions are closed.

Table 5.1 Professions registered by statute

Profession	Statutory committee controlling professional conduct
Architects	Architects Registration Board
Dentists	General Dental Council
Doctors	General Medical Council
Professions supplementary to medicine: arts therapists, biomedical scientists, chiropodists/podiatrists, clinical scientists, dieticians, hearing aid dispensers, occupational therapists, operating department practitioners, orthoptists, paramedics, physiotherapists, practitioner psychologists, prosthetists/orthotists, radiographers, speech and language therapists and social workers	Health and Care Professions Council (HCPC)
Nurses and midwives	Nursing and Midwifery Council
Opticians and optometrists	General Optical Council
Osteopaths	General Osteopathic Council
Patent attorneys	Chartered Institute of Patent Attorneys
Pharmacists, pharmacy technicians	General Pharmaceutical Council
Teachers	The National College for Teaching and Leadership

Study

Some associations give their members an opportunity to keep abreast of a particular discipline or to undertake further study in it. Such associations are especially numerous in medicine, science and applied science. Many qualifying associations also provide an information and study service for their members. Some of the more famous learned societies confer added status upon distinguished practitioners by electing them to membership or honorary membership.

Protection of Members' Interests

Some associations exist mainly to look after the interests of individual practitioners and the group. A small number are directly concerned with negotiations over salary and working conditions.

MEMBERSHIP OF PROFESSIONAL ASSOCIATIONS

Qualifying associations

The principal function of qualifying associations is to examine and qualify people who wish to become practitioners in the field with which they are concerned. As already indicated, some regulate professional conduct and many offer opportunities for further study. Membership is divided into grades, usually classified as corporate and non-corporate. Non-corporate members are those not yet admitted to full membership, mainly students; they are divided from corporate membership by barriers of age and levels of responsibility and experience. The principal requirement for admission to membership is the knowledge and ability to pass the association's exams; candidates may be exempted from the association's exams if they have acceptable alternative qualifications.

Non-corporate or affiliated members

Non-corporate members are those who are as yet unqualified or only partly qualified. They are accorded limited rights and privileges, but may not vote at meetings of the corporate body. Most associations have a student membership grade. Students are those who are preparing for the exams that qualify them for admission to corporate membership. Some associations have licentiate and graduate membership grades, which are senior to the student grade. Graduates are those who have passed the qualifying exams but lack other requirements, such as age and experience, for admission to corporate membership.

Corporate or full members

Corporate members are the fully qualified constituent members of incorporated associations. They are accorded full rights and privileges and may vote at meetings of the corporate body. Corporate membership is often divided into two grades: a senior grade of members or fellows and a general grade of associate members or associates.

Honorary members

Some associations have a special class of honorary members or fellows for distinguished members or individuals who have made an outstanding contribution to the profession in question.

Examinations and requirements

Professionals normally become corporate members by exam or exemption, with or without additional requirements. Many final professional exams are of degree standard, and a number of professional qualifications are accepted by employers as evidence of competence at operational level. Ongoing professional development is encouraged by most associations to ensure members' skills and knowledge are up to date and relevant.

The transition from the general grade of membership to the senior can be automatic in some associations (for instance, on reaching a prescribed age), but in others the higher grade is reached only after the submission of evidence of research or progress in the profession.

Qualifying exams are usually conducted in two or more stages. The first stage leads to an Intermediate or Part I qualification, the second leads to a Final or Part II or Part III qualification, which is about the standard of a degree.

Gaining professional qualifications

Prospective students can study by any of the following means:

- correspondence courses (distance learning and/or online support);

- personal attendance at the schools maintained by some associations (eg the Architectural Association School of Architecture);

- further and higher education institutions.

ACCOUNTANCY
Membership of Professional Institutions and Associations

ASSOCIATION OF ACCOUNTING TECHNICIANS

140 Aldersgate Street
London EC1A 4HY
Tel: +44 (0)20 3735 2434
Fax: 020 7397 3009
E-mail: aat@aat.org.uk
Website: www.aat.org.uk

AAT is the UK's leading qualification and membership body for accounting professionals. We have over 125,000 members including students, people working in accountancy and self-employed business owners, in more than 90 countries worldwide. Established in 1980 to ensure consistent training and regulation for accounting staff, our qualifications provide a progression route to CIMA, CIPFA, ICAS, ICAEW and ACCA.

MEMBERSHIP
Student Member
Affiliate Member
Full Member (MAAT)
Fellow Member (FMAAT)

QUALIFICATION/EXAMINATIONS
AAT Accounting Qualifications
Entry Award in Accounting (AAT Access)
Entry Certificate in Accounting
Introductory Certificate in Accounting
Introductory Diploma in Accounting and Business (16–19-year-olds)
Intermediate Diploma in Accounting
Advanced Diploma in Accounting
Advanced Certificate in Taxation and Ethics
AAT Bookkeeping
Introductory Award in Bookkeeping
Intermediate Certificate in Bookkeeping
Advanced Certificate in Bookkeeping and Ethics
AAT Computerised Accounting
Introductory Award in Computerised Accounting
Intermediate Award in Computerised Accounting
Advanced Certificate in Computerised Accounting and Ethics
AAT Small Business Courses
Introductory Award in Accounting Skills to Run Your Business
AAT Essentials (One day courses)

DESIGNATORY LETTERS
MAAT and FMAAT

ASSOCIATION OF CHARITY INDEPENDENT EXAMINERS

The Gatehouse
White Cross
South Road
Lancaster
Lancashire LA1 4XQ
Tel: 01524 34892
E-mail: info@acie.org.uk
Website: www.acie.org.uk

ACIE provides support, training, conferences, resources and qualifications for independent examiners of charity accounts throughout the UK (*subscriptions apply*). Further information at the website: **www.acie.org.uk**

Registered charity in E&W 1139609 & SC039066. Registered company limited by guarantee 7461134; registered in England at The Gatehouse, White Cross, Lancaster LA1 4XQ.

MEMBERSHIP
Affiliate
Full Member (*with category of either Associate or Fellow*)

QUALIFICATION/EXAMINATIONS
Associate (*limited re: size and type of charity by one of several authorisation bands – see website*): ACIE
Fellow (*all UK charities eligible for IE*): FCIE

DESIGNATORY LETTERS
ACIE, FCIE

CHARTERED INSTITUTE OF INTERNAL AUDITORS

13 Abbeville Mews
88 Clapham Park Road
London SW4 7BX
Tel: 020 7498 0101
Fax: 020 7978 2492
E-mail: membership@iia.org.uk
Website: www.iia.org.uk

The Chartered Institute of Internal Auditors (IIA) is the only professional body in the UK and Ireland focused exclusively on internal auditing and we are passionate about supporting, promoting and training the professionals who work in it. Every year we help internal auditors at every stage of their career with training, qualifications and technical resources.

MEMBERSHIP
Student Member
Affiliate Member
Voting Member (PIIA, CMIIA)

Head of Internal Audit Service Member
Fellow (FIIA, CFIIA)

QUALIFICATION/EXAMINATIONS
IIA Certificate in Internal Audit and Business Risk (IA Cert)
IIA Diploma (PIIA)
IIA Advanced Diploma (CMIIA)
IT Auditing Certificate

DESIGNATORY LETTERS
IA Cert, PIIA, CMIIA, FIIA, CFIIA

CIMA – THE CHARTERED INSTITUTE OF MANAGEMENT ACCOUNTANTS

26 Chapter Street
London SW1P 4NP
Tel: 020 8849 2251
E-mail: cima.contact@cimaglobal.com
Website: www.cimaglobal.com

CIMA is the employers' choice when recruiting financially qualified business leaders.

The Chartered Institute of Management Accountants, founded in 1919, is the world's leading and largest professional body of Management Accountants, with 183,000 members and students operating at the heart of business in 168 countries. CIMA works closely with employers and sponsors leading-edge research, constantly updating its qualification, professional experience requirements and continuing professional development to ensure it remains the most relevant international accountancy qualification for business.

MEMBERSHIP
Member
Associate (ACMA)
Fellow (FCMA)

QUALIFICATION/EXAMINATIONS
Certificate in Business Accounting
CIMA Professional
Certificate in Islamic Finance
Diploma in Islamic Finance

DESIGNATORY LETTERS
ACMA, FCMA

ICAEW (THE INSTITUTE OF CHARTERED ACCOUNTANTS IN ENGLAND AND WALES)

Metropolitan House
321 Avebury Boulevard
Milton Keynes MK9 2FZ
Tel: 01908 248 250
E-mail: careers@icaew.com
Website: icaew.com/careers

ICAEW is a world leading professional membership organisation that promotes, develops and supports over 140,000 chartered accountants worldwide. We provide qualifications and professional development, share our knowledge, insight and technical expertise, and protect the quality and integrity of the accountancy and finance profession.

MEMBERSHIP
ACA (Associate of the Institute of Chartered Accountants in England and Wales)
FCA (Fellow Chartered Accountant)

QUALIFICATION/EXAMINATIONS
The ICAEW chartered accountancy qualification, the ACA, is one of the most advanced learning and professional development programmes available. It has integrated components which give an in-depth understanding across accountancy, finance and business. Combined they help build the technical knowledge, professional skills and practical experience needed to become an ICAEW Chartered Accountant. There is more than one way to start the ACA, find out more at icaew.com/careers

The ICAEW Certificate in Finance, Accounting and Business (ICAEW CFAB) provides fundamental knowledge and skills in finance, accounting and business. ICAEW CFAB consists of the same six exam modules as the first level of the ACA qualification. It can be studied as a stand-alone qualification or as an entry route to the ACA. There are no entry requirements and it is achievable in as little as 12 months through online learning, self-study or classroom tuition. Find out more at icaew.com/cfab

DESIGNATORY LETTERS
ACA, FCA

ICAS (INSTITUTE OF CHARTERED ACCOUNTANTS OF SCOTLAND)

CA House
21 Haymarket Yards
Edinburgh EH12 5BH
Tel: 0131 347 0100
E-mail: caeducation@icas.com
Website: icas.com

ICAS is a professional body for around 19,000 world class business professionals who work in the UK and in more than 100 countries around the world. Our members have all achieved the internationally recognised and respected CA qualification. We are an educator, examiner, regulator, and thought leader. ICAS is the first professional body for accountants and was created by Royal Charter in 1854.

MEMBERSHIP

To qualify as a CA, trainees must enter and complete a training contract with an ICAS authorised employer for a prescribed period, normally three years. They must achieve relevant work experience requirements and key competencies, study for and pass three stages of examinations and complete a course and assignment in Business Ethics. For further information please see the ICAS website.

QUALIFICATION/EXAMINATIONS

The CA qualification syllabus contains ten subjects leading to three stages of exams.

Test of Competence (TC) contains five subjects: Financial Accounting, Principles of Auditing and Reporting, Finance, Business Management, Business Law.

Test of Professional Skills (TPS): Taxation, Advanced Finance, Financial Reporting, Assurance and Business Systems.

Test of Professional Expertise (TPE) contains a multidisciplinary case study designed to apply theoretical knowledge and practical skills to a real-life situation.

In addition to including ethics within the three levels, Business Ethics forms a standalone subject and assessment.

DESIGNATORY LETTERS

CA

INSTITUTE OF FINANCIAL ACCOUNTANTS

Burford House
44 London Road
Sevenoaks
Kent TN13 1AS
Tel: 01732 458080
Fax: 01732 455848
E-mail: mail@ifa.org.uk
Website: www.ifa.org.uk

The IFA was established in 1916 and is the oldest body of non-Chartered Accountants in the world. We represent members and students in more than 80 countries, providing qualifications for those wishing to work in financial management and accountancy, and CPD for qualified Financial Accountants, particularly in SMEs.

MEMBERSHIP

Financial Accounting Executive
Associate (AFA)

Fellow (FFA)

QUALIFICATION/EXAMINATIONS

IFE Level 4 Award for SME Tax Advisers (QCF)
IFA Level 4 Award for SME Financial Accounting (International Standards) (QCF)
IFA Level 4 Diploma for SME Financial Accountants (QCF)
IFA Level 5 Diploma for SME Financial Managers (QCF)

IFA Level 5 Diploma for SME Finance and Business Managers (QCF)

The Diploma in IFRS for Accounting Professionals and the Diploma in IFRS for Business

INTERNATIONAL ASSOCIATION OF BOOKKEEPERS

Suite 5
20 Churchill Square
Kings Hill
West Malling
Kent ME19 4YU
Tel: 0844 3303527
Fax: 0844 3303514
E-mail: mail@iab.org.uk
Website: www.iab.org.uk

The IAB specializes in providing high-quality, accredited and regulated financial and business qualifications. We continue to be the leading international membership body for professional bookkeepers. Established in 1973, we now have many thousands of students and members worldwide.

MEMBERSHIP
Associate (AIAB)
Member (MIAB)
Fellow (FIAB)

QUALIFICATION/EXAMINATIONS
Award in Bookkeeping (Level 1)
Award in Manual Bookkeeping (Level 1)
Award in Computerized Bookkeeping (Level 1)
Certificate in Bookkeeping (Level 2)
Award in Manual Bookkeeping (Level 2)
Award in Computerized Bookkeeping (Level 2)
Certificate in Bookkeeping (Level 1)
Certificate in Bookkeeping (Level 3)
Diploma in Bookkeeping (Level 3)
Certificate in Manual Bookkeeping (Level 3)
Award in Computerized Bookkeeping (Level 3)
Diploma in Accounting to International Standards (Level 4)
Certificate in Payroll (Level 1)
Certificate in Payroll (Level 2)
Award in Computerized Payroll (Level 2)
Diploma in Payroll (Level 2)
Diploma in Payroll (Level 3)
Award in Computerized Payroll (Level 1)
Award in Computerized Payroll for Business (Level 1)
Certificate in Computerized Payroll for Business (Level 2)
Certificate in Computerized Payroll for Business (Level 3)
Award in Computerized Payroll (Level 3)
Award in Computerized Accounting for Business (Level 1)
Certificate in Computerized Accounting for Business (Level 2)
Certificate in Computerized Accounting for Business (Level 3)
Diploma in Accounting and Advanced Bookkeeping (Level 3)
Diploma in Small Business Financial Management (Level 3)
Diploma in Cost and Management Accounting (Level 3)
Diploma in Financial Information for Managers (Level 4)
Diploma in Personal and Business Tax (Level 4)

DESIGNATORY LETTERS
NCF, QCF

THE ASSOCIATION OF CHARTERED CERTIFIED ACCOUNTANTS

London WC2A 3EE
Tel: 020 7059 5000
Fax: 020 7059 5050
E-mail: info@accaglobal.com
Website: www.accaglobal.com

ACCA is the largest and fastest-growing international accountancy body, with over 424,000 students and 147,000 members in 170 countries. The ACCA Qualification is an established route to professional status, and we offer continued support to our members throughout their careers.

MEMBERSHIP
Associate (ACCA)
Fellow (FCCA)

QUALIFICATION/EXAMINATIONS
Foundations in Accountancy

Certificate in International Finance Reporting
Certificate in International Finance Reporting Standard for SMEs
Diploma in International Finance Reporting
The ACCA Qualification
MBA (awarded by Oxford Brookes University; accredited by the Association of MBAs)

DESIGNATORY LETTERS
ACCA, FCCA

THE ASSOCIATION OF CORPORATE TREASURERS

68 King William Street
London EC4N 7DZ
Tel: 020 7847 2540
Fax: 020 7374 2598
E-mail: enquiries@treasurers.org
Website: www.treasurers.org

The ACT is the professional chartered body for treasury and sets the benchmark for international treasury excellence. The ACT leads the profession through its globally recognised treasury qualifications by defining standards and championing continuing professional development.

MEMBERSHIP
eAffiliate Member
Student Member
Affiliate Member
Associate Member
Fellow
Business Member

QUALIFICATION/EXAMINATIONS
Treasury qualifications pathway
Certificate in Treasury Fundamentals
Certificate in Treasury
Diploma in Treasury Management
MCT Advanced Diploma
Cash management qualifications
Award in Cash Management Fundamentals
Certificate in International Cash Management

DESIGNATORY LETTERS
CertTF, CertT, AMCT, MCT, AwardCMF, CertICM,

THE ASSOCIATION OF INTERNATIONAL ACCOUNTANTS

Staithes 3
The Watermark
Metro Riverside
Newcastle upon Tyne
Tyne & Wear NE11 9SN
Tel: 0191 493 0277
Fax: 0191 493 0278
E-mail: aia@aiaworldwide.com
Website: www.aiaworldwide.com

AIA was founded in 1928 as a global accountancy body and has recognition as a Recognised Qualifying Body for statutory auditors, supervisory status for its members in the Money Laundering Regulations 2007 and an Awarding Body in the UK. AIA is a Prescribed Body in the ROI and is recognised worldwide.

MEMBERSHIP
Student Member
Graduate Member
Academic Member
Associate (AAIA)
Fellow (FAIA)
Honorary Member
Retired Member

QUALIFICATION/EXAMINATIONS
Professional Accountancy Qualification
Recognised Professional Qualification (Statutory Audit)
QCF Level 5 Certificate in Accountancy
QCF Level 6 Diploma in Accountancy
QCF Level 7 Diploma in Professional Accountancy
Auditing Diploma
IFRS Diploma
Management Accounting & Costing Diploma
IFRS for SMEs Certificate

DESIGNATORY LETTERS
AAIA, FAIA

THE CHARTERED INSTITUTE OF PUBLIC FINANCE AND ACCOUNTANCY (CIPFA)

77 Mansell Street
London E1 8AN
Tel: 020 7543 5600
Fax: 020 7543 5700
E-mail: students@cipfa.org.uk
Website: www.cipfa.org.uk

The Chartered Institute of Public Finance and Accountancy (CIPFA) is *the* professional body for people in public finance. Our 14,000 members work throughout the public services and as the only UK professional accountancy body to specialise in public services, CIPFA's qualifications are the foundation for a career in public finance.

MEMBERSHIP
Affiliate
Associate
Full Member

QUALIFICATION/EXAMINATIONS
CIPFA Professional Qualification
Professional Qualification in Public & Corporate Accounting
Integrated Qualification for Auditors
Certificate in International Public Sector Financial Reporting
Certificate in International Public Sector Accounting Standards
Certificate in Financial Reporting for Academies

DESIGNATORY LETTERS
CPFA

THE INSTITUTE OF CERTIFIED BOOKKEEPERS

London Underwriting Centre
3 Minster Court
Mincing Lane
City of London EC3R 7DD
Tel: 0845 060 2345
Fax: 01635 298960
E-mail: info@bookkeepers.org.uk
Website: www.bookkeepers.org.uk

The ICB is the largest bookkeeping institute in the world. Our aims are to promote bookkeeping as a profession, to improve training in the principles of bookkeeping, and to establish qualifications and the award of grades of membership that recognize academic attainment, work experience and professional competence, and thereby enable qualified bookkeepers to gain recognition as an integral part of the financial world.

MEMBERSHIP
Registered Student
Affiliate
Associate Member (AICB)
Member (MICB)
Fellow (FICB)

QUALIFICATION/EXAMINATIONS
Level 1: Certificate in Basic Bookkeeping

Level 2: (Intermediate): Certificate in Computerized Bookkeeping
Level 2: (Intermediate): Certificate in Manual Bookkeeping
Level 3: (Advanced): Diploma in Computerized Bookkeeping
Level 3: (Advanced): Diploma in Manual Bookkeeping
Level 3: (Advanced): Diploma in Payroll Management
Level 3: (Advanced): Diploma in Self-Assessment Tax Returns
Level 4: (Advanced): Diploma in Financial Management (Drafting Financial Statements, Management Accounting, Personal Taxation and Business Taxation)

DESIGNATORY LETTERS
AICB, MICB, FICB

ACOUSTICS
Membership of Professional Institutions and Associations

INSTITUTE OF ACOUSTICS

St Peter's House
45–49 Victoria Street
St Albans
Hertfordshire AL1 3WZ
Tel: 01727 848195
Fax: 01727 850553
E-mail: ioa@ioa.org.uk
Website: www.ioa.org.uk

The IOA is the UK's professional body for those working in acoustics, noise and vibration, and has more than 3,000 members in research, educational, environmental, government and industrial organizations. It offers professionally recognized courses

and is licensed by the Engineering Research Council to offer registration at Chartered and Incorporated Engineer levels.

MEMBERSHIP
Student

Affiliate
Technician Member (TechIOA)
Associate Member (AMIOA)
Member (MIOA)
Fellow (FIOA)
Honorary Fellow (HonFIOA)
Incorporated Engineer (IEng)
Chartered Engineer (CEng)
Sponsor

Certificate of Competence in Environmental Noise
Measurement

Certificate of Competence in Workplace Noise Risk
Assessment
Certificate Course in the Management of Occupational Exposure to Hand–Arm Vibration
Certificate Course in Building Acoustics
Measurements
Diploma in Acoustics and Noise Control

DESIGNATORY LETTERS
TechIOA, AMIOA, MIOA, FIOA, HonFIOA, IEng,
CEng

ADVERTISING AND PUBLIC RELATIONS
Membership of Professional Institutions and Associations

CHARTERED INSTITUTE OF PUBLIC RELATIONS

52–53 Russell Square
London WC1B 4HP
Tel: 020 7631 6900
Fax: 020 7631 6944
E-mail: info@cipr.co.uk
Website: www.cipr.co.uk

The CIPR, founded in 1948, is the professional body for PR practitioners and has more than 9,000 members, to whom it offers information, advice, support and training. Our aim is to raise standards within the profession through the promotion of best practice and our members abide by our strict code of professional conduct.

MEMBERSHIP
Student
Affiliate
Associate (ACIPR)

Member (MCIPR)
Fellow (FCIPR)
Global Affiliate

QUALIFICATION/EXAMINATIONS
Foundation Award in Public Relations
Advanced Certificate
Diploma

DESIGNATORY LETTERS
ACIPR, MCIPR, FCIPR

INSTITUTE OF PRACTITIONERS IN ADVERTISING

44 Belgrave Square
London SW1X 8QS
Tel: 020 7235 7020
Fax: 020 7245 9904
E-mail: web@ipa.co.uk
Website: www.ipa.co.uk

The IPA is the UK's leading professional body for advertising, media and marketing communications agencies. We promote the services of our member agencies, which have access to a range of services and benefits, including a Legal Department, Information Centre and training courses provided by our Professional Development Department.

MEMBERSHIP
Personal Member (MIPA)
Fellow/Honorary Fellow (FIPA)
Member Agency

QUALIFICATION/EXAMINATIONS
Foundation Certificate

Advanced Certificate
LegRgs Certificate
Commercial Certificate
Search Certificate
Excellence Diploma
Eff Test

DESIGNATORY LETTERS
MIPA, FIPA

INSTITUTE OF PROMOTIONAL MARKETING

E-mail: training@theipm.org.uk
Website: www.theipm.org.uk

The Institute of Promotional Marketing represents promoters, agencies and service partners engaged in promotional marketing in the UK by protecting, promoting and progressing effective sales promotion across all media channels through its education, legal advice, awards, and other products and services.

MEMBERSHIP
Corporate Member

QUALIFICATION/EXAMINATIONS
IPM Certificate
IPM Incentive & Motivation Diploma
IPM Diploma
Legal Code Certification (LCC)

DESIGNATORY LETTERS
MISP

LONDON SCHOOL OF PUBLIC RELATIONS

118A Kensington Church Street
London W8 4BH
Tel: 020 7221 3399
Fax: 020 7243 1730
E-mail: info@lspr-education.com
Website: www.lspr-education.com

Established in 1992, the London School of Public Relations (LSPR) provides up-to-date training courses for those wishing to enter public relations as a career or for those already in PR or an information/communications job who require up-to-date practical training awarded with a professional development qualification.

LSPR provides the following courses:
  DIPLOMA:
* PR & Reputation Management
  ADVANCED CERTIFICATES:
* Business Strategy for PR
* Branding
* Corporate Social Responsibility & Sustainability
* Risk Management

* Leadership
  CERTIFICATES:
* Business Writing 2 days
* Business Writing 10 weeks
* Social Media & Online Marketing
* Press Release Writing
* Presentation Skills

Our Diploma, *PR & Reputation Management*, is awarded to delegates upon successful completion of a 5-day full-time intensive course, Monday–Friday.

The Advanced Certificate courses run for 3 days, Wednesday–Friday.

Certificate courses are intensive short courses run for 1 day on Thursday or Friday (Presentation Skills and Press Release Writing) or 2 days;

Thursday–Friday (Business Writing 2 days and Social Media & Online Marketing) and 10 weeks; one per week in the evening 6.30pm–8.30pm (Business Writing 10 weeks).

All the courses are also offered in-house for clients.

LSPR training programmes are approved and recognised by Continuous Professional Development (CPD).

LSPR operates globally with franchises, in association with international PR bodies and agencies.

MEMBERSHIP
Continuous Professional Development (CPD)

QUALIFICATION/EXAMINATIONS
- Diploma: Examination, Assessment and a Final project
- Advanced Certificates: Critical Thinking Exercises
- Certificates: Projects and Exercises

AGRICULTURE AND HORTICULTURE
Membership of Professional Institutions and Associations

INSTITUTE OF HORTICULTURE

Capel Manor College
Bullsmoor Lane
Enfield
Middlesex EN1 4RQ
Tel: 01992 707025
E-mail: ioh@horticulture.org.uk
Website: www.horticulture.org.uk

The IoH represents all those professionally engaged in horticulture in the UK and the Republic of Ireland. Our main aim is to promote the profession and its importance in food and ornamental plant production, improving the environment, providing employment and as the leisure pursuit of gardening. We are also developing CPD and mentoring schemes for our members and liaise with government and other bodies on matters of interest or concern.

MEMBERSHIP
Student Member, Affiliate, e-Affiliate, Associate (AI Hort), Member (MI Hort), Fellow (FI Hort), Group Membership

DESIGNATORY LETTERS
AI Hort, MI Hort, FI Hort

ROYAL HORTICULTURAL SOCIETY

RHS Garden Wisley
Woking
Surrey GU23 6QB
Tel: 01483 226500
E-mail: qualifications@rhs.org.uk
Website: www.rhs.org.uk

The Royal Horticultural Society is a recognized awarding body offering a range of qualifications in horticultural knowledge and skills. Part-time courses leading to RHS qualifications are offered by approved centres throughout the UK and Ireland, and by distance-learning providers. The RHS School of Horticulture provides courses in practical horticultural skills.

QUALIFICATION/EXAMINATIONS
RHS Level 1 Introductory Award in Practical Horticulture
RHS Level 1 Award in Practical Horticulture

RHS Level 2 Certificate in the Principles of Plant Growth, Propagation and Development
RHS Level 2 Certificate in the Principles of Garden Planning, Establishment and Maintenance
RHS Level 2 Certificate in the Principles of Horticulture
RHS Level 2 Certificate in Practical Horticulture
RHS Level 2 Diploma in the Principles and Practices of Horticulture

RHS Level 3 Certificate in the Principles of Plant Growth, Health and Applied Propagation
RHS Level 3 Certificate in the Principles of Garden Planning, Construction and Planting
RHS Level 3 Certificate in Practical Horticulture
RHS Level 3 Diploma in the Principles and Practices of Horticulture
Master of Horticulture (RHS)
RHS Level 3 Diploma in Horticultural Practice

THE ROYAL BOTANIC GARDEN EDINBURGH

20A Inverleith Row
Edinburgh EH3 5LR
Tel: 0131 552 7171
Fax: 01312 482901
E-mail: education@rbge.org.uk
Website: www.rbge.org.uk

The RBGE was founded in the 17th century as a physic garden, growing medicinal plants. Now it extends over four gardens boasting a rich living collection of plants, and is a world-renowned centre for plant science and education.

QUALIFICATION/EXAMINATIONS
Certificate in Botanic Illustration
Certificate in Herbology
Certificate in the Principles of Horticulture (RHS Level 2)

Certificate in Practical Field Botany
Certificate in Practical Horticulture
Diploma in Botanical Illustration
Diploma in Garden Design
Diploma in Garden History
Diploma in Herbology
HND/BSc in Horticulture with Plantsmanship
MSc in The Biodiversity and Taxonomy of Plants

AMBULANCE SERVICE
Membership of Professional Institutions and Associations

AMBULANCE SERVICE INSTITUTE

Suite 183
Maddison House
226 High Street
Croydon CR9 1DF
E-mail: enquiries@asi-international.com
Website: www.asi-international.com

The ASI is a non-union, non-political, independent institute whose membership is dedicated to raising the standards and quality of ambulance provision and thereby improving the professionalism and quality of care available to patients. Membership is open to non-NHS personnel as well as to employees of NHS Ambulance Services.

MEMBERSHIP
Student
Member (MASI)

Licentiate (LASI)
Associate (AASI)
Graduate (GASI)
Fellow (FASI)

QUALIFICATION/EXAMINATIONS
The Institute offers professional examinations and qualifications in the areas of Pre-Hospital Care,

Control and Communications, and Management, for those who desire a career in the ambulance service.

DESIGNATORY LETTERS
MASI, LASI, AASI, GASI, FASI

ARBITRATION

Membership of Professional Institutions and Associations

THE CHARTERED INSTITUTE OF ARBITRATORS

12 Bloomsbury Square
London WC1A 2LP
Tel: 020 7421 7444
Fax: 020 7404 4023
E-mail: info@ciarb.org
Website: www.ciarb.org

The CIArb is a not-for-profit, UK-registered charity with 12,000 members worldwide that exists to promote and facilitate the settlement of private disputes by arbitration and alternative dispute resolution. We provide training for arbitrators, mediators and adjudicators and act as an international centre for practitioners, policy-makers, academics and those in business concerned with the cost-effective and early settlement of disputes.

MEMBERSHIP
Associate (ACIArb)

Member (MCIArb)
Fellow (FCIArb)

QUALIFICATION/EXAMINATIONS
Introductory Certificate
Advanced Certificate
Diploma

DESIGNATORY LETTERS
ACIArb, MCIArb, FCIArb

ARCHAEOLOGY

Membership of Professional Institutions and Associations

CHARTERED INSTITUTE FOR ARCHAEOLOGISTS

Miller Building
University of Reading
Reading
Berkshire RG6 6AB
Tel: 0118 378 6446
E-mail: admin@archaeologists.net
Website: www.archaeologists.net

CIfA is the leading professional body representing archaeologists working in the UK and overseas. We

promote high professional standards and strong ethics in archaeological practice, to maximise the benefits that archaeologists bring to society. We are the authoritative and effective voice for archaeologists, bringing recognition and respect to our profession.

MEMBERSHIP
Student

Affiliate
Practitioner (PCIfA)
Associate (ACIfA)
Member (MCIfA)
Registered Organisation

ARCHITECTURE
Membership of Professional Institutions and Associations

ARCHITECTS REGISTRATION BOARD

8 Weymouth Street
London W1W 5BU
Tel: 020 7580 5861
Fax: 020 7436 5269
E-mail: info@arb.org.uk
Website: www.arb.org.uk

The ARB is the regulatory body for architects in the UK. Only individuals registered with the Board can use the title 'architect'. Applicants must have passed the recognized exams at a school of architecture in the UK (or have an equivalent non-UK professional qualification) and have at least 2 years' practical experience working under the supervision of an architect.

CHARTERED INSTITUTE OF ARCHITECTURAL TECHNOLOGISTS (CIAT)

397 City Road
London EC1V 1NH
Tel: 020 7278 2206
Fax: 020 7837 3194
E-mail: info@ciat.org.uk
Website: www.ciat.org.uk

CIAT represents professionals working and studying in the field of Architectural Technology. We are internationally recognised as the qualifying body for Chartered Architectural Technologists (MCIAT) and Architectural Technicians (TCIAT).

MEMBERSHIP
Student Member

Profile Candidate
Associate (ACIAT)
Architectural Technician (TCIAT)
Chartered Architectural Technologist (MCIAT)
Honorary Member (HonMCIAT)

DESIGNATORY LETTERS
ACIAT, TCIAT, MCIAT

ROYAL INSTITUTE OF BRITISH ARCHITECTS

66 Portland Place
London W1B 1AD
Tel: 020 7580 5533
E-mail: info@riba.org
Website: www.architecture.com

The Royal Institute of British Architects is the UK membership body for architecture and the architectural profession. We provide support for our 41,000 members worldwide in the form of training, technical services, publications and events, and set standards for the education of architects, both in the UK and overseas. We also work with government to improve the design quality of public buildings, new homes and new communities.

MEMBERSHIP
Student Member

Affiliate Member
Associate Member
Chartered Member
Fellow Member
Chartered Practice

QUALIFICATION/EXAMINATIONS
The RIBA Examination in Architecture for office-based candidates Part 1 and Part 2 (distance learning)

ART AND DESIGN
Membership of Professional Institutions and Associations

BRITISH ASSOCIATION OF ART THERAPISTS

Claremont
24–27 White Lion Street
London N1 9PD
Tel: 020 7686 4216
E-mail: info@baat.org
Website: www.baat.org

The BAAT is the professional organization for art therapists in the UK and has its own Code of Ethics of Professional Practice. We maintain a comprehensive directory of qualified art therapists and work to promote art therapy in the UK through 20 regional groups. We also have a European section and an international section.

MEMBERSHIP
Trainee Member

Associate Member
Full Member
Honorary Member
Fellow
Corporate Member

QUALIFICATION/EXAMINATIONS
The BAAT organizes a programme of CPD courses for Art Therapists. For details see the website.

D&AD

96 Hanbury Street
London E1 5JL
Tel: 020 7840 1111
Fax: 020 7840 0840
E-mail: info@dandad.co.uk
Website: www.dandad.org

Founded in 1962, D&AD is a professional association and educational charity with a membership of more than 2,000, working on behalf of the design and advertising communities. Our mission is to set creative standards, educate and inspire the next creative generation, and promote the importance of good design and advertising to business as a whole.

MEMBERSHIP
Awarded
Professional
Education Network

SOCIETY OF DESIGNER CRAFTSMEN (SDC)

24 Rivington Street
London EC2A 3DU
Tel: 020 7739 3663
E-mail: info@societyofdesignercraftsmen.org.uk
Website: www.societyofdesignercraftsmen.org.uk

The Society, which was founded in 1887 as the Arts and Crafts Exhibition Society, is the largest and oldest multi-craft society in the UK. Our aim is to emphasize designer-making where innovation, originality and quality are important; we provide promotional services and exhibiting opportunities to members.

MEMBERSHIP
Associate
Licentiate (LSDC)
Member (MSDC)

Fellow (FSDC)

QUALIFICATION/EXAMINATIONS
Membership is by direct application by an individual craftsman and assessment is on quality of craftsmanship and design.
New graduates can be assessed at New Designers or College degree show following graduation.
Application forms and criteria are on our website.

DESIGNATORY LETTERS
LSDC, MSDC, FSDC

THE BRITISH ASSOCIATION OF PAINTINGS CONSERVATOR-RESTORERS (BAPCR)

4 Caburn Crescent
Lewes
East Sussex BN7 1NR
Tel: 07989 559346
E-mail: BAPCRsecretary@gmail.com
Website: www.bapcr.org.uk

The British Association of Paintings Conservator-Restorers promotes and fosters the practice of paintings conservation in the United Kingdom and around the world.

Established in 1943, we are the oldest dedicated professional organisation for all conservator-restorers of paintings in the UK.

Our members are skilled professionals working in private practice or in established institutions.

MEMBERSHIP
Associate (Student)
Associate
Fellow

THE CHARTERED SOCIETY OF DESIGNERS

1 Cedar Court
Royal Oak Yard
Bermondsey Street
London SE1 3GA
Tel: 020 7357 8088
Fax: 020 7407 9878
E-mail: info@csd.org.uk
Website: www.csd.org.uk

The CSD, which was founded in 1930, is the professional body for designers and has more than 3,000 members. We promote sound principles of design in all areas in which design considerations apply, further design practice and encourage the study of design techniques for the benefit of the community.

MEMBERSHIP
Student Member
Associate (Assoc. CSD)
Member (MCSD)
Fellow (FCSD)

DESIGNATORY LETTERS
MCSD, FCSD

THE INDEX OF PROFESSIONAL MASTER DESIGNERS

Kensington House
33 Imperial Square
Cheltenham Spa
Gloucestershire GL50 1QZ
Tel: 08701 161823
Fax: 08702 626146
E-mail: masterdesigners@kensington-house.com

The Index was formed to provide a register of designers practising in all areas of design. Our objectives are to enable designers to achieve recognition and attain qualifications and also to accredit schools and training organizations offering suitable courses.

MEMBERSHIP
Student

Professional Designer (IPMD (DIP))
Master Designer (IPMD (MAS))

QUALIFICATION/EXAMINATIONS
Certificate of Excellence – Interior Design Students

DESIGNATORY LETTERS
IPMD (DIP), IPMD (MAS)

ASTRONOMY AND SPACE SCIENCE
Membership of Professional Institutions and Associations

THE BRITISH INTERPLANETARY SOCIETY

27/29 South Lambeth Road
London SW8 1SZ
Tel: 020 7735 3160
Fax: 020 7582 7167
E-mail: info@bis-space.com
Website: www.bis-space.com

The BIS was formed in 1933 and has been at the forefront of actively promoting new ideas on space exploration at technical, educational and popular levels for 80 years. We serve the interests of those professionally involved with space, promote fundamental space research, technology and applications, encourage technical and scientific space studies, and undertake educational activities on space topics.

MEMBERSHIP
Member
Fellow (FBIS)

DESIGNATORY LETTERS
FBIS

AVIATION
Membership of Professional Institutions and Associations

THE GUILD OF AIR PILOTS AND AIR NAVIGATORS

Cobham House
9 Warwick Court
London WC1R 5DJ
Tel: 020 7404 4032
Fax: 020 7404 4035
E-mail: gapan@gapan.org
Website: www.gapan.org

The Guild, an active Livery Company of the City of London, represents pilot and navigator interests within all areas of aviation. Most of our members are, or have been, professional licence holders, or hold a private licence. Our aims include promoting the highest standards of air safety, liaising with all authorities connected with licensing, training and legislation, providing advice and facilitating exchange of information.

MEMBERSHIP
Associate
Freeman
Upper Freeman

QUALIFICATION/EXAMINATIONS
Master Air Pilot Certificate
Master Air Navigator Certificate
Master Rearcrew Certificate

THE GUILD OF AIR TRAFFIC CONTROL OFFICERS

Membership Services
4 St Mary's Road
Bingham
Nottingham
Nottinghamshire NG13 8DW
Tel: +44 (0)1949 876405
Fax: +44 (0) 1949 876405
E-mail: caf@gatco.org
Website: www.gatco.org

Founded in 1954, GATCO is an independent professional organization that exists to promote the highest standards in all aspects of Air Traffic Management. It is dedicated to the safety of all who travel by air.

MEMBERSHIP
Student Member
ATM Support Member
Non-Operational Member
Retired Member

FISO Member
ABM(W) Member
ATCO Abroad Member
ATCO UK Member
Corporate Member

QUALIFICATION/EXAMINATIONS
Qualifying criteria apply to all membership categories. Further information should be sought from GATCO Ltd, Membership Services.

AWARDS
Membership of Professional Institutions and Associations

CONFEDERATION OF PROFESSIONAL AWARDING BODIES (COPAB)

40 Archdale Road
East Dulwich
London SE22 9HJ
Tel: 0208 693 0555
Fax: 0208 693 0555
E-mail: secretary@copab.net; profblankson@snnp.org.uk
Website: www.copab.net

DESIGNATORY LETTERS
MCOPAB

BANKING

Membership of Professional Institutions and Associations

THE CHARTERED INSTITUTE OF BANKERS IN SCOTLAND

Drumsheugh House
38B Drumsheugh Gardens
Edinburgh EH3 7SW
Tel: 0131 473 7777
Fax: 0131 473 7788
E-mail: info@charteredbanker.com
Website: www.charteredbanker.com

The Chartered Institute of Bankers in Scotland provides world-class professional qualifications for both the UK and international markets. Our vision for the financial services industry is one of professionalism. We are the only organisation in the world entitled to award the designation 'Chartered Banker' to its members.

MEMBERSHIP
Student
Affiliate
Associate (ACIBS)

Member (MCIBS)
Fellow (FCIBS)

QUALIFICATION/EXAMINATIONS
Certificate
Diploma
Advanced Diploma
Chartered Banker

DESIGNATORY LETTERS
ACIBS, MCIBS, FCIBS

THE LONDON INSTITUTE OF BANKING AND FINANCE

8th Floor
Peninsular House
36 Monument Street
London EC3R 8LJ
Tel: 0207 4447111
Fax: 0207 4447115
E-mail: customerservices@ifslearning.ac.uk
Website: www.ifslearning.ac.uk

We exist to advance banking and finance by providing outstanding education and thinking; equipping individuals with the knowledge and skills to achieve what they want in their career.

And because we've been at the heart of the sector since 1879, we create connections and build partnerships that make banking and finance more accessible.

MEMBERSHIP
Member
Student Member

Associate
Fellow
Chartered Associate
Chartered Fellow

QUALIFICATION/EXAMINATIONS
Offering a wide range of qualifications for those employed or aspiring to a career in the financial services industry, and for consumers. For details see www.libf.ac.uk

BEAUTY THERAPY AND BEAUTY CULTURE
Membership of Professional Institutions and Associations

BRITISH ASSOCIATION OF BEAUTY THERAPY AND COSMETOLOGY LTD

BABTAC Limited
Ambrose House, Meteor Court
Barnett Way
Barnwood
Gloucester GL4 3GG
Tel: 0845 250 7277
Fax: 01452 611599
E-mail: info@babtac.com
Website: www.babtac.com

BABTAC was formed in 1977 and is a non-profit-making organization for beauticians and therapists in the UK. Members work to a rigorous code of ethics and good practice, both in terms of the treatments and therapies they offer and the way they conduct their relationships with their clients. CIBTAC, an international, educational awarding body that works closely with BABTAC, offers over 30 internationally recognized diplomas in beauty and complementary therapies to accredited colleges and students in the UK and abroad.

MEMBERSHIP
Student Member
Associate Member
Full Therapist Member
Full Hairdresser Member
Salon and Spa Member
International Member

QUALIFICATION/EXAMINATIONS
BABTAC offers a programme of short courses. For details see the BABTAC website. For CIBTAC diplomas see www.cibtac.com/courses_home.htm

BRITISH INSTITUTE AND ASSOCIATION OF ELECTROLYSIS LTD

40 Parkfield Road
Ickenham
Middlesex UB10 BLW
Tel: 08445 441373
E-mail: sec@electrolysis.co.uk
Website: www.electrolysis.co.uk

The BIAE is a non-profit-making organisation that demands a high standard of skill and ethical conduct from its members, who are spread throughout the UK and overseas. Candidate Electrolysists must complete the rigorous assessments, both theoretical and practical, of the BIAE Examining Board before being accepted onto the Register.

MEMBERSHIP
Member

QUALIFICATION/EXAMINATIONS
Certificate in Remedial Electrolysis (CRE)

FEDERATION OF HOLISTIC THERAPISTS

18 Shakespeare Business Centre
Hathaway Close
Eastleigh
Hampshire SO50 4SR
Tel: 023 8062 4350
Fax: 023 8062 4396
E-mail: info@fht.org.uk
Website: www.fht.org.uk

The FHT is the leading and largest professional beauty, sports and complementary therapist association in the UK, which has been representing the interests of holistic therapists since 1962. The FHT leads the industry by offering its members a Code of Conduct and Professional Practice, public liability insurance, access to regulation, a robust CPD programme with auditing, class-leading journal, local therapist network, and comprehensive business and public affairs updates.

MEMBERSHIP
Student
Affiliate
Associate
Member
Fellow
International

QUALIFICATION/EXAMINATIONS
Please see the FHT's website.

DESIGNATORY LETTERS
MFHT, FFHT, AFHT, AfFHT

ITEC

2nd Floor, Chiswick Gate
598–608 Chiswick High Road
London W4 5RT
Tel: 020 8994 4141
Fax: 020 8994 7880
E-mail: info@itecworld.co.uk
Website: www.itecworld.co.uk

ITEC is a leading international specialist examination board, providing high quality qualifications specialising in: Beauty & Spa Therapy, Hairdressing, Complementary Therapies, Sports & Fitness and Customer Service.

QUALIFICATION/EXAMINATIONS
Beauty & Spa Therapies
Hairdressing
Complementary Therapies
Sports & Fitness
Customer Service

BIOLOGICAL SCIENCES
Membership of Professional Institutions and Associations

INSTITUTE OF BIOMEDICAL SCIENCE

12 Coldbath Square
London EC1R 5HL
Tel: 020 7713 0214
Fax: 020 7837 9658
E-mail: mail@ibms.org
Website: www.ibms.org

The IBMS is the professional body for biomedical scientists in the UK. We aim to promote and develop the role of biomedical science within healthcare to deliver the best possible service for patient care and safety.

MEMBERSHIP
eStudent
Associate
Licentiate (LIBMS)
Member (MIBMS)
Fellow (FIBMS)
Company Member

QUALIFICATION/EXAMINATIONS
Certificate of Achievement Part I and II
Certificate of Competence (also required for registration with the Health and Care Professions Council (HCPC))
Specialist Diploma in:
Cellular Pathology, Clinical Biochemistry, Clinical Immunology, Cytopathology, Haematology &

Transfusion Science, Histocompatibility & Immunogenetics (developed in conjunction with BSHI), Medical Microbiology, Transfusion Science, Virology
Diploma of Biomedical Science
Diploma of Specialist Practice
Higher Specialist Diploma in:
Cellular Pathology, Clinical Chemistry, Cytopathology, Haematology, Immunology, Histocompatibility & Immunogenetics (developed in conjunction with BSHI), Medical Microbiology, Transfusion Science, Virology
Diploma of Higher Specialist Practice
Complementary qualifications/examinations related to areas of scientific expertise (available to Members and/or Fellows)
Certificates and Diplomas of Expert Practice
Advanced Specialist Diplomas

DESIGNATORY LETTERS
LIBMS, MIBMS, FIBMS

SOCIETY OF BIOLOGY

Charles Darwin House
12 Roger Street
London WC1N 2JU
Tel: 020 7685 2550
E-mail: info@societyofbiology.org
Website: www.societyofbiology.org

The Society of Biology aims to be a single unified voice for biology: advising government and influencing policy; advancing education and professional development; supporting members; and engaging and encouraging public interest in the life sciences.

MEMBERSHIP
Associate Member (AMSB)
Member (MSB)

Fellow (FSB)
Chartered Biologist (CBiol)
Affiliate
Sudent
BioNet

DESIGNATORY LETTERS
AMSB, MSB, FSB, CBiol

BREWING

Membership of Professional Institutions and Associations

INSTITUTE OF BREWING & DISTILLING

33 Clarges Street
Mayfair
London W1J 7EE
Tel: 020 7499 8144
Fax: 020 7499 1156
E-mail: enquiries@ibd.org.uk
Website: www.ibd.org.uk

The IBD is a members' organization dedicated to the education and training needs of brewers and distillers and those in related industries. We do this by offering a range of internationally recognized qualifications and the training to support them, through either direct instruction or distance learning.

MEMBERSHIP
Member
Honorary Member
Senior Member
Fellow (FIBD)
Honorary Fellow
Corporate Member
Student Member
Member in Retirement
Certificate Member

QUALIFICATION/EXAMINATIONS
Certificate in the Fundamentals of Brewing and Packaging of Beer (FBPB) (City & Guilds Level 2)

Certificate in the Fundamentals of Distilling (FD) (City & Guilds Level 2)
General Certificate in Brewing (GCB) (City & Guilds Level 3)
General Certificate in Distilling (GCD) (City & Guilds Level 3)
General Certificate in Packaging (GCP) (City & Guilds Level 3)
Diploma in Packaging (Dipl.Pack) (City & Guilds Level 4)
General Certificate in Spirits Packaging
General Certificate in Malting
Diploma in Brewing (Dipl.Brew) (City & Guilds Level 4)
Diploma in Distilling (Dipl.Distil) (City & Guilds Level 4)
Master Brewer (MBrew)

DESIGNATORY LETTERS
Dipl.Brew, Dipl.Distil, Dipl.Pack, MBrew, FIBD, Hon FIBD

BUILDING

Membership of Professional Institutions and Associations

INSTITUTE OF ASPHALT TECHNOLOGY

PO Box 15690
BATHGATE EH48 9BT
Tel: 01506 238397
E-mail: info@instituteofasphalt.org
Website: www.instituteofasphalt.org

The IAT is the UK's professional body for persons working in asphalt technology and those interested in aspects of the manufacture, placing, technology and uses of materials containing asphalt or bitumen.

A fully audited CPD system for members has been available since 1994 and is now also offered in computerized format for ease of data entry and auditing, via members' own PCs.

MEMBERSHIP
Student
Technician (Tech.IAT)
Affiliate (AIAT)
Associate Member (AMIAT)
Member (MIAT)

Fellow (FIAT)
Honorary Fellow (Hon FIAT)

DESIGNATORY LETTERS
Tech.IAT, AIAT, AMIAT, MIAT, FIAT, Hon.FIAT   .

THE CHARTERED INSTITUTE OF BUILDING

Englemere
Kings Ride
Ascot
Berkshire SL5 7TB
Tel: 01344 630700
Fax: 01344 630777
E-mail: reception@ciob.org.uk
Website: www.ciob.org

The CIOB is the international voice of the construction industry. CIOB members are largely Construction Managers engaged in managing the development, conservation and improvement of the built environment, with a common commitment to achieving and maintaining the highest possible standards.

MEMBERSHIP
Student Member
Associate (ACIOB)
Incorporated (ICIOB)
Member (MCIOB)
Fellow (FCIOB)
Chartered Environmentalist (CENV)
Student in Employment
Educationalist
Concessionary

QUALIFICATION/EXAMINATIONS
The CIOB has routes to membership to suit a range of professionals from those with degrees or vocational qualifications to those with experience but no formal qualifications. All our members have a strong commitment to improve and develop themselves in a challenging and exciting career.

Chartered Member status is recognized internationally as the mark of a skilled professional in the construction industry. CIOB members are from a wide range of professions in the construction industry.

To find out more about our membership qualifications and joining the CIOB just visit our website www.ciob.org

The CIOB Awarding Body offers a suite of qualifications to enable site operatives to progress into management roles.

Level 3 Diploma in Site Supervisory Studies
Level 4 Certificate in Site Management
Level 4 Diploma in Site Management

The CIOB qualifications develop the skills and confidence to manage and coordinate all types of construction projects. The site management qualifications are nationally recognized and allow the learner to progress to higher education and National Vocational Qualifications (NVQs).

For more information on the Site Management Qualifications visit the website at www.ciob.org.uk/education/courseinfo/sitemanagement

DESIGNATORY LETTERS
ACIOB, ICIOB, MCIOB, FCIOB, CENV

THE INSTITUTE OF CARPENTERS

32 High Street
Wendover
Buckinghamshire HP22 6EA
Tel: 0844 879 7696
Fax: 01296 620981
E-mail: info@instituteofcarpenters.com
Website: www.instituteofcarpenters.com

The IOC was founded in 1890 to oversee training for carpenters and joiners and maintain high professional standards at a time when many feared that traditional skills were being lost. Today, while remaining committed to our original aims, we embrace many other wood craftsmen, such as shopfitters, furniture and cabinetmakers, boat builders (woodworking skills), structural post & beam carpenters (heavy structural timber framers), wheelwrights, wood carvers and wood turners, and offer professional status to those holding recognized qualifications.

MEMBERSHIP
Student
Mature Student
Affiliate

Licentiate (LIOC)
Member (MIOC)
Fellow (FIOC)
College Member
Corporate Member
Corporate Associate

QUALIFICATION/EXAMINATIONS
Foundation Examination
Intermediate Examination
Advanced Craft Examination
Fellowship Examination
Setting-Out Course

DESIGNATORY LETTERS
LIOC, MIOC, FIOC

THE INSTITUTE OF CLERKS OF WORKS AND CONSTRUCTION INSPECTORATE OF GREAT BRITAIN INC

28 Commerce Road
Lynch Wood
Peterborough PE2 6LR
Tel: 01733 405160
Fax: 01733 405161
E-mail: info@icwci.org
Website: www.icwci.org

The ICWCI is the professional body that supports quality construction through inspection. As a membership organization, we provide a support network of meeting centres, technical advice, publications and events to help keep our members up to date with the ever-changing construction industry.

MEMBERSHIP
Student

Licentiate (LICWCI)
Member (MICWCI)
Fellow (FICWCI)
Life Member
Honorary Member

DESIGNATORY LETTERS
LICWCI, MICWCI, FICWCI

BUSINESS STUDIES
Membership of Professional Institutions and Associations

ASSOCIATION OF BUSINESS RECOVERY PROFESSIONALS (R3)

8th Floor
120 Aldersgate Street
London EC1A 4JQ
Tel: 020 7566 4200
Fax: 020 7566 4224
E-mail: association@r3.org.uk
Website: www.r3.org.uk

The Association of Business Recovery Professionals (known by its brand name 'R3') is the leading professional association for insolvency, business recovery and turnaround specialists in the UK. A not-for-profit organization, it promotes best practice for professionals working with financially troubled individuals and businesses, and provides a forum for debate on key issues facing the profession.

MEMBERSHIP
New Professional (Student) Member
New Professional (Networking) Member
Associate Member (AABRP)
Full Member (MABRP)
Fellow (FABRP)

QUALIFICATION/EXAMINATIONS
R3 provides comprehensive Continuing Professional Education in the field of Insolvency and Restructuring. For details of courses see R3's website.

DESIGNATORY LETTERS
AABRP, MABRP, FABRP

INSTITUTE OF ASSESSORS AND INTERNAL VERIFIERS

PO Box 1138
Warrington WA4 9GS
Tel: 01925 485 786
E-mail: office@iavltd.co.uk
Website: www.iavltd.co.uk

The IAV is the professional organization representing assessors and internal verifiers in the UK in vocational training and assessment.

MEMBERSHIP
Affiliate Member
Associate Member
Licentiate Member

THE ACADEMY OF EXECUTIVES & ADMINISTRATORS

PO Box 93
Moreton-in-Marsh GL56 9WG
Tel: 01386 277973
E-mail: info@academyofexecutivesandadministrators.org.uk
Website: www.academyofexecutivesandadministrators.org.uk

The Academy of Executives & Administrators was founded in 2002 to give professional status and recognition to the knowledge and skills of executives and administrators. We encourage excellence and flexibility in the changing environment of executive and administrative roles, and support lifelong learning to help members fulfil their career ambitions.

MEMBERSHIP
Student Member (StudAEA)
Associate Member (AMAEA)
Member (MAEA)
Fellow (FAEA)
Companion (CAEA)

QUALIFICATION/EXAMINATIONS
Associate Diploma for Business Economists
Associate Diploma for Financial Managers
Associate Diploma for Assistant Accountants
Associate Diploma for Assistant Corporate Accountants
Associate Diploma for Trainers
Certified Administration Practitioner
Certified Executive Practitioner
Certified Budget and Planning Practitioner

THE ACADEMY OF MULTI-SKILLS

40 Archdale Road
East Dulwich
London SE22 9HJ
Tel: 07092012910
E-mail: info@academyofmulti-skillsuk.org
Website: www.academyofmulti-skillsuk.org

The Academy of Multi-Skills was founded in 1995 to give professional recognition to multi-skilled personnel, skilled trades, crafts and professions. The Academy encourages a positive and energetic attitude to the challenges of careers that require diversity, creativity and intellect, and recognizes the valuable contribution that these skills provide to society.

MEMBERSHIP
Student Member GBP 100 Stud AMS (Cert MS)
Associate GBP 200 AMAMS (Dip MS)
Full Member GBP 250 MAMS (Dip MS)
Fellow GBP 300 FAMS (Dip MS)
Doctorate Fellow GBP 3,000 DFAMS
Company GBP 500 COAMS

QUALIFICATION/EXAMINATIONS
Members may choose to enhance their qualifications via our diploma, HND, post-graduate and doctoral diploma courses.
We have arrangements with other prestigious organisations which our members may choose to join to obtain further qualifications.
Discounts are available to our members from organisations ranging from books to overseas conferences.

DESIGNATORY LETTERS
Stud AMS, AMAMS, MAMS, FAMS, DFAMS, COAMS

THE FACULTY OF SECRETARIES AND ADMINISTRATORS LIMITED

Brightstowe
Catteshall Lane
Godalming
Surrey GU7 1LL
Tel: 01483 427323
Fax: 0871 288 6935
E-mail: admin@facultyofsecretaries.org.uk
Website: www.facultyofsecretaries.co.uk

The Faculty is a professional body for corporate secretaries whose qualified designation is that of Certified Public or Corporate Secretary and since 1930 has led in promoting good but liberal governance.

The Faculty kitemark embeds the concept of reasonableness and care for others in an organisation's operation and decision taking.

MEMBERSHIP
Membership Fellows (FFCS)
Associates (AFCS)
Member (MACS)
Ordinary Member
Student Member
Licentiate (LFCS)
Corporate

QUALIFICATION/EXAMINATIONS
Part 1 The Generic Business Assessment to ONC/D Level
Part 2 Professional Papers in Company Secretarial Practice, Company Law and Management, Secretarial and Administrative Practice, Commercial Law
Part 3 Professional Meetings Law and Procedure, Company Taxation, Accountancy and Finance, Company Law
Assessment of Senior Personnel for direct entry now involves a viva voce interview and rated questions on company secretaryship as well as exemptions based on an agreed list of qualifications and a declaration of working with the general ethos of the faculty.

Single subject examinations are available and a programme for the assessment of in-house courses for company secretaries, directors and trustees. The Faculty gives credit for approved attendance at Directory of Social Change, Institute of Directors and other recognised bodies', courses on governance, leadership and management where it is clear they are beneficial to the development of caring, fair and liberal governance. The Faculty supports the aims and objectives of 'The Commonwealth' and seeks to ensure a fit with the syllabi of related bodies in Commonwealth countries.

The Society of Teachers in Business Education monitors this interview process.

The Kitemark is an assessment which an organisation can go through to establish good and liberal governance and has formats for private, public and voluntary sector organisations.

DESIGNATORY LETTERS
FFCS, AFCS, LFCS, MACS

THE INSTITUTE OF CHARTERED SECRETARIES AND ADMINISTRATORS

16 Park Crescent
London W1B 1AH
Tel: 020 7580 4741
Fax: 020 7323 1132
E-mail: studentsupport@icsaglobal.com
Website: www.icsaglobal.com

The Institute of Chartered Secretaries and Administrators is the international qualifying and membership body for the Chartered Secretary profession. With a global community of 37,000 members we provide Chartered Membership, training and a professional qualifying scheme to set you on the path to a diverse, challenging and rewarding career.

MEMBERSHIP
Affiliate
Graduate (GradICSA)
Associate (ACIS)
Fellow (FCIS)

QUALIFICATION/EXAMINATIONS
Chartered Secretaries Qualifying Scheme (CSQS)
Certificate in Offshore Finance and Administration
Diploma in Offshore Finance and Administration
Certificate in Company Secretarial Practice and Share Registration Practice
Certificate in Irish Company Secretarial Practice and Share Registration Practice
Certificate in Employee Share Plans
Postgraduate Certificate in Charity Management
ICSA Certificate in Further Education Governance

DESIGNATORY LETTERS
GradICSA, ACIS, FCIS

CATERING AND INSTITUTIONAL MANAGEMENT
Membership of Professional Institutions and Associations

BII

Wessex House
80 Park Street
Camberley
Surrey GU15 3PT
Tel: 01276 684449
E-mail: info@bii.org
Website: www.bii.org

Founded in 1981, BII is the professional body for the licensed retail sector with a remit to raise standards throughout the industry. BIIAB, the wholly owned awarding body of BII, does this through offering qualifications specifically tailored to, and designed in conjunction with, the industry.

MEMBERSHIP
There is a wide range of membership grades available, from those who have just started their careers in licensed retailing to those who have been in the industry for many years. The grade of membership awarded depends on both experience and qualifications and is determined by a points system. Member of the Hotel Catering and Management Association, HCIMA.

QUALIFICATION/EXAMINATIONS
Qualifications for licensing
Award for Designated Premises Supervisors (Level 2)
Award for Licensing Practitioners (Alcohol) (Level 2)
Award for Personal Licence Holders (Level 2)
Award for Upskilling Door Supervisors (Level 2)
Award for Upskilling Door Supervisors (Scotland)
Award in Door Supervision (Level 2)
Award in Door Supervision (Scotland)
Award in Door Supervision (Northern Ireland)
Award in CCTV Operations (Public Space Surveillance) (Scotland)
Award in Crime Scene Preservation (Level 2)
Award in Drug Awareness for Licensed Hospitality Staff (Level 2)
Award in Fire Safety (Level 2)
Scottish Certificate for Licensees (Drugs Awareness)
Award in Isle of Man Licensing Law
Award in Jersey Licensing Law
Qualifications for new licensed retail managers
Award in Licensed Retailing (Level 2)

Award in Beer and Cellar Quality (Cask and Keg) (Level 2)
Award in Beer and Cellar Quality (Keg) (Level 2)
Scottish Certificate in Licensed Retailing

Qualifications for staff development
Award in Kitchen Management (Level 3)
Award in Introduction to Employment in the Hospitality Industry (Level 1)
Professional Barperson's Qualification
Award in Conflict Management for Licensed Premises Staff (Level 2)
Award in Customer Service Excellence (Licensed Hospitality)
Award in Food Safety in Catering (Level 2)
Award in Health and Safety in the Workplace (Level 2)
Isle of Man Security Staff Qualification

Qualifications for management development

Award in Licensed Hospitality Operations (Level 2)
Certificate in Licensed Hospitality Operations (Level 2)
Certificate in Licensed Hospitality Skills (Level 2)
Award in Hospitality Business Management (Level 3)
Certificate in Hospitality Business Management (Level 3)
Certificate in Multiple Licensed Premises Management (Level 4)
Qualifications for personal and social responsibility

Award in Alcohol Awareness (Level 1)
Award in Assessment of Licensed Premises (Social Responsibility) (Level 2)
Award in Assessment of Licensed Premises (Social Responsibility) (Scotland)

GUILD OF INTERNATIONAL PROFESSIONAL TOASTMASTERS

Life President: Ivor Spencer
22 Great Mead
Denmead
Waterlooville
Hampshire PO7 6HH
Tel: 07802 250477
E-mail: info@guildoftoastmasters.co.uk
Website: www.guildoftoastmasters.co.uk

The Guild of Professional Toastmasters was established over 30 years ago to improve standards in the profession and support its members. A 5-day course is offered to prospective members, who may apply for membership upon successful completion of the course. Applications are considered by the Fellows of the Guild.

MEMBERSHIP
Fellow (FGIntPT)

DESIGNATORY LETTERS
FGIntPT

INSTITUTE OF HOSPITALITY

Trinity Court
34 West Street
Sutton
Surrey SM1 1SH
Tel: 020 8661 4900
Fax: 020 8661 4901
E-mail: awardingbody@instituteofhospitality.org
Website: www.instituteofhospitality.org

The Institute of Hospitality is the international professional body for managers and leaders in hospitality, leisure and tourism. We offer professional qualifications, accredit academic programmes of study, endorse training courses providing professional development opportunities ranging from daily operational duties to board level strategy.

Uniting Professionals, Promoting Excellence, Facilitating Learning

MEMBERSHIP
Student Member
Affiliate

Associate (AIH)
Member (MIH)
Fellow (FIH)

QUALIFICATION/EXAMINATIONS
Institute of Hospitality Level 3 Diploma in Hospitality and Toursim Management (VRQ)
Institute of Hospitality Level 4 Diploma in Advanced Hospitality and Tourism Management (VRQ)

DESIGNATORY LETTERS
AIH, MIH, FIH

CHEMISTRY

Membership of Professional Institutions and Associations

SOCIETY OF COSMETIC SCIENTISTS

Suite 5
Langham House West
Mill Street
Luton
Bedfordshire LU1 2NA
Tel: 01582 726661
Fax: 01582 405217
E-mail: gem.bektas@btconnect.com
Website: www.scs.org.uk

The main object of the Society, which was formed in 1948, is to advance the science of cosmetics. We endeavour to do this by attracting highly qualified scientists with both academic and industrial experience in cosmetics or a related science to our membership of around 900 members, and by means of our publications, educational programmes and scientific meetings.

MEMBERSHIP
Student
Affiliate
Associate Member
Member – B Grade
Member – A Grade
Honorary Member

QUALIFICATION/EXAMINATIONS
Certificate of Higher Education in Cosmetic Science

THE OIL AND COLOUR CHEMISTS' ASSOCIATION

Charnwood House
Harcourt Way
Leicester LE19 1WP
Tel: 0116 257 5488
Fax: 0116 257 5499
E-mail: admin@occa.org.uk
Website: www.occa.org.uk

OCCA, founded in 1918, is a learned society comprising individual qualified persons employed in, or associated with, the worldwide surface coatings industries. Most of our members work in a technical capacity, but there are senior personnel from throughout the surface coating industries. The word 'oil' in our title refers to vegetable oils, which once formed a major part of surface coatings' formulations.

MEMBERSHIP
Student Member
Ordinary Member
Honorary Member
Licentiate (LTSC)
Associate (ATSC)
Fellow (FTSC)
Chartered Scientist (CSci)

DESIGNATORY LETTERS
LTSC, ATSC, FTSC, CSci

THE ROYAL SOCIETY OF CHEMISTRY

Thomas Graham House
Science Park
Milton Road
Cambridge CB4 0WF
Tel: 01223 420066
Fax: 01223 423623
E-mail: membership@rsc.org
Website: www.rsc.org

The RSC is the UK professional body for chemical scientists and an international learned society for advancing the chemical sciences. With over 46,000 members worldwide and an internationally acclaimed publishing business, our activities span education and training, conferences, science policy and the promotion of the chemical sciences to the public.

MEMBERSHIP
Affiliate
Associate Member (AMRSC)
Member (MRSC)
Fellow (FRSC)

QUALIFICATION/EXAMINATIONS
NVQ Analytical Chemistry (Level 5)
Registered Scientist and Registered Science Technician
MSc in Chemical Technology and Management
Mastership in Chemical Analysis (MChemA)
Chartered Chemist (CChem)
Chartered Scientist (CSci)

DESIGNATORY LETTERS
AMRSC, MRSC, FRSC, CChem

CHIROPODY
Membership of Professional Institutions and Associations

BRITISH CHIROPODY AND PODIATRY ASSOCIATION

The New Hall
149 Bath Road
Maidenhead
Berkshire SL6 4LA
Tel: 01628 632440
Fax: 01628 674483
E-mail: membership@bcha-uk.org
Website: www.bcha-uk.org

The BChA, formed in 1959, is the largest professional organization in the UK representing the interests of independent private chiropodists / podiatrists. Since 2005 we have added foothealth practitioners to include our 7,000 members, most of whom work mainly in private practice. Those who are registered with the Health Professions Council may work in the NHS or in education.

MEMBERSHIP
Member (MSSCh & MBChA) – Podiatrists

Fellow (FSSCh) – Podiatrist
Associate members are foothealth practitioners trained by The SMAE Institute.

QUALIFICATION/EXAMINATIONS
Diploma in Podiatric Medicine (DipPodMed)
Foothealth practitioners carry the qualification – MAFHP

DESIGNATORY LETTERS
MSSCh, MBChA, FSSCh and MAFHP

Chiropody

THE INSTITUTE OF CHIROPODISTS AND PODIATRISTS

150 Lord Street
Southport
Merseyside PR9 0NP
Tel: 01704 546141
E-mail: secretary@iocp.org.uk
Website: www.iocp.org.uk

The Institute serves members throughout the whole of the profession of podiatry and podiatric medicine. Its members include chiropodists, podiatrists and podiatric surgeons, employed and self-employed at all levels of practice. The Institute certificate of membership is proof that members undertake to adhere to a strict code of ethics and professional conduct and that they have access to some of the UK's most innovative continuing professional development training.

The Institute is a democratic organisation with the election of officers both local and national being decided bi-annually by members. All members therefore play an active role in their own affairs. For more than 60 years the Institute has followed an independent line at the forefront of the profession it serves, for the progress and well-being of both the profession and the public.

The IOCP represents all levels of the profession and our CPD is open to both members and non-members, as by elevating professional standards we aim to improve public safety. We have branches throughout the UK and the Republic of Ireland, and members overseas, and hold lectures, seminars and workshops to enable members to keep up to date.

MEMBERSHIP
Full Member
Student
Associate

QUALIFICATION/EXAMINATIONS
MInstChP – Full Member
AInstFHP – Associate

THE SOCIETY OF CHIROPODISTS AND PODIATRISTS

1 Fellmongers Path
Tower Bridge Road
London SE1 3LY
Tel: 020 7234 8620
E-mail: enq@scpod.org
Website: www.scpod.org

The SCP is the professional body and trade union for registered podiatrists. Membership is restricted to those qualified for registration and the Society represents around 10,000 NHS podiatrists, private practitioners and students. We monitor standards of undergraduate education and provide opportunities for CPD for our members.

MEMBERSHIP
Member (MChS)
Associate

DESIGNATORY LETTERS
MChS

CHIROPRACTIC

Membership of Professional Institutions and Associations

MCTIMONEY CHIROPRACTIC ASSOCIATION

Crowmarsh Gifford
Wallingford
Oxfordshire OX10 8DJ
Tel: 01491 829211
E-mail: admin@mctimoney-chiropractic.org
Website: www.mctimoneychiropractic.org

The McTimoney Chiropractic Association is a professional association for Chiropractors, who in the UK are registered with the General Chiropractic Council.

MEMBERSHIP
Provisional Member
Full Member
Fellow

DESIGNATORY LETTERS
MMCA

SCOTTISH CHIROPRACTIC ASSOCIATION

1 Chisholm Avenue
Bishopton
Renfrewshire PA7 5JH
Tel: 0141 404 0260
E-mail: admin@sca-chiropractic.org
Website: www.sca-chiropractic.org

The SCA was formed in 1979 and now has more than 60 members practising in Scotland and over 120 associated members elsewhere in the UK and abroad. Our aims are to enhance the chiropractic profession in the UK, maintain high standards of professional practice, and provide advice and support to our members.

MEMBERSHIP
Member

UNITED CHIROPRACTIC ASSOCIATION

1st Floor
45 North Hill
Plymouth
Devon PL4 8EZ
Tel: 01752 658785
Fax: 01752 658786
E-mail: admin@united-chiropractic.org
Website: www.united-chiropractic.org

The UCA is a UK-based organization for qualified, professional, principal-based chiropractors, associates and students. Full membership is open to qualified, GCC-registered chiropractors from any recognized school of chiropractic.

MEMBERSHIP
Student
Associate
Affiliate

1st Year Graduate
2nd Year Graduate
Full Member
Overseas Member

THE CHURCHES

Membership of Professional Institutions and Associations

BAPTIST UNION OF SCOTLAND

48 Speirs Wharf
Glasgow G4 9TH
Tel: 0141 423 6169
Fax: 0141 424 1422
E-mail: admin@scottishbaptist.org.uk
Website: www.scottishbaptist.org.uk

The Baptist Union of Scotland was formed in 1869, when 51 churches with a total congregation of about 3,500 united. Today, with 162 churches and about 11,250 members, the Union strives for simplicity in organizational structure and promotes increasing contact between the local churches and the National Team, who function under the overall direction of the General Director.

QUALIFICATION/EXAMINATIONS
BD or BA in Theology
Graduate Diploma in Applied Theology through Work Based Learning
Graduate Diploma in Pastoral Studies
(awarded by the Scottish Baptist College, Paisley, and validated by the University of Paisley)

BRISTOL BAPTIST COLLEGE

The Promenade
Clifton Down
Clifton
Bristol BS8 3NJ
Tel: 0117 946 7050
Fax: 0117 946 7787
E-mail: reception@bristol-baptist.ac.uk
Website: www.bristol-baptist.ac.uk

The central aim of the College is to train men and women for ministry in the Church and in the world. We do this by enabling critical reflection upon the Bible and Christian theological tradition and on the contexts from which we come and within which we are placed.

QUALIFICATION/EXAMINATIONS
Certificate in Theological Studies
Diploma in Theological Studies
BA in Theological Studies
MA in Christian Theology
(all validated by the University of Bristol)

METHODIST CHURCH IN IRELAND

1 Fountainville Avenue
Belfast BT9 6AN
Tel: 028 9032 4554
Fax: 028 9023 9467
E-mail: secretary@irishmethodist.org
Website: www.irishmethodist.org

MEMBERSHIP
Candidates for training must normally have the standard of general education for university entrance. They must be accredited Local Preachers of the Methodist Church, and are examined by written papers in Biblical Studies and Theology and by oral aptitude and personality tests. After admission to training, candidates normally spend 3 years at Edgehill Theological College, Belfast, studying for a diploma or degree of Queen's University, Belfast, in New Testament Greek, Hebrew, the English Bible, Theology, Church History, Pastoral Psychology, or Homiletics. This is followed by 3 years as a probationer Minister working under a superintendent Minister. During probation the candidate continues study within a tutorial system and is examined by continuous assessment.

SCOTTISH EPISCOPAL INSTITUTE

Forbes House
21 Grosvenor Crescent
Edinburgh EH12 5EE
Tel: 0131 243 1347
E-mail: institute@scotland.anglican.org
Website: www.scotland.anglican.org

Candidates are trained for lay and ordained, stipendiary and non-stipendiary ministries in the Scottish Episcopal Church and the United Reformed Church.

The curriculum is delivered centrally through residential sessions and seminar teaching. The Diploma of Higher Education in Theology, Ministry and Mission and the BA in Theology, Ministry and Mission courses run by the Institute are validated by Common Awards/Durham University. Some students undertake degree programmes in parallel with their formation through Scottish Universities.

THE CHURCH IN WALES

St Michael's College
Llandaff
Cardiff CF5 2YJ
Tel: 029 205 63379
Fax: 029 208 38008
Website: www.stmichaels.ac.uk

The Church in Wales expects candidates for ordination and reader ministry to satisfy the requirements of recognized theological courses. University graduates usually spend at least 2 years full time (or its part time equivalent) at a theological college or course, and will be encouraged to study for a postgraduate degree.

Non-theological graduates are encouraged to study for a university degree, diploma or certificate in Theology, depending on their age and the ministry for which they are being trained. Non-graduate candidates must have at least 5 passes at GCSE and normally study for a university certificate or diploma in Theology or a degree in Theology if they have obtained the necessary grades at A level. These requirements may be modified in the case of older candidates.

THE CHURCH OF ENGLAND

Ministry Division of The Archbishops' Council
Church House
Great Smith Street
London SW1P 3AZ
Tel: 020 7898 1397
E-mail: keith.beech-gruneberg@churchofengland.org
Website: www.churchofengland.org/clergy-office-holders/ministry.aspx
www.aet-lambeth.org/

The Church of England's Ministry Division oversees training for ordination and licensed lay ministry/Reader ministry including the Common Awards created by the Church and validated by Durham University.

In addition, The Archbishop's Examination in Theology offers means of study at research degree level.

QUALIFICATION/EXAMINATIONS
Awards validated by Durham University:
Certificate of Higher Education in Theology, Ministry and Mission
Certificate of Higher Education in Christian Ministry and Mission (180 credits)
Diploma of Higher Education in Theology, Ministry and Mission
BA in Theology, Ministry and Mission
Graduate Certificate in Theology, Ministry and Mission
Graduate Diploma in Theology, Ministry and Mission
Postgraduate Certificate in Theology, Ministry and Mission
Postgraduate Diploma in Theology, Ministry and Mission
MA in Theology, Ministry and Mission
Archbishop's Examination:
Master of Philosophy
Doctor of Philosophy

THE CHURCH OF SCOTLAND

Church of Scotland Offices
121 George Street
Edinburgh EH2 4YN
Tel: 0131 225 5722
Website: www.churchofscotland.org.uk

The vision of The Church of Scotland is to be a church which seeks to inspire the people of Scotland and beyond with the Good News of Jesus Christ through enthusiastic worshipping, witnessing, nurturing and serving communities.

THE METHODIST CHURCH

Formation in Ministry Office (Initial Development of Ministries)
25 Marylebone Road
London NW1 5JR
Tel: 020 7486 5502
E-mail: helpdesk@methodistchurch.org.uk
Website: www.methodist.org.uk

Candidates for Diaconal or Presbyteral Ministry in the Methodist Church must have been members of the Methodist Church at least 2 years and are expected to offer at least 10 years of ministerial service. The first stage of preparation is Foundation Training, which requires 1 year (FT) or 2 years (PT) to complete, during which a person may apply to become a candidate for ordained ministry. The process of selection takes 6 months. To enter into training for Presbyteral Ministry, a candidate must be a trained Local Preacher, which involves taking the Methodist Local Preachers' Training Course, Faith & Worship. Deacons become members of the Methodist Diaconal and are not required to be preachers. Accepted candidates for either order receive 1 or 2 years of further theological training, which in most cases leads to a degree or diploma in Theology or Ministry. Upon completion of training, a candidate serves as a Methodist Minister for 2 years on probation before ordination. For Presbyters, the appointment may be to an itinerant appointment (stipendiary) or to a local appointment (usually non-stipendiary) or as licensed to minister in secular employment. Deacons are always itinerant.

THE MORAVIAN CHURCH IN GREAT BRITAIN AND IRELAND

Moravian Church House
5–7 Muswell Hill
London N10 3TJ
Tel: 020 8883 3409
Fax: 020 8365 3371
E-mail: office@moravian.org.uk
Website: www.moravian.org.uk

Candidates for Moravian Church Service must be members of the Moravian Church and would normally have completed the Lay Training Course and have the support of their local church committee. They should make an initial application to the Provincial Board of the Moravian Church. Their qualifications are examined by the Church Service Advisory Board, which reports on them to the Provincial Board, with whom the final decision rests. Normally the standard of education required for the work of the Ministry is a university Divinity degree or Certificate together with a thorough acquaintance with the history, principles and methods of the Moravian Church. Candidates receive guidance for the Ministry during a period of supervised service under the direction of experienced Ministers. A class of non-stipendiary Ministers has been established for those who wish to serve on a non-maintained basis. Training varies according to candidates' needs. In all cases applications should be made to the address given above.

THE PRESBYTERIAN CHURCH IN IRELAND

The Director of Ministerial Studies
Union Theological College
108 Botanic Avenue
Belfast BT7 1JT
Tel: 02890 205088
Fax: 02890 205099

Qualifications required: Under 30 – a non-theological degree; over 30 but under 40 (as reckoned on 1 October following application) – either a non-theological degree or 2 years, non-graduating Arts or 4 modules of PT BD study or 6 modules of PT study in Humanities acceptable to the Board of Studies; over 40 – not normally accepted, except in exceptional circumstances, where candidate is already possessed of good educational background and/or professional experience.

THE PRESBYTERIAN CHURCH OF WALES

Tabernacle Chapel
81 Merthyr Road
Whitchurch
Cardiff CF14 1DD
Tel: 02920 627465
Fax: 02920 616188
E-mail: swyddfa.office@ebcpcw.org.uk
Website: www.ebcpcw.org.uk

The Presbyterian Church of Wales (PCW) is a Protestant non-conformist denomination. Ordination is dependent on successful application through the local church and Presbytery to the Candidates and Training Department.

MEMBERSHIP
Ministers are ordained to the full-time, part-time or non-stipendiary ministry.

QUALIFICATION/EXAMINATIONS
Pastoral Studies course

THE ROMAN CATHOLIC CHURCH

Candidates for the priesthood in the RC Church attend a residential seminary course of at least 6 years. Among subjects studied are Philosophy, Psychology, Dogmatic and Moral Theology, Scripture, Church History, Canon Law, Liturgy, Catechetics, Communications and Pastoral Theology. Each college/seminary has its own arrangements for the university education of its students. Those who do not attend university take a final internal exam.

THE SALVATION ARMY

UK Headquarters
101 Newington Causeway
London SE1 6BN
Tel: 020 7367 4500
E-mail: info@salvationarmy.org.uk
Website: www.salvationarmy.org.uk

Salvation Army officers engaged in FT service are ordained ministers of religion, and are commissioned following a 2-year period of residential training at the William Booth College, Denmark Hill, London SE5 8BQ. This course – an HE Diploma in Salvation Army Officer Training – may now be undertaken by distance learning, or a mixture of residential and distance learning. Officers may be appointed to corps (church) work, to social services centres (for which additional professional qualifications are required) or to administrative posts.

THE SCOTTISH UNITED REFORMED AND CONGREGATIONAL COLLEGE

113 West Regent Street
Glasgow G2 2RU
Tel: 0141 248 5382
E-mail: Scottishcollege@urcscotland.org.uk
Website: www.scotland.urc.org.uk

The College is recognized as a resource centre for learning by the General Assembly of the United Reformed Church and is one of the institutions charged with responsibility for initial ministerial education.

QUALIFICATION/EXAMINATIONS
The College awards only its own certificate, which is part of the process of accreditation of ordinands as ministers of the United Reformed Church. Students, however, are normally concurrently matriculated for a degree, usually in Theology or Religious Studies, at a university.

THE UNITARIAN AND FREE CHRISTIAN CHURCHES

Essex Hall
London WC2R 3HY
Tel: 020 7240 2384
Fax: 020 7240 3089
E-mail: info@unitarian.org.uk
Website: www.unitarian.org.uk

Candidates accepted for training for the ministry in the Unitarian and Free Christian Churches take courses of training either at Manchester Academy & Harris College, Oxford (2 to 4 years' study for an Oxford degree in Theology/or Theology & Philosophy or an Oxford Certificate in Theology/Religious Studies), or at the Unitarian College (Luther King House, Brighton Grove, Rusholme, Manchester; an individually designed contextual theology course of the Partnership for Theological Education which may lead to a degree or other academic qualification validated by Chester or Manchester University). Alternative arrangements can be made for candidates wishing to study through the Welsh language. Placement work and Unitarian studies are also integral to ministerial preparation. Training normally takes 2 or more years.

THE UNITED REFORMED CHURCH

Church House
86 Tavistock Place
London WC1H 9RT
Tel: 020 7916 2020
Fax: 020 7916 2021
E-mail: urc@urc.org.uk
Website: www.urc.org.uk

Candidates for **Ministry of Word and Sacraments** must have been a member of the URC for at least 2 years. and complete a candidating process. Most then take a 3- or 4-year course of part-time or full-time academic study alongside a minimum of 800 hours of pastoral placements. The minimum required outcome is a Diploma of Higher Education, in Theology. **Church-related Community Workers** strengthen the local church's mission through community development. Candidates are required to obtain at least a Diploma in Theology and a Diploma in Community Work before being commissioned.

Lay Preacher's Certificate: The qualifying course for this takes 3 years in local groups, residential weekends, and practical work in churches.

THE WESLEYAN REFORM UNION

Church House
123 Queen Street
Sheffield S1 2DU
Tel: 0114 272 1938
E-mail: admin@thewru.co.uk
Website: www.thewru.com

The Wesleyan Reform Union has no training college of its own and encourages candidates for its Ministry to enter a Bible College for 2 or 3 years. All candidates are, however, under the personal supervision of a Union Tutor, who directs a Biblical Studies & Training Department offering fairly extensive courses. Candidates attend Headquarters once a year for an oral exam in Theology conducted by the Tutor in the presence of the Union Examination Committee; they also take written exams.

UNITED FREE CHURCH OF SCOTLAND

11 Newton Place
Glasgow G3 7PR
Tel: 01413 323435
E-mail: office@ufcos.org.uk
Website: www.ufcos.org.uk

The United Free Church of Scotland is a small presbyterian denomination which came into being in 1929. Those seeking to become candidates for the ministry should normally have been members of the denomination for at least a year. They will require to undertake a degree course in Theology.

CINEMA, FILM AND TELEVISION
Membership of Professional Institutions and Associations

BRITISH KINEMATOGRAPH SOUND AND TELEVISION SOCIETY (BKSTS)

Pinewood Studios
Pinewood Road
Iver Heath
Buckinghamshire SL0 0NH
Tel: 01753 656656
E-mail: info@bksts.com
Website: www.bksts.com

The BKSTS was founded in 1931 to serve the growing film industry and today arranges meetings, presentations, seminars, international exhibitions and conferences, as well as organizing an extensive programme of training courses, lectures, workshops and special events. We ensure that our members remain up to date with the latest techniques through master classes and our print and electronic publications.

MEMBERSHIP
Student Member
Associate Member
Full Member (MBKS)
Retired Member
Fellow (FBKS)

DESIGNATORY LETTERS
MBKS, FBKS

THE LONDON FILM SCHOOL

24 Shelton Street
Covent Garden
London WC2H 9UB
Tel: 020 7836 9642
Fax: 020 7497 3718
E-mail: info@lfs.org.uk
Website: www.lfs.org.uk

The LFS is one of the foremost independent film schools in Europe and is recognized by Skillset as a Centre of Excellence. It is a registered charity and a non-profit-making company, limited by guarantee. Since 1956 we have trained thousands of directors, cinematographers, editors and other film professionals from around the world.

QUALIFICATION/EXAMINATIONS
MA in Filmmaking (validated by London Metropolitan University)
MA in Screenwriting (validated by London Metropolitan University)
MA International Film Business
PhD Film by Practice

THE NATIONAL FILM AND TELEVISION SCHOOL

Beaconsfield Studios
Station Road
Beaconsfield
Buckinghamshire HP9 1LG
Tel: 01494 671234
Fax: 01494 674042
E-mail: info@nfts.co.uk
Website: www.nfts.co.uk

Creative Skillset Film Academy, the UK's leading film and television school, offers full-time MA and Diploma courses in all the key film and television disciplines, from Animation to VFX. Purpose-built studios include two film stages, a large television studio, and post-production facilities rivalling those of many professional companies.

QUALIFICATION/EXAMINATIONS
Diploma (in 1 of 8 disciplines)
MA in Film and Television (specializing in 1 of 13 disciplines)

CLEANING, LAUNDRY AND DRY CLEANING
Membership of Professional Institutions and Associations

BRITISH INSTITUTE OF CLEANING SCIENCE

9 Premier Court
Boarden Close
Moulton Park
Northampton
Northants NN3 6LF
Tel: 01604 678710
Fax: 01604 645988
E-mail: info@bics.org.uk
Website: www.bics.org.uk

The British Institute of Cleaning Science is the largest independent professional and educational body within the cleaning industry.

Our mission is to raise the standards of education and to build awareness of the cleaning industry, through professional standards and accredited training.

MEMBERSHIP
PBICSc
CBICSc
LBICSc

QUALIFICATION/EXAMINATIONS
Cleaning Professional Skills Suite (CPSS)
Other bespoke cleaning qualifications are also available

THE GUILD OF CLEANERS AND LAUNDERERS

56 Maple Drive
Larkhall
South Lanarkshire ML9 2AR
Tel: 01698 322669
E-mail: enquiries@gcl.org.uk
Website: www.gcl.org.uk

The Guild, formed in 1949, is a technical and professional society whose aim is to further knowledge and skill in all branches of the industry. We keep our members up to date through lectures, seminars and written reports, exchange information of mutual benefit with other organizations in the industry, and voice our opinion in relevant forums.

MEMBERSHIP
Young Guilder

Member
Associate (AGCL)
Advanced Member (AdGCL)
Licentiate (LGCL)
Fellow (FGCL)
Guild Plus Member

DESIGNATORY LETTERS
AGCL, AdGCL, LGCL, FGCL

COLOUR TECHNOLOGY
Membership of Professional Institutions and Associations

PAINTING AND DECORATING ASSOCIATION

32 Coton Road
Nuneaton
Warwickshire CV11 5TW
Tel: 024 7635 3776
Fax: 024 7635 4513
E-mail: info@paintingdecoratingassociation.co.uk
Website: www.paintingdecoratingassociation.co.uk

The PDA is a registered trade and employers' organization, catering exclusively for the needs of professional painting and decorating trade employers. The Association conducts no examinations, but all membership applications are scrutinized at branch level to ensure that only bona fide firms that agree to abide by our code of conduct are admitted.

MEMBERSHIP
Full Member
Associate

THE SOCIETY OF DYERS AND COLOURISTS

Perkin House
82 Grattan Road
Bradford BD1 2LU
Tel: 01274 725138
Fax: 01274 392888
E-mail: members@sdc.org.uk
Website: www.sdc.org.uk

An educational charity, professional body and chartered society, serving globally all aspects of the coloration industries including the textile supply chain through the knowledgeable and enthusiastic involvement of its professional members and industry partners. Recognized as the authority for colour science and technology, delivering high-quality international qualifications and training programmes.

MEMBERSHIP
Individual Voting Member, Individual Non-voting Member, Individual Student Member, Graduate Member, College Member, Company Member

QUALIFICATION/EXAMINATIONS
Fellowship (FSDC), Associateship (ASDC), Licentiateship (LSDC), Chartered Colourist (CCol)

DESIGNATORY LETTERS
FSDC, ASDC, LSDC, CCol

COMMUNICATIONS AND MEDIA
Membership of Professional Institutions and Associations

THE PICTURE RESEARCH ASSOCIATION

c/o 10 Marrick House
Mortimer Crescent
London NW6 5NY
Tel: 0771403017
E-mail: chair@picture-research.org.uk
Website: www.picture-research.org.uk

The PRA, founded in 1977, is a professional organization for picture researchers, picture editors and anyone specifically involved in the research, management and supply of visual material to the media industry. Our aims are to provide information and give support to our members, and to promote their interests and specific skills to potential employers.

MEMBERSHIP
Introductory Member
Full Member
Sponsors

QUALIFICATION/EXAMINATIONS
To qualify as a member of the Association you need a minimum of 2 years experience as a qualified picture researcher/picture editor, eg you were involved in the online search of images, working to a specific brief or project. You would have supplied both digital or analogue files for reproduction. You would also be required to have knowledge and experience of fee negotiations, clearances, copyright and licensing of photographic images from a selection of photographic sources and collections.
Sponsors: A full- or part-time employee of a picture library, picture agency or image archive who is directly involved in the supply of images to the media in general.

COMPUTING AND INFORMATION TECHNOLOGY
Membership of Professional Institutions and Associations

ASSOCIATION OF COMPUTER PROFESSIONALS

ACP
Chilverbridge House
Arlington
East Sussex BN26 6SB
Tel: 01323 871874
Fax: 01323 871875
E-mail: admin@acpexamboard.com
Website: www.acpexamboard.com

The ACP is an independent professional examining body, founded in 1984 to set and maintain standards of education that reflect the constantly changing requirements of the computer industry, both in the UK and overseas. We do so through the provision of course syllabuses and examinations to our carefully vetted training centres around the world.

MEMBERSHIP
Student
Practitioner
Graduate (GradACP)

Licentiate (LACP)
Associate (AACP)
Member (MACP)
Fellow (FACP)

QUALIFICATION/EXAMINATIONS
Please see the ACP's website for details of certificates and diplomas.

DESIGNATORY LETTERS
GradACP, LACP, AACP, MACP, FACP

BCS, THE CHARTERED INSTITUTE FOR IT

1st Floor, Block D
North Star House
North Star Avenue
Swindon
Wiltshire SN2 1FA
Tel: 01793 417417
Fax: 01793 417444
E-mail: customerservices@bcs.uk
Website: www.bcs.org

We promote wider social and economic progress through the advancement of information technology science and practice. We bring together industry, academics, practitioners and government to share knowledge, promote new thinking, inform the design of new curricula, shape public policy and inform the public.

Our vision is to be a world-class organisation for IT. Our 75,000 strong membership includes practitioners, businesses, academics and students in the UK and internationally. We deliver a range of professional development tools for practitioners and employees. A leading IT qualification body, we offer a range of widely recognised qualifications.

MEMBERSHIP
Memberships:
Associate Member (AMBCS)
Professional Member (MBCS)
Chartered IT Professional (CITP)
Fellowship (FBCS)
Student
Apprentice
Affiliate

QUALIFICATION/EXAMINATIONS

IT User Qualifications

- Computer and Online Basics – Understand the basics of how to use a computer
- Digital Skills – Develop skills for our digital world
- ECDL – Develop skills using office-based software
- e-safety – The online safety qualification for Schools
- ITQ – The flexible IT qualification – Create your own qualification, or use one of our tailor-made solutions

Higher Education Qualifications

- BCS Level 4 Certificate in IT/100/6190/2
- BCS Level 5 Diploma in IT/100/6190/3
- BCS Level 6 Professional Graduate Diploma in IT/100/6191/5

Professional Certification

- Business analysis
- Information security and CESG scheme
- Software testing
- IT service management (inc ITIL)

- Agile
- Project & programme management
- PRINCE2
- Solution development and architecture
- Consultancy
- Green IT
- Data centre management
- OpenStack software

Apprenticeships

- Cyber Intrusion Analyst
- Cyber Security Technologist
- Data Analyst
- Digital Marketer
- Infrastructure Technician
- Network Engineer
- Software Developer
- Software Tester
- Unified Communications Trouble Shooter

See the BCS website for details of other qualifications.

INSTITUTE FOR THE MANAGEMENT OF INFORMATION SYSTEMS

Suite A (Part) 2nd Floor
3 White Oak Square
London Road
Swanley
Kent BR8 7AG
Tel: 0845 850 0006
Fax: 0845 850 0007
E-mail: imis@bcs.org
Website: www.imis.org.uk

IMIS is one of the leading professional associations in the IT sector. A registered charity, it plays a prominent role in fostering greater understanding of IS management, in working to enhance the status of those engaged in the profession, and in promoting higher standards through better education and training worldwide.

MEMBERSHIP
Student Member
Practitioner Member
Licentiate Member (LIMIS)

Associate Member (AIMIS)
Full Member (MIMIS)
Fellow (FIMIS)

QUALIFICATION/EXAMINATIONS
Foundation
Diploma
Higher Diploma

DESIGNATORY LETTERS
LIMIS, AIMIS, MIMIS, FIMIS

INSTITUTION OF ANALYSTS AND PROGRAMMERS

Boundary House
Boston Road
London W7 2QE
Tel: 020 8434 3685
E-mail: admin@iap.org.uk
Website: www.iap.org.uk

The IAP is a professional organization for people who work in the development, installation and testing of business systems and computer software. Our aim is to promote high standards of competence and conduct among our members, to encourage them to develop their skills and progress their career, and to facilitate the advancement and spreading of knowledge within the profession.

MEMBERSHIP
Licentiate
Graduate (GradIAP)
Associate Member (AIAP)
Member (MIAP)
Fellow (FIAP)

DESIGNATORY LETTERS
GradIAP, AIAP, MIAP, FIAP

COUNSELLING
Membership of Professional Institutions and Associations

COUNSELLING LTD

Registered Office
5 Pear Tree Walk
Wakefield
West Yorkshire WF2 0HW
E-mail: via website
Website: www.counselling.ltd.uk

Counselling, a registered charity founded in 1998, is a membership organization for counsellors and psychotherapists in the UK that has established a network of about 2,700 affiliated CCC-registered counsellors, many of whom are able to provide occasional free or discounted face-to-face counselling with clients on low incomes.

MEMBERSHIP
Affiliate

CSCT COUNSELLING TRAINING

13 Coleshill Street
Sutton Coldfield
West Midlands B72 1SD
Tel: 0121 321 1396
Fax: 0121 355 5581
E-mail: info@counsellingtraining.com
Website: www.counsellingtraining.com

CSCT has been producing counselling training courses for over 25 years, during which time we have trained over 50,000 students. Our courses are offered PT via a network of colleges and private providers throughout the UK. Our training materials are written to the specifications of the appropriate awarding body and we provide 24-hour e-mail and telephone support from Client Services and the Academic Team.

QUALIFICATION/EXAMINATIONS
Please see the CSCT's website.

CREDIT MANAGEMENT
Membership of Professional Institutions and Associations

CHARTERED INSTITUTE OF CREDIT MANAGEMENT

The Water Mill
Station Road
South Luffenham
Oakham
Leicestershire LE15 8NB
Tel: 01780 722900
Fax: 01780 721333
E-mail: info@cicm.com
Website: www.cicm.com

CICM is the largest professional credit management organisation in Europe and the only one accredited by Ofqual as an awarding body. We represent the credit profession across trade, consumer and export credit, as well as in related activities such as collections, credit reporting, credit insurance and insolvency, promote excellence in credit management and raise awareness of its vital role in business and the community.

MEMBERSHIP
Affiliate
Associate Member (AICM)
Graduate Member (MICM(Grad))
Member (MICM)
Fellow (FICM)

Corporate Member

QUALIFICATION/EXAMINATIONS
Certificate in Credit Management
Level 3 Diploma in Credit Management
Level 5 Diploma in Credit Management
Certificate in Debt Collection
Diploma in Debt Collection
Certificate in Money and Debt Advice
Diploma in Money and Debt Advice
Certificate in High Court Enforcement (Level 4)
Diploma in High Court Enforcement (Level 4)
Diploma in High Court Enforcement (Level 5)

DESIGNATORY LETTERS
AICM, MICM (Grad), MICM, FIFA

DANCING
Membership of Professional Institutions and Associations

BRITISH BALLET ORGANIZATION

Woolborough House
39 Lonsdale Road
Barnes
London SW13 9JP
Tel: 020 8748 1241
Fax: 020 8748 1301
E-mail: info@bbo.org.uk
Website: www.bbo.org.uk

The BBO, founded in 1930, is an awarding body offering teacher training and examinations in classical ballet, tap, modern dance and jazz. We have schools throughout the UK and in several other countries.

MEMBERSHIP
Student Member

Senior Student Member
Affiliated Member
Student Teacher Member
Teacher Member

QUALIFICATION/EXAMINATIONS
Please see the BBO website for details.

IMPERIAL SOCIETY OF TEACHERS OF DANCING

Imperial House
22/26 Paul Street
London EC2A 4QE
Tel: +44 (0)20 7377 1577
Fax: +44 (0)20 7247 8829
E-mail: via website
Website: www.istd.org

The ISTD is a registered educational charity and examinations board. We aim to promote knowledge of dance, to maintain and improve teaching standards, and to qualify (by examination) teachers of dancing. Our dance techniques cover more than 12 different genres and are taught by more than 7,500 members by our members worldwide.

MEMBERSHIP
A range of 9 categories from Student to Life Membership.

QUALIFICATION/EXAMINATIONS
Please see our website www.istd.org or www.dance-teachers.org

DESIGNATORY LETTERS
ISTD

INTERNATIONAL DANCE TEACHERS' ASSOCIATION LIMITED

International House
76 Bennett Road
Brighton BN2 5JL
Tel: 01273 685652
Fax: 01273 674388
E-mail: via website
Website: www.idta.co.uk

The IDTA is one of the world's largest dance examination boards, with more than 7,000 members in 55 countries. Our aims are to promote knowledge and foster the art of dance in all its forms, to maintain and improve dancing standards, and to offer a comprehensive range of professional qualifications in all dance genres.

MEMBERSHIP
Associate (AIDTA)
Licentiate (LIDTA)
Fellow (FIDTA)

DESIGNATORY LETTERS
AIDTA, LIDTA, FIDTA

THE BENESH INSTITUTE

36 Battersea Square
London SW11 3RA
Tel: 020 7326 8031
E-mail: beneshinstitute@rad.org.uk
Website: www.benesh.org

The Benesh Institute is the international centre for Benesh Movement Notation (BMN) founded in 1962 to promote, develop and offer education in BMN. We also function as an examining body and professional centre, and are responsible for coordinating technical developments. Since 1997 The Benesh Institute has been incorporated within the Royal Academy of Dance.

QUALIFICATION/EXAMINATIONS
Certificate in Benesh Movement Notation (CBMN) (validated by the Royal Academy of Dance)
Diploma for Professional Benesh Movement Notators (DPBMN) (validated by the Royal Academy of Dance)
Associate of the Institute of Choreology (AI Chor)

DENTISTRY
Membership of Professional Institutions and Associations

BRITISH ASSOCIATION OF CLINICAL DENTAL TECHNOLOGY

44–46 Wollaton Road
Beeston
Nottingham N69 2NR
Tel: 0115 957 5370
Fax: 0115 925 4800
E-mail: info@bacdt.org.uk
Website: www.bacdt.org.uk

The CDTA provides political and educational representation for its members, who are registered with the General Dental Council and trained in designing, creating, constructing, repairing and rebasing removable appliances to ensure optimal fit, maximum comfort and general wellbeing of patients. We are committed to team dentistry and ensure that our members work to the highest professional standards.

MEMBERSHIP
Full Membership
In training Membership
Practice Membership
Multi Practice Membership

BRITISH ASSOCIATION OF DENTAL NURSES

PO Box 4, Room 200
Hillhouse International Business Centre
Thornton-Cleveleys
Lancashire FY5 4QD
Tel: 01253 338360
E-mail: admin@badn.org.uk
Website: www.badn.org.uk

The BADN represents dental nurses, whether qualified or unqualified, working in general practice, hospital, the community, the armed forces, industry, practice management or reception, and has representation on the National Examining Board, the Dental Nurses Standards and Training Advisory Board and its Registration Committee, the Joint Consultative Committee, and other bodies.

MEMBERSHIP
Associate Member
Full Member

BRITISH SOCIETY OF DENTAL HYGIENE AND THERAPY

Smile House
2 East Union Street
Rugby
Warwickshire CV22 6AJ
Tel: 01788 575050
E-mail: enquiries@bsdht.org.uk
Website: www.bsdht.org.uk

The BSDHT is the only nationally recognised body that represents dental hygienists. Join the UK's largest professional body for practising dental hygienists, those dually qualified in dental hygiene and therapy, and students of the profession. We represent your interests, influence positive change for the industry and provide information to the public. See more at: www.bsdht.org.uk/#sthash.WHpbKNhV. dpuf. We have a membership of more than 3,500, and look after their interests through liaising with the Department of Health, General Dental Council, British Dental Association and other organisations.

MEMBERSHIP
Member

DENTAL TECHNOLOGISTS ASSOCIATION

3 Kestral Court
Waterwells Drive
Waterwells Business Park
Gloucester GL2 2AT
Tel: 01452 886366
E-mail: via website
Website: www.dta-uk.org

The DTA is an organization that supports the development of the dental technology profession by encouraging and promoting education, including CPD, and for the exchange of views between dental technicians. We advise, develop and support dental technicians and maintain links with the government, other dental organizations, service providers and the public.

MEMBERSHIP
Member

GENERAL DENTAL COUNCIL

37 Wimpole Street
London W1G 8DQ
Tel: 0845 222 4141
E-mail: information@gdc-uk.org
Website: www.gdc-uk.org

The GDC regulates dental professionals in the UK. All dentists, clinical dental technicians, dental hygienists, dental nurses, dental technicians, dental therapists and orthodontic therapists must be registered with the GDC in order to work in the UK.

THE BRITISH DENTAL ASSOCIATION

64 Wimpole Street
London W1G 8YS
Tel: 020 7935 0875
Fax: 020 7487 5232
E-mail: enquiries@bda.org
Website: www.bda.org

The BDA, which was founded in 1880, is the professional association and trade union for dentists in the UK. Our aims are to advance the science, arts and ethics of dentistry, improve the UK's oral health, and promote the interests of our members. Membership, which is voluntary, stands at around 23,000, mostly in general practice.

MEMBERSHIP
Essential
Extra
Expert

DIETETICS

Membership of Professional Institutions and Associations

THE BRITISH DIETETIC ASSOCIATION

5th Floor
Charles House
148–49 Great Charles Street Queensway
Birmingham B3 3HT
Tel: 0121 200 8080
E-mail: info@bda.uk.com
Website: www.bda.uk.com

The BDA, established in 1936, is the UK's leading professional association and trade union for dietitians. Our aims are to advance the science and practice of dietetics and associated subjects, to promote education and training in the science and practice of dietetics and associated subjects, and to regulate relations between our 8,000+ members and their employers.

MEMBERSHIP
Full Member
Associate Member
Affiliate Member
Alliance Member
Student Member
International Member

DISTRIBUTION

Membership of Professional Institutions and Associations

THE CHARTERED INSTITUTE OF LOGISTICS AND TRANSPORT (UK)

Earlstrees Court
Earlstrees Road
Corby
Northamptonshire NN17 4AX
Tel: 01536 740104
Fax: 01536 740101
E-mail: membership@ciltuk.org.uk
Website: www.ciltuk.org.uk

The Chartered Institute of Logistics and Transport is the membership organisation for professionals involved in the movement of goods and people and their associated supply chains.

Members are involved in the management and design of infrastructure, systems, processes and information flows and in the management and development of effective organisations.

MEMBERSHIP
Learner
Full Time Student
Apprentice
e-Member
Affiliate
Member (MILT)
Chartered Member (CMILT)
Chartered Fellow (FCILT)

QUALIFICATION/EXAMINATIONS
Regulated qualifications cover areas within the Institute's nine Professional Sectors: Supply Chain, Transport Planning, Rail, Active Travel & Travel Planning, Bus & Coach, Ports Maritime & Waterways, Freight Forwarding, Aviation and Operations Management.

Regulated qualifications meet the regulatory requirements for the design, delivery, assessment and award of units and qualifications, and are regulated by Ofqual and/or Qualifications Wales/CCEA Accreditation, if appropriate.

Level 1 – Award
Level 2 – Award, Certificate, Diploma
Level 3 – Award, Certificate
Level 4 – Certificate
Level 5 – Award, Certificate, Diploma, Professional Diploma
Level 6 – Advanced Diploma

Non-Regulated Programmes

Humanitarian Logistics (3 programmes)
Supply Chain Practitioner Award (Foundation, Professional and Master programmes)
Certificate of Customs Competency
Certified European Logistician (Junior, Senior, Master programmes)
Certified DOPsys (Delivery, Offload and Position System) (Technician, Team Leader, Project Manager)

DESIGNATORY LETTERS
MILT, CMILT, FCILT

DRAMATIC AND PERFORMING ARTS
Membership of Professional Institutions and Associations

DRAMA UK

Woburn House
20 Tavistock Square
London WC1H 9HB
Tel: 020 3393 6141
E-mail: info@dramauk.co.uk
Website: www.dramauk.co.uk

Drama UK was formed in 2012 following the merger of the National Council for Drama Training and the Conference of Drama Schools.

We act as an advocate for quality drama training; offer advice to students of all ages; and award a quality mark to the very best drama training available.

EQUITY

Guild House
Upper St Martins Lane
London WC2H 9EG
Tel: 020 7379 6000
E-mail: info@equity.org.uk
Website: www.equity.org.uk

Equity is the UK trade union representing professional performers and other creative workers from across the entertainment, creative and cultural industries. The main function of Equity is to negotiate minimum terms and conditions of employment for its members and to represent its members' interests to the government and other bodies.

MEMBERSHIP
Student Member
Graduate Member
Full Member

THE BRITISH (THEATRICAL) ARTS

12 Deveron Way
Rise Park
Romford
Essex RM1 4UL
Tel: 01708 756263
E-mail: sally.chennelle1@ntlworld.com
Website: www.britisharts.org

The British Arts is a non-profit-making organization dedicated to maintaining and where necessary raising the standard of the teaching of Performing Arts subjects. We work to encourage a strong technical foundation combined with an understanding of professional theatrical presentation and conduct exams in Dramatic Art, Classical & Stage Ballet, Mime, Tap, Musical Theatre and Modern Dance.

MEMBERSHIP
Student Member
Companion
Associate (Teaching and Non-teaching)
Member (Teaching and Non-teaching)
Advanced Teacher Member
Fellow

QUALIFICATION/EXAMINATIONS
Please see the British Arts website.

DRIVING INSTRUCTORS
Membership of Professional Institutions and Associations

REGISTER OF APPROVED DRIVING INSTRUCTORS

The Axis Building
112 Upper Parliament Street
Nottingham NG1 6LP
Tel: 0300 200 1122
E-mail: ADIReg@dvsa.gov.uk

The Register of Approved Driving Instructors (ADI) and the licensing scheme for trainee instructors (PDI) are administered under the provisions of the Road Traffic Act 1988 by the Department for Transport (DfT). It is an offence for anyone to give professional instruction (that is instruction paid for by or in respect of the pupil) in driving a motor car unless: (a) his or her name is on the Register of Approved Driving Instructors; or (b) he or she holds a 'trainee's licence to give instruction' issued by the Registrar.

QUALIFICATION/EXAMINATIONS
Please see the GOV.UK website (www.gov.uk/apply-to-become-a-driving-instructor) for details of the qualifying examinations.

EMBALMING

Membership of Professional Institutions and Associations

INTERNATIONAL EXAMINATIONS BOARD OF EMBALMERS

146 Alexandra Road
Great Wakering
Essex SS3 0GW
Tel: 01702 218907
E-mail: admin@iebe.co.uk

The Board examines candidates who wish to become qualified members of the British Institute of Embalmers (qv), which is not itself an examining body but can provide information packs (also available from the above address) that contain lists of approved schools and accredited tutors.

THE BRITISH INSTITUTE OF EMBALMERS

Anubis House
21c Station Road
Knowle
Solihull
West Midlands B93 0HL
Tel: 01564 778991
Fax: 01564 770812
E-mail: info@bioe.co.uk
Website: www.bioe.co.uk

The BIE, founded in 1927, is an organization for professional embalmers. Its objectives include supporting and protecting the status, character and interests of embalmers, promoting the efficient tuition of persons seeking to become embalmers, and encouraging the study and practice of improved methods of embalming.

MEMBERSHIP
Member (MBIE)
Fellow (FBIE)

DESIGNATORY LETTERS
MBIE, FBIE

EMPLOYMENT AND CAREERS SERVICES
Membership of Professional Institutions and Associations

CAREER DEVELOPMENT INSTITUTE

Ground Floor
Copthall House
1 New Road
Stourbridge
West Midlands DY8 1PH
Tel: 01384 376464
E-mail: hq@thecdi.net
Website: www.thecdi.net

The CDI is the largest UK-wide professional and membership body for career development professionals. Our aim is to support members and promote access to high-quality career development services, delivered by professionally qualified staff working within an appropriate ethical framework. Suitably qualified members can join the UK Register of Career Development Professionals.

MEMBERSHIP
Student Member
Full Member
Registered Member
Retired Member
Affiliate Organisation
School Affiliate

QUALIFICATION/EXAMINATIONS
Qualification in Career Guidance (QCG)
Qualification in Career Guidance and Development (QCGD)
CDI Certificate in Career Guidance Theory (CCGT)
CDI Certificate in Careers Leadership (CCL)

RECRUITMENT AND EMPLOYMENT CONFEDERATION

Dorset House
First Floor
27–45 Stamford Street
London SE1 9NT
Tel: 020 7009 2100
E-mail: info@rec.uk.com
Website: www.rec.uk.com

The REC is the representative body for the UK's £27 billion private recruitment and staffing industry, with a membership of more than 8,000 Corporate Members comprising agencies and businesses from all sectors, and 6,000 members of the Institute of Recruitment Professionals (IRP) made up of recruitment consultants and other industry professionals.

MEMBERSHIP
Affiliate (AIRP)
Member (MIRP)
Fellow (FIRP)

QUALIFICATION/EXAMINATIONS
Certificate in Recruitment Practice (QCF)
Diploma in Recruitment Practice (QCF)
Diploma in Recruitment Management (QCF)

DESIGNATORY LETTERS
AIRP, MIRP, FIRP

ENGINEERING, AERONAUTICAL
Membership of Professional Institutions and Associations

ROYAL AERONAUTICAL SOCIETY

4 Hamilton Place
Hyde Park Corner
London W1J 7BQ
Tel: 020 7670 4300
Fax: 020 7670 4309
E-mail: raes@aerosociety.com
Website: www.aerosociety.com

The RAeS, founded in 1866 to further the science of aeronautics, is a multidisciplinary professional institution dedicated to the global aerospace community. We work on our members' behalf to promote the highest professional standards in all aerospace disciplines, to provide specialist information and act as a central forum for the exchange of ideas, and to play a leading role in influencing opinion on aviation matters.

MEMBERSHIP
Student Affiliate
Affiliate
Associate (ARAeS)
Associate Member (AMRAeS)
Member (MRAeS)
Companion (CRAeS)
Fellow (FRAeS)
Apprentice

ENGINEERING, AGRICULTURAL
Membership of Professional Institutions and Associations

BRITISH AGRICULTURAL AND GARDEN MACHINERY ASSOCIATION

Middleton House
2 Main Road
Middleton Cheney
Oxfordshire OX17 2TN
Tel: 01295 713344
Fax: 01295 711665
E-mail: info@bagma.com
Website: www.bagma.com

BAGMA is the trade association representing agricultural and garden machinery dealers in the UK. We have some 850 dealer members and 75 affiliated suppliers and allied industry companies. We offer a range of training and assessment courses through our online learning package and at approved Training and Assessment Centres.

QUALIFICATION/EXAMINATIONS
Please see the BAGMA website.

THE INSTITUTION OF AGRICULTURAL ENGINEERS

The Bullock Building
University Way
Cranfield
Bedford
Bedfordshire MK43 0GH
Tel: 01234 750876
E-mail: secretary@iagre.org
Website: www.iagre.org

The Institution of Agricultural Engineers is the professional body for engineers, scientists, technologists and managers in agriculture and the environment, agri-technology and allied landbased industries, including forestry, food engineering and technology, amenity, renewable energy, horticulture and the environment. The IAgrE also administers the Landbased Engineering Technician Accreditation schemes (LTA) for industry.

MEMBERSHIP
Student
Associate (AIAgrE)

Associate Member (AMIAgrE)
Member (MIAgrE)
Fellow (FIAgrE)
Honorary Fellow

QUALIFICATION/EXAMINATIONS
Chartered Engineer (CEng), Chartered Environmentalist (CEnv), Incorporated Engineer (IEng), Engineering Technician (EngTech)

DESIGNATORY LETTERS
AIAgrE, AMIAgrE, MIAgrE, FIAgrE

ENGINEERING, AUTOMOBILE
Membership of Professional Institutions and Associations

INSTITUTE OF AUTOMOTIVE ENGINEER ASSESSORS

The Firs
High Street
Whitchurch
Buckinghamshire HP22 4JU
Tel: 01296 642895
Fax: 01296 640044
E-mail: sally@theiaea.org
Website: www.iaea-online.org

The IAEA, a Professional Affiliate of the Engineering Council, was founded in 1932 and now represents more than 1,500 automotive engineer assessors responsible for activities such as vehicle damage assessment, accident reconstruction, investigation of mechanical failures, electrical failures and vehicle fires, providing expert witness testimony, repair assessment, car fleet surveys, and conciliation and arbitration.

MEMBERSHIP
Affiliate (AffInstAEA)
Associate (AInstAEA)
Member (MInstAEA)
Fellow (FInstAEA)
Honorary Fellow (HFInstAEA)

QUALIFICATION/EXAMINATIONS
Basic Principles of Maths & Physics Application to Accident Reconstruction
Motor Vehicle Legislation as related to Insurance Principles

Principles and Practice of Vehicle Damage Assessment
Motor Insurance
Automotive Technology

DESIGNATORY LETTERS
AffInstAEA, AInstAEA, MInstAEA, FInstAEA

THE INSTITUTE OF THE MOTOR INDUSTRY

Fanshaws
Brickendon
Hertford SG13 8PQ
Tel: 01992 511521
Fax: 01992 511548
E-mail: comms@theimi.org.uk
Website: www.motor.org.uk and www.automotivetechnician.org.uk

The IMI is the professional association for individuals working in the motor industry and exists to help individuals and employers improve professional standards and performance by qualifying, recognizing and developing people. We are the Sector Skills Council for the automotive retail industry, a Licensed Member of the Engineering Council and the governing body for Automotive Technician Accreditation (ATA) – the UK's first national voluntary assessment system for vehicle technicians.

MEMBERSHIP
Affiliate (AffIMI)

Licentiate (LIMI)
Associate (AMIMI)
Member (MIMI)
Fellow (FIMI)
For technicians only, there are two special IMI awards recognizing technical qualifications and experience:
AAE (Advanced Automotive Engineer)
CAE (Certificated Automotive Engineer)

DESIGNATORY LETTERS
AffIMI, LIMI, AMIMI, MIMI, FIMI, AAE, CAE

ENGINEERING, BUILDING SERVICES
Membership of Professional Institutions and Associations

THE CHARTERED INSTITUTION OF BUILDING SERVICES ENGINEERS

222 Balham High Road
London SW12 9BS
Tel: 020 8675 5211
Fax: 020 8675 5449
Website: www.cibse.org

CIBSE is the professional body for people involved in the design, construction, operation and maintenance of the engineering elements of a building other than its structure and enables it to operate efficiently by saving energy and contributing to a low carbon built environment. This includes heating, ventilation, air conditioning, electrical services, lighting etc.

MEMBERSHIP
Student Affiliate

Affiliate
Graduate
Companion
Licentiate (LCIBSE)
Associate (ACIBSE)
Member (MCIBSE)
Fellow (FCIBSE)
CIBSE is a licensed institution of the Engineering Council. This means that, as well as joining CIBSE, you will be Registered as a Chartered Engineer

(CEng), Incorporated Engineer (IEng) or Engineering Technician (EngTech) when you have reached the appropriate level of qualification and professional skill.

QUALIFICATION/EXAMINATIONS
Please see the CIBSE website for more information www.cibse.org

DESIGNATORY LETTERS
LCIBSE, ACIBSE, MCIBSE, FCIBSE

ENGINEERING, CHEMICAL
Membership of Professional Institutions and Associations

THE INSTITUTION OF CHEMICAL ENGINEERS

Davis Building
Railway Terrace
Rugby
Warwickshire CV21 3HQ
Tel: 01788 578214
Fax: 01788 560833
E-mail: customerservices@icheme.org
Website: www.icheme.org

The IChemE, founded in 1922, is an international professional membership organization for chemical, biochemical and process engineers, and we have some 30,000 members in more than 113 countries. We promote competence and a commitment to sustainable development, advance the discipline for the benefit of society, and support the professional development of our members.

MEMBERSHIP
Student
Affiliate

Associate Member (AMIChemE)
Member (MIChemE)
Fellow (FIChemE)
Chartered Chemical Engineer (CEng MIChemE)
Chartered Engineer (CEng)
Chartered Scientist (CSci)
Chartered Environmentalist (CEnv)
Associate Fellow

DESIGNATORY LETTERS
AMIChemE, MIChemE, FIChemE, CEng MIChemE, CEng, CSci, CEnv

ENGINEERING, CIVIL
Membership of Professional Institutions and Associations

INSTITUTION OF CIVIL ENGINEERS

1 Great George Street
Westminster
London SW1P 3AA
Tel: 020 7222 7722
E-mail: membership@ice.org.uk
Website: www.ice.org.uk

The ICE is a UK-based international organization with 80,000 members that strives to promote and progress civil engineering around the world. Our purpose is to qualify professionals engaged in civil engineering, exchange knowledge and best practice, and support our members, and in the UK we liaise with government and publish reports on civil engineering issues.

MEMBERSHIP
Student
Graduate
Affiliate

Technician Member
Associate Member (AMICE)
Member (MICE)
Companion
Fellow (FICE)

ENGINEERING, ELECTRICAL, ELECTRONIC AND MANUFACTURING
Membership of Professional Institutions and Associations

INSTITUTION OF LIGHTING PROFESSIONALS

Regent House
Regent Place
Rugby
Warwickshire CV21 2PN
Tel: 01788 576492
E-mail: info@theilp.org.uk
Website: www.theilp.org.uk

The ILP is a professional lighting association with about 2,000 members, including lighting designers, consultants and engineers. We are dedicated to excellence in lighting and to raising awareness about the important contribution of lighting in road safety, crime prevention and the environment. We support members by providing technical advice and encourage their CPD through our monthly journal and by holding a wide range of conferences, regional meetings, seminars and courses.

MEMBERSHIP
Apprentice
Student
Affiliate

Associate Member (AMILP)
Member (MILP)
Fellow (FILP)
Corporate Member
Premier Corporate Member
Engineering Technician (EngTech)
Incorporated Engineer (IEng)
Chartered Engineer (CEng)

QUALIFICATION/EXAMINATIONS
Exterior Lighting Diploma
LET Diploma in Lighting

DESIGNATORY LETTERS
AMILP, MILP, FILP, EngTech, IEng, CEng

THE INSTITUTION OF ENGINEERING AND TECHNOLOGY

Michael Faraday House
Stevenage
Hertfordshire SG1 2AY
Tel: 01438 313311
Fax: 01438 765526
E-mail: postmaster@theiet.org
Website: www.theiet.org

The IET is working to engineer a better world through our mission to inspire, inform and influence the global engineering community, supporting technology innovation to meet the needs of society. The

IET has over 163,000 members in 127 countries, with offices in Europe, North America, South Asia and Asia-Pacific.

MEMBERSHIP
Student
Associate
Member (MIET)
Fellow (FIET)

Honorary Fellow
ICT Technician (ICTTech)
Engineering Technician (EngTech)
Incorporated Engineer (IEng)
Chartered Engineer (CEng)

DESIGNATORY LETTERS
FIET, ICTTech, EngTech, IEng, CEng, MIET

ENGINEERING, ENERGY
Membership of Professional Institutions and Associations

ENERGY INSTITUTE

61 New Cavendish Street
London W1G 7AR
Tel: 020 7467 7100
Fax: 020 7255 1472
E-mail: info@energyinst.org
Website: www.energyinst.org

The EI is the chartered professional membership body for the energy industry, providing learning and networking opportunities, professional recognition and energy knowledge resources for individuals and companies worldwide. We offer professional qualifications including Chartered, Incorporated and Engineering Technician status for engineers, as well as Chartered Scientist, Chartered Energy Manager and Chartered Environmentalist.

MEMBERSHIP
Student Member
Affiliate
Graduate Member (GradEI)

Member (MEI)
Fellow (FEI)
Engineering Technician (EngTech)
Incorporated Engineer (IEng)
Chartered Engineer (CEng)
Chartered Scientist (CSci)
Chartered Environmentalist (CEnv)
Chartered Energy Manager (exclusive EI title)
Chartered Energy Engineer (exclusive EI title)
Chartered Petroleum Engineer (exclusive EI title)

DESIGNATORY LETTERS
GradEI, MEI, FEI, EngTech, IEng, CEng, CEnv, CSci

ENGINEERING, ENVIRONMENTAL
Membership of Professional Institutions and Associations

INSTITUTE OF ENVIRONMENTAL MANAGEMENT AND ASSESSMENT

Saracen House
Lincoln LN6 7AS
Tel: 01522 540069
Fax: 01522 540090
E-mail: info@iema.net
Website: www.iema.net

The IEMA is a not-for-profit membership organization that provides recognition and support to environmental professionals and promotes sustainable development through improved environmental practice and performance. We have about 15,000 individual and corporate members in 87 countries, in the public, private and non-governmental sectors.

MEMBERSHIP
Student Member
Affiliate Member
Graduate Member
Associate (AIEMA)

Full Member (MIEMA)
Fellow (FIEMA)
Chartered Environmentalist (CEnv)
Corporate Member

QUALIFICATION/EXAMINATIONS
Foundation Certificate in Environmental Management
Associate Certificate in Environmental Management
Diploma

DESIGNATORY LETTERS
AIEMA, MIEMA, FIEMA, CEnv

THE CHARTERED INSTITUTION OF WATER AND ENVIRONMENTAL MANAGEMENT

15 John Street
London WC1N 2EB
Tel: 020 7831 3110
Fax: 020 7405 4967
E-mail: via website
Website: www.ciwem.org

Founded in 1895, CIWEM is an independent professional body and registered charity with 12,000 members that advances the science and practice of water and environmental management for a clean, green and sustainable world by promoting environmental excellence and professional development and training, supplying independent advice and evidence-based opinion, and providing a forum for debate through conferences, technical meetings and its publications.

MEMBERSHIP
Student
Associate ACIWEM
Graduate
Member MCIWEM C.WEM
Fellow FCIWEM C.WEM
Environmental Partner
Chartered Engineer (CEng)
Chartered Environmentalist (CEnv)
Chartered Scientist (CSci)

QUALIFICATION/EXAMINATIONS
Online training courses in partnership with Staffordshire University, accredited university courses at 12 leading institutions, CPD modules and Rural Environmental Management Programme

DESIGNATORY LETTERS
CEng, CEnv, CSi, C.WEM

THE SOCIETY OF ENVIRONMENTAL ENGINEERS

The Manor House
High Street
Buntingford
Hertfordshire SG9 9AB
Tel: 01763 271209
Fax: 01763 273255
E-mail: office@environmental.org.uk
Website: www.environmental.org.uk

The SEE, founded in 1959, is a professional society that promotes awareness of the discipline of environmental engineering (the measurement, modelling, control and simulation of all types of environment). We provide members with information, training and representation within this field and encourage communication and good practice in quality, reliability, and cost-effective product development and manufacture.

MEMBERSHIP
Student
Member
Corporate Member
Engineering Technician (EngTech)
Incorporated Engineer (IEng)
Chartered Engineer (CEng)

DESIGNATORY LETTERS
EngTech, IEng, CEng

ENGINEERING, FIRE
Membership of Professional Institutions and Associations

ASSOCIATION OF PRINCIPAL FIRE OFFICERS

9–11 Pebble Close
Amington
Tamworth
Staffordshire B77 4RD
Tel: 01827 302300
Fax: 01827 302399
E-mail: enquiries@apfo.org.uk
Website: www.apfo.org.uk

The APFO is the staff association of the most senior Fire Officers in the UK. Our objectives are: to represent and promote the interests of members in conditions of service and legal and employment matters; to negotiate and promote the settlement of disputes involving members; to provide assistance to members and their dependants in exceptional circumstances; and to provide support to members in matters concerning employment or a work-related injury.

MEMBERSHIP
Associate Member
Lifetime Past Member

CHIEF FIRE OFFICERS' ASSOCIATION

9–11 Pebble Close
Amington
Tamworth
Staffordshire B77 4RD
Tel: 01827 302300
Fax: 01827 302399
Website: www.cfoa.org.uk

The CFOA is a professional membership association of the most senior fire officers in the UK. We provide independent advice to the government, local authorities and others. Our aim is to reduce loss of life, personal injury and damage to property by improving the quality of fire fighting, rescue, fire protection and fire prevention in the UK.

MEMBERSHIP
Member

THE INSTITUTION OF FIRE ENGINEERS

IFE House
64–66 Cygnet Court
Timothy's Bridge Road
Stratford-upon-Avon CV37 9NW
Tel: 01789 261 463
Fax: 01789 296 426
E-mail: info@ife.org.uk
Website: www.ife.org.uk

The IFE, founded in 1918, is a non-profit-making professional body for fire professionals and has more than 12,000 members worldwide. Our aim is to encourage and improve the science and practice of fire extinction, fire prevention and fire engineering, to enhance technical networks, and to give advice and support to our members for the benefit of the community at large.

MEMBERSHIP
Student
Affiliate Member
Technician (TIFireE)
Graduate (GIFireE)
Associate (AIFireE)
Member (MIFireE)

Fellow (FIFireE)
Engineering Technician (EngTech)
Incorporated Engineer (IEng)
Chartered Engineer (CEng)
Affiliate Organization

QUALIFICATION/EXAMINATIONS
IFE Certificate in Fire Science, Operations and Safety (Level 2)
IFE Certificate in Fire Science, Operations, Fire Safety and Management (Level 3)
IFE Diploma in Fire Science and Fire Safety (Level 3)

DESIGNATORY LETTERS
TIFireE, GIFireE, AIFireE, MIFireE, FIFireE, EngTech, IEng, CEng

ENGINEERING, GAS

Membership of Professional Institutions and Associations

THE INSTITUTION OF GAS ENGINEERS AND MANAGERS

IGEM House
High Street
Kegworth
Derbyshire DE74 2DA
Tel: 0844 375 4436
Fax: 01509 678198
E-mail: general@igem.org.uk
Website: www.igem.org.uk

IGEM is licensed by EC(UK) and serves a wide range of professionals in the UK and international gas industry through membership and technical standards, having a diverse membership ranging from university students to qualified professionals. Anyone working or interested in the gas industry can form positive connections to enhance their career through IGEM.

MEMBERSHIP
Student Member
Associate (AIGEM)

Associate Member (AMIGEM)
Graduate Member (GradIGEM)
Member Manager (MIGEM)
Technician Member (Eng Tech (MIGEM))
Incorporated Member (I Eng (MIGEM))
Chartered Member (C Eng (MIGEM))
Fellow (C Eng (FIGEM))

DESIGNATORY LETTERS
MIGEM, Eng Tech (MIGEM), I Eng (MIGEM), C Eng (MIGEM), C Eng (FIGEM)

ENGINEERING, GENERAL

Membership of Professional Institutions and Associations

ASSOCIATION OF COST ENGINEERS

Lea House
Sandbach
Cheshire CW11 1XL
Tel: 01270 764798
Fax: 01270 766180
E-mail: enquiries@acoste.org.uk
Website: www.acoste.org.uk

The ACostE represents the professional interests of those with responsibility for the prediction, planning and control of resources for engineering, manufacturing and construction. As a Professional Affiliate of The Engineering Council, we can propose suitably qualified members for the award of the titles of Chartered Engineer (CEng) and Incorporated Engineer (IEng).

MEMBERSHIP
Student
Associate (AA Cost E)
Companion (Companion A Cost E)
Graduate (Grad A Cost E)
Member (MA Cost E)
Fellow (FA Cost E)
Honorary Fellow (Hon FA Cost E)

Certified Cost Engineer (CCE)
Engineering Technician (EngTech)
Incorporated Engineer (IEng)
Chartered Engineer (CEng)

DESIGNATORY LETTERS
AA Cost E, Companion A Cost E, Grad A Cost E, MA
Cost E, FA Cost E, CCE, EngTech, IEng, CEng

INSTITUTE OF MEASUREMENT AND CONTROL

87 Gower Street
London WC1E 6AF
Tel: 020 7387 4949
Fax: 020 7388 8431
E-mail: membership@instmc.org
Website: www.instmc.org

The IMC is a multidisciplinary body that brings together thinkers and practitioners from the many disciplines that have a common interest in measurement and control. Our object is to promote for the public benefit, by all available means, the general advancement of the science and practice of measurement and control technology and its application.

MEMBERSHIP
Student Member
Affiliate Member
Associate Member
Member (MemInstMC)
Fellow (FInstMC)
Honorary Fellow (HonFInstMC)

SEMTA – THE SECTOR SKILLS COUNCIL FOR SCIENCE, ENGINEERING AND MANUFACTURING TECHNOLOGIES

14 Upton Road
Watford
Hertfordshire WD18 0JT
Tel: 0845 643 9001
E-mail: via website
Website: www.semta.org.uk

Semta is part of the Skills for Business network of 25 employer-led Sector Skills Councils in the UK and works with employers in the aerospace, automotive, electrical, electronics, marine, mechanical, metals and science & bioscience sectors to ascertain their current and future skills needs and provide short- and long-term solutions to meet those needs.

THE ENGINEERING COUNCIL

2nd Floor
246 High Holborn
London WC1V 7EX
Tel: 020 3206 0500
Fax: 020 3206 0501
Website: www.engc.org.uk

The Engineering Council holds the national registers of Engineering Technicians (EngTech), Incorporated Engineers (IEng), Chartered Engineers (CEng) and Information and Communications Technology Technicians (ICTTech). We set and maintain internationally recognised standards of competence and ethics, ensuring that employers, government and society can have confidence in registrants' skills and commitment.

DESIGNATORY LETTERS
EngTech, IEng, CEng, ICTTech

WOMEN'S ENGINEERING SOCIETY

Michael Faraday House
Six Hills Way
Stevenage
Herts SG1 2AY
Tel: 01438 765506
E-mail: info@wes.org.uk
Website: www.wes.org.uk

The WES, founded in 1919, is a professional, not-for-profit network of women engineers, scientists and technologists, who offer inspiration, support and professional development. Working in partnership, we campaign to encourage women to participate and achieve as engineers, scientists and as leaders.

MEMBERSHIP
Student Member

Associate
Full Member (MWES)
Fellow
Company Member

DESIGNATORY LETTERS
WES

ENGINEERING, MARINE
Membership of Professional Institutions and Associations

THE INSTITUTE OF MARINE ENGINEERING, SCIENCE AND TECHNOLOGY

33 Aldgate High Street
London EC3N 1EN
Tel: +44 (0)20 7382 2600
Fax: +44 (0)20 7382 2670
E-mail: via website
Website: www.imarest.org

The IMarEST, established in 1889, is the leading international membership body and learned society for marine professionals and has more than 15,000 members worldwide. We have a strong international presence, with a network of 50 international branches, affiliations with major marine societies around the world, representation on the key marine technical committees and non-governmental status at the International Maritime Organization.

Membership Categories

IMarEST membership is open to everyone with an interest in the marine world across scientific, engineering and technological disciplines and applications.

Categories of membership are available to those who are seeking professional recognition, those who are currently studying or just starting out in their careers, or those who simply have a general interest in the IMarEST and its activities. There are no academic requirements for Non-corporate Membership of the IMarEST. However, professionals seeking Corporate Membership will require certain academic qualifications according to the type of membership being sought.

Corporate Membership Categories

Fellow (FIMarEST)

Fellows are those who qualify for the category of Member and have demonstrated to the satisfaction of Council a level of knowledge and understanding, competence and commitment involving superior responsibility for the conceptual design, management or the execution of important work in a marine related profession, and have given a commitment to abide by the Institute's Code of Professional Conduct.

Member (MIMarEST)

Members are those who qualify for the category of Associate Member and have demonstrated to the satisfaction of Council that they have achieved a position of professional standing having normally been professionally engaged in the marine sector for a period of 5 years that includes significant responsibility and have given a commitment to abide by the Institute's Code of Professional Conduct.

Associate Member (AMIMarEST)

Associate Members are those demonstrating to the satisfaction of Council that they have achieved a position as a technician, or are professionally engaged in Initial Professional Development or occupy an occupational role in the marine sector, and have given a commitment to abide by the Institute's Code of Professional Conduct.

Non-corporate Membership Categories

Affiliate

Affiliates may either be those with an interest in, or who may contribute to, the activities of the Institute; or persons who, in the opinion of Council, can contribute to, or wish to have access to, the technical services of the Institute, being resident in a recognized overseas territory and also members of a professional society with which the Institute has a reciprocal arrangement.

Student (SIMarEST)

Student members are those enrolled on a programme of further or higher education accredited or recognized by the IMarEST.

Professional Registration

In addition to membership, the IMarEST is licensed to provide a range of registers covering the fields of engineering, science and technology. In addition, the IMarEST's Royal Charter empowers the Institute to offer registers designed to meet the specific needs of the marine profession. Corporate members can become registered (chartered) as follows:

Engineers

Chartered Engineer (CEng)
Chartered Marine Engineer (CMarEng)
Incorporated Engineer (IEng)
Incorporated Marine Engineer (IMarEng)
Engineering Technician (EngTech)
Marine Engineering Technician (MarEngTech)

Scientists

Chartered Scientist (CSci)
Chartered Marine Scientist (CMarSci)
Registered Marine Scientist (RMarSci)
Marine Technician (MarTech)

Technologists

Chartered Marine Technologist (CMarTech)
Registered Marine Technologist (RMarTech)
Marine Technician (MarTech)

SIMarEST, AMIMarEST, MIMarEST, FIMarEST

ENGINEERING, MECHANICAL
Membership of Professional Institutions and Associations

INSTITUTION OF MECHANICAL ENGINEERS

1 Birdcage Walk
Westminster
London SW1H 9JJ
Tel: 020 7222 7899
E-mail: enquiries@imeche.org
Website: www.imeche.org

The IMechE is a professional engineering body with about 80,000 members. Our aims are to promote sustainable energy and engineering sustainable supply, economic growth while mitigating and adapting to climate change and the depletion of natural resources, and safe, efficient transport systems to ensure less congestion and emissions, and to inspire, prepare and support tomorrow's engineers so we can respond to society's changes.

MEMBERSHIP
Affiliate

Associate Member (AMIMechE)
Member (MIMechE)
Fellow (FIMechE)
Engineering Technician (EngTech)
Incorporated Engineer (IEng)
Chartered Engineer (CEng)

DESIGNATORY LETTERS
AMIMechE, MIMechE, FIMechE, EngTech, IEng, CEng

ENGINEERING, MINING
Membership of Professional Institutions and Associations

INSTITUTE OF EXPLOSIVES ENGINEERS

Ground Floor, Unit 1
Greyfriars Business Park
Frank Foley Way
Stafford
Staffordshire ST16 2ST
Tel: 01785 594136
E-mail: vicki.hall@iexpe.org
Website: www.iexpe.org

The Institute of Explosives Engineers promotes the occupational competency, education and professional standing of those who work with explosives and provides consultative facilities for organizations and government departments within the explosives field.

MEMBERSHIP
Student
Associate (AIExpE)
Member (MIExpE)

Fellow (FIExpE)
Company
Company Affiliate

QUALIFICATION/EXAMINATIONS
CEng, IEng, Eng Tech

DESIGNATORY LETTERS
AIExpE, MIExpE, FIExpE

THE INSTITUTE OF MATERIALS, MINERALS AND MINING (IOM³)

1 Carlton House Terrace
London SW1Y 5DB
Tel: 020 7451 7300
Fax: 020 7839 1702
E-mail: via website
Website: www.iom3.org

IOM³ is a major UK engineering institution whose activities encompass the whole materials cycle, from exploration and extraction, through characterization, processing, forming, finishing and application, to product recycling and land reuse. We promote and develop all aspects of materials science and engineering, geology, mining and associated technologies, mineral and petroleum engineering and extraction metallurgy, as a leading authority in the worldwide materials and mining community.

MEMBERSHIP
Student
Graduate
Affiliate
Member (MIMMM)
Fellow (FIMMM)
Associate (AIMMM)
Technician (Eng Tech)

DESIGNATORY LETTERS
MIMMM, FIMMM, AIMMM, Eng Tech

THE INSTITUTE OF QUARRYING

McPherson House
8a Regan Way
Chetwynd Business Park
Chilwell
Nottingham NG9 6RZ
Tel: 0115 972 9995
E-mail: mail@quarrying.org
Website: www.quarrying.org

The Institute of Quarrying, which dates from 1917, is the international professional body for quarrying, construction materials and related extractive and processing industries, and has 6,000 members in some 50 countries. Our aim is to improve all aspects of operational performance through education and training at every level.

MEMBERSHIP
Student
Associate

Technical Member (TMIQ)
Member (MIQ)
Fellow (FIQ)

QUALIFICATION/EXAMINATIONS
Diploma in Quarry Technology
Professional Examination

DESIGNATORY LETTERS
TMIQ, MIQ, FIQ

ENGINEERING, NUCLEAR

Membership of Professional Institutions and Associations

THE NUCLEAR INSTITUTE

CK International House
1–6 Yarmouth Place
London WJ1 7BU
Tel: 020 3475 4701
E-mail: admin@nuclearinst.com
Website: www.nuclearinst.com

The NI (a Nominated Body of the UK Engineering and Science Councils) is the only professional membership body for the Nuclear Sector. We organize lectures, seminars and events at a regional and national level, have a vibrant young generation network and provide opportunities for career development and networking.

MEMBERSHIP
Student Member
Learned Member
Graduate Member
Technician Member (TNucI)
Associate Member (AMNucI)
Member (MNucI)
Fellow (FNucI)

New Structure from Jan 2016:
Affiliate (formerly Student)
Associate (formerly Learned and Graduate Members)
Member (MNucI)(incorporating Member, Associate Member and Technician Member)
Fellows (FNucI)
*Member and Fellow Grades require interview to assess competency and professional standards against The Nuclear Deltaxxx

QUALIFICATION/EXAMINATIONS
The Nuclear Deltaxxx

DESIGNATORY LETTERS
MNucI, FNucI

ENGINEERING, REFRACTORIES

Membership of Professional Institutions and Associations

INSTITUTE OF REFRACTORIES ENGINEERING

575 Trentham Road
Burton
Stoke on Trent
Staffs ST3 3BN
Tel: 01782 310 234
Fax: 01782 310 234
E-mail: secretary@ireng.org
Website: www.ireng.org

The IRE is a non-profit-making organization dedicated to fostering the science, technology and skills of refractories engineering and to serving the needs of refractories engineers worldwide. Our members have a background in R&D, design, engineering, manufacturing and installation contracting in the iron & steel, cement, non-ferrous, glass, chemical/petrochemical incineration, power generation, ceramics/bricks and similar industries.

MEMBERSHIP
Student
Associate Member (AMI Ref Eng)
Member (MI Ref Eng)

Fellow (FI Ref Eng)

DESIGNATORY LETTERS
AMI Ref Eng, MI Ref Eng, FI Ref Eng

ENGINEERING, REFRIGERATION
Membership of Professional Institutions and Associations

THE INSTITUTE OF REFRIGERATION

Kelvin House
76 Mill Lane
Carshalton
Surrey SM5 2JR
Tel: 020 8647 7033
E-mail: ior@ior.org.uk
Website: www.ior.org.uk

The IOR is the professional body for the refrigeration and air conditioning industries. We promote the technical advancement and perfection of refrigeration, air conditioning and heat pumps, and the minimization of its effects on the environment, encourage the extension of refrigeration, air conditioning and heat pump services for the benefit of the community, and provide advice, CPD and support to our members.

MEMBERSHIP
Student and Young Persons
Technician TMInstRAffiliate

Associate Member (AMInstR)
Fellow (FMInstR)Member (MInstR)
Service Engineering Section
Air Conditioning and Heat Pump Institute of the IOR

QUALIFICATION/EXAMINATIONS
REAL Zero CPD, REAL Skills Europe CPD, REAL Alternative
Engineering Council Registration

DESIGNATORY LETTERS
AMInstR, TMInstR, MInstR, FInstR

ENGINEERING, ROAD, RAIL AND TRANSPORT
Membership of Professional Institutions and Associations

INSTITUTE OF HIGHWAY ENGINEERS

De Morgan House
58 Russell Square
London WC1B 4HS
Tel: 020 7436 7487
Fax: 020 7436 7488
E-mail: secretary@theihe.org
Website: www.theihe.org

The IHE is the main professional body for highway and traffic professionals. We are run by engineers for engineers and technicians, and work to keep the standards of the profession high, to safeguard the interests of our members, and to ensure that their contribution is recognised.

MEMBERSHIP
Student Member
Apprentice Member (AppIHE)
Affiliate Member
Associate Member (AMIHE)
Member (MIHE)
Fellow (FIHE)
Engineering Technician (EngTech)
Incorporated Engineer (IEng)
Chartered Engineer (CEng)

QUALIFICATION/EXAMINATIONS
Prof Cert in Traffic Sign Design

Prof Cert in Traffic Signal Control
Prof Cert in Highway Development Management
Prof Cert in Highway Maintenance
Prof Cert for Winter Services Decision Makers and Managers
Prof Cert in Road Safety Engineering
Prof Cert in Cycling Infrastructure Design
Prof Cert in Public Realm
Prof Cert in Temporary Traffic Management
Prof Cert in Asset Management

DESIGNATORY LETTERS
AMIHE, MIHE, FIHE, EngTech, IEng, CEng

INSTITUTION OF RAILWAY SIGNAL ENGINEERS

4th Floor
1 Birdcage Walk
Westminster
London SW1H 9JJ
Tel: 020 7808 1180
Fax: 020 7808 1196
E-mail: hq@irse.org
Website: www.irse.org

The Institution of Railway Signal Engineers, known more usually as the IRSE, is an international organization, active throughout the world. It is the professional institution for all those engaged or interested in railway signalling and telecommunications and allied disciplines. Membership is open to anyone engaged or interested in the management, planning, design, installation, telecommunications or associated equipment.

MEMBERSHIP
Student

Associate
Accredited Technician
Associate Member
Member
Fellow
Companion

QUALIFICATION/EXAMINATIONS
Professional Examination

DESIGNATORY LETTERS
AMIRSE, MIRSE, FIRSE, CompIRSE

SOCIETY OF OPERATIONS ENGINEERS

22 Greencoat Place
London SW1P 1PR
Tel: 020 7630 1111
Fax: 020 7630 6677
E-mail: soe@soe.org.uk
Website: www.soe.org.uk

SOE is a professional membership organisation representing more than 16,000 individuals and companies in the engineering industry. It was formed in 2000 by the merger of the Institute of Road Transport Engineers (IRTE) and the Institution of Plant Engineers (IPlantE). The Society's third Professional Sector, the Bureau of Engineer Surveyors (BES), joined in 2004.

MEMBERSHIP
Associate Member (AMSOE)
Member (MSOE)
Fellow (FSOE)

Engineering Technician (EngTech)
Incorporated Engineer (IEng)
Chartered Engineer (CEng)

THE CHARTERED INSTITUTION OF HIGHWAYS AND TRANSPORTATION

119 Britannia Walk
London N1 7JE
Tel: 020 7336 1555
Fax: 020 7336 1556
E-mail: info@ciht.org.uk
Website: www.ciht.org.uk

The CIHT is a learned society and membership organization concerned with the planning, design, construction, maintenance and operation of land-based transport systems and infrastructure. CIHT provides professional development and networking opportunities to members, with routes to qualifications, cutting-edge technical conferences and exciting social events.

MEMBERSHIP
Student

Associate Member (AMCIHT)
Member (MCIHT)
Fellow (FCIHT)

QUALIFICATION/EXAMINATIONS
Transport Planning Professional (TPP) status (awarded jointly with the Transport Planning Society (TPS))

DESIGNATORY LETTERS
AMCIHT, MCIHT, FCIHT

ENGINEERING, SHEET METAL
Membership of Professional Institutions and Associations

INSTITUTE OF SHEET METAL ENGINEERING

102 Richmond Drive
Perton
Wolverhampton
West Midlands WV6 7UQ
Tel: 07891 499146
E-mail: ismesec@googlemail.com
Website: www.isme.org.uk

The ISME is a learned body with individual membership open to those employed in the sheet metal and associated industries and corporate membership open to relevant companies. Our aims are to promote the science of working and using sheet metal by providing opportunities for the exchange of ideas and information, and to encourage the professional development of our members.

MEMBERSHIP
Student Member
Member (MISME)
Fellow (FISME)
Corporate Member

DESIGNATORY LETTERS
MISME, FISME

ENGINEERING, STRUCTURAL
Membership of Professional Institutions and Associations

THE INSTITUTION OF STRUCTURAL ENGINEERS

47–58 Bastwick Street
London EC1V 3PS
Tel: 020 7235 4535
Fax: 020 7235 4294
E-mail: membership@istructe.org
Website: www.istructe.org

The Institution of Structural Engineers, founded in 1908, is the world's largest membership organization dedicated to the art and science of structural engineering. Our aims include: maintaining professional standards for structural engineering; ensuring continued technical excellence; advancing safety, creativity and innovation; and promoting a sustainable approach to both the structural engineering profession and the built environment.

MEMBERSHIP
Student
Graduate
Technician (TIStructE)
Associate Member (AMIStructE)
Associate (AIStructE)
Chartered Member (MIStructE)
Fellow (FIStructE)

DESIGNATORY LETTERS
TIStructE, AMIStructE, AIStructE, MIStructE, FIStructE

ENGINEERING, WATER
Membership of Professional Institutions and Associations

INSTITUTE OF WATER

4 Carlton Court
Team Valley
Gateshead
Tyne and Wear NE11 0AZ
Tel: 0191 422 0088
Fax: 0191 422 0087
E-mail: info@instituteofwater.org.uk
Website: www.instituteofwater.org.uk

The IW is the only institute concerned with the UK water industry. Our aim is to promote high standards of integrity, conduct and ethics, and to provide our members with an opportunity for CPD and growth through sharing knowledge, experience and networking opportunities.

MEMBERSHIP
Student Member
Associate Member
Full Member
Fellow
Honorary Member
Engineering Technician (EngTech)
Incorporated Engineer (IEng)
Chartered Engineer (CEng)
Chartered Environmentalist (CEnv)
Company Member

DESIGNATORY LETTERS
EngTech, IEng, CEng, CEnv

ENGINEERING DESIGN
Membership of Professional Institutions and Associations

THE INSTITUTION OF ENGINEERING DESIGNERS

Courtleigh
Westbury Leigh
Westbury
Wiltshire BA13 3TA
Tel: 01373 822801
Fax: 01373 858085
E-mail: via website
Website: www.ied.org.uk

Established in 1945, the IED represents 4,000 members worldwide working in engineering design, product design and CAD. Benefits include a bimonthly journal, access to an extensive library, legal advice helpline, local branch activities, and guidance and support to registration with the EC(UK) for suitably qualified members.

MEMBERSHIP
IED membership has two divisions: Engineering Design, and Product Design and Technology.

Each division has a range of membership grades: Student Member (StudIED), Graduate/Diplomate Member (GradIED/DipIED), Competent Draughting Associate (CDAIED), Associate (AIED), Member (MIED), Fellow (FIED), Affiliate

QUALIFICATION/EXAMINATIONS
Registration with EC(UK) for suitably qualified members

DESIGNATORY LETTERS
AIED, MIED, FIED

ENVIRONMENTAL SCIENCES
Membership of Professional Institutions and Associations

CHARTERED INSTITUTE OF ECOLOGY AND ENVIRONMENTAL MANAGEMENT

43 Southgate Street
Winchester
Hampshire SO23 9EH
Tel: 01962 868626
E-mail: enquiries@cieem.net
Website: www.cieem.net

Founded in 1991 to advance the science, technology and practice of ecology, environmental management and sustainable development to further conservation and the enhancement of biodiversity through education, training, study and research. CIEEM now has more than 5,000 members drawn from local authorities, government agencies, industry, environmental consultancy, teaching/research and NGOs.

MEMBERSHIP
Supporter Member

Student Member
Qualifying Member
Graduate Member (Grad CIEEM)
Associate Member (ACIEEM)
Full Member (MCIEEM)
Fellow (FCIEEM)

DESIGNATORY LETTERS
Grad CIEEM, ACIEEM, MCIEEM, FCIEEM

EXPORT
Membership of Professional Institutions and Associations

THE INSTITUTE OF EXPORT

Export House
Minerva Business Park
Lynch Wood
Peterborough PE2 6FT
Tel: 01733 404400
E-mail: via website
Website: www.export.org.uk

Established since 1935 offering training and professional qualifications to those working within international trade. We are the only professional institute in the UK offering qualifications ranging from the new 14–19 Diploma up to a level 5 Diploma as well as standard and bespoke training courses for individuals and companies.

MEMBERSHIP
Affiliate
Student
Associate
Member MIEx (Grad)
Member MIEx
Fellow
Business

QUALIFICATION/EXAMINATIONS
Diploma in International Trade (DIT)
Certified International Trade Advisor (CIT)
Advanced Certificate in International Trade (ACIT)
Young International Trader (YIT)
Certificate in International Trade (CIT)
Foundation Degree (FdA)

FISHERIES MANAGEMENT
Membership of Professional Institutions and Associations

INSTITUTE OF FISHERIES MANAGEMENT

PO Box 679
Hull
East Yorkshire HU5 9AX
Tel: 0845 388 7012
E-mail: info@ifm.org.uk
Website: www.ifm.org.uk

The Institute of Fisheries Management is an international organization of persons sharing a common interest in the modern and sustainable management of recreational and commercial fisheries. It is a non-profit-making body and is a constituent body of the Society for the Environment.

MEMBERSHIP
Subscriber
Student Member
Associate Member (AMIFM)
Registered Member (MIFM)
Fellow (FIFM)
Honorary Fellow (Hon FIFM)
Corporate Member
Honorary Member (Hon MIFM)

QUALIFICATION/EXAMINATIONS
Certificate
Diploma (accredited by The Open University)

DESIGNATORY LETTERS
AMIFM, MIFM, FIFM, Hon FIFM, Hon MIFM

FLORISTRY
Membership of Professional Institutions and Associations

BRITISH FLORIST ASSOCIATION

PO Box 674
Wigan
Lancashire WN1 9LL
Tel: 0844 800 7299
E-mail: via website
Website: www.britishfloristassociation.org

The BFA, founded in 1951, is an awarding body that promotes the highest standards in professional floristry. We are responsible for preparing and setting the highest floristry qualifications and for designing programmes for the training of SOF judges and examiners. We provide help, advice and information to our more than 1,000 members, who include business owners, florists, training providers, and students.

MEMBERSHIP
Florist Individual
Student
Corporate
Associate
College Member
Honorary Member

FOOD SCIENCE AND NUTRITION
Membership of Professional Institutions and Associations

INSTITUTE OF FOOD SCIENCE AND TECHNOLOGY

5 Cambridge Court
210 Shepherd's Bush Road
London W6 7NJ
Tel: 020 7603 6316
E-mail: info@ifst.org
Website: www.ifst.org

IFST is the leading independent qualifying body for food professionals in Europe and the only professional body in the UK concerned with all aspects of food science and technology. As a registered charity we are independent of government, industry, lobby or special interest groups.

MEMBERSHIP
Associate

Member (MIFST)
Fellow (FIFST)
Chartered Scientist (CSci)
Registered Scientist (RSci)
Registered Science Technician (RSciTech)
Professional Food Sensory Group

DESIGNATORY LETTERS
MIFST, FIFST, CSci, RSci, RSciTech

FORESTRY AND ARBORICULTURE
Membership of Professional Institutions and Associations

INSTITUTE OF CHARTERED FORESTERS

59 George Street
Edinburgh EH2 2JG
Tel: 0131 240 1425
Fax: 0131 240 1424
E-mail: icf@charteredforesters.org
Website: www.charteredforesters.org

The ICF is the Royal Chartered body for foresters and arboriculturists in the UK. We have over 1,000 members, to whom we offer advice, guidance and support. We also strive to foster a greater public understanding and awareness of the profession, as the environment and its management become more relevant to everyone.

MEMBERSHIP
Student Member

Supporter
Associate Member
Professional Member (MICFor)
Fellow (FICFor)

QUALIFICATION/EXAMINATIONS
Professional Membership Entry (PME) exam

DESIGNATORY LETTERS
MICFor, FICFor

THE ARBORICULTURAL ASSOCIATION

The Malthouse
Stroud Green
Standish
Stonehouse
Gloucestershire GL10 3DL
Tel: 01242 522152
Fax: 01242 577766
E-mail: admin@trees.org.uk
Website: www.trees.org.uk

The Arboricultural Association, founded in 1964, is the leading body in the UK for the amenity tree care professional in either civic or commercial employment at craft, technical, supervisory, managerial or consultancy level. There are currently over 2,000 members of The Arboricultural Association in a variety of membership classes.

MEMBERSHIP
Student Member
Ordinary Member
Associate Member

Technician Member
Professional Member
Fellow
Fellow Retired
Corporate Member

QUALIFICATION/EXAMINATIONS
Arboricultural Association Approved Contractor
Arboricultural Association Registered Consultant

DESIGNATORY LETTERS
TechArborA, MArborA, FArborA

THE ROYAL FORESTRY SOCIETY

The Hay Barns
Home Farm Drive
Upton Estate
Banbury OX15 6HU
Tel: 01295 678588
Fax: 01295 670798
E-mail: rfshq@rfs.org.uk
Website: www.rfs.org.uk

The RFS was founded in 1882 and now has over 3,600 members. We are an educational charity dedicated to promoting the wise management of trees and woodlands, and to increasing understanding of forestry. We publish a popular journal, the *Quarterly Journal of Forestry,* arrange outdoor meetings, organize woodland study tours in the UK and overseas, run courses in forestry and arboriculture, and manage model woodlands.

MEMBERSHIP
Individual Member
Corporate Member
Student Member

QUALIFICATION/EXAMINATIONS
RFS Certificate in Arboriculture (Level 2)
RFS Certificate in Forestry (Level 2)
RFS Certificate in Silviculture (Level 3)

FOUNDRY TECHNOLOGY AND PATTERN MAKING
Membership of Professional Institutions and Associations

THE INSTITUTE OF CAST METALS ENGINEERS

National Metalforming Centre
47 Birmingham Road
West Bromwich
West Midlands B70 6PY
Tel: 01216 016979
Fax: 01216 016981
E-mail: info@icme.org.uk
Website: www.icme.org.uk

The ICME is the professional body for those in the castings and associated industry. It was formed in 1904, granted its first Royal Charter in 1921, a Third Supplemental Charter in 1994 and changed its name in 2001. The granting of the Third Supplemental Charter aligned its membership requirements with those of the EC(UK).

MEMBERSHIP
Student
Member (MICME)

Professional Member (Prof MICME)
Fellow (FICME)
Engineering Technician (EngTech)
Incorporated Engineer (IEng)
Chartered Engineer (CEng)
European Engineer (EurIng)

DESIGNATORY LETTERS
MICME, Prof MICME, FICME, EngTech, IEng, CEng, EurIng

FREIGHT FORWARDING
Membership of Professional Institutions and Associations

BRITISH INTERNATIONAL FREIGHT ASSOCIATION (BIFA)

Redfern House
Browells Lane
Feltham
Middlesex TW13 7EP
Tel: 020 8844 2266
E-mail: bifa@bifa.org
Website: www.bifa.org

BIFA is the principal trade association providing representation, training and support to British companies engaged in the international movement of freight to and from the UK by air, rail, road and sea. It is a not-for-profit organisation. Members are encouraged to contribute to the running of the Association.

MEMBERSHIP
Associate Member
Trade Member

FUNDRAISING
Membership of Professional Institutions and Associations

INSTITUTE OF FUNDRAISING

Park Place
12 Lawn Lane
London SW8 1UD
Tel: 020 7840 1000
Fax: 020 7840 1001
E-mail: enquiries@institute-of-fundraising.org.uk
Website: www.institute-of-fundraising.org.uk

The Institute of Fundraising is the professional body for fundraisers in the UK, representing over 5,000 individual fundraisers and 340 organisations. We offer professional support, act as a voice for fundraisers and promote best practice. We offer professional qualifications and training, and the annual IoF National Convention is the largest fundraising conference of its type in Europe.

MEMBERSHIP
Associate
Full Member (MInstF)
Fully Certificated Member MInstF(Cert)
Diploma Qualified Member MInstF(Dip)
Organisational Member

QUALIFICATION/EXAMINATIONS
Introductory Certificate in Fundraising
Certificate in Fundraising
Diploma in Fundraising
Advanced Diploma in Fundraising (in development)
Certificate in Direct Marketing

DESIGNATORY LETTERS
MInstF, MInstF(Cert), MInstF(Dip), FInstF,
FInstF(Cert), FInstF(Dip)

FUNERAL DIRECTING, BURIAL AND CREMATION ADMINISTRATION
Membership of Professional Institutions and Associations

NATIONAL ASSOCIATION OF FUNERAL DIRECTORS

618 Warwick Road
Solihull
West Midlands B91 1AA
Tel: 0845 230 1343
Fax: 0121 711 1351
E-mail: info@nafd.org.uk
Website: www.nafd.org.uk

The NAFD, founded in 1905, is an independent trade association whose members include more than 3,200 funeral homes throughout the UK, suppliers to the profession, and overseas funeral directing businesses. We provide support to our members and offer informed opinion to government.

MEMBERSHIP
Funeral Director (Category A) Member

Supplier (Category B) Member
Overseas Member

QUALIFICATION/EXAMINATIONS
Diploma in Funeral Arranging and Administration (Dip.FAA)
Diploma in Funeral Directing (Dip.FD)

NATIONAL ASSOCIATION OF MEMORIAL MASONS

1 Castle Mews
Rugby
Warwickshire CV21 2AL
Tel: 01788 542264
Fax: 01788 542276
E-mail: enquiries@namm.org.uk
Website: www.namm.org.uk

The NAMM was formed in 1907 to promote excellence and craftsmanship within the memorial masonry trade. Our services to members include training, business advice, technical advice, promotion, a legal helpline, a conciliation and arbitration service, trade exhibitions and a conference. We protect members' interests through representation to the British Standards Institution (BSI) and the Burial & Cemeteries Advisory Group (BCAG).

MEMBERSHIP
Individual Associate Member
Affiliate Member
Full Retail and Wholesale Members
Company Associate Member
Corporate Associate Member
Overseas Member
Overseas Affiliate Member

THE INSTITUTE OF BURIAL AND CREMATION AUTHORITIES

ICCM National Office & Training Centre
City of London Cemetery
Aldersbrook Road
Manor Park
London E12 5DQ
Tel: 020 8989 4661
Fax: 020 8989 6112
E-mail: iccmjulie@gmail.com
Website: www.iccm-uk.com

Accredited education and training opportunities for those working in cemeteries and crematori.

Best practice guidance and policy for burial and cremation authorities.

MEMBERSHIP
Member (MICCM)
Associate Member (AICCM)
Fellow (FICCM)
Corporate
Associate Corporate

QUALIFICATION/EXAMINATIONS
Diploma – Fully Accredited NHC in Cemetery & Crematorium Management and the Management of Natural Burial Grounds
Cemetery Operatives Training Scheme – A comprehensive suite of City & Guilds accredited qualifications
Crematorium Technicians Training Scheme – BTEC accredited qualifications for crematory staff

DESIGNATORY LETTERS
MICCM, AICCM, FICCM

FURNISHING AND FURNITURE
Membership of Professional Institutions and Associations

FLOORING INDUSTRY TRAINING ASSOCIATION

4c St Marys Place
The Lace Market
Nottingham NG1 1PH
Tel: 0115 9506836
E-mail: info@fita.co.uk
Website: www.fita.co.uk

FITA was set up and is fully supported by the CFA and the NICF to provide training for the floor-covering industry. We have a fully equipped training centre at Loughborough, where the majority of our courses are run. We also offer tailor-made courses to suit individual specifications and requirements.

QUALIFICATION/EXAMINATIONS
FITA Training Courses
The Flooring Industry Flooring Association was set up by, and is fully supported by the CFA and NICF to provide training.

FITA has a fully equipped training centre at Loughborough in Leicestershire where the majority of our standard courses are run. FITA also offers tailor-made courses to suit your specifications and requirements, quotations on request.
FITA instructors have all passed assessments and knowledge exams and are supported on courses by technicians with specialist knowledge from the trade. FITA also enjoys the support of a considerable number of suppliers who freely donate materials, accessories and tools.

Fully trained staff are an asset to any company. The outlay for training courses far outweighs the initial cost.

Please be sure to book early to reserve your place on a course. Go to our Course Dates page for details of our latest courses and the training centres where they are being held.

Training courses considered suitable for Domestic Installers

Carpet Fitting – Basic
Carpet Fitting – Intermediate
Domestic Sheet Vinyl Fitting
Profitable Measuring and Quoting
Subfloor Preparation – Domestic

Training courses considered suitable for Commercial Installers

Commercial Vinyl Fitting – Advanced
Commercial Vinyl Fitting – Basic
Commercial Vinyl Fitting – Intermediate
Cost Effective Estimating and Planning

Linoleum Installation – Intermediate
Subfloor Preparation – Commercial

Training courses considered suitable for Domestic & Commercial Installers

Carpet Fitting – Advanced
Laminate and Wood Fitting – Basic
Linoleum Installation – Basic
Moisture – Preventing floor failures
Resilient / Luxury Vinyl Tile Fitting – Advanced
Resilient / Luxury Vinyl Tile Fitting – Basic
Wood Fitting – Advanced
Wood Fitting – Intermediate
Wood Sanding and Finishing

Assessments designed for FITA QA Accreditation

QA Card Adhered Carpet Assessment
QA Card Carpet Tile Assessment
QA Card Floating Timber Assessment
QA Card Resilient Sheet Assessment
QA Card Subfloor Preparation Assessment
QA Card Vinyl Tile Assessment

NATIONAL INSTITUTE OF CARPET AND FLOORLAYERS

4c St Marys Place
The Lace Market
Nottingham NG1 1PH
Tel: 0115 9583077
Fax: 0115 9412238
E-mail: info@nicfltd.org.uk
Website: www.nicfltd.org.uk

The NICF furthers the interests of its members by promoting excellence in the field of carpet and floorlaying and providing a range of benefits, products and services.

MEMBERSHIP
Master Fitter Member
Fitter Member

Trainee Fitter Member
Retailer Member
Associate Member
Patron Member

QUALIFICATION/EXAMINATIONS
Fitter qualification assessment
Master Fitter qualification assessment

GEMMOLOGY AND JEWELLERY
Membership of Professional Institutions and Associations

THE GEMMOLOGICAL ASSOCIATION OF GREAT BRITAIN

21 Ely Place
London EC1N 6TD
Tel: 020 7404 3334
Fax: 020 7404 8843
E-mail: information@gem-a.com
Website: www.gem-a.com

The Gemmological Association of Great Britain (Gem-A), a UK-registered charity, is the world's longest established provider of gem and jewellery education, our first diploma having been awarded in 1913. We are committed to promoting the study of gemmology and to providing CPD to our members – an international community of gem professionals and enthusiasts.

MEMBERSHIP
Member

Fellow (FGA)
Diamond Member (DGA)
Corporate Member

QUALIFICATION/EXAMINATIONS
Foundation Certificate in Gemmology
Diploma in Gemmology
Diamond Diploma

DESIGNATORY LETTERS
FGA, DGA

THE NATIONAL ASSOCIATION OF JEWELLERS

78A Luke Street
London EC2A 4XG
Tel: 020 7613 4445
E-mail: info@naj.co.uk
Website: www.naj.co.uk

The NAJ serves and supports the jewellery industry of Great Britain and Ireland. We promote high professional standards among our members, who must adhere to a code of professional practice. In return, we offer them advice, support and learning and development in the form of distance learning courses and short courses.

MEMBERSHIP
Alumni Member
Allied Member

Affiliate Member
Ordinary Member

QUALIFICATION/EXAMINATIONS
Professional Jewellers' Diploma (JET 1 Certificate)
Professional Jewellers' Diploma (JET 2 Diploma)
Professional Jewellers' Management Diploma
Professional Jewellers' Business Development Diploma
Certificate of Appraisal Theory (CAT)

GENEALOGY
Membership of Professional Institutions and Associations

SOCIETY OF GENEALOGISTS

14 Charterhouse Buildings
Goswell Road
London EC1M 7BA
Tel: 020 7251 8799
Fax: 020 7250 1800
E-mail: info@sog.org.uk
Website: www.sog.org.uk

The Society (founded 1911) is the National Family History Centre. A registered educational charity, it was founded to encourage and foster the study, science and knowledge of genealogy. This it does chiefly through its library, publications and extensive education programme of courses and events. It currently does not hold exams.

MEMBERSHIP
Member
Fellow (FSG)
Honorary Fellow (FSG Hon)

DESIGNATORY LETTERS
FSG, FSG Hon

THE HERALDRY SOCIETY

53 Hitchin Street
Baldock
Herts SG7 6AQ
Tel: 01869 246188
E-mail: memsec@theheraldrysociety.com
Website: www.theheraldrysociety.com

The Heraldry Society is a registered charity that aims to encourage interest in heraldry through publications, lectures, visits and related activities. Members receive *The Heraldry Gazette*, which contains heraldic news and comments, and Society information quarterly. We maintain contact with heraldic societies in many parts of the UK and abroad.

MEMBERSHIP
Associate Member
Ordinary Member

Fellow (FHS)
Honorary Fellow (Hon FHS)

QUALIFICATION/EXAMINATIONS
Elementary Certificate
Intermediate Certificate
Advanced Certificate
Diploma (DipHS)

DESIGNATORY LETTERS
FHS, Hon FHS

THE INSTITUTE OF HERALDIC AND GENEALOGICAL STUDIES

79–82 Northgate
Canterbury
Kent CT1 1BA
Tel: 01227 768664
Fax: 01227 765617
E-mail: registrar@ihgs.ac.uk
Website: www.ihgs.ac.uk

The IHGS, founded in 1961, is an independent educational charitable trust that offers a wide range of courses on family history, heraldry and related historical subjects, and has an extensive library, archive and research facilities. We also offer a genealogical and heraldic research service.

MEMBERSHIP
Associate Member
Graduate Member

QUALIFICATION/EXAMINATIONS
Correspondence Course in Genealogy

Correspondence Course in Heraldry
Online Course in Genealogy
Certificate in Genealogy
Higher Certificate in Genealogy
Diploma in Genealogy
Licentiateship in Heraldry and Genealogy
Online Course in Heraldry

DESIGNATORY LETTERS
Dip Gen, LHG, FHG

GEOGRAPHY
Membership of Professional Institutions and Associations

ROYAL GEOGRAPHICAL SOCIETY (WITH THE INSTITUTE OF BRITISH GEOGRAPHERS)

1 Kensington Gore
London SW7 2AR
Tel: 020 7591 3000
Fax: 020 7591 3001
E-mail: via website
Website: www.rgs.org

The RGS-IBG is the learned society and professional body for geography. We aim to foster an understanding and informed enjoyment of our world: developing, supporting and promoting geographical research, expeditions and fieldwork, education, public engagement, and providing geography input to policy.

MEMBERSHIP
Young Geographer

Member
Postgraduate Fellow
Fellow
Chartered Geographer (CGeog)
Corporate Member

DESIGNATORY LETTERS
FRGS, CGeog

GEOLOGY
Membership of Professional Institutions and Associations

THE GEOLOGICAL SOCIETY

Burlington House
Piccadilly
London W1J 0BG
Tel: 020 7434 9944
Fax: 020 7439 8975
E-mail: enquiries@geolsoc.org.uk
Website: www.geolsoc.org.uk

The Geological Society, founded in 1807, is the UK's national organization for professional Earth scientists. The normal grade of membership is Fellow. Students may become Candidate Fellows. Members of the public not eligible for any other status may join as Friends.

MEMBERSHIP
Friend
Candidate Fellow
Fellow
Chartered Geologist

DESIGNATORY LETTERS
FGS, CGeol

GLASS TECHNOLOGY
Membership of Professional Institutions and Associations

BRITISH SOCIETY OF SCIENTIFIC GLASSBLOWERS

Unit W1, MK2 Business Centre
Barton Road
Bletchley
Milton Keynes
Buckinghamshire MK2 3HU
Tel: 01908 821191
Fax: 01908 821195
E-mail: sales@biochemglass.co.uk
Website: www.bssg.co.uk

The Society was founded in 1960 for the benefit of those engaged in Scientific Glassblowing and its associated professions, and to uphold and further the status of Scientific Glassblowers. We welcome written submissions to our quarterly journal, which is circulated to members.

MEMBERSHIP
Associate
Student Member

Fellow
Full Member
Master
Honorary Member
Retired Member
Overseas Member

DESIGNATORY LETTERS
Master MBSSG, Fellow FBSSG

SOCIETY OF GLASS TECHNOLOGY

9 Churchill Way
Chapeltown
Sheffield
South Yorkshire S35 2PY
Tel: 0114 2634455
Fax: 0871 8754085
E-mail: info@sgt.org
Website: www.sgt.org

The objects of the Society of Glass Technology are to encourage and advance the study of the history, art, science, design, manufacture, after treatment, distribution and end use of glass of any and every kind.

MEMBERSHIP
Personal Member
Fellow (FSGT)
Fellow Emeritus
Honorary Fellow (HonFSGT)
Centenary Honorary Fellow (CentHonFSGT) only three and only in 2016, our centenary year.

Corporate Member

QUALIFICATION/EXAMINATIONS
Peer review by the Board of Fellows.
2016 is the SGT centenary and some Centenary Honorary Fellows will be created. These will be in addition to the limit of 12 for Honorary Fellows. Decided by the Board of Fellows as normal.

DESIGNATORY LETTERS
FSGT, HonFSGT

HAIRDRESSING
Membership of Professional Institutions and Associations

HABIA

Oxford House
Sixth Avenue
Sky Business Park, Robin Hood Airport
Doncaster
South Yorkshire DN9 3GG
Tel: 0845 6 123555
Fax: 01302 774949
E-mail: info@habia.org
Website: www.habia.org

Habia is the government-appointed standards-setting body for hair, beauty, nails, spa therapy, barbering and African-type hair, and creates the standards that form the basis of all qualifications, including NVQs, SVQs, apprenticeships, diplomas and foundation degrees, as well as industry codes of practice.

MEMBERSHIP
Habia offers a membership programme for training providers (Habia Members) and a wider, free membership for industry professionals and educators.

THE GUILD OF HAIRDRESSERS

Archway House
Barnsley S71 1AQ
Tel: 01226 786555
Fax: 01226 208300

The Guild of Hairdressers dates back to 1340, when it was part of the Guild of Barbers and Surgeons. Then in the late 16th century, when the surgeons split off, it became the Guild of Hairdressers, Wigmakers and Perfumers. Today it still exists for the benefit of its members, who adhere to a code of ethics and to whom it provides help and advice.

HEALTH AND HEALTH SERVICES
Membership of Professional Institutions and Associations

BRITISH OCCUPATIONAL HYGIENE SOCIETY

5/6 Melbourne Business Court
Millennium Way
Pride Park
Derby DE24 8LZ
Tel: 01332 298101
Fax: 01332 298099
E-mail: admin@bohs.org
Website: www.bohs.org

BOHS is the Chartered Society for Worker Health Protection – one of the largest occupational hygiene societies in Europe and the only professional society representing qualified occupational hygienists in the UK. BOHS provides internationally recognised qualifications, scientific conferences and membership services, and has almost 1,800 members in 56 countries.

MEMBERSHIP
Individual
Student
Affiliate (corporate)
Retired
Associate (AFOH)
Licentiate (LFOH)
Chartered Member (CMFOH)
Specialist Member (MFOH(S))
Chartered Fellow (CFFOH)

QUALIFICATION/EXAMINATIONS
Since 1953, BOHS has been the only organisation dedicated to occupational hygiene, and to be awarded a Royal Charter – in recognition of its unique and pre-eminent role as the leading authority in occupational disease prevention. This also means that BOHS is the only occupational hygiene organisation to offer the opportunity to achieve 'Chartered Occupational Hygienist' status, via its professional development route: the BOHS Faculty of Occupational Hygiene sets, develops and maintains the professional standards of occupational hygienists. It is also an internationally recognised, and the only UK-based, examining board for qualifications in occupational hygiene. BOHS qualifications are widely regarded as the industry standard, and are recognised by HSE, UKAS and IOHA, and by national and international institutions, organisations and employers.

DESIGNATORY LETTERS
AFOH, LFOH, CMFOH, CFFOH

CHARTERED INSTITUTE OF ENVIRONMENTAL HEALTH

Chadwick Court
15 Hatfields
London SE1 8DJ
Tel: 020 7827 5800
Fax: 020 7806 0666
E-mail: via website
Website: www.cieh.org

The CIEH is an Awarding Organisation providing Ofqual regulated qualifications in Food Safety, Health & Safety, First Aid, Environmental Protection and Fire Safety.

MEMBERSHIP
Student Member
Associate
Accredited Associate
Graduate Member
Voting Member
Fellow
Chartered Environmental Health Practitioner

QUALIFICATION/EXAMINATIONS
The CIEH offers a range of Ofqual-regulated qualifications at four levels in health and safety, food safety, environmental protection, fire safety and education and training.

CHARTERED INSTITUTE OF ERGONOMICS & HUMAN FACTORS

Elms Court
Elms Grove
Loughborough
Leicestershire LE11 1RG
Tel: 07736 893350
E-mail: iehf@ergonomics.org.uk
Website: www.ergonomics.org.uk

Chartered Institute of Ergonomics & Human Factors, founded in 1949, is a UK-based professional society for ergonomists worldwide. We encourage and maintain high standards of professional practice through education, accreditation and development, promote the interests of our members across government, academia, business and industry, and raise awareness of ergonomics in general.

MEMBERSHIP
Student Member
Associate Member
Graduate Member
Registered Member
Fellow
Technical Member
Retired Member

INSTITUTE OF HEALTH PROMOTION AND EDUCATION

c/o Dawn Wills
20 Mardley Avenue
Welwyn
Hertfordshire AL6 0UD
Tel: c/o 01438 840040
E-mail: admin@ihpe.org.uk
Website: www.ihpe.org.uk

The IHPE was established 50 years ago to bring together professionals with a common interest in health education and promotion to share their experience, ideas and information. Our members come from a diverse range of backgrounds, including nursing, midwifery, health visiting, medicine, dentistry, public health, stress management, psychology and teaching.

MEMBERSHIP
Student Member
Associate Member (AIHPE)
Full Member (MIHPE)
Fellow (FIHPE)
Corporate Member

DESIGNATORY LETTERS
MIHPE, AIHPE, FIHPE

INSTITUTE OF HEALTH RECORDS AND INFORMATION MANAGEMENT

Marshall House
Heanor Gate Road
Heanor
Derbyshire DE75 7RG
Tel: 01773 713927
Fax: 01773 713927
E-mail: ihrim@zen.co.uk
Website: www.ihrim.co.uk

IHRIM was founded in 1948, primarily as an educational body, to provide qualifications as well as career and professional assistance to members. We encourage professionalism and high standards among our members who work in the fields of health records, information management, clinical coding and information governance.

MEMBERSHIP
Student
Affiliate
Licentiate
Certificated Member (CHRIM)
Accredited Clinical Coder (ACC)

Associate (AHRIM)
Fellow (FHRIM)
Corporate Affiliate

QUALIFICATION/EXAMINATIONS
Certificate of Technical Competence
Foundation exam
Certificate exam
Diploma exam
National Clinical Coding Qualification

DESIGNATORY LETTERS
CHRIM, ACC, AHRIM, FHRIM

INSTITUTE OF HEALTHCARE ENGINEERING AND ESTATE MANAGEMENT

2 Abingdon House
Cumberland Business Centre
Northumberland Road
Portsmouth PO5 1DS
Tel: 023 92 823186
Fax: 023 92 815927
E-mail: office@iheem.org.uk
Website: www.iheem.org.uk

The Institute of Healthcare Engineering and Estate Management (IHEEM) is a Professional Engineering Institute, a specialist institute for the Healthcare Estates Sector.

The Institute counts among its members employees of both public and private healthcare providers, as well as those employed in private sector engineering and consultancy firms and practices.

MEMBERSHIP
Graduate (GIHEEM)
Associate Member (AMIHEEM)
Technician (TIHEEM)
Member (MIHEEM)
Fellow (FIHEEM)

DESIGNATORY LETTERS
GIHEEM, AMIHEEM, TIHEEM, MIHEEM, FIHEEM

INSTITUTE OF HEALTHCARE MANAGEMENT

John Snow House
59 Mansell Street
London E1 8AN
Tel: 020 7265 7321
Fax: 020 7265 7301
E-mail: education@ihm.org.uk
Website: www.ihm.org.uk

The IHM is the professional organization for managers throughout healthcare, including the NHS, independent providers, healthcare consultants and the armed forces. Our focus is on improving patient/user care by publishing standards of management practice, promoting the IHM Code (which covers behavioural and ethical aspects of management practice) and establishing a CPD framework for our members.

MEMBERSHIP
Associate Member
Full Member (MIHM)

QUALIFICATION/EXAMINATIONS
Certificate in Health Management Studies (CertHMS)
Certificate in Health Services Management (CertHSM)
Certificate in Managing Health Services (CertMHS)
Certificate in Managing Health & Social Care (CertMHSC)
Diploma in Health Services Management (DipHSM)

DESIGNATORY LETTERS
MIHM, FIHM, CIHM

THE ROYAL SOCIETY FOR PUBLIC HEALTH

John Snow House
59 Mansell Street
London E1 8AN
Tel: 020 7265 7300
Fax: 020 7265 7301
E-mail: via website
Website: www.rsph.org.uk

The RSPH was formed in October 2008 by the merger of the Royal Society for the Promotion of Health (RSPH/RSH) and the Royal Institute of Public Health (RIPH). We offer a wide range of vocationally related qualifications in the fields of food safety and nutrition, hygiene, health and safety, pest control, health promotion and the built environment.

MEMBERSHIP
Associate (ARSPH)

Licentiate (LRSPH)
Member (MRSPH)
Fellow (FRSPH)
Student

QUALIFICATION/EXAMINATIONS
Please see the RSPH's website.

DESIGNATORY LETTERS
ARSPH, LRSPH, MRSPH, FRSPH

HORSES AND HORSE RIDING
Membership of Professional Institutions and Associations

EQUESTRIAN QUALIFICATIONS GB LTD

Equestrian Qualifications GB Ltd
Equestrian House
Abbey Park
Kenilworth
Warwickshire CV8 2XZ
Tel: 02476 840544
Fax: 02476 840501
E-mail: enquiry@equestrian-qualifications.org.uk
Website: www.equestrian-qualifications.org.uk

EQL offers vocational and work-based qualifications for the Equestrian Industry. We work in partnership with a variety of organisations to develop and award qualifications for grooms, stable managers and coaches. Our qualifications include UKCC qualifications, British Horse Society qualifications, Work Based Diplomas, Scottish Vocational Qualifications and Equestrian Tourism Qualifications.

QUALIFICATION/EXAMINATIONS
Our Awards include:
BHS Horse Knowledge and Care Level 1 – Level 4
BHS Riding Exams Level 1 – Level 4

BHS Coaching and Teaching Exams Level 2 – Level 5
UKCC Certificates in Coaching (specialist routes) Level 1 – Level 3
Work Based Diplomas
Scottish Vocational Qualifications

The BHS also offers higher level qualifications for BHS Instructor and Fellowship of the BHS, as well as those for the recreational horse owner.

EQL website: www.equestrian-qualifications.org.uk
BHS website: www.bhs.org.uk

HOUSING

Membership of Professional Institutions and Associations

THE CHARTERED INSTITUTE OF HOUSING

Octavia House
Westwood Way
Coventry CV4 8JP
Tel: 024 7685 1700
E-mail: membership.services@cih.org
Website: www.cih.org

The CIH is the professional body for people involved in housing and communities. We are a registered charity and not-for-profit organization. We have a diverse and growing membership of over 22,000 people – both in the public and private sectors – living and working in over 20 countries on five continents across the world.

MEMBERSHIP
Offering two grades of membership we look to support members at all stages of their career:
CIH Member
CIH Chartered Member
Visit www.cih.org/membership to find out more about CIH membership.

QUALIFICATION/EXAMINATIONS
Certificate Courses
The CIH offers a range of certificated courses at Levels 2, 3 and 4 delivered at various centres across the UK. They are also available by online learning.
Professional Qualifications
The CIH Professional Qualification can be achieved at either undergraduate or postgraduate level, FT or PT.
Please see the CIH's website for details.

DESIGNATORY LETTERS
CIH Members: CIH Member or CIHM, CIH Chartered Members: CIH Chartered Member or CIHCM (existing Fellows can continue to use FCIH and Honorary Members can use (Hon).

INDEXING

Membership of Professional Institutions and Associations

SOCIETY OF INDEXERS

Woodbourn Business Centre
10 Jessell Street
Sheffield S9 3HY
Tel: 01142 449561
E-mail: admin@indexers.org.uk
Website: www.indexers.org.uk

The Society of Indexers is the professional body for indexing in the UK and Ireland, and exists to promote indexing, the quality of indexes and the profession of indexing. We offer information to publishers and other organizations on commissioning indexes and our online directory 'Indexers Available' provides an up-to-date guide to indexers currently working in a wide range of fields.

MEMBERSHIP
Student Member
Member
Professional Member (MSocInd)
Advanced Professional Member (MSocInd(Adv))
Fellow (FSocInd)
Corporate Member

QUALIFICATION/EXAMINATIONS
Training in Indexing course
Advanced Test
Fellowship index submission

DESIGNATORY LETTERS
MSocInd, MSocInd(Adv), FSocInd

INDUSTRIAL SAFETY
Membership of Professional Institutions and Associations

BRITISH SAFETY COUNCIL

70 Chancellors Road
London W6 9RS
Tel: 020 8741 1231
Fax: 0844 583 4731
E-mail: info@britsafe.org
Website: www.britsafe.org

The BSC is one of the world's leading health and safety organizations. Our mission is to keep people healthy and safe at work. Our range of charitable initiatives, such as free health and safety qualifications for school children, is supported by a broad mix of commercial activities centred on membership, training, auditing and qualifications.

MEMBERSHIP
UK Member
International Member

QUALIFICATION/EXAMINATIONS
Award in COSHH Risk Assessment (Level 2)
Award in DSE Risk Assessment (Level 2)
Award in Fire Risk Assessment (Level 2)
Award in Manual Handling Risk Assessment (Level 2)
Award in Risk Assessment (Level 2)
Award in Supervising Staff Safely (Level 2)
Certificate in Occupational Health and Safety (Level 3)
Diploma in Occupational Health and Safety (Level 6)
International Certificate in Occupational Health and Safety
International Diploma in Occupational Health and Safety
Entry Level Award in Workplace Hazard Awareness
Award in Health and Safety at Work (Level 1)
Certificate in Fire Safety and Risk Management
National Certificate in Construction Health and Safety

HEALTH & SAFETY EXECUTIVE APPROVED MINING QUALIFICATIONS

Mining Qualifications, The Health & Safety Executive
2nd Floor, Foundry House
3 Millsands, Riverside Exchange
Sheffield
South Yorkshire S3 8NH
Tel: 0114 291 2394
Fax: 0114 291 2399
E-mail: sarah.johnson@hse.gsi.gov.uk
Website: www.hse.gov.uk/mining

The HSE issues First and Second Class Certificates of Qualification as required under the Management and Administration of Safety and Health at Mines Regulations (MASHAM) 1993 for the appointment of a manager and undermanager respectively, in mines of coal, shale and fireclay in the UK. It also issues certificates to Mining Mechanical and Mining Electrical Engineers, Mechanics and Electricians Class I and Class II, Mines Surveyor, and Mines Deputy. For details see: www.hse.gov.uk/mining

INTERNATIONAL INSTITUTE OF RISK AND SAFETY MANAGEMENT

Suite 7a
77 Fulham Palace Road
London W6 8JA
Tel: 020 8741 9100
Fax: 020 8741 1349
E-mail: info@iirsm.org
Website: www.iirsm.org

The IIRSM is a professional body for health & safety practitioners and specialists in associated professions. Our aim is to advance professional standards in accident prevention and occupational health throughout the world. We have more than 8,100 members, in the UK and over 70 other countries, to whom we provide support and offer advice via a technical helpline.

MEMBERSHIP
Student

Affiliate
Associate (AIIRSM)
Member (MIIRSM)
Specialist Member (SIIRSM)
Fellow (FIIRSM)
Specialist Fellow (SFIIRSM)

DESIGNATORY LETTERS
AIIRSM, MIIRSM, SIIRSM, FIIRSM, SFIIRSM

NEBOSH (THE NATIONAL EXAMINATION BOARD IN OCCUPATIONAL SAFETY AND HEALTH)

Dominus Way
Meridian Business Park
Leicester LE19 1QW
Tel: (+44) 116 263 4700
Fax: (+44) 116 282 4000
E-mail: info@nebosh.org.uk
Website: www.nebosh.org.uk

NEBOSH offers globally recognized qualifications designed to meet the health, safety, environmental and risk management needs of all places of work. Courses leading to NEBOSH qualifications attract over 50,000 candidates annually in over 120 countries around the world.

MEMBERSHIP
NEBOSH's National General Certificate, National Certificate in Fire Safety and Risk Management, National Certificate in Construction Health and Safety, and the International General Certificate are all accepted as meeting the academic requirements to apply for Technical Membership (Tech IOSH) of the Institution of Occupational Safety and Health (IOSH).

In partnership with the Association for Project Safety (APS) the NEBOSH National and International Certificates in Construction Health and Safety meet the headline entrance criteria requirements for Construction Safety Associate membership (AaPS).

In addition holders of either the NEBOSH National or International Diploma in Occupational Health and Safety and either the NEBOSH National or International Certificate in Construction Health and Safety meet the headline qualification entrance criteria requirements for Registered Construction Safety Practitioner (RMaPS).

NEBOSH environmental management qualifications are now being accepted by CIWEM (The Chartered Institution of Water and Environmental Management) as meeting its membership requirements.

The NEBOSH Certificate in Environmental Management will be accepted for its new Technician Membership grade entitling the use of post-nominal designation (TechCIWEM).

The NEBOSH National Diploma in Environmental Management fulfils the qualification requirements for non-chartered Member of CIWEM (MCIWEM). Progression on to chartered membership is a further opportunity.

The NEBOSH Certificate in Environmental Management meets the academic criteria to gain the globally recognised IEMA Associate (AIEMA) membership, whilst holders of the NEBOSH National Diploma in Environmental Management will be eligible to apply for IEMA Practitioner (PIEMA) level membership.

NEBOSH's National Diploma and International Diploma are accepted as meeting the requirements to apply for Graduate Membership (Grad IOSH) of the Institution of Occupational Safety and Health (IOSH).

A NEBOSH Diploma provides a sound basis for progression to MSc level: a number of UK universities offer MSc programmes that accept the National Diploma as a full or partial entry requirement.

The new Masters of Research (MRes) Degree is open to holders of a NEBOSH Diploma who wish to further their career in Health and Safety and/or Environment. It will be delivered by distance learning through research directly relevant to the candidate's own work.

QUALIFICATION/EXAMINATIONS
NEBOSH Environmental Awareness at Work Qualification
NEBOSH Health and Safety at Work Qualification
NEBOSH Health, Safety and Environment in the Process Industries Qualification
NEBOSH National Certificate in Construction Health and Safety
NEBOSH Certificate in Environmental Management
NEBOSH National Certificate in Fire Safety and Risk Management
NEBOSH National General Certificate in Occupational Health and Safety
NEBOSH International General Certificate in Occupational Health and Safety
NEBOSH International Technical Certificate in Oil and Gas Operational Safety
NEBOSH National Certificate in the Management of Health and Well-being at Work
NEBOSH International Certificate in Construction Health and Safety
NEBOSH International Certificate in Fire Safety and Risk Management
NEBOSH National Diploma in Environmental Management
NEBOSH National Diploma in Occupational Health and Safety
NEBOSH International Diploma in Occupational Health and Safety
Masters programmes in partnership with the University of Hull
MRes in Occupational Health and Safety Management
MRes in Occupational Health, Safety and Environmental Management
MRes in Environmental Management
MSc in Occupational Health and Safety Management
MSc in Occupational Health, Safety and Environmental Management
MSc in Environmental Management
NEBOSH Diploma in Regulatory Health and Safety – developed for the Health and Safety Executive for all new UK HSE Inspectors

DESIGNATORY LETTERS
DipNEBOSH, EnvDipNEBOSH

THE INSTITUTION OF OCCUPATIONAL SAFETY AND HEALTH

The Grange
Highfield Drive
Wigston
Leicestershire LE18 1NN
Tel: 0116 257 3100
Fax: 0116 257 3101
E-mail: membership@iosh.co.uk
Website: www.iosh.co.uk

Our membership totals over 44,000 – we are the focal point for health and safety professionals working in a diverse range of organisations.

Founded in 1945 IOSH is an independent, not-for-profit organization setting professional standards, supporting and developing members, and providing authoritative advice and guidance on health and safety issues.

MEMBERSHIP
Affiliate Member
Associate Member
Technical Member (Tech IOSH)
Graduate Member (Grad IOSH)

Chartered Member (CMIOSH)
Chartered Fellow (CFIOSH)

QUALIFICATION/EXAMINATIONS
For qualifications that meet our academic requirements for our designatory categories of membership please see the IOSH website: http:// www.iosh.co.uk/ Membership/About-membership/Qualifications.aspx

DESIGNATORY LETTERS
AIOSH, Tech IOSH, Grad IOSH, CMIOSH, CFIOSH

INSURANCE AND ACTUARIAL WORK
Membership of Professional Institutions and Associations

ASSOCIATION OF AVERAGE ADJUSTERS

c/o RTI Ltd
2nd Floor, International House
1 St Katharine's Way
London E1W 1UN
Tel: 020 748 1250
E-mail: aaa@rtiForensics.com
Website: www.average-adjusters.com

The AAA was founded in 1869 to promote correct principles in the adjustment of marine insurance claims and general average, uniformity of practice among average adjusters and the maintenance of good professional conduct. It ensures the independence and impartiality of its members by imposing a strict code of conduct and has close links with other international associations and insurance markets.

MEMBERSHIP
Subscriber

Associate
Fellow

QUALIFICATION/EXAMINATIONS
The Association's examination consists of 6 modules. Passes in Modules A1 & A2 are required for Associateship, passes in Modules F3, F4, F5 and F6 for Fellowship. For details see the Association's website.

THE CHARTERED INSTITUTE OF LOSS ADJUSTERS

51–55 Gresham Street
London EC2V 7HQ
Tel: 020 7216 7580
E-mail: info@cila.co.uk
Website: www.cila.co.uk

The CILA, which was founded in 1941, is the professional body representing the claims specialists who investigate, negotiate and agree the conclusion of insurance and other claims on behalf of insurers and policyholders. We safeguard the interests of our members and maintain the high standards of the profession by requiring them to abide by our code of professional conduct.

MEMBERSHIP
Student Member

Ordinary Member
Certificate Member (Cert CILA)
Associate (ACILA)
Fellow (FCILA)
Honorary Member

QUALIFICATION/EXAMINATIONS
ACILA examination

DESIGNATORY LETTERS
Cert CILA, Dip CILA, ACILA, FCILA

THE CHARTERED INSURANCE INSTITUTE

42–48 High Road
South Woodford
London E18 2JP
Tel: 020 8989 8464
Fax: 020 8530 3052
E-mail: customer.serv@cii.co.uk
Website: www.cii.co.uk

The CII is the premier professional body for those working in the insurance and financial services industry. We are dedicated to promoting higher standards of competence and integrity through the provision of relevant qualifications for employees at all levels across all sectors of the industry.

MEMBERSHIP
Ordinary Member
Qualified Member
Associate Member (ACII)
Fellow (FCII)

QUALIFICATION/EXAMINATIONS
Award in Financial Planning
Certificate in Equity Release
Certificate in Financial Planning
Certificate in Insurance
Certificate in Life and Pensions

Certificate in Mortgage Advice
Diploma in Financial Planning
Diploma in Insurance
Advanced Diploma in Financial Planning
Advanced Diploma in Insurance
Award for the Foundation Insurance Test
Award in General Insurance
Award in London Market Insurance
Award in Customer Service Insurance
Award in Financial Administration
Award in Bancassurance
Award in Investment Planning
Certificate in Contract Wording
Certificate in Insurance and Financial Services
Certificate in London Market Insurance Specialisation
Certificate in Discretionary Investment Management
Certificate in Paraplanning
Certificate in Securities Advice and Dealing

Certificate in Investment Operations
Diploma in Regulated Financial Planning
MSc in Insurance and Risk Management
MSc in Wealth Management

DESIGNATORY LETTERS
ACII, FCII

THE FACULTY AND INSTITUTE OF ACTUARIES

Faculty of Actuaries
Maclaurin House
18 Dublin Street
Edinburgh EH1 3PP
Tel: 0131 240 1313
E-mail: faculty@actuaries.org.uk
Website: www.actuaries.org.uk

Institute of Actuaries
Staple Inn Hall
High Holborn
London WC1V 7QJ
Tel: 020 7632 2111
E-mail: institute@actuaries.org.uk

Napier House
4 Worcester Street
Oxford OX1 2AW
Tel: 01865 268211
E-mail: institute@actuaries.org.uk

Actuaries are experts in assessing the financial impact of tomorrow's uncertain events. They enable financial decisions to be made with more confidence by analysing the past, modelling the future, assessing the risks involved, and communicating what the results mean in financial terms.

MEMBERSHIP
Student Member
Affiliate Member

Associate (AFA or AIA)
Fellow (FFA or FIA)
Honorary Fellow

QUALIFICATION/EXAMINATIONS
Certificate in Financial Mathematics

DESIGNATORY LETTERS
AFA, AIA, FFA, FIA

JOURNALISM
Membership of Professional Institutions and Associations

NATIONAL COUNCIL FOR THE TRAINING OF JOURNALISTS

NCTJ Training Ltd
The New Granary
Newport
Saffron Walden
Essex CB11 3PL
Tel: 01799 544014
Fax: 01799 544015
E-mail: info@nctj.com
Website: www.nctj.com

The NCTJ provides a range of multimedia journalism training products and services in the UK, including: accredited courses; apprenticeships; qualifications and examinations; awards; careers information; distance learning; short courses and CPD; information and research; publications and events. We play an influential role in all areas of journalism education and training.

QUALIFICATION/EXAMINATIONS
Certificate in Foundation Journalism
Apprenticeship Standard for Junior Journalists
Diploma in Journalism
National Qualification in Journalism (NQJ)

THE CHARTERED INSTITUTE OF JOURNALISTS

2 Dock Offices
Surrey Quays Road
London SE16 2XU
Tel: 020 7252 1187
Fax: 020 7232 2302
E-mail: memberservices@cioj.co.uk
Website: www.cioj.co.uk

The CIoJ, which dates back to 1884, is a professional body and trade union for journalists. We expect our members to uphold high standards in the way they work and to adhere to a strict code of conduct, and in return we champion journalistic freedom, protect their interests in the workplace and campaign for better working conditions.

MEMBERSHIP
Student Member
Affiliate Member
Trainee Member
Full Member
International Member

DESIGNATORY LETTERS
MCIJ – Member, FCIJ – Fellow

LAND AND PROPERTY
Membership of Professional Institutions and Associations

RICS (ROYAL INSTITUTION OF CHARTERED SURVEYORS)

Parliament Square
London SW1P 3AD
Tel: 024 7686 8555
Fax: 020 7334 3811
E-mail: contactrics@rics.org
Website: www.rics.org/careers

RICS, an independent, not-for-profit organization, has around 100,000 qualified members and more than 50,000 students and trainees in some 140 countries, and provides the world's leading professional qualification in land, property, construction and associated environmental issues. We accredit over 600 courses at leading universities worldwide and provide impartial, authoritative advice on key issues for business, society and governments.

MEMBERSHIP
Student
Associate (AssocRICS)
Member (MRICS)
Fellow (FRICS)

DESIGNATORY LETTERS
AssocRICS, MRICS, FRICS

THE COLLEGE OF ESTATE MANAGEMENT

Whiteknights
Reading
Berkshire RG6 6AW
Tel: 0118 921 4696
Fax: 0118 921 4620
E-mail: enquiries@cem.ac.uk
Website: www.cem.ac.uk

The College of Estate Management is the leading provider of supported distance learning for real estate and construction professionals. We have been playing a key role in the property world for over 90 years. At any one time we have over 4,000 students based all over the world.

QUALIFICATION/EXAMINATIONS
BCSC Diploma in Shopping Centre Management
BSc(Hons) Building Surveying
BSc(Hons) Construction Management
BSc(Hons) Estate Management

BSc(Hons) Property Management
BSc(Hons) Quantity Surveying
Postgraduate Diploma/MSc Conservation of the Historic Environment
Postgraduate Diploma/MSc Surveying
MBA Real Estate and Construction Management
Postgraduate Diploma/MSc Facilities Management
Postgraduate Diploma/MSc Property Investment
RICS Professional Membership Graduate Route – Adaptation 1

THE INSTITUTE OF REVENUES, RATING AND VALUATION

Northumberland House
5th Floor
303–306 High Holborn
London WC1V 7JZ
Tel: 020 7831 3505
Fax: 020 7831 2048
E-mail: education@irrv.org.uk
Website: www.irrv.org.uk

The Institute offers professional and technical qualifications for all those whose professional work is concerned with local authority revenues and benefits, valuation for rating, property taxation and the appeals procedure. Our qualifications are widely recognized throughout the profession.

MEMBERSHIP
Student Member
Affiliate Member
Graduate Member
Technician Member (Tech IRRV)
Corporate Member (IRRV)
Diploma Member (IRRV Dip)

Honours Member (IRRV Hons)
Honorary Member
Fellow (FIRRV)

QUALIFICATION/EXAMINATIONS
Level 3 Certificate in Local Taxation and Benefits OR Business Rates
Level 3 Local Taxation & Benefits (RQF)
Professional Diploma in Local Taxation and Benefits Honours

DESIGNATORY LETTERS
Tech IRRV, IRRV, IRRV (Dip), IRRV(Hons), FIRRV

THE NATIONAL FEDERATION OF PROPERTY PROFESSIONALS AWARDING BODY

Arbon House
6 Tournament Court
Edgehill Drive
Warwick CV34 6LG
Tel: 0845 250 6008
Fax: 01926 417789
E-mail: quals@nfopp.co.uk
Website: www.nfopp-awardingbody.co.uk

The **NFOPP Awarding Body** is committed to raising standards within agency through the provision of accredited, nationally recognized qualifications. We are recognized by the Qualifications and Examinations Regulator (Ofqual) and Welsh Government and we have to follow strict guidelines and maintain quality standards in the provision of all our qualifications.

MEMBERSHIP
For membership details of the following organizations please refer to the relevant website:
APIP: www.apip.co.uk

ARLA: www.arla.co.uk
ICBA: www.icba.uk.com
NAEA: www.naea.co.uk
NAVA: www.nava.org.uk

QUALIFICATION/EXAMINATIONS
NFoPP **Level 2 Award** in Introduction to Residential Property Management Practice (QCF)
NFoPP **Level 3 Technical Award** in Commercial Property Agency (QCF)
NFoPP **Level 3 Technical Award** in Real Property Auctioneering (QCF)

NFoPP **Level 3 Technical Award** in Residential Letting and Property Management (QCF)

NFoPP **Level 3 Technical Award** in Residential Letting and Property Management Northern Ireland (QCF)

NFoPP **Level 3 Technical Award** in Sale of Residential Property (QCF)

NFoPP **Level 3 Technical Award** in Chattels Auctioneering (QCF)

NFoPP **Level 3 Technical Award** in Residential Inventory Management & Practice (QCF)

NFoPP **Level 4 Certificate** in Residential Letting & Property Management (QCF)

NFoPP **Level 4 Certificate** in Sale of Residential Property (QCF)

NFoPP **Level 4 Certificate** in Commercial Property Agency (QCF)

NFoPP **Level 6 Technical Award** in Sale of Residential Property Scotland (SCQF)

NFoPP **Level 6 Technical Award** in Residential Letting & Property Management Scotland (SCQF)

THE PROPERTY CONSULTANTS SOCIETY

Basement Office
Surrey Court
1 Surrey Street
Arundel
West Sussex BN18 9DT
Tel: 01903 883787
E-mail: info@propertyconsultantssociety.org
Website: www.propertyconsultantssociety.org

The Property Consultants Society is a non-profit-making organization that offers advice to qualified surveyors, architects, valuers, auctioneers, land and estate agents, master builders, construction engineers, accountants and members of the legal profession to help them to undertake their property consultancy in a competent, legitimate and publicly acceptable way.

MEMBERSHIP
Student (SPCS)
Licentiate (LPCS)
Associate (APCS)
Fellow (FPCS)
Honorary Member

DESIGNATORY LETTERS
SPCS, LPCS, APCS, FPCS

LANDSCAPE ARCHITECTURE
Membership of Professional Institutions and Associations

LANDSCAPE INSTITUTE

Charles Darwin House
107 Gray's Inn Road
London WC1X 8TZ
Tel: 020 7685 2640
E-mail: membership@landscapeinstitute.org
Website: www.landscapeinstitute.org

The LI is an educational charity and chartered body responsible for protecting, conserving and enhancing the natural and built environment for the benefit of the public. We champion well-designed and well-managed urban and rural landscape. Our 6,000 members include chartered landscape architects, academics and scientists working for local authorities, government agencies and in private practice, and students.

MEMBERSHIP
Student Member
Affiliate Member
Licentiate Member
Chartered Member (CMLI)
Fellow (FLI)
Academic Member
Academic Fellow

QUALIFICATION/EXAMINATIONS
Pathway to Chartership oral examination conferring
chartered professional status (CMLI)

DESIGNATORY LETTERS
CMLI, FLI

LANGUAGES, LINGUISTICS AND TRANSLATION
Membership of Professional Institutions and Associations

INSTITUTE OF TRANSLATION & INTERPRETING

Milton Keynes Business Centre
Foxhunter Drive
Linford Wood
Milton Keynes MK14 6GD
Tel: 01908 325250
Fax: 01908 325259
E-mail: info@iti.org.uk
Website: www.iti.org.uk

The Institute of Translation & Interpreting is one of the primary sources of information on these services to government, industry, the media and the general public. We promote the highest standards, providing guidance to those entering the profession and advice to those who offer language services and to their customers.

MEMBERSHIP
Associate (AITI)
Student

Qualified Member (MITI)
Corporate Member
Fellow

QUALIFICATION/EXAMINATIONS
Applicants for qualified membership must take an exam (translators) or attend an interview (interpreters).

THE CHARTERED INSTITUTE OF LINGUISTS

Saxon House
48 Southwark Street
London SE1 1UN
Tel: 020 7940 3100
Fax: 020 7940 3101
E-mail: info@iol.org.uk
Website: www.iol.org.uk

The Chartered Institute of Linguistics, founded in 1910, is a respected language assessment and accredited awarding body, with about 6,500 members. Our aims include promoting the learning and use of modern languages, improving the status of all professional linguistics, and ensuring the maintenance of high professional standards through adherence to our code of conduct.

MEMBERSHIP
Registered Student
Associate Member (ACIL)
Member (MCIL)

Fellow (FCIL)
Chartered Linguist (CL)

QUALIFICATION/EXAMINATIONS
Certificate in Bilingual Skills (CBS)
Diploma in Public Service Interpreting (DPSI)

International Diploma in Bilingual Translation (IDBT)
Diploma in Translation (DipTrans)

DESIGNATORY LETTERS
ACIL, MCIL, FCIL, CL

THE GREEK INSTITUTE

29 Onslow Gardens
London N21 1DY
Tel: 020 8360 7968
Fax: 020 8360 7968
E-mail: info@greekinstitute.co.uk
Website: www.greekinstitute.co.uk

The Greek Institute, which was founded in 1969, is a non-profit-making cultural organization that promotes Modern Greek studies and culture through lectures, publications, literary competitions, Greek cultural evenings and the award of Certificates and a Diploma which are recognized by many UK universities as equivalent to GCSE and GCE A level Modern Greek.

MEMBERSHIP
Member
Associate (AGI)
Fellow (FGI)

QUALIFICATION/EXAMINATIONS
Certificate in Greek Conversation – Basic Stage: Levels 1 and 2
Certificate in Greek Conversation – Intermediate Stage: Levels 3 and 4
Certificate in Greek Conversation – Higher Stage: Levels 5 and 6
Preliminary Certificate
Intermediate Certificate
Advanced Certificate
Diploma in Greek Translation (DipGrTrans)

DESIGNATORY LETTERS
AGI, FGI

LAW

ENGLAND AND WALES

MAGISTRATES

The President of the Courts of England and Wales, The Lord Chief Justice, is head of the Judiciary. He is responsible for the welfare, training and deployment of magistrates, for approving the names of the candidates recommended for appointment and for disciplinary action, short of removal. He also has responsibility for the protection of judicial independence and for working to ensure that the magistracy reflects the diversity of society as a whole.

There are key qualities that a magistrate must possess: good character, understanding and effective communication, social awareness, maturity and a sense of fairness, sound judgement, commitment and reliability. Magistrates do not sit exams nor do they have to be legally qualified.

Before sitting in court, magistrates must undertake some basic training, which includes structured observations in court. This covers practice and procedure in court, structured decision making, sentencing, and so on. New magistrates are assigned a mentor for the first year or so. Core training also involves visits to penal institutions to equip magistrates with the key knowledge they need. Consolidation training takes place at the end of the first year; this is designed to help magistrates plan for their ongoing development and prepare for their first appraisal which takes place about 12 to 18 months after appointment. Magistrates only sit in adult courts when first appointed. Having got that experience they may apply to sit in youth courts and family courts and have to undertake more training before they can sit.

Ongoing training and development includes appraisals which take place every three years, continuation training which takes place once every three years, usually before appraisals, update training on new legislation and procedures and threshold training which accompanies each development in a magistrate's role.

The Magistrates Association has more information about magistrates (www.magistrates-association.org.uk).

JUDGES

All judicial office holders are Her Majesty's Judges and as such all appointments are made by the Queen or her Ministers. All candidates for judicial appointment in England and Wales have been selected by the independent Judicial Appointments Commission (JAC, website: jac.judiciary.gov.uk), which passes its recommendations to the Lord Chancellor for approval. The key statutory responsibilities of the JAC are to select candidates solely on merit; to select only people of good character; to have regard to the need to encourage diversity in the range of people available for selection for appointments.

Once the JAC's selections have been received, the actual appointments are made in slightly different ways depending on the type of post. The Lord Chancellor appoints Deputy District Judges and most members of tribunals. The 30,000 unpaid magistrates who are selected by local Advisory Committees, not by the JAC, are also appointed by The Lord Chancellor. The Queen appoints High Court and Circuit Judges, Masters, Registrars and District Judges, District Judges (Magistrates Courts) and Recorders on the advice of the Lord Chancellor. A special panel convened by the JAC appoints the Lord Chief Justice. The Queen appoints Heads of Division, Court of Appeal judges and senior judges with lengthy judicial experience, on the recommendation of a selection panel convened by the JAC. Scotland and Northern Ireland have their own separate court systems, with their own arrangements for appointing members of the judiciary.

The Supreme Court (http://supremecourt.uk) has jurisdiction over the whole of the UK, so its Justices are not selected by the JAC, which is an England and Wales body. Rather, a special committee is set up, which is made up of the three judicial appointments bodies from around the UK (England and Wales, Scotland and Northern Ireland), who recommend a name to Ministers. The Queen appoints the Justices on the basis of advice from the Prime Minister.

Candidates for appointment as Justices of the Supreme Court must have held high judicial office for two years or must have been practising barristers or solicitors of the senior courts for at least 15 years (www.supremecourt.uk/faqs.html#1d). More information about judges can be found at the Courts and Tribunals Judiciary website: www.judiciary.gov.uk

OFFICERS OF THE COURT

Officers of the Court include judicial and administrative staff; the former include Masters and Registrars, the latter secretaries and clerks to the judges and the staff who administer the court service. Details are given in *The English Legal System*, 17th edition, 2016–17 (Routledge). Qualifications for the judicial offices vary somewhat, but most appointments are limited to established barristers and solicitors.

THE LEGAL PROFESSION

The legal profession consists of two branches. Each performs distinct duties, although there is a degree of overlap in some aspects of their work.

Solicitors undertake all ordinary legal business for their clients (with whom they are in direct contact). They may also appear on behalf of a client in the magistrates and county courts and tribunals, and with specialist training are able to represent them in the higher courts (Crown Court, High Court and Court of Appeal). The website for the Law Society contains further information (www.lawsociety.org.uk).

Barristers (known collectively as the Bar and collectively and individually as Counsel) advise on legal problems submitted by solicitors and conduct cases in court when instructed by a solicitor; only barristers or qualified solicitor advocates may represent clients in the higher courts. More information on barristers can be found on The Bar Council website (www.barcouncil.org.uk).

LEGAL EXECUTIVES

Both graduates and non-graduates can work in a legal office with the option of qualifying as a solicitor through further vocational training. Chartered Legal Executive lawyers are 'authorised persons' undertaking 'reserved legal activities' alongside, for example, solicitors and barristers. As a general rule, a Chartered Legal Executive lawyer is able to undertake all the same work that may be undertaken by a solicitor, with some conditions. The Chartered Institute of Legal Executives website has information on becoming a legal executive and the work they can undertake (www.cilex.org.uk).

CORONERS

Coroners must be barristers, solicitors or legally qualified medical practitioners of not less than five years standing. They are appointed by local authorities. There are approximately 95 coroner areas in England and Wales; each area is locally funded and resourced by local authorities. Coroners are independent judicial officers. When not engaged in coronal duties, coroners (apart from whole-time coroners) continue in their legal or medical practices. The Chief Coroner is head of the coroner system, assuming overall responsibility and providing national leadership for coroners in England and Wales. He oversees the implementation of the Coroner and Justice Act 2009. Further information from the Coroners Society of England and Wales, website: www.coronersociety. org.uk and the Crown Prosecution Service website: www.cps.gov.uk/legal/a_to_c/coroners/#a02.

BARRISTERS

Qualification as a barrister at the Bar of England and Wales

There are three stages that must be completed to qualify as a barrister. The academic stage consists of an undergraduate degree in law or in any other subject with a minimum of a 2:2. For those with an undergraduate degree in a subject other than law a one-year conversion course (CPE/GDL) must be completed.

Before commencing the vocational stage candidates must join one of the four Inns and then undertake the Bar Professional Training Course (BPTC), which is either one year full time or two years part time. The main skills taught on the BPTC are: casework skills, legal research, fact management, general written skills including opinion-writing (that is, giving written advice) and drafting, management and interpersonal skills including conference skills (interviewing clients), resolution of disputes out of court (ReDOC) and advocacy (court or tribunal appearances). The main areas of legal knowledge taught on the BPTC are: civil litigation, evidence and remedies, criminal litigation, evidence and sentencing, professional ethics, and two optional subjects or one double optional subject selected from a choice of at least six.

Three centralised assessments are set by a Central Examinations Board, which is comprised of experienced legal practitioners and academics appointed by the Bar Standards Board (BSB). The subjects that are centrally assessed are Civil Litigation, Evidence and Remedies, Criminal Litigation, Evidence and Sentencing and Professional Ethics. Applicants will also have to take the Bar Course Aptitude Test. It aims to test critical thinking and reasoning, but does not test legal knowledge. Practice tests are available on the BSB website. The Aptitude Test will ensure that those undertaking the BPTC have the required skills to succeed.

Once the BPCT has been successfully completed candidates are called to the Bar by their Inn. The Pupillage Stage consists of one year spent in an authorized pupillage training organization. Pupillage is divided into two parts: the non-practising six months (also known as the first six) and the practising six months (also known as the second six).

To find out more about all three stages of qualification as a barrister visit www.barcouncil.org. uk and www.barstandardsboard.org.uk

SOLICITORS

Qualification as a solicitor in England and Wales

To practise as a solicitor in England and Wales a person must have been admitted as a solicitor, his or her name having been entered on the Roll of Solicitors, and must hold a practising certificate issued by The Solicitors Regulation Authority (SRA) (Solicitors Regulation Authority, The Cube, 199 Wharfside Street, Birmingham B1 1RN; Tel: 0370 606 2555; www.sra.org.uk).

The SRA is the independent regulatory body of the Law Society of England and Wales. People will be admitted as solicitors only if they have passed the appropriate academic and vocational course and have completed a training contract and Professional Skills course, or have transferred from another jurisdiction or the Bar. The SRA controls the training of solicitors. Most solicitors become members of the Law Society, but membership is not compulsory. Intending solicitors other than Fellows of the Chartered Institute of Legal Executives (CILEx), Justices Clerk's Assistants and qualified lawyers from overseas, are required to serve a period of training with a practising solicitor after they have completed the legal practice course.

All new entrants to the profession are required to complete a Disclosure and Barring Service (DBS) standard disclosure prior to admission. Candidates wishing to start training must enrol as a student with the SRA and satisfy it that they have successfully completed the academic stage of training and there are no issues that may call their character and suitability into question.

It is not necessary for the first degree to be in law as about 20 per cent of solicitors qualify via the non-law graduate route. The key stages of this are:

- degree in any subject;
- Common Professional Examination/Graduate Diploma in Law;
- Legal Practice course;
- practice-based training incorporating the Professional Skills course;
- admission to the roll of solicitors.

THE COMMON PROFESSIONAL EXAMINATION (CPE) OR GRADUATE DIPLOMA IN LAW (GDL)

The seven taught modules are the foundation subjects prescribed by the Joint Academic Stage Board on behalf of the Law Society and General Council of the Bar: Criminal Law, Contract Law, the Law of Tort, Equity and Trusts, Public Law, European Union Law and Property Law. For an up-to-date list of course providers for the CPE, use the training provider search in the student section on the SRA website: www.sra.org.uk

THE LEGAL PRACTICE COURSE

Stage 1 covers core practice areas: Litigation, Property Law and Practice (PLP), Business Law and Practice (BLP); Course Skills: Research, Writing, Drafting, Interviewing and Advising, and Advocacy (these skills form an integral part of the compulsory and elective subjects) and also Professional Conduct and Regulation, Taxation and Wills and Administration of Estates. Stage 2 covers three vocational electives chosen from a range of corporate client or private client topics (the range of electives available can differ from institution to institution). An up-to-date list of course providers for the LPC is available using the training provider search in the student section on the SRA website: www.sra.org.uk

TRAINING CONTRACT

The training contract to be served by all intending solicitors, other than Fellows of the Institute of Legal Executives and Justices Clerk's Assistants, is usually two years full time or a part-time study training contract that normally lasts between three and four years. During this period the trainee works and is studying the last two years of a part-time qualifying law degree, the part-time Common Professional Examination course and/or the part-time Legal Practice Course.

The law graduate who holds a qualifying law degree must complete the Legal Practice course at a recognized institution, and then serve under the training contract, usually for two years. The non-law graduate must first pass the Common Professional Exam (CPE) or the Postgraduate Diploma in Law, having attended either a one-year full-time or two-year part-time preparatory course. He or she may then serve under the training contract for two years after completion of a Legal Practice Course. A Professional Skills course must be attended and successfully completed during the training contract.

Fellows of the Institute of Chartered Legal Executives (CILEx) may obtain partial or full exemptions from the CPE and Justices Clerk's Assistants courses by virtue of similar subjects passed in their Fellowship exams or the Diploma in Magisterial Law. After passing or being exempted from the CPE, the Fellow/ Justices Clerk's Assistant may be exempt from serving under a training contract following successful completion of a Legal Practice Course. A Professional Skills course must be taken prior to application for admission.

THE PROFESSIONAL SKILLS COURSE

The aim of the Professional Skills course is to build on the foundations laid in the Legal Practice Course so as to develop a trainee's professional skills. Providers of the course, trainees and their employers are encouraged to regard the course as the first stage of a trainee's lifetime professional development.

Built upon the Legal Practice Course, the course provides training in three subject areas: financial and business skills; advocacy and communication skills; client care and professional standards. Elective topics will also be chosen, which fall within one or more of these three core areas. All trainees have to complete all sections of the course satisfactorily before being admitted. The course consists of face-to-face instruction on the core subjects, for a minimum of 18 hours each for financial and business skills and advocacy and communication skills, and a minimum of 12 hours for client care and professional standards. The elective topics require a minimum total of 24 hours, of which a minimum of 12 hours must be face-to-face. The instruction must be completed during the training contract. The PSC is offered by accredited external course providers.

APPRENTICESHIPS

Legal apprenticeships have been introduced as alternative way to gain legal qualifications. While working for an employer, an apprentice can qualify as a solicitor, a legal executive or a paralegal. During the apprenticeship a combination of classroom and work-based learning is undertaken and the apprentice receives a salary. The minimum entry requirements can be found on the Law Society's website: www.lawsociety.org.uk. The apprenticeship lasts from five to six years. The apprentice is assessed by timed examination and a work-based assessment. The apprentice then takes a standardised practical legal exam in the last six months of the apprenticeship in order to qualify. Further information is available on the SRA's website and www.getingofar.gov.uk

QUALIFIED LAWYERS FROM OTHER JURISDICTIONS

Lawyers from certain foreign jurisdictions can apply for admission under the Qualified Lawyers Transfer Scheme Regulations 2011. They need to obtain a QLTS Certificate of Eligibility, but may be entitled to exemption from some or all of the QLTS assessments if they are:

- a lawyer qualified in the EEA/EU/Switzerland and seeking to qualify via Directive 2005/36/EC (recognition of professional qualifications)
- a lawyer qualified in Northern Ireland or Scotland
- a barrister who has qualified in England and Wales who has completed a pupillage.

The Solicitors Regulation Authority has appointed Kaplan QLTS as the assessment organization for the operation of the assessments (http://qlts.kaplan.co.uk) and the assessments are only available at Kaplan QLTS. The assessments are usually only available twice a year and take place in London. The email address for queries regarding eligibility is contact-centre@sra.org.uk.

EU, Northern Irish and Scottish lawyers and barristers qualified in England and Wales follow a different transfer process and should get in touch with the SRA Contact Centre for further information. SRA Contact Centre Tel: 0370 606 2555 (International callers: +44 (0)121 329 6800); Website: www.sra.org.uk/contact-us

All international applicants must satisfy the requirements and pass the QLTS Assessments. The Assessments are in two parts: Part 1 is a multiple choice test designed to test Part A of the SRA's Day One Outcomes, namely the knowledge of law expected of a newly qualified solicitor of England and Wales and consists of 180 questions; Part 2, is an Objective Structured Clinical Examination (OSCE). For the OSCE, candidates are examined in the skills of interviewing, advocacy/oral presentations, legal research, legal drafting and legal writing in business, civil and criminal litigation, property and probate.

EEA, Northern Irish and Scottish lawyers, and barristers qualified in England and Wales will be individually assessed against the Day One Outcomes. All transferees are required to prove their character and suitability to be a solicitor by taking the SRA Suitability Test. Candidates who have passed the LPC can get exemption from the Part 1 (MCT) assessment.

Prospective candidates wanting more information on QLTS can consult the website www.sra.org.uk/solicitors/qlts/key-features.page for guidance, or contact the SRA on 0370 606 2555 (International callers: +44(0)121 329 6800); Website: www.sra.org.uk/contact-us

SCOTLAND

The Court of Session, High Court of Justiciary, Sheriff Courts and Justice of the Peace Courts are administered by the Scottish Court service, an Executive Agency of the Scottish Government. For further information on Scottish Courts go to www.scotcourts.gov.uk

THE LEGAL PROFESSION

The profession consists of solicitors and advocates.

Qualification as a Solicitor in Scotland

Solicitors in Scotland have their names inserted in a Roll of Solicitors and are granted annual Certificates entitling them to practise by The Law Society of

Scotland, contact details: Atria One, 144 Morrison Street, Edinburgh EH3 8EX; Tel: 0131 226 7411; e-mail: lawscot@lawscot.org.uk; website: www.lawscot.org.uk; Education and Careers e-mail: careers@lawscot.org.uk.

For any queries relating to qualifying as a solicitor in Scotland, including LLB/diploma providers, diploma validity, traineeships, admission as a solicitor, entrance certificates and training contracts, alternative routes to qualification and requalifying into Scotland, contact legaleduc@lawscot.org.uk.

A Certificate is granted to candidates who have passed approved exams, completed a term of practical training and been admitted as solicitors.

THE QUALIFYING EXAMINATIONS

The standard route to qualification is the LLB (the Ordinary degree is a three-year course, the Honours is four years) followed by the Diploma in Professional Legal Practice (Professional Education and Training Stage 1: PEAT 1) and then the traineeship, the period of paid in-office training working towards the standard of the qualified solicitor (Professional Education and Training Stage 2: PEAT 2). Outcomes in professionalism, professional ethics and standards, professional communication and business, commercial, financial and practice awareness apply across both PEAT 1 and 2, linking them and providing real clarity across the two stages.

All trainees are required to undertake Trainee Continuing Professional Development (TCPD). All solicitors are required to undertake CPD for a minimum of 20 hours each year. To support solicitors in their CPD activities, the Society provides basic templates, which can be completed online, to assist with identifying training needs, recording CPD undertaken and evaluating the outcome of the training. A wide range of activities are acceptable as CPD, including structured and formalized one-to-one training, coaching and online training.

An alternate route to qualifying as a solicitor in Scotland is by a combination of the Law Society's own examinations and three years pre-Diploma training. To be eligible to sit the Law Society's examinations, non-law graduates must find full-time employment as a pre-Diploma trainee with a qualified solicitor practising in Scotland. A pre-Diploma training contract lasts for three years. During the period of the training contract, a pre-Diploma trainee will study for the Law Society's examinations. The two routes to qualification (degree and Law Society exams) merge at this point as all intending solicitors are required to complete the Diploma in Professional Legal Practice. Upon successful completion of the Diploma the graduate will enter into a two-year post-Diploma training contract with a qualified solicitor practising in Scotland.

Transfer tests are in place for solicitors from England, Wales, Northern Ireland and other parts of the European Union who wish to requalify as Scottish solicitors.

Qualification as an advocate in Scotland

Barristers in Scotland are called Advocates. Scottish Advocates are not only members of the Faculty of Advocates but also members of the College of Justice and officers of the Court. The procedure for the admission of Intrants is subject in part to the control of the Court and in part to the control of the Faculty; the Court is responsible for most of the formal procedures and the Faculty for the exams and periods of professional training. To become an Intrant, applicants must produce evidence that they hold one of the following standard of degree: a degree with Honours, Second Class (Division 2) or above, in Scottish Law at a Scottish university, or a degree in Scottish Law at a Scottish university together with a degree with Honours, Second Class (Division 2) or above, in another subject at a UK university or an ordinary degree with distinction in Scottish Law at a Scottish university. A Diploma in Legal Practice from a Scottish University is also required, although in exceptional cases this requirement may be waived.

In order to go through the various stages of qualification and training, applicants must matriculate as intrants to the Faculty. Matriculation involves making an application to the Court of Session and to the Faculty.

An Intrant must also comply with the professional training required by the Faculty, which consists of a period of 21 months training in a solicitors office (although the Faculty recommends a traineeship of 24 months). Subject-for-subject exemptions are granted to Intrants who have passed exams at this standard in the course of a curriculum for a law degree at a Scottish university. Every Intrant must pass or be exempted from exams in the compulsory subjects and two optional subjects. In addition, and prior to the commencement of pupillage (also known as devilling) every Intrant must sit the Faculty's entrant examination in Evidence, Practice and Procedure. If successfully passed, the Intrant can then commence his or her pupillage.

During the first five or six weeks of pupillage pupils undertake the Foundation course. After about three months of work with their devil master, the pupils will participate in the February Skills course, comprising a series of performance workshops involving the use of documents in evidence, the conduct of a procedure roll discussion, workshops on judicial review, section 275 applications and working with expert evidence. Shortly before admission, the pupils attend the May Preparation for Practice course, covering workshops on vulnerable witnesses, longer motions, reclaiming motions, negotiation and mediation, as well as carrying out civil and criminal appeals before a serving judge.

Intrants who have passed all the necessary exams and undergone the necessary professional training as well as successfully completing their pupillage may apply to be admitted to membership of the Faculty and are admitted at a public meeting of the Faculty.

Once admitted, Intrants are introduced to the Court by the Dean of Faculty, make a Declaration of Allegiance to the Sovereign in open Court and are then admitted by the Court to the public office of Advocate. For further information on becoming an advocate contact Faculty of Advocates, Parliament House, Edinburgh EH1 1RF; Tel: 0131 226 5071; e-mail: admissions@advocates.org.uk; website: www.advocates.org.uk

NORTHERN IRELAND

As in England and Wales, the superior courts are the Supreme Court, Court of Appeal, the High Court and the Crown Court. The latter is an exclusively criminal court. The Court of Appeal hears appeals on points of law in civil and criminal cases from all courts. Appeals lie from the Court of Appeal to the Supreme Court.

Inferior Courts: as in England and Wales, the county courts are principally civil courts, but in Northern Ireland they also hear appeals from conviction in the Magistrates Courts for summary offences.

Magistrates Courts: these deal principally with minor criminal offences (summary offences) and are presided over by Resident Magistrates (stipendiaries). Resident Magistrates are appointed by the Crown on the advice of the Lord Chancellor.

Coroners: coroners in Northern Ireland must be barristers or solicitors who have practised for not less than five years. They are appointed by the Lord Chancellor.

THE LEGAL PROFESSION

The legal profession in Northern Ireland consists of barristers and solicitors belonging to professional bodies organized on similar lines to those in England and Wales.

Qualification as a barrister in Northern Ireland

The path to becoming a barrister in Northern Ireland will differ depending on where you study, qualify and complete your pupillage training. There are different pathways for those who have trained as barristers in Northern Ireland, the Republic of Ireland or England and Wales. A different procedure exists for solicitors who wish to requalify as barristers or those who wish to transfer from European jurisdictions. Full information can be found at www.barofni.com/page/becoming-a-barrister

To qualify to practise as a barrister in Northern Ireland a candidate who has trained in Northern Ireland must have a recognized law degree of 2.1

honours standard or higher, or equivalent. The candidate must then complete the Bar Post-Graduate Diploma in Professional Legal Studies at the Institute of Professional Legal Studies, Queen's University, Belfast (IPLS). Finally the candidate must call to the Bar of Northern Ireland and complete a 12-month pupillage. Enquiries about the Bar can be made to the Bar Council Office, The Bar Library, 91 Chichester Street, Belfast BT1 3JQ; Tel: 028 9024 1523; website: www.barofni.com).

Qualification as a solicitor in Northern Ireland

The solicitors' professional body in Northern Ireland is the Law Society of Northern Ireland (Law Society House, 96 Victoria Street, Belfast BT1 3GN; Tel: 028 9023 1614; e-mail: enquiry@lawsoc-ni.org; website: www.lawsoc-ni.org). It has overall responsibility for education and admission to the profession.

Admission to training is generally dependent upon possession of a recognized law degree from a university. Law graduates must attend a two-year vocational apprenticeship course at the Institute of Professional Legal Studies, The Queen's University of Belfast, 10 Lennoxvale, Belfast, BT9 5BY; Tel: 028 9097 5567; e-mail: iplsenquiries@qub.ac.uk. On completion of the two-year apprenticeship newly qualified solicitors receive restricted practising certificates, which means that although they are fully qualified they cannot practise on their own account or in partnership for at least two more years.

Non-law graduates must satisfy the Society that they possess an acceptable degree in a discipline other than law and have attained a satisfactory level of legal knowledge in areas such as: Constitutional Law, Law of Tort, Law of Contract, Criminal Law, Equity, Land Law and Law of Evidence; that they have been offered a place in the Institute; and that they have obtained a Master (a solicitor with whom the applicant proposes to serve his or her apprenticeship).

Membership of Professional Institutions and Associations

CHARTERED INSTITUTE OF LEGAL EXECUTIVES (CILEX)

Kempston Manor
Kempston
Bedford MK42 7AB
Tel: 01234 841000
E-mail: membership@cilex.org.uk
Website: www.cilex.org.uk

The Chartered Institute of Legal Executives (CILEx) is the professional association which represents 20,000 Chartered Legal Executive lawyers, paralegals and other legal practitioners. Our role is to enhance the position and standing of Chartered Legal Executive lawyers in the legal profession. For more than 50 years, we have been offering unparalleled access to a flexible career in law. We work closely with Government and the Ministry of Justice and are recognised in England and Wales as one of the three core approved regulators of the legal profession alongside barristers and solicitors.

MEMBERSHIP
Student Member
Affiliate Member
Associate Member (ACILEx)
Graduate Member (GCILEx)
Chartered Legal Executive Lawyer (FCILEx)

QUALIFICATION/EXAMINATIONS
Level 1 Award/Certificate/Diploma in Legal Studies
Level 2 Award/Certificate/Diploma in Legal Studies
Level 2 Certificate/Diploma for Legal Secretaries
Level 3 Certificate/Diploma for Legal Secretaries
Level 3 Professional Diploma in Law and Practice
Level 3 Certificate in Law and Practice
Level 3 Certificate in Civil Litigation
Level 3 Certificate in Family Practice
Level 3 Certificate in Employment Practice
Level 3 Certificate in Private Client Practice
Level 3 Certificate in Property
Level 3 Diploma in Providing Legal Services
Level 4 Diploma in Commercial Litigation
Level 4 Diploma in Debt Recovery and Insolvency
Level 4 Diploma in Personal Injury Litigation
Level 4 Diploma in Providing Legal Services
Level 4 Extended Diploma in Personal Injury Litigation
Level 6 Certificate in Law
Level 6 Higher Diploma in Law and Practice
Graduate Fast-track Diploma (Level 6)

DESIGNATORY LETTERS
ACILEx, GCILEx, FCILEx

COUNCIL FOR LICENSED CONVEYANCERS

16 Glebe Road
Chelmsford
Essex CM1 1QG
Tel: 01245 349599
Fax: 01245 341300
E-mail: clc@clc-uk.org
Website: www.clc-uk.org

The CLC was established under the provisions of the Administration of Justice Act 1985 as the Regulatory Body for Licensed Conveyancers. Our purpose is to set entry standards and regulate the profession of Licensed Conveyancers effectively. CLC regulates Probate services provided by its licensed practitioners. CLC is an authorised regulator for ABS.

MEMBERSHIP
Student
Licensed Conveyancer

Probate Practitioner
ABS

Finals
Practical Training

QUALIFICATION/EXAMINATIONS
Foundation

THE ACADEMY OF EXPERTS

3 Gray's Inn Square
Gray's Inn
London WC1R 5AH
Tel: 020 7430 0333
Fax: 020 7430 0666
E-mail: admin@academy-experts.org
Website: www.academy-experts.org

The Academy of Experts, multidisciplinary body established in 1987 to establish and promote high objective standards for those acting as expert witnesses. We act as an accrediting and professional body, offering training, technical guidance and representation. In addition we promote cost-efficient dispute resolution, maintaining a register of qualified dispute resolvers.

MEMBERSHIP
Associate Member

Associate Member (AMAE)
Full Member (MAE)
Fellow (FAE)
Practising Corporate Member
Dispute Resolver Member

QUALIFICATION/EXAMINATIONS
There are examinations for upgrade.

DESIGNATORY LETTERS
AMAE, MAE, FAE, QDR

THE INSTITUTE OF LEGAL FINANCE AND MANAGEMENT (ILFM)

2nd Floor
Marlowe House
109 Station Road
Sidcup
Kent DA15 7ET
Tel: 020 8302 2867
Fax: 020 8302 7481
E-mail: kim.freeman@ilfm.org.uk
Website: www.ilfm.org.uk

The ILFM, which was founded in 1978, is a non-profit-making professional body dedicated to the education and support of specialist financial and administrative personnel working within the legal community. We encourage the development of our members' skills through educational courses, training workshops, seminars, conferences and our bimonthly magazine, *Legal Abacus*.

MEMBERSHIP
Ordinary Member

Diploma Member (ILFM (Dip))
Associate Member (AILFM)
Fellow Member (FILFM)
Affiliated Professional Member

QUALIFICATION/EXAMINATIONS
Diploma
Associate
Fellow

DESIGNATORY LETTERS
DILFM (Dip), AILFM, FILFM

THE LAW SOCIETY OF SCOTLAND

Atria One
144 Morrison Street
Edinburgh EH3 8EX
Tel: 0131 226 7411
Fax: 0131 225 2934
E-mail: lawscot@lawscot.org.uk
Website: www.lawscot.org.uk

The Law Society of Scotland is the membership organisation of Scottish solicitors. We promote the interests of the profession and of the public in relation to the profession. Our services include providing initial career advice, overseeing legal education in Scotland, handling admissions to the profession, monitoring trainees, providing post-qualifying legal education, and administering courses and examinations for the Society of Law Accountants in Scotland.

MEMBERSHIP
All practising solicitors in Scotland must be members of the Society and must hold a current Practising Certificate which is issued by the Society.
Students stuyding the LLB or Diploma can become Student Associates free of charge. Visit www.lawscot.org.uk/students for more information

QUALIFICATION/EXAMINATIONS
Please see the Law Society of Scotland's website.

LEISURE AND RECREATION MANAGEMENT
Membership of Professional Institutions and Associations

CHARTERED INSTITUTE FOR THE MANAGEMENT OF SPORT AND PHYSICAL ACTIVITY (CIMSPA)

Sportpark Loughborough University
3 Oakwood Drive
Loughborough
Leicestershire LE11 3QF
Tel: 01509 226474
Fax: 01509 226475
E-mail: info@cimspa.co.uk
Website: www.cimspa.co.uk

CIMSPA is the membership body for sport and physical activity professionals. We promote high standards and provide CPD as well as a wide range of training courses to our members in-house and at venues across the UK. We also work hard to influence government policy on behalf of our members.

MEMBERSHIP
Student Member
Affiliate Member
Associate Member
Member
Fellow
Companion
Chartered Member
Chartered Fellow
Retired Member

QUALIFICATION/EXAMINATIONS
National Pool Plant Operators Certificate
National Pool Plant Foundation Certificate
National Spa Pool Operators Certificate
Supervisory Management Certificate
Fitness Management Certificate
Health and Safety Management Certificate
Higher Professional Diploma in Sport and Recreation Management

Online Continuing Professional Development (CPD) (Entrance and Supervisory Level)

Online Continuing Professional Development (CPD) (Management Level)

Certificate in Leisure Operations (QCF) (1st4sport Level 2)

NVQ Award in Mechanical Ride Operation (QCF) (1st4sport Level 2)

NVQ Certificate in Active Leisure, Learning and Well-being Operational Services (QCF) (1st4sport Level 2)

Certificate in Leisure Management (QCF) (1st4sport Level 3)

NVQ Diploma in Leisure Management (QCF) (1st4sport Level 3)

NVQ Diploma in Sports Development (QCF) (1st4sport Level 3)

Award in Introductory Work in the Outdoors (QCF) (1st4sport Level 2)

NVQ Diploma in Outdoor Programmes (QCF) (1st4sport Level 3)

Award in Coordinating Sports Volunteers (QCF) (1st4sport Level 3)

Certificate in Managing Sports Volunteers (QCF) (1st4sport Level 3)

DESIGNATORY LETTERS
NPPO, RoPPPS, CPD, QCF

INSTITUTE OF GROUNDSMANSHIP

28 Stratford Office Village
Walker Avenue
Wolverton Mill East
Milton Keynes MK12 5TW
Tel: 01908 312511
Fax: 01908 311140
E-mail: iog@iog.org
Website: www.iog.org

The Institute of Groundsmanship is the only membership organisation supporting the whole of the grounds care industry. Serving the industry for more than 80 years, we provide a range of quality products, services and events including education, training and membership services, the national SALTEX exhibition, local information days, an annual conference and awards programme.

MEMBERSHIP
Student Member
Facility/Organisation Member
E-Member
Individual Member
Corporate and Corporate PLUS Member

QUALIFICATION/EXAMINATIONS
For details see: www.iog.org/training-training-courses.asp

LIBRARIANSHIP AND INFORMATION WORK
Membership of Professional Institutions and Associations

CHARTERED INSTITUTE OF LIBRARY AND INFORMATION PROFESSIONALS

7 Ridgmount Street
London WC1E 7AE
Tel: 020 7255 0500
Fax: 020 7255 0501
E-mail: memberservices@cilip.org.uk
Website: www.cilip.org.uk

CILIP is the professional body representing library, knowledge and information professionals in the UK.

MEMBERSHIP
Certified Affiliate (ACLIP)
Chartered Member (MCLIP)
Chartered Fellow (FCLIP)
Revalidated Affiliate, Member or Fellow
Student Membership

QUALIFICATION/EXAMINATIONS
Application for levels of professional registration is through the submission of a portfolio of evidence meeting published criteria. Please contact the Institute for further information.

DESIGNATORY LETTERS
ACLIP, MCLIP, FCLIP

MANAGEMENT
Membership of Professional Institutions and Associations

ASSOCIATION FOR PROJECT MANAGEMENT

Ibis House
Regent Park
Summerleys Road
Princes Risborough
Buckinghamshire HP27 9LE
Tel: 0845 458 1944
E-mail: via website
Website: www.apm.org.uk

The association is a registered charity with over 19,500 individual and 500 corporate members making it the largest professional body of its kind in Europe. APM's mission statement is 'to develop and promote the professional disciplines of project and programme management for the public benefit'.

MEMBERSHIP
Student Member
Associate Member
Full Member (MAPM)
Fellow (FAPM)
Corporate Member
Honorary Member/ Fellow (HonFAPM)

QUALIFICATION/EXAMINATIONS
Introductory Certificate in Project Management (IC)
APMP
APMP for PRINCE2 Practitioners
Practitioner Qualification (PQ)
Risk level 1
Risk level 2
Pan sector standard:
Registered Project Professional (RPP)
Higher Apprenticeship:
Higher Apprenticeship in Project Management

DESIGNATORY LETTERS
MAPM, FAPM, HonFAPM, RPP

ASSOCIATION OF CERTIFIED COMMERCIAL DIPLOMATS (ACCD)

Commercial Diplomats Regulation Authority
ACCD Global Headquarters
Central Administration Office
PO Box 50561, Canary Wharf
London E16 3WY
Tel: +44(0)8445 864249
E-mail: enquiries@chartereddiplomats.org.uk
Website: www.commercialdiplomats.org.uk

Association of Certified Commercial Diplomats is the first independent accreditation, awarding and regulation authority, and extraterritorial global professional awarding body for commercial diplomats and diplomatic institutions. The umbrella of ACCD covers ambassadors, representatives of government, trade commissioners, advisors and negotiators, arbitrators, negotiators of IIAs, policy-makers & government officials, commercial judges, arbitrators, involved in trade, commercial and/or investment issues, commercial counsellors, IIA experts, academia, private sector & NGO representatives, officials in government ministries, parastatals, corporations, academic, public and private institutions worldwide. Its principal objectives are to provide accreditation and regulation, and to advance the interests of its members as qualified, certified and competent commercial diplomats. As the global voice, ACCD has overall responsibility, including the setting of policy and guidelines, as well as the qualification and accreditation procedures for the commercial diplomatic profession. ACCD is non-partisan, not-for-profit, independent of government, and uniquely the professional regulatory body for diplomatic institutions of higher learning providing advanced postgraduate, doctoral, and postdoctoral programmes on commercial judicial diplomatic affairs.

MEMBERSHIP
REGULATED FULL MEMBERSHIP
Associate
Member
Fellow

QUALIFICATION/EXAMINATIONS
ACCD REGULATED POSTGRADUATE EXAMINATIONS AND QUALIFICATIONS
Certificate of Competency
Advanced Certificate of Competency
Master Certificate of Competency
Advanced Master Certificate of Competency
ACCD REGULATED ACADEMIC QUALIFICATIONS
Master of Commercial Diplomacy
Doctor of Commercial Diplomacy
ACCD REGULATED ACCREDITATIONS
Associate Expert (AE)
Qualified Policy Advocate (QA)
Qualified Certified Diplomat (QCD)
Chartered Diplomat (C. Dipl)

DESIGNATORY LETTERS
ACDipl, MCD, MCDipl, M.Arb, DCD, DCDipl, FCDipl, QA, QCD, C. Dipl

AUA

AUA National Office
University of Manchester
Sackville Street Building
Manchester M60 1QD
Tel: 0161 275 2063
Fax: 0161 275 2036
E-mail: aua@aua.ac.uk
Website: www.aua.ac.uk

As a member-led organization with over 3,500 members, AUA promotes best practice in higher education management and exists to advance and promote professional recognition and development of those who work in higher and further education by encouraging and fostering sound methods of leadership, management and administration, through a range of professional development initiatives.

AUA members are individually and collectively committed to:

- the continuous development of their own and others' professional knowledge, skills and practices;
- actively championing equality of educational and professional opportunity;
- the advancement of higher education through the robust application of professional knowledge, skills and practices;
- the highest standards of fair, ethical and transparent professional behaviours.

AUA is at the forefront of professional development in higher education and has developed a sector-wide framework to support the development of professional services colleagues. Through continuing professional development, individuals, teams and institutions can foster skills and behaviours associated with the profession. AUA also holds the largest professional development annual conference in the UK higher education calendar.

MEMBERSHIP
Member (MAUA)
Accredited Member (AAUA)
Fellow (FAUA)
Honorary Member (FAUA)
Student Member (MAUA)

QUALIFICATION/EXAMINATIONS
Postgraduate Certificate in Professional Practice (PG Cert)
This programme is validated by The Open University and credits from the course can be used on a number of MA courses.

BRITISH INSTITUTE OF FACILITIES MANAGEMENT

Number One Building
The Causeway
Bishop's Stortford
Hertfordshire CM23 2ER
Tel: #44 (0)1279 712651
Fax: #44 (0)1279 712669
E-mail: qualifications@bifm.org.uk
Website: www.bifm.org.uk

The BIFM is the professional body for facilities management (FM). Founded in 1993, the Institute provides information, education, training and networking services for over 17,000 members – both individual professionals and employers. The BIFM is the professional body responsible for promoting excellence in facilities management for the benefit of practitioners, the economy and society.

MEMBERSHIP
Affiliate
Associate (ABIFM)
Member (MBIFM)
Certified Member (CBIFM)
Fellow (FBIFM)
Corporate Member

QUALIFICATION/EXAMINATIONS
BIFM Level 2 Certificate in Facilities Services
BIFM Level 2 Certificate in Facilities Services Principles
BIFM Level 3 Award in Facilities Management
BIFM Level 3 Certificate in Facilities Management
BIFM Level 3 Certificate in Facilities Management Practice
BIFM Level 3 Diploma in Facilities Management

BIFM Level 4 Award in Facilities Management
BIFM Level 4 Certificate in Facilities Management
BIFM Level 4 Diploma in Facilities Management
BIFM Level 5 Award in Facilities Management
BIFM Level 5 Certificate in Facilities Management
BIFM Level 5 Diploma in Facilities Management
BIFM Level 6 Award in Facilities Management
BIFM Level 6 Certificate in Facilities Management
BIFM Level 6 Extended Diploma in Facilities Management
BIFM Level 7 Certificate in Facilities Management
BIFM Level 7 Extended Diploma in Facilities Management

DESIGNATORY LETTERS
ABIFM, MBIFM, CBIFM, FBIFM

BUSINESS MANAGEMENT ASSOCIATION

2 Old College Court
29 Priory Street
Ware
Hertfordshire SG12 0DE
Tel: 0871 231 1689
E-mail: enquiries@businessmanagement.org.uk
Website: www.businessmanagement.org.uk

The Business Management Association is a professional body for business owners and managers. We promote the aims and interests of the small business sector internationally, provide information and advice to our members, encourage networking between members, and seek to provide members with advanced knowledge, skill and qualifications in several aspects of management.

MEMBERSHIP
Affiliate (AffBMA)
Associate (ABMA)
Member (MBMA)
Fellow (FBMA)

Companion (CBMA)
Certified Manager (CertMgr)
Certified Master of Management (CMMgt)
Certified Master of Business Administration (CMBA)
Certified Doctor of Business Administration (CDBA)

QUALIFICATION/EXAMINATIONS
Entrepreneurs Award (EA)
Diploma In Business Management (DipBMA)

DESIGNATORY LETTERS
AffBMA, ABMA, MBMA, FBMA, CBMA, CertMgr, CMMgt, CMBA, CDBA, MCBMA, FCBMA

DIPLOMATIC ACADEMY OF EUROPE AND THE ATLANTIC

Institution for the Training of Commercial Diplomats
ACCD Global Headquarters
PO Box 50561, Canary Wharf
Greater London E16 3WY

Diplomatic Academy of Europe and the Atlantic is an authoritative knowledge-based international professional diplomatic institution whose activities include advanced research, training and development, provision of postgraduate and post-qualification commercial diplomatic education, and contribution to responsible commercial diplomatic practice and service. It is a key independent extraterritorial diplomatic organization established for the advancement and development of greater knowledge and skills in commercial diplomacy. DAEA offers a complete portfolio of specialized mandatory postgraduate programmes on commercial diplomacy.

MEMBERSHIP
Fellow of the Diplomatic Academy (FDA)

QUALIFICATION/EXAMINATIONS
MANDATORY EXAMINATIONS
Qualified Policy Advocate
Qualified Certified Diplomat
Chartered Diplomat
QUALIFICATIONS
Advanced Certificate of Competency
Master Certificate of Competency
Master of Commercial Diplomacy

DESIGNATORY LETTERS
ACDipl, MCDipl, DCD, FCD

FACULTY OF PROFESSIONAL BUSINESS AND TECHNICAL MANAGEMENT

PO Box 93
Moreton-in-Marsh GL56 9WG
Tel: 01386 277973
E-mail: info@pbtm.org.uk
Website: www.pbtm.org.uk

FPBTM was founded in 1983 to forge the link between business and technology. We give professional recognition to the knowledge and skills of managers in business and technology, supporting lifelong learning to help members fulfil their career ambitions and develop their potential.

MEMBERSHIP
Student Member (SFPBTM)
Technician Member (TMFPBTM)
Associate Member (AMFPBTM)
Member (MFPBTM)
Fellow (FFPBTM)
Companion (CFPBTM)

INSTITUTE OF ADMINISTRATIVE MANAGEMENT

Coppice House
Halesfield 7
Telford
Shropshire TF7 4NA
Tel: 01952 585387
E-mail: info@instam.org
Website: www.instam.org

The IAM is the leading professional body and part of the IQ group who is a UK government-recognized awarding body for those involved in the administration and management of business.

MEMBERSHIP
Affiliate
Associate (AInstAM)
Member (MInstAM)
Fellow (FInstAM)
IAM Student
Non-IAM Student

QUALIFICATION/EXAMINATIONS
IQ IAM Level 2 Diploma in Team Leading
IQ IAM Level 2 Diploma in Business Administration
IQ IAM Level 3 Diploma in Business Administration
IQ IAM Level 3 Diploma in Management
IQ IAM Level 4 Award in Administration for Executive Assistants
IQ IAM Level 4 NVQ Diploma in Management
IQ IAM Level 4 Diploma in Business & Administrative Management
IQ IAM Level 4 NVQ Diploma in Business Administration
IQ IAM Level 5 Diploma in Business & Administrative Management
IQ IAM Level 5 NVQ Diploma in Management and Leadership
IQ IAM Level 6 Diploma in Business and Administrative Management
IQ IAM Level 6 Diploma in Business Management

IQ IAM Level 3 Certificate in Business and Administrative Management (VRQ)
IQ IAM Level 3 Certificate in Professional PA and Administration Skills (VRQ)
IQ IAM Level 4 Certificate in Office and Administration Management (VRQ)

DESIGNATORY LETTERS
AInstAM, MInstAM, FInstAM

INSTITUTE OF CONSULTING

4th Floor
2 Savoy Court
Strand
London WC2R 0EZ
Tel: 020 7497 0580
Fax: 020 7497 0463
E-mail: welcome@ibconsulting.org.uk
Website: www.iconsulting.org.uk

The Institute of Consulting was formed in 2007 by the merger of the Institute of Business Advisers and the Institute of Management Consultancy, and we are the professional body for business consultants and advisers. Our aim is to raise the standards of professional practice in support of better business performance.

MEMBERSHIP
Student
Affiliate
Associate (AIBC)
Member (MIBC)
Fellow (FIBC)
Certified Business Advisor (CBA)
Certified Management Consultant (CMC)
Practice Member (corporate membership)

QUALIFICATION/EXAMINATIONS
Award in Professional Consulting (Level 5) (QCF)
Certificate in Professional Consulting (Level 5) (QCF)
Diploma in Professional Consulting (Level 5) (QCF)
Award in Business Support (Level 5) (QCF)
Certificate in Business Support (Level 5) (QCF)
Diploma in Business Support (Level 5) (QCF)
Award in Professional Consulting (Level 7) (QCF)
Certificate in Professional Consulting (Level 7) (QCF)
Diploma in Professional Consulting (Level 7) (QCF)
Certified Management Consultant Award (CMC)
Certified Business Advisor Award (CBA)

DESIGNATORY LETTERS
AIBC, MIBC, FIBC

INSTITUTE OF DIRECTORS

116 Pall Mall
London SW1Y 5ED
Tel: 020 7766 2601
E-mail: professionaldev@iod.com
Website: www.iod.com/development

The IoD represents professional leaders, with individual members ranging from entrepreneurs of start-up companies to CEOs of multinational organizations. The Institute's principal objectives are to advance the interests of its members as company directors, and to provide them with business facilities and a variety of services.

MEMBERSHIP
Student
Associate Member

Member (MIoD)
Fellow (FIoD)
Chartered Director (C Dir)

QUALIFICATION/EXAMINATIONS
Certificate in Company Direction (CertIoD)
Diploma in Company Direction (DipIoD)
Chartered Director (C Dir)

DESIGNATORY LETTERS
MIoD, FIoD, C Dir

INSTITUTE OF LEADERSHIP & MANAGEMENT

Stowe House
Netherstowe
Lichfield
Staffordshire WS13 6TJ
Tel: 01543 266867
Fax: 01543 266893
E-mail: customer@i-l-m.com
Website: www.i-l-m.com

The ILM supports, develops and informs leaders and managers at every stage of their career. With our broad range of industry-leading qualifications, membership services and learning resources, the ILM provides flexible development solutions that can be blended to meet the specific needs of employers and learners.

MEMBERSHIP
Studying Member
Professional Member

QUALIFICATION/EXAMINATIONS
Management
Principles of Team Leading including Foundation Award in Management Practice (Level 2)
Award, Certificate in Effective Team Member Skills (Level 2)
Award, Certificate in Leadership and Team Skills (Level 2)
NVQ Certificate in Team Leading (Level 2)

Certificate in Team Leading (Level 2)
NVQ Certificate in Management (Level 3)
Certificate in Effective Management (Level 3)
Certificate in Principles of Leadership and Management (Level 3)
Award, Certificate and Diploma in Leadership and Management (Level 4)
Diploma in Principles of Leadership and Management (Level 5)
NVQ Diploma in Management (Level 5)
Award in Management (Level 6)
NVQ Diploma in Management (Level 7)
Diploma in Strategic Leadership and Executive Management (Level 7)
Award, Certificate and Diploma in Executive Management (Level 7)
Leadership
Certificate in Leadership (Level 3)
Award in Leadership (Level 4)
Award, Certificate and Diploma in Strategic

Leadership (Level 7)

Leadership and Management

Award, Certificate and Diploma in Leadership and Management (Level 3)

Award, Certificate and Diploma in Leadership and Management (Level 5)

Coaching and Mentoring

Certificate in Coaching and Mentoring (Level 3)

Certificate and Diploma in Coaching and Mentoring (Level 5)

Certificate and Diploma in Coaching Supervision (Level 7)

Certificate and Diploma in Executive Coaching and Leadership Mentoring (Level 7)

Specialist Management Qualifications

Environmental Management

Facilities Management

Equality and Diversity

Managing Volunteers

Sales Management

Waste Management

Business and Enterprise

Certificate in Enterprise (Level 2)

Award and Certificate in Enterprise and Entrepreneurship (Level 3)

Award in Management (Level 5)

Certificate and Diploma in Social Enterprise Support (Level 5)

Specialist Management Qualifications

Operational management

Service improvement

Waste management

Equality and diversity

Volunteer management

Management consultancy

Staff and organisational development

Quality improvement

Scottish Vocational Qualifications (SVQs)

SVQ 2 in Team Leading (Scottish Level 5)

SVQ 3 in Management (Scottish Level 7)

SVQ 4 in Management (Scottish Level 9)

SVQ 5 in Management (Scottish Level 11)

INSTITUTE OF MANAGEMENT SERVICES

Brooke House
24 Dam Street
Lichfield
Staffordshire WS13 6AA
Tel: 01543 266909
Fax: 01543 257848
E-mail: admin@ims-productivity.com
Website: www.ims-productivity.com

QUALIFICATION/EXAMINATIONS
IMS Certificate

DESIGNATORY LETTERS
AMS, MMS, FMS

INSTITUTE OF VALUE MANAGEMENT

PO Box 101
Ledbury
Herefordshire HR8 9JW
Tel: 01531 631444
E-mail: secretary@ivm.org.uk
Website: www.ivm.org.uk

The Institute aims to establish Value Management as an all-encompassing strategy for achieving value in every sector of the economy and to provide support in the innovative use of value management techniques.

MEMBERSHIP
Corporate – This grade is for organizations that use or promote value management and want to make a corporate statement to that effect. A Corporate Member may nominate up to 10 members of staff

who will have full voting rights. Corporate members may use the designatory letters AIVM (or MIVM if they meet the requirements and make a successful application).

Student – This grade is for students studying full time for a UK qualification. Student members are not eligible to use any designatory letters.

Trainee – This grade is for individuals who have completed either an IVM accredited Foundation Course in Value Management in the previous 6 months or a Management of Value (MoV) Foundation Course in the previous 6 months. Trainee membership is limited to two years. Trainee Members are not eligible to use designatory letters.

Associate – This grade is open to individuals who have a demonstrable interest in Value Management and who either promote, use or are associated with Value Management. Associate Members may use the designatory letters AIVM.

Member – This grade is open to individuals who have considerable sector knowledge and skills in their profession and who meet at least one of the following requirements:
- Have successfully completed an IVM accredited VM2 Course
- Hold a QVA or CVA qualification
- Have successfully completed a Management of Value (MoV) Practitioner course
- Have a minimum of 3 years' experience working in a Value Management environment
- Hold a relevant professional qualification in Lean, Benefits or Project Management
Members may use the post nominals MIVM

Fellow – Fellowship of the Institute of Value Management is the most senior grade available and is reserved for those who have reached the highest echelons in their career. It is open to those who meet at least one of the following requirements:
- Have demonstrated significant experience or contribution to the field of Value Management
- Hold a current PVM qualification

Fellows may use the post nominals FIVM

QUALIFICATION/EXAMINATIONS
IVM Certification Board – The IVM's Certification Board is an independent body whose role is to implement and control the certification and training policies developed by the IVM and the European Governing Board (EGB), representing all the European value associations.

Certification Levels
There are three levels of recognised certification based on experience and knowledge:
- Qualified Value Associate (QVA) – (Europe)
- Professional in Value Management (PVM) – (Europe). This qualification signals competence to lead value studies in a variety of environments and contribute to the development of VM strategies.
- Trainer in Value Management (TVM) – (Europe). In order to develop competence to train to an appropriate standard, the qualification of Trainer in Value Management (TVM) has been introduced. This qualification is only available for PVMs with at least 2 years experience, who have completed an approved train the trainer course.

DESIGNATORY LETTERS
AIVM, MIVM, FIVM, HFIVM

INTERNATIONAL PROFESSIONAL MANAGERS ASSOCIATION

5 Starnes Court
Union Street
Maidstone
Kent ME14 1EB
Tel: 01622 672867
Fax: 01622 755149
E-mail: admin@ipma.co.uk
Website: www.ipma.co.uk

The IPMA is an international examining, licensing and regulatory professional body, which, through its qualifying examinations, enables practising managers to participate in and be part of the process of improving managerial performance and effectiveness in all areas of business, industry and public administration.

MEMBERSHIP
Student Member
Graduate Member (GRD PMA)
Licentiate Member (LMPMA)
Certified Associate (AMPMA)
Certified Member (MPMA)
Certified Fellow (FPMA)

QUALIFICATION/EXAMINATIONS
Certified International Professional Manager (CIPM) examinations
Foundation: Economics, Legal Environment of Business, Information Communication and Technology, Business Management, Statistical Methods for Business, Principles of Finance

Intermediate: Business Marketing, Entrepreneurship, Corporate Law, Management Accounting, Advanced Management Practice, Managing People
Professional Level 1: Human Resource Management, Management Decision Making, Organisational Behaviour, Information Systems Management, Operations Management
Professional Level 2: Business Policy and Strategic Management, Corporate Finance and Risk Management, Organisation Change and Development, Multinational Business Management, Case Study and a Project

DESIGNATORY LETTERS
GRD PMA, LMPMA, AMPMA, MPMA, FPMA, CIPM

THE ASSOCIATION OF BUSINESS EXECUTIVES

5th Floor, CI Tower
St Georges Square
New Malden
Surrey KT3 4TE
Tel: 020 8329 2930
Fax: 020 8329 2945
E-mail: info@abeuk.com
Website: www.abeuk.com

ABE is a professional membership body and examination board. We develop business and management qualifications at Levels 4, 5, 6 & 7 on the QCF framework. ABE's range of OFQUAL accredited qualifications provide progression routes to degree and Master's programmes worldwide.

MEMBERSHIP
Affiliate Member
Student Member
Associate Member (AMABE)
Member (MABE)
Fellow (FABE)

QUALIFICATION/EXAMINATIONS
Diploma Levels 4, 5 and 6 in:
Business Management
Management of Information Systems (Pathway)
Financial Management (Pathway)
Human Resource Management
Marketing Management
Travel, Tourism and Hospitality Management
Diploma in Business Development (Level 7)
Diploma in Business Start-Up and Entrepreneurship (Level 4)

DESIGNATORY LETTERS
AMABE, MABE, FABE

THE CAMBRIDGE ACADEMY OF MANAGEMENT

Royal Arsenal Gatehouse
Beresford Square
Woolwich
London SE18 6AR
Tel: 0844 284 7190
E-mail: admin@camuk.org
Website: www.camuk.org.uk

The Cambridge Academy of Management (CAM) is a professional, autonomous, not-for-profit institution established to foster the concept of UK management education made available to all internationally. CAM is built on the foundation of promoting state-of-the-art knowledge and expertise in all facets of management education, training and development for the global educational arena.

MEMBERSHIP
Associate Category (ACAM)
Member Category (MCAM)
Fellowship Category (FCAM)

QUALIFICATION/EXAMINATIONS
All programmes offered by Cambridge Academy of Management are accredited by Quality Assurance Commission UK. Programmes offered:
CAM International Foundation Diploma
CAM International Certificate in Restaurant & Catering Management
CAM International Diploma in Business Management
CAM International Diploma in Business (Restaurant & Catering Management)
CAM International Diploma in Business (Tourism Management)
CAM International Advanced Diploma in Business Management
CAM International Advanced Diploma in Business (Restaurant & Catering Management)
CAM International Advanced Diploma in Business (Tourism Management)
CAM International Postgraduate Diploma in Hospitality Management
CAM International Postgraduate Diploma in Business
CAM International Postgraduate Diploma in Business with Specialization in: Marketing, Finance, Human Resource

THE CHARTERED MANAGEMENT INSTITUTE

Customer Service Department
Management House
Cottingham Road
Corby
Northants NN17 1TT
Tel: 01536 204222
Fax: 01536 201651
E-mail: enquiries@managers.org.uk
Website: www.managers.org.uk

CMI is the only chartered professional body in the UK dedicated to promoting the highest standards of management and leadership excellence. With a member community of over 130,000, CMI gives managers and leaders, and their organisations, the skills they need to improve their performance and create an impact.

MEMBERSHIP
Affiliate
Associate (ACMI)
Member (MCMI)
Fellow (FCMI)
Chartered Member (CMgr MCMI)
Chartered Fellow (CMgr FCMI)
Companion (CCMI)

The breadth and depth of our management and leadership qualification portfolio is unmatched. We have over 80 individual qualifications ranging from team leading, strategic management to coaching and mentoring to name a few.

To support your development we have a wide range of online and hardcopy resources and materials, including ManagementDirect and Pathways Workbooks. With CMI Membership you can also enjoy benefits of a Career Development Centre, mentoring and professional development.

We have a network of more than 500 Centres delivering our qualifications so you can always find somewhere to study that's convenient for you.

DESIGNATORY LETTERS
ACMI, MCMI, FCMI, CMgr MCMI, CMgr FCMI, CCMI

THE INSTITUTE OF COMMERCIAL MANAGEMENT

ICM House
Yeoman Road
Ringwood
Hampshire BH24 3FA
Tel: 01202 490555
E-mail: info@icm.education
Website: www.icm.education

Established in 1975, the Institute is the leading professional body for Commercial and Business Development Managers. It provides examining and assessment services for those undertaking business and management studies and offers in excess of 200 programmes. The Institute works with public and private sector education and training providers in more than 100 countries.

MEMBERSHIP
Student Membership

QUALIFICATION/EXAMINATIONS
ICM Awards cover the following areas: Accounting & Finance; Business Studies; Commercial Management; Hospitality Management; Human Resource Development; Journalism; Legal Studies; Management Studies; Maritime Management; Marketing Management; Sales Management; Travel & Tourism

THE INSTITUTE OF MANAGEMENT SPECIALISTS

PO Box 93
Moreton-in-Marsh GL56 9WG
Tel: 01386 277973
E-mail: info@instituteofmanagementspecialists.org.uk
Website: www.instituteofmanagementspecialists.org.uk

The Institute of Management Specialists was founded in 1971 to give professional recognition to the knowledge and skills of managers and specialists. The Institute encourages management excellence and specialist expertise, and supports lifelong learning to help members fulfil their career ambitions.

Specialised Manager Awards are available in a range of specialised areas and IMS offers a CPD (Continuous Professional Development) programme leading to Certified Specialist Manager status.

MEMBERSHIP
Student Member (StudIMS)

Associate Member (AMIMS)
Member (MIMS)
Fellow (FIMS)
Companion (CompIMS)

QUALIFICATION/EXAMINATIONS
Diploma of Management
Executive Diploma in Business Leadership and Management
Professional Diploma in Project Management Development

THE SOCIETY OF BUSINESS PRACTITIONERS

PO Box 11
Sandbach
Cheshire CW11 3GE
Tel: 01270 526339
Fax: 01270 526339
E-mail: info@mamsasbp.org.uk
Website: www.mamsasbp.org.uk

SBP is an International Examination Board founded in 1956 by experienced educationalists and executives to fulfil a need to set standards in business practice achieved by examinations/assessments. Inexperienced and mature students should be able to follow careers in further education and/or be proficient in employment and receive the benefits of membership.

MEMBERSHIP
Student (StuSBP)
Member (MSBP)
Certified Professional Manager (CPMSBP)
Honorary Fellow
Professional Memberships *(Senior Professional Qualifications)*
Associateship (ASBP)
Licentiateship (LSBP)
Graduateship (GSBP)
Fellowship (FSBP)
These are certified competency-based Membership Awards open to persons occupied in business practice who are considered suitable by the Membership Committee.
CPD programmes are also offered for the Asia region.

QUALIFICATION/EXAMINATIONS
Diploma in Business Administration
Advanced Diploma in Business Administration
PGDip in Business Administration
PGDip in International Marketing
Diploma in Computer Studies
Advanced Diploma in Computer Studies
GradDip in IT & E-Commerce
GradDip in Entrepreneurship
Advanced Diploma in Accounting
Diploma & Advanced Diploma in Marketing Management (Joint Award with the Managing & Marketing Sales Association)

DESIGNATORY LETTERS
StuSBP, MSBP, CPMSBP, ASBP, LSBP, GSBP, FSBP

MANUFACTURING
Membership of Professional Institutions and Associations

THE INSTITUTE OF MANUFACTURING

PO Box 93
Moreton-in-Marsh GL56 9WG
Tel: 01386 277973
E-mail: info@instituteofmanufacturing.org.uk
Website: www.instituteofmanufacturing.org.uk

The Institute of Manufacturing was founded in 1978 to give professional recognition to the knowledge and skills of people in all aspects of manufacturing. The Institute supports lifelong learning to help members fulfil their career ambitions and develop their potential.

MEMBERSHIP
Student Member (StudIManf)
Associate Member (AMIManf)
Member (MIManf)
Fellow (FIManf)
Companion (CompIManf)

QUALIFICATION/EXAMINATIONS
Associate Diploma in Manufacturing
Executive Diploma in Manufacturing
Certified Manufacturing Practitioner

Certificate in Public Speaking
Certificate in Negotiation
Certificate of Professional Competence

MARKETING AND SALES
Membership of Professional Institutions and Associations

LONDON CENTRE OF MARKETING

Buckingham House West
Stanmore
London HA7 4EB
Tel: 020 8385 7766
Fax: 020 8385 7755
E-mail: info@lcmuk.com
Website: www.lcmuk.com

The London Centre of Marketing is an Ofqual accredited, non-political, Awarding Organisation based in London, which exists with the sole aim of providing internationally recognised professional qualifications in marketing and marketing management.

MEMBERSHIP
We offer three types of memberships:
1. Associate (ALCM)
2. Member (MLCM)
3. Fellow (FLCM)

QUALIFICATION/EXAMINATIONS
Diploma, Higher Diploma, Professional Diploma, Graduate Diploma and Postgraduate Dipolma in:
Business Management & Marketing
Human Resource Development & Marketing
Sales & Marketing Management
Travel & Tourism Marketing
Public Relations & Marketing
Entrepreneurship & Marketing

DESIGNATORY LETTERS
ALCM/MLCM/FLCM

MANAGING AND MARKETING SALES ASSOCIATION EXAMINATION BOARD

PO Box 11
Sandbach
Cheshire CW11 3GE
Tel: 01270 526339
Fax: 01270 526339
E-mail: info@mamsasbp.org.uk
Website: www.mamsasbp.org.uk

MAMSA is an international Examination Board offering qualifications in Sales, Marketing and Management and its senior specialist Diploma in Marketing Strategy. The importance of 'Customer Service' is emphasized throughout all the programmes.

MEMBERSHIP
Graduate (GradMAMSA)
Graduate Affiliate (GradAfMAMSA)
Professional (MMAMSA)
Fellow (FMAMSA)

QUALIFICATION/EXAMINATIONS
Standard Diploma in Salesmanship
Certificate in Sales Marketing
Higher Diploma in Marketing
Advanced Diploma in Sales Management
Certificate in Marketing Strategy
Diploma in Marketing Strategy & Management
(Hypothesis/Thesis)

Diploma in Sales and Marketing Practices (Joint
Award with the Society of Business Practitioners)
A CPD programme is also offered

DESIGNATORY LETTERS
GradMAMSA, GradAfMAMSA, MMAMSA,
FMAMSA

MRS (THE MARKET RESEARCH SOCIETY)

The Old Trading House
15 Northburgh Street
London EC1V 0JR
Tel: 020 7490 4911
Fax: 020 7490 0608
E-mail: profdevelopment@mrs.org.uk
Website: www.mrs.org.uk

With members in more than 50 countries, MRS is the world's leading authority on research and business intelligence. For those who need, use, generate or interpret the evidence essential to making good decisions for commercial and public policy. MRS is an awarding body for vocationally related qualifications in research.

MEMBERSHIP
Student Member
Member (MMRS)
Certified Member (CMRS)

Fellow (FMRS)
Honorary Fellow (Hon. FMRS)

QUALIFICATION/EXAMINATIONS
MRS Certificate in Market and Social Research
MRS Certificate in Interviewing Skills
MRS Advanced Certificate in Market and Social Research Practice
MRS Diploma in Market and Social Research Practice

DESIGNATORY LETTERS
MMRS, CMRS, FMRS, Hon. FMRS

THE CHARTERED INSTITUTE OF MARKETING

Moor Hall
Maidenhead
Berkshire SL6 9QH
Tel: 01628 427120
Fax: 01628 427158
E-mail: qualifications@cim.co.uk
Website: www.cim.co.uk/learningzone

The Chartered Institute of Marketing is the leading international professional marketing body, with 47,000 members worldwide. We aim to improve the skills of marketing practitioners, enabling them to deliver exceptional results for their organization. Qualifications from Introductory to Chartered postgraduate level are offered to anyone wanting to develop their career in marketing.

MEMBERSHIP
Affiliate (Studying/Professional)
Associate (ACIM)
Member (MCIM)
Fellow (FCIM)
Chartered Marketer

QUALIFICATION/EXAMINATIONS
Professional Certificate in Marketing

Professional Diploma in Marketing
Chartered Postgraduate Diploma in Marketing
Diploma in Marketing Communications
Diploma in Digital Marketing
Professional Diploma in Marketing for Business Services and Solutions
Diploma in Digital Marketing (Mobile)
Diploma in Digital Marketing (Metrics and Analytics)
Diploma in Digital Marketing (Media and Branding)

Certificate in Professional Sales Practice
Advanced Certificate in Professional Sales Management Practice
Advanced Certificate in Account Management Practice
Intensive Diploma on Strategic Sales Practice

DESIGNATORY LETTERS
ACIM, MCIM, FCIM

THE INSTITUTE OF DIRECT AND DIGITAL MARKETING

1 Park Road
Teddington
Middlesex TW11 0AR
Tel: 020 8164 0277
E-mail: enquiries@theidm.com
Website: www.theidm.com

The Institute of Direct and Digital Marketing is the UK's only government-approved Institute for the professional development of direct and digital marketers, offering a broad range of practitioner-taught training courses and professional marketing qualifications. It is also a membership organisation, providing status, knowledge and networking opportunities to senior marketers.

MEMBERSHIP
Affiliate Member
Associate Member
Member
Fellow
Corporate Member

QUALIFICATION/EXAMINATIONS
MSc in Digital Marketing

MSc in Marketing Management
Postgraduate Diploma in Digital Marketing
Postgraduate Diploma in Digital Marketing with B2B
Postgraduate Diploma in Direct and Digital Marketing
Postgraduate Diploma in Direct and Digital Marketing with B2B
Professional Diploma in Digital Marketing
Professional Diploma in Direct and Digital Marketing
Certificate in Social Media
Certificate in Email Marketing
Certificate in Search Marketing
Award in Digital Copywriting
Award in Data Management
Award in Direct and Digital Marketing
Award in Mobile Marketing

THE INSTITUTE OF SALES AND MARKETING MANAGEMENT (ISMM)

Basepoint Business & Innovation Centre
Unit 22A, 110 Butterfield
Great Marlings
Luton
Bedfordshire LU2 8DL
Tel: 01582 840001
E-mail: education@ismm.co.uk
Website: www.ismm.co.uk

Founded in 1911, the ISMM is the worldwide representative body for sales people. To help members improve their skills set the ISMM provide qualifications, approved by Ofqual, the UK Government's regulatory body for education. Written by qualified and experienced sales professionals they cover the salesperson's career right up to sales director level.

MEMBERSHIP
Affiliate
Associate (AInstSMM)
Member (MInstSMM)
Fellow (FInstSMM)
Companion (CInstSMM)

QUALIFICATION/EXAMINATIONS
Level 1 Award in Selling Lawfully and Ethically
Level 1 Award in Understanding the Sales Cycle
Level 1 Award in Understanding Marketing
Level 1 Award in Communication Skills in Sales
Level 1 Award in Sales and Marketing
Level 2 Award in Understanding Laws and Ethics of Selling
Level 2 Award in Understanding Marketing
Level 2 Award in Understanding Buyer Behaviour
Level 2 Award in Sales Targets
Level 2 Award in Selling to Customers
Level 2 Award in Understanding Selling to Customers
Level 2 Award in Telesales
Level 2 Certificate in Sales and Marketing
Level 3 Award in Preparing and Delivering a Sales Presentation
Level 3 Award in Handling Objections, Negotiating and Closing Deals
Level 3 Award in Understanding Influences on Buyer Behaviour
Level 3 Award in Understanding customer segmentation and profiling

Level 3 Award in Understanding sales and marketing in organisations
Level 3 Award in Using market information for sales
Level 3 Award in Time and territory management for sales people
Level 3 Award in Planning for professional development
Level 3 Award in Prospecting for new business
Level 3 Award in Sales pipeline management
Level 3 Certificate in Sales and Marketing
Level 3 Diploma in Sales and Marketing
Level 4 Award in Managing responsible selling
Level 4 Award in Understanding segmentation, targeting and positioning
Level 4 Award in Managing a sales team
Level 4 Award in Operational sales planning
Level 4 Award in Sales negotiations
Level 4 Award in Analysing the marketing environment
Level 4 Award in Finance for sales managers
Level 4 Award in Writing and delivering a sales proposal
Level 4 Certificate in Sales and Marketing Management
Level 4 Diploma in Sales and Marketing Management
Level 5 Award in Understanding and developing customer accounts
Level 5 Award in Understanding the integrated functions of sales and marketing
Level 5 Award in Sales forecasts and target setting
Level 5 Award in Leading a team
Level 5 Award in Motivation and compensation for sales teams
Level 5 Award in Coaching and mentoring
Level 5 Award in Designing, planning and managing sales territories
Level 5 Award in Analysing the financial potential and performance of customer accounts
Level 5 Award in Relationship management for account managers

Level 5 Award in Bid and tender management for account managers
Level 5 Award in Developing a product portfolio
Level 5 Certificate in Sales and Account Management
Level 5 Diploma in Sales and Account Management
Level 6 Award in Leading a culture for responsible selling
Level 6 Award in Leadership and management in sales
Level 6 Award in Planning and implementing sales and marketing strategy
Level 6 Award in Salesforce organisation

Level 6 Award in Sales forecasting and budgeting
Level 6 Award in Developing strategic relationships with major customers
Level 6 Award in Managing sales-related change
Level 6 Award in Developing and using customer insight
Level 6 Certificate in Strategic Sales Management
Level 6 Diploma in Strategic Sales Management

DESIGNATORY LETTERS
AInstSMM, MInstSMM, FInstSMM

MARTIAL ARTS
Membership of Professional Institutions and Associations

INSTITUTE OF MARTIAL ARTS AND SCIENCES

1 Henrietta Street
Bolton
Lancashire BL3 4HL
Tel: 07792 214993
E-mail: admin@instituteofmartialartsandsciences.com
Website: www.instituteofmartialartsandsciences.com

The IMAS is a professional institute for martial artists, dedicated to education and research in the martial arts and offering memberships, accredited training and qualifications, and university degrees in martial arts studies. IMAS publishes a quarterly, peer reviewed journal, and an annual yearbook containing its research articles.

MEMBERSHIP
Affiliate
Student
Associate (AIMAS)
Member (MIMAS)
Fellow (FIMAS)

QUALIFICATION/EXAMINATIONS
Accredited instructor training in partnership with the Teaching and Learning Academy
Specialist courses for police/security professionals
Higher Educational opportunities include: Graduate of the Institute of Martial Arts and Sciences (Grad. IMAS); BA(Hons); Masters by Research (MRes); Doctoral studies (PhD) available through our associated university in the UK

DESIGNATORY LETTERS
Grad.IMAS, BA(Hons), MRes, PhD

MASSAGE AND ALLIED THERAPIES
Membership of Professional Institutions and Associations

BRITISH MEDICAL ACUPUNCTURE SOCIETY

BMAS House
3 Winnington Court
Winnington Street
Northwich
Cheshire CW8 1AQ
Tel: 01606 786782
Fax: 01606 786783
E-mail: admin@medical-acupuncture.co.uk
Website: www.medical-acupuncture.co.uk

The BMAS was formed in 1980 as an association of medical practitioners interested in acupuncture and we now have a membership of more than 2,500 registered doctors and allied health professionals who practise acupuncture alongside more conventional techniques. We believe that acupuncture has an important role to play in healthcare and promote its use as a therapy following orthodox medical diagnosis by suitably trained practitioners. We run training programmes in the UK for doctors, dentists and other healthcare professionals.

MEMBERSHIP
Member
Accredited Member
Dental/Veterinary Member
Retired Member
Affiliated
Overseas Member

QUALIFICATION/EXAMINATIONS
Certificate of Basic Competence (CoBC)
Diploma of Medical Acupuncture (DipMedAc)

LCSP REGISTER OF REMEDIAL MASSEURS AND MANIPULATIVE THERAPISTS

38A High Street
Lowestoft
Suffolk NR32 1HY
Tel: 01502 563344
Fax: 01502 582220
E-mail: admin@lcsp.uk.com
Website: www.lcsp.uk.com

The Register accepts practitioners who currently work in Massage, Sports / Remedial Massage or Manipulative Therapy. Applicants must have completed a course of education at an establishment whose training meets or exceeds the National Occupational Standards. The Register offers heavily discounted comprehensive medical malpractice insurance, business support, regular communications and CPD.

MEMBERSHIP
Student Member
Associate Member (LCSP (Assoc))
Full Member (LCSP (Phys))
Affiliate
Fellow (FLCSP)
Honorary Member

DESIGNATORY LETTERS
LCSP (Assoc), LCSP (Phys), FLCSP

NORTHERN INSTITUTE OF MASSAGE LTD

14–16 St Mary's Place
Bury
Greater Manchester BL9 0DZ
Tel: 0161 797 1800
E-mail: information@nim.co.uk
Website: www.nim.co.uk

The NIM was founded in 1924 and offers professional training in Remedial Massage, Advanced Remedial Massage, and Manipulative Therapy. We also offer a number of CPD seminars and short courses to supplement our main training programme. Research is carried out mostly by therapists on patients from their own clinics or by students completing university courses.

QUALIFICATION/EXAMINATIONS
Advanced Remedial Massage Diploma
Manipulative Therapy Diploma

SOCIETY OF HOMEOPATHS

11 Brookfield Duncan Close
Moulton Park
Northampton NN3 6WL
Tel: 01604 817890
Fax: 01604 648848
E-mail: info@homeopathy-soh.org
Website: www.homeopathy-soh.org

The Society of Homeopaths was established in 1978 and is now the largest organization registering professional homeopaths in Europe. Our vision is 'homeopathy for all' and we aim to achieve this both by supporting our members and by raising the profile of homeopathy in general.

MEMBERSHIP
Subscriber
Student Member
Student Clinical Member
Registered Member (RSHom)

DESIGNATORY LETTERS
RSHom

MATHEMATICS
Membership of Professional Institutions and Associations

EDINBURGH MATHEMATICAL SOCIETY

School of Mathematics, Edinburgh University
James Clerk Maxwell Building
Mayfield Road
Edinburgh EH9 3JZ
Tel: 01316 505060
Fax: 01316 506553
E-mail: queries@maths.ed.ac.uk
Website: www.maths.ed.ac.uk

The EMS, founded in 1883, is the principal mathematical society for the academic community in Scotland as well as mathematicians in industry and commerce. We organize meetings, publish a journal and support mathematical activities through various funds.

MEMBERSHIP
Ordinary Member
Reciprocal Member
Honorary Member

THE INSTITUTE OF MATHEMATICS AND ITS APPLICATIONS

Catherine Richards House
16 Nelson Street
Southend-on-Sea
Essex SS1 1EF
Tel: 01702 354020
Fax: 01702 354111
E-mail: post@ima.org.uk
Website: www.ima.org.uk

The IMA, founded in 1964, is the UK's learned society for mathematics and its applications. We promote mathematical research, education and careers, and the use of mathematics in business, industry and commerce. In 1990 the Institute was incorporated by Royal Charter and subsequently granted the right to award the status of Chartered Mathematician, Chartered Scientist and Chartered Mathematics Teacher.

MEMBERSHIP
Student

Affiliate
Associate Member (AMIMA)
Member (MIMA)
Fellow (FIMA)
Chartered Mathematician (CMath)
Chartered Mathematics Teacher (CMathTeach)
Chartered Scientist (CSci)

DESIGNATORY LETTERS
AMIMA, MIMA, FIMA, CMath, CMathTeach, CSci

THE MATHEMATICAL ASSOCIATION

259 London Road
Leicester LE2 3BE
Tel: 01162 210013
Fax: 01162 122835
E-mail: office@m-a.org.uk
Website: www.m-a.org.uk

The MA dates from 1871 and supports and improves the teaching and learning of mathematics and its applications, and provides opportunities for communication and collaboration between teachers and students of mathematics. We publish a number of books, journals and magazines, hold an annual conference and regional meetings, and organize CPD events for our members. We also confer with government re the curriculum and assessment.

MEMBERSHIP
Student Member
Personal Member
Institutional Member

MEDICAL HERBALISM
Membership of Professional Institutions and Associations

THE NATIONAL INSTITUTE OF MEDICAL HERBALISTS

Clover House
James Court
South Street
Exeter
Devon EX1 1EE
Tel: 01392 426022
Fax: 01392 498963
E-mail: info@nimh.org.uk
Website: www.nimh.org.uk

The NIMH is the UK's leading professional organization of qualified medical herbal practitioners. We maintain high standards of practice and patient care, and work to promote the benefits of western herbal medicine. We provide codes of conduct, ethics and practice, and represent the profession, patients and the public through participation in external processes.

MEMBERSHIP
Member (MNIMH) Membership is open to graduates holding a BSc(Hons) degree in Herbal Medicine from Lincoln College or University of Westminster. There is also a student affiliate membership scheme for those who are undergraduates of either of the above schools.

QUALIFICATION/EXAMINATIONS
The NIMH has historically managed its own accreditation process, with universities currently offering a BSc(Hons) degree in Herbal Medicine at Lincoln College and University of Westminster.
From 2011 accreditation of the above courses transferred to The European Herbal and Traditional Medicine Practitioners Association (EHTPA), as an umbrella body of Professional Herbal Medicine Associations, although graduates will continue to be eligible to apply for NIMH membership.

DESIGNATORY LETTERS
MNIMH, FNIMH

MEDICAL SECRETARIES
Membership of Professional Institutions and Associations

ASSOCIATION OF MEDICAL SECRETARIES, PRACTICE MANAGERS, ADMINISTRATORS AND RECEPTIONISTS

Tavistock House North
Tavistock Square
London WC1H 9LN
Tel: 020 7387 6005
Fax: 020 7388 2648
E-mail: info@amspar.co.uk
Website: www.amspar.com

AMSPAR is a professional membership and educational organization. We work with City & Guilds to provide non-clinical qualifications for health administration within the UK qualification frameworks. We aim to promote quality and coherence in the delivery of qualifications, and encourage and support standards of excellence in the pursuit of continuous professional development and lifelong learning.

MEMBERSHIP
Associate Member (AAMS)
Member (MAMS)
Fellow (FAMS)

QUALIFICATION/EXAMINATIONS
The Level 5 Diploma in Primary Care & Health Management
The Level 5 Certificate in Primary Care & Health Management
The Level 3 Diploma for Medical Secretaries
The Level 3 Certificate in Medical Administration
The Level 3 Certificate in Medical Terminology
The Level 3 Award in Legal Aspects of Medical Administration
The Level 3 Award in Medical Principles for the Administrator
The Level 3 Award in Medical Word Processing
The Level 3 Award in Production of Medical Documents from Recorded Speech
The Level 2 Diploma in Medical Administration
The Level 2 Certificate in Medical Administration
The Level 2 Award in Medical Terminology
The Level 2 Award in Working in the NHS
The Level 2 Award in Medical Word Processing
The Level 2 Award in Production of Medical Documents from Recorded Speech
The Level 3 Advanced Technical Diploma in Medical Administration
The Level 2 Technical Certificate in Medical Administrative Support

DESIGNATORY LETTERS
AAMS, MAMS, FAMS

MEDICINE

A student who wishes to qualify as a doctor in the UK must first obtain a primary qualification. Medical students in the UK typically study for five years to receive their medical degrees or for four years on a graduate-entry accelerated course. There are also courses offered for candidates with non-science subjects to offer at A level (or equivalent) that include the pre-medical year. The pre-medical year is a preliminary course in chemistry, physics and biology and lasts normally 30 weeks. Each medical school sets its own entry requirements, and may require applicants to complete clinical aptitude tests.

After graduation, a trainee doctor will enter the two-year Foundation Programme. There is a national application process for entry to the F1 year, but trainees successfully completing this year move into F2 without having to compete for a place. The trainee is provisionally registered with a licence to practise with the General Medical Council (GMC) while completing the first year and full registration is awarded upon completion of year one.

The F1 year aims to provide experience in a broad range of settings prior to full GMC registration. Regular work-based assessments take place, and trainees must maintain a national learning portfolio in order to progress.

The F2 year usually consists of four varied three-month placements giving trainees the opportunity to try a number of different specialities before making a decision about which specialty training programme

they would like to pursue. More information can be found at www.nhscareers.nhs.uk

The GMC is charged with the responsibility under the Medical Act 1983 of keeping a register of all duly qualified medical practitioners. General Medical Council, Regent's Place, 350 Euston Road, London NW1 3JN; Tel: 0161 923 6602; e-mail: gmc@gmc-uk. org; website: www.gmc-uk.org. For information on how to apply to join the register, see www.gmc-uk. org/doctors/applications.asp

PRIMARY QUALIFICATIONS

The GMC decides which universities are entitled to issue medical degrees. Qualifying examinations are examinations held for the granting of one or more primary medical qualifications (PMQs) by any one of the bodies or combinations of bodies in the United

Kingdom that are included in a list maintained by the GMC and published on the GMC's website (www. gmc-uk.org/education/undergraduate/awarding_bodies.asp).

LICENSING AND REVALIDATION

Doctors must be registered with a licence to practise with the General Medical Council (GMC) and hold a licence to practise medicine in the UK. The licence to practise gives a doctor the legal authority to undertake certain activities in the UK, for example prescribing, signing death or cremation certificates and holding certain medical posts (such as working as a doctor in the NHS). Any person whose fitness to practise is not impaired and who a) holds one or more primary United Kingdom qualifications and has satisfactorily completed an acceptable programme for provisionally registered doctors; or b) being a national of any relevant European State, holds one or more primary European qualifications,

is entitled to be registered as a fully registered medical practitioner. Doctors who do not work in the UK, or who do not undertake any activities for which a licence is required, do not need to hold a licence to practise and can continue to be registered without a licence.

Revalidation ensures that all licensed doctors demonstrate on an ongoing basis that they are up to date and fit to practise in their chosen field and able to provide a good level of care. Licensed doctors have to revalidate, usually every five years, by having regular appraisals based on the GMC's core guidance for doctors, *Good Medical Practice*.

Membership of Professional Institutions and Associations

COLLEGE OF OPERATING DEPARTMENT PRACTITIONERS

130 Euston Road
London NW1 2AY
Tel: 0870 121 5414
E-mail: office@codp.org
Website: www.codp.org.uk

The CODP is the professional body for Operating Department Practitioners. It is a membership, not-for-profit organization that sets standards of education for the pre-registration aspect of the profession and promotes the enhancement of knowledge and skills,

in the context of the multidisciplinary team, through regional, national and international networks.

MEMBERSHIP
Student Member
Association Member
Full College Member

ROYAL COLLEGE OF GENERAL PRACTITIONERS

30 Euston Square
London NW1 2FB
Tel: 020 3188 7400
Fax: 020 3188 7401
E-mail: info@rcgp.org.uk
Website: www.rcgp.org.uk

The aims of the College are to encourage, foster and maintain the highest possible standards in general medical practice. Full entry to the College is by exam undertaken whilst in training for General Practice, or assessment as a qualified GP.

MEMBERSHIP
Associate in Training
Associate
Member (MRCGP)
Fellow (FRCGP)

International Member (MRCGP[INT])
Undergraduate medical students and Foundation programme students may register with the College's Student Forum, which exposes the students to life in general practice.

QUALIFICATION/EXAMINATIONS
Assessment for Membership of the RCGP (MRCGP)

DESIGNATORY LETTERS
MRCGP, FRCGP

ROYAL COLLEGE OF OBSTETRICIANS AND GYNAECOLOGISTS

27 Sussex Place
London NW1 4RG
Tel: 020 7772 6200
E-mail: library@rcog.org.uk
Website: www.rcog.org.uk

The RCOG encourages the study and advancement of the science and practice of obstetrics and gynae-cology. We do this through postgraduate medical education and training development, and the pub-lication of clinical guidelines and reports on aspects of the specialty and service provision. The RCOG International Office works with other international organizations to help lower maternal morbidity and mortality in under-resourced countries.

MEMBERSHIP
Affiliate
Associate
Diplomate

Trainee – pre-membership
Member without Examination (MRCOG)
Member (MRCOG)
Fellow (FRCOG)
Fellow *honoris causa*
Fellow *ad eumdem* (FRCOG)
Honorary Fellow (FRCOG)

QUALIFICATION/EXAMINATIONS
MRCOG (Membership Exam)
FRCOG (Diploma)

DESIGNATORY LETTERS
MRCOG, FRCOG

ROYAL SOCIETY OF MEDICINE

1 Wimpole Street
London W1G 0AE
Tel: 020 7290 2900
Fax: 020 7290 2992
E-mail: membership@rsm.ac.uk
Website: www.rsm.ac.uk

The RSM, founded in 1805, is a medical charity that promotes the exchange of information and ideas in medical science. We provide a broad range of educational activities and opportunities for doctors, dentists, veterinary surgeons, students of these disciplines and allied healthcare professionals, organize conferences, and publish books and journals through our publishing division, RSM Press.

MEMBERSHIP
Student
Associate
Fellow
Corporate

QUALIFICATION/EXAMINATIONS
NONE

DESIGNATORY LETTERS
N/A

THE FEDERATION OF ROYAL COLLEGES OF PHYSICIANS OF THE UNITED KINGDOM

MRCP(UK)
11 St Andrews Place
Regent's Park
London NW1 4LE
Tel: +44 (0)20 3075 1248
E-mail: policy.officer@mrcpuk.org
Website: www.mrcpuk.org

The Federation is a partnership between the Royal College of Physicians of Edinburgh, the Royal College of Physicians and Surgeons of Glasgow and the Royal College of Physicians of London. Working together, the colleges develop and deliver membership and specialty examinations that are recognized around the world as quality benchmarks.

MEMBERSHIP
Membership of the Royal Colleges of Physicians (MRCP(UK)): Once candidates have successfully completed their final part of the examination they must then submit and complete the Form of Faith as a testimonial for election to membership.

QUALIFICATION/EXAMINATIONS
The Federation is responsible for a portfolio of examinations: MRCP(UK) Diploma (Membership of the Royal Colleges of Physicians of the United Kingdom): Candidates for the MRCP(UK) Diploma may enter through the Royal College of Physicians of Edinburgh, the Royal College of Physicians and Surgeons of Glasgow, the Royal College of Physicians of London, or through the online application system. There are three components to the MRCP(UK) Diploma. The part 1 examination has a two-paper format. Each paper is 3 hours in duration and contains 100 multiple choice questions in one from five (best of five) format, where a candidate chooses the best answer from five possible answers. The part 2 written examination has a three-paper format. All papers in the MRCP(UK) part 2 written examination are 3 hours in duration and contain up to 100 multiple choice questions. The questions will usually have a clinical scenario, may include the results of investigations and may be illustrated. The part 2 clinical examination (PACES) consists of five clinical stations, each assessed by two independent examiners. Candidates will start at any one of the five

stations, and then move round the carousel of stations at 20-minute intervals until they have completed the cycle. There is a 5-minute period between each station. Candidates may apply to sit the MRCP(UK) part 1 examination provided they graduated at least 12 months in advance of the examinations date (and have had at least 12 months' experience in medical employment). Candidates who have passed the part 1 examination can proceed to complete the remaining components. The MRCP(UK) Examination provides valid, reliable evidence of attainment in knowledge, clinical skills and behaviour, and is a mandatory component of assessment for Core Medical Training (CMT). The Specialty Certificate Examinations (SCEs): The Federation of Royal Colleges of Physicians of the UK, in association with Specialist Societies, has developed a programme to deliver Specialty Certificate Examinations within the new specialist training structure. The aim of these national assessments is to ensure that trainees have sufficient knowledge of their specialty to practise safely and competently as consultants. The Specialty Certificate Examination is delivered in computer-based format (referred to as CBT) at a Pearson VUE test centre. Each paper is based on the MRCP(UK) written paper format and contains 100 multiple choice questions in 'best of five' format. A Specialty Certificate Examination is a compulsory component of assessment for Certificate of Completion of Training (CCT) for all UK trainees whose specialist training began in or after August 2007 and is in one of the following specialties: Acute Medicine, Dermatology; Endocrinology and Diabetes; Gastroenterology; Geriatric Medicine; Infectious Diseases; Medical Oncology; Nephrology; Neurology; Palliative Medicine; Respiratory Medicine and Rheumatology.

DESIGNATORY LETTERS
MRCP(UK)

THE INSTITUTE OF CLINICAL RESEARCH

10 Cedar Court
Grove Park
White Waltham Road
Maidenhead
Tel: 0845 521 0056
E-mail: info@icr-global.org
Website: www.icr-global.org

The ICR was founded in 1978 and is now the largest professional clinical research body in Europe and India. Our aim is to promote knowledge and understanding by engaging with the healthcare community and the general public, to support and facilitate communication between our members, and to provide opportunities for learning and development to enhance professional competence.

MEMBERSHIP
Affiliate

Registered Member (RICR)
Professional Member (MICR)
Fellow (FICR)
Honorary Fellow (Hon FICR)

QUALIFICATION/EXAMINATIONS
Please see the ICR's website.

DESIGNATORY LETTERS
RICR, MICR, FICR, HonFICR

THE ROYAL COLLEGE OF ANAESTHETISTS

Churchill House
35 Red Lion Square
London WC1R 4SG
Tel: 020 7092 1500
Fax: 020 7092 1730
E-mail: info@rcoa.ac.uk
Website: www.rcoa.ac.uk

The RCoA, which dates from 1948, is the professional body responsible for the specialty of anaesthesia throughout the UK. Our principal responsibility is to ensure the quality of patient care through the maintenance of standards in anaesthesia, pain medicine and critical care. We set and run examinations, and provide CPD for all practising anaesthetists.

MEMBERSHIP
Trainee
Affiliate
Associate Member

Member (MRCA)
Associate Fellow
Fellow *ad eundem* (FRCA)
Fellow (FRCA)
Honorary Fellow (FRCA)

QUALIFICATION/EXAMINATIONS
FRCA Examinations (FRCA)

DESIGNATORY LETTERS
MRCA, FRCA

THE ROYAL COLLEGE OF PATHOLOGISTS

2 Carlton House Terrace
London SW1Y 5AF
Tel: 020 7451 6700
E-mail: info@rcpath.org
Website: www.rcpath.org

The College aims to advance the science and practice of pathology, to provide public education, to promote research in pathology and to disseminate the results.

MEMBERSHIP
Affiliate Member
Associate
Diplomate Member (DipRCPath)
Fellow (FRCPath)

QUALIFICATION/EXAMINATIONS
Training programmes are approved for all pathology specialities and sub-specialities. The exact examination arrangements vary for each speciality but they will all involve a Part 1 and a Part 2 which include, inter alia, written, practical and oral components. In addition the College offers a Diploma in Cytopathology, a Diploma in Dermatopathology and a Diploma in Forensic Pathology. Further details may be obtained from the Examinations Department or the College's website.

DESIGNATORY LETTERS
DipRCPath, FRCPath

THE ROYAL COLLEGE OF PHYSICIANS AND SURGEONS OF GLASGOW

232–242 St Vincent Street
Glasgow G2 5RJ
Tel: 0141 2216072
Fax: 0141 2211804
E-mail: exams@rcpsg.ac.uk
Website: www.rcpsg.ac.uk

The Royal College of Physicians and Surgeons of Glasgow (RCPSG) welcomes professionals from a diverse range of disciplines. At present, our collegiate body includes Physicians, Surgeons, professionals in Dentistry, Travel Medicine, Podiatric Medicine and other professions allied to medicine. The College aims to provide career support to our membership through education, training, professional development, examinations and assessment, whilst acting as a charity and leading voice on health issues in order to set the highest standards of health care.

MEMBERSHIP
Fellow   FRCP(Glasg)/   FRCS(Glasg)/   FDS RCPS(Glasg)/   FFTM   RCPS(Glasg)/   FFPM RCPS(Glasg)
Member MRCPS(Glasg)/ MFDS RCPS(Glasg)/ MRCS(Glasg)/   MRCS(ENT)(Glasg)/   MFTM RCPS(Glasg)/ MFPM RCPS(Glasg)

Associate Member
Affiliate Member
Student Member

QUALIFICATION/EXAMINATIONS
Diploma in Dermatology (Dip Derm)
Diploma in Otolaryngology – Head and Neck Surgery (DOHNS)
Diploma in Travel Medicine (DipTravMed)
Diploma in Expedition and Wilderness Medicine
Postgraduate Diploma in Clinical Education
Diploma of Membership of the Royal Colleges of Physicians of the United Kingdom (MRCP(UK))

Diploma of Membership of the Royal College of Surgeons (MRCS(Glasg))
Diploma of Membership of the Royal College of Surgeons (MRCS(ENT)(Glasg))
Diploma of Membership of the Faculty of Dental Surgery (MFDS RCPS(Glasg))
Diploma of Membership in (dental specialty) (M(dental specialty) RCPS(Glasg)
Diploma of Membership of the Faculty of Travel Medicine (MFTM RCPS(Glasg))
Diploma of Membership of the Faculty of Podiatric Medicine (MFPM RCPS(Glasg))
Diploma of Fellowship of the Royal College of Physicians and Surgeons of Glasgow in Ophthalmology (FRCS(Glasg))
Diploma of Fellowship of the Royal College of Physicians and Surgeons of Glasgow (FDS (dental specialty) RCPS(Glasg))
Diploma of Fellowship of the Royal College of Physicians and Surgeons of Glasgow (FRCSGlasg (surgical specialty))
Diploma of Fellowship of the Faculty of Travel Medicine (FFTM RCPS(Glasg))
Diploma of Fellowship of the Faculty of Podiatric Medicine (FFPM RCPS(Glasg))

DESIGNATORY LETTERS
MFDS   RCPS(Glasg),   MFTM   RCPS(Glasg),
MRCP(UK),   MRCS(Glasg),   MRCS(ENT)(Glasg),
MRCPS(Glasg), MFPM RCPS(Glasg), M(dental specialty) RCPS(Glasg)/ FRCP(Glasg)/ FRCS(Glasg)/ FRCSGlasg(surgical specialty)/ FDS RCPS(Glasg)/ FRCS(Urol)(Glasg), FFTM RCPS(Glasg)

THE ROYAL COLLEGE OF PHYSICIANS OF EDINBURGH

9 Queen Street
Edinburgh EH2 1JQ
Tel: 01312 257324
E-mail: l.tedford@rcpe.ac.uk
Website: www.rcpe.ac.uk

The RCPE promotes the highest standards in internal medicine in the UK and internationally. Along with our sister Colleges in Glasgow and London we oversee the membership examination of the Royal Colleges of Physicians, MRCP(UK), enabling doctors to enter higher specialist training, leading eventually to a Certificate of Completion of Specialist Training (CCST).

MEMBERSHIP
Student + Foundation
Associate
Collegiate Member (MRCPE)
Fellow (FRCPE)

QUALIFICATION/EXAMINATIONS
MRCP(UK)
Specialty Certificate Examinations

DESIGNATORY LETTERS
MRCPE, FRCPE

THE ROYAL COLLEGE OF PHYSICIANS OF LONDON

11 St Andrews Place
Regent's Park
London NW1 4LE
Tel: +44 (0)20 3075 1649
E-mail: via website
Website: www.rcplondon.ac.uk

The Royal College of Physicians of London offers a Diploma in Geriatric Medicine (DGM) Examination and a Diploma in Tropical Medicine and Hygiene, run in conjunction with the London School of Tropical Medicine and Hygiene.

MEMBERSHIP
The Royal College of Physicians of London runs the MRCP(UK) Examination which is the MRCP(UK) membership examination. As the examination is run in conjunction with two other Royal Colleges of Physicians, this examination and the membership qualification MRCP(UK) are listed in this directory under *The Federation of Royal Colleges of Physicians.*

QUALIFICATION/EXAMINATIONS
Diploma in Geriatric Medicine The Diploma in Geriatric Medicine is designed to give recognition of competence in the provision of care of older people to General Practitioner vocational trainees, staff physicians and others working in non-consultant career posts in Departments of Geriatric Medicine, and other doctors with interests in or responsibilities for the care of older people.

The Diploma in Geriatric Medicine is available to all registered doctors. It is not primarily directed towards career geriatricians, but is generally to family doctors, psycho-geriatricians and indeed any doctor involved in the care of older people.

The Diploma in Geriatric Medicine is in two parts, the first of which is a written examination of multiple choice (best of 5) questions, lasting 2 hours and 30 minutes normally held twice a year at the Royal College of Physicians of London.

The second part is a Clinical Examination also held twice a year at various clinical centres in England and Wales. The clinical examination is a four-station standardized examination similar to an Objective Standard Clinical Examination (OSCE).

Diploma in Tropical Medicine and Hygiene The Diploma in Tropical Medicine and Hygiene is intended to test the knowledge required of physicians who wish to practise medicine effectively in developing countries.

Candidates for the Diploma in Tropical Medicine & Hygiene must hold a primary medical qualification recognized by the Royal College of Physicians of London.

The Royal College of Physicians of London will accept applications from candidates who are in the process of completing, or have completed within the last 5 years, the Tropical Medicine courses in London, Liverpool, Sheffield and Glasgow, which are recognized as appropriate training centres for the examination. The examination is held once a year over 2 days (unless required for a viva) and is conducted in the following sections: A **Practical Section** lasting 2 hours and 30 minutes consists of a mixture of microscopy specimens, including 20 'spot' questions that are set up on a microscope for identification. Other specimens require the candidate to use the microscopes themself. They are mainly parasitological and may include faecal, blood and haematological preparations together with some entomological specimens. A **Written Section** (3 hours and 20 minutes in total) consists of three papers. The **Clinical Paper** (1 hour) contains 18 compulsory questions. The first 16 are based on clinical pictures – usually of patients with abnormal physical signs; but occasionally laboratory slides, X-rays, or epidemiological data may be shown. There will be 2 or 3 questions on each, asking (for example) identification, diagnosis, further investigation, treatment etc. Each of these 16 questions is worth a maximum of 5 marks. The last 2 questions (17 and 18) are brief clinical cases, with 2 or 3 questions (again concentrating on diagnosis or differential diagnosis, investigation and treatment). The **Multiple Choice Question Paper** (1 hour and 20 minutes) consists of 40 multiple choice questions designed to test the knowledge of tropical medicine and hygiene over a wide area. The **Preventative Medicine Paper** (1 hour including 5 minutes reading time) consists of 10 questions of which the candidate must choose 5. Each question may have several parts, covering all aspects of preventative medicine and international community health in a tropical context.

There is also an **Oral ('Viva') Examination** for borderline candidates. The examination is conducted by two examiners. The first part of the examination (10 minutes) is a discussion of an illustrated clinical case history, which candidates are allowed to study for 10 minutes before the examination. The second part of the examination (10 minutes) consists of more general questions.

THE ROYAL COLLEGE OF PSYCHIATRISTS

21 Prescot Street
London E1 8BB
Tel: 020 7235 2351
Fax: 020 3701 2761
E-mail: reception@rcpsych.ac.uk
Website: www.rcpsych.ac.uk

The RCPsych is the professional and educational body for psychiatrists in the UK and Ireland. We are committed to improving the understanding of psychiatry and mental health, and are at the forefront in setting and achieving the highest standards through education, training and research. We actively promote psychiatry as a career, and provide guidance and support to our members and associates.

MEMBERSHIP
Pre-Membership Psychiatric Trainee
New Associate
Affiliate
Specialist Associate
Member (MRCPsych)

Fellow (FRCPsych)
Honorary Fellow
International Associate

QUALIFICATION/EXAMINATIONS
MRCPsych qualifying exams
Paper A – The Scientific and Theoretical Basis of Psychiatry
Paper B – Critical Review and the Clinical Topics in Psychiatry
CASC – Clinical Assessment of Skills and Competencies

DESIGNATORY LETTERS
MRCPsych, FRCPsych

THE ROYAL COLLEGE OF RADIOLOGISTS

63 Lincoln's Inn Fields
London WC2A 3JW
Tel: 020 7405 1282
E-mail: enquiries@rcr.ac.uk
Website: www.rcr.ac.uk

The Royal College of Radiologists (RCR) leads, supports and educates in medical imaging and cancer treatment. RCR sets and maintains the standards for entry to, and practice in, the specialties of clinical oncology and clinical radiology and shapes their future development for the benefit of patients. The College works to advance the science and practice of radiology and oncology. It furthers public awareness and education, and promotes study and research through setting professional standards of practice. It also sets the curriculum for the two specialties ensuring that high educational standards are met in the interests of safe and responsible practice.

MEMBERSHIP
Junior Member
Associate
Trainee
Member
Fellow (FRCR)
Honorary Member/Fellow (Hon MRCR/Hon FRCR)

QUALIFICATION/EXAMINATIONS
First FRCR Examination
Final FRCR Examination
Diploma in Dental and Maxillofacial Radiology (DDMFR)

DESIGNATORY LETTERS
FRCR, Hon MRCR, Hon FRCR

THE ROYAL COLLEGE OF SURGEONS OF EDINBURGH

Nicolson Street
Edinburgh EH8 9DW
Tel: 0131 527 1600
Fax: 0131 557 6406
E-mail: mail@rcsed.ac.uk
Website: www.rcsed.ac.uk

The Royal College of Surgeons of Edinburgh, which dates from 1505, is dedicated to the maintenance and promotion of the highest standards of surgical practice, through education, training and rigorous examination, and its liaison with external medical bodies. Today, with more than 20,000 Fellows and Members, we pride ourselves also on our innovation and adaptability.

MEMBERSHIP
Affiliate

Associate
Member (MRCSEd)
Fellow (FRCSEd)

QUALIFICATION/EXAMINATIONS
Please see the Royal College of Surgeons of Edinburgh website.

DESIGNATORY LETTERS
MRCSEd, FRCSEd

THE ROYAL COLLEGE OF SURGEONS OF ENGLAND

35–43 Lincoln's Inn Fields
London WC2A 3PE
Tel: 020 7405 3474
E-mail: membership@rcseng.ac.uk
Website: www.rcseng.ac.uk

The Royal College of Surgeons of England is committed to enabling surgeons to achieve and maintain the highest standards of surgical practice and patient care. We examine trainees, supervise the training of and provide support and advice for surgeons, promote and support surgical research in the UK, and liaise with the DoH, health authorities, Trusts and hospitals in the UK and other medical and academic organizations worldwide.

MEMBERSHIP
Affiliate
Associate
Fellow *ad eundem*
Membership *ad eundem*
Specialty Membership

QUALIFICATION/EXAMINATIONS
Please see the Royal College of Surgeons of England website.

THE WORSHIPFUL SOCIETY OF APOTHECARIES OF LONDON

Apothecaries' Hall
Black Friars Lane
London EC4V 6EJ
Tel: 020 7236 1180
Fax: 020 7329 3177
E-mail: via website
Website: www.apothecaries.org

The Society of Apothecaries of London was incorporated by Royal Charter in 1617 and allowed to prepare and sell drugs for medicinal purposes, laying the foundations of the British pharmaceutical industry. Later, apothecaries were permitted to prescribe and dispense medicines, becoming the forerunners of today's GPs. Now the Society is primarily an examining body.

QUALIFICATION/EXAMINATIONS
PGDip in Forensic Medical Sciences (DFMS)
PGDip in Genitourinary Medicine (Dip GU Med)
PGDip in the History of Medicine (DHMSA)
PGDip in HIV Medicine (Dip HIV Med)
PGDip in the Medical Care of Catastrophes (DMCC)
PGDip in Medical Jurisprudence (Pathology) (DMJ[Path])
PGDip in the Philosophy of Medicine (DPMSA)

METALLURGY
Membership of Professional Institutions and Associations

INSTITUTE OF CORROSION

Barratt House
Kingsthorpe Road
Northampton NN2 6EZ
Tel: 01604 438222
E-mail: admin@icorr.org
Website: www.icorr.org

The Institute of Corrosion has since 1959 been serving the corrosion science, technology and engineering community in the fight against corrosion, which costs the UK around 4 per cent of GNP per annum. We promote the establishment and promotion of sound corrosion management practice, the advancement of cost-effective corrosion control measures, and a sustained effort to raise corrosion awareness at all stages of design, fabrication and operation.

MEMBERSHIP
Student Member
Ordinary Member
Technical Member (TICorr)
Professional Member (MICorr)
Fellow Member (FICorr)
Engineering Technician (EngTech)

Incorporated Engineer (IEng)
Chartered Engineer (CEng)
Chartered Scientist (CSci)

QUALIFICATION/EXAMINATIONS
Cathodic Protection Technician (Level 1)
Senior Cathodic Protection Technician (Level 2)
Senior Cathodic Protection Engineer (Level 3)
Painting Inspector (ICorr Levels 1, 2 and 3)
Coating Inspector (ICorr Levels 1, 2 and 3)
FireProofing Inspector Level 2
Insulation Inspector Level 2
Hot Dip Galvanizing Inspector Level 2

DESIGNATORY LETTERS
TICorr, MICorr, FICorr, EngTech, IEng, CEng

THE INSTITUTE OF METAL FINISHING

Exeter House
48 Holloway Head
Birmingham B1 1NQ
Tel: 01216 227387
Fax: 01216 666316
E-mail: exeterhouse@instituteofmetalfinishing.org
Website: www.uk-finishing.org.uk

The IMF, founded in 1925, provides a focus for surface engineering and finishing activities worldwide through the fulfilment of technical, educational and professional needs at all levels for individuals and companies involved in the coatings industry. We promote R&D within the industry and CPD for our members, cooperate with other institutes, and liaise with legislative bodies to influence decision making.

MEMBERSHIP
Student
Affiliate
Associate (AssocIMF)
Technician (TechIMF)
Licentiate (LIMF)
Member (MIMF)
Fellow (FIMF)
Engineering Technician (EngTech)
Sustaining Member (company)

QUALIFICATION/EXAMINATIONS
Foundation Certificate
Technician Certificate
Advanced Technician Certificate

DESIGNATORY LETTERS
AssocIMF, TechIMF, LIMF, MIMF, FIMF, EngTech

METEOROLOGY AND CLIMATOLOGY
Membership of Professional Institutions and Associations

MET OFFICE COLLEGE

Met Office
Fitzroy Road
Exeter
Devon EX1 3PB
Tel: 01392 885680
Fax: 01392 885681
E-mail: enquiries@metoffice.gov.uk
Website: www.metoffice.gov.uk

The Meteorological Office College is part of the Met Office and is located in Exeter, Devon. We provide meteorological training for our own staff and to meteorological services worldwide, as places become available on a fee-paying basis.

QUALIFICATION/EXAMINATIONS
Level 3 Diploma in Meteorological Observing (QCF)

Level 4 Certificate for a Meteorological Forecasting Technician (QCF)
Level 5 Diploma in Meteorological Forecasting (QCF)
Level 5 Award in Meteorological Briefing (QCF)
Level 5 Certificate in Meteorological Broadcasting (QCF)
Level 6 Diploma in Flood Forecasting (QCF)

ROYAL METEOROLOGICAL SOCIETY

104 Oxford Road
Reading RG1 7LL
Tel: 0118 956 8500
Fax: 0118 956 8571
E-mail: info@rmets.org
Website: www.rmets.org

The RMetS is the learned and professional society for anyone whose profession or interests are connected with weather and climate. It administers the NVQs of the profession and is the accreditation body for the status of Chartered Meteorologist. Its principal aim is the advancement of the understanding of weather and climate for the benefit of everyone.

MEMBERSHIP
Student

Associate Fellow
Fellow (FRMetS)
Honorary Member
Chartered Meteorologist (CMet)
School Member
Corporate Member

DESIGNATORY LETTERS
FRMetS, CMet

MICROSCOPY
Membership of Professional Institutions and Associations

THE ROYAL MICROSCOPICAL SOCIETY

37/38 St Clements
Oxford OX4 1AJ
Tel: 01865 254760
Fax: 01865 791237
E-mail: info@rms.org.uk
Website: www.rms.org.uk

The RMS, which dates from 1839, is an international scientific society dedicated to advancing the science of microscopy and the interests of its 1,400 members, who range from individuals interested in microscopy to scientists and company members representing manufacturers and suppliers of microscopes, other equipment and services.

MEMBERSHIP
Ordinary Member
Fellow (FRMS)
Corporate Member

DESIGNATORY LETTERS
FRMS

MUSEUM AND RELATED WORK
Membership of Professional Institutions and Associations

MUSEUMS ASSOCIATION

42 Clerkenwell Close
London EC1R 0AZ
Tel: 020 7566 7800
E-mail: info@museumsassociation.org
Website: www.museumsassociation.org

The MA is the oldest museums association in the world, set up in 1889 to guard the interests of museums and galleries. Today, we have 5,200 individual members, 600 institutional members and 250 corporate members. Our aim is to enhance the value of museums to society by sharing knowledge, developing skills, inspiring innovation and providing leadership.

MEMBERSHIP
Student
Volunteer
Professional Member
Associate (AMA)
Corporate Member
Institutional Member

DESIGNATORY LETTERS
AMA

MUSIC
Membership of Professional Institutions and Associations

ABRSM (ASSOCIATED BOARD OF THE ROYAL SCHOOLS OF MUSIC)

24 Portland Place
London W1B 1LU
Tel: 020 7636 5400
Fax: 020 7637 0234
E-mail: abrsm@abrsm.org
Website: www.abrsm.org

ABRSM's mission is to motivate musical achievement. We aim to support the development of learners and teachers in music education worldwide and to celebrate their achievements. We do this through authoritative and internationally recognized assessments, publications and professional development support for teachers, and through charitable donations.

MEMBERSHIP
Licentiate (LRSM)
Fellow (FRSM)

QUALIFICATION/EXAMINATIONS
Certificate of Teaching (CT ABRSM)
Diploma in Instrumental/Vocal Teaching (DipABRSM)
Diploma in Music Direction (DipABRSM)
Diploma in Music Performance (DipABRSM)

Please see the ABRSM website for details of other examinations and awards.

DESIGNATORY LETTERS
CT ABRSM, DipABRSM, LRSM, FRSM

INCORPORATED SOCIETY OF MUSICIANS

10 Stratford Place
London WIC 1AA
Tel: 020 7629 4413
Fax: 020 7408 1538
E-mail: membership@ism.org
Website: www.ism.org

The ISM, a non-profit-making organization founded in 1882, is the UK's professional body for musicians. We promote the art of music and the interests of musicians through campaigns, support and practical advice. Members also receive our monthly in-house magazine, *Music Journal*, which includes news and information on CPD.

MEMBERSHIP
Student Member
Associate Member
Full Member
Corporate Member
Graduate Member

MUSICAL INSTRUMENT TECHNOLOGY
Membership of Professional Institutions and Associations

PIANOFORTE TUNERS' ASSOCIATION

PO Box 230
Hailsham
East Sussex BN27 9EA
Tel: 0845 602 8796
E-mail: secretary@pianotuner.org.uk
Website: www.pianotuner.org.uk

The PTA is a professional body committed to improving standards, and applicants for membership must pass a theoretical and practical examination to prove their ability as a qualified piano tuner or technician. We publish a regular newsletter and hold an Annual Convention and General Meeting in different towns around Britain, to which members and aspiring non-members are invited.

MEMBERSHIP
Student
Patron
Associate
Technician Member
Member
Subscriber

THE INCORPORATED SOCIETY OF ORGAN BUILDERS

The Tower
7 Lower Port View
SALTASH
Cornwall PL12 4BY
Tel: 01752-842027
Fax: 01752-842027
E-mail: secretary@isob.co.uk
Website: www.isob.co.uk

The ISOB was founded in 1947 to advance the science and practice of organ building, to provide a central organization for organ builders, and to provide for the better definition and protection of the profession by a system of examinations and the issue of certificates and distinctions. We hold regular meetings and conferences around the UK and overseas.

MEMBERSHIP
Student Member

Ordinary Member (MISOB)
Associate Member (AISOB)
Fellow (FISOB)
Counsellor (CISOB)
Companion

DESIGNATORY LETTERS
MISOB, AISOB, FISOB, CISOB

NAVAL ARCHITECTURE
Membership of Professional Institutions and Associations

THE ROYAL INSTITUTION OF NAVAL ARCHITECTS

8–9 Northumberland Street
London WC2N 5DA
Tel: 020 7235 4622
Fax: 020 7259 5912
E-mail: membership@rina.org.uk
Website: www.rina.org.uk

The RINA is an internationally renowned professional institution whose members are involved at all levels in the design, construction, maintenance and operation of marine vessels and structures. Our members are widely represented in industry, universities and colleges, and maritime organizations in over 90 countries.

MEMBERSHIP
Student Member
Associate (AssocRINA)
Associate Member (AMRINA)
Member (MRINA)
Fellow (FRINA)

DESIGNATORY LETTERS
AssocRINA, AMRINA, MRINA, FRINA

NAVIGATION, SEAMANSHIP AND MARINE QUALIFICATIONS
Membership of Professional Institutions and Associations

THE NAUTICAL INSTITUTE

202 Lambeth Road
London SE1 7LQ
Tel: 020 7928 1351
Fax: 020 7401 2817
E-mail: sec@nautinst.org
Website: www.nautinst.org

The Nautical Institute is the international representative body for maritime professionals involved in the control of sea-going ships with an interest in nautical matters. It provides a wide range of services to enhance the professional standing and knowledge of members who are drawn from all sectors of the maritime world.

MEMBERSHIP
Honorary Fellow
Fellow (FNI)
Associate Fellow (AFNI)
Member (MNI)
Associate Member (AMNI)

QUALIFICATION/EXAMINATIONS
Harbour Master's Certificate
Pilotage Certificate
Command Diploma
International Sail Endorsement Scheme

DESIGNATORY LETTERS
FNI, AFNI, MNI, AMNI

THE ROYAL INSTITUTE OF NAVIGATION

1 Kensington Gore
London SW7 2AT
Tel: 020 7591 3134
Fax: 020 7591 3131
E-mail: admin@rin.org.uk
Website: www.rin.org.uk

The RIN is a learned society with charitable status. Our aims are: to unite those with a professional or personal interest in any aspect of navigation in one unique body; to further the development of navigation in every sphere; and to increase public awareness of both the art and science of navigation, how it has shaped the past, how it impacts our world today, and how it will affect the future.

MEMBERSHIP
Junior Associate Member
Student

Associate
Member (MRIN)
Associate Fellow (AFRIN)
Fellow (FRIN)
Affiliate Club
Affiliate College or University
Corporate Member
Small Business

DESIGNATORY LETTERS
MRIN, AFRIN, FRIN

NON-DESTRUCTIVE TESTING
Membership of Professional Institutions and Associations

THE BRITISH INSTITUTE OF NON-DESTRUCTIVE TESTING

Newton Building
St George's Avenue
Northampton NN2 6JB
Tel: 01604 89 3811
Fax: 01604 89 3861
E-mail: info@bindt.org
Website: www.bindt.org

The BINDT was formed in 1976 from the merger of the Society of Non-Destructive Examination (SONDE) and the Society of Industrial Radiology and Allied Methods of Non-Destructive Testing, later renamed the NDT Society of Great Britain (NDTS), both formed in 1954. Our aim is to promote and advance the science and practice of non-destructive testing, condition monitoring, diagnostic engineering and all other materials and quality testing disciplines.

MEMBERSHIP
Student Member
Affiliate

Practitioner Member (PInstNDT)
Graduate Member (GInstNDT)
Member (MInstNDT)
Fellow (FInstNDT)
Engineering Technician (EngTech)
Incorporated Engineer (IEng)
Chartered Engineer (CEng)
Licensed Engineering Practitioner
Associate Member (corporate)

DESIGNATORY LETTERS
PInstNDT, GInstNDT, MInstNDT, FInstNDT, EngTech, IEng, CEng

NURSERY NURSING
Membership of Professional Institutions and Associations

COUNCIL FOR AWARDS IN CHILDREN'S CARE AND EDUCATION

Apex House
81 Camp Road
St Albans
Hertfordshire AL1 5GB
Tel: 0845 347 2123
Fax: 01727 818618
E-mail: info@cache.org.uk
Website: www.cache.org.uk

CACHE is an Awarding Body that designs courses and qualifications in the care and education of children and young people. Our courses, which are widely available, range from entry level to advanced qualifications for sector professionals. We regularly lobby the government and other agencies to raise the quality and professionalism of child care.

QUALIFICATION/EXAMINATIONS
Please see the CACHE website.

THE SOCIETY OF NURSERY NURSING PRACTITIONERS

40 Archdale Road
East Dulwich
London SE22 9HJ
Tel: 0208 693 0555
Fax: 0208 693 0555
E-mail: info@snnp.org.uk
Website: www.snnp.org.uk

The Society is the only professional examining body in the field. Incorporated in 1991, it caters for the interests and aspirations of childminders, nursery nurses and all those who look after children and young people from birth to age 5. It also exists to raise the flagging professional image of nursery nurses.

MEMBERSHIP
Graduate (GSNNP)
Associate (ASNNP)
Fellow (FSNNP)

QUALIFICATION/EXAMINATIONS
The examinations in Early Childhood Studies are in three stages: Certificate, Advanced Certificate and Diploma. The subjects for all the examinations are the same but the questions are set and marked at the appropriate level. The subjects are:
Care of the sick child and special needs

Data investigation and interpretation
Early childhood play and learning
First aid and safety
Legal aspects of child care, health and community care
Management in the Early Years (Diploma level)
Managing self evaluation reflection
Observation, assessment and the young child
Overview of growth and development
Practice in service in child care
Pregnancy, birth and child development
Preparing for employment with young children
Protecting children from abuse
Social and psychological development
Working with parents and young children
Course work on a topic selected by the student

DESIGNATORY LETTERS
GSNNP, ASNNP, FSNNP

NURSING AND MIDWIFERY
Membership of Professional Institutions and Associations

THE NURSING & MIDWIFERY COUNCIL

23 Portland Place
London W1B 1PZ
Tel: 020 7333 9333
E-mail: UKenquiries@nmc-uk.org
Website: www.nmc-uk.org

We are the nursing and midwifery regulator for England, Wales, Scotland, Northern Ireland and the Islands. We exist to safeguard the health and well-being of the public.

OCCUPATIONAL THERAPY
Membership of Professional Institutions and Associations

COLLEGE OF OCCUPATIONAL THERAPISTS

106–114 Borough High Street
Southwark
London SE1 1LB
Tel: 020 7357 6480
Fax: 020 7450 2299
E-mail: membership@cot.co.uk
Website: www.cot.org.uk

The College of Occupational Therapists is the professional body for occupational therapy in the UK. The College has over 31,000 members and represents the profession nationally and internationally. COT accredits pre-registration occupational therapy degree programmes in 32 UK Universities.

MEMBERSHIP
Student Member
Associate
Discounted Associate
Professional Member
Discounted Professional Member
Self-employed Member
Retired Member
Overseas Member

QUALIFICATION/EXAMINATIONS
BA(Hons)
PG Dip
MSc

OPTICIANS (DISPENSING)

Dispensing opticians must be registered with the General Optical Council (GOC, 10 Old Bailey, London EC4M 7NG; Tel: 020 7580 3898; e-mail: goc@optical.org; website: www.optical.org). The GOC publishes registers of all optometrists, dispensing opticians, student opticians and optical businesses that are qualified and fit to practise, train or carry on business.

Qualification takes three years in total, and can be completed by combining a distance learning course or day release while working as a trainee under the supervision of a qualified and GOC-registered optician. Alternatively students can do a two-year full-time course followed by one year of supervised practice with a qualified and registered optician. The GOC has approved training courses in dispensing optics at the following institutions in the UK: Anglia Ruskin University, Association of British Dispensing Opticians (ABDO) College (Distance Learning Institute), Bradford College, City and Islington College, City University and Glasgow Caledonian University. All routes are assessed by final ABDO examinations. On successful completion of training you must register with the GOC in order to practise in the UK. Once qualified, you will need to undertake a minimum amount of continuing education and training to remain on the register. All registered dispensing opticians have to renew their registration each year: this is called 'retention'.

The approved training course for the contact lens specialty is run by ABDO College and City and Islington College. For further information contact the ABDO College (Tel: 01227 738 829 option 1; email: info@abdocollege.org.uk) or City and Islington College (Tel: 020 7700 9200; email: courseinfo@candi.ac.uk).

If you qualify as a dispensing optician and have worked in practice as a qualified dispensing optician for at least two years, the University of Bradford offers a career progression course that enables you to graduate with a degree in optometry by undertaking 6 months of distance-learning followed by 12 months of study at the University (Tel: 01274 236296; email: admissions-life@bradford. ac.uk).

Continuing education and training is a statutory requirement for all fully-qualified dispensing opticians. The CET scheme is a points-based scheme that runs over a three-year cycle. All full registrants must earn a minimum number of CET points by the end of each cycle to stay on the registers.

Nationals of EU/EEA countries who have gained optical quailfications in an EU/EEA country can apply to another EU/EEA country to have their qualifications recognised.

ENTRY REQUIREMENTS

Requirements vary according to the college or university, but typically five GCSEs at Grade C or above, to include Mathematics, English and Science and perhaps two or three A Levels at a minimum of a Grade D or equivalent are required. Relevant work experience will also be considered.

For further details contact the admissions tutor or check the website of the university you wish to apply to.

Membership of Professional Institutions and Associations

ASSOCIATION OF BRITISH DISPENSING OPTICIANS

199 Gloucester Terrace
London W2 6LD
Tel: 020 7298 5100
E-mail: general@abdolondon.org.uk
Website: www.abdo.org.uk

The ABDO is the qualifying body for dispensing opticians in the UK. Our aims are to advance the science and art of dispensing optics, to further the education and training of dispensing opticians, and to support and promote the interests of the profession.

MEMBERSHIP
Student Member
Associate Member
Full Member
Fellow (FBDO)

Elder

QUALIFICATION/EXAMINATIONS
Certificate in Contact Lens Practice (Level 6)
Diploma in The Assessment & Management of Low Vision (Level 6)
Diploma in Ophthalmic Dispensing (Level 6)
Diploma in Advanced Contact Lens Practice (Level 7)
Diploma in Spectacle Lens Design (Level 7)

DESIGNATORY LETTERS
FBDO

ASSOCIATION OF CONTACT LENS MANUFACTURERS

PO Box 735
Devizes
Wiltshire SN10 3TQ
Tel: 01380 860418
Fax: 01380 860863
E-mail: secgen@aclm.org.uk
Website: www.aclm.org.uk

The ACLM was founded in 1962 to publicize the work of UK contact lens manufacturers, to develop new products and to raise standards. Today we represent the manufacturers of the vast majority of prescription contact lenses and lens care products sold in the UK, and provide a cohesive voice for our members.

MEMBERSHIP
Member

OPTOMETRY

Careers in optometry are overseen by the General Optical Council (10 Old Bailey, London EC4M 7NG; Tel: 020 7580 3898; e-mail: goc@optical.org; website: www.optical.org). You can study for an undergraduate optometry degree from one of nine GOC-approved institutions in the UK: Anglia Ruskin University, Aston University, the University of Bradford, Cardiff University, City University, Glasgow Caledonian University, Plymouth University, the University of Manchester and the University of Ulster.

LENGTH OF COURSE
Usually four years in total (five in Scotland): a full-time three-year (four-year in Scotland) degree course, followed by one year's salaried pre-registration training with a practice under the guidance of a GOC-registered optometrist. This includes a series of assessments, set by the College of Optometry, or the University of Manchester, throughout the placement. Trainees must have gained a degree in Optometry at 2:2 or above and have a valid Certificate of Clinical Competency in order to enter a pre-registration placement. Trainees whose certificate has expired or who fail to achieve a 2:2 in their degree must successfully complete the GOC's Optometry Progression Scheme before entering a pre-registration placement.

ENTRY REQUIREMENTS
You will normally need five GCSEs (or equivalent) at grade C or above, one of which should be English; often maths and physics or double science are also required. You will normally be required to have three A Level passes/approximately 320 UCAS tariff points from the following subjects: physics, biology, chemistry or mathematics. Requirements vary between universities, so be sure to check the university's prospectus and/or consult the relevant admission tutors.

REGISTRATION
On successful completion of the pre-registration period of training, which includes work-based assessment and a final assessment on the Stage 2 core competencies for optometry, the qualified optometrist must register with the GOC in order to practise.

Nationals of EU/EEA countries who have gained optical qualifications in an EU/EEA country can apply to another EU/EEA country to have their qualifications recognised. For people who gained their qualification outside the EU/EEA the requirements for registration as an optometrist in the UK are detailed on the GOC website.

Membership of Professional Institutions and Associations

ASSOCIATION OF OPTOMETRISTS

2 Woodbridge Street
London EC1R 0DG
Tel: 020 7549 2000
Fax: 020 7251 8315
E-mail: postbox@aop.org.uk
Website: www.aop.org.uk

The AOP serves its members by promoting and protecting them, providing them with relevant services, representing and supporting them, enhancing their professional and business effectiveness, and expanding the role of optometry in primary and secondary eyecare.

MEMBERSHIP
Student Member
Honorary Member
Dispensing Associate
Full Member

ORTHOPTICS

Membership of Professional Institutions and Associations

BRITISH AND IRISH ORTHOPTIC SOCIETY

Salisbury House
Station Road
Cambridge CB1 2LA
Tel: 01353 66 55 41
E-mail: bios@orthoptics.org.uk
Website: www.orthoptics.org.uk

Orthoptists diagnose and treat problems with visual development and binocular vision (how the eyes work together as a pair), and eye movement disorders. They are experts in childhood vision screening. Most orthoptists in the UK work in the Ophthalmology Clinics of acute hospitals, treating patients with stroke, glaucoma, reading difficulties, neurological disorders, low vision and other conditions.

MEMBERSHIP
Student, Full, Associate

QUALIFICATION/EXAMINATIONS
Degrees in orthoptics are offered by Liverpool University (www.liv.ac.uk), Sheffield University (www.sheffield.ac.uk) and Glasgow Caledonian University (www.gcu.ac.uk)

OSTEOPATHY AND NATUROPATHY
Membership of Professional Institutions and Associations

BRITISH OSTEOPATHIC ASSOCIATION

3 Park Terrace
Manor Road
Luton
Bedfordshire LU1 3HN
Tel: 01582 488455
Fax: 01582 481533
E-mail: boa@osteopathy.org
Website: www.osteopathy.org

The BOA was formed in 1998 as a result of the merger of the British Osteopathic Association, the Osteopathic Association of Great Britain and the Guild of Osteopaths. We provide opportunities for individual and professional development in osteopathic practice and promote the highest standards of osteopathic education and research.

MEMBERSHIP
Student Member
1st/2nd/3rd/4th Year Graduate Member
Full Member
Overseas Member

PATENT AGENCY
Membership of Professional Institutions and Associations

THE CHARTERED INSTITUTE OF PATENT ATTORNEYS

95 Chancery Lane
London WC2A 1DT
Tel: 020 7405 9450
Fax: 020 7430 0471
E-mail: mail@cipa.org.uk
Website: www.cipa.org.uk

CIPA is the professional, training and examining body for patent attorneys in the UK. From 2010 the IP Regulation Board, an independent body within the CIPA, sets the standards for regulation of the profession. Trainees, all technical graduates, also study for the qualification to practise before the European Patent Office.

MEMBERSHIP
Student Member
Associate

Fellow
British Overseas Member
Foreign Member

QUALIFICATION/EXAMINATIONS
Qualifying examination for registration as a Patent Attorney

DESIGNATORY LETTERS
RPA, CPA

PENSION MANAGEMENT
Membership of Professional Institutions and Associations

THE PENSIONS MANAGEMENT INSTITUTE

PMI House
4–10 Artillery Lane
London E1 7LS
Tel: 020 7247 1452
Fax: 020 7375 0603
E-mail: via website
Website: www.pensions-pmi.org.uk

The Pensions Management Institute is the professional body that promotes standards of excellence and lifetime learning for pensions professionals and trustees through its qualifications, membership and ongoing support services. For further details please visit our website.

MEMBERSHIP
Student Membership
Certificate Membership
Diploma Membership
Associate Membership
Fellowship
Affiliate Membership
Trustee Group Membership

QUALIFICATION/EXAMINATIONS
Award in Pensions Essentials (APE)

Certificate in Pensions Essentials (CPE)
Certificate in Pension Calculations (CPC)
Certificate in Pensions Administration (CPA)
Diploma in Pensions Administration (DPA)
Retirement Provision Certificate (RPC)
Certificate in Pensions Automatic Enrolment (CPAE)
Diploma in Retirement Provision (DRP)
Diploma in Employee Benefits and Retirement Savings (DEBRS)
Diploma in International Employee Benefits (DipIEB)
Diploma in Regulated Retirement Advice (DRRA)
Advanced Diploma in Retirement Provision (ADRP)
Awards in Pensions Trusteeship (APT)

DESIGNATORY LETTERS
CertPMI, DipPMI, APMI, FPMI

PERSONNEL MANAGEMENT
Membership of Professional Institutions and Associations

CHARTERED INSTITUTE OF PERSONNEL AND DEVELOPMENT

151 The Broadway
Wimbledon
London SW19 1JQ
Tel: +44(0)20 8612 6208
Fax: +44(0)20 8612 6201
E-mail: membershipenquiry@cipd.co.uk
Website: www.cipd.co.uk

The CIPD is the world's largest Chartered HR and development professional body. With 135,000 members across 120 countries it supports and develops those responsible for the management and development of people within organisations.

MEMBERSHIP
Affiliate Member
Student Member
Associate Member (Assoc CIPD)
Chartered Member (MCIPD)

Chartered Fellow (FCIPD)
Academic Member
For further information see: www.cipd.co.uk/
membership

QUALIFICATION/EXAMINATIONS
CIPD qualifications are available at three levels:
Level 3 Foundation
Level 5 Intermediate
Level 7 Advanced
In three different sizes:

Awards
Certificates
Diplomas
For more information and to find out where to study
CIPD qualifications visit: www.cipd.co.uk/
qualifications

DESIGNATORY LETTERS
Assoc CIPD, Chartered MCIPD, Chartered FCIPD,
CCIPD

THE INSTITUTE OF CONTINUING PROFESSIONAL DEVELOPMENT

Royal Institute of Chartered Surveyors
Parliament Square
London SW1P 3AD
Tel: 020 7695 1673
E-mail: info@cpdinstitute.org
Website: www.cpdinstitute.org

The Institute of Continuing Professional Development is part of the Continuing Professional Development Foundation, an educational charitable trust providing high-quality and broad-ranging CPD since 1981. We serve the public interest by helping to raise the effectiveness of professionals through the promotion of CPD as an important and integral element of lifelong learning.

MEMBERSHIP
Member (MInstCPD)
Fellow (FInstCPD)

DESIGNATORY LETTERS
MInstCPD, FInstCPD

UK EMPLOYEE ASSISTANCE PROFESSIONALS ASSOCIATION

PO Box 7966
Wilson
Derby DE1 0XP
E-mail: info@eapa.org.uk
Website: www.eapa.org.uk

The UK Employee Assistance Professionals Association represents the interests of professionals concerned with employee assistance, psychological health and wellbeing in the UK. Members include external and internal EAP providers, purchasers, counsellors, consultants and trainers.

MEMBERSHIP
♦ Registered Internal Provider: £1,200 per annum

♦ Registered External Provider: £1,200 per annum
♦ Non Registered Provider: £500 per annum
♦ Consultant Associate Member: £300 per annum
♦ Associate Member: £150 per annum
♦ Individual Member: £50 per annum
♦ Student Member: £25 per annum

PHARMACY

Membership of Professional Institutions and Associations

GENERAL PHARMACEUTICAL COUNCIL

1 Lambeth High Street
London SE1 7JN
Tel: 020 7735 9141
Fax: 020 7735 7629
E-mail: enquiries@rpsgb.org
Website: www.pharmacyregulation.org

The RPSGB, which dates from 1841, is the professional body for pharmacists and pharmacy technicians in England, Scotland and Wales. Our primary objectives are to lead, regulate, develop and represent the profession. We promote advancement of the science and practice of pharmacy, and pharmaceutical education and knowledge, and liaise with government and other bodies in the interests of our members.

MEMBERSHIP
Pharmacy Technician
Pharmacist
Student

DESIGNATORY LETTERS
MRPharmS, FRPharmS

THE PHARMACEUTICAL SOCIETY OF NORTHERN IRELAND

73 University Street
Belfast BT7 1HL
Tel: 028 9032 6927
Fax: 028 9043 9919
E-mail: info@psni.org.uk
Website: www.psni.org.uk

The Pharmaceutical Society of Northern Ireland, founded in 1925, is the regulatory and professional body for pharmacists in Northern Ireland. It maintains a register of more than 2,000 pharmacists and over 500 pharmacy premises, and sets and promotes the standards for pharmacists' admission to and remaining on the register, thereby protecting public safety.

MEMBERSHIP
Trainee
Member

QUALIFICATION/EXAMINATIONS
Registration Examination

PHOTOGRAPHY

Membership of Professional Institutions and Associations

ASSOCIATION OF PHOTOGRAPHERS (AOP)

21 Downham Road
London N1 5AA
Tel: 020 7739 6669
E-mail: info@aophoto.co.uk
Website: www.the-aop.org

The AOP was founded in 1968 to promote the highest standards throughout the industry and to improve the rights of all professional photographers based in the UK. Our membership currently comprises 1,800 photographers and photographic assistants, and we are supported by photographers' agents, printers, and manufacturers and suppliers of photographic equipment.

MEMBERSHIP
Student Member
Assistant Member
Photographer (full) Member
Agent Member
College Member
Affiliated Company

BRITISH INSTITUTE OF PROFESSIONAL PHOTOGRAPHY

The Coach House
The Firs, High Street
Whitchurch
Aylesbury
Buckinghamshire HP22 4SJ
Tel: 01296 642020
Fax: 01296 641553
E-mail: info@bipp.com
Website: www.bipp.com

The BIPP is the qualifying body for professional photographers in the UK. We provide support, training and qualifications for photographers across all types of photography, and organize a number of regional activities and events. A not-for-profit organization, we ensure that professional standards are met and maintained.

MEMBERSHIP
Open to full- or part-time professional photographers. Join as a Provisional member (maximum of 1 year) and work towards gaining a professional qualification. Friends' & Student membership is also available.

QUALIFICATION/EXAMINATIONS
Three tiers of qualification:
Licentiateship (LBIPP)
Associateship (ABIPP)
Fellowship (FBIPP)
BIPP is also aligned with the BA Hons in Photography through the OCA. Full details of the qualifications criteria can be found at www.bipp.com

DESIGNATORY LETTERS
LBIPP, ABIPP, FBIPP

MASTER PHOTOGRAPHERS ASSOCIATION

Jubilee House
1 Chancery Lane
Darlington
Co Durham DL1 5QP
Tel: 01325 356555
Fax: 01325 357813
E-mail: general@mpauk.com
Website: www.mpauk.com

The MPA was founded in 1952 and is now the UK's only organization for FT, qualified professional photographers. We have more than 2,000 members, who enjoy a range of benefits, including education, qualifications, informative regional meetings, business building promotions and marketing support, and abide by the Association's Code of Conduct.

MEMBERSHIP
Licentiate (LMPA)
Associate (AMPA)
Fellow (FMPA)

QUALIFICATION/EXAMINATIONS
The Diploma in Photographic Practice (DipPP) is recognized by SkillSet, as a benchmark competence mapped to the Photo Imaging National Standards: it is available to all qualified members and is an assessment process of professional photographic business and personal skills.

DESIGNATORY LETTERS
LMPA, AMPA, FMPA, DipPP

THE ROYAL PHOTOGRAPHIC SOCIETY

Fenton House
122 Wells Road
Bath
Somerset BA2 3AH
Tel: 01225 325733
E-mail: reception@rps.org
Website: www.rps.org

The RPS was founded in 1853. It is an educational charity and membership organisaton with the aim of promoting photography and supporting photographers. It realises these through exhibitions, workshops and courses and a distinctions and qualifications programme. It lobbies on behalf of photographers and photography. Membership is open to anyone.

MEMBERSHIP
Member
Family
Student
65 and over
25 and under
Disabled
Overseas

QUALIFICATION/EXAMINATIONS
Licentiate (LRPS)
Associate (ARPS)
Fellowship (FRPS)
Qualified Imaging Scientist and Licentiate (QIS LRPS)
Graduate Imaging Scientist and Associate (GIS ARPS)
Accredited Imaging Scientist and Associate (AIS ARPS)
Accredited Senior Imaging Scientist and Fellow (ASIS FRPS)
Qualified in Imaging in the Creative Industries (QICI & LRPS)
Graduate in Imaging in the Creative Industries (GICI & ARPS)

Accredited in Imaging in the Creative Industries (AICI & ARPS)

Accredited Senior in Imaging in the Creative Industries (ASICI FRPS)

Creative Industries Qualification

DESIGNATORY LETTERS
LRPS, ARPS, FRPS

PHYSICS
Membership of Professional Institutions and Associations

INSTITUTE OF PHYSICS AND ENGINEERING IN MEDICINE

Fairmount House
230 Tadcaster Road
York YO24 1ES
Tel: 01904 610821
Fax: 01904 612279
E-mail: office@ipem.org.uk
Website: www.ipem.ac.uk

The IPEM is dedicated to bringing together physical science, engineering and clinical professionals in academia, healthcare services and industry to share knowledge, advance science and technology, and inform and educate the public, with the purpose of improving the understanding, detection and treatment of disease and the management of patients.

MEMBERSHIP
Student Member

Affiliate
Associate
Medical Member (MedMIPEM)
Medical Fellow (MedFIPEM)
Corporate Member (MIPEM)
Fellow (FIPEM)
International

DESIGNATORY LETTERS
MedMIPEM, MedFIPEM, IIPEM, MIPEM, FIPEM

THE INSTITUTE OF PHYSICS

76 Portland Place
London W1B 1NT
Tel: 020 7470 4800
Fax: 020 7470 4848
E-mail: physics@iop.org
Website: www.iop.org

The IOP is a scientific charity devoted to increasing the practice, understanding and application of physics. We have a worldwide membership of over 36,000 and are a leading communicator of physics-related science to all audiences, from specialists through to government and the general public. Our publishing company, IOP Publishing, is a world leader in scientific publishing and the electronic dissemination of physics.

MEMBERSHIP
Student Member
Affiliate
Associate Member (AMInstP)
Member (MInstP)
Fellow (FInstP)
Chartered Physicist (CPhys)
IOPi Member

DESIGNATORY LETTERS
AMInstP, MInstP, FInstP, CPhys

PHYSIOTHERAPY
Membership of Professional Institutions and Associations

THE CHARTERED SOCIETY OF PHYSIOTHERAPY

14 Bedford Row
London WC1R 4ED
Tel: 0207 306 6666
E-mail: via website
Website: www.csp.org.uk

The CSP is the professional, educational and trade union body for the UK's 52,000 chartered physiotherapists, physiotherapy students and assistants. In order to become a member of the CSP it is necessary to have undertaken a qualification recognized by the Health and Care Professions Council (HCPC) – see: www.hcpc-uk.org

MEMBERSHIP
Student Member
Associate
Member (MCSP)
Fellow (FCSP)

DESIGNATORY LETTERS
MCSP, FCSP

PLUMBING
Membership of Professional Institutions and Associations

CHARTERED INSTITUTE OF PLUMBING AND HEATING ENGINEERING

64 Station Lane
Hornchurch
Essex RM12 6NB
Tel: 01708 472791
Fax: 01708 448987
E-mail: info@ciphe.org.uk
Website: www.ciphe.org.uk

The CIPHE, founded in 1906, is the professional body for the UK plumbing and heating industry. Our membership of around 12,000 is made up of individuals from a wide range of backgrounds and includes consultants, specifiers, designers, public health engineers, lecturers, trainers, trainees and practitioners, as well as manufacturers and distributors.

MEMBERSHIP
Trainee
Affiliate
Companion (CompCIPHE)

Associate (ACIPHE)
Member (MCIPHE)
Fellow (FCIPHE)

QUALIFICATION/EXAMINATIONS
Apprentice, Journeyman and Master Plumber Certificate (awarded jointly with the Worshipful Company of Plumbers and the City & Guilds of London Institute)

DESIGNATORY LETTERS
CompCIPHE, ACIPHE, MCIPHE, FCIPHE

PRINTING

Membership of Professional Institutions and Associations

PROSKILLS UK

Unit 24 East Central
127 Olympic Avenue
Milton Park
Abingdon
Oxfordshire OX14 4SA
Tel: 01235 833844
E-mail: info@proskills.co.uk
Website: www.proskills.co.uk

Proskills UK is the bridge between employers and government on skills and training. Employer-led representing key industries including: Building Products, Coatings, Furniture, Furnishings & Interiors, Glass & Related Industries, Health and Safety Paper, Printing and Wood industries, which make up a third of the UK manufacturing sector. We help to raise the profile of the sector, set the skills standards and qualifications and ensure that the skills and funding system delivers against the current and future needs of the industries.

QUALIFICATION/EXAMINATIONS
Please see the Proskills UK website.

THE INSTITUTE OF PAPER, PRINTING AND PUBLISHING (IP3)

Claremont House
70–72 Alma Road
Windsor
Berks SL4 3EZ
Tel: 0870 330 8625
Fax: 0870 330 8615
E-mail: info@ip3.org.uk
Website: www.ip3.org.uk

IP3 is the professional body representing the interests of individuals within the paper, printing and publishing sector. It was formed in 2005 from the merger of the Institute of Paper, the Institute of Printing and the Institute of Publishing, and brought together more than 2,000 members and a wealth of knowledge.

MEMBERSHIP
Student
Associate (AIP3)
Member (MIP3)
Fellow (FIP3)

QUALIFICATION/EXAMINATIONS
Certificate

DESIGNATORY LETTERS
AIP3, MIP3, FIP3

PROFESSIONAL INVESTIGATION

Membership of Professional Institutions and Associations

THE INSTITUTE OF PROFESSIONAL INVESTIGATORS

Claremont House
70–72 Alma Road
Windsor
Berkshire SL4 3EZ
Tel: 0870 330 8622
Fax: 0870 330 8612
E-mail: admin@ipi.org.uk
Website: www.ipi.org.uk

The IPI was founded in 1976 as a professional body, catering primarily for the work and educational needs of professional investigators of all types and all specializations. We encourage members' CPD and require them to adhere to the Institute's strict code of ethics, and we promote the recognition of professional investigation as a profession by government, legislative bodies and the public.

MEMBERSHIP
Associate
Member (MIPI)
Student

Fellow (FIPI)

QUALIFICATION/EXAMINATIONS
The Institute provides an interactive online Foundation Course for students and others interested in becoming part of the investigative industry; this course also provides a refresher course for those who need to update their specialization and/or interest in other areas of investigative work.

DESIGNATORY LETTERS
MIPI, FIPI

PSYCHOANALYSIS

Membership of Professional Institutions and Associations

THE BRITISH PSYCHOANALYTICAL SOCIETY

Byron House
112a Shirland Road
London W9 2BT
Tel: 020 7563 5000
Fax: 020 7563 5001
E-mail: admin@iopa.org.uk
Website: www.psychoanalysis.org.uk

The British Psychoanalytical Society has c500 members and c60 candidates for membership. Our aims include: to support the development of psychoanalytical knowledge as a general theory of mind, to further the clinical and scientific standards of psychoanalysis, and to train high-quality psychoanalytical professionals in sufficient numbers to develop the profession.

MEMBERSHIP
Associate Member
Full Member
Fellow

PSYCHOLOGY
Membership of Professional Institutions and Associations

BRITISH PSYCHOLOGICAL SOCIETY

St Andrews House
48 Princess Road East
Leicester LE1 7DR
Tel: 0116 254 9568
Fax: 0116 227 1314
E-mail: enquiries@bps.org.uk
Website: www.bps.org.uk

Psychology is the scientific study of people, the mind and behaviour. The British Psychological Society is the representative body for psychology and psychologists in the UK. We are responsible for the development, promotion and application of psychology for the public good.

MEMBERSHIP
Student Member
Graduate Member (MBPsS)
Associate Fellow (AFBPsS)
Fellow (FBPsS)
Honorary Fellow (HonFBPsS)
Affiliate
Chartered Membership (CPsychol)
Subscriber
e-Subscriber

QUALIFICATION/EXAMINATIONS
Statement of Equivalence in Clinical Psychology (SoE)
Qualification in Educational Psychology (Scotland) (Stage 2)
Qualification in Forensic Psychology (Stage 2) (QFP)
Qualification in Clinical Neuropsychology (QiCN)
Qualification in Counselling Psychology (QCoP)
Qualification in Health Psychology (Stage 2)
Qualification in Occupational Psychology (QOccPsych)
Qualification in Sport & Exercise Psychology (QSEP)

DESIGNATORY LETTERS
MBPsS, AFBPsS, FBPsS, CPsychol, HonMBPsS, HonFBPsS, SoE

PSYCHOTHERAPY
Membership of Professional Institutions and Associations

ASSOCIATION OF CHILD PSYCHOTHERAPISTS

Unit 7, 19–23 Wedmore Street
London N19 4RU
Tel: 020 7281 8479
E-mail: admin@childpsychotherapy.org.uk
Website: www.childpsychotherapy.org.uk

The ACP is the main professional body for psychoanalytic child and adolescent psychotherapists in the UK. Our members work with children and young people as well as their parents, families and wider networks, treating a wide range of difficulties ranging from problems with sleeping and bed-wetting to eating disorders, self-harm, depression and anxiety.

MEMBERSHIP
Member

BRITISH ASSOCIATION FOR COUNSELLING AND PSYCHOTHERAPY

BACP House
15 St John's Business Park
Lutterworth
Leicestershire LE17 4HB
Tel: 01455 883300
Fax: 01455 550243
E-mail: bacp@bacp.co.uk
Website: www.bacp.co.uk

BACP is the largest and broadest body within the sector and participates in the development of counselling and psychotherapy at an international level. Our work with large and small organizations ranges from advising schools on how to set up a counselling service to assisting the NHS on service provision, working with voluntary agencies and supporting independent practitioners.

MEMBERSHIP
Individual Member
Registered Member (MBACP)
Senior Accredited Member (Snr Accred)
Student Member
Affiliate Member
Associate Member
Member (MBACP)
Accredited Member (MBACP Accred)
Fellow (FBACP)

QUALIFICATION/EXAMINATIONS
We run workshops for members and accredit individual counsellors/psychotherapists, supervisors, counselling services and training courses. For details see our website.

DESIGNATORY LETTERS
MBACP, MBACP (Accred), FBACP, Snr Accred

BRITISH ASSOCIATION FOR THE PERSON CENTRED APPROACH

BAPCA
PO Box 143
Ross-on-Wye
Herefordshire HR9 9AH
Tel: 01989 763863
E-mail: via website
Website: www.bapca.org.uk

The BAPCA was founded in 1989 as a non-religious, non-profit-making organization with the aim of advancing education in Client-Centred Psychotherapy and Counselling and the Person-Centred Approach through its publications and website, and cooperation with other national and international organizations with similar goals.

MEMBERSHIP
Individual Member
Joint Member
International Member
Institutional Member

BRITISH PSYCHOTHERAPY FOUNDATION

37 Mapesbury Road
London NW2 4HJ
Tel: 020 8452 9823
E-mail: mail@bap-psychotherapy.org
Website: www.bap-psychotherapy.org

The BAP is one of the longest established and largest independent providers of Jungian analytic and psychoanalytic psychotherapy for adults and children in the UK. We have been training psychoanalytic and Jungian psychotherapists for nearly 60 years, and our members work in the NHS, the corporate and voluntary sectors and as private practitioners.

MEMBERSHIP
Member

QUALIFICATION/EXAMINATIONS
Certificate/Diploma/MSc in Psychodynamics of Human Development (jointly with Birkbeck College, University of London)
DPsych in Child and Adolescent Psychotherapy (jointly with Birkbeck College, University of London)

CAMBRIDGE COLLEGE OF HYPNOTHERAPY

7 Bold Street
Warrington WA1 1DN
Tel: 01925 659303
E-mail: info@thecch.com
Website: www.hypnotherapytraining.org.uk

The CCH offers training to become a professional hypnotherapist. The course is accredited by the NCH, HA, APHP, NGH and NRAH. No formal qualifications are required to enrol on the course. What is required is a willingness to learn, a sense of humour and a genuine compassion and liking for people from all paths in life. This can be a very rewarding new or second career or a supplement to your current work / lifestyle. In addition to the College Diploma, it is possible to gain the HPD (Hypnotherapy Practitioner Diploma) which is awarded by ncfe and also possible to gain a Diploma awarded by the National Guild of Hypnotists in the USA. The HPD is at NVQ level 4/5 and has transferable credits of 45 for a first year degree with the Open University.

QUALIFICATION/EXAMINATIONS
Intermediate Practitioner Certificate
Diploma in Therapeutic Hypnosis (DipTHP)

DESIGNATORY LETTERS
DipTHP

NATIONAL COLLEGE OF HYPNOSIS AND PSYCHOTHERAPY

PO Box 5779
Loughborough
Leicestershire LE12 5ZF
Tel: 0845 257 8735
E-mail: enquiries@nchp.org.uk
Website: www.hypnotherapyuk.net

The NCHP is a not-for-profit organization founded in 1977 and now offers accredited hypnotherapy training, hypnosis training and psychotherapy training at weekends in Leicester, London, Manchester and Oxford. We also provide a programme of 1- and 2-day workshops and seminars, and (where appropriate) distance-learning courses.

MEMBERSHIP
United Kingdom Council for Psychotherapy
European Association for Psychotherapy
European Association for Hypno-Psychotherapy

QUALIFICATION/EXAMINATIONS
Foundation Course

Certificate in Hypno-Psychotherapy (CHP(NC))
Diploma in Hypno-Psychotherapy (DHP(NC))
Advanced Diploma in Hypno-Psychotherapy (ADHP(NC))

NATIONAL COUNCIL OF PSYCHOTHERAPISTS

PO Box 541
Keighley BD21 9DS
Tel: 0800 170 1250
E-mail: info@thencp.org
Website: www.ncphq.co.uk

The National Council is a registering and accrediting body for psychotherapists, counsellors and coaches within the UK and also, through the International Council, the rest of the world.

Members can join the Council regardless of which discipline and where they completed their training.

MEMBERSHIP
Accredited Member (MNCP Accred)
Member (MNCP)
Fellow (FNCP)

DESIGNATORY LETTERS
ANCP, LNCP, MNCP, FNCP

THE FOUNDATION FOR PSYCHOTHERAPY AND COUNSELLING

5 Maidstone Buildings Mews
72–76 Borough High Street
London SE1 1GN
Tel: 0207 378 7392
E-mail: membership@thefpc.org.uk
Website: www.thefoundation-uk.org

The Foundation for Psychotherapy and Counselling was formed during the 1970s as the graduate body of WPF Therapy (the largest charitable provider of counselling and psychotherapy in England) and now has some 700 fully trained and qualified members, most of whom are in private practice.

MEMBERSHIP
Member

THE NATIONAL REGISTER OF HYPNOTHERAPISTS AND PSYCHOTHERAPISTS

Ground Floor
34 Altrincham Road
Wilmslow
Cheshire SK9 5ND
Tel: 0161 635 3530
E-mail: admin@nrhp.co.uk
Website: www.nrhp.co.uk

NRHP (est 1985) – a professional association of qualified hypno-psychotherapists who trained with a UKCP-accredited training organisation. Members are required to adhere to a code of ethics and carry appropriate insurance. We publish a Directory of Practitioners and offer a public referral service via our website and office. Member of the UKCP.

MEMBERSHIP
Student

Associate 1 (NRHP(Assoc 1))
Associate 2 (NRHP(Assoc 2))
Associate 3 (NRHP(Assoc 3))
Full Member (MNRHP)
Fellow (FNRHP)

DESIGNATORY LETTERS
NRHP(Assoc 1), NRHP(Assoc 2), NRHP(Assoc 3), MNRHP, FNRHP

UK COUNCIL FOR PSYCHOTHERAPY (UKCP)

2nd Floor Edward House
2 Wakley Street
London EC1V 7LT
Tel: 020 7014 9955
Fax: 020 7014 9977
E-mail: info@ukcp.org.uk
Website: www.psychotherapy.org.uk

UKCP is the leading professional body for the education, training, accreditation and regulation of psychotherapists and psychotherapeutic counsellors. Our register is accredited by the government's Professional Standards Authority. As part of our commitment to protecting the public, we work to improve access to psychotherapy, to support and disseminate research, to improve standards and to respond effectively to complaints against our members.

PURCHASING AND SUPPLY
Membership of Professional Institutions and Associations

THE CHARTERED INSTITUTE OF PROCUREMENT & SUPPLY

Easton House
Easton on the Hill
Stamford
Lincolnshire PE9 3NZ
Tel: 01780 756777
Fax: 01780 751610
E-mail: press@cips.org
Website: www.cips.org

The Chartered Institute of Procurement & Supply (CIPS) is the world's largest procurement and supply professional organisation. It is the worldwide centre of excellence on purchasing and supply management issues. CIPS has a global community of 115,000 in 150 different countries, including senior business people, high-ranking civil servants and leading academics. The activities of purchasing and supply chain professionals have a major impact on the profitability and efficiency of all types of organisation and CIPS offers corporate solutions packages to improve business profitability.

MEMBERSHIP
Student Member

Affiliate
Certificate Member
Diploma Member
Associate Member
Full Member (MCIPS)
Fellow (FCIPS)
Chartered Professional in procurement and supply

QUALIFICATION/EXAMINATIONS
Please see website: www.cips.org

DESIGNATORY LETTERS
MCIPS, FCIPS, Chartered Professional in procurement and supply

QUALITY ASSURANCE
Membership of Professional Institutions and Associations

THE CHARTERED QUALITY INSTITUTE

2nd Floor North
Chancery Exchange
10 Furnival Street
London EC4A 1AB
Tel: 020 7245 6722
Fax: 020 7245 6788
E-mail: membership@thecqi.org
Website: www.thecqi.org

The CQI is the chartered body for quality management professionals. Established in 1919, we gained a Royal Charter in 2006 and became the CQI shortly afterwards. Our vision is to place quality at the heart of every organization; we promote the benefits of quality management to industry, disseminate quality knowledge and resources, provide qualifications and training, and assess quality competence.

MEMBERSHIP
Student
Associate Member (ACQI)

Practitioner (PCQI)

Member, Chartered Quality Professional (MCQI, CQP)

Fellow, Chartered Quality Professional (FCQI, CQP)

QUALIFICATION/EXAMINATIONS

Level 3 Certificate in Quality Management (QCF)

Level 5 Certificate in Systems Management (QCF)

Level 5 Certificate in Assuring Service & Product Quality (QCF)

Level 5 Certificate in Managing Supply Chain Quality (QCF)

Level 5 Certificate in Quality Improvement for Business (QCF)

Level 5 Certificate in Quality Management Systems Audit (QCF)

Level 5 Diploma in Quality Management (QCF)

DESIGNATORY LETTERS

MCQI, CQP; FCQI, CQP

RADIOGRAPHY
Membership of Professional Institutions and Associations

THE SOCIETY OF RADIOGRAPHERS

207 Providence Square
Mill Street
London SE1 2EW
Tel: 020 7740 7200
Fax: 020 7740 7233
E-mail: via website
Website: www.sor.org

The Society of Radiographers, founded in 1920, represents diagnostic and therapeutic radiographers in the UK. Associated professionals working in medical imaging, radiation therapy and oncology are also welcome. It is responsible for their professional, educational, public and workplace interests. Together with the College of Radiographers, our charitable subsidiary, our efforts are directed towards education, research and other activities in support of the science and practice of radiography.

MEMBERSHIP

We have a range of membership options, including student, associate professional, healthcare support worker and assistant practitioner, retired and international membership options.

RETAIL
Membership of Professional Institutions and Associations

FOOD AND DRINK TRAINING AND EDUCATION COUNCIL LTD (FTC)

Icon Business Centre
4100 Park Approach
Leeds
West Yorkshire LS15 8GB
Tel: 0113 3970 398
E-mail: ftc@foodtraining.org.uk
Website: www.foodtraining.org.uk

Food and drink training and education council (ftc) formerly known as Meat Training Council (MTC). Ftc is a food industry skills-focused charity, dedicated to working collaboratively to build a world class food industry in the UK. We are involved in a range of practical and impactful charitable work to help support our industry in competing with the greatest nations in the world. We are the parent company of FDQ, a specialist food industry awarding organisation.

INSTITUTE OF MASTERS OF WINE

24 Fitzroy Square
London W1T 6EP
Tel: 020 7383 9130
Fax: 020 7383 9139
E-mail: peter@mastersofwine.org
Website: www.mastersofwine.org

The Institute of Masters of Wine is a membership body that represents the interests of its members (Masters of Wine), administers the MW Examination, and runs an education programme in preparation for the examination. We also hold a number of events throughout the year, including seminars and tastings, master classes, discussions and, every 4 years, a symposium, most of which are open to the public.

MEMBERSHIP
Master of Wine (MW)

QUALIFICATION/EXAMINATIONS
Master of Wine Examination

DESIGNATORY LETTERS
MW

THE BRITISH ANTIQUE DEALERS' ASSOCIATION

20 Rutland Gate
London SW7 1BD
Tel: 020 7589 4128
Fax: 020 7581 9083
E-mail: info@bada.org
Website: www.bada.org

BADA, which was founded in 1918, is the trade association for antique dealers in Britain. Our vetted members are elected for their high business standards and expertise, and adhere to a strict code of practice; we provide safeguards for members of the public who deal with our members, including independent arbitration if a dispute arises.

MEMBERSHIP
Member

THE GUILD OF ARCHITECTURAL IRONMONGERS

BPF House
6 Bath Place
Rivington Street
London EC2A 3JE
Tel: 0207 033 2480
Fax: 0207 033 2486
E-mail: info@gai.org.uk
Website: www.gai.org.uk

The GAI represents the interests of architectural ironmongers and manufacturers of architectural ironmongery. We develop, promote and protect standards of integrity and excellence, and encourage academic study relating to the industry, operating an Institute for individual members to facilitate their continuous professional development. We liaise with various bodies on matters affecting the industry.

MEMBERSHIP
Affiliate Member
Associate Member
Full Member
Registered Architectural Ironmonger (Reg AI)

QUALIFICATION/EXAMINATIONS
The GAI provides a 3-year incremental training programme. Students are examined each year and must pass each year in turn before progressing to the next. A Certificate is awarded to successful students each year, culminating in the GAI Diploma (Dip GAI) on successful completion of year 3.

DESIGNATORY LETTERS
Reg AI

THE INSTITUTE OF BUILDERS MERCHANTS

1180 Elliot Court
Coventry Business Park
Herald Avenue
Coventry CV5 6UB
Tel: 01767 650662
E-mail: admin@iobm.co.uk
Website: www.iobm.co.uk

To improve through seminars and website articles, the technical and general knowledge of persons engaged in builders' merchants; to verify management training courses with providers; to acknowledge personal achievements and award diplomas, certificates and other distinctions; to encourage the need for knowledge, integrity and efficiency in the builders' merchants industry.

MEMBERSHIP
Student
Associate
Member
Fellow
Corporate Supporter

QUALIFICATION/EXAMINATIONS
University Degree
The Institute of Builders Merchants Business Studies Course
The Builders Merchants Federation Diploma in Merchanting
Higher National Certificate (HNC) in Business Studies
Higher National Diploma (HND) in Business Studies
NVQ Level 4
Company management programmes as approved by the Board of Governors

THE SOCIETY OF SHOE FITTERS

c/o The Anchorage
28 Admirals Walk
Hingham
Norfolk NR9 4JL
Tel: 01953 851171
Fax: 01953 851190
E-mail: secretary@shoefitters-uk.org
Website: www.shoefitters-uk.org

The Society of Shoe Fitters, a non-profit organisation since 1959. Freely assists public and industry with footwear/fitting/foothealth enquiries via website, help line and leaflets. Teaches professional shoe fitting via five-month course, also instore training and application for experienced shoe fitters. Provides

National Shoe Fitting Week and lobbies government for better health education.

MEMBERSHIP
Student Member
Associate Member
Member (MSSF)
Fellow (FSSF)
Associate Member (corporate membership)

QUALIFICATION/EXAMINATIONS
One-day on-site courses – certificate only
Five-month course leading to membership qualification
Entrance Examination and Entrance Application for experienced shoe fitters leading to qualification

DESIGNATORY LETTERS
MSSF, FSSF

SECURITY
Membership of Professional Institutions and Associations

THE SECURITY INSTITUTE

1 The Courtyard
Caldecote
Warwickshire CV10 0AS
E-mail: info@security-institute.org
Website: www.security-institute.org

The Security Institute promotes professionalism in the security world through its professional grades of membership, and encourages a proper understanding of the value of the security function by management. Membership can be an employment prerequisite, and successful students of the Certificate, Diploma and Advance Diploma enjoy enhanced credibility and automatic membership.

MEMBERSHIP
Affiliate/Student
Graduate
Associate (ASyI)

Member (MSyI)
Fellow (FSyI)
Chartered Security Professional (CSyP)

QUALIFICATION/EXAMINATIONS
Certificate in Security Management (Level 3)
Diploma in Security Management (Level 5)
Advanced Diploma in Security Management (Level 7)

DESIGNATORY LETTERS
ASyI, MSyI, FSyI, CSyP

SOCIAL WORK AND PROBATION

SOCIAL WORK
Social work is a career for people who like people and much of a social worker's time is spent working in the community, helping support and protect people who are vulnerable and at risk. They work with people who are experiencing social and emotional problems and their families if they are affected. They may help people who use services to claim benefits, plan budgets, obtain legal advice or deal with other local authority departments. Social workers undertake assessment in relation to childcare, mental health and criminal justice. Depending on individual needs, a social worker may arrange

services such as home care assistance or hospital treatment.

HEALTH AND CARE PROFESSIONS COUNCIL
The role of the Health and Care Professions Council (HCPC) is to protect the public. It does this by developing and monitoring strategy and policy for the HCPC, and ensuring that the organization fulfils its functions under the Health and Social Work Professions Order 2001. The Council has 12 members made up of 6 registrant and 6 lay members. The HCPC also runs committees to help the Council with its work. Four statutory committees have been set up to establish and monitor standards of education and

training and to deal with fitness to practise issues. In addition, the Council has established two non-statutory committees to provide it with advice and guidance on specific issues.

The HCPC is a regulator and keeps a register of health and care professionals who meet their standards for their training, professional skills, behaviour and health. It is an offence for someone to claim they are registered with the HCPC when they are not or to use a protected title they are not entitled to use. Each of the professions regulated by the HCPC have at least one professional title that must be registered.

The HCPC accredits universities that offer social work qualifications at both qualifying and post-qualifying levels, and quality-assures all social work courses.

EDUCATION AND TRAINING

Social workers need a breadth of skills, as they will act as an adviser, advocate, counsellor and listener. There are various routes to becoming a social worker, but you will need to gain a professional qualification in social work (usually at degree level) either on a full-time or part-time basis. This is offered at undergraduate and postgraduate masters level. It is also possible to take a degree course combining social work with mental health or learning disability nursing. To find HCPC-approved degree courses visit www.hcpc-uk.org/education/programmes/register

Students following a social work course may be eligible for a bursary from the Department of Health.

For further information visit the NHS Business Authority website: www.nhsbsa.nhs.uk/837.aspx and the Gov.UK website: www.gov.uk/social-work-bursaries

REGISTRATION

Social work regulation in the UK is covered by the HCPC in England, The Care Council for Wales in Wales, the Scottish Social Services Council (SSSC) in Scotland and the Northern Ireland Social Care Council (NISCC) in Northern Ireland. It is possible to register with more than one regulator.

For further details, contact The Health and Care Professions Council, Park House, 184 Kennington Park Road, London SE11 4BU; Tel: 0300 500 6184; Fax: 020 7820 9684; e-mail: registration@hcpc-uk.org; website: www.hcpc-uk.org

For information about social work training and registration in Scotland, contact Scottish Social Services Council, Compass House, 11 Riverside Drive, Dundee DD1 4NY; Tel: 0345 6030 891; website: www.sssc.uk.com (online contact form).

For information about social work training and registration in Wales, contact Care Council for Wales, South Gate House, Wood Street, Cardiff CF10 1EW; Tel: 0300 3033 444; e-mail: info@ccwales.org.uk; website: www.ccwales.org.uk

For information about social work training and registration in Northern Ireland, contact Northern Ireland Social Care Council, 7th Floor, Millennium House, 19--25 Great Victoria Street, Belfast BT2 7AQ; Tel: 028 9536 2600; e-mail: info@niscc.hscni.net; website: www.niscc.info

Membership of Professional Institutions and Associations

THE BRITISH ASSOCIATION OF SOCIAL WORKERS

16 Kent Street
Birmingham B5 6RD
Tel: 0121 6223911
Fax: 0121 6224860
E-mail: membership@basw.co.uk
Website: www.basw.co.uk

The BASW is the largest professional association representing social work and social workers in the UK. Whether you are qualified or not, experienced or just entering the profession, we are here to help, support, advise and campaign on your behalf.

MEMBERSHIP
Student Member
Affiliate
Member (4 categories)
Retired Member
Overseas Member

SOCIOLOGY
Membership of Professional Institutions and Associations

BRITISH SOCIOLOGICAL ASSOCIATION

Bailey Suite, Palatine House
Belmont Business Park
Belmont
Durham DH1 1TW
Tel: 0191 383 0839
Fax: 0191 383 0782
E-mail: enquiries@britsoc.org.uk
Website: www.britsoc.co.uk

The BSA was founded in 1951 to promote sociology in the UK. Our members include researchers, teachers, students and practitioners in a variety of fields. We provide a network of communication to all who are concerned with the promotion and use of sociology and sociological research.

SPEECH AND LANGUAGE THERAPY
Membership of Professional Institutions and Associations

ROYAL COLLEGE OF SPEECH AND LANGUAGE THERAPISTS

2 White Hart Yard
London SE1 1NX
Tel: 020 7378 1200
E-mail: info@rcslt.org
Website: www.rcslt.org

The RCSLT is the professional body for speech and language therapists and support workers. We set, promote and maintain high standards in education, clinical practice and ethical conduct. Our national campaigning work aims to improve services for people with speech, language, communication and swallowing needs and to influence health, education and social care policies.

MEMBERSHIP
Student Member
Newly Qualified Member
Full Member
Fellow (FRCSLT)
Honorary Fellow (Hon FRCSLT)

DESIGNATORY LETTERS
FRCSLT, Hon FRCSLT

SPORTS SCIENCE
Membership of Professional Institutions and Associations

LONDON SCHOOL OF SPORTS MASSAGE

28 Station Parade
Willesden Green
London NW2 4NX
Tel: 020 8452 8855
Fax: 020 8452 4524
E-mail: via website
Website: www.lssm.com

The LSSM, founded in 1989, was the first to provide specialist training in Sport & Remedial Massage. We offer vocational training for those who want to develop a professional career in massage therapy and were instrumental in setting up the Institute of Sport & Remedial Massage (ISRM), which is the professional body promoting our needs and aspirations as clinical therapists.

MEMBERSHIP
Member

QUALIFICATION/EXAMINATIONS
Introductory Massage Workshop
Professional Diploma in Clinical Sport & Remedial Massage Therapy (BTEC Level 5)

STATISTICS
Membership of Professional Institutions and Associations

THE ROYAL STATISTICAL SOCIETY

12 Errol Street
London EC1Y 8LX
Tel: 020 7638 8998
E-mail: rss@rss.org.uk
Website: www.rss.org.uk

The RSS is the learned society and professional body for statistics and statisticians in the UK. We have over 7,000 members worldwide, and are active in a wide range of areas both directly and indirectly relating to the study and application of statistics.

MEMBERSHIP
Student Member
Fellow

Affiliate
Graduate Statistician (GradStat)
Chartered Statistician (CStat)

QUALIFICATION/EXAMINATIONS
Ordinary Certificate in Statistics
Higher Certificate in Statistics
Graduate Diploma in Statistics

DESIGNATORY LETTERS
GradStat, CStat

STOCKBROKING AND SECURITIES
Membership of Professional Institutions and Associations

CFA SOCIETY OF THE UK

2nd Floor
135 Canon Street
London EC4N 5BP
Tel: 020 7280 9620
Fax: 020 7280 9636
E-mail: info@cfauk.org
Website: www.cfauk.org

The CFA Society of the UK was formerly the UK Society of Investment Professionals (UKSIP) and was renamed in 2007. Our aim is to promote the development of the investment profession in the UK through the promotion of the highest standards of ethical behaviour and the provision of education, professional development, information, career support and advocacy to our members.

MEMBERSHIP
IMC Member
Candidate Member
Affiliate Member
Regular Member

QUALIFICATION/EXAMINATIONS
Investment Management Certificate (IMC)

THE CHARTERED INSTITUTE FOR SECURITIES & INVESTMENT

8 Eastcheap
London EC3M 1AE
Tel: 020 7645 0600
E-mail: customersupport@cisi.org
Website: www.cisi.org.uk

The Chartered Institute for Securities & Investment is the largest professional body for practitioners in stockbroking, derivatives markets, investment management, corporate finance, operations and related activities, having over 44,000 members.

MEMBERSHIP
Student Member
Affiliate
Associate (ACSI)
Member (MCSI)
Chartered Member (Ch. MCSI)
Fellow (FCSI)
Chartered Fellow (Ch. FCSI)

QUALIFICATION/EXAMINATIONS
Introduction to Investment
Islamic Finance Qualification
IT in Investment Operations
Risk in Financial Services
Combating Financial Crime

Global Financial Compliance
Investment Operations Certificate (IOC) also known as Investment Administration Qualification (IAQ)
Certificate in Corporate Finance
Certificate in Investments
Certificate in Private Client Investment Advice & Management
International Certificate in Wealth Management
Investment Advice Diploma
Advanced Certificate in Global Securities Operations
Advanced Certificate in Operational Risk
Diploma in Investment Compliance
Diploma in Investment Operations
CISI Diploma
CISI Masters in Wealth Management
Fundamentals of Financial Services
International Introduction to Investment
Diploma in Finance, Risk & Investment
Certificate in Finance Risk & Decision Making

Certificate for Introduction to Securities & Investment

Level 3 Certificate in Investment Management

Level 3 International Certificate in Investment Management

Level 4 Certificate in Investment Management

DESIGNATORY LETTERS
ACSI, MCSI, Ch. MCSI, FCSI, Ch. FCSI

SURGICAL, DENTAL AND CARDIOLOGICAL TECHNICIANS
Membership of Professional Institutions and Associations

THE BRITISH INSTITUTE OF DENTAL AND SURGICAL TECHNOLOGISTS

4 Thompson Green
Shipley
West Yorkshire BD17 7PR
Tel: 0115 9683 182
E-mail: via website
Website: www.bidst.org

The BIDST has been established for over 70 years and exists to provide a vehicle for the continuing education of technicians within the spheres of dental and surgical technology. It is our aim to make membership of the Institute an aspiration for all technicians, raising standards and portraying an image of professionalism which professional technicians deserve.

MEMBERSHIP
Affiliate (Overseas)
Affiliate (DCP)
Affiliate (Student)
Associate
Member
Fellow
Corporate Member

DESIGNATORY LETTERS
LBIDST, FBIDST

SURVEYING
Membership of Professional Institutions and Associations

CHARTERED ASSOCIATION OF BUILDING ENGINEERS

Lutyens House
Billing Brook Road
Weston Favell
Northampton
Northamptonshire NN3 8NW
Tel: 44 (0)1604 404 121
E-mail: info@cbuilde.com
Website: www.cbuilde.com

The ABE is the professional body for those specializing in the technology of building and the management processes by which buildings are designed, constructed, renewed and maintained. Our objectives are to promote and advance the planning, design, construction, maintenance and repair of the built environment; to maintain a high standard of professional practice; and to encourage cooperation between professionals.

MEMBERSHIP
Student
Technician
Training Affiliate
Academic Affiliate
Associate Member (ABEng)
Graduate Member (GradBEng)
Corporate Member (MBEng)
Corporate Fellow (FBEng)
Honorary Fellow (HonFBEng)

QUALIFICATION/EXAMINATIONS
ABBE Level 3 NVQ Diploma in Town Planning Technical Support (QCF)
ABBE Level 3 NVQ Diploma in Conservation Technical Support (QCF)
ABBE Level 3 NVQ Diploma in Building Control Technical Support (QCF)
ABBE Level 6 NVQ Diploma in Building Control (QCF)

ABBE Level 6 NVQ Diploma in Town Planning (QCF)
Edexcel Level 3 NVQ Diploma in Construction Site Supervision (Construction) (QCF)
Edexcel Level 3 NVQ Diploma in Construction Contracting Operations (QCF)
Edexcel Level 6 NVQ Diploma in Construction Contracting Operations (QCF)
Edexcel Level 6 NVQ Diploma in Construction Site Management (Construction) (QCF)
Edexcel Level 6 NVQ Diploma in Senior Site Inspection (QCF)
Edexcel Level 6 NVQ Diploma in Built Environment Design Management (QCF)
Edexcel Level 7 NVQ Diploma in Built Environment Design and Consultancy Practice (QCF)
Edexcel Level 7 NVQ Diploma in Construction Senior Management (QCF)

DESIGNATORY LETTERS
ABEng, GradBEng, MBEng, FBEng

SWIMMING INSTRUCTION
Membership of Professional Institutions and Associations

THE SWIMMING TEACHERS' ASSOCIATION

Anchor House
Birch Street
Walsall
West Midlands WS2 8HZ
Tel: 01922 645097
Fax: 01922 720628
E-mail: sta@sta.co.uk
Website: www.sta.co.uk

The STA is dedicated to the preservation of human life by the teaching of swimming, lifesaving and survival techniques to as many people as possible, both in the UK and internationally. We offer a range of specialist training programmes and qualifications, which are used in more than 25 countries worldwide, and liaise with other organizations concerned with swimming teaching and water safety.

MEMBERSHIP
Junior Member
Associate Member (ASTA)
Qualified Member (MSTA)
Corporate Member

QUALIFICATION/EXAMINATIONS
STA Level 2 Award in Swimming Teaching (QCF)
STA Level 2 Certificate in Swimming Teaching (QCF)
STA Level 1 Award for Pool to Open Water Swimming Coaching (QCF)
STA Level 2 Award for Open Water Swimming Coaching (QCF)
STA Level 2 Award in Aquatic Teaching – People with Disabilities (QCF)
STA Level 2 Award in Aquatic Teaching – Baby & Pre-School (QCF)
STA Level 1 Award in Pool Emergency Procedures (QCF)
STA Level 2 Award for Pool Responder (QCF)
STA Level 2 Award for Pool Lifeguard (QCF)

STA Level 2 Award in Emergency First Aid at Work (QCF)

STA Level 2 Award in Paediatric First Aid (QCF)

STA Level 2 Award in Activity First Aid (QCF)

STA Level 2 Award in Swimming Pool Water Testing (QCF)

STA Level 2 Award in Swimming Pool Water Treatment (QCF)

STA Level 3 Award in Pool Plant Operations (QCF)

STA Level 3 Award in Preparing to Teach in the Lifelong Learning Sector (QCF)

STA Level 4 Award in Preparing to Teach in the Lifelong Learning Sector (QCF)

STA Professional Award in Teaching Swimming at SCQF Level 6

STA Professional Certificate in Teaching Swimming

STA Professional Award in Aquatic Teaching – Baby and Pre-School at SCQF Level 6

STA Professional Award in Pool Emergency Procedures at SCQF Level 6

STA Professional Award for Pool Responder at SCQF Level 7

STA Professional Award for Pool Lifeguard at SCQF Level 7

STA Award in Emergency First Aid at Work at SCQF Level 5

STA Award in First Aid at Work at SCQF Level 6

DESIGNATORY LETTERS
ASTA, MSTA

TAXATION
Membership of Professional Institutions and Associations

SOCIETY OF TRUST & ESTATE PRACTITIONERS

Artillery House (South)
11–19 Artillery Row
London SW1P 1RT
Tel: +44 (0)20 7340 0500
Fax: +44 (0)20 7340 0501
E-mail: step@step.org
Website: www.step.org

The Society of Trust and Estate Practitioners (STEP) is the worldwide professional association for practitioners dealing with family inheritance and succession planning. The Society helps to improve public understanding of the issues families face in this area and promotes education and high professional standards among its members.

MEMBERSHIP
Full members of STEP are the most experienced and senior practitioners in the field of trusts and estates.

QUALIFICATION/EXAMINATIONS
STEP Diplomas and Certificates are recognised as essential qualifications and TEPs are sought after by employers. A portfolio of courses has been designed to enhance your career, including the STEP Diploma for England & Wales (Trusts and Estates), STEP Diploma for Ireland, STEP Diploma for Scotland, STEP Diploma in International Trust Management and the STEP Diploma for Accountants & Tax Practitioners. The Certificate series includes the STEP Advanced Certificate in Family Business Advising, the STEP Certificate for Financial Services (Trusts and Estate Planning) and many more.

DESIGNATORY LETTERS
STEP

THE ASSOCIATION OF TAXATION TECHNICIANS

1st Floor
Artillery House
11–19 Artillery Row
London SW1P 1RT
Tel: 020 7340 0551
E-mail: info@att.org.uk
Website: www.att.org.uk

The ATT was founded in 1989 in recognition of the increasing demand for tax services and the development of tax practice as a professional activity in its own right. Our primary aim is to provide an appropriate qualification for individuals who undertake such work, and we now have more than 10,500 members, affiliates and registered students.

MEMBERSHIP
Member

QUALIFICATION/EXAMINATIONS
Certificate of Competency

DESIGNATORY LETTERS
ATT

THE CHARTERED INSTITUTE OF TAXATION

First Floor
11–19 Artillery Row
London SW1P 1RT
Tel: 020 7340 0550
E-mail: via website
Website: www.tax.org.uk

The CIOT, which dates from 1930, is the professional body for Chartered Tax Advisers and has 14,300 members. Our aims are to promote education in and the study of the administration and practice of taxation, and to achieve a better, more efficient, tax system for all affected by it – taxpayers, advisers and the authorities.

MEMBERSHIP
Member (CTA)

QUALIFICATION/EXAMINATIONS
Chartered Tax Adviser (CTA) examination
Advanced Diploma in International Taxation (ADIT)
VAT Compliance Diploma (VCD) (offered by the Institute of Indirect Taxation)

DESIGNATORY LETTERS
CTA, ATII, FTII

TAXI DRIVERS
Membership of Professional Institutions and Associations

TAXI DRIVERS (LONDON)

Cab drivers and cab proprietors in the Metropolitan Police District and City of London are licensed by an Assistant Commissioner of the Metropolitan Police, through the Public Carriage Office at 15 Penton Street, Islington N1 9PU. A cab driver's licence is valid for 3 years and a cab proprietor's licence for 1 year.

TEACHING/EDUCATION

Initial qualifications in the UK

Qualified Teacher Status

To obtain a teaching appointment as a qualified teacher in maintained schools and non-maintained special schools in England and Wales, it is necessary to have Qualified Teacher Status (QTS). To be qualified, teachers must have satisfactorily completed an approved course of initial teacher training (ITT), and to be able to teach in maintained schools in England must have successfully completed their induction period (there are similar arrangements for teaching in Scotland, Wales and Northern Ireland). The National College for Teaching and Leadership (NCTL), an executive agency of the Department for Education, is the awarding body for QTS.

Qualified Teacher Learning and Skills

Qualified Teacher Learning and Skills (QTLS) status is recognised in law as equal to QTS for teaching in schools. The Society for Education and Training (SET) provides QTLS which you can gain by successfully completing professional formation -- a process that enables you to demonstrate the ability to use effectively the skills and knowledge acquired whilst training to be a teacher and also the application of the occupational standards required of a teacher.

To apply for QTLS, you need an initial teacher training qualification at Level 5, for example, equivalent to the Diploma to Teach in the Lifelong Learning Sector (DTLLS) or Diploma in Education and Training (DET). You are also required to demonstrate numeracy and literacy qualifications at (or above) Level 2.

The Society for Education and Training also offers a recognition route to QTLS for members with substantial teaching experience but who do not hold a recognised teaching qualification. Visit the SET website for more information: https://set.et-foundation.co.uk. The Society for Education and Training, 157–197 Buckingham Palace Road, London, SW1W 9SP; telephone: 0800 093 9111 (free) or 020 3092 5001 (local call); email: membership.enquiries@etfoundation.co.uk.

Teacher training courses

Initial teacher training courses in England and Wales are provided by accredited training providers mainly through university departments of education. Courses available include Bachelor of Arts or Bachelor of Science with QTS, Bachelor of Education (BEd) for undergraduates, and Postgraduate Certificates of Education (PGCEs) for graduates.

Undergraduate training courses generally take three or four years full time, or four to six years part time. However, if you have undergraduate credits from previous study you may be able to complete a course in two years. A PGCE generally lasts one year full time, or up to two years part time.

There are also some employment-based routes into teaching. The School Direct Programme allows schools to recruit trainees with the expectation that they will go on to work in the school or group of schools in which they have been trained, though there is no guarantee of employment. There are more than 100 schools offering places. Courses generally last for one year full time.

School Direct offers two separate training options: the School Direct Training Programme and the School Direct Training Programme (salaried). The School Direct Training Programme (salaried) is open to graduates with three or more years' career experience (there may be exceptions for some subjects). Trainees will be employed as unqualified teachers with a salary subsidised by The National College for Teaching and Leadership. Trainees on a School Direct Training Programme will have to pay tuition fees to cover the cost of the course, but home and EU trainees will be eligible for a tuition fee loan to cover these costs and you might be eligible for funding through training bursaries or scholarships. For more information, see The National College for Teaching and Leadership, School Direct (https://www.gov.uk/government/organisations/national-college-for-teaching-and-leadership). With School Direct, you are selected for training by a school or group of schools in partnership with a university or SCITT.

School-centred initial teacher training (SCITT) is training in a school environment for those with a UK degree or an equivalent qualification. SCITT programmes are designed and delivered by groups of neighbouring schools and colleges; they are usually full time for one year. Taught by experienced, practising teachers, and often tailored towards local teaching needs, all SCITT courses lead to QTS. Many, though not all, will also award you a PGCE validated by a higher education institution. There are consortia of schools and colleges running SCITT courses all over England. These groups provide all kinds of SCITT, covering primary, middle years and the full range of secondary subjects. Application for SCITT courses is usually through UCAS (www.ucas.com/ucas/teacher-training).

Teach First offers a two-year Leadership Development Programme for those interested in an employment-based route into teaching. Teach First enables graduates with a 2:1 or a First to spend two years working in secondary and primary schools in low income communities while earning a full-time salary. It offers the programme in different regions in the UK; during the application process you will be able to state your local area preference but they recommend that you be open minded about local area and understand that they will prioritise the needs of the schools and their children over the preferences of applicants. A PGCE is awarded on completion of the course. Candidates have to demonstrate a high proficiency in eight core competencies throughout this process to ensure they can achieve real impact for pupils: Humility, respect and empathy, interaction, leadership, planning and organising, problem solving, resilience, self-evaluation, and knowledge of Teach First and their academic subjects. Visit the Teach First website for further information: www.teachfirst.org.uk.

There are also other ways into teaching, including Troops to Teachers, Researchers in Schools and Assessment Only. Further details can be found at https://getintoteaching.education.gov.uk/explore-my-options/teacher-training-routes.

The qualification of Professional Graduate Diploma in Education (PGDE) is a one-year postgraduate degree course leading to registration as a primary or secondary school teacher in Scotland (see www.teachinscotland.org). Alternatively it is possible to undertake a four-year undergraduate degree course in education. In Scotland there are seven universities that offer teacher training courses: University of Aberdeen, University of Dundee, University of Edinburgh, University of Stirling, University of Glasgow, University of Strathclyde and University of the West of Scotland. For more information on how to apply for a teaching course in Scotland contact the Universities and Colleges Admissions System (UCAS), Tel: 0371 468 0469, www.ucas.com/ucas/teacher-training. The General Teaching Council for Scotland is also a useful source of information: www.gtcs.org.uk.

The Education Workforce Council (EWC) is the independent regulator in Wales for teachers in maintained schools, Further Education teachers and learning support staff in both school and FE settings. Contact details: EWC 9th Floor Eastgate House, 35--43 Newport Road, Cardiff, CF24 0AB; Tel: 029 20460099; Fax: 029 20475850; e-mail: information@ewc.wales; website: www.ewc.wales. EWC is responsible for administering the award of Qualified Teacher Status (QTS) in Wales, on behalf of the Welsh Government. The main ways to gain QTS in Wales are completion of a course of teacher training at an accredited institution in Wales (see www.teachertrainingcymru.org/home) or completion of employment-based training under the Graduate Teacher Programme (GTP). GTP programmes in Wales are managed and delivered by three regional centres of teacher training and education on behalf of the Welsh Government. Their contact details can be found at http://teachertrainingcymru.org/4

Initial Teacher Education (ITE) in Northern Ireland consists of the Postgraduate Certificate of Education course, approved by the Department of Education Northern Ireland, or a four-year BEd(Hons) course, which leads to recognition as a schoolteacher in Northern Ireland (see www.education-ni.gov.uk).

Qualifications for admission to training

Higher education institutions offering undergraduate ITT or ITE courses will set admissions criteria, typically two good A levels (or equivalent qualifications). Entrants to PGCE and other graduate training courses will require a relevant UK Bachelor's degree or a recognized equivalent and be expected to demonstrate a standard equivalent to GCSE grade C in English and mathematics (in Wales grade B, or equivalent is required), and additionally a standard equivalent to GCSE grade C in a science subject for those wishing to train to teach primary school children. Trainees who have undertaken their initial teacher training in England must pass professional skills tests in numeracy and literacy before starting the course. These tests cover core skills that teachers need in their jobs and QTS cannot be awarded until they are passed. If you are undertaking initial teacher training in Wales, you are not required to complete the skills tests in order to be awarded QTS.

There are various funding options available to support you throughout your teacher training. These include tax-free scholarships and bursaries. Your eligibility for financial support, and the amount you can expect to receive, generally depends on the subject you choose to teach, the class of your degree, and sometimes other qualifications and experience are taken into account too.

The National College for Teaching and Leadership

The National College for Teaching and Leadership is the executive agency of the Department for

Education (DfE). It is the body responsible for ITT in England and the award of QTS. It has two key aims: improving the quality of the education workforce; and helping schools to help each other to improve. NCTL works with schools to develop an education system supported locally by partnerships and led by the best head teachers. For information about the College, visit www.gov.uk/government/organisations/national-college-for-teaching-and-leadership.

General Teaching Councils

General Teaching Councils exist in Wales (EWC), Scotland (GTCS) and Northern Ireland (GTCNI). These councils hold registers of qualified teachers and also act as disciplinary bodies. You can find out more from their respective websites: EWC: www.ewc.wales; GTCS: www.gtcs.org.uk; GTCNI: www.gtcni.org.uk

Applications

Applications for undergraduate and postgraduate courses are made through UCAS. For courses in Northern Ireland visit the Department for Education on Northern Ireland's website (www.education-ni.gov.uk). You can find out more about training to teach from the following websites: UCAS: www.ucas.com; The National College for Teaching and Leadership: www.gov.uk/government/organisations/national-college-for-teaching-and-leadership and https://getintoteaching.education.gov.uk for queries relating to becoming a teacher, initial teacher training, recruitment opportunities or provision of relevant training.

TECHNICAL COMMUNICATIONS
Membership of Professional Institutions and Associations

THE INSTITUTE OF SCIENTIFIC AND TECHNICAL COMMUNICATORS (ISTC LTD)

Airport House
Purley Way
Croydon CR0 0XZ
Tel: 020 8253 4506
Fax: 020 8253 4510
E-mail: istc@istc.org.uk
Website: www.istc.org.uk

The ISTC is a non-profit-making organization and the largest UK body representing professional communicators and information designers. Our aims include improving standards of scientific and technical communication, promoting scientific and technical communication as a career, supporting our members, and consulting, cooperating and collaborating with other bodies that share our ideals.

MEMBERSHIP
Student
Associate
Junior
Member (MISTC)
Fellow (FISTC)
Business Affiliate

DESIGNATORY LETTERS
MISTC, FISTC

TEXTILES
Membership of Professional Institutions and Associations

THE TEXTILE INSTITUTE

8th Floor St James' Buildings
79 Oxford Street
Manchester M1 6FQ
Tel: 0161 2371188
Fax: 0161 2361991
E-mail: tiihq@textileinst.org.uk
Website: www.textileinstitute.org

The Textile Institute covers all disciplines – from technology and production to design, development and marketing – relating to fibres, fabrics, clothing, footwear, and interior and technical textiles.

MEMBERSHIP
Student
Individual
Licentiate (LTI)

Associate (CText ATI)
Fellow (CText FTI)
Companion
Honorary Fellow
Corporate

DESIGNATORY LETTERS
LTI, CText ATI, CText FTI

TIMBER TECHNOLOGY
Membership of Professional Institutions and Associations

WOOD TECHNOLOGY SOCIETY

The Boilerhouse
Springfield Business Park
Caunt Road
Grantham
Lincs NG31 7FZ
Tel: 01476 513880
Fax: 01476 513899
E-mail: emily.drury@iom3.org
Website: www.iom3.org/content/wood-technology

The Wood Technology Society (IWSc – a Division of the Institute of Materials, Minerals and Mining), formerly the Institute of Wood Science, is the professional body for the timber and allied industries. We promote and encourage a better understanding of timber, wood-based materials and associated timber processes, and are the UK examining body, awarding qualifications at Foundation, Certificate and Diploma level.

MEMBERSHIP
Student Member
Affiliate Member

Technician (EngTech)
Fellow (FIMMM)
Professional Member (MIMMM)
Graduate (Grad IMMM)
Corporate Member

QUALIFICATION/EXAMINATIONS
Level 2 Award in Timber and Panel Products (QCF)
Certificate
Diploma

DESIGNATORY LETTERS
TIWSc, LIWSc, MIWSc, FIWSc

TOWN AND COUNTRY PLANNING
Membership of Professional Institutions and Associations

ROYAL TOWN PLANNING INSTITUTE

41 Botolph Lane
London EC3R 8DL
Tel: 020 7929 9494
E-mail: education@rtpi.org.uk
Website: www.rtpi.org.uk

The RTPI is the largest professional institute for planners in Europe, with over 23,000 members. As well as promoting spatial planning, we develop and shape policy affecting the built environment, work to raise professional standards and support members through their education, training and career development.

MEMBERSHIP
Chartered Town Planner (MRTPI)
Fellow (FRTPI)
Associate Member (AssocRTPI)
Legal Associate (LARTPI)
Licentiate Member
Student Member
Retired Member
Affiliate
Honorary Member

QUALIFICATION/EXAMINATIONS
From January 2017 all routes to become a Chartered Town Planner are competency based and applicants must submit an Assessment of Professional Competence.
There are a range of educational pathways to Chartered Membership although the majority of applicants will have studied an accredited planning degree. Please see www.rtpi.org.uk/findacourse for a list of accredited training providers.

DESIGNATORY LETTERS
MRTPI, FRTPI, LARTPI, AssocRTPI

TRADING STANDARDS
Membership of Professional Institutions and Associations

THE CHARTERED TRADING STANDARDS INSTITUTE

1 Sylvan Court
Sylvan Way
Southfields Business Park
Basildon
Essex SS15 6TH
Tel: 01268 582200
Fax: 01268 582225
E-mail: institute@tsi.org.uk
Website: www.tradingstandards.uk

The CTSI, formed in 1881, is a not-for-profit membership association representing trading standards professionals in both the public and private sectors in the UK and overseas. CTSI encourages honest enterprise and business, and helps safeguard the economic, environmental, health and social well-being of consumers.

MEMBERSHIP
Student Member
Affiliate Member
Associate Member (ACTSI)
Full Member (MCTSI)
Chartered Trading Standards Practitioner (CTSP)
Fellow (FCTSI)

Corporate Affiliate
International

QUALIFICATION/EXAMINATIONS
The Trading Standards Qualifications Framework consists of:
Certificate of Competence
Core Skills in Consumer Affairs and Trading Standards

Module Certificate in Consumer Affairs and Trading Standards
Diploma in Consumer Affairs and Trading Standards
Higher Certificate in Consumer Affairs and Trading Standards
Higher Diploma in Consumer Affairs and Trading Standards

DESIGNATORY LETTERS
ACTSI, MCTSI, CTSP, FCTSI

TRANSPORT
Membership of Professional Institutions and Associations

INSTITUTE OF TRANSPORT ADMINISTRATION

The Old Studio
25 Greenfield Road
Westoning
Bedfordshire MK45 5JD
Tel: 01525 634940
Fax: 01525 750016
E-mail: director@iota.org.uk
Website: www.iota.org.uk

The primary aim of IoTA is to broaden and improve the knowledge, skills and experience of its members in the practice of efficient road, rail, air and sea transport. We are one of the few professional bodies still recognized within the terms of the Road Traffic 1968 (Statutory Instrument 78), wherein it is permitted to proffer qualified opinion as to the professional competence of its members. Established in 1944, the Institute continues to set new benchmark standards for the industry; promoting a policy of Experience Teaches.

MEMBERSHIP
Student (StInstTA)
Associate (AInstTA)
Honorary Member
Associate Member (AMInstTA)
Member (MInstTA)
Fellow (FInstTA)
Patron Scheme for Companies

DESIGNATORY LETTERS
StInstTA, AInstTA, AMInstTA, MInstTA, FInstTA

THE INSTITUTE OF TRAFFIC ACCIDENT INVESTIGATORS

Column House
London Road
Shrewsbury
Shropshire SY2 6NN
Tel: 08456 212066
E-mail: gensec@itai.org
Website: www.itai.org

The Institute provides a means of communication, education, representation and regulation in the field of Traffic Accident Investigation. Our main aim is to provide a forum for spreading knowledge and enhancing expertise among those engaged in the discipline. Members include police officers, lecturers in higher education and private practitioners.

MEMBERSHIP
Affiliate

Associate (AITAI)
Member (MITAI)

DESIGNATORY LETTERS
AITAI, MITAI

TRAVEL AND TOURISM
Membership of Professional Institutions and Associations

CONFEDERATION OF TOURISM AND HOSPITALITY

37 Duke Street
London W1U 1LN
Tel: 020 7258 9850
Fax: 020 7258 9869
E-mail: info@cthawards.com
Website: www.cthawards.com

The Confederation of Tourism and Hospitality is an awarding body approved by Ofqual, and registered on the QCA's National Qualifications Framework. We were established in 1982 to provide recognized standards of management and vocational training appropriate to the needs of the hotel and travel industries, via our syllabuses, examinations and awards.

MEMBERSHIP
Student Member
Professional Member (MCTH)
Honorary Fellow (FCTH)

QUALIFICATION/EXAMINATIONS
Level 2 Diploma in English Communication Skills (QCF)

Level 3 Diploma in Communication and Research Skills (QCF)
Level 3 Diploma in Tourism and Hospitality (QCF)
Level 4 Diploma in Hospitality Management (QCF)
Level 4 Diploma in Tourism Management (QCF)
Level 5 Diploma in Hospitality Management (QCF)
Level 5 Diploma in Tourism Management (QCF)
Level 6 Diploma in Hospitality and Tourism Management (QCF)
Level 7 Diploma in Hospitality and Tourism Management (QCF)

DESIGNATORY LETTERS
MCTH, FCTH

INSTITUTE OF TRAVEL AND TOURISM

PO Box 217
Ware
Hertfordshire SG12 8WY
Tel: 0844 4995 653
Fax: 0844 4995 654
E-mail: enquiries@itt.co.uk
Website: www.itt.co.uk

The ITT, founded in 1956, is a professional membership body for individuals employed in the travel and tourism industry. We provide support and guidance for our members throughout their career and offer

them CPD and training to maintain standards for the benefit of the industry as a whole.

MEMBERSHIP
Student Member

Introductory Member
Affiliate Member
Member
Member (MInstTT)
Fellow
Fellow (FInstTT)
University/College Member

Group Member
Corporate Member
Retired Member

DESIGNATORY LETTERS
MInstTT, FInstTT

THE TOURISM MANAGEMENT INSTITUTE

c/o Hon Secretary, Dr Cathy Guthrie, FTMI, FTS
18 Cuninghill Avenue
Inverurie
Aberdeenshire AB51 3TZ
Tel: 01467 620769
E-mail: secretary@tmi.org.uk
Website: www.tmi.org.uk

TMI is the professional body for tourism destination managers. Its network of 250+ members shares information via website, conferences, e-mails and newsletters. The TMI CPD programme aims to support destination management professionals throughout their career. TMI HE Course Recognition gives students & lecturers assurance of industry engagement, relevance and employability.

MEMBERSHIP
Student
Associate (ATMI)
Member (MTMI)
Fellow (FTMI)

DESIGNATORY LETTERS
ATMI, MTMI, FTMI

THE TOURISM SOCIETY

Queens House
55–56 Lincoln's Inn Fields
London WC2A 3BH
Tel: 020 7269 9693
Fax: 020 7404 2465
E-mail: admin@tourismsociety.org
Website: www.tourismsociety.org

The Tourism Society, founded in 1977, is the professional membership body for people working in all sectors of tourism. We strive to drive up standards of professionalism and act as an advocate of tourism to the government and the public and private sectors, and liaise with other tourism professionals worldwide. We also provide advice, support and networking opportunities to our 1,200 or so members.

MEMBERSHIP
Student
Full Member (MTS)
Fellow (FTS)
Overseas/Retired Member
Group Member
Corporate Member
Graduate

DESIGNATORY LETTERS
MTS, FTS

VETERINARY SCIENCE
Membership of Professional Institutions and Associations

BRITISH VETERINARY ASSOCIATION

7 Mansfield Street
London W1G 9NQ
Tel: 020 7636 6541
Fax: 020 7908 6349
E-mail: bvahq@bva.co.uk
Website: www.bva.co.uk

The BVA is the representative body for the veterinary profession in the UK and has more than 11,500 members. We promote and support the interests of our members and the animals under their care, liaise with the government and are the leading provider of veterinary information to the media and general public.

MEMBERSHIP
Student Member
Associate Member
Full Member
Overseas Member

ROYAL COLLEGE OF VETERINARY SURGEONS

Belgravia House
62–64 Horseferry Road
London SW1P 2AF
Tel: 020 7222 2001
Fax: 020 7222 2004
E-mail: info@rcvs.org.uk
Website: www.rcvs.org.uk

The RCVS is the regulatory body for veterinary surgeons and veterinary nurses in the UK. We aim to enhance society through improved animal health and welfare. We do this by setting, upholding and advancing the educational, ethical and clinical standards of veterinary surgeons and veterinary nurses.

MEMBERSHIP
Member (MRCVS)

Fellow (FRCVS)
Registered veterinary nurse (RVN)

QUALIFICATION/EXAMINATIONS
Certificate in Advanced Veterinary Practice (CertAVP)
Diploma in Advanced Veterinary Nursing (DipAVN)

DESIGNATORY LETTERS
MRCVS, FRCVS, RVN

SOCIETY OF PRACTISING VETERINARY SURGEONS

The Governor's House
Cape Road
Warwick CV34 5DJ
Tel: 01926 410454
Fax: 01926 411350
E-mail: office@spvs.org.uk
Website: www.spvs.org.uk

The SPVS was founded in 1933 with the aim of promoting the interests of veterinary surgeons in private practice. We are a non-territorial division of the British Veterinary Association. Our remit is to advise on all aspects of managing the business of a clinical veterinary practice, and we hold one-day, weekend and week-long courses and an annual congress.

MEMBERSHIP
Student Member
Graduate Member
Practice Member
Retired Member

WASTES MANAGEMENT
Membership of Professional Institutions and Associations

CHARTERED INSTITUTION OF WASTES MANAGEMENT

9 Saxon Court
St Peter's Gardens
Marefair
Northampton NN1 1SX
Tel: 01604 620426
Fax: 01604 621339
E-mail: membership@ciwm.co.uk
Website: www.ciwm.co.uk

The CIWM represents more than 6,000 waste management professionals – predominantly in the UK but also overseas. We promote education, training and research in the scientific, technical and practical aspects of waste management for the safeguarding of the environment, and set and strive to maintain high standards for individuals working in the waste management industry.

MEMBERSHIP
Student Member
Technician Member (TechMCIWM)
Associate Member (AssocMCIWM)
Graduate Member (GradMCIWM)

Licentiate (LCIWM)
Member (MCIWM)
Fellow (FCIWM)
Affiliated Organization

QUALIFICATION/EXAMINATIONS
CIWM Training Services specializes in developing and providing waste management training for individuals and organizations. Each year we organize more than 70 courses. For details see the website.

DESIGNATORY LETTERS
TechMCIWM, AssocMCIWM, GradMCIWM, LCIWM, MCIWM, FCIWM

WATCH AND CLOCK MAKING AND REPAIRING
Membership of Professional Institutions and Associations

THE BRITISH HOROLOGICAL INSTITUTE LIMITED

Upton Hall
Upton
Newark
Nottinghamshire NG23 5TE
Tel: 01636 813795
Fax: 01636 812258
E-mail: via website
Website: www.bhi.co.uk

The BHI, which was formed in 1858 to promote horology, is a professional body with about 3,000 members worldwide. We provide education and specialist training, set recognized standards of excellence in workmanship and professional conduct, and support our members in their work, making, repairing and servicing clocks and watches.

MEMBERSHIP
Associate
Member (MBHI)

Fellow (FBHI)

QUALIFICATION/EXAMINATIONS
Diploma in Clock and Watch Servicing (Level 3)
Diploma in the Servicing and Repair of Clocks / Watches (Level 4)
Diploma in the Repair, Restoration and Conservation of Clocks / Watches (Level 5)

DESIGNATORY LETTERS
MBHI, FBHI

WELDING
Membership of Professional Institutions and Associations

THE WELDING INSTITUTE

Granta Park
Great Abington
Cambridge CB21 6AL
Tel: 01223 899000
E-mail: professional@twi.co.uk
Website: www.theweldinginstitute.com

The Welding Institute is the engineering institution for welding and joining professionals. We are committed to promoting the importance of welding/materials joining technology, given its importance as a key industrial technology governing the reliability and safety of many products, and to the advancement of education, training and CPD for our members.

MEMBERSHIP
Associate (AWeldI)

Technician (TechWeldI)
Member (MWeldI)
Fellow (FWeldI)
Engineering Technician (EngTech)
Incorporated Engineer (IEng)
Chartered Engineer (CEng)

DESIGNATORY LETTERS
AWeldI, TechWeldI, MWeldI, FWeldI, EngTech, IEng, CEng

WELFARE

Membership of Professional Institutions and Associations

INSTITUTE OF WELFARE

PO Box 5570
Stourbridge DY8 9BA
Tel: 0800 0 32 37 25
E-mail: info@instituteofwelfare.co.uk
Website: www.instituteofwelfare.co.uk

The Institute of Welfare was founded in 1945 and exists to promote the highest possible standards in the delivery of welfare to those who need it. We make representations to government, undertake research on welfare issues, encourage and facilitate the exchange of information, and provide opportunities for those engaged in welfare work to pursue CPD.

MEMBERSHIP
Affiliate Member
Member (MIW)
Fellow (FIW)
Companion (CIW)

DESIGNATORY LETTERS
MIW, FIW, CIW

Part 6

Bodies Accrediting Independent Institutions

THE BRITISH ACCREDITATION COUNCIL FOR INDEPENDENT FURTHER AND HIGHER EDUCATION (BAC)

BAC is a registered charity that was established in 1984 to act as the national accrediting body for independent further and higher education. It is independent of both government and of the colleges it accredits.

A college that is accredited by BAC undergoes a thorough inspection every three or four years, with an interim visit in the middle of the accreditation cycle. BAC accreditation is not only available to colleges in the United Kingdom, there are now accredited colleges in 11 countries around the world. At present BAC accredits or approves 201 colleges in the United Kingdom and 25 overseas. Lists of accredited colleges are published each year; full details can be viewed on the BAC website (www.the-bac.org).

BAC has a close relationship with the accreditation scheme operated by Accreditation UK (in the field of English as a Foreign Language) and is a member of ENQA, the European Association for Quality Assurance in Higher Education. It maintains close links with The British Council, UK Council for International Student Affairs (UKCISA), UK NARIC, OFQUAL and the Federation of Awarding Bodies (FAB) and The Accreditation Body for Language Services (ABLS). In 2015 it was admitted onto the European Quality Assurance Register for Higher Education (EQAR).

Accreditation by BAC is recognized by the UK Visas and Immigration (UKVI) department of the Home Office as a qualifying requirement for institutions to enrol visa students.

Contact details for BAC are: BAC, Ground Floor, 14 Devonshire Square, London, EC2M 4YT; Tel: 0300 330 1400; Fax: 0300 330 1401; e-mail: info@the-bac.org; website: www.the-bac.org

THE BRITISH COUNCIL

The British Council runs the Accreditation UK scheme in partnership with English UK for the inspection and accreditation of organizations that provide courses in English as a Foreign Language (EFL) in Britain. The British Council aims to make quality language materials available to learners and teachers all over the world, and they offer over three million UK examinations worldwide, helping people gain access to trusted qualifications to support their career and study prospects.

Under the terms of the scheme, institutions are inspected rigorously every four years in the areas of management, resources and environment, teaching and learning, welfare and student services and care of under 18s. The scheme also includes a system of random spot-checking. The management and policy of the scheme are conducted by an independent board while a separate independent committee reviews inspectors' reports.

The majority of recognized schools are also members of English UK, which insists on British Council accreditation as a criterion for membership. In addition, all English UK members, of which there are around 450, are required to abide by the Association's Code of Practice and Regulations. English UK exists to raise the high standards of its members even further through conferences, training courses and publications. The association also represents the interests of members and students to government bodies, and promotes international student mobility.

Further information on the Accreditation UK scheme may be obtained from the Accreditation Unit, British Council, Bridgewater House, 58 Whitworth Street, Manchester M1 6BB;

Tel: 0161 957 7755; or use the online enquiry form at www.britishcouncil.org/contact; website: www.britishcouncil.org/education/accreditation

Further information on English UK may be obtained from English UK, 219 St John Street, London EC1V 4LY; Tel: 020 7608 7960; Fax: 020 7608 7961; e-mail: info@englishuk.com; website: www.englishuk.com

THE OPEN AND DISTANCE LEARNING QUALITY COUNCIL (ODLQC)

ODLQC was established in 1968 as the Council for the Accreditation of Correspondence Colleges, a joint initiative of the then Labour government and representatives of the sector. It is the principal accrediting body for a wide variety of providers of open and distance learning (ODL) in the UK, from commercial colleges to professional and public-sector institutions. Now independent, it nevertheless continues to have the informal support of government. ODLQC promotes quality by:

- establishing standards of education and training in ODL;
- recognizing good quality provision, wherever it occurs;
- supporting and protecting the interests of learners;
- encouraging the improvement of existing methods and the development of new ones;
- linking ODL with other forms of education and training;
- promoting wider recognition of the value of ODL.

Accreditation includes a rigorous assessment of educational provision, covering materials, tutorial support, publicity, contractual arrangements with learners and general administrative procedures, each of which is measured against the Council's published benchmark standards. If accredited, the provider is monitored on a regular basis and reassessed at least once every three years.

The Council promotes those colleges that it accredits, which are by definition quality providers of ODL, and acts as honest broker in matching accredited colleges to potential markets. A list of accredited providers is included on the Council's website: www.odlqc.org.uk. The Council also seeks to protect the interests of learners by promoting the importance of accreditation, and by offering advice and support directly to learners. At the same time, knowledge of good practice is disseminated more widely, and quality encouraged wherever ODL occurs.

The Council consists of members drawn from professional and public bodies involved in education, as well as representatives of accredited providers, and has strong links with other bodies in the sector, both in the UK and abroad.

All enquiries should be through the contact form on the website: www.odlqc.org.uk

THE COUNCIL FOR INDEPENDENT EDUCATION (CIFE)

CIFE was founded in 1973 to promote strict adherence by independent sixth-form and tutorial colleges to the highest standards of academic and professional integrity and to provide an inspection service for these colleges. All member colleges must be accredited by the British Accreditation Council for Independent Further and Higher Education (BAC), and/or the Independent Schools Inspectorate (ISI). CIFE colleges all undergo regular inspection by the Department for Education

They are also inspected either by the British Accreditation Council, the Independent Schools Inspectorate, or both. Ofsted (Office for Standards in Education) check college-provided accommodation and student welfare. Candidate membership is available for up to three years for colleges that are seeking BAC or ISI accreditation and otherwise satisfy CIFE's exacting membership criteria. All colleges must also abide by stringent codes of conduct and practice; the character and presentation of their published exam results are subject to regulation, and the accuracy of the information must be validated by BAC as academic auditor to CIFE. Full members are subject to reinspection by their accrediting bodies. There are 19 colleges in full or candidate membership of CIFE at present, spread throughout England but with concentrations in London and Oxford.

CIFE colleges offer a wide range of GCSE, A and AS level courses. In addition, some CIFE colleges offer English language tuition for students from overseas, and degree-level tuition. Most colleges also provide A level and GCSE revision courses during the Easter holidays. Further information on CIFE may be obtained from the CIFE website: www.cife.org.uk; Tel: 020 8767 8666; e-mail: enquiries@cife.org.uk

Part 7

Study Associations and the 'Learned Societies'

Study associations consist of people who wish to increase their knowledge of a particular subject or range of subjects; they may be professionals or amateurs. Some associations consist almost entirely of specialists (e.g. the Royal Statistical Society); others (e.g. the Royal Geographical Society and the Zoological Society of London) have a more general membership. The learned societies usually have two grades of membership: fellows and members. Some also admit group members (such as schools or libraries), known as corporate members, and junior associate, corresponding and overseas members, who pay lower subscriptions. Some also elect honorary fellows or members. The members of some societies may use designatory letters, but this does not mean that the holder is 'qualified' in the same sense as a doctor or a chartered accountant.

Membership of some learned societies is by election, and is commonly accepted as distinguishing the candidate by admission to an exclusive group. Candidates may be selected in respect of pre-eminence in their subject or in the public service. The chief associations of this type are the Royal Society (founded in 1660 and granted Royal Charters in 1662 and 1663), the Royal Academy of Arts (founded in 1768) and the British Academy (granted the Royal Charter in 1902).

The Royal Society (www.royalsociety.org)was established to improve 'natural knowledge' and is mainly concerned with pure and applied science and technology. Election to Fellowship (FRS) is regarded as one of the highest distinctions. The society elects Fellows, Foreign Members, Royal Fellows and Honorary Fellows. The Royal Academy (www.royalacademy.org.uk) was established to cultivate and improve the arts of painting, sculpture and architecture. There are two main grades of membership: Academicians (RAs) (including Senior Academicians) and the Honorary RAs, Honorary Fellows and Honorary Members. The British Academy (www.britac.ac.uk) is the UK's national academy for the humanities and the social sciences. It is the counterpart to the Royal Society that exists to serve the natural sciences. The Academy has Fellows (FBA), Corresponding Fellows and a small number of Honorary Fellows.

A list of learned societies and study associations can be found below.

OCCUPATIONAL ASSOCIATIONS

The occupational associations do not qualify practitioners but organize them. Some coordinate the activities of specialists and others promote the individual and collective interests of professionals working in a wider area. Both types also seek to safeguard the public interest and to offer an educational service to their members. The latter type of association is especially numerous among teachers (e.g. the National Union of Teachers (NUT), the Educational Institute of Scotland (EIS), NASWUT (the National Association of Schoolmasters/Union of Women Teachers) and the National Association of Head Teachers (NAHT)), and is represented in the medical profession by the British Medical Association.

LIST OF STUDY ASSOCIATIONS AND LEARNED SOCIETIES

This list largely excludes qualifying bodies, which are covered in Part 5. The date on the left is that of foundation or adoption of title.

Agriculture and related subjects

1926	Agricultural Economics Society (AES)	1839	Royal Agricultural Society of England
1952	British Agricultural History Society		(now part of Innovation for
1945	British Grassland Society		Agriculture)
1944	British Society of Animal Science	1882	Royal Forestry Society
	(BSAS)	1784	Royal Highland and Agricultural
1947	British Society of Soil Science		Society of Scotland (RHASS)
1921	Commonwealth Forestry Association	1804	Royal Horticultural Society (RHS)
	(CFA)	1854	Royal Scottish Forestry Society
1927	Herb Society of Great Britain	1904	Royal Welsh Agricultural Society
1925	Institute of Chartered Foresters (ICF)		(RWAS)
1938	Institution of Agricultural Engineers	1943	Society of Dairy Technology
	(IAgrE)	1945	The Soil Association
1947	International Fertiliser Society (IFS)		

Anthropology and related subjects

1963	African Studies Association of the UK	1972	Japan Foundation
	(ASAUK)	1891	Japan Society
1979	Association for the Study of Modern	1843	Royal Anthropological Institute of
	and Contemporary France		Great Britain and Ireland (the RAI)
1982	Association for the Study of Modern	1823	Royal Asiatic Society of Great Britain
	Italy		and Ireland
1946	Association of Social Anthropologists	1868	Royal Commonwealth Society (RCS)
	of the UK and Commonwealth	1901	Royal Society for Asian Affairs
1985	British Association for Irish Studies		(RSAA)
	(BAIS)	1936	Saltire Society
1974	British Association for Japanese	1977	Society for Caribbean Studies (SCS)
	Studies	1964	Society for Latin American Studies
1972	British Association for South Asian		(SLAS)
	Studies (BASAS)	1969	Society for Libyan Studies
1961	British Institute of Persian Studies	1983	Society for the Promotion of Byzantine
	(BIPS)		Studies
1973	British Society for Middle Eastern	1879	Society for the Promotion of Hellenic
	Studies (BRISMES)		Studies
1981	European Association for Jewish	1910	Society for the Promotion of Roman
	Studies (EAJS)		Studies
1878	Folklore Society	1969	University Association for
1943	Hispanic and Luso Brazilian Council		Contemporary European Studies
	(Canning House)		(UACES)
1974	International Association for the Study	1892	Viking Society for Northern Research
	of German Politics (IASGP)		

Archaeology and related subjects

1924	Ancient Monuments Society	1948	British Institute at Ankara (BIAA)
1979	Association for Environmental	1846	Cambrian Archaeological Association
	Archaeology (AEA)	1944	Council for British Archaeology
1843	British Archaeological Association	1838	Ecclesiological Society
	(BAA)	1882	Egypt Exploration Society
1996	British Epigraphy Society		

1855	London and Middlesex Archaeological Society (LAMAS)	1843	Royal Archaeological Institute
1865	Palestine Exploration Fund (PEF)	1967	Society for Post-Medieval Archaeology (SPMA)
1908	Prehistoric Society		

Art and Design

1974	Association of Art Historians (AAH)	1754	Royal Society for the Encouragement of Arts, Manufactures and Commerce (RSA)
1910	Contemporary Art Society		
1915	Design and Industries Association	1904	Royal Society of British Sculptors
1950	International Institute for Conservation of Historic and Artistic Works	1904	Royal Society of Marine Artists (RSMA)
		1895	Royal Society of Miniature Painters, Sculptors and Gravers
1888	National Society for Education in Art and Design (NSEAD)		
		1884	Royal Society of Painter-Printmakers
1898	Pastel Society	1891	Royal Society of Portrait Painters
1768	Royal Academy of Arts	1804	Royal Watercolour Society
1814	Royal Birmingham Society of Artists (RBSA)	1919	Society of Graphic Fine Art (SGFA)
		1952	Society of Portrait Sculptors
1883	Royal Institute of Oil-Painters (ROI)	1952	United Society of Artists
1831	Royal Institute of Painters in Watercolours	1955	William Morris Society
1826	Royal Scottish Academy of Art and Architecture		

Biology and related subjects

1936	Association for the Study of Animal Behaviour (ASAB)	1931	Society for Applied Microbiology (SfAM)
1904	Association of Applied Biologists (AAB)	1911	The Biochemical Society
		1913	The British Ecological Society (BES)
1968	Biomedical Engineering Society (BMES)	1896	The British Mycological Society
		1858	The British Ornithologists' Union (BOU)
1836	Botanical Society of Scotland		
1836	Botanical Society of the British Isles (BSBI)	1959	The British Society for Cell Biology (BSCB)
1896	British Bryological Society (BBS)	1933	The British Trust for Ornithology (BTO)
1929	Freshwater Biological Association (FBA)		
		1937	The Systematics Association
1889	Marine Biological Association (MBA)	1826	Zoological Society of London (ZSL)
1833	Royal Entomological Society		

Chemistry

1918	Oil and Colour Chemists' Association (OCCA)	1881	Society of Chemical Industry (SCI)
		1897	Society of Leather Technologists and Chemists (SLTC)
1980	Royal Society of Chemistry (RSC)		

Economics, Statistics and related subjects

1992	Chartered Association of Business Schools	1902	Royal Economic Society (RES)
		1834	Royal Statistical Society (RSS)
1927	Economic History Society	1897	Scottish Economic Society (SES)
1955	Institute of Economic Affairs (IEA)		

Engineering and related subjects

1997	Chartered Institute of Ergonomics and Human Factors	1866	Royal Aeronautical Society
		1916	Royal Incorporation of Architects in Scotland (RIAS)
1966	Concrete Society		
1946	Forum for the Built Environment (fbe) (formerly the Faculty of Building)	1860	Royal Institution of Naval Architects (RINA)
1997	Faculty of Party Wall Surveyors	1916	Society of Automotive Engineers (SAE)
1978	Institute of Concrete Technology (ICT)		
2006	Institution of Engineering and Technology (IET)	1958	Society of Environmental Engineers
		2003	The Energy Institute (EI)
1976	Royal Academy of Engineering (RAEng)	1899	Town and Country Planning Association (TCPA)

Geography, Geology and related subjects

1963	British Cartographic Society (BCS)	1971	Institution of Environmental Sciences (IES)
1949	British Geotechnical Society (BGA)		
1940	British Society of Rheology (BSR)	1876	Mineralogical Society of Great Britain and Ireland
1923	English Place-Name Society (EPNS) (University of Nottingham)		
		1847	Palaeontographical Society
1931	Gemmological Association of Great Britain (Gem-A)	1957	Paleontological Association
		1830	Royal Geographical Society (RGS)
1893	Geographical Association (GA)	1997	Royal Institute of Navigation (RIN)
1807	Geological Society of London	1884	Royal Scottish Geographical Society (RSGS)
1858	Geologists' Association (GA)		
1846	Hakluyt Society		

History and related subjects

1902	British Academy	1961	Institute of Heraldic and Genealogical Studies (IHGS)
1952	British Agricultural History Society (BAHS)		
		1921	Institute of Historical Research (IHR)
1888	British Record Society	1893	Jewish Historical Society of England
1932	British Records Association (BRA)	1964	London Record Society
1947	British Society for the History of Science (BSHS)	1920	Newcomen Society for the Study of the History of Engineering and Technology
1988	Centre for Metropolitan History (CMH)		
		1921	Oriental Ceramic Society (OCS)
1864	Early English Texts Society (EETS)	1868	Royal Historical Society (RHS)
1964	Furniture History Society (FHS)	1836	Royal Numismatic Society
1869	Harleian Society	1869	Royal Philatelic Society, London (RPSL)
1885	Huguenot Society of Great Britain and Ireland		
		1953	Scottish Genealogy Society
		1886	Scottish History Society

1897	Scottish Record Society	1707	Society of Antiquaries of London
1976	Social History Society	1780	Society of Antiquaries of Scotland
1921	Society for Army Historical Research	1956	Society of Architectural Historians in Great Britain (SAHGB)
1910	Society for Nautical Research		
1967	Society for Renaissance Studies	1911	Society of Genealogists
1970	Society for the Social History of Medicine (SSHM)	1906	The Historical Association
		1958	Victorian Society

Languages

1883	Alliance Française	1910	Chartered Institute of Linguists (CIOL)
1891	An Comunn Gaidhealach		
1981	Association for French Language Studies (AFLS)	1991	Instituto Cervantes
		1964	National Association for the Teaching of English (NATE)
1932	Association for German Studies in Great Britain and Ireland (AGS)	1993	University Council of Modern Languages (UCML)
1990	Association for Language Learning (ALL)	1988	Women in German Studies (WIGS)

Law

1958	British Institute of International and Comparative Law (BIICL)	1920	Royal Institute of International Affairs (Chatham House)
1972	Intellectual Property Bar Association	1965	Scottish Law Commission
1922	Law Society of Northern Ireland	1887	Selden Society (Queen Mary University)
1949	Law Society of Scotland		

Literature and Arts

1959	Yr Academi Gymreig (The Welsh Academy)	1904	Classical Association
		2009	Deans and Leaders of Arts, Social Sciences and Humanities (DASSH-UK)
1973	Alliance of Literary Societies (ALS)		
1969	Art Libraries Society (ARLIS/UK & Ireland)	1902	Dickens Fellowship
		1890	Edinburgh Bibliographical Society
1970	Association for Scottish Literary Studies (ASLS)	1906	English Association (University of Leicester)
1989	Association of Independent Libraries (AIL)	1886	Francis Bacon Society Inc
1892	Bibliographical Society	1960	H. G. Wells Society
1992	British Association for Information and Library Education and Research (BAILER)	1997	Historical Novel Society
		1973	Joseph Conrad Society
		1997	Leeds Philosophical and Literary Society
1975	British Comparative Literature Association (BCLA)		
		1906	Malone Society
1933	British Film Institute (BFI)	1781	Manchester Literary and Philosophical Society
1960	British Society of Aesthetics (BSA)		
1893	Bronte Society	1995	Philip Larkin Society
1949	Cambridge Bibliographical Society	1842	Philological Society
1935	Charles Lamb Society (CLB)		

1909	Poetry Society	2004	Society of College, National and University Libraries (SCONUL)
1820	Royal Society of Literature		
1884	Society of Authors	1968	Thomas Hardy Society

Management

1986	British Academy of Management (BAM)

Mathematics and Physics

1924	Astronomical Society of Edinburgh (ASE)	1927	British Institute of Radiology (BIR)
		1933	British Interplanetary Society (BIS)
1890	British Astronomical Association (BAA)	1871	Mathematical Association (MA)
		1820	Royal Astronomical Society (RAS)
1966	British Biophysical Society (BBS)	1850	Royal Meteorological Society (RMetS)

Medicine (including Psychology)

1887	Anatomical Society (AS)	1948	British Geriatrics Society (BGS)
1957	Association for Child and Adolescent Mental Health (ACAMH)	1832	British Medical Association (BMA)
		1950	British Neuropathological Society (BNS)
1957	Association for the Study of Medical Education (ASME)	1953	British Occupational Hygiene Society (BOHS)
1932	Association of Anaesthetists of GB and Ireland (AAGBI)	1965	British Orthodontic Society (BOS)
1933	Association of British Neurologists (ABN)	1918	British Orthopaedic Association (BOA)
1953	Association of Clinical Biochemistry and Laboratory Medicine (ACB)	1901	British Psychological Society (BPS)
		1948	British Society for Allergy and Clinical Immunology (BSACI)
1927	Association of Clinical Pathologists (ACP)	2011	British Association for Cytopathology (BAC)
1920	Association of Surgeons of GB and Ireland (ASGBI)	1937	British Society of Gastroenterology (BSG)
1971	BASO – The Association for Cancer Surgery	1960	British Society for Haematology (BSH)
1959	British Academy for Forensic Science (BAFS)	1947	British Society for Research on Ageing (BSRA)
2003	British Association for Sexual Health and HIV (BASHH)	1945	British Thoracic Society (BTS)
		2014	Chartered Institute of Ergonomics and Human Factors
1977	British Association of Clinical Anatomists (BACA)	1959	Chartered Society of Forensic Sciences
1950	British Association of Forensic Medicine (BAFM)	1934	Diabetes UK
		1946	Experimental Psychology Society (EPS)
1962	British Association of Oral Surgeons (BAOS)	1950	Faculty of Homeopathy
2008	British Association of Otohinolaryngology (ENT UK)	1819	Hunterian Society
		2014	Institute of Osteopathy (iO)
1954	British Association of Paediatric Surgeons (BAPS)	1924	Institute of Psychoanalysis
		1969	Institute of Occupational Medicine (IOM)
1945	British Association of Urological Surgeons (BAUS)		

1964	Institute of Pharmacy Management (IPM)	2008	Royal Society for Public Health (RSPH)
1773	Medical Society of London	1805	Royal Society of Medicine (RSM)
1901	Medico-Legal Society	1907	Royal Society of Tropical Medicine and Hygiene (RSTMH)
1941	Nutrition Society		
1906	Pathological Society of Great Britain and Ireland	1946	Society for Endocrinology
		1950	Society for Reproduction and Fertility (SRF)
1875	Royal Environmental Health Institute of Scotland (REHIS)	1884	Society for the Study of Addiction (SSA)
1734	Royal Medical Society		
1931	Royal Pharmaceutical Society of Great Britain (RPS)	1926	Society of British Neurological Surgeons

Music

1977	Alkan Society	1888	Plainsong and Medieval Music Society (PMMS)
1979	British Music Society		
1971	Chopin Society	1874	Royal Musical Association (RMA)
1932	English Folk Dance and Song Society (efdss)	1955	Welsh Music Guild
1882	Incorporated Society of Musicians (ISM)		

Philosophy

1880	Aristotelian Society	1781	Manchester Literary and Philosophical Society
1984	British Society for the History of Philosophy (BSHP)		
		1913	Philosophical Society of England
1819	Cambridge Philosophical Society	1925	Royal Institute of Philosophy
1990	Friedrich Nietzsche Society (FNS)	1802	Royal Philosophical Society of Glasgow
1979	Hegel Society of Great Britain (HSGB)		

Politics

1975	British International Studies Association (BISA)	1987	Institute of Welsh Affairs
		1974	International Association for the Study of German Politics (ISAGP)
1951	David Davies Memorial Institute of International Studies (Aberystwyth University)	1950	Political Studies Association (PSA)
		1868	Royal Commonwealth Society
1884	Electoral Reform Society (ERS)	1920	Royal Institute of International Affairs (Chatham House)
1945	Federal Trust for Education and Research		

Science general

1831	British Science Association (BSA)	1799	Royal Institution of Great Britain (Ri)
1947	British Society for the History of Science (BSHS)	1660	Royal Society
		1783	Royal Society of Edinburgh
1960	British Society for the Philosophy of Science (BSPS)		

Theology and Religious Studies

1908	Baptist Historical Society	1981	European Association for Jewish Studies (EAJS)
1954	British Association for the Study of Religions (BASR)	1903	Friends Historical Society
1904	Canterbury and York Society	1972	United Reformed Church History Society (Westminster College)
1904	Catholic Record Society		
1961	Ecclesiastical History Society (EHS)	1893	Wesley Historical Society

General Index

Note: In addition to the abbreviations listed at the beginning of the book, the following are used throughout the index; FE – Further Education; HE – Higher Education. Universities are listed under locations eg: Aberdeen, University of